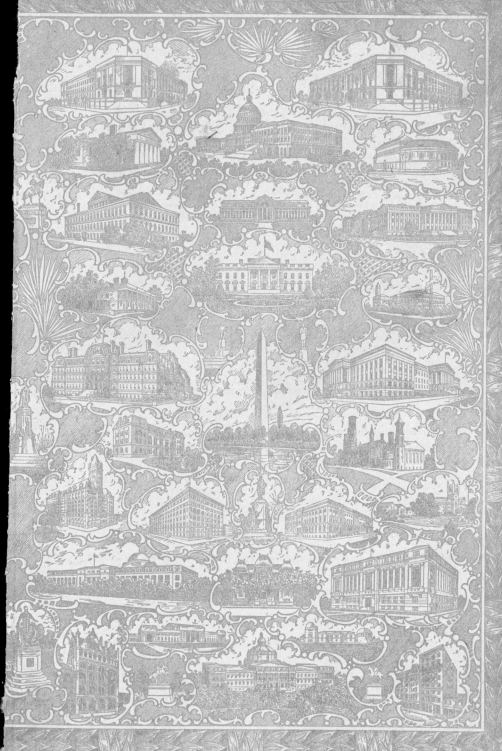

Supreme Court

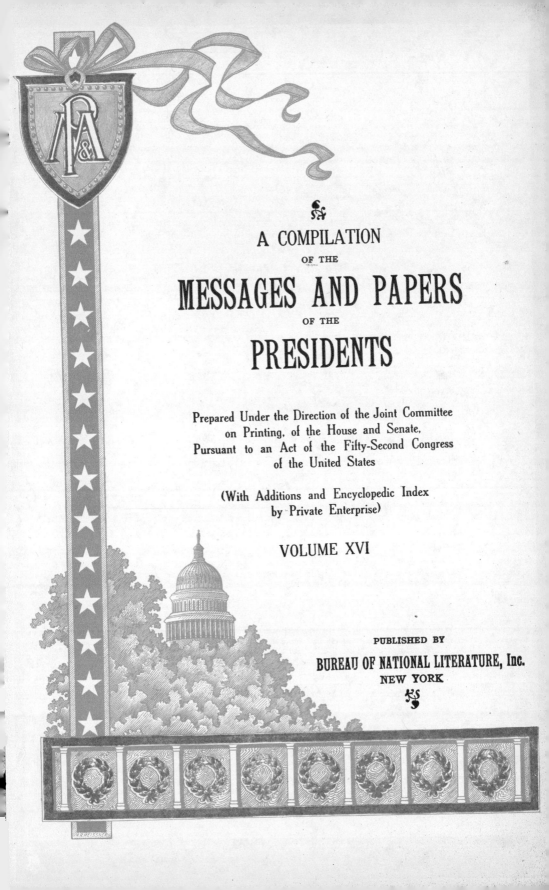

A COMPILATION

OF THE

MESSAGES AND PAPERS

OF THE

PRESIDENTS

Prepared Under the Direction of the Joint Committee
on Printing, of the House and Senate,
Pursuant to an Act of the Fifty-Second Congress
of the United States

(With Additions and Encyclopedic Index
by Private Enterprise)

VOLUME XVI

PUBLISHED BY

BUREAU OF NATIONAL LITERATURE, Inc.
NEW YORK

ILLUSTRATIONS IN VOLUME SIXTEEN

Again, on February 4, 1881, a select committee of the Senate recommended the passage of a similar bill, and made a report, in which, while approving the separation of the three branches, the executive, legislative, and judicial, they point out as a reason for the proposed change that, although having a separate existence, the branches are " to cooperate, each with the other, as the different members of the human body must cooperate, with each other in order to form the figure and perform the duties of a perfect man."

The report concluded as follows:

This system will require the selection of the strongest men to be heads of departments and will require them to be well equipped with the knowledge of their offices. It will also require the strongest men to be the leaders of Congress and participate in debate. It will bring these strong men in contact, perhaps into conflict, to advance the public weal, and thus stimulate their abilities and their efforts, and will thus assuredly result to the good of the country.

If it should appear by actual experience that the heads of departments in fact have not time to perform the additional duty imposed on them by this bill, the force in their offices should be increased or the duties devolving on them personally should be diminished. An undersecretary should be appointed to whom could be confided that routine of administration which requires only order and accuracy. The principal officers could then confine their attention to those duties which require wise discretion and intellectual activity. Thus they would have abundance of time for their duties under this bill. Indeed, your committee believes that the public interest would be subserved if the Secretaries were relieved of the harassing cares of distributing clerkships and closely supervising the mere machinery of the departments. Your committee believes that the adoption of this bill and the effective execution of its provisions will be the first step toward a sound civil-service reform which will secure a larger wisdom in the adoption of policies and a better system in their execution.

(Signed)   GEO. H. PENDLETON.
W. B. ALLISON.
D. W. VOORHEES.
J. G. BLAINE.
M. C. BUTLER.
JOHN J. INGALLS.
O. H. PLATT.
J. T. FARLEY.

It would be difficult to mention the names of higher authority in the practical knowledge of our Government than those which are appended to this report.

POSTAL SAVINGS BANK SYSTEM

The Postal Savings Bank System has been extended so that it now includes 4,004 fourth-class post offices, as well as 645 branch offices and stations in the larger cities. There are now 12,812 depositories at which patrons of the system may open accounts. The number of depositors is 300,000 and the amount of their deposits is approximately $28,000,000, not including $1,314,140 which has been withdrawn by depositors for the purpose of buying postal savings bonds. Experience demonstrates the value of dispensing with the pass-book and introducing in its place a certificate of deposit. The gross income of the postal savings system for the fiscal year ending June 30, 1913, will amount to $700,000 and the interest payable to depositors to $300,000. The cost of supplies, equipment, and salaries is $700,000. It thus appears that the system lacks $300,000 a year of paying interest and expenses. It is estimated, however, that when the deposits have reached the sum of $50,000,000, which at the present rate they soon will do, the system will be self-sustaining. By law the postal savings funds deposited at each post office are required to be redeposited in local banks. State and national banks to the number of 7,357 have qualified as depositories for these funds. Such deposits are secured by bonds aggregating $54,000,000. Of this amount, $37,000,000 represent municipal bonds.

PARCEL POST

In several messages I have favored and recommended the adoption of a system of parcel post. In the postal appropriation act of last year a general system was provided and its installation was directed by the 1st of January. This has entailed upon the Post Office Department a great deal of very heavy labor, but the Postmaster General informs me that on the date selected, to wit, the 1st of January, near at hand, the department will be in readiness to meet successfully the requirements of the public.

CLASSIFICATION OF POSTMASTERS

A trial, during the past three years, of the system of classifying fourth-class postmasters in that part of the country lying between the Mississippi River on the west, Canada on the north, the Atlantic Ocean on the east, and Mason and Dixon's line on the south has been sufficiently satisfactory to justify the postal authorities in recommending the extension of the order to include all the fourth-class postmasters in the country. In September, 1912, upon the suggestion of the Postmaster General, I directed him to prepare an order which should put the system in effect, except in Alaska, Guam, Hawaii, Porto Rico, and Samoa. Under date of October 15 I issued such an order which affected 36,000 postmasters. By the order the post offices were divided into groups A and B. Group A includes all postmasters whose compensation is $500 or more, and group B those whose compensation is less than that sum. Different methods are pursued in the selection of the postmasters for group A and group B. Criticism has been made of this order on the ground that the motive for it was political. Nothing could be further from the truth.

The order was made before the election and in the interest of efficient public service. I have several times requested Congress to give me authority to put first-, second-, and third-class postmasters, and all other local officers, including internal-revenue officers, customs officers, United States marshals, and the local agents of the other departments under the classification of the civil-service law by taking away the necessity for confirming such appointments by the Senate. I deeply regret the failure of Congress to follow these recommendations. The change would have taken out of politics practically every local officer and would have entirely cured the evils growing out of what under the present law must always remain a remnant of the spoils system.

COMPENSATION TO RAILWAYS FOR CARRYING MAILS

It is expected that the establishment of a parcel post on January 1st will largely increase the amount of mail matter to be transported by the railways, and Congress should be prompt to provide a way by which they may receive the additional compensation to which they will be entitled. The Postmaster General urges that the department's plan for a complete readjustment of the system of paying the railways for carrying the mails be adopted, substituting space for weight as the principal factor in fixing compensation. Under this plan it will be possible to determine without delay what additional payment should be made on account of the parcel post. The Postmaster General's recommendation is based on the results of a far-reaching investigation begun early in the administration with the object of determining what it costs the railways to carry the mails. The statistics obtained during the course of the inquiry show that while many of the railways, and particularly the large systems, were making profits from mail transportations, certain of the lines were actually carrying the mails at a loss. As a result of the investigation the department, after giving the subject careful consideration, decided to urge the abandonment of the present plan of fixing compensation on the basis of the weight of the mails carried, a plan that has proved to be exceedingly expensive and in other respects unsatisfactory. Under the method proposed the railway companies will annually submit to the department reports showing what it costs them to carry the mails, and this cost will be apportioned on the basis of the car space engaged, payment to be allowed at the rate thus determined in amounts that will cover the cost and a reasonable profit. If a railway is not satisfied with the manner in which the department apportions the cost in fixing compensation, it is to have the right, under the new plan, of appealing to the Interstate Commerce Commission. This feature of the proposed law would seem to insure a fair treatment of the railways. It is hoped that Congress will give the matter immediate attention and that the method of compensation recommended by the department or some other suitable plan will be promptly authorized.

DEPARTMENT OF THE INTERIOR

The Interior Department, in the problems of administration included within its jurisdiction, presents more difficult questions than any other. This has been due perhaps to temporary causes of a political character, but more especially to the inherent difficulty in the performance of some of the functions which are assigned to it. Its chief duty is the guardianship of the public domain and the disposition of that domain to private ownership under homestead, mining, and other laws, by which patents from the Government to the individual are authorized on certain conditions. During the last decade the public seemed to become suddenly aware that a very large part of its domain had passed from its control into private ownership, under laws not well adapted to modern conditions, and also that in the doing of this the provisions of existing law and regulations adopted in accordance with law had not been strictly observed, and that in the transfer of title much fraud had intervened, to the pecuniary benefit of dishonest persons. There arose thereupon a demand for conservation of the public domain, its protection against fraudulent diminution, and the preservation of that part of it from private acquisition which it seemed necessary to keep for future public use. The movement, excellent in the intention which prompted it, and useful in its results, has nevertheless had some bad effects, which the western country has recently been feeling and in respect of which there is danger of a reaction toward older abuses unless we can attain the golden mean, which consists in the prevention of the mere exploitation of the public domain for private purposes while at the same time facilitating its development for the benefit of the local public.

The land laws need complete revision to secure proper conservation on the one hand of land that ought to be kept in public use and, on the other hand, prompt disposition of those lands which ought to be disposed in private ownership or turned over to private use by properly guarded leases. In addition to this there are not enough officials in our Land Department with legal knowledge sufficient promptly to make the decisions which are called for. The whole land-laws system should be reorganized, and not until it is reorganized, will decisions be made as promptly as they ought, or will men who have earned title to public land under the statute receive their patents within a reasonably short period. The present administration has done what it could in this regard, but the necessity for reform and change by a revision of the laws and an increase and reorganization of the force remains, and I submit to Congress the wisdom of a full examination of this subject, in order that a very large and important part of our people in the West may be relieved from a just cause of irritation.

I invite your attention to the discussion by the Secretary of the Interior of the need for legislation with respect to mining claims, leases of coal lands in this country and in Alaska, and for similar disposition of oil, phosphate, and potash lands, and also to his discussion of the proper use to be made of water-power sites held by the Government. Many of these lands are now being withheld from use by the public under the general withdrawal act which was passed by the last Congress. That act was not for the purpose of disposing of the question, but it was for the purpose of preserving the lands until the question could be solved. I earnestly urge that the matter is of the highest importance to our western fellow citizens and ought to command the immediate attention of the legislative branch of the Government.

Another function which the Interior Department has to perform is that of the guardianship of Indians. In spite of everything which has been said in criticism of the policy of our Government toward the Indians, the amount of wealth which is now held by it for these wards per capita shows that the Government has been generous; but the management of so large an estate, with the great variety of circumstances that surround each tribe and each case, calls for the exercise of the highest business discretion, and the machinery provided in the Indian Bureau for the discharge of this function is entirely inadequate. The position of Indian commissioner demands the exercise of business ability of the first order, and it is difficult to secure such talent for the salary provided.

The condition of health of the Indian and the prevalence in the tribes of curable diseases has been exploited recently in the press. In a message to Congress at its last session I brought this subject to its attention and invited a special appropriation, in order that our facilities for overcoming diseases among the Indians might be properly increased, but no action was then taken by Congress on the subject, nor has such appropriation been made since.

The commission appointed by authority of the Congress to report on proper method of securing railroad development in Alaska is formulating its report, and I expect to have an opportunity before the end of this session to submit its recommendations.

DEPARTMENT OF AGRICULTURE

The far-reaching utility of the educational system carried on by the Department of Agriculture for the benefit of the farmers of our country calls for no elaboration. Each year there is a growth in the variety of facts which it brings out for the benefit of the farmer, and each year confirms the wisdom of the expenditure of the appropriations made for that department.

PURE-FOOD LAW

The Department of Agriculture is charged with the execution of the pure-food law. The passage of this encountered much opposition from manufacturers and others who feared the effect upon their business of the enforcement of its provisions. The opposition aroused the just indignation of the public, and led to an intense sympathy with the severe and rigid enforcement of the provisions of the new law. It had to deal in many instances with the question whether or not products of large business enterprises, in the form of food preparations, were deleterious to the public health; and while in a great majority of instances this issue was easily determinable, there were not a few cases in which it was hard to draw the line between a useful and a harmful food preparation. In cases like this when a decision involved the destruction of great business enterprises representing the investment of large capital and the expenditure of great energy and ability, the danger of serious injustice was very considerable in the enforcement of a new law under the spur of great public indignation. The public officials charged with executing the law might do injustice in heated controversy through unconscious pride of opinion and obstinacy of conclusion. For this reason President Roosevelt felt justified in creating a board of experts, known as the Remsen Board, to whom in cases of much importance an appeal might be taken and a review had of a decision of the Bureau of Chemistry in the Agricultural Department. I heartily agree that it was wise to create this board in order that injustice might not be done. The questions which arise are not generally those involving palpable injury to health, but they are upon the narrow and doubtful line in respect of which it is better to be in some error not dangerous than to be radically destructive. I think that the time has come for Congress to recognize the necessity for some such tribunal of appeal and to make specific statutory provision for it. While we are struggling to suppress an evil of great proportions like that of impure food, we must provide machinery in the law itself to prevent its becoming an instrument of oppression, and we ought to enable those whose business is threatened with annihilation to have some tribunal and some form of appeal in which they have a complete day in court.

AGRICULTURAL CREDITS

I referred in my first message to the question of improving the system of agricultural credits. The Secretary of Agriculture has made an investigation into the matter of credits in this country, and I commend a consideration of the information which through his agents he has been able to collect. It does not in any way minimize the importance of the proposal, but it gives more accurate information upon some of the phases of the question than we have heretofore had.

DEPARTMENT OF COMMERCE AND LABOR

I commend to Congress an examination of the report of the Secretary of Commerce and Labor, and especially that part in which he discusses the office of the Bureau of Corporations, the value to commerce of a proposed trade commission, and the steps which he has taken to secure the organization of a national chamber of commerce. I heartily commend his view that the plan of a trade commission which looks to the fixing of prices is altogether impractical and ought not for a moment to be considered as a possible solution of the trust question.

The trust question in the enforcement of the Sherman antitrust law is gradually solving itself, is maintaining the principle and restoring the practice of competition, and if the law is quietly but firmly enforced, business will adjust itself to the statutory requirements, and the unrest in commercial circles provoked by the trust discussion will disappear.

PANAMA-PACIFIC INTERNATIONAL EXPOSITION

In conformity with a joint resolution of Congress, an Executive proclamation was issued last February, inviting the nations of the world to participate in the Panama-Pacific International Exposition to be held at San Francisco to celebrate the construction of the Panama Canal. A sympathetic response was immediately forthcoming, and several nations have already selected the sites for their buildings. In furtherance of my invitation, a special commission visited European countries during the past summer, and received assurance of hearty cooperation in the task of bringing together a universal industrial, military, and naval display on an unprecedented scale. It is evident that the exposition will be an accurate mirror of the world's activities as they appear 400 years after the date of the discovery of the Pacific Ocean.

It is the duty of the United States to make the nations welcome at San Francisco and to facilitate such acquaintance between them and ourselves as will promote the expansion of commerce and familiarize the world with the new trade route through the Panama Canal. The action of the State governments and individuals assures a comprehensive exhibit of the resources of this country and of the progress of the people. This participation by State and individuals should be supplemented by an adequate showing of the varied and unique activities of the National Government. The United States can not with good grace invite foreign governments to erect buildings and make expensive exhibits while itself refusing to participate. Nor would it be wise to forego the opportunity to join with other nations in the inspiring interchange of ideas tending to promote intercourse, friendship, and commerce. It is the duty of the Government to foster and build up commerce through the canal, just as it was the duty of the Government to construct it.

I earnestly recommend the appropriation at this session of such a sum as will enable the United States to construct a suitable building, install a governmental exhibit, and otherwise participate in the Panama-Pacific International Exposition in a manner commensurate with the dignity of a nation whose guests are to be the people of the world. I recommend also such legislation as will facilitate the entry of material intended for exhibition and protect foreign exhibitors against infringement of patents and the unauthorized copying of patterns and designs. All aliens sent to San Francisco to construct and care for foreign buildings and exhibits should be admitted without restraint or embarrassment.

THE DISTRICT OF COLUMBIA AND THE CITY OF WASHINGTON

The city of Washington is a beautiful city, with a population of 352,936, of whom 98,667 are colored. The annual municipal budget is about $14,000,000. The presence of the National Capital and other governmental structures constitutes the chief beauty and interest of the city. The public grounds are extensive, and the opportunities for improving the city and making it still more attractive are very great. Under a plan adopted some years ago, one half the cost of running the city is paid by taxation upon the property, real and personal, of the citizens and residents, and the other half is borne by the General Government. The city is expanding at a remarkable rate, and this can only be accounted for by the coming here from other parts of the country of well-to-do people who, having finished their business careers elsewhere, build and make this their permanent place of residence.

On the whole, the city as a municipality is very well governed. It is well lighted, the water supply is good, the streets are well paved, the police force is well disciplined, crime is not flagrant, and while it has purlieus and centers of vice, like other large cities, they are not exploited, they do not exercise any influence or control in the government of the city, and they are suppressed in as far as it has been found practicable. Municipal graft is inconsiderable. There are interior courts in the city that are noisome and centers of disease and the refuge of criminals, but Congress has begun to clean these out, and progress has been made in the case of the most notorious of these, which is known as " Willow Tree Alley." This movement should continue.

The mortality for the past year was at the rate of 17.80 per 1,000 of both races; among the whites it was 14.61 per thousand, and among the blacks 26.12 per thousand. These are the lowest mortality rates ever recorded in the District.

One of the most crying needs in the government of the District is a tribunal or public authority for the purpose of supervising the corporations engaged in the operation of public utilities. Such a bill is pending in Congress and ought to pass. Washington should show itself under the direction of Congress to be a city with a model form of government, but as long as such authority over public utilities is withheld from the municipal government, it must always be defective.

Without undue criticism of the present street railway accommodations, it can be truly said that under the spur of a public utilities commission they might be substantially improved.

While the school system of Washington perhaps might be bettered in the economy of its management and the distribution of its buildings, its usefulness has nevertheless greatly increased in recent years, and it now offers excellent facilities for primary and secondary education.

From time to time there is considerable agitation in Washington in favor of granting the citizens of the city the franchise and constituting an elective government. I am strongly opposed to this change. The history of Washington discloses a number of experiments of this kind, which have always been abandoned as unsatisfactory. The truth is this is a city governed by a popular body, to wit, the Congress of the United States, selected from the people of the United States, who own Washington. The people who come here to live do so with the knowledge of the origin of the city and the restrictions, and therefore voluntarily give up the privilege of living in a municipality governed by popular vote. Washington is so unique in its origin and in its use for housing and localizing the sovereignty of the Nation that the people who live here must regard its peculiar character and must be content to subject themselves to the control of a body selected by all the people of the Nation. I agree that there are certain inconveniences growing out of the government of a city by a national legislature like Congress, and it would perhaps be possible to lessen these by the delegation by Congress to the District Commissioners of greater legislative power for the enactment of local laws than they now possess, especially those of a police character.

Every loyal American has a personal pride in the beauty of Washington and in its development and growth. There is no one with a proper appreciation of our Capital City who would favor a niggardly policy in respect to expenditures from the National Treasury to add to the attractiveness of this city, which belongs to every citizen of the entire country, and which no citizen visits without a sense of pride of ownership. We have had restored by a Commission of Fine Arts, at the instance of a committee of the Senate, the original plan of the French engineer L'Enfant for the city of Washington, and we know with great certainty the course which the improvement of Washington should take. Why should there be delay in making this improvement in so far as it involves the extension of the parking system and the construction of greatly needed public buildings? Appropriate buildings for the State Department, the Department of Justice, and the Department of Commerce and Labor have been projected, plans have been approved, and nothing is wanting but the appropriations for the beginning and completion of the structures. A hall of archives is also badly needed, but nothing has been done toward its construction, although the land for it has long been bought and paid for. Plans have been made for the union of Potomac Park with the valley of Rock Creek and Rock Creek Park, and the necessity for the connection between the Soldiers' Home and Rock Creek Park calls for no comment. I ask again why there should be delay in carrying out these plans. We have the money in the Treasury, the plans are national in their scope, and the improvement should be treated as a national project. The plan will find a hearty approval throughout the country. I am quite sure, from the information which I have, that, at comparatively small expense, from that part of the District of Columbia which was retroceded to Virginia, the portion including the Arlington estate, Fort Myer, and the palisades of the Potomac can be acquired by purchase and the jurisdiction of the State of Virginia over this land ceded to the Nation. This ought to be done.

The construction of the Lincoln Memorial and of a memorial bridge from the base of the Lincoln Monument to Arlington would be an appropriate and symbolic expression of the union of the North and the South at the Capital of the Nation. I urge upon Congress the appointment of a commission to undertake these national improvements, and to submit a plan for their execution; and when the plan has been submitted and approved, and the work carried out, Washington will really become what it ought to be—the most beautiful city in the world.

WM. H. TAFT.

SPECIAL MESSAGE.

[On Fur Seals.]

THE WHITE HOUSE, *January 8, 1913.*

To the Senate and House of Representatives:

At the last session of Congress an act was adopted to give effect to the fur-seal treaty of July 7, 1911, between Great Britain, Japan, Russia, and the United States, in which act was incorporated a provision establishing a five-year period during which the killing of seals upon the Pribilof Islands is prohibited. Prior to the passage of this act, I pointed out in my message to Congress, on August 14 last, the inadvisability of adopting legislation the effect of which was to require this Government to suspend the killing of surplus male seals on land before it was actually proved by the test of experience and scientific investigation that such suspension of killing was necessary for the protection and preservation of the seal herd. I also pointed out in that message that the other Governments interested might justly complain if this Government by prohibiting all land killing should deprive them of their expected share of the skins taken on land, unless we can show by satisfactory evidence that this course was adopted as the result of changed conditions justifying a change in our previous attitude on the subject. As was then anticipated, the other parties interested have now objected to the suspension thus imposed on the ground that it is contrary to the spirit, if not the letter, of the treaty, inasmuch as under existing conditions a substantial number of male seals not required for breeding purposes can be killed annually without detriment to the reproductive capacity of the herd. The same objection was raised by the other Governments interested under this convention while the bill was awaiting my signature, after its passage by Congress, but I refrained from vetoing it because at that time several thousand sealskins had already been taken on the islands and were ready for distribution in accordance with the requirements of the treaty, so that the suspension of land killing would not actually become effective until the following year, and I was satisfied that the information resulting from a study of the condition of the herd during the past summer would put this Government in possession of facts which would either lead to the amendment of the act at this session of Congress, or enable this Government to justify a temporary suspension of land killing; and apart from this particular provision, the act was needed to give effect to our treaty obligations.

It now appears that under the operation of the fur-seal convention during the past year the condition and size of the herd has improved to an extent which seems to indicate that there is now no necessity, and therefore no justification, for the suspension of all land killing of male seals, as required by the act under consideration.

Last season's reports from the officials in charge on the Pribilof Islands show that the herd which the year before contained at the highest estimate not more than 140,000 seals, now numbers upward of 215,000 by actual count, showing in one season an increase of at least 75,000 seals. This increase is largely due to the protection afforded by the treaty to the breeding female seals, which last summer numbered nearly 82,000, many thousands of which, except for the treaty, would have been slaughtered by pelagic sealers, and as every breeding female adds one pup to the herd each year, over 81,000 new pups were added last season. Moreover, instead of losing 10,000 or 15,000 of these pups through starvation as heretofore on account of the slaughter of the nursing mothers by pelagic sealers, this summer by actual count the number of dead pups found on the rookeries was only 1,060.

It is evident from these reports that there has been a very remarkable increase in the size of the herd in one season under the operation of this convention and that a large part of this increase consists of female seals, upon which the future increase of the herd depends.

The present condition of the herd shows that there will be about 100,000 breeding female seals in the herd next summer, each one of which will produce one pup, and in the following year the female pups born last summer, amounting in accordance with the laws of nature to one-half of the total number of the year's pups, will pass into the breeding class, subject to losses from natural mortality, thus adding a possible 40,000 more, which would bring the total up in the neighborhood of 140,000 breeding female seals; and so on from year to year the reproductive strength of the herd will increase in almost geometrical progression, so that we can confidently count on having the present size of the herd doubled and trebled within a very short period.

All that is required to fulfill these expectations is to protect absolutely the female seals and set aside an adequate number of male seals for breeding purposes. The protection and preservation of the herd does not require the protection and preservation of the surplus male seals not needed for breeding purposes. Owing to the polygamous habits of the seals, the increase in the number of these surplus bachelor seals can in no conceivable way increase the birth rate or the reproductive capacity of the herd. Seals of this class contribute nothing to the welfare of the herd, and in some ways they are a distinct detriment as a disturbing element on the rookeries and as consumers of food, which is bound to become scarcer as the size of the herd increases. These nonbreeding males, therefore, are of no value as members of the herd except to furnish skins for the market in place of those heretofore taken by pelagic sealers, and in this connection it should be noted that the value of their skins for commercial purposes diminishes after they are 4 years old and ceases altogether after the age of 5 or 6.

It is right and necessary that the killing of all seals in the herd other than the nonbreeding males should be absolutely prohibited not only for five years but forever. Land killing has been and always must be strictly limited by law to male seals, so that female seals would never be included in land killing in any event. Pelagic sealing, on the other hand, always has been chiefly directed against female seals, thus diminishing the size of the herd not merely by the number actually killed each year but also by an equal number of nursing pups killed by starvation and by the loss of the countless number of unborn pups which would have been added to the herd the following year and in succeeding years. Pelagic sealing has now been stopped, but it must be remembered that the United States alone was powerless to stop it. An international agreement was necessary for that purpose, and has at last been secured after difficult and protracted negotiations resulting in the present convention with Great Britain, Japan, and Russia, who have now joined with us in prohibiting pelagic sealing, and whose cooperation is necessary to make that prohibition effective. To secure such an agreement has been the aim of the United States throughout the entire period covered by the fur-seal controversy, and from the point of view of the United States this prohibition against pelagic sealing is the most important feature of the present convention. In order, however, to secure its adoption by Great Britain and Japan it was necessary for the United States to agree to give each of them a share of the proceeds of the annual increase of the American herd with the assurance, as an inducement, that a large annual increase available for commercial purposes would result from the abandonment of pelagic sealing. As stated in my former message to Congress on this subject—

" Ever since the question of land killing of seals was subjected to scientific investigation, soon after the fur-seal controversy arose, nearly 25 years ago, this Government has invariably insisted throughout the protracted and almost continuous diplomatic negotiations which have ensued for the settlement of this controversy that the progressive diminution of the herd was due to the killing of seals at sea, and that if pelagic sealing was discontinued the polygamous habits of the seals would make it possible to kill annually on land a large number of surplus males without detriment to the reproductive capacity of the herd and without interfering with the normal growth of the size of the herd. The position thus taken by the United States has always been put forward and relied on by the United States in urging that an international agreement should be entered into prohibiting pelagic sealing; and it is obvious that one of the considerations which induced Great Britain and Japan to enter into this convention prohibiting their subjects from pelagic sealing was the expectation that the position thus taken by the United States was well founded and that the skins falling to the share of those Governments from the land killing of seals, as provided for in this convention, would compensate them for abandoning the taking of sealskins at sea."

It was well understood by all the parties in entering into this convention that the result aimed at was to increase the annual reproductive capacity of the herd so that a larger number of sealskins might be taken each year for commercial purposes without injury to the welfare of the herd.

It is evident from these considerations that the United States is in honor bound under this convention to permit the killing annually for commercial purposes of male seals not required as a reserve for breeding before they have passed beyond the age when their skins cease to have a commercial value.

The question of how many male seals should be reserved each year for breeding purposes can readily be determined. In the act under consideration, as it passed the House and before it was amended in the Senate, there was a provision that hereafter only 3-year-old males shall be killed, and that there shall be reserved from among the finest and most perfect seals of that age not fewer than 2,000 in 1913, 2,500 in 1914, 3,000 in 1915, 3,500 in 1916, and 4,000 each year from 1917 to 1921, inclusive, and 5,000 each year thereafter during the continuance of the convention. These figures were arrived at after full and careful investigation by the House Committee on Foreign Affairs and it appears from the committee reports accompanying this act that these figures were intended to be and were regarded as large enough to be on the safe side. It would be more appropriate and convenient to leave the decision of this question to the Secretary of Commerce and Labor, subject to the limitation, which might properly be imposed, that each year before any commercial killing is done there should be marked and set aside or reserved from among the finest and best of the males of 3 years of age such number as is necessary, in his judgment, to provide an ample breeding reserve of males. In any event it is evident that the determination of the number of male seals to be reserved each year for this purpose will present no difficulty; and in this connection it should be noted, as stated in my former message on this subject, that—

" since the fur-seal business has been taken over by the Government and no private interests are now concerned in making a profit out of it, there is no urgent necessity for imposing by legislation stringent limitations upon land killing."

The only provision in the convention authorizing the United States to limit or suspend land killing is the reservation in Article X that nothing therein contained shall restrict the right of the United States at any time and from time to time to suspend altogether the taking of sealskins on its islands and to impose such restrictions and regulations upon the total number of skins to be taken in any season, and the manner and times and places of taking them, " as may be necessary to protect and preserve the seal herd or increase its number." It is clear from the terms of the convention that the right thus reserved to the United States to regulate or suspend land killing is not an arbitrary right, but can be exercised only when necessary to protect or preserve or increase the herd. It is also clear that this provision must be read in connection with the main purpose of the convention, and that the right reserved should be exercised in aid of that purpose. It has already been shown that the result aimed at by this convention was to increase the annual reproductive capacity of the herd, so that a larger number of sealskins might be taken each year for commercial purposes without injury to the welfare of the herd. It follows, therefore, that when a limitation or suspension of land killing would interfere with, rather than promote, this purpose of the convention there would then be not only no necessity but no justification for such limitation or suspension.

The argument has been advanced that in addition to the right thus reserved the convention recognized an absolute right in the United States arbitrarily to suspend all land killing, because, according to this argument, another clause of the convention fixes a measure of damages to be paid each year to the other parties whenever the United States prohibits all land killing. The clause referred to is found in Article XI, which provides that in case the United States shall absolutely prohibit all land killing of seals, then it shall pay to Great Britain and Japan each the sum of $10,000 annually in lieu of their share of skins during the years when no killing is allowed. It is evident, however, from an examination of the other provisions of the same clause of the convention that these $10,000 payments can not be, and were not intended to be, regarded as a measure of damages, because Great Britain and Japan are required to repay them to the United States with interest at 4 per cent out of the proceeds of their share of the skins taken whenever land killing is resumed. A payment which is subsequently to be refunded clearly is not a measure of damages. Moreover, even if this provision could be regarded as fixing a measure of damages, that in itself would not justify the United States in arbitrarily imposing those damages upon Great Britain and Japan. These provisions requiring the $10,000 payments to be made when land killing is suspended and to be refunded when killing is resumed clearly have an ulterior purpose; otherwise they are wholly unnecessary, for the same result would have been accomplished with much greater simplicity by omitting them altogether. The ulterior purpose becomes perfectly clear when we consider that under the laws in force when the treaty was made it was within the power of the Secretary of Commerce and Labor to suspend land killing altogether whenever in his opinion the welfare of the herd required such action. The evident purpose, therefore, of this requirement for making substantial payments when land killing was suspended, was to prevent the suspension of land killing by executive action unless Congress was prepared to appropriate the money necessary for making such payments. It was undoubtedly assumed that the necessity for adopting legislation appropriating the money to make these payments would lead to a careful investigation of whether or not the actual condition of the herd warranted a total suspension of land killing, and that the appropriation would not be made unless the investigation produced satisfactory evidence that such suspension of killing was absolutely necessary within the requirements of the treaty.

In view of the present condition of the herd and the very marked increase in its size and particularly in the number of female seals, which has resulted from the operation of this convention during a single year, and which, as above shown, is to be attributed almost wholly to the protection afforded by the prohibition against pelagic sealing, I recommend to Congress the immediate consideration of whether or not the complete suspension of land killing imposed by this act is now necessary for the protection and preservation of the herd, and for increasing its number within the meaning and for the purposes of the convention. If no actual necessity is found for such suspension then it is not justified under the convention, and the act should be amended accordingly.

As stated in my annual message to Congress in December last, it is important that in case there is any uncertainty as to the real necessity for suspending all land killing, this Government should yield on that point rather than give the slightest ground for the charge that we have been in any way remiss in observing our treaty obligations. I also wish to impress upon Congress that, as stated in my former message on this subject, it is essential in dealing with it not only to fulfill the obligations imposed upon the United States by the letter and the spirit of the convention, but also to consider the interests of the other parties to the convention, for their cooperation is necessary to make it an effective and permanent settlement of the fur-seal controversy.

WM. H. TAFT.

SPECIAL MESSAGE

[Transmitting Reports of the Commission on Economy and Efficiency.]

THE WHITE HOUSE, *January 8, 1913.*

To the Senate and House of Representatives:

I submit for the information of Congress the report of the commission appointed by me to carry on the work authorized under act of appropriation of June 25, 1910, which made available $100,000—

To enable the President, by the employment of accountants and experts * * * to more effectively inquire into the methods of transacting the public business * * * with a view of inaugurating new or changing old methods * * * so as to attain greater efficiency and economy therein, and to ascertain and recommend to Congress what changes in law may be necessary to carry into effect such results of his inquiry as can not be carried into effect by Executive action alone.

Pursuant to this authority a preliminary investigation was instituted under the Secretary to the President with a view to determining what ground should be covered and what staff and organization would be required. This preliminary inquiry was carried on until March, 1911, when, at my request, the term of the appropriation was extended to June 30, 1912, and $75,000 was added.

Of this $175,000 made available for the first two years the amount expended for the preliminary inquiry was $12,252.14, leaving $162,-747.86 available for the 15 months remaining after March 8, 1911, when the commission was organized. By special message of January 17, 1912, I requested that $250,000 be made available for the current fiscal year. Only $75,000, however, was appropriated, and to this was attached a restriction to the effect that not more than three salaries could be paid in excess of $4,000 per annum, thereby forcing a complete reorganization of the commission. At the same time the Congress by special resolution requested a report from the commission with recommendations on the organization and work of the Patent Office—this to be submitted to Congress not later than December 10, or a little over three months after the resolution was passed. Although $10,000 additional was appropriated for this purpose, it was impossible within the time to organize a special staff which could do such a highly technical piece of work. A further limitation to constructive work has been found in the short period for which funds have been made available. Many of the problems of administration which should be gone into require months of constant attention. The commission has not felt free to undertake work which could not be reported on before the expiration of the appropriation, and the appropriation for the current fiscal year was not passed until August 24, the authority expiring June 30 following. I mention these facts to indicate some of the handicaps under which the commission has labored in prosecuting one of the most difficult, far-reaching, technical inquiries that has ever been undertaken, and one from which economies have already been realized many times greater than the cost.

In planning the work to be done by the commission the first controlling fact was that there was no basis in information for judgment as to what changes should be made or what would be the effect of any recommended change, no matter how simple it might at first appear. As was stated in my message of January 17, 1912, on the subject:

This vast organization has never been studied in detail as one piece of administrative mechanism. Never have the foundations been laid for a thorough consideration of the relations of all of its parts. No comprehensive effort has been made to list its multifarious activities or to group them in such a way as to present a clear picture of what the Government is doing. Never has a complete description been given of the agencies through which these activities are performed. At no time has the attempt been made to study all of these activities and agencies with a view to the assignment of each activity to the agency best fitted for its performance, to the avoidance of duplication of plant and work, to the integration of all administrative agencies of the Government, so far as may be practicable, into a unified organization for the most effective and economical dispatch of public business.

The only safe course, therefore, was first to obtain accurate knowledge of the vast administrative mechanism of the Government; get a clear notion of what the officers and agents of the Government were doing in all of its departments, bureaus, and subdivisions; find out how each part of the service was organized for performing its activities, what methods are being employed, what results are being obtained, where there are duplications of work and plant, wherein the organization and methods are ill adapted or ill adjusted.

In each case, as first drafts of descriptive reports have been completed by the commission, they first have been submitted to the services whose organization and work are involved, so that this part of the work has been a joint product of all services. This has been done for the double purpose of having a statement of fact that is beyond controversy, and to lay the foundation for the consideration of the critical comments and constructive suggestions that have followed.

To the present time 85 reports have been submitted which carry recommendations. Fifteen of these reports, most of which recommend constructive legislation, have already been sent to Congress, viz.:

1. Outlines of organization of the Government. Submitted January 17, 1912 (published as H. Doc. 458).

2. The centralization of the distribution of Government publications. Submitted February 5, 1912 (published in S. Doc. 293).

3. The use of window envelopes in the Government service. Submitted February 5, 1912 (published in S. Doc. 293).

4. The use of the photographic process for copying printed and written documents, maps, drawings, etc. Submitted February 5, 1912 (published in S. Doc. 293).

5. Methods of appointment. Submitted April 4, 1912 (published in H. Doc. 670).

6. The consolidation of the Bureau of Lighthouses of the Department of Commerce and Labor and the Life-Saving Service of the Department of the Treasury. Submitted April 4, 1912 (published in H. Doc. 670).

7. The Revenue-Cutter Service of the Department of the Treasury. Submitted April 4, 1912 (published in H. Doc. 670).

8. The accounting offices of the Treasury, with recommendations for the consolidation of the six auditors' offices into one. Submitted April 4, 1912 (published in H. Doc. 670).

9. The Returns Office of the Department of the Interior. Submitted April 4, 1912 (published in H. Doc. 670).

10. Travel expenditures. Submitted April 4, 1912 (published in H. Doc. 670).

11. Memorandum of conclusions concerning the principles which should govern the handling and filing of correspondence. Submitted April 4, 1912 (published in H. Doc. 670).

12. Supplementary report on the centralization of the distribution of Government publications. Submitted April 4, 1912 (published in H. Doc. 670).

13. The use of outlines of organization of the Government. Submitted April 4, 1912 (published in H. Doc. 670).

14. Report on the retirement of superannuated employees. Submitted May 6, 1912 (published as H. Doc. 732).

15. Report on "The Need for a National Budget." Submitted June 27, 1912 (published as H. Doc. 854).

The reports of the commission already submitted which call for Executive action relate to a variety of subjects. Included in these reports are recommendations: For the modification of orders and practices related to the administration of the civil-service law; the installation of a uniform system of accounting and reporting; forms and instructions for the preparation and submission of a budget; the use of window envelopes; the introduction of labor-saving office devices; more economical Government housing; better lighting, heating, ventilation, and sanitation; the better utilization of waste; the more economical disposition of obsolete and condemned stores and other property; the discontinuance of the jurat in the preparation of claims for reimbursement; the promulgation of rules governing travel expenditures.

With respect to many of these, affirmative action has been taken, but in nearly every case it is necessary to proceed slowly with the making of changes, which have already been ordered, as it necessarily requires months to make any change which broadly affects the service without causing so much confusion as to seriously interfere with the transaction of Government business.

On December 9 I transmitted the report of the commission, with its recommendations, on the organization and work of the Patent Office. This report is printed as House Document No. 1110. I am transmitting herewith 11 other reports, the recommendations contained in which have my approval, as follows:

1. Business methods of the office of The Adjutant General of the War Department.
2. The handling and filing of correspondence in the Mail and Record Division of the office of the Chief of Engineers.
3. The handling and filing of correspondence and the doing of statistical work in the Bureau of Insular Affairs.
4. The handling and filing of correspondence in the office of the Surgeon General.
5. The handling and filing of correspondence in the office of the Signal Corps.
6. The handling and filing of correspondence in the office of the Chief of Ordnance.
7. The handling and filing of correspondence in the Mail and Record Division of the Department of Justice.
8. Methods of keeping efficiency records of employees in the National Bank Redemption Agency of the Department of the Treasury.
9. Report on the electric lighting of Federal buildings of the Department of the Treasury.
10. On the establishment of an independent public health service.
11. The recovery of fiber stock of canceled paper money.

The first six of these reports have been the result of intensive study of methods employed in the offices of the War Department at Washington, which point to detail reductions in cost which may affect the appropriations for 1914. These, together with the recommendations of the Secretary of War, are sent for your information. In the opinion of the commission, an estimated saving of over $400,000 a year can ultimately be made by favorable action on the changes in methods which are recommended in the six offices of the War Department alone.

One report above listed relates to the question of personnel. This is important both in its relation to efficiency of organization and economy of work. A number of other reports, containing recommendations for changes in the details of methods which, in the opinion of the commission, will produce marked savings in annual cost of transacting the business of the offices investigated are in the hands of the services interested. These will be sent for the information of the Congress as soon as action has been taken or other conclusion has been reached.

The report on electric lighting of public buildings is significant of the inattention to administrative details in a subdivision of the service which is charged with the operation and maintenance of several hundred Government buildings. Until this inquiry was begun no attempt had been made in this office to find out what was even the gross expenditures for operation as distinct from maintenance, or capital outlays, either for each building or for the whole service, and there were no means provided for knowing the heating, lighting, cleaning, or other costs as subdivisions of operation. The head of the office was presumably interested in construction; the primary responsibility of the department was for the care and custody of funds; the result was that no attention was given to the development of the information essential to the central direction and control over operative services. And it may be said that the condition found in this office is typical of the condition found in many of the operative services. The report covers only a partial inquiry into lighting efficiency.

The report submitted relative to the recovery of fiber stock of canceled paper money proposes that the method of macerating this stock which has been in use for about 40 years be discontinued and that more modern methods be adopted. Under modern methods of treating this paper stock it is deinked and defibered with but a small loss of pulp, and such stock when recovered can be used in the manufacture of new money paper, at a saving, as compared with the present method of macerating and sale, of about $100,000 per annum.

While during the time and with the staff available it has not been possible to make final detailed reports on more than a few of the hundreds of offices at Washington, and in only one office outside of Washington has work of this character been undertaken, the reports which are submitted will serve to illustrate the character of results which may follow an extensive investigation of office technique and procedure. It is further to be noted that the offices which have been reported on are those which have been frequently under scrutiny. From what is known of the offices outside of Washington it is thought that it is in this field that the largest opportunities for economy will be found—partly due to the fact that these offices have not been brought under scrutiny, and partly due to the fact that a large number of them are dominated by political appointees.

As illustrating the relative importance of services outside of Washington, it is of interest to note that the cost of clerk hire at the New York post office alone is more than that incurred in the Departments of War, Navy, State, Justice, and Commerce and Labor at Washington; that in the customhouse at New York the cost of clerk hire is greater than in any one department at Washington.

In my opinion the technique and procedure of every branch and office of the Government should be submitted to the same painstaking examination as has been given to those on which reports have been made. To do this, however, ample funds must be provided. As stated in previous messages to Congress on the subject, there is no greater service that can be rendered to the country than that of the continuance of the work of the commission until some form of organization is provided for continuously doing this kind of work under the Executive. I have asked, therefore, that $250,000 be provided for the continuation of the investigation which has been so well begun, and that these funds be made available March 4. In my opinion this is not a matter in which the Congress should assume that public money will be unwisely spent. At a total cost of about $230,000 during the 21 months covered by the work of the commission, facts have been developed and recommendations have been made that, if followed up, will result in savings of millions of dollars each year. This has been done under the handicap of inadequate funds and uncertainty of continuation, which interfered with the making of plans which could not be completely executed within a few months. It would be very much to the advantage of the administration if the President were authorized to spend whatever amount he may deem to be necessary within the next two years, the only condition attached being that he render an account of expenditures.

WM. H. TAFT.

[NOTE: Accompanying this message was the report of the commission's inquiries and work relating to the organization and personnel of the various executive departments of the government, as well as their functions and activities, including the budget, accounting and standardization of office equipment and service, both individual and by groups; inquiries and work relating to navigation, health, statistical cartographic and survey services and relating to the subject of a central accounting and auditing service; a complete report of the business methods of the Adjutant General's office; the handling and filing of correspondence and the doing of statistical work in the Mail and Record division of the office of the Chief of Engineers, the Bureau of Insular Affairs, the Signal Corps and Chief of Ordnance of the War Department, the Mail and Record division of the Department of Justice, and the methods of keeping efficiency records of employees in the National Bank Redemption Agency of the Treasury, and a report on the lighting of the buildings in the same department.

The commission recommended that a permanent central executive control be established to maintain uniform methods and to develop expertness and efficiency and to harmonize the relations between the bureaus and departments, to the end that duplication of work and conflicts of jurisdiction might be avoided and time saved.

Frederick A. Cleveland, Walter W. Warwick and Merritt O. Chance were the commissioners.]

SPECIAL MESSAGE.

[Transmitting certified copies of franchises granted by the Executive Council of Porto Rico.]

THE WHITE HOUSE, *January 9, 1913.*

To the Senate and House of Representatives:

As required by section 32 of the act of Congress approved April 12, 1900, entitled "An act temporarily to provide revenues and a civil government for Porto Rico, and for other purposes," I transmit herewith certified copies of franchises granted by the Executive Council of Porto Rico, which are described in the accompanying letter from the Secretary of War transmitting them to me. Such of these as relate to railroad, street railway, telegraph, and telephone franchises, privileges, or concessions have been approved by me, as required by the joint resolution of May 1, 1900 (31 Stat., 715).

WM. H. TAFT.

Following is the substance of the letter from the Secretary of War:

To the PRESIDENT: I have the honor to inclose herewith, for transmission to Congress, two certified copies of franchises granted by the Executive Council of Porto Rico, as follows: Granting to Thomas D. Mott, Jr., authority to construct, maintain, and operate a system for the manufacture, distribution, and sale of gas; approved by the Governor, July 30, 1912, and amended Oct. 23, 1912. Granting to the municipality of Fajardo permission to take 30 liters of water per second from the Fajardo River; approved July 30, 1912. Granting a revocable permit to Pavenstedt Land Co. to take and use for irrigation purposes 286 liters of water per second from the Tanama River; approved Aug. 10, 1912. Granting to the Porto Rico Railway, Light & Power Co. the right to reconstruct and widen its bridge over the San Antonio Channel and to extend its double track to a point approximately 234 feet west of Stop Eleven; approved Aug. 27, 1912. Granting to the Fajardo Development Co., a corporation organized under the laws of the State of Connecticut, the right to construct, maintain, and operate a railway between the towns of Mameyes, Luquillo, Fajardo, Ceiba, and Naguabo in the Island of Porto Rico; approved Aug. 27, 1912. Repealing an ordinance granting to the Robbins-Ripley Co. authority to construct, maintain, and operate a pier on the harbor shore of San Juan; approved Sept. 4, 1912. Granting a revocable permit to Francisco Antongiorgi to take and use for irrigation purposes 1½ liters of water per second from the Brook Cristales, municipality of Yauco; approved Oct. 12, 1912. Granting a revocable permit to the Porto Rico Railway, Light & Power Co. to take and use for industrial purposes 1 liter of water per second from the Hondo River, Bayamon; approved Oct. 23, 1912. Granting to Sosthenes Behn the right to construct, maintain, and operate a system of long-distance telephone lines between the towns of Carolina and Hormigueros and other intervening towns and cities, together with local telephone systems in certain of said towns and local stations at other points, and authorizing the Porto Rico General Telephone Co. to construct, maintain, and operate telephone systems in San Juan, Mayaguez, and the eastern end of the Island; approved Dec. 12, 1912.

Very respectfully,   HENRY L. STIMSON, *Secretary of War.*

SPECIAL MESSAGE.

[Transmitting report from the Secretary of State concerning claims of American citizens growing out of joint naval operations of the United States and Great Britain in and about the Town of Apia, in the Samoan Islands, March, April, and May, 1899.]

THE WHITE HOUSE, *Washington, January 10, 1913.*

To the Senate and the House of Representatives:

I transmit herewith a report by the Secretary of State of the action taken by him in pursuance of the act of Congress approved June 23, 1910, authorizing and directing him to ascertain the " amounts due, if any, respectively, to American citizens on claims heretofore filed in the Department of State, growing out of the joint naval operations of the United States and Great Britain in and about the town of Apia, in the Samoan Islands, in the months of March, April, and May, 1899, * * * and report the same to Congress."

Accompanying the report of the Secretary of State is the report of the officer who, pursuant to the Secretary's direction, visited the Samoan Islands for the purpose of collecting evidence regarding the claims mentioned. Of the total amount of American claims, of about $64,677.88, payment of $14,811.42 is recommended by the agent. This finding is approved by the Secretary of State, who submits for the consideration of Congress the question of an immediate appropriation for the payment of the claims recommended.

WM. H. TAFT.

Letter of submittal from the Secretary of War:

To the PRESIDENT: I have the honor to submit, with a view to its transmission to Congress, the accompanying report, together with copies of the evidence collected, relative to the action taken by this department in response to the act of Congress approved June 23, 1910, authorizing and directing me to ascertain the " amounts due, if any, respectively, to American citizens on claims heretofore filed in the Department of State, growing out of the joint naval operations of the United States and Great Britain in and about the town of Apia, in the Samoan Islands, in the months of March, April, and May, 1899, * * * and report the same to Congress." For carrying into effect this act there was appropriated in the diplomatic and consular appropriation act approved March 3, 1911, the sum of $750.

Pursuant to my instructions of April 15, 1911, Mr. Joseph R. Baker, of the solicitor's office of this department, visited the Samoan Islands during the summer of 1911 and remained there for about two months collecting evidence regarding the claims in question. Under date of Oct. 12, 1911, Mr. Baker submitted his report in the matter, including recommendations as to the amount properly payable, if any, on each of such respective claims. This report and the evidence in writing collected by Mr. Baker have been carefully considered by the department, and the conclusion has been reached that the amounts indicated by him are to be regarded as equitably due the various claimants.

By decision given at Stockholm Oct. 14, 1902, by His Majesty Oscar II, then King of Sweden and Norway, to whom the matter had been referred by the convention of Nov. 7, 1899, between the United States, Great Britain, and Germany, it was held that the Governments of the United States and Great Britain were responsible for the losses caused by certain military action, found by the arbitrator to be unwarranted, in the Samoan Islands in the spring of 1899, namely: (1) The bringing back of the Malietoans (to the island of Upolu) and the distribution to them of arms and ammunition; (2) the bombardment; (3) the military operations on shore; and (4) the stopping of the street traffic in Apia. There was reserved for future decision " the question as to the extent to which the two Governments or each of them may be considered responsible for such losses."

However, such further decision was never made nor requested, inasmuch as it was agreed upon by the United States and Great Britain that each Government should pay one-half the amounts found to be due to the citizens or subjects of other powers and should deal alone with the claims of its own nationals.

The German Government, after an interchange of several notes on the subject, finally signified through the German ambassador in Washington its acceptance of the offer of $40,000 in full settlement of the claims, and thereafter Congress appropriated as the moiety of the United States in payment thereof the sum of $20,000.

The French and Danish claims were resubmitted, and the respective sums of $6,782.26 and $1,520 were paid thereon. Congress appropriated in each case for the moiety of the United States, as it did also in the cases of the Swedish and Norwegian claims, upon which were paid, respectively, $750 and $400.

The department is advised that after its contribution to the payment of the said claims of persons of other nationalities the Government of Great Britain several years ago reimbursed its own subjects in the sum of £3,645 for similar losses.

It appears to follow, then, that the American claimants alone, as a class (aside from the native Samoans), remain unpaid for the losses suffered in these Samoan troubles, and it would seem that the equities of the situation require that provision should be made without delay for such payment where it is shown to be deserved.

Investigation by the department reveals that, generally speaking, the American claims are of the same character as those of other nationalities. The total amount of the American claims is about $64,677.88 and the total amount recommended for payment is $14,811.42.

In conclusion, to show by an eyewitness the condition of affairs in Samoa immediately after the war in question, I desire to quote the following extracts from the report of Hon. Bartlett Tripp, the American representative upon the commission which composed affairs in Samoa following the war:

> The country surrounding Apia indeed had much the appearance of a battle field at the time of our arrival * * *. The shells from the war vessels fired to dislodge the forces of Mataafa had left their marks upon the houses and plantations surrounding the town and within a radius of 3 miles from the inner harbor, while the lawless acts of looting and foraging parties from either camp had left them a scene of devastation and desolation which always succeeds the invasion of armed forces of savage and civilized men * * *. The white people whose homes had been pillaged and who had sought refuge in Apia, under the guns of the men-of-war, despondingly awaited events which might again bring peace, and the inhabitants of the unhappy town, whose houses had been unluckily struck by the shells of a friendly fleet, and who sought shelter upon the shore, were about equally divided in their words of censure for the hostile forces of the natives and the vessels of their own fleet. (Foreign Relations, 1899, pp. 621, 622, and 649.)

Respectfully submitted,   P. C. KNOX, *Secretary of State.*

SPECIAL MESSAGE.

[Transmitting, in response to Senate resolution of January 2, 1913, a memorandum of the Secretary of State submitting a report by the Consul General at Berlin relative to the Friedmann Cure for Tuberculosis.]

THE WHITE HOUSE, *January 16, 1913.*

To the Senate of the United States:

I transmit herewith a memorandum of the Secretary of State, inclosing a report prepared by the consul general at Berlin in regard to the Friedmann cure for tuberculosis.

The report is sent in reply to a resolution of the Senate in January 2, 1913, by which I am requested to submit to the Senate the results of any investigation of the Friedmann cure made or being made by the American consul general in Germany or any other officer of the United States.

WM. H. TAFT.

Secretary Knox's letter of submittal follows:

To the PRESIDENT: The undersigned, the Secretary of State, has the honor to lay before the President, in accordance with a resolution of the Senate of the United States of January 2, 1913, a copy of a dispatch from the consul general at Berlin, Germany, transmitting a report in regard to the Friedmann cure for tuberculosis.   P. C. KNOX, *Secretary of State.*

January 15, 1913.

REPORT ON THE FRIEDMANN CURE FOR TUBERCULOSIS

AMERICAN CONSULATE GENERAL,
Berlin, Germany, December 31, 1912.

The Secretary of State, Washington, D. C.:

SIR: On November 6th last Dr. Friedrich Franz Friedmann, of Berlin, in a lecture delivered before the Berlin Medical Society (Berliner medizinische Gesellschaft) announced that he has discovered a remedy for tuberculosis. The treatment consists in the injection of a solution prepared by the doctor himself, which he claims contains living nonvirulent bacilli taken from cold-blooded animals in contradistinction to the virulent organisms contained in Koch's Tuberkulin and other tuberculosis remedies. Up to November 18th last Dr. Friedmann claims to have treated 1,182 cases, mostly children, and that the inoculation has proved a success.

In the discussions which followed the lecture some of the most prominent Berlin physicians expressed their surprise at the favorable results obtained by Dr. Friedmann in his treatment of their tuberculosis patients. Other doctors claimed that equally favorable results have been obtained by the Koch and other tuberculosis cures. It is the consensus of opinion of the Berlin medical profession that the results of the new treatment can not be definitely acknowledged till facilities have been offered to the various physicians to observe the effects of the preparation under their own administrations and then only after sufficient time has elapsed to determine whether or not the cures or the instances of amelioration of the condition of the patient are permanent. Owing to the comparatively short period which has elapsed since the new treatment has been tried fears have been expressed lest the nonvirulent organisms when injected into the human system may become virulent and cause an outbreak of the disease.

Dr. Friedmann has stated that at present the new preparation can not be given to the medical profession at large, as he has not the proper facilities for the manufacture of the remedy, but as soon as possible the solution will be furnished to medical experts to enable them to administer the cure to their own patients.

In answer to a request for information made recently by this consulate general, Dr. Friedmann replied as follows:

My remedy for the time being has not yet been given out to any one. For the present, patients will be treated only under my personal direction in my Institute for Tuberculosis and Scrofulosis at 49 Lutzowstrasse, Berlin. I am unable to say just yet how soon my remedy will be available in America.

My institute is not a hospital, but room and board may be had elsewhere in Berlin at usual prices by those who come for treatment.

It is impossible to give an estimate of length of time necessary for treatment without examination. Where cases are not too far advanced treatment usually covers a period of several weeks.

The following is an opinion of the new remedy given by one of the local physicians:

In November of this year Dr. Friedmann delivered a lecture to the Berlin Medical Association in which he announced that he had discovered a new preparation for the treatment of tuberculosis. In his lecture he stated that the new remedy would not only cure cases of tuberculosis which were already well defined, but also that he could prevent the disease by inoculation, especially in small children. There already exists up to the present time various preparations which we call " sera," by the injection of which tuberculosis has been fought. The first serum was made by the celebrated Robert Koch and consisted of dead tuberculosis bacilli. The other preparations which have appeared since were also obtained by the emulsion of dead tuberculosis bacilli. The preparation of Dr. Friedmann consists of living nonvirulent bacilli taken from cold-blooded animals, such as turtles; that is to say, of living tuberculosis bacilli which have lost their virulence or poisonous quality if injected into the human body.

Friedmann claimed that he has treated many hundred cases by himself and with the assistance of several Berlin physicians and has had a great success. The cases which he presented to the Berlin Medical Association showed, indeed, a great improvement, but that the cures are permanent can only be determined in the future. It is certain that similar success has been obtained with other preparations, therefore it is very difficult to give a definite opinion as to the new discovery; first, because Dr. Friedmann does not specify the method by which his preparation is made, and, secondly, because he has not given his material to other doctors to enable them to prove his statements. In all events, the medical profession is very skeptical in regard to this cure, as Friedmann uses living or even weakened tuberculosis bacilli, and nobody can state with certainty at this time that these bacilli, if injected into the human body, do not become virulent. My opinion is as follows:

It is very possible that successful results have actually been obtained by the use of the Friedmann preparation, but, before the results can be accepted as definite by the medical profession at large, it will be necessary to have an experience with the preparation for several years by other doctors besides Dr. Friedmann. Under the present conditions I, as well as many other doctors, would abstain from treatment with the new preparation.

Copies of the Berliner Klinische Wochenschrift are forwarded as annexes to this report. In No. 47, of Nov. 18, 1912, on pages 2214 to 2217, the lectures of Dr. Friedmann are given in the original text, and on pages 2241 to 2246 the discussion which followed the lecture. In No. 49, of Dec. 2, 1912, on pages 2329 to 2335, the discussion is concluded.

A. M. THACKARA,
American Consul General.

SPECIAL MESSAGE.

[Transmitting the Sixty-third Annual Report of the Board of Directors of the Panama Railroad for fiscal year ending June 30, 1912.]

THE WHITE HOUSE, *January 22, 1913.*

To the Senate and House of Representatives:

I transmit herewith, for the information of Congress, the Sixty-third Annual Report of the Board of Directors of the Panama Railroad Co. for the fiscal year ending June 30, 1912.

WM. H. TAFT.

SIXTY-THIRD ANNUAL REPORT OF THE PANAMA RAILROAD CO., JUNE 30, 1912.
PANAMA RAILROAD CO.,
New York, N. Y., November 1, 1912.

To the stockholders of the Panama Railroad Co.:

I respectfully submit for your consideration a report of the company's financial condition and operations for the 12 months from July 1, 1911, to June 30, 1912.

The sums heretofore advanced by the United States Government, amounting to $4,185,047.03, were not decreased by payments during the fiscal period ending June 30, 1912; the total payments previously made on account amounted to $937,714.92, leaving a total balance due of $3,247,332.11.

Congressional enactment (sec. 2 of the sundry civil service act, approved March 4, 1911), by which this company was released from further payments on account of principal or interest upon its indebtedness to the United States Government until further action by Congress, is still in effect.

The company's operations for the period covered by this report, after meeting the total cost of operation, together with fixed charges aggregating $39,954.12, and charges for depreciation of rolling stock, floating and plant equipment, amounting to $232,489.20, resulted in net income of $1,762,049.22.

Of net income, as above stated, $1,385,568.25 was applied to additions and betterments of plant and equipment.

GEO. W. GOETHALS,
President.

BOARD OF DIRECTORS—George W. Goethals, F. C. Boggs, C. A. Devol, E. A. Drake, Clarence R. Edwards, Oswald H. Ernst, Mordecai T. Endicott, D. DuB. Gaillard, H. F. Hodges, H. H. Rousseau, Richard Reid Rogers, W. L. Sibert, E. T. Wilson.

OFFICERS—George W. Goethals, president; E. A. Drake, vice president; H. F. Hodges, second vice president; J. A. Smith, general superintendent; Sylvester Deming, treasurer; T. H. Rossbottom, assistant to vice president, and secretary; V. M. Newton, auditor; R. W. Hart, local auditor, F. C. Boggs, general purchasing officer, Eugene T. Wilson, commissary; Wendell L. Simpson, commissary purchasing agent; Roland Allwork, superintending engineer; F. Mears, chief engineer; H. I. Bawden, terminal superintendent; Richard Reid Rogers, general counsel. General offices.—No. 24 State Street, New York.

SPECIAL MESSAGE.

[Recommending Appropriation for the Fourth International Congress of School Hygiene to be held in Buffalo, N. Y., August 25 to 30, 1913.]

THE WHITE HOUSE, *January 22, 1913.*

To the Senate and House of Representatives:

On the 19th of August last Congress passed the following resolution:

Resolved by the Senate and House of Representatives of the United States of America in Congress assembled, That the President of the United States is hereby requested to direct the Secretary of State to issue invitations to foreign governments to participate in the Fourth International Congress on School Hygiene, to be held in Buffalo, New York, August twenty-fifth to thirtieth, nineteen hundred and thirteen: *Provided,* That no appropriation shall be granted at any time hereafter in connection with said congress.

At the time the resolution was passed there were three gentlemen in Buffalo whose means and whose interest in the congress were such that the people of Buffalo had every reason to believe that the expense of the congress would be contributed by these, their citizens. Since that time the three citizens have died, and there is no written obligation on the part of their estates to meet the necessary expenses.

I recommend the appropriation of $30,000 (to which the citizens of Buffalo will have to add a substantial sum) as a contribution of the Government to the fund necessary to make the reception of the congress accord with what we regard as American hospitality.

Personally I am very much opposed to any invitation of this sort at the instance of the Government in which the Government does not assume all the expenses of entertainment. Other countries much less able than the United States never extend an invitation of this sort without having proper preparation for the reception of the guests of the nation.

In the peculiar circumstances of the present resolution I urgently recommend the appropriation of the sum mentioned to enable the obligation of the invitation to be properly met. The proviso in the resolution was an unfortunate one, in my judgment, but whether it was so or not, under the circumstances it offers no reason for Congress not to take the proper course.

WM. H. TAFT.

SPECIAL MESSAGE.

[Transmitting report on the Transportation Question in the Territory of Alaska, etc.]

THE WHITE HOUSE, *February 6, 1913.*

To the Senate and House of Representatives:

In accordance with the provisions of section 18 of an act of Congress approved August 24, 1912, I appointed a commission—

to conduct an examination into the transportation question in the Territory of Alaska; to examine railroad routes from the seaboard to the coal fields and to the interior and navigable waterways; to secure surveys and other information with respect to railroads, including cost of construction and operation; to obtain information in respect to the coal fields and their proximity to railroad routes; and to make report of the facts to Congress on or before the first day of December, nineteen hundred and twelve, or as soon thereafter as may be practicable, together with their conclusions and recommendations in respect to the best and most available routes for railroads in Alaska which will develop the country and the resources thereof for the use of the people of the United States.

Under the requirements of the act, this commission consisted of—

an officer of the Engineer Corps of the United States Army, a geologist in charge of Alaska surveys, an officer in the Engineer Corps of the United States Navy, and a civil engineer who has had practical experience in railroad construction and has not been connected with any railroad enterprise in said Territory.

The date when the act was passed was late in the summer season, thus allowing a very limited time for the preparation of a report for presentation at the present session of Congress. Nevertheless, within a week after the act was approved the commission had been appointed, as follows: Maj. Jay J. Morrow, Corps of Engineers, United States Army, chairman; Alfred H. Brooks, geologist in charge of Division of Alaskan Mineral Resources, Geological Survey, vice chairman; Civil Engineer Leonard M. Cox, United States Navy. Colin M. Ingersoll, consulting railroad engineer, New York City. This commission has transmitted to me a report, which is herewith submitted to Congress in accordance with the provisions of the act. An examination of this report discloses that the following are among the more important of the findings of the commission:

The Territory of Alaska contains large undeveloped mineral resources, extensive tracts of agricultural and grazing lands, and the climate of a large part of the Territory is favorable to permanent settlement and industrial development. The report contains much specific information and many interesting details with regard to these resources. It finds that they can be developed and utilized only by the construction of railways which shall connect tidewater on the Pacific Ocean with the two great inland waterways, the Yukon and the Kuskokwim Rivers. The resources of the inland region and especially of these great river basins are almost undeveloped because of lack of transportation facilities. The Yukon and Kuskokwim Rivers system include some 5,000 miles of navigable water, but these are open to commerce only about three months in the year. Moreover, the mouths of these two rivers on Bering Sea lie some 2,500 miles from Puget Sound, thus involving a long and circuitous route from the Pacific Coast States. The transportation of freight to the mouths of these rivers and thence upstream will always be so expensive and confined to so limited a season as to forbid any large industrial advancement for the great inland region now entirely dependent on these circuitous avenues of approach.

From these considerations the commission finds that railway connections with open ports on the Pacific are not only justified, but imperative if the fertile regions of inland Alaska and its mineral resources are to be utilized; but that with such railway connections a large region will be opened up to the homesteader, the prospector, and the miner. So far as the limited time available has permitted the commission has investigated, and in its report describes all of the railway routes which have been suggested for reaching the interior, including the ocean terminals of these routes. The relative advantages and disadvantages of these routes are compared. The principal result of this comparison may be stated to be that railroad development in Alaska should proceed first by means of two independent railroad systems, hereafter to be connected and supplemented as may be justified by future development. One of these lines should connect the valley of the Yukon and its tributary, the Tanana, with tidewater; and the other should be devoted to the development and needs of the Kuskokwim and the Susitna.

The best available route for the first railway system is that which leads from Cordova by way of Chitina to Fairbanks; and the best available route for the second is that which leads from Seward around Cook Inlet to the Iditarod. The first should be connected with the Bering coal field and the second with the Matanuska coal field. Other routes and terminals are discussed, but are found not to have the importance or availability for the development of the Territory possessed by the two mentioned. Thus, the route extending inland from Haines, in southeastern Alaska, has value for local development, though chiefly on the Canadian side of the boundary, but the distance to Fairbanks is found to be too great to permit of its being used as a trunk line to the Yukon waters. The route from Iliamna Bay also has value for local use, but is too far to the southwest to permit of its use as a trunk line into the interior. The proposed terminals at Katalla and Controller Bay are found to be very expensive both as to construction and maintenance, besides furnishing very inferior harbors. The route inland from Valdez is at a disadvantage because it would not serve any of the coal fields, although as hereafter noted Valdez is regarded by the commission as an important alternative terminal in the possible future development of the Chitina-Fairbanks route.

The investigations of the commission indicate that the route from Cordova by way of Chitina to Fairbanks would furnish the best trunk line to the Yukon and Tanana waters: (1) Because Cordova has distinct advantages as a harbor; (2) because this route requires the shortest actual amount of construction, but chiefly (3) because the better grades possible on this route should give the lowest freight rates into the Tanana Valley. The Copper River & Northwestern Railroad is now constructed from Cordova to Chitina and thence up the Chitina River. The commission recommends the building of a railway from Chitina to Fairbanks, 313 miles, estimated to cost $13,971,000, with the provision that if this railway is built by other interests than those controlling the Copper River & Northwestern Railroad, and if an equitable traffic arrangement can not be made with it, connection should be made with Valdez by the Thompson Pass route, 101 miles, estimated to cost $6,101,479.

The commission finds that Cordova offers the best present ocean terminal for the Bering River coal. The commission also points out that it would not be economical to haul the Matanuska coal to either Valdez or Cordova, and that therefore the logical outlet for that field is Seward. If commercial development of these two fields should disclose that the quality of the coal is the same in both, the Bering River field would have the advantage of greater proximity to open tidewater. A branch line from the Copper River Railway to the Bering River field, a distance of 38 miles, at an estimated cost of $2,054,000, is recommended to afford an outlet for the coal on Prince William Sound and into the Copper River Valley and the region where there is at present the largest market for Alaska coal.

The commission finds that a railway from Chitina to Fairbanks will not solve the transportation problem of Alaska, because it will not give access to the Matanuska coal field, the fertile lands and mineral wealth of the lower Susitna, or the great Kuskokwim basin. This province properly belongs to an independent railway system based on the harbor at Seward. The commission recommends a railway from Kern Creek, the present inland terminal of the Alaska Northern Railway, to the Susitna River (distance, 115 miles; estimated cost, $5,209,000), with a branch line to the Matanuska coal field (distance, 38 miles; estimated cost, $1,618,000); and an extension of the main line through the Alaska Range to the Kuskokwim River (distance, 229 miles; estimated cost, $12,760,000).

The entire railways thus recommended will constitute two independent systems involving 733 miles of new construction at a cost of $35,000,000. Eventually these systems will be tied together and there will be earlier demands for branch and local lines as the country develops. One of these systems will find an outlet to the coast over the Copper River & Northwestern Railroad; the other over the Alaska Northern. If these new lines are constructed by others than those financially interested in these two railroads respectively, satisfactory traffic arrangements would have to be made with them. If the new railways recommended should be constructed by the Government, the question is necessarily presented as to whether the Government should acquire the whole or any part of the existing lines, or either of them, or should endeavor to make appropriate traffic agreements. Much would depend upon whether the Government would operate its own railroads or would make operating agreements with those operating existing lines. The commission has not discussed these questions for the reason pointed out in its report that the act of Congress omits questions of this sort from those upon which the commission was instructed to report:

The report of the commission contains the following statement:

Its instructions from Congress do not contemplate that any recommendation should be made as to how railroads in Alaska should be constructed, i. e., by private corporate ownership or by one of the many forms in use whereby Government assistance is rendered. The commission disavows any intention of making such recommendations, believing that Congress, in its wisdom, desired to reserve to itself the solution of that problem; but it has been impossible to form any estimates of costs of operation without some assumption as to the interest rate on the capital required for construction. This interest rate would obviously differ in two cases—construction by Government or bond guaranty, and construction by private capital. Moreover, were construction carried on by private capital unassisted, the necessity of earning sufficient income to pay operating expenses and interest on bonded indebtedness might make it the duty of the directors of the corporation to impose rates on traffic that would seriously retard the development which the Territory so greatly needs.

The commission has therefore been forced to base its studies upon two hypotheses, viz.: That the capital necessary for construction is obtained at 6 per cent interest, assumed as possible if construction is carried out by private corporate ownership unassisted; and that capital is obtained at 3 per cent interest, assumed as possible if the construction is done either by the Government itself or by private capital with bonded indebtedness guaranteed both as to principal and interest.

On similar grounds the commission did not feel justified in discussing the use of the Panama Canal machinery and equipment or in including in its estimates the effect of such use; but a list of the machinery and equipment available at Panama is given in an appendix.

Upon the assumption that the railroad from Chitina to Fairbanks is built by private capital, eliminating promotion profit, but assuming the necessity of earning 6 per cent on the capital invested, it is the judgment of the commission that on estimated available traffic the road could be operated from Cordova to Fairbanks without loss at a passenger rate of 7 cents per mile and an average freight rate of 8 cents per ton-mile. This would mean a through freight rate of $36.94 per ton from Cordova to Fairbanks and a through passenger rate of $31.15. It is the opinion of the commission that—

an average freight rate exceeding 5 cents per ton-mile and passenger rate in excess of 6 cents per mile would defeat the immediate object of the railroad, namely, the expeditious development of the interior of Alaska, and, furthermore, would introduce the question as to whether or not the Seattle-Cordova-Fairbanks freight route would be able to compete with the present all-water route via the Yukon River system, except on shipments in which the time element is of such importance as to warrant the payment of a higher freight rate.

To meet the requirements of expeditious development and water competition the estimate of the commission involves a through freight rate from Cordova to Fairbanks at $22.25 per ton, and a through passenger rate of $26.70. The report further says:

Were the road to be constructed by the Government, or by private corporate ownership with a Government guaranty of principal and interest on bonded indebtedness, the capital required should be obtained at a much lower rate of interest, thus materiallly reducing the annual expenditures.

Using 3 per cent on the investment as fixed charges, and omitting mileage tax of $100, on the assumption that this tax would not be

VIEWS OF THE ENGLISH AND GERMAN FLEETS

GERMAN AND ENGLISH FLEETS.

The historian of the great European War will record, and contemporary historians are recording, that the deciding factors in the conflict were wrapped up in the control of the seas. Despite several severe naval engagements (which are described in the article European War in the Encyclopedic Index), the main fleets of the nations involved did not exchange broadsides. The main German fleet did not challenge England's control of the seas, nor her absolute blockade of the ports of the Central Powers; and the Imperial German Government retaliated only by the ruthless use of her large fleet of submarines. The accompanying picture is especially interesting in that it shows aeroplanes hovering over the English men-of-war; for there can be little doubt that aircraft were of inestimable value in preventing the destruction of the English ships by bombs from German Zeppelins.

levied in the case of a Government owned or aided road, the commission estimates that the road would pay on the basis of a passenger rate of 6 cents per mile, and a freight rate of 5.49 cents per ton-mile, making the average through freight rate from Cordova to Fairbanks $24.43 per ton and the through passenger rate $26.70. I give these figures as illustrations. The report contains similar estimates of freight and passenger rates and traffic for the road recommended from Seward to the Kuskokwim.

After recommending the construction of the two principal systems and their extensions already mentioned, the commission states, in conclusion that it—

is unanimously of the opinion that this development should be undertaken at once, and prosecuted with vigor; that it can not be accomplished without providing the railroads herein recommended under some system which will insure low transportation charges and the consequent rapid settlement of this new land and the utilization of its great resources.

The necessary inference from the entire report is that in the judgment of the commission its recommendations can certainly be carried out only if the Government builds or guarantees the construction costs of the railroads recommended. If the Government is to guarantee the principal and interest of the construction bonds, it seems clear that it should own the roads, the cost of which it really pays. This is true whether the Government itself should operate the roads or should provide for their operation by lease or operating agreement. I am very much opposed to Government operation, but I believe that Government ownership with private operation under lease is the proper solution of the difficulties here presented.

I urge the prompt and earnest consideration of this report and its recommendations.

WM. H. TAFT.

VETO MESSAGE.

[Transmitting, without approval, " An Act to Regulate the Immigration of Aliens to and the Residence of Aliens in the United States."]

THE WHITE HOUSE, *Washington, February 14, 1913.*

To the Senate:

I return herewith, without my approval, Senate Bill No. 3175.

I do this with great reluctance. The bill contains many valuable amendments to the present immigration law which will insure greater certainty in excluding undesirable immigrants.

The bill received strong support in both Houses and was recommended by an able commission after an extended investigation and carefully drawn conclusions.

But I can not make up my mind to sign a bill which in its chief provision violates a principle that ought, in my opinion, to be upheld in dealing with our immigration. I refer to the literacy test. For the reasons stated in Secretary Nagel's letter to me, I can not approve that test. The Secretary's letter accompanies this.

WM. H. TAFT.

Department of Commerce and Labor,

Washington, February 12, 1913.

My Dear Mr. President: On the 4th instant Mr. Hilles, by your direction, sent me Senate bill 3175, " An act to regulate the immigration of aliens to and the residence of aliens in the United States," with the request that I inform you at my earliest convenience if I know of any objection to its approval. I now return the bill with my comments. The following are some of the objections that have been raised:

First. No exception has been made in behalf of Hawaii.

Second. The provision that persons shall be excluded who can not become eligible under existing law to become citizens of the United States by naturalization is obscure, because it leaves unsettled the question as to who are to be regarded as white persons. But this is merely a perpetuation of the uncertainty which is now to be found in the naturalization law.

Third. The provision that the Secretary may determine in advance upon application whether it is necessary to import skilled labor in any particular instance, that this decision shall be held in abeyance for 30 days, and that in the meantime anyone objecting may appeal to the district court to try de novo such question of necessity is unsatisfactory. The provision for the appeal to the courts is probably unconstitutional, but even if the entire provision proves ineffective the law will be left substantially where it is, and so this does not constitute a grave objection to the bill.

Fourth. The provision that the Secretary may detail immigrant inspectors and matrons for duty on vessels carrying immigrants or immigrant passengers is objected to by foreign countries, but inasmuch as this is left to the discretion of the Secretary, and it is understood, for illustration, that Italy insists upon such practice with respect to all steamship companies taking immigrants from her shores, it does not seem to me that this is a controlling objection.

Fifth. The provision in section 7, with respect to the soliciting of immigration by steamship companies, vests the Secretary with somewhat drastic authority by way of imposing fines and denying the right of a steamship company to land alien immigrant passengers. Again, this is not mandatory, and therefore does not go to the heart of the bill.

It appears to me that all these and similar objections might well have been considered in committee and may become the subject of future consideration by Congress, but, fairly considered, they are of incidental importance only and furnish no sufficient reason for disapproving this bill.

With respect to the literacy test I feel compelled to state a different conclusion. In my opinion, this is a provision of controlling importance, not only because of the immediate effect which it may have upon immigration and the embarrassment and cost it may impose upon the service, but because it involves a principle of far-reaching consequence with respect to which your attitude will be regarded with profound interest.

The provision as it now appears will require careful reading. In some measure the group system is adopted—that is, one qualified immigrant may bring in certain members of his family—but the effect seems to be that a qualified alien may bring in members of his family who may themselves be disqualified, whereas a disqualified member would exclude all dependent members of his family no matter how well qualified they might otherwise be. In other words, a father who can read a dialect might bring in an entire family of absolutely illiterate people, barring his sons over 16 years of age, whereas a father who can not read a dialect would bring about the exclusion of his entire family, although every one of them can read and write.

Furthermore, the distinction in favor of the female members of the family as against the male members does not seem to me to rest upon sound reason. Sentimentally, of course it appeals, but industrially considered it does not appear to me that the distinction is sound. Furthermore, there is no provision for the admission of aliens who have been domiciled here, and who have simply gone abroad for a visit. The test would absolutely exclude them upon return.

In the administration of this law very considerable embarrassment will be experienced. This at least is the judgment of members of the immigration force upon whose recommendations I rely. Delay will necessarily ensue at all ports, but on the borders of Canada and Mexico that delay will almost necessarily result in great friction and constant complaint. Furthermore, the force will have to be very considerably increased, and the appropriation will probably be in excess of present sums expended by as much as a million dollars. The force of interpreters will have to be largely increased and, practically speaking, the bureau will have to be in a position to have an interpreter for any kind of language or dialect of the world at any port at any time. Finally, the interpreters will necessarily be foreigners, and with respect to only a very few of the languages or dialects will it be possible for the officials in charge to exercise anything like supervision.

I am of the opinion that this provision can not be defended upon its merits. It was originally urged as a selective test. For some time recommendations in its support upon that ground have been brought to our attention. The matter has been considered from that point of view, and I became completely satisfied that upon that ground the test could not be sustained. The older argument is now abandoned, and in the later conferences, at least, the ground is taken that the provision is to be defended as a practical measure to exclude a large proportion of undesirable immigrants from certain countries. The measure proposes to reach its result by indirection, and is defended purely upon the ground of practical policy, the final purpose being to reduce the quantity of cheap labor in this country. I can not accept this argument. No doubt the law would exclude a considerable percentage of immigration from southern Italy, among the Poles, the Mexicans, and the Greeks. This exclusion would embrace probably in large part undesirable but also a great many desirable people, and the embarrassment, expense, and distress to those who seek to enter would be out of all proportion to any good that can possibly be promised for this measure.

My observation leads me to the conclusion that, so far as the merits of the individual immigrant are concerned, the test is altogether overestimated. The people who come from the countries named are frequently illiterate because opportunities have been denied them. The oppression with which these people have to contend in modern times is not religious, but it consists of a denial of the opportunity to acquire reading and writing. Frequently the attempt to learn to read and write the language of the particular people is discouraged by the Government, and these immigrants in coming to our shores are really striving to free themselves from the conditions under which they have been compelled to live.

So far as the industrial conditions are concerned, I think the question has been superficially considered. We need labor in this country, and the natives are unwilling to do the work which the aliens come over to do. It is perfectly true that in a few cities and localities there are congested conditions. It is equally true that in very much larger areas we are practically without help. In my judgment, no sufficiently earnest and intelligent effort has been made to bring our wants and our supply together, and so far the same forces that give the chief support to this provision of the new bill have stubbornly resisted any effort looking to an intelligent distribution of new immigration to meet the needs of our vast country. In my judgment, no such drastic measure based upon a ground which is untrue and urged for a reason which we are unwilling to assert should be adopted until we have at least exhausted the possibilities of a rational distribution of these new forces.

Furthermore, there is a misapprehension as to the character of the people who come over here to remain. It is true that in certain localities newly-arrived aliens live under deplorable conditions. Just as much may be said of certain localities that have been inhabited for a hundred years by natives of this country. These are not the general conditions, but they are the exceptions. It is true that a very considerable portion of immigrants do not come to remain, but return after they have acquired some means, or because they find themselves unable to cope with the conditions of a new and aggressive country. Those who return for the latter reason relieve us of their own volition of a burden. Those who return after they have acquired some means certainly must be admitted to have left with us a consideration for the advantage which they have enjoyed. A careful examination of the character of the people who come to stay and of the employment in which a large part of the new immigration is engaged will, in my judgment, dispel the apprehension which many of our people entertain. The census will disclose that with rapid strides the foreign-born citizen is acquiring the farm lands of this country. Even if the foreign-born alone is considered, the percentage of his ownership is assuming a proportion that ought to attract the attention of the native citizens. If the second generation is included it is safe to say that in the Middle West and West a majority of the farms are to-day owned by foreign-born people or they are descendants of the first generation. This does not embrace only the Germans and the Scandinavians, but is true in large measure, for illustration, of the Bohemians and the Poles. It is true in surprising measure of the Italians; not only of the northern Italians, but of the southern.

Again, an examination of the aliens who come to stay is of great significance. During the last fiscal year 838,172 aliens came to our shores, although the net immigration of the year was only a trifle above 400,000. But, while we received of skilled labor 127,016, and only 35,898 returned; we received servants 116,529, and only 13,449 returned; we received farm laborers 184,154, and only 3,978 returned, it appears that laborers came in the number of 135,726, while 209,279 returned. These figures ought to demonstrate that we get substantially what we most need, and what we can not ourselves supply, and that we get rid of what we least need and what seems to furnish, in the minds of many, the chief justification for the bill now under discussion.

The census returns show conclusively that the importance of illiteracy among aliens is overestimated, and that these people are prompt after their arrival to avail of the opportunities which this country affords. While, according to the reports of the Bureau of Immigration, about 25 per cent of the incoming aliens are illiterate, the census shows that among the foreign-born people of such States as New York and Massachusetts where most of the congestion complained of has taken place, the proportion of illiteracy represents only about 13 per cent.

I am persuaded that this provision of the bill is in principle of very great consequence, and that it is based upon a fallacy in undertaking to apply a test which is not calculated to reach the truth and to find relief from a danger which really does not exist. This provision of the bill is new, and it is radical. It goes to the heart of the measure. It does not permit of compromise, and, much as I regret it, because the other provisions of the measure are in most respects excellent and in no respect really objectionable, I am forced to advise that you do not approve this bill. Very sincerely, yours,

CHARLES NAGEL, *Secretary.*

SPECIAL MESSAGE.

[Transmitting reports on the extension of 2-cent letter postage to Norway, Sweden, Denmark, and The Netherlands.]

THE WHITE HOUSE, *March 1, 1913.*

To the House of Representatives:

In response to the resolution of the House of Representatives of February 20, 1913, requesting the President of the United States—

if not incompatible with the public interest, to transmit to the House of Representatives all information that may be in his possession or the possession of the Department of State or the Post Office Department as to the practicability of extending a 2-cent letter postage rate, similar to that in force with Great Britain and Germany, to Norway, Sweden, Denmark, and the Netherlands, and whether offers or intimations of a willingness on the part of any of said countries to establish such postal rates have been received, and if received, what action was taken in that behalf and the reason therefor—

I transmit herewith reports by the Secretary of State and the Postmaster General upon the subject matter.

WM. H. TAFT.

DEPARTMENT OF STATE, *Washington, February 28, 1913.*

To the President:

The undersigned Secretary of State, to whom was referred a copy of the resolution adopted in the House of Representatives on February 20, 1913, has the honor to report that there is no information in the possession of the Department of State as to the practicability of extending the 2-cent letter postage rate and that no offers or intimations of a willingness on the part of Norway, Sweden, Denmark, and the Netherlands to establish such postal rates have been received by it.

P. C. KNOX, *Secretary.*

POST OFFICE DEPARTMENT, *Washington, February 26, 1913.*

To the Postmaster General:

Replying to your inquiry in connection with House resolution 809 I have the honor to state as follows:

The agreement with Great Britain for a 2-cent letter rate of postage became operative October 1, 1908. The agreement with Germany applying only to letters exchanged between the United States and Germany by sea direct became operative January 1, 1909. Both of the agreements were exceptional and experimental, and no similar agreements except that with the colony of Newfoundland have been concluded since. Proposals for similar agreements received from other countries, including Denmark and Norway, have been replied to uniformly to the effect that the department is not prepared to extend the 2-cent letter rate to any other countries. No proposals for a 2-cent letter rate appear to have been received from either the Netherlands or Sweden.

Letters from this country for Norway, Sweden, Denmark, and The Netherlands, unless dispatched by slow steamers not used for the conveyance of such letters, would be required to pass in transit over one or more intervening countries in which this department would have to pay the transit charges fixed by the Universal Postal Convention, which would make the 2-cent rate on letters for those countries less advisable than the 2-cent rate on letters for Great Britain and Germany, which involves this department in no charges for intermediary transit.

It is estimated that during the fiscal year ended June 30, 1912, the agreements with Great Britain and Germany resulted in the loss of postal revenue to this department amounting to $899,961.92, assuming that the same number of letters would have been dispatched at the regular postal-union rate as were actually dispatched at the 2-cent rate.

In view of the loss of revenue involved and of possible changes in international postage rates which may result from the next Universal Postal Congress which will be held at Madrid in the spring of 1914, it is not deemed practicable or desirable to conclude agreements for 2-cent letter postage at this time with Norway, Sweden, Denmark, the Netherlands, or any other foreign country.

JOSEPH STEWART,
Second Assistant Postmaster General.

SPECIAL MESSAGE.

[On the subject of relations between the United States and the Republic of Colombia.]

THE WHITE HOUSE, *Washington, March 1, 1913.*

To the Senate and the House of Representatives:

I transmit herewith for the information of the Congress a report made to me on February 20, 1913, by the Secretary of State, on the subject of relations between the United States and the Republic of Colombia.

WM. H. TAFT.

DEPARTMENT OF STATE,
Washington, February 20, 1913.

To the President:

In the report which I had the honor to submit to you on May 17, 1912, and which was transmitted in your message of May 22, 1912, to the Senate in response to the Senate's resolution of March 1, 1912, requesting the transmission of correspondence with the Government of Colombia, I stated that the possibility of finding any reasonable means to put an end to the remaining ill feeling between the Republic of Colombia and the United States had, by your direction, long been the subject of study by the department. That study having culminated in the program approved by your letter of November 30, 1912, I deem it my duty now to report upon the outcome of the efforts which the department had made to carry out that program and thereby to replace the relations of the two countries in a state of cordial friendship and mutual confidence. That program was the result of the exhaustive study and earnest endeavors which, by your direction, had engaged the attention of the department from the beginning of the administration, in accordance with your conviction and that of the department that, so far as consistent with the dignity and honor of the United States and with the principles of justice when applied to the true facts, no effort should be spared in seeking to restore American-Colombian relations to a footing of completely friendly feeling.

Before discussing the generous advances of this Government, which I regret have been, I think so mistakenly, rebuffed by the Government at Bogota, it will be convenient by way of recapitulation to sketch, in a measure, the antecedents of the recent attempts of the department to reach the hoped-for adjustment. Inasmuch, however, as the present report is not submitted with a view to its transmission to the Congress, nor intended as a complete survey of the very extensive and complex historical background of the subject, I shall endeavor to confine it within reasonable limits, which would not be possible if the vast amount of material on the subject now on file in the department were to be included or exhaustively summarized.

The necessity for some brief review of what had preceded is enhanced by the fact that the subject of arbitration, now again urged by Colombia, is intimately associated with political problems affecting the status of Panama, and the efforts of the Government of the United States to bring about an adjustment of concatenated questions in which, as a party directly interested because of its rights in regard to the Panama Canal, this Government is the more deeply concerned.

It seems obvious that, even assuming that any tangible issue for arbitration between the United States and Colombia could be made out, evidently no terms of arbitral submission could be entertained which might call in question the right of Panama to exist as a sovereign State.

At this point it should be recalled that Colombian proposals of arbitration, inadmissible for this and other reasons, have twice been rejected by this Government after full consideration by two former Secretaries of State, Mr. Hay and Mr. Root.

Mr. Hay, writing to Gen. Reyes on January 5, 1904, said:

Entertaining these feelings, the Government of the United States would gladly exercise its good offices with the Republic of Panama, with a view to bringing about some arrangement on a fair and equitable basis. For the acceptance of your proposal of a resort to The Hague tribunal this Government perceives no occasion. Indeed, the questions presented in your "statement of grievances" are of a political nature such as nations of even the most advanced ideas as to international arbitration have not proposed to deal with by that process. Questions of foreign policy and of the recognition or nonrecognition of foreign States are of a purely political nature and do not fall within the domain of judicial decision; and upon these questions this Government has in the present paper defined its position.

Mr. Root, writing to a succeeding Colombia minister on February 10, 1906, said:

The real gravamen of your complaint is this espousal of the cause of Panama by the people of the United States. No arbitration could deal with the real rights and wrongs of the parties concerned unless it were to pass upon the question whether the cause thus espoused was just—whether the people of Panama were exercising their just rights in declaring and maintaining their independence of Colombian rule.

We assert and maintain the affirmative upon that question. We assert that the ancient State of Panama, independent in its origin and by nature and history a separate political community, was confederated with the other States of Colombia upon terms which preserved and continued its separate sovereignty; that it never surrendered that sovereignty; that in the year 1885 the compact which bound it to the other States of Colombia was broken and terminated by Colombia, and the Isthmus was subjugated by force; that it was held under foreign domination to which it had never consented; and that it was justly entitled to assert its sovereignty and demand its independence from a rule which was unlawful, oppressive, and tyrannical. We cannot ask the people of Panama to consent that this right of theirs, which is vital to their political existence, shall be submitted to the decision of any arbitrator. Nor are we willing to permit any arbitrator to determine the political policy of the United States in following its sense of right and justice by espousing the cause of this weak people against the stronger Government of Colombia, which had so long held them in unlawful subjection.

There is one other subject contained in your note which I can not permit to pass without notice. You repeat the charge that the Government of the United States took a collusive part in fomenting or inciting the uprising upon the Isthmus of Panama which ultimately resulted in the revolution. I regret that you should see fit to thus renew an aspersion upon the honor and good faith of the United States in the face of the positive and final denial of the fact contained in Mr. Hay's letter of January 5, 1904. You must be well aware that the universally recognized limitations upon the subjects proper for arbitration forbid that the United States should submit such a question to arbitration. In view of your own recognition of this established limitation, I have been unable to discover any justification for the renewal of this unfounded assertion.

It is important to note also that the Government of Colombia has never to this day presented anything even approaching a question justiciable by arbitration, it being a universally recognized principle that neither indefinite nor purely political matters are of a nature to be arbitrated.

It is perhaps useful to advert somewhat more to the background of previous events. On January 22, 1903, was signed at Washington the treaty between the United States and Colombia, known as the Hay-Herran treaty, for the construction of an interoceanic canal by the United States. This treaty, although essentially conforming to the proposals of Colombia, besides being eminently just and even generous, was enthusiastically welcomed by its direct beneficiaries, the people of the Panaman Isthmus. In Bogota it was coldly received. At the first signs of opposition in the Colombian Congress discontent and resentment were manifested in Panama. As the possibility of the treaty's being rejected at Bogota grew to a probability, the idea of regaining their historical autonomy awakened and became strong in the minds of Panamans. The contingency of secession was openly discussed and advocated. Months before the event the representatives of Panama in the Congress at Bogota raised their voices in unheeded warning. The certainty, which soon became evident, that the canal treaty would be rejected proved their warning true. The bloodless revolution of November 3, 1903, followed, with instant success. Within 48 hours from the proclamation of Panaman independence the last vestige of Colombian authority on the Isthmus had disappeared and the people of Panama, through the unanimous vote of their municipalities, had ratified the Republic.

Imbued with the inherited spirit of territorial nationality and the recollection of their ancient geographical entity, the keen interest of the Panaman people in the establishment of interoceanic transit through their territory is readily comprehensible and it is no cause for surprise that they were impatient of the obstacles set by the Government at Bogota, through its rejection of the Hay-Herran treaty, in the way of the accomplishment of the stupendous work of the canal. The feelings of the people of Panama were early shown through the declaration made by their representative in the Colombian Congress and echoed by other farsighted members, that a failure to ratify the canal treaty would be followed immediately by a separatist revolution. It was a matter of common notoriety in the city of Bogota that such an outcome of the rejection of the treaty was inevitable. Although amply forewarned, the authorities at Bogota appear to have courted the impending result. The Colombian President contributed to bring it about by his amazing departure from the practice of nations in failing even to recommend for approval a treaty signed under the explicit direction of its President on behalf of the sovereign State by its empowered agent. In the light of the manifested spirit of the people of Panama, it is evidently quite superfluous to allege that this revolutionary sentiment was fomented by persons in the United States. Outside pressure, even by interested private parties, would seem to have been a work of supererogation, even if its existence were a fact. The separation became a patent certainty from the moment the Colombian executive and Congress foredoomed the treaty to failure.

The Government of the United States, being satisfied that a de facto government, republican in form and without substantial opposition from its own people, had been there established, extended its recognition to the new Republic of Panama on November 6, 1903. From almost the very day in November, 1903, that Panama regained the attribute of self-government which that State had possessed without question from the time of emancipation from Spanish domination to the time of its incorporation by conquest into the centralized Government of Colombia, the Government of the United States bent its earnest efforts toward effecting a just and practical settlement to which Panama, equally with the United States and Colombia, should be a party.

The earlier representations of the Colombian Government, after the recognition of the Republic of Panama and the conclusion of the canal treaty, did not urge arbitration, except by way of alternative submission of pending questions to an impartial court should a diplomatic arrangement not be feasible. These representations were made up of complaints and charges against the United States with imputation of violation of treaty and general bad faith. Colombia then insisted upon reparation being made by the Government of the United States. This is shown by the correspondence heretofore published.

As an element of the proposed negotiation for a conventional settlement a suggestion of arbitration was made which looked to " the settlement of the claims of a material order which either Colombia or Panama by mutual agreement may reasonably bring forward against the other as a consequence of facts preceding or following the declaration of independence of Panama." This proposition, as formulated, was favored by Secretary Hay, together with the proposal that a plebiscite should determine whether the people of the Isthmus preferred allegiance to the Republic of Panama or to the Republic of Colombia (Mr. Hay to Gen. Reyes, Jan. 13, 1904). Both these proposals were considered in the subsequent negotiations of the tripartite treaties, which aimed to settle all claims " of a material order " between Colombia and Panama and which were, in terms, largely responsive to the Colombian demands in this regard; but the only subject to be submitted to arbitration under the abortive treaty between Colombia and Panama signed by Messrs. Cortes and Arosemena was the boundary line in the long-disputed district of Jurado. No provisions for a Panaman plebiscite appeared therein. Even that proposed alternative of arbitration thus disappeared when the parties to the controversy reached the conventional accord formulated in the tripartite treaties of January 9, 1909.

The negotiations of these treaties with the United States and Panama for the adjustment of all questions between the three parties were proposed by the Government of Colombia itself.

The negotiations stretched over a period of some three years, being interrupted from time to time by fresh demands on the part of Colombia and hampered in their course by what seemed a very inconsistent reversion of the Colombian plenipotentiaries of the time to attempt to create issues any bases for which had in effect been set aside by Colombia's own proposal to settle the material questions involved. On one occasion the obstructive tactics of the Colombian plenipotentiary were virtually disavowed by his recall and the substitution of another more in accord with the policies of his Government.

The issue had thus been early narrowed to the question of compensation for the losses and injuries pleaded by Colombia, and, it being undeniable that Colombia had suffered by failure to reap a share of the benefits of the canal, the Government of the United States was entirely willing to take this consideration into account, and to endeavor to accommodate the conflicting interests of the three parties by the conventional fixation of a just measure of compensation, in money or in material equivalence. Throughout the whole discussion the course of the United States was marked by kindly forbearance and equitable generosity. The result was the signature on January 9, 1909, of three treaties, one between the United States and the Republic of Colombia, one between the United States and the Republic of Panama, and one between Colombia and Panama, all three being interdependent, to stand or fall together. The treaties between the United States and the respective Republics of Colombia and of Panama received the advisory and consenting approval of the Senate on the respective dates of February 24 and March 3, 1909. That between Colombia and Panama was ratified by the Republic of Panama January 27, 1909, while the treaty with the United States was ratified by Panama three days later.

It seems unnecessary for the purposes of this report to narrate the elaborate negotiations which preceded the signature of the " tripartite " treaties. The Senate, in executive session, was apprised of the processes by which the conventional results were reached and the nature of those results is made apparent by the text of the three instruments. That their provisions sought to deal, adequately, justly, and in the only practical manner so far suggested, with the international problems growing out of the secession of Panama and out of the assumption by the United States of the great work of constructing the canal, would appear to be evident to the unprejudiced mind. The interests and honor of the three countries were, throughout the negotiation, jealously guarded by their respective plenipotentiaries, and their agreement on all vital points was a confirmatory safeguard.

Nevertheless, negotiated as these treaties were at the instance of Colombia, and framed as they were with every desire to accommodate their terms to the just expectations of Colombia; and although they were accepted by the Colombian cabinet, which made repeated efforts to bring about conditions favorable to their approval by the Congress, the treaties still remain unacted upon.

It thus remained for the Colombian Government to hold up the treaties, to propose the nullification of all the negotiations which had led up to their conclusion and which it had invited, and to suggest entrance upon new negotiations with the United States alone. This suggestion the United States then declined to accept, holding that the "tripartite" treaties must stand or fall together and that no such substitutionary arrangement could be considered without the harmonious agreement of all three parties. In the same attitude, the Colombian Government, without seeking the consent of the United States to enter, after these two rebuffs, upon a discussion of an entirely different character, sought to revert to its former proposal of some kind of settlement by arbitration.

The next proposal of Colombia, on January 5, 1910, was that the United States and Panama should agree to submit to a plebiscite the question of the separation of Panama with the promise that the interests of the United States in the Canal Zone should not be affected by the result. This proposal as made was considered intangible and impracticable, although, as late as March 26, 1910, it appears to have been the subject of an informal suggestion of the Colombian minister, coupled with the promise that if the vote should be unfavorable to the status of Panama the Government of Colombia would formally recognize the acts of Panama in the canal matter.

Again the suggestion of arbitration in somewhat more tangible form appears in the shape of a confidential memorandum, under date of November 30, 1910, expressing the view of Señor Olaya, the Colombian minister for foreign affairs, that, as the provision of Article XXXV of the treaty of 1846 in regard to the guarantee by the United States of Colombian sovereignty over the territory of the Isthmus was differently interpreted by the two Governments, the question whether the acts of the United States on the Isthmus in 1903 were not in harmony with the engagements of Article XXXV, appeared to be a judicial issue proper for arbitral determination. This informal suggestion appeared to involve proposals already rejected by Secretaries Hay and Root. It did not, moreover, materialize in a shape admitting of discussion, and was lost to sight when, about the same time, a new turn was given to the matter by the suggestion of the Colombian foreign office that, with a few changes ("more apparent than real") the treaties might be approved. No tangible proposal was offered, however, as to the changes desired, although it was intimated in January, 1911, that they might import confirmation of Colombia's claim to the ownership of the Panama Railway and of alleged rights and interests in any canal contract or concession granted by Colombia. This intimation, like others put forward during 1910, never reached the stage of diplomatic discussion.

Still another phase supervened when, on March 28, in view of the statement alleged to have been made by ex-President Roosevelt in an address delivered at Berkeley, Cal., on March 23, to the effect that "he took the Canal Zone," the Colombian minister, Señor Borda, construing this reported utterance as an admission that his nation had been "gratuitously, profoundly, and unexpectedly offended and injured," demanded that the dignity and honor of Colombia should "receive satisfaction." No diplomatic discussion of this incident ensued.

At the end of May, 1911, Señor Borda took leave of the President, and returned to Colombia, being replaced by Gen. Pedro Nel Ospina, who presented his credentials May 31, 1911.

No record exists of any effort by this new minister of Colombia to reach an understanding in regard to the Panama controversy or the tripartite treaties until his note of November 25, 1911. In that note he recited "the utter unlikelihood" of a diplomatic settlement of the Panaman issues; characterized the attempt to regulate the situation by the direct agreement embodied in the tripartite treaties of 1909 as "most unfortunate," owing to the adverse sentiment of the Colombian people which had brought about the expatriation of the head of the Government and of the plenipotentiary (Señor Cortes) by whom they were signed; asserted that it had been demonstrated practically that the desired settlement of the existing differences could not be reached by direct agreement, and urged resort to the decision of an impartial tribunal as to the interpretation to be given to that part of the still existing treaty of 1846, by which the United States, in return for valuable concessions, assumed the obligations to guarantee to New Granada (now Colombia) "the rights of sovereignty and property which she has and possesses, over the territory of the Isthmus of Panama."

In conformity with usage, it was to be expected that the envoy would follow up such a communication by seeking personal conference with the Secretary of State to clear the way for formal treatment of a proposal alike so important and so vaguely comprehensive. As a matter of course, and as a part of the public duty of his office, the Secretary of State was and is, at all times, ready to hold such conference with a foreign representative, knowing the advantage to both parties in such a case, of thoroughly understanding each other's views before their expression in official correspondence. Moreover, a just regard for the sensibilities of a nation with which this Government sincerely desires to maintain friendly intercourse naturally made the Secretary of State averse to making a categorical refusal of the proposition, while on the other hand the vagueness of the proposal, like the nature of some of its implications, forbade its academic discussion without a more distinct understanding of its true scope. Gen. Nel Ispina, however, held aloof from the Department of State.

Matters were in this posture when, on the eve of the departure of the Secretary of State on a mission of good will and earnest amity toward the several Republics of the Caribbean, a kindly personal intimation of the pleasure it would afford the Secretary to include Colombia in his itinerary was met by the assertion that such a visit would be "inopportune." Included in this reply to an urbane note were arguments and also accusations tending to impugn the honor and good faith of the United States. It is gratifying to know that this singular course of the minister was taken on his own initiative and was reprobated by his Government. The incident was not of international moment, but it was closed by the spontaneous recall of the envoy by his Government, leaving nothing in the path of that good understanding which this country desires to maintain with its fellow Republic.

It is thus seen that the request of Colombia for arbitration has only recently advanced from the status of a suggested contingent alternative, as a resort in case of failure to attain a diplomatic adjustment, to that of a request predicated on the impossibility of such a direct settlement, an impossibility, if it be one, only because of the act of the Colombian Government in twice repudiating settlements already agreed upon on two occasions by the procedure usual in the intercourse of nations.

It is also to be seen that, while the request takes the same form as the earlier suggested contingent alternative and appears to confine the subject matter of arbitration to ascertainment of the true intent of an isolated clause of Article XXXV of the treaty of 1846, a decision in that regard would revive the old charges and bring them into the arbitral proceedings.

It does not seem timely or pertinent to the purposes of this message to discuss these charges, which were exhausted in the correspondence of 1904 and

1905, and which were necessarily laid aside when the two Governments entered upon negotiations for a friendly adjustment of their differences, with the result of agreement upon conventional terms of settlement. It suffices to say that the thirty-fifth article of the treaty of 1846 is necessarily to be construed as a whole, that the reciprocal obligations of the United States and Colombia were framed to enable this country to enjoy and maintain the enjoyment of the privileges of free uninterrupted isthmian transit, and that the transit was to be kept open by the United States upon occasion, free from disturbance from within or aggression from without. The stipulation which the Colombian Government isolates from its context and seeks to make the sole basis of its contention is in its essence a part of the rights reserved to the United States in order to secure to itself the tranquil and constant enjoyment of the advantages of the transit.

While it is styled as being in compensation for these advantages and in return for the general commercial privileges accorded by the convention, it is perfectly clear that, like the " perfect neutrality " of the Isthmus, the guarantee of the rights of sovereignty and property is to the end " that the free transit from the one to the other sea may not be interrupted or embarrassed in any future time while this treaty exists." And here it may not be out of place to observe that the neutrality of the Isthmus is not its international-law neutrality. The word neutrality has many meanings and shades of meaning besides its strictly technical sense of impartiality between alien belligerents, and is too often indefinitely or irrelevantly employed. In this instance, the obvious sense is that the territory covered by the transit is not to be allowed to become an arena of foreign assault or internal disturbance that may impair the tranquil enjoyment of its use. The United States has exercised the right to prevent such interruption in the past upon occasion, sometimes with the consent of Colombia, sometimes without it, sometimes at the request of Colombia herself in times of civil disturbance, and in the latter case not in fulfillment of any supposed duty to uphold the authority of the titular Government of the territory, but to prevent disorderly interference with the transit. Indeed, the very acts of the United States upon the Isthmus of which Colombia complained comport fully with the right and duty of the United States under the treaty of 1846 to keep the line of transit free from the paralyzing disturbance of civil war, just as it would have been a right and duty to prevent its being a prey of alien rapacity in violation of the territorial rights of its own nationals.

When a new American minister, Mr. James T. Du Bois, was sent to Colombia, in the latter half of 1911, he was informed of the desire of the United States to find some means consistent with its dignity and honor whereby an end might be put to the ill-feeling of Colombia. The view of this Government that, as a condition precedent to any real hope of this desirable result, there should be some modification of attitude in the direction of reasonableness on the part of the Colombian Government was explained, and much time was given by Mr. Du Bois to a careful study of the relations between the two countries. In the summer of 1912 he returned from Bogota to confer with the Department of State as to how a just and fair settlement of our differences with Colombia could be reached.

A program having been evolved which was thought fully responsive to all the needs of the situation, as fresh evidence of the sincere desire of the United States to allay once for all the ill-feeling existing in Colombia, the minister was given full instructions and proceeded to his post. In view of the experience of this Government in seeing adjustments carefully made twice shattered by the failure of their final acceptance at Bogota, it was felt that any fresh formal proposals should certainly emanate from the Colombian Government. The minister was therefore authorized simply to make known through informal and confidential conversations certain bases which, if reduced to the form of proposals made to the United States by the Government of Colombia, would receive sympathetic consideration by this Government as forming a practical means of complete adjustment of all existing differences with Colombia.

The program which the minister laid before the Colombian Government in the tentative and informal manner indicated comprised the following points:

(1) That if Colombia would ratify the Root-Cortes and Cortes-Arosemena treaties as they stood the United States would be willing to sign an additional convention paying to Colombia $10,000,000 for a permanent option for the construction of an interoceanic canal through Colombian territory and for the perpetual lease of the islands of St. Andrews and Old Providence. In the event that the Colombian Government felt that on account of their relationship with Panama there existed difficulties in which they might desire the assistance of the United States the minister was to intimate that there might be added a stipulation that the United States would be willing to use its good offices with the Government of Panama for the purpose of securing an amicable adjustment by arbitration or otherwise of the Colombia-Panama boundary dispute and of any other matters pending between the two countries. Again, if such a proposal by Colombia seemed impossible the minister was instructed to intimate that in addition to the foregoing the Government of the United States would be willing to conclude with Colombia a convention submitting to arbitration the question of the ownership of the reversionary rights in the Panama Railway, which the Colombian Government asserts that it possesses, and looking to proper indemnity should the Colombian contention be sustained.

(2) In the event that the Colombian Government should be strongly averse to making a proposal involving the ratification of the Cortes-Arosemena treaty with Panama, then the minister was to intimate that this Government would be willing to consider the foregoing proposal, even with certain amendments. These amendments were to be: First, the addition of a protocol whereby the United States would undertake to use its good offices on behalf of Colombia in the adjustment of boundary questions between it and Panama; and second, a convention whereby the Root-Cortes treaty between Colombia and the United States should be amended to the extent of eliminating its interdependence upon the Cortes-Arosemena treaty while preserving to Colombia the important advantages it would give that country in reference to the use of the Panama Canal—one effect of this charge being that Colombia would have either definitively to forego the payment of $2,500,000 to be made it under the original tripartite arrangement, or at least to forego such payment until such future time, if ever, when the Colombian Government might find it convenient to ratify the Cortes-Arosemena treaty.

The minister returned to Bogota on January 15, 1913, and at once proceeded to carry out his instructions.

The foregoing constituted the complete program of the extreme limits to which, in the judgment of the department, the Government of the United States would be justified, from any point of view, in going in the rather extraordinary efforts thus undertaken to eliminate once for all all causes of friction, whether justified or not, between the two countries.

The lease of Colombia's rights in two small Caribbean Islands was included as a possible safeguard in the matter of canal defense and for the purpose, regardful of Colombia's dignity, of clothing the discussion with a larger aspect of mutuality of consideration. The option for an interoceanic canal through Colombian territory where there has been, from time to time, recrudescent discussion of such a possible canal project in the Atrato region was introduced in accordance with the same policy which actuated the Government of the United States in encouraging the recent convention with Nicaragua, although the probability of such an undertaking in that region is regarded as far more remote than is true with reference to the Nicaraguan route. In pursuance of the same broad policy of setting at rest once for all all talk of any rival interoceanic canal not controlled by the United States, the department was convinced of the desirability of such a convention, which, like the lease of the islands above mentioned, offered further opportunity to give semblance of consideration for the payment proposed.

The remainder of the program is quite simple and offers to give to Colombia all the advantages given by the tripartite treaties and in a manner most considerate of the present Colombian feeling toward the Republic of Panama, while, at the same time, as is of paramount necessity, jealously guarding the fixed rights and interests of the United States, which, of course, could not be permitted to be called in question.

On January 20, Mr. Du Bois had a preliminary conversation with the President of Colombia and informally discussed with him the first alternative of the program, viz., that including the ratification by Colombia of the tripartite treaties. He was informed by the President that he could not and would not consent to recommend to the Colombian Congress ratification of the Arosemena-Cortes treaty. In reply to an inquiry from the minister whether he should proceed to offer the second alternative, he was informed by the Secretary of State that he could do so if and when he was absolutely satisfied that the decision of the Colombian President was final, it being understood that the United States could not consider any other or further concession than indicated in the second form of the program.

The minister then proceeded further with his conversations, and on January 27, 1913, telegraphed to the Secretary of State that the proposition for the perpetual lease of the islands of Old Providence and St. Andrews was embarrassing to the Colombian Government, being regarded as practically a sale of the islands, which could not be ratified. Inquiry was made by the minister for his information and guidance whether a liberal option for coaling, airship, and wireless stations on one or both of the islands, together with a 60-year option on the Atrato Canal route would be acceptable to the United States. The minister in reply was cautioned to avoid making any proposals, which should logically come from the Government of Colombia, but was informed that if he could assure the Department of State that that Government would accept and the Colombian Congress ratify the agreement, without seeking any additional concessions, should this Government be willing to accept coaling stations instead of the perpetual lease of the islands, the proposal would be considered. With respect to placing a time limit on the canal-route option he was instructed that he should discourage positively any thought on the part of Colombia that a 60-year term would be acceptable if the United States were to pay any such figure as was named in his instructions.

The next information received from the minister was contained in a telegram, dated January 31, 1913, and was to the effect that the Colombian Government seemed determined to treat with the incoming Democratic administration.

These friendly, considerate, and conciliatory efforts to put the relations between the United States and Colombia on a more cordial basis having thus failed, the minister at Bogota was instructed by telegraph on February 7, 1913, to drop the matter after communicating to the Colombian President a personal note as follows:

Although your excellency will doubtless appreciate that those intimations which I have been able to give of the nature of a proposal which, if made by Colombia, would be considered by my Government naturally had reference only to the time at which I had the honor to make them, nevertheless, in order to avoid even a remote possibility of misunderstanding, I am directed to make it entirely clear to your excellency that nothing which has transpired in these purely personal and informal conversations is to be regarded as any indication of what may be the future disposition of the Government of the United States or as committing my Government in any respect whatever, my efforts to arrive at some definite conclusion having, to my regret, come to naught.

The minister has informed the department that after final discussion he has presented a note in the above sense.

The most recent telegrams from the minister show that quite aside from his instructions and acting upon his personal responsibility, Mr. Du Bois, as a matter of curiosity, sounded the Colombian Government still further in order to elicit a clearer idea of its pretentions. It was intimated to the minister that if the Colombian Government would make proposals in accordance with his informal suggestions a revolution would, in its opinion, result.

Continuing in his evident personal desire to sound, if possible, the limits of Colombian pretentions, the minister also inquired whether an offer of $10,000,-000 without the considerations which had been suggested would be acceptable. To this he was informed that it would not; that all his suggestions fell short by far of what Colombia could accept. To his inquiry, what terms Colombia would accept, the reply was: "The arbitration of the whole Panama question or a direct proposition from the United States to compensate Colombia for all the moral, physical, and financial losses sustained by it because of the separation of Panama." This, it was intimated, was the last word of the Colombian Government.

The very latest telegram from Mr. Du Bois shows that in a subsequent interview he took it upon himself informally to ask whether if the United States should, without requesting options or privileges of any kind, offer Colombia $25,000,000, its good offices with Panama, the arbitration of the question of reversionary rights in the Panama Railway, and preferential rights of the canal, the Government would accept; to which he was answered in the negative.

Included in this most recent telegraphic correspondence is a statement of the impression of the legation at Bogota that the Colombian Government cherishes the expectation that the incoming administration will arbitrate the entire Panama question, or will directly compensate Colombia for the value of the territory of Panama, the Panama Railway, the railroad annuities, and the contract with the French Canal Co.

I merely mention the results of these personal inquiries made by Mr. Du Bois, as I have said, in his personal capacity and without any authority, because they throw so much light upon the Colombian obsession with regard to this whole subject. This attitude resulting in the rebuff of generous overtures by the United States is undoubtedly due in a great measure to a radical misconception of real public opinion in the United States, engendered probably by reiterated criticism in certain uninformed quarters leveled at the policy of this Government at the very time it was bending every effort to adjust its relations with Colombia and required for such adjustment an atmosphere of calm instead of one of captious attack and unreasoning encouragement of an arbitrary attitude on the part of the foreign country with which it was dealing.

Feeling that this Government has made every effort consistent with the honor, dignity, and interests of the United States in its sincere aim to bring about a state of better feeling on the part of the Government of Colombia, it is with regret that I have to report that these efforts are thus far still met by a desire for impossible arbitrations, and so have proved unavailing unless, indeed, they may yet prove fruitful in the course of time of a more reasonable and friendly attitude on the part of Colombia.

Meanwhile, the Government of Colombia would appear to have closed the door to any further overtures on the part of the United States.

P. C. Knox, *Secretary.*

SPECIAL MESSAGE.

[Transmitting plan of reorganization of the Customs Service and detailed estimate of expenses of the same.]

The White House, *March 4, 1913.*

To the Senate and House of Representatives:

Whereas, by virtue of the provision of chapter 355 of the acts of 1912, approved August 24, 1912, being " An act making appropriations for sundry civil expenses of the Government for the fiscal year ending June thirtieth, nineteen hundred and thirteen, and for other purposes," I was authorized to reorganize the customs service and cause estimates to be submitted therefor on account of the fiscal year 1914, reducing the total cost of said service for said fiscal year by an amount not less than $350,000, and I was further authorized in making such reorganization and reduction in expenses to abolish or consolidate collection districts, ports and subports of entry and delivery, to discontinue needless offices and employments, to reduce excessive rates of compensation below amounts fixed by law or Executive order, and to do all such other and further things that in my judgment may be necessary to make such reorganization effective and within the said limit of cost; and

Whereas it was further provided that such reorganization should be communicated to Congress at its next regular session and should constitute for the fiscal year 1914, and until otherwise provided by Congress, the permanent organization of the customs service: Now, therefore,

It is hereby ordered and communicated that the following plan shall be the organization of the customs service for the said fiscal year 1914, and unless otherwise provided by Congress the permanent organization of the custom service:

In lieu of all customs-collection districts, ports, and subports of entry and ports of delivery now or heretofore existing there shall be forty-nine customs-collection districts and ports of entry as follows:

1—Maine and New Hampshire. 2—Eastern Vermont. 3—Western Vermont. 4—Massachusetts. 5—Rhode Island. 6—Connecticut. 7—St. Lawrence. 8—Rochester. 9—Buffalo. 10—New York. 11—Philadelphia. 12—Pittsburgh 13—Maryland. 14—Virginia. 15—North Carolina. 16—South Carolina. 17—Georgia. 18—Florida. 19—Mobile. 20—New Orleans. 21—Sabine. 22—Galveston. 23—Laredo. 24—El Paso. 25—Eagle Pass. 26—Arizona. 27—Southern California. 28—San Francisco. 29—Oregon. 30—Washington. 31—Alaska. 32—Hawaii. 33—Montana and Idaho. 34—Dakota. 35—Minnesota. 36—Duluth and Superior. 37—Wisconsin. 38—Michigan. 39—Chicago. 40—Indiana. 41—Ohio. 42—Kentucky. 43—Tennessee. 44—Iowa. 45—St. Louis. 46—Omaha. 47—Colorado. 48—Utah and Nevada. 49—Porto Rico.

SUMMARY OF EXPENDITURES:

For compensation (including salaries of the Board of General Appraisers)	$9,597,017.10
For rents and contingent expenses	699,132.00
Salaries and expenses of special agents, special inspectors, customs agents, and confidential agents	318,616.91
Printing and stationery	37,000.00
Witnesses before Board of General Appraisers	5,000.00
Miscellaneous expenses on direct settlement	25,000.00
	$10,681,766.01

Deduct for difference between detailed estimates and actual expenditures by reason of vacancies, suspensions, etc. (The difference between the detailed estimates and the actual expenditures for the past three years has averaged, approximately, $300,000 per year) 300,000.00

$10,381,766.01

WM. H. TAFT.

VETO MESSAGE.

[Transmitting to the House of Representatives, without approval, "An act making appropriations for the sundry civil expenses of the Government for the fiscal year ending June 30, 1914, and for other purposes."]

THE WHITE HOUSE, *March 4, 1913*

To the House of Representatives:

I return without my approval the bill H. R. 28775, being "An act making appropriations for the sundry civil expenses of the Government for the fiscal year ending June 30, 1914, and for other purposes."

My reasons for failing to approve this important appropriation bill are found in a provision which has been added to that appropriating

$300,000 for the enforcement of the antitrust laws in the following language:

> *Provided, however,* That no part of this money shall be spent in the prosecution of any organization or individual for entering into any combination or agreement having in view the increasing of wages, shortening of hours or bettering the condition of labor, or for any act done in furtherance thereof not in itself unlawful; *Provided further,* That no part of this appropriation shall be expended for the prosecution of producers of farm products and associations of farmers who cooperate and organize in an effort to and for the purpose to obtain and maintain a fair and reasonable price for their products.

This provision is class legislation of the most vicious sort. If it were enacted as substantive law and not merely as a qualification upon the use of moneys appropriated for the enforcement of the law, no one, I take it, would doubt its unconstitutionality. A similar provision in the laws of the State of Illinois was declared by the Supreme Court to be an invasion of the guaranty of the equal protection of the laws contained in the fourteenth amendment of the Constitution of the United States in the case of Connelly *v.* Union Sewer Pipe Co. (184 U. S., 540), although the only exception in that instance from the illegality of organizations and combinations, etc., declared by that statute, was one which exempted agriculturists and live stock raisers in respect of their products or live stock in hand from the operation of the law leaving them free to combine to do that which, if done by others, would be a crime against the State.

The proviso is subtly worded so as in a measure to conceal its full effect by providing that no part of the money appropriated shall be spent in the prosecution of any organization or individual " for entering into any combination or agreement *having in view* the increasing of wages, shortening of hours, or bettering the condition of labor, * * * etc." So that any organization formed with the beneficent purpose described in the proviso might later engage in a conspiracy to destroy by force, violence, or unfair means any employer or employees who failed to conform with its requirements, and yet because of its originally avowed lawful purpose it would be exempt from prosecution so far as prosecution depended upon the moneys appropriated by this act, no matter how wicked, how cruel, how deliberate the acts of which it was guilty. So, too, by the following sentence in the act, such an organization would be protected from prosecution " for any act done in furtherance " of " the increasing of wages, shortening of hours, or bettering the condition of labor," not in itself unlawful. But under the law of criminal conspiracy acts lawful in themselves may become the weapons whereby an unlawful purpose is carried out and accomplished. (Shawnee Compressed Coal *v.* Anderson, 209 U. S., 423–434; Aikens *v.*

Wisconsin, 195 U. S., 194–206; Swift *v.* United States, 196 U. S., 375–396; U. S. *v.* Reading Company, Dec. 16, 1912.)

The further proviso that the appropriation shall not be used in the prosecution of producers of farm products and associations of farmers who coöperate and organize in an effort to obtain and maintain a fair and reasonable price for their products is apparently designed to encourage or, at least, to discourage the prosecutions of organizations having for their purpose the artificial enhancement of the prices of food products, and thus to avoid the effect of the construction given to the antitrust law in the case of United States *v.* Patten, decided January 6, 1913.

At a time when there is widespread complaint of the high cost of living it certainly would be anomalous to put on the statute books of the United States an act in effect preventing the prosecution of combinations of producers of farm products for the purpose of artificially controlling prices; and the evil is not removed, although it may be masked, by referring to the purpose of the organization as " to obtain and maintain *a fair and reasonable price* for their products."

An amendment almost in the language of this proviso, so far as it refers to organizations for the increasing of wages, etc., was introduced in the Sixty-first Congress, passed the House, was rejected in the Senate, and after a very full discussion in the House failed of enactment. Representative Madison, speaking in favor of the amendment which struck out the proviso, characterized it as an attempt " to write into the law so far as this particular measure is concerned, a legalization of the secondary boycott. * * * The laws of this country," he pointed out, " are liberal to the workingman. He can strike, he can agree to strike, he can act under a leader in a strike, and he can apply the direct boycott; but when it comes to going further and so acting as to impede and obstruct the natural and lawful course of trade in this country, then the law says he shall stop. And all in the world that this antitrust act does is to apply to him that simple and proper rule that he, too, as well as the creators of trusts and monopolies, shall not obstruct the natural and ordinary course of trade in the United States of America." " I believe," he added, " in the high aims, motives, and patriotism of the American workingmen and do not believe that rightly understanding this amendment they would ask us to write it into the law of this Republic." (Congressional Record, p. 8850, 61st Cong., 2d sess.)

It is because I am unwilling to be a party to writing such a provision into the laws of this Republic that I am unable to give my assent to a bill which contains this provision.

WM. H. TAFT.

QUESTIONS.

1. What is an injunction, and what would be the result of depriving the courts of their power to issue same? Page 7378.

2. What Supreme Court decisions define the scope of the anti-trust law of 1890? Page 7644.

3. What was Taft's proposal for increasing the efficiency of the Navy? Page 7473.

4. What was Taft's plan for Government supervision and control of mineral lands? Page 7534.

5. What was Taft's reason for withdrawing oil, gas, and phosphate lands, and Alaska coal lands from entry? Page 7534.

6. What plan was proposed for expediting decisions of land cases under the Interior Department? Pages 7489, 7531.

7. What was the rate of interest in the value of farm products in the period between 1891 and 1910? Page 7537.

8. What measure did Taft recommend to protect the seal herds of Alaska? Page 7477.

9. What was Taft's idea of a secondary boycott? Page 7378.

10. When was the last monarchy in Portugal overthrown? Page 7495.

SUGGESTIONS.

President Taft favored a Government-owned railroad in Alaska, which has since become a reality. His conservative view on Government ownership generally is woven into his discussion. Page 7721.

The suggestion that the Government aid in building an Alaskan railroad appears to have been made first by Roosevelt. Pages 6920, 7019. (See also Alaska, Encyclopedic Index.)

Read Taft's discussion of maximum and minimum tariffs. Page 7501. Also other tariff discussions, page 7393, and particularly his encomium on the Payne-Aldrich Act. Page 7403.

It is interesting to read the President's reasons, given in 1912, for the creation of the Commerce Court, page 7756, which he had first recommended more than two years before. Page 7442.

Taft's discussions on the Foreign Policy are elaborate. (For page references see Foreign Relations under Taft, William H., Encyclopedic Index.)

NOTE.

For further suggestions on Taft's administration see Taft, William H., Encyclopedic Index.

By reading the Foreign Policy of each President, and by scanning the messages as to the state of the nation, a thorough knowledge of the history of the United States will be acquired from the most authentic sources; because, as has been said, "Each President reviews the past, depicts the present and forecasts the future of the nation."

Woodrow Wilson

March 4, 1913—March 4, 1921

Messages, Proclamations, Executive Orders, and Addresses to Congress and the People

SEE ENCYCLOPEDIC INDEX.

The Encyclopedic Index is not only an index to the other volumes, not only a key that unlocks the treasures of the entire publication, but it is in itself an alphabetically arranged brief history or story of the great controlling events constituting the History of the United States.

Under its proper alphabetical classification the story is told of every great subject referred to by any of the Presidents in their official Messages, and at the end of each article the official utterances of the Presidents themselves are cited upon the subject, so that you may readily turn to the page in the body of the work itself for this original information.

Next to the possession of knowledge is the ability to turn at will to where knowledge is to be found.

Woodrow Wilson

ELLEN LOUISE AXSON WILSON, EDITH BOLLING GALT WILSON

ELLEN LOUISE AXSON, like her husband, was a child of the sunny Southland. She was born in Savannah, Ga., the daughter of Reverend Samuel E. Axson, a Presbyterian clergyman. She received her education in Shorter College, Rome, Ga., where the family had removed from Savannah, and it was during a year's study of art in New York that she was wooed and won by Woodrow Wilson. They were married in 1885, in the house in Savannah where the bride had been born. Mrs. Wilson was a talented artist, and her paintings, especially her landscapes, were known to the discerning as some of the finest products of American art. But it was as wife and mother that Mrs. Wilson's talents found their chief outlet. She was an untiring personification of the hospitality of the South, and her household was a never-failing source of inspiration to those who were privileged to enter it. With her three daughters, Jessie Woodrow (later Mrs. Francis Sayre), Eleanor (later Mrs. William G. McAdoo), and Margaret, she permeated the White House with a beautiful home-like atmosphere, and her endeavors for the improvement of housing conditions in Washington, especially among the negroes, earned her the undying gratitude of the poor of that city. She died on August 6, 1914.

EDITH BOLLING GALT was born in Wytheville, Virginia, the same state which has given birth to so many of our Presidents, including Woodrow Wilson. Her father was a prominent lawyer of Virginia, and his daughter's tastes for art and literature were developed to their fullest expression in the little Virginia town. In 1896, she married Mr. Norman Galt, and removed to Washington, where her charm and graciousness soon won her a place of distinction in the social life of the capital, although she lived very quietly after the death of her husband in 1907. The announcement of her engagement to President Wilson was made on October 6, 1915, and they were married on December 19, 1915, spending their honeymoon in Hot Springs, Virginia. Mrs. Wilson succeeded the President's oldest daughter, Miss Margaret Wilson, in the administration of the social duties of the White House, and her hospitality has enriched the social life of Washington, while her thoughtfulness and devotion have done much to lighten the burdens which have weighed down the President in the momentous period of the European War.

WOODROW WILSON

The most succinct and discriminating appraisal ever made of Woodrow Wilson was by Senator Williams of Mississippi, when the Senator spoke of the President as long-visioned, deep-visioned, and tender-visioned.

Flung into American politics at a time of confusion and upheaval, where the radical and reactionary elements were trying in vain to diagnose the ills of society and to prescribe the appropriate remedies, Woodrow Wilson by the compelling clarity of his program brought order out of chaos, fused refractory elements, and with unmistakable directness pointed the inviting paths of a new national life.

For his appointed task the elements in the chief executive were kindly mixed. Though elected from the state of New Jersey, he was born in Virginia. While his adult life had rendered him not immune to the pulsing industrial life of the great industrial and manufacturing communities in which his mature lot was cast, his boyhood in the South had kept him alive to the vital and simpler needs and habits of a great agricultural section, all but impoverished by the Civil War, but instinct with the elemental political virtues of the early Republic.

His predilection for public affairs found no congenial vent in the active practice of the law, which he renounced as fast becoming not a profession but a trade. Turning his back on the law, he betook himself to the severe apprenticeship of scholarship; and in the unremunerative labor of teaching and writing won his livelihood.

Among students of American social and constitutional history his incisive views soon challenged attention. At a time when the formalistic study of the text of statutes was supposed to constitute the equipment of the great constitutional lawyer, he boldly challenged this great popular superstition.

While historians almost without exception had theretofore maintained that the doctrine of federal powers as it was constituted after the Civil War had been the precise idea entertained by the Fathers, he showed convincingly that the earlier balance of opinion had inclined toward the views of state sovereignty; that it was rather the weight of experience and commercial evolution which had made national supremacy imperative; and that Webster, the great expounder of the Constitution, was right, not as a historian but primarily as a prophet.

When the doctrine of checks and balances in government and the three-fold division of governmental powers were supposed to constitute almost a divine revelation in the political art, he stoutly insisted that the Constitution is not reverenced by blind worship; that the separation of governmental powers—the much lauded opposition of the executive to the legislature, and of both to the judiciary—divided and scattered responsibility, precluded the harmonious functioning of administration, beclouded the popular understanding of politics; and that the fear of a fanciful tyranny had too often made for the real supremacy of the invisible government of an irresponsible machine.

The growth of the common law he had early appraised at its real value as the gradual development of policy to subserve and accommodate the real but changing needs of the people. His sudden emergence into the politics of his adopted state and his elevation to the governorship were signalized by a reconstitution of industrial law under his compelling leadership. The workman's compensation act and similar legislation, and the relegation of private and corporate interests to effective legal control in the interest of the commonwealth transformed the policy of the state.

Elected to the presidency in anticipation of effectuating a constructive policy of domestic reforms, he encountered at the very outset the menace of serious foreign complications.

The knowledge of the scholar, however, was not in his case sicklied o'er with the pale cast of hesitation or dismay. His adherents in Congress were welded together into a cohesive legion of harmonious and "forward looking" supporters. The long deferred and complex program of establishing a scientific banking and currency law was pushed to successful conclusion. Revenue legislation was reshaped with the intent of exorcising therefrom the last lurking vestiges of privilege to special interests. And our great federal charter, the Constitution, was invigorated by freeing the federal government from hampering limitations upon the raising of revenue by income taxation; and by placing the choice of United States senators directly in the hands of the electorate.

In his Mexican policy the President set himself resolutely to prevent interference in the domestic chaos which vexed and rent that unhappy country. The influence of financial interests with Mexican investments failed to swerve him from his resolve; and whatever the criticism evoked, his policy cemented the friendship and won the confidence of the South American republics.

While the cloud to the south still hung ominous, there was launched the cataclysm of the World War. True to his determination to preserve peace, he insisted at the outset upon the maintenance of strict neutrality. When at last it became only too painfully evident that the submarine policy of the German government had become a war against mankind, that American ships had been sunk and American lives taken, he whole-heartedly accepted the status of belligerent that had been forced upon the nation. With the united support of Congress and the people, he set himself unflaggingly to the effective prosecution of the war. The following year saw the Central Powers broken and defeated, and the armistice signed. The President immediately undertook the herculean task of contriving that a similar world disaster should never recur. It was due to his fundamental insistence that the Treaty of Versailles was centered around a new covenant, that of the League of Nations, which seeks to guarantee universal peace. Stricken down during his heroic advocacy of this far-reaching project for world betterment and unable to secure its approval by the United States Senate, he still stands as the creator of the League of Nations and of the ideals which it embodies. No other American has exerted so intimate and powerful an influence upon the nations of Europe and of the world.

Winthrop More Daniels

7866-D

WOODROW WILSON

THOMAS WOODROW WILSON was born of Scotch-Irish ancestry on December 28, 1856, in Staunton, Virginia, where his father was a Presbyterian clergyman. His early education was obtained largely in Augusta, Georgia, after which he attended Davidson College, in North Carolina, for a year. He entered Princeton University in 1875 and was graduated with the bachelor of arts degree in 1879. He then attended the law school of the University of Virginia until January 1, 1882. In that year he was admitted to the bar, but after an unsuccessful attempt to practise law in Atlanta, he decided to devote his career to the study and practise of political science.

He entered The Johns Hopkins University as a graduate student in 1883 and his thesis on Congressional government in the United States attracted immediate and intense interest. He began teaching at Bryn Mawr College in 1885, in which year he married Ellen Louise Axson. They had three daughters. In 1886 he received his degree of doctor of philosophy from Johns Hopkins, in 1888 joined the faculty of Wesleyan and two years later was appointed a professor at Princeton.

In 1902, he became the president of Princeton, and soon thereafter began attempts to democratize its educational processes. By 1910, however, he had suffered defeat in his plans for the administration of the University and in that year he accepted the nomination for governor of New Jersey from the Democratic Party, with which he had been affiliated for some time. His election to the governorship and his able administration of it made him available as a Presidential candidate. Largely through the efforts of William J. Bryan, he was nominated for the Presidency on the forty-sixth ballot by the Democratic Convention in Baltimore in 1912 and was elected the twenty-eighth President of the United States.

His first term as President was marked by much domestic legislation, including revision of the tariff and the currency system, and by attempts to keep neutral in the World War. His first wife died on August 6, 1914, and on December 18, 1915, he married Mrs. Edith Bolling Galt. Renominated in 1916, he defeated the Republican candidate, Charles E. Hughes, by a very narrow margin. The United States entered the World War in April, 1917, and Wilson soon became a world figure through his formulation of peace terms and his advocacy of a league of nations to prevent wars.

Wilson attended the Peace Conference of Paris in person, but the peace treaty which he there signed failed of ratification by the Senate. He suffered a stroke of paralysis in the summer of 1919, and thereafter, until his death as a private citizen in Washington on February 3, 1924, lived in physical invalidism. He was buried in Washington.

INAUGURAL ADDRESS.

[Delivered at Washington, March 4, 1913.]

There has been a change of government. It began two years ago, when the House of Representatives became Democratic by a decisive majority. It has now been completed. The Senate about to assemble will also be Democratic. The offices of President and Vice-President have been put into the hands of Democrats. What does the change mean? That is the question that is uppermost in our minds to-day. That is the question I am going to try to answer, in order, if I may, to interpret the occasion.

It means much more than the mere success of a party. The success of a party means little except when the Nation is using that party for a large and definite purpose. No one can mistake the purpose for which the Nation now seeks to use the Democratic Party. It seeks to use it to interpret a change in its own plans and point of view. Some old things with which we had grown familiar, and which had begun to creep into the very habit of our thought and of our lives, have altered their aspect as we have latterly looked critically upon them, with fresh, awakened eyes; have dropped their disguises and shown themselves alien and sinister. Some new things, as we look frankly upon them, willing to comprehend their real character, have come to assume the aspect of things long believed in and familiar, stuff of our own convictions. We have been refreshed by a new insight into our own life.

We see that in many things that life is very great. It is incomparably great in its material aspects, in its body of wealth, in the diversity and sweep of its energy, in the industries which have been conceived and built up by the genius of individual men and the limitless enterprise of groups of men. It is great, also, very great, in its moral force. Nowhere else in the world have noble men and women exhibited in more striking forms the beauty and the energy of sympathy and help-fulness and counsel in their efforts to rectify wrong, alleviate suffering, and set the weak in the way of strength and hope. We have built up, moreover, a great system of government, which has stood through a long age as in many respects a model for those who seek to set liberty upon foundations that will endure against fortuitous change, against storm and accident. Our life contains every great thing, and contains it in rich abundance.

But the evil has come with the good, and much fine gold has been corroded. With riches has come inexcusable waste. We have squandered a great part of what we might have used, and have not stopped to conserve the exceeding bounty of nature, without which our genius for enterprise would have been worthless and impotent, scorning to be careful, shamefully prodigal as well as admirably efficient. We have been proud of our industrial achievements, but we have not hitherto stopped thoughtfully enough to count the human cost, the cost of lives snuffed out, of energies overtaxed and broken, the fearful physical and spiritual cost to the men and women and children upon whom the dead weight and burden of it all has fallen pitilessly the years through. The groans and agony of it all had not yet reached our ears, the solemn, moving undertone of our life, coming up out of the mines and factories and out of every home where the struggle had its intimate and familiar seat. With the great Government went many deep secret things which we too long delayed to look into and scrutinize with candid, fearless eyes. The great Government we loved has too often been made use of for private and selfish purposes, and those who used it had forgotten the people.

At last a vision has been vouchsafed us of our life as a whole. We see the bad with the good, the debased and decadent with the sound and vital. With this vision we approach new affairs. Our duty is to cleanse, to reconsider, to restore, to correct the evil without impairing the good, to purify and humanize every process of our common life without weakening or sentimentalizing it. There has been something crude and heartless and unfeeling in our haste to succeed and be great. Our thought has been " Let every man look out for himself, let every generation look out for itself," while we reared giant machinery which made it impossible that any but those who stood at the levers of control should have a chance to look out for themselves. We had not forgotten our morals. We remembered well enough that we had set up a policy which was meant to serve the humblest as well as the most powerful, with an eye single to the standards of justice and fair play, and remembered it with pride. But we were very heedless and in a hurry to be great.

We have come now to the sober second thought. The scales of heedlessness have fallen from our eyes. We have made up our minds to square every process of our national life again with the standards we so proudly set up at the beginning and have always carried at our hearts. Our work is a work of restoration.

We have itemized with some degree of particularity the things that ought to be altered and here are some of the chief items: A tariff which cuts us off from our proper part in the commerce of the world, violates the just principles of taxation, and makes the Government a facile instrument in the hands of private interests; a banking and currency system based upon the necessity of the Government to sell its bonds fifty years ago and perfectly adapted to concentrating cash and restricting credits; an industrial system which, take it on all its sides, financial as well as administrative, holds capital in leading strings, •

254

restricts the liberties and limits the opportunities of labor, and exploits without renewing or conserving the natural resources of the country; a body of agricultural activities never yet given the efficiency of great business undertakings or served as it should be through the instrumentality of science taken directly to the farm, or afforded the facilities of credit best suited to its practical needs; watercourses undeveloped, waste places unreclaimed, forests untended, fast disappearing without plan or prospect of renewal, unregarded waste heaps at every mine. We have studied as perhaps no other nation has the most effective means of production, but we have not studied cost or economy as we should either as organizers of industry, as statesmen, or as individuals.

Nor have we studied and perfected the means by which government may be put at the service of humanity, in safeguarding the health of the Nation, the health of its men and its women and its children, as well as their rights in the struggle for existence. This is no sentimental duty. The firm basis of government is justice, not pity. These are matters of justice. There can be no equality or opportunity, the first essential of justice in the body politic, if men and women and children be not shielded in their lives, their very vitality, from the consequences of great industrial and social processes which they can not alter, control, or singly cope with. Society must see to it that it does not itself crush or weaken or damage its own constituent parts. The first duty of law is to keep sound the society it serves. Sanitary laws, pure food laws, and laws determining conditions of labor which individuals are powerless to determine for themselves are intimate parts of the very business of justice and legal efficiency.

These are some of the things we ought to do, and not leave the others undone, the old-fashioned, never-to-be-neglected, fundamental safeguarding of property and of individual right. This is the high enterprise of the new day: To lift everything that concerns our life as a Nation to the light that shines from the hearthfire of every man's conscience and vision of the right. It is inconceivable that we should do this as partisans; it is inconceivable we should do it in ignorance of the facts as they are or in blind haste. We shall restore, not destroy. We shall deal with our economic system as it is and as it may be modified, not as it might be if we had a clean sheet of paper to write upon; and step by step we shall make it what it should be, in the spirit of those who question their own wisdom and seek counsel and knowledge, not shallow self-satisfaction or the excitement of excursions whither they can not tell. Justice, and only justice, shall always be our motto.

And yet it will be no cool process of mere science. The Nation has been deeply stirred, stirred by a solemn passion, stirred by the knowledge of wrong, of ideals lost, of government too often debauched and made an instrument of evil. The feelings with which we face this new age of right and opportunity sweep across our heartstrings like some air out of God's own presence, where justice and mercy are reconciled and the judge and the brother are one. We know our task to be no mere task of politics but a task which shall search us through and through, whether we be able to understand our time and the need of our people, whether we be indeed their spokesmen and interpreters, whether we have the pure heart to comprehend and the rectified will to choose our high course of action.

This is not a day of triumph; it is a day of dedication. Here muster, not the forces of party, but the forces of humanity. Men's hearts wait upon us; men's lives hang in the balance; men's hopes call upon us to say what we will do. Who shall live up to the great trust? Who dares fail to try? I summon all honest men, all patriotic, all forward-looking men, to my side. God helping me, I will not fail them, if they will but counsel and sustain me!

ADDRESS.

[Delivered in the chamber of the House of Representatives at a joint session of the two Houses of Congress at the beginning of the First Session (special) of the Sixty-third Congress, April 8, 1913.]

Mr. Speaker, Mr. President, Gentlemen of the Congress:

I am very glad indeed to have this opportunity to address the two Houses directly and to verify for myself the impression that the President of the United States is a person, not a mere department of the Government hailing Congress from some isolated island of jealous power, sending messages, not speaking naturally and with his own voice—that he is a human being trying to cooperate with other human beings in a common service. After this pleasant experience I shall feel quite normal in all our dealings with one another.

I have called the Congress together in extraordinary session because a duty was laid upon the party now in power at the recent elections which it ought to perform promptly, in order that the burden carried by the people under existing law may be lightened as soon as possible and in order, also, that the business interests of the country may not be kept too long in suspense as to what the fiscal changes are to be to which they will be required to adjust themselves. It is clear to the whole country that the tariff duties must be altered. They must be changed to meet the radical alteration in the conditions of our economic life which the country has witnessed within the last generation. While the whole face and method of our industrial and commercial life were being changed beyond recognition the tariff schedules have remained what they were before the change began or have moved in the direction they were given when no large circumstance of our industrial development was what it is to-day. Our task is to square them with the actual facts. The sooner that is done the sooner we shall escape from suffering from the facts and the sooner our men of business will be free to thrive by the law of nature (the nature of free business) instead of by the law of legislation and artificial arrangement.

We have seen tariff legislation wander very far afield in our day— very far indeed from the field in which our prosperity might have had a normal growth and stimulation. No one who looks the facts squarely in the face or knows anything that lies beneath the surface of action can fail to perceive the principles upon which recent tariff legislation has been based. We long ago passed beyond the modest notion of "protecting" the industries of the country and moved boldly forward to the idea that they were entitled to the direct patronage of the Government. For a long time—a time so long that the men now active in public policy hardly remember the conditions that preceded it—we have sought in our tariff schedules to give each group of manufacturers or producers what they themselves thought that they needed in order to maintain a practically exclusive market as against the rest of the world. Consciously or unconsciously, we have built up a set of privileges and exemptions from competition behind which it was easy by any, even the crudest, forms of combination to organize monopoly; until at last nothing is normal, nothing is obliged to stand the tests of efficiency and economy, in our world of big business, but everything thrives by concerted arrangement. Only new principles of action will save us from a final hard crystallization of monopoly and a complete loss of the influences that quicken enterprise and keep independent energy alive.

It is plain what those principles must be. We must abolish everything that bears even the semblance of privilege or of any kind of artificial advantage, and put our business men and producers under the stimulation of a constant necessity to be efficient, economical, and enterprising, masters of competitive supremacy, better workers and merchants than any in the world. Aside from the duties laid upon articles which we do not, and probably can not, produce, therefore, and the duties laid upon luxuries and merely for the sake of the revenues they yield, the object of the tariff duties henceforth laid must be effective competition, the whetting of American wits by contest with the wits of the rest of the world.

It would be unwise to move toward this end headlong, with reckless haste, or with strokes that cut at the very roots of what has grown up amongst us by long process and at our own invitation. It does not alter a thing to upset it and break it and deprive it of a chance to change. It destroys it. We must make changes in our fiscal laws, in our fiscal system, whose object is development, a more free and whole-some development, not revolution or upset or confusion. We must build up trade, especially foreign trade. We need the outlet and the enlarged field of energy more than we ever did before. We must build up industry as well, and must adopt freedom in the place of artificial stimulation only so far as it will build, not pull down. In deal-ing with the tariff the method by which this may be done will be a matter of judgment, exercised item by item. To some not accustomed to the excitements and responsibilities of greater freedom our meth-ods may in some respects and at some points seem heroic, but remedies may be heroic and yet be remedies. It is our business to make sure that they are genuine remedies. Our object is clear. If our motive is above just challenge and only an occasional error of judgment is chargeable against us, we shall be fortunate.

We are called upon to render the country a great service in more matters than one. Our responsibility should be met and our methods should be thorough, as thorough as moderate and well considered, based upon the facts as they are, and not worked out as if we were beginners. We are to deal with the facts of our own day, with the facts of no other, and to make laws which square with those facts. It is best, indeed it is necessary, to begin with the tariff. I will urge nothing upon you now at the opening of your session which can ob-scure that first object or divert our energies from that clearly defined duty. At a later time I may take the liberty of calling your attention to reforms which should press close upon the heels of the tariff changes, if not accompany them, of which the chief is the reform of our banking and currency laws; but just now I refrain. For the pres-ent, I put these matters on one side and think only of this one thing— of the changes in our fiscal system which may best serve to open once more the free channels of prosperity to a great people whom we would serve to the utmost and throughout both rank and file.

I thank you for your courtesy.

CALIFORNIA'S ALIEN LAND LAW.

The California Legislature in 1913 was subjected to much criticism by citizens of other States on account of the introduction of a bill, the principal provisions of which were:

No alien who is ineligible to citizenship shall be permitted to acquire and hold land in California for a period of more than one year after the date of such ac-quisition.

No corporation, the majority of stock of which is held by aliens who are ineligible to citizenship, shall be permitted to acquire and hold land except for one year.

Governor Hiram Johnson, in answer to the criticism, said:

" Californians are unable to understand why an act admittedly within the jurisdiction of the California Legislature, like the passage of an alien land bill, creates tumult, confusion, and criticism, and why this local act of undoubted right becomes an international question. Of course, the California Legislature would not attempt to contravene any treaty of the Nation, nor to do more than has been done by the Federal Government itself and many other States.

" Our Legislature is now considering an alien land bill in general language and not discriminatory. If terms are used which are claimed to be discriminatory, those very terms long since were made so by many enactments and by the laws of the Nation itself. Broadly speaking, many States have endeavored to prevent the ownership of land by those ineligible to citizenship.

" The United States by statute provided that no alien or person who is not a citizen of the United States, or who has not declared his intention to become a citizen of the United States, shall acquire title to land, etc., and relative to the District of Columbia the United States statutes contain the same inhibition.

" Arizona in 1912 passed an act that no person other than a citizen of the United States, or who had declared his intention to become such, shall hereafter acquire any land, etc.

" The State of Washington prevented the acquisition or holding of lands by those who are ' incapable of becoming citizens of the United States.'

" Illinois has enacted that an alien may hold title for the period of six years, and then, if he shall not have become a citizen of the United States, proceedings shall be commenced for the sale of the land, and the proceeds shall go to the State.

" Minnesota provides that no person, unless he be a citizen of the United States, or has declared his intention to become a citizen, shall acquire land.

" Missouri has a similar enactment. Kentucky, Oklahoma, and Texas all have laws of like character.

" Japan, until 1910, had an absolute law against alien ownership and in effect has it yet. What the United States Government has done, what has been done by many States of the Union, what has been done by Japan, all of which admittedly has been done in pursuance of unquestioned power and undoubted right— is now attempted to be done by the State of California, and no reason can logically exist for sundering friendly relations with any power, or for offense and threats by any nation.

" The character of the present California Legislature is the guarantee that only legislation deemed absolutely essential for the preservation of the State and the protection of its people—legislation having its precedent in the enactments of the National Government and the various States—will be passed. And such measures as may be enacted will be considered thoroughly, calmly, judicially and without prejudice or discrimination."

Senator Isidor Rayner on December 12, 1906, speaking to a resolution he had introduced declaring it to be the opinion of the Senate that there was no provision in the treaty between the United States and Japan that related to or in any manner interfered with the right of the State of California to conduct and administer its system of public schools in accordance with its own legislation, said:

" I admit that the United States can enter into any treaty with any foreign power in reference to any subject embraced in the Constitution. I deny, however, that it possesses any inherent right to make a treaty, and I claim that the treaty-making power lies in grant and not in sovereignty and must be construed in pari materia with all the other clauses of the instrument that must be governed by the principles of international law, its usages, and its practices, as those principles, usages, and practices appertain to our form of constitutional government. I utterly deny that we have any right to make a treaty that violates the Constitution or deprives the States of their reserved rights to conduct their local affairs, over which the Federal Government has no jurisdiction, and which they alone have the right to administer according to their own constitutions and statutes."

This resolution had particular reference to the exclusion of Japanese from the public schools of California, which gave rise at that time to international complications.

Applying Senator Rayner's argument to the present situation, the contention would be that if the existing treaty between the United States and Japan interferes with the right vested in the State of California to make its own land laws, then that treaty is unconstitutional and cannot be enforced.

The importance of the proposed alien land legislation by the State of California was emphasized by an appeal from the President of the United States to the Governor of California as follows:

LETTER TO GOVERNOR OF CALIFORNIA.

WASHINGTON, D. C., *April 22, 1913.*

I speak upon the assumption, which I am sure is well founded, that the people of California do not desire their Representatives—and that their Representatives do not wish or intend—in any circumstances to embarrass the Government of the United States in its dealings with a nation with whom it has most earnestly and cordially sought to maintain relations of genuine friendship and good will, and that least of all do they desire to do anything that might impair treaty obligations or cast a doubt upon the honor and good faith of the Nation and its Government.

I therefore appeal with the utmost confidence to the people, the Governor, and the Legislature of California to act in the matter now under consideration in a manner that cannot from any point of view be fairly challenged or called in question. If they deem it necessary to exclude all aliens who have not declared their intentions to become citizens from the privileges of land ownership they can do so along lines already followed in the laws of many of the other States and of many foreign countries, including Japan herself. Insidious discrimination will inevitably draw in question the treaty obligations of the Government of the United States.

I register my very earnest and respectful protest against discrimination in this case, not only because I deem it my duty to do so as the Chief Executive of the Nation, but also, and the more readily, because I believe the people and the legislative authorities of California will generously respond the moment the matter is frankly presented to them as a question of National policy and of National honor. If they have ignored this point of view, it is, I am sure, because they did not realize what and how much was involved.

WOODROW WILSON.

Gov. Johnson's message to the President in reply was as follows:

SACRAMENTO, CAL., *April 22, 1913.*

The President, Washington, D. C.:

Immediately upon receipt of your telegram of this date, it was transmitted to both houses of the Legislature. I think I may assure you it is the desire of the majority of the members of the Legislature to do nothing in the matter of alien land bills that shall be embarrassing to our own Government or offensive to any other. It is the design of these legislators specifically to provide in any act that nothing therein shall be construed as affecting or impairing any rights secured by treaty, although from the legal standpoint this is deemed unnecessary.

If any act be passed, it will be general in character relating to those who are ineligible to citizenship, and the language employed will be that which has its precedent and sanction in statutes which now exist upon the subject.

I speak, I think, for the majority of the Senate of California; certainly I do for the voting power of the State, when I convey to you our purpose to co-operate fully and heartily with the National Government and to do only that which is admittedly within our province without intended offense or invidious discrimination.

HIRAM W. JOHNSON.

Secretary of State Bryan was sent by the President to California to counsel with the State authorities, and at a conference of the Governor, the Lieutenant-Governor and the members of the Legislature Mr. Bryan delivered the views of President Wilson on the proposed alien land legislation. The Secretary said California might exercise the fullness of her right as a State and enact a rigid law barring Orientals from land ownership, but such action would be against the wishes of the National Administration.

The Secretary of State counseled delay, and as various alternatives suggested that a new treaty with Japan might be sought; that a commission might be appointed to investigate the alien situation with the aid of the President, and finally that if an alien land law seemed imperative its terms should not be such as to give offense.

A compromise measure which had been drafted by Attorney General Webb at Governor Johnson's suggestion, dropped the phrase "ineligible to citizenship," which was declared by Secretary Bryan to be odious to the Japanese. The principal features of the bill were as follows:

1. All aliens eligible to citizenship may acquire and hold land in the same manner as citizens of the United States.

2. All other aliens may acquire and hold land "in the manner and to the extent and for the purposes prescribed by any treaty now existing between the Government of the United States and the nation or country of which such alien is a citizen or subject."

3. Corporations composed of aliens other than those who are eligible to citizenship may acquire and hold land only according to the terms of existing treaties.

4. Present holdings of aliens, regardless of their rights of citizenship, are protected.

5. The State specifically reserves its sovereign right to enact any and all laws relating to the acquisition or holding of real property by aliens.

In drafting the compromise measure Attorney General Webb worked upon the theory that there could be no objection to writing into the statute the specific limitations of the Japanese treaty of 1911

The bill reaches its purpose in two ways:

First—On the death of an alien land owner the bill provides that his ownership ceases and that the property must be taken over by the Probate Court and sold to the highest bidder. Under its terms an alien cannot bequeath real property except to a citizen. The proceeds from the sale of such land are distributed to the heirs by the court.

Second—No leases whatsoever are permitted. Originally it was planned to permit leases covering a maximum period of three to five years, but the Webb act denies this opportunity for colonization by aliens and provides that any lease of agricultural lands is subject to escheat to the State on the day it is begun. To make this more effective the bill provides that when suit is begun to escheat such leases the court shall appraise the lease, sell the property at a forced sale and pay the value of the lease to the State. The remainder of the proceeds shall go to the citizen owner of the land.

Substantially, it is true that the ineligibility to citizenship of the Japanese and Chinese is the keynote of the Webb bill, said Governor Johnson, and if it is determined by the courts of last resort that these aliens could become citizens, then, of course, they would not be affected by this act.

However, up to this time it never has been suggested that the Japanese were eligible to citizenship, and the language of the federal statutes seems very clear on this point.

By the President of the United States of America:

A PROCLAMATION

[The Preservation and Protection of Fur Seals and Sea Otter.]

Whereas, By the first article of the Convention between the Governments of the United States, Great Britain, Japan and Russia for the preservation and protection of the fur seals and sea otter which frequent the waters of the North Pacific Ocean, concluded at Washington July 7, 1911, it is provided as follows:

The High Contracting Parties mutually and reciprocally agree that their citizens and subjects respectively, and all persons subject to their laws and treaties, and their vessels, shall be prohibited, while this Convention remains in force, from engaging in pelagic sealing in the waters of the North Pacific Ocean, north of the thirtieth parallel of north latitude and including the Seas of Bering, Kamchatka, Okhotsk and Japan, and that every such person and vessel offending against such prohibition may be seized, except within the territorial jurisdiction of one of the other Powers, and detained by the naval or other duly commissioned officers of any of the Parties to this Convention, to be delivered as soon as practicable to an authorized official of their own nation at the nearest point to the place of seizure, or elsewhere as may be mutually agreed upon; and that the authorities of the nation to which such person or vessel belongs alone shall have jurisdiction to try the offense and impose the penalties for the same; and that the witnesses and proofs necessary to establish the offense, so far as they are under the control of any of the Parties to this Convention, shall also be furnished with all reasonable promptitude to the proper authorities having jurisdiction to try the offense.

And, WHEREAS, By an Act entitled "An Act to give effect to the Convention between the Governments of the United States, Great Britain, Japan and Russia for the preservation and protection of the fur seals and sea otter which frequent the waters of the North Pacific Ocean, concluded at Washington July seventh, nineteen hundred and eleven," approved August 24, 1912, it is provided that the President of the United States shall determine by proclamation when the other parties to said Convention, by appropriate legislation or otherwise, shall have authorized the naval or other officers of the United States, duly commissioned and instructed by the President to that end to arrest, detain, and deliver to the proper officers of such parties, vessels and subjects under their jurisdiction, offending against said Convention or any statute or regulation made by those Governments to enforce said Convention; and that his determination shall be conclusive upon the question.

Now, THEREFORE, I, WOODROW WILSON, President of the United States of America, by virtue of the power and authority conferred upon me by the said Act approved August 24, 1912, do hereby declare that satisfactory information has been received by me that the Governments of Great Britain, Japan and Russia have authorized the naval or other officers of the United States to arrest, detain, and deliver to the proper officers of such Governments, respectively, all persons and vessels subject to their jurisdiction, offending against said Convention, or against any statute or regulation made by those Governments to enforce its provisions; and I do further declare that from and after the date of this Proclamation any person or vessel subject to the jurisdiction of the United States offending or being about to offend against the prohibitions of said Convention, or of said Act, or of the regulations made thereunder, may be seized and detained by the naval or other duly commissioned officers of any of the parties to the said Convention other than the United States, except within the territorial jurisdiction of one of the other of said parties, on condition, however, that such person or vessel so seized and detained shall be delivered as soon as practicable at the nearest point to the place of seizure, with the witnesses and proofs necessary to establish the offenses so far as they are under the control of such party, to the proper official of the

United States, whose courts alone shall have jurisdiction to try the offense and impose the penalties for the same.

In Witness Whereof I have hereunto set my hand and caused the seal of the United States to be affixed.

[SEAL.] Done at the city of Washington this thirty-first day of May, in the year of our Lord one thousand nine hundred and thirteen, and of the Independence of the United States of America the one hundred and thirty-seventh.

WOODROW WILSON.

By the President:

W. J. BRYAN, *Secretary of State.*

ADDRESS

[Delivered by President Wilson at a joint session of the two Houses of Congress, June 23, 1913.]

Mr. Speaker, Mr. President, Gentlemen of the Congress:

It is under the compulsion of what seems to me a clear and imperative duty that I have a second time this session sought the privilege of addressing you in person. I know, of course, that the heated season of the year is upon us, that work in these chambers and in the committee rooms is likely to become a burden as the season lengthens, and that every consideration of personal convenience and personal comfort, perhaps, in the cases of some of us, considerations of personal health even, dictate an early conclusion of the deliberations of the session; but there are occasions of public duty when these things which touch us privately seem very small; when the work to be done is so pressing and so fraught with big consequence that we know that we are not at liberty to weigh against it any point of personal sacrifice. We are now in the presence of such an occasion. It is absolutely imperative that we should give the business men of this country a banking and currency system by means of which they can make use of the freedom of enterprise and of individual initiative which we are about to bestow upon them.

We are about to set them free; we must not leave them without the tools of action when they are free. We are about to set them free by removing the trammels of the protective tariff. Ever since the Civil War they have waited for this emancipation and for the free opportunities it will bring with it. It has been reserved for us to give it to them. Some fell in love, indeed, with the slothful security of their dependence upon the Government; some took advantage of the shelter of the nursery to set up a mimic mastery of their own within its walls.

Now both the tonic and the discipline of liberty and maturity are to ensue. There will be some readjustments of purpose and point of view. There will follow a period of expansion and new enterprise, freshly conceived. It is for us to determine now whether it shall be rapid and facile and of easy accomplishment. This it can not be unless the resourceful business men who are to deal with the new circumstances are to have at hand and ready for use the instrumentalities and conveniences of free enterprise which independent men need when acting on their own initiative.

It is not enough to strike the shackles from business. The duty of statesmanship is not negative merely. It is constructive also. We must show that we understand what business needs and that we know how to supply it. No man, however casual and superficial his observation of the conditions now prevailing in the country, can fail to see that one of the chief things business needs now, and will need increasingly as it gains in scope and vigor in the years immediately ahead of us, is the proper means by which readily to vitalize its credit, corporate and individual, and its originative brains. What will it profit us to be free if we are not to have the best and most accessible instrumentalities of commerce and enterprise? What will it profit us to be quit of one kind of monopoly if we are to remain in the grip of another and more effective kind? How are we to gain and keep the confidence of the business community unless we show that we know how both to aid and to protect it? What shall we say if we make fresh enterprise necessary and also make it very difficult by leaving all else except the tariff just as we found it? The tyrannies of business, big and little, lie within the field of credit. We know that. Shall we not act upon the knowledge? Do we not know how to act upon it? If a man can not make his assets available at pleasure, his assets of capacity and character and resource, what satisfaction is it to him to see opportunity beckoning to him on every hand, when others have the keys of credit in their pockets and treat them as all but their own private possession? It is perfectly clear that it is our duty to supply the new banking and currency system the country needs, and it will need it immediately more than it has ever needed it before.

The only question is, When shall we supply it—now, or later, after the demands shall have become reproaches that we were so dull and so slow? Shall we hasten to change the tariff laws and then be laggards about making it possible and easy for the country to take advantage of the change? There can be only one answer to that question. We must act now, at whatever sacrifice to ourselves. It is a duty which the circumstances forbid us to postpone. I should be recreant to my deepest convictions of public obligation did I not press it upon you with solemn and urgent insistence.

The principles upon which we should act are also clear. The country has sought and seen its path in this matter within the last few years—sees it more clearly now than it ever saw it before—much more clearly than when the last legislative proposals on the subject were made. We must have a currency, not rigid as now, but readily, elastically responsive to sound credit, the expanding and contracting credits of everyday transactions, the normal ebb and flow of personal and corporate dealings. Our banking laws must mobilize reserves; must not permit the concentration anywhere in a few hands of the monetary resources of the country or their use for speculative purposes in such volume as to hinder or impede or stand in the way of other more legitimate, more fruitful uses. And the control of the system of banking and of issue which our new laws are to set up must be public, not private, must be vested in the Government itself, so that the banks may be the instruments, not the masters, of business and of individual enterprise and initiative.

The committees of the Congress to which legislation of this character is referred have devoted careful and dispassionate study to the means of accomplishing these objects. They have honored me by consulting me. They are ready to suggest action. I have come to you, as the head of the Government and the responsible leader of the party in power, to urge action now, while there is time to serve the country deliberately and as we should, in a clear air of common counsel. I appeal to you with a deep conviction of duty. I believe that you share this conviction. I therefore appeal to you with confidence. I am at your service without reserve to play my part in any way you may call upon me to play it in this great enterprise of exigent reform which it will dignify and distinguish us to perform and discredit us to neglect.

ADDRESS

[Delivered by President Wilson at Gettysburg, Pa., July 4, 1913.]

Friends and Fellow Citizens:

I need not tell you what the battle of Gettysburg meant. These gallant men in blue and gray sit all about us here. Many of them met upon this ground in grim and deadly struggle. Upon these famous fields and hillsides their comrades died about them. In their presence it were an impertinence to discourse upon how the battle went, how it ended, what it signified! But 50 years have gone by since then, and I crave the privilege of speaking to you for a few minutes of what those 50 years have meant.

What *have* they meant? They have meant peace and union and vigor, and the maturity and might of a great nation. How wholesome and healing the peace has been! We have found one another again as brothers and comrades in arms, enemies no longer, generous friends rather, our battles long past, the quarrel forgotten—except that we shall not forget the splendid valor, the manly devotion of the men then arrayed against one another, now grasping hands and smiling into each other's eyes. How complete the union has become and how dear to all of us, how unquestioned, how benign and majestic, as State after State has been added to this our great family of free men! How handsome the vigor, the maturity, the might of the great Nation we love with undivided hearts; how full of large and confident promise that a life will be wrought out that will crown its strength with gracious justice and with a happy welfare that will touch all alike with deep contentment! We are debtors to those 50 crowded years; they have made us heirs to a mighty heritage.

But do we deem the Nation complete and finished? These venerable men crowding here to this famous field have set us a great example of devotion and utter sacrifice. They were willing to die that the people might live. But their task is done. Their day is turned into evening. They look to us to perfect what they established. Their work is handed on to us, to be done in another way but not in another spirit. Our day is not over; it is upon us in full tide.

Have affairs paused? Does the Nation stand still? Is what the 50 years have wrought since those days of battle finished, rounded out, and completed? Here is a great people, great with every force that has ever beaten in the lifeblood of mankind. And it is secure. There is no one within its borders, there is no power among the nations of the earth, to make it afraid. But has it yet squared itself with its own great standards set up at its birth, when it made that first noble, naive appeal to the moral judgment of mankind to take notice that a government had now at last been established which was to serve men, not masters? It is secure in everything except the satisfaction that its life is right, adjusted to the uttermost to the standards of righteousness and humanity. The days of sacrifice and cleansing are not closed. We have harder things to do than were done in the heroic days of war, because harder to see clearly, requiring more vision, more calm balance of judgment, a more candid searching of the very springs of right.

Look around you upon the field of Gettysburg! Picture the array, the fierce heats and agony of battle, column hurled against column, battery bellowing to battery! Valor? Yes! Greater no man shall see in war; and self-sacrifice, and loss to the uttermost; the high recklessness of exalted devotion which does not count the cost. We are made by these tragic, epic things to know what it costs to make a nation—the blood and sacrifice of multitudes of unknown men lifted to a great stature in the view of all generations by knowing no limit to their manly willingness to serve. In armies thus marshaled from the ranks of free men you will see, as it were, a nation embattled, the leaders and the led, and may know, if you will, how little except in form its action differs in days of peace from its action in days of war.

May we break camp now and be at ease? Are the forces that fight for the Nation dispersed, disbanded, gone to their homes forgetful of the common cause? Are our forces disorganized, without constituted leaders, and the might of men consciously united because we contend, not with armies, but with principalities and powers and wickedness in high places? Are we content to lie still? Does our union mean sympathy, our peace contentment, our vigor right action, our maturity self-comprehension and a clear confidence in choosing what we shall do? War fitted us for action, and action never ceases.

I have been chosen the leader of the Nation. I can not justify the choice by any qualities of my own, but so it has come about, and here I stand. Whom do I command? The ghostly hosts who fought upon these battlefields long ago and are gone? These gallant gentlemen stricken in years whose fighting days are over, their glory won? What are the orders for them, and who rallies them? I have in my mind another host, whom these set free of civil strife in order that they might work out in days of peace and settled order the life of a great Nation. That host is the people themselves, the great and the small, without class or difference of kind or race or origin; and undivided in interest, if we have but the vision to guide and direct them and order their lives aright in what we do. Our constitutions are their articles of enlistment. The orders of the day are the laws upon our statute books. What we strive for is their freedom, their right to lift themselves from day to day and behold the things they have hoped for, and so make way for still better days for those whom they love who are to come after them. The recruits are the little children crowding in. The quartermaster's stores are in the mines and forests and fields, in the shops and factories. Every day something must be done to push the campaign forward; and it must be done by plan and with an eye to some great destiny.

How shall we hold such thoughts in our hearts and not be moved? I would not have you live even to-day wholly in the past, but would wish to stand with you in the light that streams upon us now out of that great day gone by. Here is the nation God has builded by our hands. What shall we do with it? Who stands ready to act again and always in the spirit of this day of reunion and hope and patriotic fervor? The day of our country's life has but broadened into morning. Do not put uniforms by. Put the harness of the present on. Lift your eyes to the great tracts of life yet to be conquered in the interest of righteous peace, of that prosperity which lies in a people's heart and outlasts all wars and errors of men. Come, let us be comrades and soldiers yet, to serve our fellow men in quiet counsel, where the blare of trumpets is neither heard nor heeded and where the things are done which make blessed the nations of the world in peace and righteousness and love.

ADDRESS

[Delivered by President Wilson at a joint session of the two Houses of Congress, August 27, 1913.]

Gentlemen of the Congress:

It is clearly my duty to lay before you, very fully and without reservation, the facts concerning our present relations with the Republic of Mexico. The deplorable posture of affairs in Mexico I need not describe, but I deem it my duty to speak very frankly of what this Government has done and should seek to do in fulfillment of its obligation to Mexico herself, as a friend and neighbor, and to American citizens whose lives and vital interests are daily affected by the distressing conditions which now obtain beyond our southern border.

Those conditions touch us very nearly. Not merely because they lie at our very doors. That of course makes us more vividly and more constantly conscious of them, and every instinct of neighborly interest and sympathy is aroused and quickened by them; but that is only one element in the determination of our duty. We are glad to call ourselves the friend of Mexico, and we shall, I hope, have many an occasion, in happier times as well as in these days of trouble and confusion, to show that our friendship is genuine and disinterested, capable of sacrifice and every generous manifestation. The peace, prosperity, and contentment of Mexico mean more, much more, to us than merely an enlarged field for our commerce and enterprise. They mean an enlargement of the field of self-government and the realization of the hopes and rights of a nation with whose best aspirations, so long suppressed and disappointed, we deeply sympathize. We shall yet prove to the Mexican people that we know how to serve them without first thinking how we shall serve ourselves.

But we are not the only friends of Mexico. The whole world desires her peace and progress; and the whole world is interested as never before. Mexico lies at last where all the world looks on. Central America is about to be touched by the great routes of the world's trade and intercourse running free from ocean to ocean at the Isthmus. The future has much in store for Mexico, as for all the States of Central America; but the best gifts can come to her only if she be ready and free to receive them and to enjoy them honorably. America in particular—America north and south and upon both continents—waits upon the development of Mexico; and that development can be sound and lasting only if it be the product of a genuine freedom, a just and ordered government founded upon law. Only so can it be peaceful or fruitful of the benefits of peace. Mexico has a great and enviable future before her, if only she choose and attain the paths of honest constitutional government.

The present circumstances of the Republic, I deeply regret to say, do not seem to promise even the foundations of such a peace. We have waited many months, months full of peril and anxiety, for the conditions there to improve, and they have not improved. They have grown worse, rather. The territory in some sort controlled by the provisional authorities at Mexico City has grown smaller, not larger. The prospect of the pacification of the country, even by arms, has seemed to grow more and more remote; and its pacification by the authorities at the capital is evidently impossible by any other means than force. Difficulties more and more entangle those who claim to constitute the legitimate government of the Republic. They have not made good their claim in fact. Their successes in the field have proved only temporary. War and disorder, devastation and confusion, seem to threaten to become the settled fortune of the distracted country. As friends we could wait no longer for a solution which every week seemed further away. It was our duty at least to volunteer our good offices—to offer to assist, if we might, in effecting some arrangement which would bring relief and peace and set up a universally acknowledged political authority there.

Accordingly, I took the liberty of sending the Hon. John Lind, formerly governor of Minnesota, as my personal spokesman and representative, to the City of Mexico, *with the following instructions:*

Press very earnestly upon the attention of those who are now exercising authority or wielding influence in Mexico the following considerations and advice:

The Government of the United States does not feel at liberty any longer to stand inactively by while it becomes daily more and more evident that no real progress is being made towards the establishment of a government at the City of Mexico which the country will obey and respect.

The Government of the United States does not stand in the same case with the other great Governments of the world in respect of what is happening or what is likely to happen in Mexico. We offer our good offices, not only because of our genuine desire to play the part of a friend, but also because we are expected by the powers of the world to act as Mexico's nearest friend.

We wish to act in these circumstances in the spirit of the most earnest and disinterested friendship. It is our purpose in whatever we do or propose in this perplexing and distressing situation not only to pay the most scrupulous regard to the sovereignty and independence of Mexico—that we take as a matter of course to which we are bound by every obligation of right and honor—but also to give every possible evidence that we act in the interest of Mexico alone, and not in the interest of any person or body of persons who may have personal or property claims in Mexico which they may feel that they have the right to press. We are seeking to counsel Mexico for her own good, and in the interest of her own peace, and not for any other purpose whatever. The Government of the United States would deem itself discredited if it had any selfish or ulterior purpose in transactions where the peace, happiness, and prosperity of a whole people are involved. It is acting as its friendship for Mexico, not as any selfish interest, dictates.

The present situation in Mexico is incompatible with the fulfillment of international obligations on the part of Mexico, with the civilized development of Mexico herself, and with the maintenance of tolerable political and economic conditions in Central America. It is upon no common occasion, therefore, that the United States offers her counsel and assistance. All America cries out for a settlement.

A satisfactory settlement seems to us to be conditioned on—

(*a*) An immediate cessation of fighting throughout Mexico, a definite armistice solemnly entered into and scrupulously observed;

(*b*) Security given for an early and free election in which all will agree to take part;

(*c*) The consent of Gen. Huerta to bind himself not to be a candidate for election as President of the Republic at this election; and

(*d*) The agreement of all parties to abide by the results of the election and co-operate in the most loyal way in organizing and supporting the new administration.

The Government of the United States will be glad to play any part in this settlement or in its carrying out which it can play honorably and consistently with international right. It pledges itself to recognize and in every way possible and proper to assist the administration chosen and set up in Mexico in the way and on the conditions suggested.

Taking all the existing conditions into consideration, the Government of the United States can conceive of no reasons sufficient to justify those who are now attempting to shape the policy or exercise the authority of Mexico in declining the offices of friendship thus offered. Can Mexico give the civilized world a satisfactory reason for rejecting our good offices? If Mexico can suggest any better way in which to show our friendship, serve the people of Mexico, and meet our international obligations, we are more than willing to consider the suggestion.

Mr. Lind executed his delicate and difficult mission with singular tact, firmness, and good judgment, and made clear to the authorities at the City of Mexico not only the purpose of his visit but also the spirit in which it had been undertaken. But the proposals he submitted were rejected, in a note the full text of which I take the liberty of laying before you.

I am led to believe that they were rejected partly because the authorities at Mexico City had been grossly misinformed and misled upon two points. They did not realize the spirit of the American people in this matter, their earnest friendliness and yet sober determination that some just solution be found for the Mexican difficulties; and they did not believe that the present administration spoke through Mr. Lind, for the people of the United States. The effect of this unfortunate misunderstanding on their part is to leave them singularly isolated and without friends who can effectually aid them. So long as the misunderstanding continues we can only await the time of their awakening to a realization of the actual facts. We can not thrust our good offices upon them. The situation must be given a little more time to work itself out in the new circumstances; and I believe that only a little while will be necessary. For the circumstances are new. The rejection of our friendship makes them new and will inevitably bring its own alterations in the whole aspect of affairs. The actual situation of the authorities at Mexico City will presently be revealed.

Meanwhile, what is it our duty to do? Clearly, everything that we do must be rooted in patience and done with calm and disinterested deliberation. Impatience on our part would be childish, and would be fraught with every risk of wrong and folly. We can afford to exercise the self-restraint of a really great nation which realizes its own strength and scorns to misuse it. It was our duty to offer our active assistance. It is now our duty to show what true neutrality will do to enable the people of Mexico to set their affairs in order again and wait for a further opportunity to offer our friendly counsels. The door is not closed against the resumption, either upon the initiative of Mexico or upon our own, of the effort to bring order out of the confusion by friendly co-operative action, should fortunate occasion offer.

While we wait, the contest of the rival forces will undoubtedly for a little while be sharper than ever, just because it will be plain that an end must be made of the existing situation, and that very promptly; and with the increased activity of the contending factions will come, it is to be feared, increased danger to the noncombatants in Mexico as well as to those actually in the field of battle. The position of outsiders is always particularly trying and full of hazard where there is civil strife and a whole country is upset. We should earnestly urge all Americans to leave Mexico at once, and should assist them to get away in every way possible—not because we would mean to slacken in the least our efforts to safeguard their lives and their interests, but because it is imperative that they should take no unnecessary risks when it is physically possible for them to leave the country. We should let every one who assumes to exercise authority in any part of Mexico know in the most unequivocal way that we shall vigilantly watch the fortunes of those Americans who can not get away, and shall hold those responsible for their sufferings and losses to a definite reckoning. That can be and will be made plain beyond the possibility of a misunderstanding.

For the rest, I deem it my duty to exercise the authority conferred upon me by the law of March 14, 1912, to see to it that neither side to the struggle now going on in Mexico receive any assistance from this side the border. I shall follow the best practice of nations in the matter of neutrality by forbidding the exportation of arms or munitions of war of any kind from the United States to any part of the Republic of Mexico—a policy suggested by several interesting precedents and certainly dictated by many manifest considerations of practical expediency. We can not in the circumstances be the partisans of either party to the contest that now distracts Mexico, or constitute ourselves the virtual umpire between them.

I am happy to say that several of the great Governments of the world have given this Government their generous moral support in urging upon the provisional authorities at the City of Mexico the acceptance of our proffered good offices in the spirit in which they were made. We have not acted in this matter under the ordinary principles of international obligation. All the world expects us in such circumstances to act as Mexico's nearest friend and intimate adviser. This is our immemorial relation towards her. There is nowhere any serious question that we have the moral right in the case or that we are acting in the interest of a fair settlement and of good government, not for the promotion of some selfish interest of our own. If further motive were necessary than our own good will towards a sister Republic and our own deep concern to see peace and order prevail in Central America, this consent of mankind to what we are attempting, this attitude of the great nations of the world towards what we may attempt in dealing with this distressed people at our doors, should make us feel the more solemnly bound to go to the utmost length of patience and forbearance in this painful and anxious business. The steady pressure of moral force will before many days break the barriers of pride and prejudice down, and we shall triumph as Mexico's friends sooner than we could triumph as her enemies— and how much more handsomely, with how much higher and finer satisfactions of conscience and of honor!

Reply of Senor Gamboa to Proposals of the American Government Conveyed Through Hon. John Lind

MEXICO, *August 16, 1913.*

SIR: On the 6th instant, pursuant to telegraphic instructions from his Government, the chargé d'affaires ad interim of the United States of America verbally informed Mr. Manuel Garza Aldape, then in charge of the department of foreign affairs, of your expected arrival in this Republic with a mission of peace. As fortunately neither then nor to-day has there existed a state of war between the United States of America and the United Mexican States, my Government was very much surprised to learn that your mission near us should be referred to as one of peace. This brought forth the essential condition which my Government ventured to demand in its unnumbered note of the 6th instant addressed to the aforesaid chargé d'affaires—"that if you do not see fit to properly establish your official character" your sojourn could not be pleasing to us according to the meaning which diplomatic usage gives to this word.

Fortunately, from the first interview I had the pleasure to have with you, your character as confidential agent of your Government was fully established, inasmuch as the letter you had the kindness to show me, though impersonally addressed, was signed by the President of the United States, for whom we entertain the highest respect.

It is not essential at this time, Mr. Confidential Agent, that I should recall the whole of our first conversation. I will say, however, that I found you to be a well-informed man and animated by the sincerest wishes that the unfortunate tension of the present relations between your Government and mine should reach a prompt and satisfactory solution.

During our second interview, which, like the first one of the 14th instant, was held at my private ([1]), you saw fit, after all intent, honest and frank exchange of opinion concerning the attitudes of our respective Governments which did not lead us to any decision, to deliver to me the note containing the instructions, also signed by the President of the United States. Duly authorized by the President of the Republic, pursuant to the unanimous approval of the Cabinet, which was convened for the purpose, I have the honor to make a detailed reply to such instructions.

The Government of Mexico has paid due attention to the advice and considerations expressed by the Government of the United States; has done this on account of three principal reasons: First, because, as stated before, Mexico entertains the highest respect for the personality

[1] Omission.

of His Excellency Woodrow Wilson; second, because certain European and American Governments, with which Mexico cultivates the closest relations of international amity, having in a most delicate, respectful way, highly gratifying to us, made use of their good offices to the end that Mexico should accord you a hearing, inasmuch as you were the bearer of a private mission from the President of the United States; and, third, because Mexico was anxious, not so much to justify its attitude before the inhabitants of the Republic in the present emergency, the great majority of whom and by means of imposing and orderly manifestations, have signified their adhesion and approval, as to demonstrate in every way the justice of its cause.

The imputation contained in the first paragraph of your instructions that no progress has been made toward establishing in the capital of Mexico a Government that may enjoy the respect and obedience of the Mexican people is unfounded. In contradiction with their gross imputation, which is not supported by any proofs, principally because there are none, it affords me pleasure to refer, Mr. Confidential Agent, to the following facts which abound in evidence and which to a certain extent must be known to you by direct observation. The Mexican Republic, Mr. Confidential Agent, is formed by 27 States, 3 Territories, and 1 Federal District, in which the supreme power of the Republic has its seat. Of these 27 States, 18 of them, the 3 Territories, and the Federal District (making a total of 22 political entities) are under the absolute control of the present Government, which, aside from the above, exercises its authority over almost every port in the Republic and, consequently, over the custom houses therein established. Its southern frontier is open and at peace. Moreover, my Government has an army of 80,000 men in the field, with no other purpose than to insure complete peace in the Republic, the only national aspiration and solemn promise of the present provisional President. The above is sufficient to exclude any doubt that my Government is worthy of the respect and obedience of the Mexican people, because the latter's consideration has been gained at the cost of the greatest sacrifice and in spite of the most evil influences.

My Government fails to understand what the Government of the United States of America means by saying that it does not find itself in the same case with reference to the other nations of the earth concerning what is happening and is likely to happen in Mexico. The conditions of Mexico at the present time are, unfortunately, neither doubtful nor secret; it is afflicted with an internal strife which has been raging almost three years, and which I can only classify in these lines as a fundamental mistake. With reference to what might happen in Mexico neither you, Mr. Confidential Agent, nor I nor anyone else can prognosticate, because no assertion is possible on incidents which have not occurred. On the other hand, my Government greatly appreciates the good offices tendered to it by the Government of the United States of America in the present circumstances; it recognizes that they are inspired by the noble desire to act as a friend as well as by the wishes of all the other Governments which expect the United States to act as Mexico's nearest friend. But if such good offices are to be of the character of those now tendered to us we should have to decline them in the most categorical and definite manner.

Inasmuch as the Government of the United States is willing to act in the most disinterested friendship, it will be difficult for it to find a more propitious opportunity than the following: If it should only watch that no material and monetary assistance is given to rebels who find refuge, conspire, and provide themselves with arms and food on the other side of the border; if it should demand from its minor and local authorities the strictest observance of the neutrality laws, I assure you, Mr. Confidential Agent, that the complete pacification of this Republic would be accomplished within a relatively short time.

I intentionally abstain from replying to the allusion that it is the purpose of the United States of America to show the greatest respect for the sovereignty and independence of Mexico, because, Mr. Confidential Agent, there are matters which not even from the standpoint of the idea itself could be given an answer in writing.

His Excellency Mr. Wilson is laboring under a serious delusion when he declares that the present situation of Mexico is incompatible with the compliance of her international obligations, with the development of its own civilization, and with the required maintenance of certain political and economical conditions tolerable in Central America. Strongly backing that there is a mistake, because to this date no charge has been made by any foreign Government accusing us of the above lack of compliance, we are punctually meeting all of our credits; we are still maintaining diplomatic missions cordially accepted in almost all the countries of the world, and we continue to be invited to all kinds of international congresses and conferences. With regard to our interior development, the following proof is sufficient, to wit, a contract has just been signed with Belgian capitalists which means to Mexico the construction of something like 5,000 kilometers of railway. In conclusion, we fail to see the evil results, which are prejudicial only to ourselves, felt in Central America by our present domestic war. In one thing I do agree with you, Mr. Confidential Agent, and it is that the whole of America is clamoring for a prompt solution of our disturbances, this being a very natural sentiment if it is borne in mind that a country which was prosperous only yesterday has been suddenly caused to suffer a great internal misfortune.

Consequently Mexico can not for one moment take into consideration the four conditions which His Excellency Mr. Wilson has been pleased to propose through your honorable and worthy channel. I must give you the reasons for it: An immediate suspension of the struggle in Mexico, a definite armistice " solemnly constructed and scrupulously observed " is not possible, as to do this it would be necessary that there should be some one capable of proposing it without causing a profound offense to civilization, to the many bandits who, under this or that pretext, are marauding toward the south and committing the most outrageous depredations; and I know of no country in the world, the United States included, which may have ever dared to enter into agreement or to propose an armistice to individuals who, perhaps on account of a physiological accident, can be found all over the world beyond the pale of the divine and human laws. Bandits, Mr. Confidential Agent, are not admitted to armistice; the first action against them is one of correction, and when this, unfortunately, fails, their lives must be severed for the sake of the biological and fundamental principle that the useful sprouts should grow and fructify.

With reference to the rebels who style themselves " Constitutionalists," one of the representatives of whom has been given an ear by Members of the United States Senate, what could there be more gratifying to us than if convinced of the precipice to which we are being dragged by the resentment of their defeat, in a moment of reaction they would depose their rancor and add their strength to ours, so that all together we would undertake the great and urgent task of national reconstruction? Unfortunately, they do not avail themselves of the amnesty law enacted by the provisional government immediately after its inauguration, but, on the contrary, well-known rebels holding elective positions in the capital of the Republic or profitable employments, left the country without molestation, notwithstanding the information which the Government had that they were going to foreign lands to work against its interests, many of whom have taken upon themselves the unfortunate task of exposing the mysteries and infirmities from which we are suffering, the same as any other human congregations.

Were we to agree with them to the armistice suggested, they would *ipso facto,* recognize their belligerency, and this is something which can not be done for many reasons which can not escape the perspicacity of the Government of the United States of America, which to this day, and publicly, at least, has classed them as rebels just the same as we have. And it is an accepted doctrine that no armistice can be concerted with rebels.

The assurance asked of my Government that it should promptly convene to free elections is the most evident proof and the most unequivocal concession that the Government of the United States considers it legally and solidly constituted and that it is exercising, like all those of its class, acts of such importance as to indicate the perfect civil operation of a sovereign nation. Inasmuch as our laws already provide such assurance, there is no fear that the latter may not be observed during the coming elections, and while the present Government is of a provisional character it will cede its place to the definite Government which may be elected by the people.

The request that Gen. Victoriano Huerta should agree not to appear as a candidate for the Presidency of the Republic in the coming elections can not be taken into consideration, because, aside from its strange and unwarranted character, there is a risk that the same might be interpreted as a matter of personal dislike. This point can only be decided by Mexican public opinion when it may be expressed at the polls.

The pledge that all parties should agree beforehand to the results of the election and to co-operate in the most loyal manner to support and organize the new administration is something to be tacitly supposed and desired, and that the experience of what this internal strife means to us in loss of life and the destruction of property will cause all contending political factions to abide by the results; but it would be extemporaneous to make any assertion in this respect, even by the most experienced countries in civil matters, inasmuch as no one can forecast or foresee the errors and excesses which men are likely to commit, especially under the influence of political passion. We hasten to signify our appreciation to the United States of America because they agree from to-day to recognize and aid the future which we, the Mexican people, may elect to rule our destinies. On the other hand, we greatly deplore the present tension in our relations with your country, a tension which has been produced without Mexico having afforded the slightest cause therefor. The legality of the government of Gen. Huerta can not be disputed. Article 85 of our political constitution provides:

If at the beginning of a constitutional term neither the President nor the Vice-President elected present themselves, or if the election has not been held and the results thereof declared by the 1st of December, nevertheless, the President whose term has expired will cease in his functions, and the secretary for foreign affairs shall immediately take charge of the Executive power in the capacity of provisional President; and if there should be no secretary for foreign affairs, or if he should be incapacitated, the Presidency shall devolve on one of the other secretaries pursuant to the order provided by the law establishing their number. The same procedure shall be followed when, in the case of the absolute or temporary absence of the President the Vice-President fails to appear, when on leave of absence from his post if he should be discharging his duties, and when in the course of his term the absolute absence of both functionaries should occur.

Now, then, the facts which occurred are the following: The resignation of Francisco I. Madero, constitutional President, and Jose Maria Pino Suarez, constitutional Vice-President of the Republic. These resignations having been accepted, Pedro Lascurain, Minister for Foreign Affairs, took charge by operation of law of the vacant executive power, appointing, as he had the power to do, Gen. Victoriano Huerta to the post of Minister of the Interior. As Mr. Lascurain soon afterwards resigned, and as his resignation was immediately accepted by Congress, Gen. Victoriano Huerta took charge of the executive power, also by operation of law, with the provisional character and under the constitutional promise already complied with to issue a call for special elections. As will be seen, the point of issue is exclusively one of constitutional law in which no foreign nation, no matter how powerful and respectable it may be, should mediate in the least.

Moreover, my Government considers that at the present time the recognition of the Government of Gen. Huerta by that of the United States of America is not concerned, inasmuch as facts which exist on their own account are not and can not be susceptible of recognition. The only thing which is being discussed is a suspension of relations as abnormal and without reason; abnormal, because the ambassador of the United States of America, in his high diplomatic investiture and appearing as dean of the foreign diplomatic corps accredited to the Government of the Republic, congratulated Gen. Huerta upon his elevation to the Presidency, continued to correspond with this department by means of diplomatic notes, and on his departure left the first secretary of the embassy of the United States of America as chargé d'affaires ad interim, and the latter continues here in the free exercise of his functions; and without reason, because, I repeat, we have not given the slightest pretext.

The confidential agent may believe that solely because of the sincere esteem in which the people and the Government of the United States of America are held by the people and Government of Mexico, and because of the consideration which it has for all friendly nations (and especially in this case for those which have offered their good offices), my Government consented to take into consideration, and to answer as briefly as the matter permits, the representations of which you are the bearer. Otherwise, it would have rejected them immediately because of their humiliating and unusual character, hardly admissible even in a treaty of peace after a victory, inasmuch as in a like case any nation which in the least respects itself would do likewise. It is because my Government has confidence in that when the justice of its cause is reconsidered with serenity and from a lofty point of view by the present President of the United States of America, whose sense of morality and uprightness are beyond question, that he will withdraw from his attitude and will contribute to the renewal of still firmer bases for the relations of sincere friendship and good understanding forcibly imposed upon us throughout the centuries by our geographical nearness, something which neither of us can change, even though we would so desire, by our mutual interests and by our share of activity in the common sense of prosperity, welfare, and culture, in regard to which we are pleased to acknowledge that you are enviably ahead of us.

With reference to the final part of the instructions of President Wilson, which I beg to include herewith and which say, "If Mexico can suggest any better way in which to show our friendship, serve the people of Mexico, and meet our international obligations, we are more than willing to consider the suggestion," that final part causes me to propose the following equally decorous arrangement: One, that our ambassador be received in Washington; two, that the United States of America send us a new ambassador without previous conditions.

And all this threatening and distressing situation will have reached a happy conclusion; mention will not be made of the causes which might carry us, if the tension persists, to no one knows what incalculable extremities for two peoples who have the unavoidable obligation to continue being friends, provided, of course, that this friendship is based upon mutual respect, which is indispensable between two sovereign entities wholly equal before law and justice.

In conclusion, permit me, Mr. Confidential Agent, to reiterate to you the assurances of my perfect consideration.

F. GAMBOA,
Secretary for Foreign Affairs of the Republic.

By the President of the United States of America:

A PROCLAMATION

[Regulations for the Protection of Migratory Birds.]

WHEREAS, an Act of Congress approved March fourth, nineteen hundred and thirteen, entitled "An Act making appropriations for the Department of Agriculture for the fiscal year ending June thirtieth, nineteen hundred and fourteen" (37 Stat., 847), contains provisions as follows:

All wild geese, wild swans, brant, wild ducks, snipe, plover, woodcock, rail, wild pigeons, and all other migratory game and insectivorous birds which in their northern and southern migrations pass through or do not remain permanently the entire year within the borders of any State or Territory, shall hereafter be deemed to be within the custody and protection of the Government of the United States, and shall not be destroyed or taken contrary to regulations hereinafter provided therefor.

The Department of Agriculture is hereby authorized and directed to adopt suitable regulations to give effect to the previous paragraph by prescribing and fixing closed seasons, having due regard to the zones of temperature, breeding habits, and times and line of migratory flight, thereby enabling the department to select and designate suitable districts for different portions of the country, and it shall be unlawful to shoot or by any device kill or seize and capture migratory birds within the protection of this law during said closed seasons, and any person who shall violate any of the provisions or regulations of this law for the protection of migratory birds shall be guilty of a misdemeanor and shall be fined not more than $100 or imprisoned not more than ninety days, or both, in the discretion of the court.

The Department of Agriculture, after the preparation of said regulations, shall cause the same to be made public, and shall allow a period of three months in which said regulations may be examined and considered before final adoption, permitting, when deemed proper, public hearings thereon, and after final adoption shall cause the same to be engrossed and submitted to the President of the United States for approval: *Provided, however,* That nothing herein contained shall be deemed to affect or interfere with the local laws of the States and Territories for the protection of non-migratory game or other birds resident and breeding within their borders, nor to prevent the States and Territories from enacting laws and regulations to promote and render efficient the regulations of the Department of Agriculture provided under this statute.

WHEREAS, the Department of Agriculture has duly prepared suitable regulations to give effect to the foregoing provisions of said Act and after the preparation of said regulations has caused the same to be made public and has allowed a period of three months in which said regulations might be examined and considered before final adoption and has permitted public hearings thereon;

And, WHEREAS, the Department of Agriculture has adopted the regulations hereinafter set forth and after final adoption thereof has caused the same to be engrossed and submitted to the President of the United States for approval;

Now, THEREFORE, I, WOODROW WILSON, President of the United States of America, by authority in me vested do hereby proclaim and make known the following regulations for carrying into effect the foregoing provisions of said Act:

REGULATION 1. DEFINITIONS.

For the purposes of these regulations the following shall be considered migratory game birds:

(*a*) Anatidæ or waterfowl, including brant, wild ducks, geese, and swans.

(*b*) Gruidæ or cranes, including little brown, sandhill, and whooping cranes.

(*c*) Rallidæ or rails, including coots, gallinules, and sora and other rails.

(*d*) Limicolæ or shore birds, including avocets, curlew, dowitchers, godwits, knots, oyster catchers, phalaropes, plover, sandpipers, snipe, stilts, surf birds, turnstones, willet, woodcock, and yellowlegs.

(*e*) Columbidæ or pigeons, including doves and wild pigeons.

For the purposes of these regulations the following shall be considered migratory insectivorous birds:

(*f*) Bobolinks, catbirds, chickadees, cuckoos, flickers, flycatchers, grosbeaks, humming birds, kinglets, martins, meadowlarks, nighthawks or bull bats, nuthatches, orioles, robins, shrikes, swallows, swifts, tanagers, titmice, thrushes, vireos, warblers, waxwings, whippoorwills, woodpeckers, and wrens, and all other perching birds which feed entirely or chiefly on insects.

REGULATION 2. CLOSED SEASON AT NIGHT.

A daily closed season on all migratory game and insectivorous birds shall extend from sunset to sunrise.

REGULATION 3. CLOSED SEASON ON INSECTIVOROUS BIRDS.

A closed season on migratory insectivorous birds shall continue to December 31, 1913, and each year thereafter shall begin January 1 and continue to December 31, both dates inclusive, provided that nothing in this or any other of these regulations shall be construed to prevent the issue of permits for collecting birds for scientific purposes in accordance with the laws and regulations in force in the respective States and Territories and the District of Columbia; and provided further that the closed season on reedbirds or ricebirds in Maryland, the District of Columbia, Virginia and South Carolina shall begin November 1 and end August 31 next following, both dates inclusive.

REGULATION 4. FIVE-YEAR CLOSED SEASONS ON CERTAIN GAME BIRDS.

A closed season shall continue until September 1, 1918, on the following migratory game birds: Band-tailed pigeons, little brown, sandhill, and whooping cranes, swans, curlew, and all shorebirds except the black-breasted and golden plover, Wilson or jack snipe, woodcock, and the greater and lesser yellowlegs.

A closed season shall also continue until September 1, 1918, on wood ducks in Maine, New Hampshire, Vermont, Massachusetts, Rhode Island, Connecticut, New York, New Jersey, Pennsylvania, West Virginia, Ohio, Indiana, Illinois, Michigan, Wisconsin, Minnesota,

Iowa, Kansas, California, Oregon, and Washington; on rails in California and Vermont; and on woodcock in Illinois and Missouri.

REGULATION 5. CLOSED SEASON ON CERTAIN NAVIGABLE RIVERS.

A closed season shall continue between January 1 and December 31, both dates inclusive, of each year, on all migratory birds passing over or at rest on any of the waters of the main streams of the following navigable rivers, to wit: The Mississippi River between Minneapolis, Minn., and Memphis, Tenn.; and the Missouri River between Bismarck, N. Dak., and Nebraska City, Nebr.; and on the killing or capture of any of such birds on or over the shores of any of said rivers, or at any point within the limits aforesaid, from any boat, raft, or other device, floating or otherwise, in or on any such waters.

REGULATION 6. ZONES.

The following zones for the protection of migratory game and insectivorous birds are hereby established:

Zone No. 1, the breeding zone, comprising States lying wholly or in part north of latitude 40° and the Ohio River and including Maine, New Hampshire, Vermont, Massachusetts, Rhode Island, Connecticut, New York, New Jersey, Pennsylvania, Ohio, Indiana, Illinois, Michigan, Wisconsin, Minnesota, Iowa, North Dakota, South Dakota, Nebraska, Colorado, Wyoming, Montana, Idaho, Oregon, and Washington—25 States.

Zone No. 2, the wintering zone, comprising States lying wholly or in part south of latitude 40° and the Ohio River and including Delaware, Maryland, the District of Columbia, West Virginia, Virginia, North Carolina, South Carolina, Georgia, Florida, Alabama, Mississippi, Tennessee, Kentucky, Missouri, Arkansas, Louisiana, Texas, Oklahoma, Kansas, New Mexico, Arizona, California, Nevada, and Utah—23 States and the District of Columbia.

REGULATION 7. CONSTRUCTION.

For the purposes of regulations 8 and 9, each period of time therein prescribed as a closed season shall be construed to include the first day and to exclude the last day thereof.

REGULATION 8. CLOSED SEASONS IN ZONE No. 1.

Closed seasons in Zone No. 1 shall be as follows:

Waterfowl.—The closed season on waterfowl shall be between December 16 and September 1 next following, except as follows:

Exceptions: In Massachusetts the closed season shall be between January 1 and September 15.

In New York, except Long Island, the closed season shall be between December 16 and September 16.

On Long Island and in Oregon and Washington the closed season shall be between January 16 and October 1.

In New Jersey the closed season shall be between February 1 and November 1; and

In Minnesota, North Dakota, South Dakota, and Wisconsin the closed season shall be between December 1 and September 7.

Rails.—The closed season on rails, coots, and gallinules shall be between December 1 and September 1 next following, except as follows:

Exceptions: In Massachusetts, New Hampshire, and Rhode Island the closed season shall be between December 1 and August 15.

In Connecticut, Michigan, and New York, and on Long Island the closed season shall be between December 1 and September 16.

In Minnesota, North Dakota, South Dakota, and Wisconsin the closed season shall be between December 1 and September 7; and

In Oregon and Washington the closed season shall be between January 16 and October 1.

Woodcock.—The closed season on woodcock shall be between December 1 and October 1 next following, except as follows:

Exceptions: In Connecticut, Massachusetts, and New Jersey the closed season shall be between December 1 and October 10.

In Rhode Island the closed season shall be between December 1 and November 1; and

In Pennsylvania and on Long Island the closed season shall be between December 1 and October 15.

Shore birds.—The closed season on black-breasted and golden plover, jack-snipe or Wilson snipe, and greater and lesser yellowlegs shall be between December 16 and September 1 next following, except as follows:

Exceptions: In Maine, Massachusetts, New Hampshire, Rhode Island, and on Long Island the closed season shall be between December 1 and August 15.

In New York, except Long Island, the closed season shall be between December 1 and September 16.

In Minnesota, North Dakota, South Dakota, and Wisconsin the closed season shall be between December 1 and September 7; and

In Oregon and Washington the closed season shall be between December 16 and October 1.

REGULATION 9. CLOSED SEASONS IN ZONE No. 2.

Closed seasons in Zone No. 2 shall be as follows:

Waterfowl.—The closed season on waterfowl shall be between January 16 and October 1 next following, except as follows:

Exceptions: In Delaware, Maryland, Virginia, North Carolina, Alabama, Mississippi, Louisiana, and Texas the closed season shall be between February 1 and November 1.

In the District of Columbia, Kansas, New Mexico, and West Virginia the closed season shall be between December 16 and September 1.

In Florida, Georgia, and South Carolina the closed season shall be between February 16 and November 20.

In Missouri and Nevada the closed season shall be between January 1 and September 15; and

In Arizona and California the closed season shall be between February 1 and October 15.

Rails.—The closed season on rails, coots, and gallinules shall be between December 1 and September 1 next following, except as follows:

Exceptions: In Tennessee and Utah the closed season shall be between December 1 and October 1.

In Missouri the closed season shall be between January 1 and September 15.

In Louisiana the closed season shall be between February 1 and November 1; and

In Arizona and California the closed season on coots shall be between February 1 and October 15.

Woodcock.—The closed season on woodcock shall be between January 1 and November 1, except as follows:

Exceptions: In Delaware and Louisiana the closed season shall be between January 1 and November 15.

In West Virginia the closed season shall be between December 1 and October 1; and

In Georgia the closed season shall be between January 1 and December 1.

Shore birds.—The closed season on black-breasted and golden plover, jack-snipe or Wilson snipe, and greater and lesser yellowlegs shall be between December 16 and September 1 next following, except as follows:

Exceptions: In Florida, Georgia, and South Carolina the closed season shall be between February 1 and November 20.

In Alabama, Louisiana, Mississippi, and Texas the closed season shall be between February 1 and November 1.

In Tennessee the closed season shall be between December 16 and October 1.

In Arizona and California the closed season shall be between February 1 and October 15; and

In Utah the closed season on snipe shall be between December 16 and October 1, and on plover and yellowlegs shall be until September 1, 1918.

REGULATION 10. HEARINGS.

Persons recommending changes in the regulations or desiring to submit evidence in person or by attorney as to the necessity for such changes should make application to the Secretary of Agriculture. Whenever possible hearings will be arranged at central points, and due

THE INAUGURATION OF WOODROW WILSON

notice thereof given by publication or otherwise as may be deemed appropriate. Persons recommending changes should be prepared to show the necessity for such action and to submit evidence other than that based on reasons of personal convenience or a desire to kill game during a longer open season.

In Witness Whereof, I have hereunto set my hand and caused the seal of the United States to be affixed.

[SEAL.]
DONE at the city of Washington, this first day of October in the year of our Lord one thousand nine hundred and thirteen and of the Independence of the United States the one hundred and thirty-eighth.

WOODROW WILSON.

By the President:
W. J. BRYAN, *Secretary of State.*

BY THE PRESIDENT OF THE UNITED STATES OF AMERICA:

A PROCLAMATION

[Cabrillo National Monument.]

WHEREAS, by section 2 of an Act of Congress approved June 8, 1906 (34 Stat. 225), the President was authorized " in his discretion, to declare by public proclamation historic landmarks, historic and prehistoric structures, and other objects of historic or scientific interest that are situated upon the lands owned or controlled by the Government of the United States to be national monuments, and may reserve as a part thereof parcels of land, the limits of which in all cases shall be confined to the smallest area compatible with the proper care and management of the objects to be protected ";

And WHEREAS, when Cabrillo sailed into San Diego Bay on the 28th day of September, 1542, Point Loma was the first land sighted; and The Order of Panama, an organization composed of representative citizens of Southern California, has applied for permission to construct a heroic statue of Juan Rodriguez Cabrillo, the discoverer of California, on Point Loma which lies within the military reservation of Fort Rosecrans, California, and has requested that a suitable site be set apart for such monument;

Now THEREFORE, I, WOODROW WILSON, President of the United States of America, under authority of the said Act of Congress, do hereby reserve as a site for the said monument, the following described parcel of land situated on Point Loma within the limits of the military reservation of Fort Rosecrans, California, and do hereby declare and

255

proclaim the same to be a national monument to commemorate the discovery of California by Juan Rodriguez Cabrillo, on the 28th day of September, 1542, viz.:

Beginning at a monument 53 ft. from southeast corner of the Old Lighthouse, Point Loma (true az. 6° 26'): thence, true az. 292° 50', 25 feet; thence, true az. 234° 09', 36 feet; thence, true az. 210° 47', 35 feet; thence, true az. 191° 14', 53 feet; thence, true az. 175° 56', 57 feet; thence, true az. 159° 26', 33 feet; thence, true az. 138° 29', 115 feet; thence, true az. 7° 39', 170 feet; thence, true az. 349° 56'; 43 feet; thence, true az. 337° 58', 25 feet; thence, true az. 332° 14', 35 feet, to the point of beginning; containing 21,910 square feet, more or less.

The area above comprises all the parcel of ground within the loop of the Point Loma Boulevard where it encircles the Old Lighthouse, but does not include any of the roadway.

In Witness Whereof, I have hereunto set my hand and caused the seal of the United States to be affixed.

[SEAL.] DONE at the City of Washington this fourteenth day of October, in the year of our Lord one thousand nine hundred and thirteen, and of the Independence of the United States the one hundred and thirty-eighth.

WOODROW WILSON.

By the President:
W. J. BRYAN, *Secretary of State.*

BY THE PRESIDENT OF THE UNITED STATES OF AMERICA:

A PROCLAMATION

[Thanksgiving—1913.]

THE season is at hand in which it has been our long respected custom as a people to turn in praise and thanksgiving to Almighty God for His manifold mercies and blessings to us as a nation. The year that has just passed has been marked in a peculiar degree by manifestations of His gracious and beneficent providence. We have not only had peace throughout our own borders and with the nations of the world but that peace has been brightened by constantly multiplying evidences of genuine friendship, of mutual sympathy and understanding, and of the happy operation of many elevating influences both of ideal and of practice. The nation has been prosperous not only but has proved its capacity to take calm counsel amidst the rapid movement of affairs and deal with its own life in a spirit of candor, righteousness, and comity. We have seen the practical completion of a great work at the Isthmus of Panama which not only exemplifies the nation's abundant resources to accomplish what it will and the distinguished skill and capacity of its public servants but also promises the beginning of a new age, of new contacts, new neighborhoods, new sympathies, new bonds, and new achievements of co-operation and peace. " Righteousness exalteth a nation " and " peace on earth, good will towards men " furnish the only foundations upon which can be built the lasting achievements of the human spirit. The year has brought us the satisfactions of work well done and fresh visions of our duty which will make the work of the future better still.

Now, THEREFORE, I, WOODROW WILSON, President of the United States of America, do hereby designate Thursday the twenty-seventh of November next as a day of thanksgiving and prayer, and invite the people throughout the land to cease from their wonted occupations and in their several homes and places of worship render thanks to Almighty God.

In Witness Whereof, I have hereunto set my hand and caused the seal of the United States to be affixed.

DONE at the City of Washington this twenty-third day of October, in the year of our Lord one thousand nine hundred and thirteen, and of the independence of the United [SEAL.] States of America the one hundred and thirty-eighth.

WOODROW WILSON.

By the President:

W. J. BRYAN, *Secretary of State.*

EXECUTIVE ORDER.

[To Regulate the Carrying of Arms in the Canal Zone.]

THE WHITE HOUSE, *November 7, 1913.*

By virtue of the authority vested in me, I hereby establish the following order for the Canal Zone:

Section 1. Anyone who carries on or about his person any firearm, dirk, dagger or other knife manufactured or sold for the purpose of offence or defence, or any slungshot, sword-cane or any knuckles made of metal or other hard substance, shall be punished by fine of not less than Five Dollars nor more than Twenty-five Dollars, or by imprisonment in jail of not less than five days nor more than thirty days, or by both such fine and imprisonment in the discretion of the court, and during such time of imprisonment such offender may be put to work upon any public work in the Canal Zone.

In addition to the punishment herein prescribed for unlawfully carrying arms, the courts shall adjudge the seizure and confiscation of the arms unlawfully carried by the offending party and the same shall be disposed of in such manner as the Head of the Department of Civil Administration shall determine.

Section 2. The preceding section shall not apply to a person engaged in the military or naval service of the United States or as a peace officer or officer authorized to execute judicial process of the United States or the Canal Zone, or in carrying mail or engaged in the collection or custody of funds of the United States or the Canal Zone, nor to a member of a gun or pistol club for the promotion of target practice, a certified copy of the constitution and by-laws of which has been approved by the Head of the Department of Civil Administration, and filed with the Collector of Revenues, when such member is going to or from a target range, and engaged in practice at the target range. For the purposes of this order, a certificate of membership in the gun or pistol club shall be issued by the organization and approved by the Head of the Department of Civil Administration, and shall entitle the holder to carry firearms as provided for in this section.

Neither shall the preceding section apply to any person authorized to have or carry arms by permit granted under the terms and conditions named in section 3 hereof.

Section 3. The Head of the Department of Civil Administration may authorize the granting of permits to have and carry arms as follows:

1. To hunt upon the public lands of the Canal Zone, or upon the lands of private persons when authorized by the latter.

2. To have arms in residences, offices, business places and plantations; and to watchmen or overseers of plantations, factories, warehouses, docks or piers.

Applications for such permits shall be made to the Head of the Department of Civil Administration and shall state the full name, residence and occupation of the applicant, and if the applicant is a minor it shall not be granted without the written consent of his parent or guardian.

The Head of the Department of Civil Administration shall satisfy himself by due inquiry that the applicant is a proper person to have a permit to carry arms, and he may grant or deny the application as to him may seem proper.

When an application is granted by the Head of the Department of Civil Administration for a permit to hunt he shall file the application, with his approval endorsed thereon, with the Collector of Revenues, who shall issue a permit to the applicant upon his paying the Collector of Revenues a fee of one dollar, to be covered into the Treasury of the Canal Zone Government.

The hunting permits issued by virtue of this order shall authorize the holder thereof to have, use or carry a gun, rifle or other similar long arm for hunting purposes during the fiscal year for which the permit is issued, provided, however, that such permit may be revoked at any time for cause by the Head of the Department of Civil Administration.

Section 4. Anyone who engages in hunting without first obtaining the permit provided for in this order shall be subject to a fine not exceeding Twenty-five dollars or imprisonment in jail not exceeding ten days, provided, however, that persons engaged in the land or naval forces of the United States shall not be required to obtain a permit to hunt upon the public lands of the Canal Zone.

Section 5. Penalties for infringements of this order imposed upon intoxicated or disorderly persons shall be in addition to the punishments authorized by law for such intoxicated or disorderly conduct.

Section 6. Sections 449 to 460, both inclusive, of the Penal Code, the Executive Order of December 1, 1909, issued by the Secretary of War by authority of the President, amending Section 450 and 456 of the Penal Code, and the Executive Order of the Secretary of War, issued by authority of the President, dated November 3, 1911, amending Section 456 of the Penal Code as amended by the Executive Order above mentioned, and all other laws, orders and decrees in conflict with this order are hereby repealed.

Section 7. This order shall take effect thirty days from and after its publication in the Canal Record.

WOODROW WILSON.

EXECUTIVE ORDER.

[Fixing the Rate of Interest on Money.]

THE WHITE HOUSE, *November 11, 1913.*

By virtue of the authority vested in me I hereby establish the following Executive Order for the Canal Zone:

Section 1. No rate of interest shall be allowed in excess of six per centum per annum upon any contract for the use or detention of money, unless the same is in writing and the interest agreed upon must not exceed twelve per centum per annum.

Section 2. All contracts whatsoever which may in any way, directly or indirectly, violate the preceding section by stipulating for a greater rate of interest than twelve per centum per annum, shall be void and of no effect for the amount or value of the interest only; but the principal sum of money or value of the contract may be received and recovered.

Section 3. When the interest received or collected for the use or detention of money exceeds the rate of twelve per centum per annum, it shall be deemed to be usurious, and the person or persons paying the same, or their legal representatives, may recover from the person, firm or corporation receiving such interest, the amount of the interest so received or collected, in any court of competent jurisdiction, within two years from the date of the payment of such interest.

Section 4. No evidence of usury shall be received on the trial of any case unless the same shall be pleaded and verified by the affidavit of the party wishing to avail himself of such defense.

Section 5. This order shall take effect thirty days from and after its publication in the Canal Record.

WOODROW WILSON.

FIRST ANNUAL ADDRESS.

[Delivered at a Joint Session of the two Houses of Congress, December 2, 1913.]

Gentlemen of the Congress:

In pursuance of my constitutional duty to "give to the Congress information of the state of the Union," I take the liberty of addressing you on several matters which ought, as it seems to me, particularly to engage the attention of your honorable bodies, as of all who study the welfare and progress of the Nation.

I shall ask your indulgence if I venture to depart in some degree from the usual custom of setting before you in formal review the many matters which have engaged the attention and called for the action of the several departments of the Government or which look to them for early treatment in the future, because the list is long, very long, and would suffer in the abbreviation to which I should have to subject it. I shall submit to you the reports of the heads of the several departments, in which these subjects are set forth in careful detail, and beg that they may receive the thoughtful attention of your committees and of all Members of the Congress who may have the leisure to study them. Their obvious importance, as constituting the very substance of the business of the Government, makes comment and emphasis on my part unnecessary.

The country, I am thankful to say, is at peace with all the world, and many happy manifestations multiply about us of a growing cordiality and sense of community of interest among the nations, foreshadowing an age of settled peace and good will. More and more readily each decade do the nations manifest their willingness to bind themselves by solemn treaty to the processes of peace, the processes of frankness and fair concession. So far the United States has stood at the front of such negotiations. She will, I earnestly hope and confidently believe, give fresh proof of her sincere adherence to the cause of international friendship by ratifying the several treaties of arbitration awaiting renewal by the Senate. In addition to these, it has been the privilege of the Department of State to gain the assent, in principle, of no less than 31 nations, representing four-fifths of the population of the world, to the negotiation of treaties by which it shall be agreed that whenever differences of interest or of policy arise which can not be resolved by the ordinary processes of diplomacy they shall be publicly analyzed, discussed, and reported upon by a tribunal chosen by the parties before either nation determines its course of action.

There is only one possible standard by which to determine controversies between the United States and other nations, and that is compounded of these two elements: Our own honor and our obligations to the peace of the world. A test so compounded ought easily to be made to govern both the establishment of new treaty obligations and the interpretation of those already assumed.

There is but one cloud upon our horizon. That has shown itself to the south of us, and hangs over Mexico. There can be no certain prospect of peace in America until Gen. Huerta has surrendered his usurped authority in Mexico; until it is understood on all hands, indeed, that such pretended governments will not be countenanced or dealt with by the Government of the United States. We are the friends of constitutional government in America; we are more than its friends, we are its champions; because in no other way can our neighbors, to whom we would wish in every way to make proof of our friendship, work out their own development in peace and liberty. Mexico has no Government. The attempt to maintain one at the City of Mexico has broken down, and a mere military despotism has been set up which has hardly more than the semblance of national authority. It originated in the usurpation of Victoriano Huerta, who, after a brief attempt to play the part of constitutional President, has at last cast aside even the pretense of legal right and declared himself dictator. As a consequence, a condition of affairs now exists in Mexico which has made it doubtful whether even the most elementary and fundamental rights either of her own people or of the citizens of other countries resident within her territory can long be successfully safeguarded, and which threatens, if long continued, to imperil the interests of peace, order, and tolerable life in the lands immediately to the south of us. Even if the usurper had succeeded in his purposes, in despite of the constitution of the Republic and the rights of its people, he would have set up nothing but a precarious and hateful power, which could have lasted but a little while, and whose eventual downfall would have left the country in a more deplorable condition than ever. But he has not succeeded. He has forfeited the respect and the moral support even of those who were at one time willing to see him succeed. Little by little he has been completely isolated. By a little every day his power and prestige are crumbling and the collapse is not far away. We shall not, I believe, be obliged to alter our policy of watchful waiting. And then, when the end comes, we shall hope to see constitutional order restored in distressed Mexico by the concert and energy of such of her leaders as prefer the liberty of their people to their own ambitions.

I turn to matters of domestic concern. You already have under consideration a bill for the reform of our system of banking and currency, for which the country waits with impatience, as for something fundamental to its whole business life and necessary to set credit free from arbitrary and artificial restraints. I need not say how earnestly I hope for its early enactment into law. I take leave to beg that the whole energy and attention of the Senate be concentrated upon it till the matter is successfully disposed of. And yet I feel that the request is not needed—that the Members of that great House need no urging in this service to the country.

I present to you, in addition, the urgent necessity that special provision be made also for facilitating the credits needed by the farmers of the country. The pending currency bill does the farmers a great service. It puts them upon an equal footing with other business men and masters of enterprise, as it should; and upon its passage they will find themselves quit of many of the difficulties which now hamper them in the field of credit. The farmers, of course, ask and should be given no special privilege, such as extending to them the credit of the Government itself. What they need and should obtain is legislation which will make their own abundant and substantial credit resources available as a foundation for joint, concerted local action in their own behalf in getting the capital they must use. It is to this we should now address ourselves.

It has, singularly enough, come to pass that we have allowed the industry of our farms to lag behind the other activities of the country in its development. I need not stop to tell you how fundamental to the life of the Nation is the production of its food. Our thoughts may ordinarily be concentrated upon the cities and the hives of industry, upon the cries of the crowded market place and the clangor of the factory, but it is from the quiet interspaces of the open valleys and the free hillsides that we draw the sources of life and of prosperity, from the farm and the ranch, from the forest and the mine. Without these every street would be silent, every office deserted, every factory fallen into disrepair. And yet the farmer does not stand upon the same footing with the forester and the miner in the market of credit. He is the servant of the seasons. Nature determines how long he must wait for his crops, and will not be hurried in her processes. He may give his note, but the season of its maturity depends upon the season when his crop matures, lies at the gates of the market where his products are sold. And the security he gives is of a character not known in the broker's office or as familiarly as it might be on the counter of the banker.

The Agricultural Department of the Government is seeking to assist as never before to make farming an efficient business, of wide co-operative effort, in quick touch with the markets for foodstuffs. The farmers and the Government will henceforth work together as real partners in this field, where we now begin to see our way very clearly and where many intelligent plans are already being put into execution. The Treasury of the United States has, by a timely and well-considered distribution of its deposits, facilitated the moving of the crops in the present season and prevented the scarcity of available funds too often experienced at such times. But we must not allow ourselves to depend upon extraordinary expedients. We must add the means by which the farmer may make his credit constantly and easily available and command when he will the capital by which to support and expand his business. We lag behind many other great countries of the modern world in attempting to do this. Systems of rural credit have been studied and developed on the other side of the water while we left our farmers to shift for themselves in the ordinary money market. You have but to look about you in any rural district to see the result, the handicap and embarrassment which have been put upon those who produce our food.

Conscious of this backwardness and neglect on our part, the Congress recently authorized the creation of a special commission to study the various systems of rural credit which have been put into operation in Europe, and this commission is already prepared to report. Its report ought to make it easier for us to determine what methods will be best suited to our own farmers. I hope and believe that the committees of the Senate and House will address themselves to this matter with the most fruitful results, and I believe that the studies and recently formed plans of the Department of Agriculture may be made to serve them very greatly in their work of framing appropriate and adequate legislation. It would be indiscreet and presumptuous in anyone to dogmatize upon so great and many-sided a question, but I feel confident that common counsel will produce the results we must all desire.

Turn from the farm to the world of business which centers in the city and in the factory, and I think that all thoughtful observers will agree that the immediate service we owe the business communities of the country is to prevent private monopoly more effectually than it has yet been prevented. I think it will be easily agreed that we should let the Sherman anti-trust law stand, unaltered, as it is, with its debatable ground about it, but that we should as much as possible reduce the area of that debatable ground by further and more explicit legislation; and should also supplement that great act by legislation which will not only clarify it but also facilitate its administration and make it fairer to all concerned. No doubt we shall all wish, and the country will expect, this to be the central subject of our deliberations during the present session; but it is a subject so many-sided and so deserving of careful and discriminating discussion that I shall take the liberty of addressing you upon it in a special message at a later date than this. It is of capital importance that the business men of this country should be relieved of all uncertainties of law with regard to their enterprises and investments and a clear path indicated which they can travel without anxiety. It is as important that they should be relieved of embarrassment and set free to prosper as that private monopoly should be destroyed. The ways of action should be thrown wide open.

I turn to a subject which I hope can be handled promptly and without serious controversy of any kind. I mean the method of selecting nominees for the Presidency of the United States. I feel confident that I do not misinterpret the wishes or the expectations of the country when I urge the prompt enactment of legislation which will provide for primary elections throughout the country at which the voters of the several parties may choose their nominees for the Presidency without the intervention of nominating conventions. I venture the suggestion that this legislation should provide for the retention of party conventions, but only for the purpose of declaring and accepting the verdict of the primaries and formulating the platforms of the parties; and I suggest that these conventions should consist not of delegates chosen for this single purpose, but of the nominees for Congress, the nominees for vacant seats in the Senate of the United States, the Senators whose terms have not yet closed, the national committees, and the candidates for the Presidency themselves, in order that platforms may be framed by those responsible to the people for carrying them into effect.

These are all matters of vital domestic concern, and besides them, outside the charmed circle of our own national life in which our affections command us, as well as our consciences, there stand out our obligations toward our territories over sea. Here we are trustees. Porto Rico, Hawaii, the Philippines, are ours, indeed, but not ours to do what we please with. Such territories, once regarded as mere possessions, are no longer to be selfishly exploited; they are part of the domain of public conscience and of serviceable and enlightened statesmanship. We must administer them for the people who live in them and with the same sense of responsibility to them as toward our own people in our domestic affairs. No doubt we shall successfully enough bind Porto Rico and the Hawaiian Islands to ourselves by ties of justice and interest and affection, but the performance of our duty toward the Philippines is a more difficult and debatable matter. We can satisfy the obligations of generous justice toward the people of Porto Rico by giving them the ample and familiar rights and privileges accorded our own citizens in our own territories and our obligations toward the people of Hawaii by perfecting the provisions for self-government already granted them, but in the Philippines we must go further. We must hold steadily in view their ultimate independence, and we must move toward the time of that independence as steadily as the way can be cleared and the foundations thoughtfully and permanently laid.

Acting under the authority conferred upon the President by Congress, I have already accorded the people of the islands a majority in both houses of their legislative body by appointing five instead of four native citizens to the membership of the commission. I believe that in this way we shall make proof of their capacity in counsel and their sense of responsibility in the exercise of political power, and that the success of this step will be sure to clear our view for the steps which are to follow. Step by step we should extend and perfect the system of self-government in the islands, making test of them and modifying them as experience discloses their successes and their failures; that we should more and more put under the control of the native citizens of the archipelago the essential instruments of their life, their local instrumentalities of government, their schools, all the common interests of their communities, and so by counsel and experience set up a government which all the world will see to be suitable to a people whose affairs are under their own control. At last, I hope and believe, we are beginning to gain the confidence of the Filipino peoples. By their counsel and experience, rather than by our own, we shall learn how best to serve them and how soon it will be possible and wise to withdraw our supervision. Let us once find the path and set out with firm and confident tread upon it and we shall not wander from it or linger upon it.

A duty faces us with regard to Alaska which seems to me very pressing and very imperative; perhaps I should say a double duty, for it concerns both the political and the material development of the Territory. The people of Alaska should be given the full Territorial form of government, and Alaska, as a storehouse, should be unlocked. One key to it is a system of railways. These the Government should itself build and administer, and the ports and terminals it should itself control in the interest of all who wish to use them for the service and development of the country and its people.

But the construction of railways is only the first step; is only thrusting in the key to the storehouse and throwing back the lock and opening the door. How the tempting resources of the country are to be exploited is another matter, to which I shall take the liberty of from time to time calling your attention, for it is a policy which must be worked out by well-considered stages, not upon theory, but upon lines of practical expediency. It is part of our general problem of conservation. We have a freer hand in working out the problem in Alaska than in the States of the Union; and yet the principle and object are the same, wherever we touch it. We must use the resources of the country, not lock them up. There need be no conflict or jealousy as between State and Federal authorities, for there can be no essential difference of purpose between them. The resources in question must be used, but not destroyed or wasted; used, but not monopolized upon any narrow idea of individual rights as against the abiding interests of communities. That a policy can be worked out by conference and concession which will release these resources and yet not jeopard or dissipate them, I for one have no doubt; and it can be done on lines of regulation which need be no less acceptable to the people and governments of the States concerned than to the people and Government of the Nation at large, whose heritage these resources are. We must bend our counsels to this end. A common purpose ought to make agreement easy.

Three or four matters of special importance and significance I beg that you will permit me to mention in closing.

Our Bureau of Mines ought to be equipped and empowered to render even more effectual service than it renders now in improving the conditions of mine labor and making the mines more economically productive as well as more safe. This is an all-important part of the work of conservation; and the conservation of human life and energy lies even nearer to our interests than the preservation from waste of our material resources.

We owe it, in mere justice to the railway employees of the country, to provide for them a fair and effective employers' liability act; and a law that we can stand by in this matter will be no less to the advantage of those who administer the railroads of the country than to the advantage of those whom they employ. The experience of a large number of the States abundantly proves that.

We ought to devote ourselves to meeting pressing demands of plain justice like this as earnestly as to the accomplishment of political and economic reforms. Social justice comes first. Law is the machinery for its realization and is vital only as it expresses and embodies it.

An international congress for the discussion of all questions that affect safety at sea is now sitting in London at the suggestion of our own Government. So soon as the conclusions of that congress can be learned and considered we ought to address ourselves, among other things, to the prompt alleviation of the very unsafe, unjust, and burdensome conditions which now surround the employment of sailors and render it extremely difficult to obtain the services of spirited and competent men such as every ship needs if it is to be safely handled and brought to port.

May I not express the very real pleasure I have experienced in co-operating with this Congress and sharing with it the labors of common service to which it has devoted itself so unreservedly during the past seven months of uncomplaining concentration upon the business of legislation? Surely it is a proper and pertinent part of my report on "the state of the Union" to express my admiration for the diligence, the good temper, and the full comprehension of public duty which has already been manifested by both the Houses; and I hope that it may not be deemed an impertinent intrusion of myself into the picture if I say with how much and how constant satisfaction I have availed myself of the privilege of putting my time and energy at their disposal alike in counsel and in action.

SPECIAL ADDRESS.

[Additional Legislation for the Control of Trusts and Monopolies. Delivered at a Joint Session of the two Houses of Congress, January 20, 1914.]

Gentlemen of the Congress:

In my report "on the state of the Union," which I had the privilege of reading to you on the 2d of December last, I ventured to reserve for discussion at a later date the subject of additional legislation regarding the very difficult and intricate matter of trusts and monopolies. The time now seems opportune to turn to that great question; not only because the currency legislation, which absorbed your attention and the attention of the country in December, is now disposed of, but also because opinion seems to be clearing about us with singular rapidity in this other great field of action. In the matter of the currency it cleared suddenly and very happily after the much-debated Act was passed; in respect of the monopolies which have multiplied about us and in regard to the various means by which they have been organized and maintained it seems to be coming to a clear and all but universal agreement in anticipation of our action, as if by way of preparation, making the way easier to see and easier to set out upon with confidence and without confusion of counsel.

Legislation has its atmosphere like everything else, and the atmosphere of accommodation and mutual understanding which we now breathe with so much refreshment is matter of sincere congratulation. It ought to make our task very much less difficult and embarrassing than it would have been had we been obliged to continue to act amidst the atmosphere of suspicion and antagonism which has so long made it impossible to approach such questions with dispassionate fairness. Constructive legislation, when successful, is always the embodiment of convincing experience, and of the mature public opinion which finally springs out of that experience. Legislation is a business of interpretation, not of origination; and it is now plain what the opinion is to which we must give effect in this matter. It is not recent or hasty opinion. It springs out of the experience of a whole generation. It has clarified itself by long contest, and those who for a long time battled with it and sought to change it are now frankly and honorably yielding to it and seeking to conform their actions to it.

The great business men who organized and financed monopoly and those who administered it in actual everyday transactions have year after year, until now, either denied its existence or justified it as necessary for the effective maintenance and development of the vast business processes of the country in the modern circumstances of trade and manufacture and finance; but all the while opinion has made head against them. The average business man is convinced that the ways of liberty are also the ways of peace and the ways of success as well; and at last the masters of business on the great scale have begun to yield their preference and purpose, perhaps their judgment also, in honorable surrender.

What we are purposing to do, therefore, is, happily, not to hamper or interfere with business as enlightened business men prefer to do it, or in any sense to put it under the ban. The antagonism between business and government is over. We are now about to give expression to the best business judgment of America, to what we know to be the business conscience and honor of the land. The Government and business men are ready to meet each other half way in a common effort to square business methods with both public opinion and the law. The best informed men of the business world condemn the methods and processes and consequences of monopoly as we condemn them; and the instinctive judgment of the vast majority of business men everywhere goes with them. We shall now be their spokesmen. That is the strength of our position and the sure prophecy of what will ensue when our reasonable work is done.

When serious contest ends, when men unite in opinion and purpose, those who are to change their ways of business joining with those who ask for the change, it is possible to effect it in the way in which prudent and thoughtful and patriotic men would wish to see it brought about, with as few, as slight, as easy and simple business readjustments as possible in the circumstances, nothing essential disturbed, nothing torn up by the roots, no parts rent asunder which can be left in wholesome combination. Fortunately, no measures of sweeping or novel change are necessary. It will be understood that our object is *not* to unsettle business or anywhere seriously to break its established courses athwart. On the contrary, we desire the laws we are now about to pass to be the bulwarks and safeguards of industry against the forces that have disturbed it. What we have to do can be done in a new spirit, in thoughtful moderation, without revolution of any untoward kind.

We are all agreed that "private monopoly is indefensible and intolerable," and our programme is founded upon that conviction. It will be a comprehensive but not a radical or unacceptable programme and these are its items, the changes which opinion deliberately sanctions and for which business waits:

It waits with acquiescence, in the first place, for laws which will effectually prohibit and prevent such interlockings of the *personnel* of the directorates of great corporations—banks and railroads, industrial, commercial, and public service bodies—as in effect result in making those who borrow and those who lend practically one and the same, those who sell and those who buy but the same persons trading with one another under different names and in different combinations, and those who affect to compete in fact partners and masters of some whole field of business. Sufficient time should be allowed, of course, in which to effect these changes of organization without inconvenience or confusion.

Such a prohibition will work much more than a mere negative good by correcting the serious evils which have arisen because, for example, the men who have been the directing spirits of the great investment banks have usurped the place which belongs to independent industrial management working in its own behoof. It will bring new men, new energies, a new spirit of initiative, new blood, into the management of our great business enterprises. It will open the field of industrial development and origination to scores of men who have been obliged to serve when their abilities entitled them to direct. It will immensely hearten the young men coming on and will greatly enrich the business activities of the whole country.

In the second place, business men as well as those who direct public affairs now recognize, and recognize with painful clearness, the great harm and injustice which has been done to many, if not all, of the great railroad systems of the country by the way in which they have been financed and their own distinctive interests subordinated to the interests of the men who financed them and of other business enterprises which those men wished to promote. The country is ready, therefore, to accept, and accept with relief as well as approval, a law which will confer upon the Interstate Commerce Commission the power to superintend and regulate the financial operations by which the railroads are henceforth to be supplied with the money they need for their proper development to meet the rapidly growing requirements of the country for increased and improved facilities of transportation. We can not postpone action in this matter without leaving the railroads exposed to many serious handicaps and hazards; and the prosperity of the railroads and the prosperity of the country are inseparably connected. Upon this question those who are chiefly responsible for the actual management and operation of the railroads have spoken very plainly and very earnestly, with a purpose we ought to be quick to accept. It will be one step, and a very important one, toward the necessary separation of the business of production from the business of transportation.

The business of the country awaits also, has long awaited and has suffered because it could not obtain, further and more explicit legislative definition of the policy and meaning of the existing antitrust law. Nothing hampers business like uncertainty. Nothing daunts or discourages it like the necessity to take chances, to run the risk of falling under the condemnation of the law before it can make sure just what the law is. Surely we are sufficiently familiar with the actual processes and methods of monopoly and of the many hurtful restraints of trade to make definition possible, at any rate up to the limits of what experience has disclosed. These practices, being now abundantly disclosed, can be explicitly and item by item forbidden by statute in such terms as will practically eliminate uncertainty, the law itself and the penalty being made equally plain.

And the business men of the country desire something more than that the menace of legal process in these matters be made explicit and intelligible. They desire the advice, the definite guidance and information which can be supplied by an administrative body, an interstate trade commission.

The opinion of the country would instantly approve of such a commission. It would not wish to see it empowered to make terms with monopoly or in any sort to assume control of business, as if the Government made itself responsible. It demands such a commission only as an indispensable instrument of information and publicity, as a clearing house for the facts by which both the public mind and the managers of great business undertakings should be guided, and as an instrumentality for doing justice to business where the processes of the courts or the natural forces of correction outside the courts are inadequate to adjust the remedy to the wrong in a way that will meet all the equities and circumstances of the case.

Producing industries, for example, which have passed the point up to which combination may be consistent with the public interest and the freedom of trade, can not always be dissected into their component units as readily as railroad companies or similar organizations can be. Their dissolution by ordinary legal process may oftentimes involve financial consequences likely to overwhelm the security market and bring upon it breakdown and confusion. There ought to be an administrative commission capable of directing and shaping such corrective processes, not only in aid of the courts but also by independent suggestion, if necessary.

Inasmuch as our object and the spirit of our action in these matters is to meet business half way in its processes of self-correction and disturb its legitimate course as little as possible, we ought to see to it, and the judgment of practical and sagacious men of affairs everywhere would applaud us if we did see to it, that penalties and punishments should fall, not upon business itself, to its confusion and interruption, but upon the individuals who use the instrumentalities of business to do things which public policy and sound business practice condemn. Every act of business is done at the command or upon the initiative of some ascertainable person or group of persons. These should be held individually responsible and the punishment should fall upon them, not upon the business organization of which they make illegal use. It should be one of the main objects of our legislation to divest such persons of their corporate cloak and deal with them as with those who do not represent their corporations, but merely by deliberate intention break the law. Business men the country through would, I am sure, applaud us if we were to take effectual steps to see that the officers and directors of great business bodies were prevented from bringing them and the business of the country into disrepute and danger.

Other questions remain which will need very thoughtful and practical treatment. Enterprises, in these modern days of great individual fortunes, are oftentimes interlocked, not by being under the control of the same directors, but by the fact that the greater part of their corporate stock is owned by a single person or group of persons who are in some way intimately related in interest. We are agreed, I take it, that holding *companies* should be prohibited, but what of the controlling private ownership of individuals or actually co-operative groups of individuals? Shall the private owners of capital stock be suffered to be themselves in effect holding companies? We do not wish, I suppose, to forbid the purchase of stocks by any person who pleases to buy them in such quantities as he can afford, or in any way arbitrarily to limit the sale of stocks to bona fide purchasers. Shall we require the owners of stock, when their voting power in several companies which ought to be independent of one another would constitute actual control, to make election in which of them they will exercise their right to vote? This question I venture for your consideration.

There is another matter in which imperative considerations of justice and fair play suggest thoughtful remedial action. Not only do many of the combinations effected or sought to be effected in the industrial world work an injustice upon the public in general; they also directly and seriously injure the individuals who are put out of business in one unfair way or another by the many dislodging and exterminating forces of combination. I hope that we shall agree in giving private individuals who claim to have been injured by these processes the right to found their suits for redress upon the facts and judgments proved and entered in suits by the Government where the Government has upon its own initiative sued the combinations complained of and won its suit, and that the statute of limitations shall be suffered to run against such litigants only from the date of the conclusion of the Government's action. It is not fair that the private litigant should be obliged to set up and establish again the facts which the Government has proved. He can not afford, he has not the power, to make use of such processes of inquiry as the Government has command of. Thus shall individual justice be done while the processes of business are rectified and squared with the general conscience.

I have laid the case before you, no doubt as it lies in your own mind, as it lies in the thought of the country. What must every candid man say of the suggestions I have laid before you, of the plain obligations of which I have reminded you? That these are new things for which the country is not prepared? No; but that they are old things, now familiar, and must of course be undertaken if we are to square our laws with the thought and desire of the country. Until these things are done, conscientious business men the country over will be unsatisfied. They are in these things our mentors and colleagues. We are now about to write the additional articles of our constitution of peace, the peace that is honor and freedom and prosperity.

EXECUTIVE ORDER.

[To Prevent the Corrupt Influencing of Agents, Employees or Servants in the Canal Zone.]

THE WHITE HOUSE, *January 21, 1914.*

By virtue of the authority vested in me I hereby establish the following Executive order for the Canal Zone:

Section 1. It shall be unlawful for any person to give, offer or promise to an agent, employee or servant, any gift or gratuity whatever without the knowledge and consent of the principal, employer or master of such agent, employee or servant with intent to influence his action in relation to the business of his principal, employer, or master;

or for any agent, employee or servant, without the knowledge and consent of his principal, employer or master, to request or accept a gift, or gratuity, or the promise of any gift or gratuity whatever beneficial to himself, under an agreement or with an understanding that he shall act in any particular manner in respect to the business of his principal, employer, or master; or for any agent, employee or servant authorized to procure materials, supplies or other articles either by purchase or contract for his principal, employer or master, or to employ servants or labor for his principal, employer or master, to request or accept or agree to accept, for himself or another, directly or indirectly, a commission, discount or bonus from the person who makes the sale or contract, or furnishes such materials, supplies or articles or from the person who renders such service or labor; or for any person to give or offer to such agent, employee, or servant such commission, discount or bonus.

A violation of any of the provisions of this order shall be punished by a fine of not less than ten dollars nor more than five hundred dollars, or by imprisonment in jail for not more than one year, or both such fine and imprisonment in the discretion of the Court.

Sec. 2. This order shall take effect thirty days from and after its publication in the Canal Record.

WOODROW WILSON.

EXECUTIVE ORDER.

[To Prevent Fire-hunting at Night, and Hunting by Means of a Spring or Trap in the Canal Zone, and to Repeal the Executive Order of September 8, 1909.]

THE WHITE HOUSE, *January 27, 1914.*

By virtue of the authority vested in me I hereby establish the following order for the Canal Zone.

Section 1. Every person who shall hunt at night, between the hours of sunset and sunrise, with the aid or use of a lantern, torch, bonfire, or other artificial light, or who shall hunt by the use of a gun or other firearm intended to be discharged by an animal or bird, by means of a spring or trap, or other similar mechanical device, shall be guilty of a misdemeanor.

The penalties imposed by this Order shall be in addition to the punishments authorized by the law against carrying arms without a permit.

Sec. 2. The Executive Order of September 8, 1909, amending Section 454 of the Penal Code of the Canal Zone, is hereby repealed.

SEC. 3. This order shall take effect thirty days from and after its publication in the Canal Record.

WOODROW WILSON.

EXECUTIVE ORDER.

[To Establish a Permanent Organization for the Operation and Government of the Panama Canal.]

THE WHITE HOUSE, *January 27, 1914.*

By virtue of the authority vested in me, I hereby enact the following order, creating a permanent organization for the Panama Canal, under the Act of Congress "To provide for the opening, maintenance, protection and operation of the Panama Canal and the sanitation and government of the Canal Zone," approved August 24, 1912.

Section 1. The organization for the completion, maintenance, operation, government and sanitation of the Panama Canal and its adjuncts and the government of the Canal Zone shall consist of the following departments, offices and agencies, and such others as may be established by the Governor of the Panama Canal on the Isthmus or elsewhere with the approval of the President, all to be under the direction of the Governor, subject to the supervision of the Secretary of War.

DEPARTMENT OF OPERATION AND MAINTENANCE.

There shall be a Department of Operation and Maintenance under the immediate supervision and direction of the Governor of the Panama Canal. This Department shall be charged with the construction of the Canal and with its operation and maintenance when completed, including all matters relating to traffic of the Canal and its adjuncts, and the operation and maintenance of beacons, lights and lighthouses; the supervision of ports and waterways, including pilotage; the admeasuring and inspecting of vessels, including hulls and boilers; the operation and maintenance of the Panama Railroad upon the Isthmus, including telephone and telegraph systems; the operation of locks, coaling plants, shops, dry-docks and wharves; office engineering, including meteorology and hydrography; the construction of buildings and sanitary and municipal engineering, including the construction and maintenance of drainage ditches, streets, roads and bridges.

PURCHASING DEPARTMENT.

There shall be a Purchasing Department under the supervision and direction of the Governor. This department shall be charged with the purchase of all supplies, machinery or necessary plant.

SUPPLY DEPARTMENT.

There shall be a Supply Department, under the supervision and direction of the Chief Quartermaster. This department shall store and distribute all material and supplies for use of the Panama Canal and of its employees; and for other departments of the Government on the

Isthmus and their employees; and for vessels of the United States and for other vessels, when required. The Supply Department shall operate commissaries, hotels and messes; shall be in charge of the maintenance of buildings, the assignment of quarters and the care of grounds; shall recruit and distribute unskilled labor; and shall have charge of the necessary animal transportation.

ACCOUNTING DEPARTMENT.

There shall be an Accounting Department under the supervision and direction of the Auditor, with an assistant in the United States. The duties of the department shall include all general bookkeeping, auditing and accounting, both for money and property, costkeeping, the examination of payrolls and vouchers, the inspection of time books and of money and property accounts, the preparation of statistical data, and the administrative examination of such accounts as are required to be submitted to the United States Treasury Department; and the collection, custody and disbursement of funds for the Panama Canal and the Canal Zone. These same duties shall be performed for the Panama Railroad Company on the Isthmus when not inconsistent with the charter and by-laws of that Company. The department shall be charged with the handling of claims for compensation on account of personal injuries and of claims for damages to vessels. Within the limits fixed by law, the duties and financial responsibilities of the officers and employees charged with the receipt, custody, disbursement, auditing and accounting for funds and property shall be prescribed in regulations issued by the Governor, with the approval of the President. The Auditor shall maintain such a system of bookkeeping as will enable him to furnish at any time full, complete and correct information in regard to the status of appropriations made by Congress, the status of all other funds, and the amounts of net profits on all operations, which are to be covered into the Treasury as required by the Panama Canal Act.

HEALTH DEPARTMENT.

There shall be a Health Department under the supervision and direction of the Chief Health Officer. This department shall be charged with all matters relating to maritime sanitation and quarantine in the ports and waters of the Canal Zone and in the harbors of the cities of Panama and Colon, and with land sanitation in the Canal Zone, and sanitary matters in said cities in conformity with the Canal Treaty between the United States and the Republic of Panama and existing agreements between the two governments thereunder, and all matters relating to hospitals and charities.

EXECUTIVE SECRETARY.

There shall be an Executive Secretary who, under the direction of the Governor of the Panama Canal, shall be charged with the supervision of all matters relating to the keeping of time of employees; to postoffices, customs, taxes and excises, excepting the collection thereof; police and prison; fire protection; land office; schools, clubs and law library; the custody of files and records; and the administration of estates of deceased and insane employees. He shall, in person or through one of his assistants, perform the duties of a Shipping Commissioner. He shall conduct all correspondence and communications between the authorities of the Canal Zone and the Government of the Republic of Panama and such other correspondence as may be given him in charge by the Governor. He shall have charge of the seal of the Government of the Canal Zone and shall attest such acts of the Government as are required by law to be performed and done under the seal.

The duties herein prescribed for the foregoing departments, offices and agencies will be assigned to divisions or bureaus thereunder by the Governor of the Panama Canal, as the necessities therefor arise. Each of the foregoing departments shall discharge such further duties as may be assigned to it from time to time by the Governor; and the Governor, with the approval of the President, may transfer from time to time specific duties from one department to another.

Sec. 2. The organization provided for in Section 1 shall be, in general, in accordance with the outline chart accompanying the memorandum of January 27, 1914, entitled "Memorandum to Accompany Executive Order of January 27, 1914, Providing for a Permanent Organization for the Panama Canal," and officers from certain departments shall be detailed in accordance with that memorandum.

Sec. 3. This order shall take effect from and after the 1st day of April, 1914, from which date the Isthmian Canal Commission, together with the present organization for the Panama Canal and the Canal Zone, shall cease to exist, in accordance with the terms of the above-mentioned Act of Congress.

WOODROW WILSON.

MEMORANDUM TO ACCOMPANY EXECUTIVE ORDER OF JANUARY 27, 1914, PROVIDING FOR A PERMANENT ORGANIZATION FOR THE PANAMA CANAL.

In construing and carrying out the foregoing order, I direct that it be done with the following considerations in view:

I have deemed it advisable for reasons of efficiency, economy and good administration to have all the activities connected with the Panama Canal under the supervision of one Cabinet officer.

The troops which will be stationed on the Canal Zone for the protection of the Panama Canal are under the Secretary of War; the Panama Canal Act provides that in time of war an Officer of the Army shall, upon the order of the President, have exclusive authority over the operation of the Panama Canal and the Government of the Canal Zone; the construction of the Canal has been successfully carried on under the supervision of the Secretary of War; the logical conclusion is, therefore, that the supervision of the operations of the Panama Canal under the permanent organization should be under the Secretary of War.

It is directed that officers shall be detailed for certain duties from the several departments as follows:

As Engineer of Maintenance, an Officer of the Corps of Engineers, U. S. Army, who shall act as Governor in the absence or disability of the Governor of the Panama Canal.

As Superintendent of Transportation, an Officer of the U. S. Navy.

As Electrical Engineer, an Officer of the Corps of Engineers, U. S. Army.

As Captains of the Terminal Ports, Officers of the U. S. Navy.

As Superintendent of Shops and Dry Docks, a Naval Constructor, U. S. Navy.

As Chief Health Officer, an Officer of the Medical Corps, U. S. Army.

As Superintendent of Hospitals, an Officer of the Medical Corps, U. S. Army.

As Chief Officer of the Quarantine Division, an Officer of the U. S. Bureau of the Public Health.

As Chief Quartermaster, an Officer of the Quartermaster Corps, U. S. Army.

The organization is to be in general accordance with the chart accompanying this memorandum, except that all of the various divisions and sub-divisions need not be established until in the opinion of the Governor it is desirable to do so, the organization being expanded gradually as the necessities of the work require.

WOODROW WILSON.

EXECUTIVE ORDER.

[Providing Conditions of Employment for the Permanent Force for the Panama Canal, the Canal Zone, the Panama Railroad, etc.]

THE WHITE HOUSE, *February 2, 1914.*

By virtue of the authority vested in me by law, it is hereby ordered that the general conditions of employment governing employees on the

Isthmus of Panama, necessary for the completion, care, management, maintenance, sanitation, government and operation of the Panama Canal, the Canal Zone, the Panama Railroad, and other adjuncts, shall be as follows:

APPOINTMENT AND COMPENSATION.

1. The salaries or compensation of employees shall in no instance exceed by more than twenty-five per centum the salaries or compensation paid for the same or similar services to persons employed by the Government in Continental United States, as determined by the Governor of the Panama Canal.

2. Service must be satisfactory to the head of the department in which employed, and employees are subject to the regulations of the Governor.

3. The compensation and conditions of employment of persons employed in the United States will be specified in provisional appointments. The compensation of such persons will begin upon date of embarkation at port of departure from the United States, and they will be granted free transportation from port of departure, including meals on the steamer, but no compensation or expenses for the journey to the port; but former employees from the United States whose next preceding service with the Panama Canal was less than one year shall be paid only from date of entry into service on the Isthmus, and will be allowed only such reduced rates of transportation to the Isthmus as may be available for Government employees. Employees appointed at an hourly rate will be paid for the period of transit to the Isthmus on the basis of an eight hour day exclusive of Sundays. Except in case of discharge or other separation from the service beyond the employee's control, payment of salary from date of embarkation to date of arrival on the Isthmus will not be made unless service on the Isthmus continues for thirty days.

4. All officers and employees in the service of the Panama Canal except those who are to perform the duties of clerk, bookkeeper, stenographer, typewriter, surgeon, physician, trained nurse, or draftsman, shall be exempt from examination under Civil Service rules, and appointments to clerical positions on the Isthmus of Panama paying $75.00 per month or less may also be made without examination. Officers and employees now in the service of the Panama Railroad Company on the Isthmus may be transferred to and retained in the service of the Panama Canal without examination, whenever any work now performed independently by the Panama Railroad is consolidated with similar work performed by the Panama Canal.

5. When employees in the present organization are transferred to the permanent organization, they shall retain their seniority as regards questions of Civil Service, quarters, and other privileges or considera-

tions; provided, however, that the seniority granted to employees by this order shall not be operative in any case so as to form any claim involving the payment of funds of the United States.

6. All employees who receive over $75.00 per month or over 40c. per hour must be citizens of the United States or the Republic of Panama, and such citizens will be given preference for employment in all grades. Aliens may not be employed in such grades unless

(a) they have occupied similar positions during the construction of the Canal for two years or more, or

(b) in case of emergency, in which latter case they must be replaced by citizens of the United States or Republic of Panama as early as practicable.

7. The Governor shall prescribe regulations, when not otherwise fixed in this order, setting forth the qualifications necessary for appointment of the various classes of employees, including physical fitness for work on the Isthmus. The age limit shall in all cases be under 45 years, but the Governor may waive this limit when in his judgment such action is for the good of the service.

8. All appointments shall be made by the Governor of the Panama Canal, or by his authority, except the district judge, district attorney, marshal, clerk of district court and his assistant.

9. Assignment to duty is vested in the respective heads of the departments, and employees will be expected to perform such duties as may properly be assigned to them. The Governor may discharge an employee at any time for cause, and terminate a provisional appointment when the exigencies of the service so require.

10. The Government reserves the right to pay in any money the value or parity of which is guaranteed by the United States.

11. Employees whose salaries are fixed on a monthly or annual basis will receive no pay for overtime work.

12. Employees above the grade of laborer, appointed with rates of pay per hour or per day, will not be employed over eight hours in any one calendar day, except in case of emergency. The time such employees work over eight hours in one calendar day, and time worked on Sundays and regularly authorized holidays, including January 1st, February 22d, May 30th, July 4th, Labor Day, Thanksgiving Day, and December 25th, shall be considered overtime, for which time and one-half will be allowed. Such employees who work on the days prior and subsequent to the holidays specifically named above will be allowed their regular pay for eight hours for such days, in addition to pay for any work performed.

13. An employee whose compensation while on duty carries with it subsistence will not be entitled to same or commutation thereof while on leave of absence, and no commutation of quarters shall be paid.

TRANSPORTATION.

14. Employees and dependent members of their families will be granted the regular Government rate upon commercial steamship lines with which arrangements for such rates can be made. While the United States operates a steamship line, either directly or through the Panama Railroad Company, employees and the dependent members of their families will be granted transportation at the same rates and under the same conditions as are at present in effect. The rates and conditions are subject to change at any time in the discretion of the Governor.

15. After three years' service, employees who are citizens of the United States will be entitled to free transportation for themselves only, on termination of service, to any port of the United States, except that when such transportation costs the Government more than $40.00 the employee must pay the excess.

16. Employees on the gold roll will be granted one complimentary round-trip pass on the Panama Railroad each calendar month. Mileage books for use of such employees and dependent members of their families or relatives temporarily residing with them, will be furnished at one-half regular tariff rates.

QUARTERS.

17. Where practicable, such bachelor quarters on the Isthmus as may be available from time to time will be assigned all employees desiring them. Family quarters, when available, will be assigned under such rules as may be prescribed by the Governor. A charge will be made for rent, fuel, and electric current at such time and in accordance with such regulations as the President may hereafter establish.

MEDICAL CARE.

18. Employees injured will be compensated in accordance with such regulations as are prescribed by law.

19. All employees in cases of illness or injury will receive free medical care and attendance in the hospitals, except in cases of alcoholism or venereal disease. If medical attendance is furnished in quarters, a charge may be made under regulations to be prescribed by the Governor. Employees will be charged for medical care and attendance furnished members of their families at the hospitals and at their quarters at such rates and under such regulations as may be prescribed by the Governor.

LEAVE REGULATIONS.

20. All employees who are citizens of the United States, and aliens whose compensation is more than $75.00 per month or 40c. per hour, shall be entitled to leave privileges.

21. Leave will be divided into three classes, viz.: (1) annual leave, (2) cumulative leave, and (3) travel leave.

ANNUAL LEAVE.

22. Twenty-four days annual leave will be allowed each employee for each year after entry into service and, if not granted prior to the close of the year, is forfeited and may not be accumulated, except that any annual leave remaining to an employee's credit in a year in which he is granted cumulative leave may be added to the cumulative leave if taken within two months after the close of his service year.

23. The service year shall date from the day on which an employee's pay in the permanent organization begins.

24. Absences of one-half day or more, when regularly authorized, will be charged against annual leave; also absences on account of illness or injury, upon the certificate of an authorized physician in the service of the Panama Canal, except that in the following classes of cases no payment shall be made for time lost, but the time shall be charged against the annual leave:

    (a) Illness due to the fault of the employee, as venereal disease and alcoholism.

    (b) Injury due to the employee's wilful intention to bring about the injury or death of himself or another.

    (c) Elective surgical operations to relieve conditions existing prior to service on the Isthmus.

25. In the case of hourly or per diem employees annual leave on account of sickness or injury shall be based upon a day of eight hours.

26. Not more than fourteen days annual leave may be taken during the first six months of a service year. In case of illness or injury in the first six months, to cover which no annual leave remains to the employee's credit, the time lost will be charged against the annual leave remaining for the year, and payment will be made after completing ten months of the service year. After the entire twenty-four days annual leave has been used, additional leave in that service year on account of illness or injury will be deducted from the cumulative leave for that year and when the cumulative leave becomes due the employee will be paid.

27. After exhausting both annual and cumulative leave for the year, additional absence on account of illness or injury will be without pay, except such compensation as may be prescribed by law for employees receiving personal injuries.

CUMULATIVE LEAVE.

28. Thirty days cumulative leave will be allowed each employee paid on a monthly or annual basis for each year of his service, and twenty

days to each employee paid on an hourly basis. This leave will be due after completing ten months' service each year and may be taken when the employee's service can be spared. It may be taken annually or left to accumulate to the credit of the employee, provided, however, that leave may not be accumulated for more than three years. If it is not desired to take the entire leave accumulated, the leave earned for the first year, or the first and second years, may be taken, provided that no employee, except at termination of service, may be granted more than ninety days leave with pay at one time. Employees will be paid for cumulative leave at the rate earned when the leave became due at the end of the tenth month of each respective year.

29. In case an employee serves part of a year on the monthly or annual basis and part on the hourly basis, he will be allowed twenty days cumulative leave, except that if he has served eight months or more on the monthly or annual basis during the year he will be granted thirty days cumulative leave.

TRAVEL LEAVE.

30. Employees who travel to points outside the tropics, when on cumulative leave, will be allowed seven days additional leave (or travel leave) with full pay. Travel leave may be allowed approximately once a year and is not cumulative.

31. Employees will be compensated for travel leave and annual leave taken in conjunction with cumulative leave at the rate earned when cumulative leave last became due.

32. After accumulating leave for three years, an employee ceases to earn additional cumulative leave until he is granted all or part of the cumulative leave already earned, unless he shall enter on cumulative leave within two months after completing the third year, or be ordered by the Governor to defer taking leave for official reasons.

33. When an employee's services are terminated on account of misconduct or unsatisfactory service, any annual leave due and travel leave will be forfeited, and cumulative leave will also be forfeited unless written notification has been given that the employee has accumulated the leave, or the four months period within which the employee may enter on leave has passed. Such written notice must be given by employees as soon as possible after cumulative leave becomes due.

34. When an employee's service is terminated, a cash payment in commutation of leave will be made to him for the number of days' cumulative leave due, plus the annual leave due. In the event of his death his estate will be paid the sum due.

35. Employees must enter on cumulative leave within four months after the date when it becomes due, except when accumulated, or unless otherwise authorized by the Governor.

36. Employees must report from leave within one week after the authorized leave expires or forfeit pay for the leave. In case of unavoidable delay, the Governor will decide whether the circumstances warrant an exception to this rule.

37. No restrictions are placed on the localities where leave may be spent.

38. Any employee transferred from the present force to the permanent operating force will be paid at the time of transfer, in addition to his regular compensation, the amount he would have received in payment for leave had he been separated from the service at the time of transfer.

39. Leave may be taken only at the convenience of heads of departments, who may direct an employee to accumulate his leave if necessary for the conduct of the work.

40. Leave without pay may be granted by the Governor to all employees, including laborers, for such period as may be prescribed by him.

OFFICE HOURS AND HOURS OF LABOR.

41. Office hours and hours of labor will be fixed by the Governor within the limits prescribed by law.

42. This order shall take effect from and after the 1st day of April, 1914.

WOODROW WILSON.

By the President of the United States of America.

A PROCLAMATION.

[Exportation of Arms or Munitions of War to Mexico.]

Whereas, by a Proclamation of the President issued on March 14, 1912, under a Joint Resolution of Congress approved by the President on the same day, it was declared that there existed in Mexico conditions of domestic violence which were promoted by the use of arms or munitions of war procured from the United States; and

Whereas, by the Joint Resolution above mentioned it thereupon became unlawful to export arms or munitions of war to Mexico except under such limitations and exceptions as the President should prescribe:

Now, therefore, I, WOODROW WILSON, President of the United States of America, hereby declare and proclaim that, as the conditions on which the Proclamation of March 14, 1912, was based have essentially changed, and as it is desirable to place the United States with reference to the exportation of arms or munitions of war to Mexico in the same position as other Powers, the said Proclamation is hereby revoked.

In witness whereof, I have hereunto set my hand and caused the seal of the United States to be affixed.

Done at the City of Washington this third day of February, in the year of our Lord one thousand nine hundred and fourteen, [SEAL] and of the Independence of the United States the one hundred and thirty-eighth.

WOODROW WILSON.

By the President:

W. J. BRYAN, *Secretary of State.*

EXECUTIVE ORDER.

[To Establish a Washington Office of The Panama Canal, to Provide Temporarily for the Organization, Officials and Employees Thereof, and to Continue in Force for The Panama Canal, Rules, Regulations, and Executive Orders which may have been made for the Isthmian Canal Commission.]

THE WHITE HOUSE, *March 2, 1914.*

By virtue of the authority vested in me it is hereby ordered:

Section 1. That an office of The Panama Canal is established in the City of Washington in the District of Columbia.

Sec. 2. That the Washington Office of The Panama Canal shall be the office of general records in the United States, and shall succeed to the custody, care and preservation of all the records and files of the Isthmian Canal Commission, to be retained and preserved in the United States on and after April 1, 1914, and shall also succeed to and become chargeable with all property of every kind and character purchased for the Washington Office of the Isthmian Canal Commission, which is on hand April 1, 1914.

Sec. 3. That the Washington Office of The Panama Canal shall be the headquarters and the principal office of the Purchasing Department of The Panama Canal. The head of the Purchasing Department of The Panama Canal, under the direction of the Governor, shall have administrative control of the Washington Office of The Panama Canal. He shall be subject to orders and supervision of the Chief of Engineers of the U. S. Army to such extent as may be directed by the Secretary of War. He shall be General Purchasing Officer for The Panama Canal, and shall also act as the Chief of the Washington Office of The Panama Canal.

Sec. 4. That until further ordered, the Washington Office of The Panama Canal shall have the same organization as to offices and departments (except the Office of the Assistant Examiner of Accounts and the Disbursing Office) as the Washington Office of the Isthmian Canal Commission shall have on March 31, 1914. The number, class and salaries of officials and employees in each of the offices and departments, except as hereinafter provided, shall be the same as those authorized for the Washington Office of the Isthmian Canal Commission on March 31, 1914, and any change in the salary of any position, or in the number of positions in any office or department, shall be made only as now provided by law. The officers and employees, except as hereinafter provided, shall perform the same class of duties that they may be assigned to on March 31, 1914.

Sec. 5. That the Assistant Auditor provided for in Executive Order No. 1885, dated January 27, 1914, shall be appointed April 1, 1914. His salary shall be fixed by the Governor. He shall perform such duties of the Accounting Department to be performed in the United States, as may be assigned to him by the Auditor, and also such other duties of a general nature as may be assigned to him by the Chief of the Washington Office of The Panama Canal.

On and after April 1, 1914, there shall be transferred to the Assistant Auditor, and he shall be charged with the custody, care and preservation of, all records and property of the Disbursing Officer and of the Assistant Examiner of Accounts of the Isthmian Canal Commission, with which those officers shall be charged on March 31, 1914.

The Chief of the Washington Office may, however, transfer to and place in the custody of the Disbursing Clerk, hereinafter provided for, such of the property and records above described, as he may deem to be essential to enable the Disbursing Clerk to properly perform his duties under this order, but the Disbursing Clerk shall not be permitted, without specific authority from the Chief of Office, to keep a separate set of records and files. He shall be required to rely upon, and consult when necessary, the records and files in the office of the Assistant Auditor, in verifying the legality of claims and accounts submitted to him for payment, or to verify the details of any collection for which he is required to account. Disbursements will be made by the Disbursing Clerk only after examination of the claim or account in the office of the Assistant Auditor.

Such of the officers and employees employed in the office of the Assistant Examiner of Accounts and the Disbursing Office of the Isthmian Canal Commission on March 31, 1914, as the Governor determines to retain, shall be transferred to and employed in the Accounting Department in the United States, and their salaries fixed at such amounts as the Governor deems just and reasonable.

There shall be a Disbursing Clerk for that part of the Accounting Department in the United States, who shall perform similar duties to those that are required to be performed by the Collector and Paymaster on the Isthmus, in so far as there are such duties to be performed in the United States, and shall be subject to the same supervision by the Assistant Auditor, as the Collector and Paymaster on the Isthmus are by the Auditor. He shall give bond in such amount as may be fixed by the Governor, or by his authority.

Such of the officers and employees as are transferred to and employed in the Accounting Department in the United States, shall be distributed between the office of the Assistant Auditor and that of the Disbursing Clerk, respectively, as the needs of the service require. They shall perform such duties as may be assigned to them by proper authority. They shall be subject to similar financial responsibilities, and to the same general rules and regulations that have been prescribed for like officers and employees employed in the Accounting Department on the Isthmus.

It is the purpose of this order, and it shall be so construed, as to require the Assistant Auditor of The Panama Canal to examine all claims and accounts before their payment by the Disbursing Clerk; to carry on all general correspondence in relation to claims and accounts required to be conducted by the Accounting Department in the United States; to prepare all vouchers and certify to the validity of all claims and accounts before they are submitted to the Disbursing Clerk for payment; to furnish to the Disbursing Clerk all necessary data to enable that officer to make reply to any exceptions that may be taken to his account by the Auditor for the War Department; to keep all general records required to be kept in the Accounting Department in the United States; to make all reports as to statistical data required to be sent to the Auditor on the Isthmus; to give an administrative examination to all accounts of the Disbursing Clerk before they are transmitted to the Auditor; to make an administrative examination of all claims which are to be submitted to the Auditor for direct settlement; to keep a complete record of all collections to be made and all moneys received by the Disbursing Clerk; to certify to the correctness of the Disbursing Clerk's accounts for collections; to see that bills collectible are issued and collections made in all proper cases; to have charge of all general files which are required to be kept by the Accounting Department in the United States; and to perform such other duties as may be assigned to him by the Auditor, or the Chief of the Washington Office.

Sec. 6. That any person holding appointment or employment in or under the Washington Office of the Isthmian Canal Commission on March 31, 1914, shall be eligible for appointment to, or employment in a like position in or under the Washington Office of The Panama Canal, created by this order, and all except those employed in the Accounting Department, will be considered to be transferred and appointed to such like position in or under the Washington Office of The Panama Canal, as of April 1, 1914, without further order or

PRESIDENT WOODROW WILSON AND CABINET

FIRST OFFICIAL PHOTOGRAPH OF PRESIDENT WOODROW WILSON AND HIS CABINET TAKEN IN THE CABINET ROOM AT THE CAPITOL, WASHINGTON, D. C., MARCH 6TH.

In the background from left to right,
President Woodrow Wilson,
William G. McAdoo, Secretary of the Treasury,
Jas. McReynolds, Attorney General,
Josephus Daniels, Secretary of the Navy,
David F. Houston, Secretary of Agriculture,
William B. Wilson, Secretary of Labor,
William C. Redfield, Secretary of Commerce.

In the foreground from left to right,
William Jennings Bryan, Secretary of State,
Lindley M. Garrison, Secretary of War,
Albert J. Burleson, Postmaster General, and
Franklin K. Lane, Secretary of Interior.

appointment. The oath of office shall be taken by all officials and employees of the Washington Office.

Sec. 7. This order shall remain in force as a provisional order only, for the establishment of the Washington Office of The Panama Canal, until an order for the permanent organization of such office shall have been made.

Sec. 8. All rules, regulations and executive orders, not inconsistent with the provisions of this order and the Executive Orders of January 27, and February 2, 1914, heretofore made for the Isthmian Canal Commission, and applicable to conditions that will exist under these orders, shall be and are hereby continued in full force and effect, as rules, regulations, and executive orders for the government of officers and employees of The Panama Canal and the transaction of the business of The Panama Canal.

WOODROW WILSON.

SPECIAL ADDRESS.

[Recommending Repeal of that Provision of the Panama Canal Act which Exempts Vessels Engaged in the Coastwise Trade of the United States from Payment of Tolls. Delivered at a Joint Session of the two Houses of Congress, March 5, 1914.]

Gentlemen of the Congress:

I have come to you upon an errand which can be very briefly performed, but I beg that you will not measure its importance by the number of sentences in which I state it. No communication I have addressed to the Congress carried with it graver or more far-reaching implications as to the interest of the country, and I come now to speak upon a matter with regard to which I am charged in a peculiar degree, by the Constitution itself, with personal responsibility.

I have come to ask you for the repeal of that provision of the Panama Canal Act of August 24, 1912, which exempts vessels engaged in the coastwise trade of the United States from payment of tolls, and to urge upon you the justice, the wisdom, and the large policy of such a repeal with the utmost earnestness of which I am capable.

In my own judgment, very fully considered and maturely formed, that exemption constitutes a mistaken economic policy from every point of view, and is, moreover, in plain contravention of the treaty with Great Britain concerning the canal concluded on November 18, 1901. But I have not come to urge upon you my personal views. I have come to state to you a fact and a situation. Whatever may be our own differences of opinion concerning this much debated measure, its meaning is not debated outside the United States. Everywhere else the language of the treaty is given but one interpretation, and that interpretation precludes the exemption I am asking you to repeal.

We consented to the treaty; its language we accepted, if we did not originate it; and we are too big, too powerful, too self-respecting a nation to interpret with a too strained or refined reading the words of our own promises just because we have power enough to give us leave to read them as we please. The large thing to do is the only thing we can afford to do, a voluntary withdrawal from a position everywhere questioned and misunderstood. We ought to reverse our action without raising the question whether we were right or wrong, and so once more deserve our reputation for generosity and for the redemption of every obligation without quibble or hesitation.

I ask this of you in support of the foreign policy of the administration. I shall not know how to deal with other matters of even greater delicacy and nearer consequence if you do not grant it to me in ungrudging measure.

SPECIAL MESSAGE.

[Asking Congress to Authorize the Use of the Land and Naval Forces to Maintain the Dignity and Authority of the United States in Mexico and Compel Respect for the American Flag.—Read Before the Assembled House and Senate, April 20, 1914.]

Gentlemen of the Congress:

It is my duty to call your attention to a situation which has arisen in our dealings with Gen. Victoriano Huerta at Mexico City which calls for action, and to ask your advice and co-operation in acting upon it.

On April 9th a Paymaster of the U. S. S. *Dolphin* landed at the Iturbide bridge landing at Tampico with a whaleboat and boat's crew to take off certain supplies needed by his ship, and while engaged in loading the boat was arrested by an officer and squad of men of the army of General Huerta. Neither the Paymaster nor any one of the boat's crew was armed. Two of the men were in the boat when the arrest took place, and were obliged to leave it and submit to be taken into custody, notwithstanding the fact that the boat carried, both at her bow and at her stern, the flag of the United States. The officer who made the arrest was proceeding up one of the streets of the town with his prisoners when met by an officer of higher authority, who ordered him to return to the landing and await orders, and within an hour and a half from the time of the arrest orders were received from the commander of the Huertista forces at Tampico for the release of the Paymaster and his men.

The release was followed by apologies from the commander, and later by an expression of regret by General Huerta himself. General Huerta urged that martial law obtained at the time at Tampico; that orders had been issued that no one should be allowed to land at the Iturbide bridge, and that our sailors had no right to land there. Our naval commanders at the port had not been notified of any such prohibition, and, even if they had been, the only justifiable course open to the local authorities would have been to request the Paymaster and his crew to withdraw and to lodge a protest with the commanding officer of the fleet. Admiral Mayo regarded the arrest as so serious an affront that he was not satisfied with the apologies offered, but demanded that the flag of the United States be saluted with special ceremony by the military commander of the port.

The incident can not be regarded as a trivial one, especially as two of the men arrested were taken from the boat itself—that is to say, from the territory of the United States; but had it stood by itself, it might have been attributed to the ignorance or arrogance of a single officer.

Unfortunately, it was not an isolated case. A series of incidents have recently occurred which can not but create the impression that the representatives of General Huerta were willing to go out of their way to show disregard for the dignity and rights of this Government, and felt perfectly safe in doing what they pleased, making free to show in many ways their irritation and contempt.

A few days after the incident at Tampico an orderly from the U. S. S. *Minnesota* was arrested at Vera Cruz while ashore in uniform to obtain the ship's mail, and was for a time thrown into jail. An official dispatch from this Government to its embassy at Mexico City was withheld by the authorities of the telegraphic service until peremptorily demanded by our *Chargé d'Affaires* in person.

So far as I can learn, such wrong and annoyances have been suffered to occur only against representatives of the United States. I have heard of no complaints from other governments of similar treatment. Subsequent explanations and formal apologies did not and could not alter the popular impression, which it is possible it had been the object of the Huertista authorities to create, that the Government of the United States was being singled out, and might be singled out with impunity, for slights and affronts in retaliation for its refusal to recognize the pretensions of General Huerta to be regarded as the Constitutional Provisional President of the Republic of Mexico.

The manifest danger of such a situation was that such offenses might grow from bad to worse until something happened of so gross and intolerable a sort as to lead directly and inevitably to armed conflict. It was necessary that the apologies of General Huerta and his representatives should go much further, that they should be such as to attract the attention of the whole population to their significance, and such as to impress upon General Huerta himself the necessity of seeing to it that no further occasion for explanations and professed regrets should arise. I, therefore, felt it my duty to sustain Admiral Mayo in the whole of his demand and to insist that the flag of the United States should be saluted in such a way as to indicate a new spirit and attitude on the part of the Huertistas.

Such a salute General Huerta has refused, and I have come to ask your approval and support in the course I now purpose to pursue.

This Government can, I earnestly hope, in no circumstances be forced into war with the people of Mexico. Mexico is torn by civil strife. If we are to accept the tests of its own Constitution, it has no government. General Huerta has set his power up in the City of Mexico, such as it is, without right and by methods for which there can be no justification. Only part of the country is under his control.

If armed conflict should unhappily come as a result of his attitude of personal resentment toward this Government, we should be fighting only General Huerta and those who adhere to him and give him their support, and our object would be only to restore to the people of the distracted republic the opportunity to set up again their own laws and their own government.

But I earnestly hope that war is not now in question. I believe that I speak for the American people when I say that we do not desire to control in any degree the affairs of our sister republic. Our feeling for the people of Mexico is one of deep and genuine friendship, and everything that we have so far done or refrained from doing has proceeded from our desire to help them, not to hinder or embarrass them. We would not wish even to exercise the good offices of friendship without their welcome and consent.

The people of Mexico are entitled to settle their own domestic affairs in their own way, and we sincerely desire to respect their right. The present situation need have none of the grave complications of interference if we deal with it promptly, firmly, and wisely.

No doubt I could do what is necessary in the circumstances to enforce respect for our Government without recourse to the congress, and yet not exceed my constitutional powers as President; but I do not wish to act in a matter possibly of so grave consequence except in close conference and co-operation with both the Senate and House. I therefore come to ask your approval that I should use the armed forces of the United States in such ways and to such an extent as may be necessary to obtain from General Huerta and his adherents the fullest recognition of the rights and dignity of the United States, even amid the distressing conditions now unhappily obtaining in Mexico.

There can in what we do be no thought of aggression or of selfish aggrandizement. We seek to maintain the dignity and authority of the United States only because we wish always to keep our great influence unimpaired for the uses of liberty, both in the United States and wherever else it may be employed for the benefit of mankind.

By the President of the United States of America.

A PROCLAMATION.

[Protection Against Domestic Violence in Colorado.]

Whereas, it is provided by the Constitution of the United States that the United States shall protect every State in this Union, on application of the legislature, or of the executive (when the legislature can not be convened), against domestic violence;

And Whereas, the Governor of the State of Colorado has represented that domestic violence exists in said State which the authorities of said State are unable to suppress; and has represented that it is impossible to convene the legislature of the State in time to meet the present emergency;

And Whereas, the laws of the United States require that in all cases of insurrection in any State or of obstruction to the laws thereof, whenever in the judgment of the President it becomes necessary to use the military forces to suppress such insurrection or obstruction to the laws, he shall forthwith by proclamation command such insurgents to disperse, and retire peaceably to their respective abodes within a limited time:

Now, Therefore, I, Woodrow Wilson, President of the United States, do hereby admonish all good citizens of the United States, and all persons within the territory and jurisdiction of the United States against aiding, countenancing, abetting, or taking part in such unlawful proceedings; and I do hereby warn all persons engaged in or connected with said domestic violence and obstruction of the laws to disperse and retire peaceably to their respective abodes on or before the thirtieth day of April, instant.

In testimony whereof, I have hereunto set my hand, and caused the seal of the United States to be affixed.

Done at the city of Washington, this twenty-eighth day of April, in the year of our Lord nineteen hundred and fourteen, [SEAL] and of the Independence of the United States of America the one hundred and thirty-eighth.

WOODROW WILSON.

By the President:

W. J. Bryan,
  Secretary of State.

EXECUTIVE ORDER

[Relating to Salaries of Consular Officers.]

THE WHITE HOUSE, *April 30, 1914.*

Paragraphs 492 and 561 of the Consular Regulations of 1896 are hereby amended to read as follows:

Paragraph 492. Salaried officers.—Consuls-general and consuls receiving salaries fixed by law are entitled to compensation at the rate of their respective salaries, as follows:

1. Beginning not prior to the date of the oath of office, for time occupied in receiving instructions in the United States, or by special direction of the Department of State, at consulates-general or consulates other than those to which they shall have been appointed, not exceeding in all thirty days.—R. S., sec. 1740.

2. For the time actually and necessarily occupied in transit, by the most convenient route, between the places of their residence and their posts, not, however, to exceed the time fixed in paragraph 478. This applies both to transit from the United States and to transit to the United States at the termination of service, unless the officer dies, or is recalled for malfeasance, or resigns in anticipation of such recall. The time during which a consul may be unavoidably detained at his post while waiting for a conveyance to the United States, after delivering up the office, may be included in his home transit so far as not to exceed in all the maximum time fixed in paragraph 478. In the event that the appointee is not in the United States at the time of appointment no allowance of salary will be made except for the period actually and necessarily occupied in transit in reaching his post of duty, and the time which he may be especially directed by the Department of State to spend at a consulate-general or consulate other than that to which he shall have been appointed, receiving instructions in the performance of consular duties, not exceeding thirty days.

3. From the date of entry upon official duty at their posts to the date when they cease to perform the duties of the office. This provision extends also to the time, after arrival at their posts, while awaiting the receipt of the exequatur or permission to act.—R. S., sec. 1740.

Paragraph 561. Receiving instructions.—The first salary account will be stated for the time, not exceeding thirty days, during which the consular officer is receiving his instructions. (Form No. 106.) The time cannot begin prior to the date of the oath of office. (Paragraph 492.) This draft therefor is drawn before departure. A certificate (Form No. 107) of the number of days occupied in receiving instructions should accompany the account.

WOODROW WILSON.

ADDRESS

[Delivered at the New York Navy Yard in Brooklyn, May 11, 1914, at the Funeral Service over the Remains of Seventeen Sailors and Marines who Lost Their Lives at the Taking of Vera Cruz, Mexico.]

After Secretary Daniels of the Navy had presented to him a roll of the dead, President Wilson said:

Mr. Secretary:

I know that the feelings which characterize all who stand about me and the whole nation at this hour are not feelings which can be suitably expressed in terms of attempted oratory or eloquence. They are things too deep for ordinary speech. For my own part, I have a singular mixture of feelings. The feeling that is uppermost is one of profound grief that these lads should have had to go to their death, and yet there is mixed with that grief a profound pride that they should have gone as they did, and, if I may say it out of my heart, a touch of envy of those who were permitted so quietly, so nobly, to do their duty.

Have you thought of it, men? Here is the roster of the navy, the list of the men, officers, and enlisted men and marines, and suddenly there swim nineteen stars out of the list—men who have suddenly gone into a firmament of memory, where we shall always see their names shine; not because they called upon us to admire them, but because they served us, without asking any questions and in the performance of a duty which is laid upon us as well as upon them.

Duty is not an uncommon thing, gentlemen. Men are performing it in the ordinary walks of life all around us all the time, and they are making great sacrifices to perform it. What gives men like these peculiar distinction is not merely that they did their duty, but that their duty had nothing to do with them or their own personal and peculiar interests. They did not give their lives for themselves. They gave their lives for us, because we called upon them as a nation to perform an unexpected duty. That is the way in which men grow distinguished and that is the only way, by serving somebody else than themselves. And what greater thing could you serve than a nation such as this we love and are proud of? Are you sorry for these lads? Are you sorry for the way they will be remembered? Does it not quicken your pulses to think of the list of them? I hope to God none of you may join the list, but if you do, you will join an immortal company.

So while we are profoundly sorrowful and while there goes out of our hearts a very deep and affectionate sympathy for the friends and relatives of these lads who for the rest of their lives shall mourn them, though with a touch of pride, we know why we do not go away from this occasion cast down but with our heads lifted and our eyes on the future of this country, with absolute confidence of how it will be worked out. Not only upon the mere vague future of this country, but the immediate future.

We have gone down to Mexico to serve mankind if we can find out the way. We do not want to fight the Mexicans. We want to serve the Mexicans if we can, because we know how we would like to be free and how we would like to be served if there were friends standing by ready to serve us. A war of aggression is not a war in which it is a grand thing to die, but a war of service is a thing in which it is a proud thing to die.

Notice that these men were of our blood. I mean of our American blood, which is not drawn from any one country, which is not drawn from any one stock, which is not drawn from any one language of the modern world, but free men everywhere have sent their sons and their brothers and their daughters to this country in order to make that great compounded nation which consists of all the sturdy elements and of all the best elements of the whole globe. I listened again to this list with a profound interest at the mixture of names, for the names bear the marks of the several national stocks from which these men came. But they are not Irishmen or Germans or Frenchmen or Hebrews any more. They were not when they went to Vera Cruz; they were American, every one of them, and with no difference in their Americanism because of the stock from which they came.

Therefore, they were in a peculiar sense of our blood and they proved it by showing that they were of our spirit—that no matter what their derivation, no matter where their people came from, they thought and wished and did the things that were American, and the flag under which they served was a flag in which all the blood of mankind is united to make a free nation.

War, gentlemen, is only a sort of dramatic representation, a sort of dramatic symbol of a thousand forms of duty. I never went into battle, I never was under fire, but I fancy that there are some things just as hard to do as to go under fire. I fancy that it is just as hard to do your duty when men are sneering at you as when they are shooting at you. When they shoot at you they can only take your natural life; when they sneer at you they can wound your heart, and men who are brave enough, steadfast enough, steady in their principles enough, to go about their duty with regard to their fellow-men, no matter whether there are hisses or cheers, men who can do what Rudyard Kipling in one of his poems wrote, "meet with triumph and disaster and treat those two impostors just the same," are men for a nation to be proud of. Morally speaking, disaster and triumph are impostors. The cheers of the moment are not what a man ought to think about, but the verdict of his conscience and the conscience of mankind.

So when I look at you I feel as if I also and we all were enlisted men. Not enlisted in your particular branch of the service, but enlisted to serve the country, no matter what may come, what though we may waste our lives in the arduous endeavor. We are expected to put the utmost energy of every power that we have into the service of our fellow-men, never sparing ourselves, not condescending to think of what is going to happen to ourselves, but ready, if need be, to go to the utter length of complete self-sacrifice.

As I stand and look at you to-day and think of these spirits that have gone from us, I know that the road is clearer for the future. These boys have shown us the way, and it is easier to walk on it because they have gone before and shown us how. May God grant to all of us that vision of patriotic service which here in solemnity and grief and pride is borne in upon our hearts and consciences.

By the President of the United States of America
A PROCLAMATION
[Mother's Day.]

Whereas, By a Joint Resolution approved May 8, 1914, "designating the second Sunday in May as Mother's Day, and for other purposes," the President is authorized and requested to issue a proclamation calling upon the government officials to display the United States flag on all government buildings, and the people of the United States to display the flag at their homes or other suitable places on the second Sunday in May as a public expression of our love and reverence for the mothers of our country;

And Whereas, By the said Joint Resolution it is made the duty of the President to request the observance of the second Sunday in May as provided for in the said Joint Resolution;

Now, Therefore, I, Woodrow Wilson, President of the United States of America, by virtue of the authority vested in me by the said Joint Resolution, do hereby direct the government officials to display the United States flag on all government buildings and do invite the people of the United States to display the flag at their homes or other suitable places on the second Sunday in May as a public expression of our love and reverence for the mothers of our country.

Done at the City of Washington this ninth day of May, in the year of our Lord one thousand nine hundred and fourteen, and [seal.] of the Independence of the United States the one hundred and thirty-eighth.

By the President: WOODROW WILSON.

William Jennings Bryan, *Secretary of State.*

ADDRESS.

[Delivered at the unveiling of the Statue to the Memory of Commodore John Barry at Washington, May 16, 1914.]

Mr. Secretary, Ladies and Gentlemen:

I esteem it a privilege to be present on this interesting occasion, and I am very much tempted to anticipate some part of what the orators of the day will say about the character of the great man whose memory we celebrate. If I were to attempt an historical address, I might, however, be led too far afield. I am going to take the liberty, therefore, of drawing a few inferences from the significance of this occasion.

I think that we can never be present at a ceremony of this kind, which carries our thoughts back to the great Revolution, by means of which our Government was set up, without feeling that it is an occasion of reminder, of renewal, of refreshment, when we turn our thoughts again to the great issues which were presented to the little Nation which then asserted its independence to the world; to which it spoke both in eloquent representations of its cause and in the sound of arms, and ask ourselves what it was that these men fought for. No one can turn to the career of Commodore Barry without feeling a touch of the enthusiasm with which he devoted an originating mind to the great cause which he intended to serve, and it behooves us, living in this age when no man can question the power of the Nation, when no man would dare to doubt its right and its determination to act for itself, to ask what it was that filled the hearts of these men when they set the Nation up.

For patriotism, ladies and gentlemen, is in my mind not merely a sentiment. There is a certain effervescence, I suppose, which ought to be permitted to those who allow their hearts to speak in the celebration of the glory and majesty of their country, but the country can have no glory and no majesty unless there be a deep principle and conviction back of the enthusiasm. Patriotism is a principle, not a mere sentiment. No man can be a true patriot who does not feel himself shot through and through with a deep ardor for what his country stands for, what its existence means, what its purpose is declared to be in its history and in its policy. I recall those solemn lines of the poet Tennyson in which he tries to give voice to his conception of what it is that stirs within a nation: "Some sense of duty, something of a faith, some reverence for the laws ourselves have made, some patient force to change them when we will, some civic manhood firm against the crowd;" steadfastness, clearness of purpose, courage, persistency, and that uprightness which comes from the clear thinking of men who wish to serve not themselves but their fellow men.

What does the United States stand for, then, that our hearts should be stirred by the memory of the men who set her Constitution up? John Barry fought, like every other man in the Revolution, in order that America might be free to make her own life without interruption or disturbance from any other quarter. You can sum the whole thing up in that, that America had a right to her own self-determined life; and what are our corollaries from that? You do not have to go back to stir your thoughts again with the issues of the Revolution. Some of the issues of the Revolution were not the cause of it, but merely the occasion for it. There are just as vital things stirring now that concern the existence of the Nation as were stirring then, and every man who worthily stands in this presence should examine himself and see whether he has the full conception of what it means that America should live her own life. Washington saw it when he wrote his farewell address. It was not merely because of passing and transient circumstances that Washington said that we must keep free from entangling alliances. It was because he saw that no country had yet set its face in the same direction in which America had set her face. We can not form alliances with those who are not going our way; and in our might and majesty and in the confidence and definiteness of our own purpose we need not and we should not form alliances with any nation in the world. Those who are right, those who study their consciences in determining their policies, those who hold their honor higher than their advantage, do not need alliances. You need alliances when you are not strong, and you are weak only when you are not true to yourself. You are weak only when you are in the wrong; you are weak only when you are afraid to do the right; you are weak only when you doubt your cause and the majesty of a nation's might asserted.

There is another corollary. John Barry was an Irishman, but his heart crossed the Atlantic with him. He did not leave it in Ireland. And the test of all of us—for all of us had our origin on the other side of the sea—is whether we will assist in enabling America to live her separate and independent life, retaining our ancient affections, indeed, but determining everything that we do by the interests that exist on this side of the sea. Some Americans need hyphens in their names, because only part of them has come over; but when the whole man has come over, heart and thought and all, the hyphen drops of its own weight out of his name. This man was not an Irish-American; he was an Irishman who became an American. I venture to say if he voted he voted with regard to the questions as they looked on this side of the water and not as they affected the other side; and that is my infallible test of a genuine American, that when he votes or when he acts or when he fights his heart and his thought are centered nowhere but in the emotions and the purposes and the policies of the United States.

This man illustrates for me all the splendid strength which we brought into this country by the magnet of freedom. Men have been drawn to this country by the same thing that has made us love this country—by the opportunity to live their own lives and to think their own thoughts and to let their whole natures expand with the expansion of a free and mighty Nation. We have brought out of the stocks of all the world all the best impulses and have appropriated them and Americanized them and translated them into the glory and majesty of a great country.

So, ladies and gentlemen, when we go out from this presence we ought to take this idea with us that we, too, are devoted to the purpose of enabling America to live her own life, to be the justest, the most progressive, the most honorable, the most enlightened Nation in the world. Any man that touches our honor is our enemy. Any man who stands in the way of the kind of progress which makes for human freedom can not call himself our friend. Any man who does not feel behind him the whole push and rush and compulsion that filled men's hearts in the time of the Revolution is no American. No man who thinks first of himself and afterwards of his country can call himself an American. America must be enriched by us. We must not live upon her; she must live by means of us.

I, for one, come to this shrine to renew the impulses of American democracy. I would be ashamed of myself if I went away from this place without realizing again that every bit of selfishness must be purged from our policy, that every bit of self-seeking must be purged from our individual consciences, and that we must be great, if we would be great at all, in the light and illumination of the example of men who gave everything that they were and everything that they had to the glory and honor of America.

EXECUTIVE ORDER.

[To create a committee to formally and officially open the Panama Canal.]

THE WHITE HOUSE, *May 20, 1914.*

By virtue of authority vested in me by the Act approved April 6, 1914, entitled "An Act Making appropriations to supply urgent deficiencies in appropriations for the fiscal year nineteen hundred and fourteen and for prior years, and for other purposes," a committee of six members is hereby created to arrange and provide suitable ceremonies for the official and formal opening of the Panama Canal, as is provided for in Section 4 of the Panama Canal Act. The committee shall be composed of persons who were members of the Isthmian Canal Commission. The committee shall be known and referred to as the "Committee for the Formal and Official Opening of the Panama Canal." It shall have a chairman and vice-chairman, but shall perform its duties under the direction of the Governor of the Panama Canal.

The persons named below are hereby appointed members of this committee.

Colonel George W. Goethals, U. S. A.
Honorable Richard L. Metcalfe.
General William C. Gorgas, U. S. A.
Colonel H. F. Hodges, U. S. A.
Lieutenant-Colonel William L. Sibert, U. S. A.
Civil Engineer H. H. Rousseau, U. S. N.

Colonel George W. Goethals, now Governor of the Panama Canal, shall be Chairman of this committee.

Honorable Richard L. Metcalfe shall be Vice-Chairman.

The members of said committee shall each receive salary at the rate of ten thousand dollars per annum from April 1, 1914, to December 31, 1914, inclusive, and such necessary traveling and living expenses during the period from April 1, 1914, to January 31, 1915, when on duty connected with the work of providing for formally and officially opening the Panama Canal, as may be approved by the Secretary of War. The salary fixed as above shall include any salary to which any member of this committee may be entitled by reason of his appointment to or employment in any other position under the United States for the period above provided for, and the amount of such salary shall be deducted from the salary fixed as above. The salary to be paid May 31, 1914, shall be equal to two months' pay in a lump sum, less the amount of any other salary for the months of April and May, 1914. The word "salary" as used herein, in determining the amount to be deducted, shall not be construed to include additional emoluments, but shall be confined to actual pay.

The committee is authorized to spend such sums as may be available for printing, postage, correspondence, employment of clerks, and other necessary expenses connected with formally and officially opening the Panama Canal, as may be approved by the Secretary of War.

The payments authorized hereunder shall be made by such disbursing officer of the Panama Canal as the Governor shall designate.

The Secretary of War shall provide the manner in which the amount to be expended for traveling, living and other expenses authorized by him shall be certified to, and, when such expenditures are so certified to, they shall be paid for without further vouchers therefor.

WOODROW WILSON.

ADDRESS.

[Delivered May 30, 1914, at the Grand Army of the Republic Memorial Day services in Arlington (Va.) National Cemetery.]

LADIES AND GENTLEMEN: I have not come here to-day with a prepared address. The committee in charge of the exercises of the day have graciously excused me on the grounds of public obligations from preparing such an address, but I will not deny myself the privilege of joining with you in an expression of gratitude and admiration for the men who perished for the sake of the Union. They do not need our praise. They do not need that our admiration should sustain them. There is no immortality that is safer than theirs. We come not for their sakes but for our own, in order that we may drink at the same springs of inspiration from which they themselves drank.

A peculiar privilege came to the men who fought for the Union. There is no other civil war in history, ladies and gentlemen, the stings of which were removed before the men who did the fighting passed from the stage of life. So that we owe these men something more than a legal re-establishment of the Union. We owe them the spiritual re-establishment of the Union as well; for they not only reunited States, they reunited the spirits of men. That is their unique achievement, unexampled anywhere else in the annals of mankind, that the very men whom they overcame in battle join in praise and gratitude that the Union was saved. There is something peculiarly beautiful and peculiarly touching about that. Whenever a man who is still trying to devote himself to the service of the Nation comes into a presence like this, or into a place like this, his spirit must be peculiarly moved. A mandate is laid upon him which seems to speak from the very graves themselves. Those who serve this Nation, whether in peace or in war, should serve it without thought of themselves. I can never speak in praise of war, ladies and gentlemen; you would not desire me to do so.

But there is this peculiar distinction belonging to the soldier, that he goes into an enterprise out of which he himself can not get anything at all. He is giving everything that he hath, even his life, in order that others may live, not in order that he himself may obtain gain and prosperity. And just so soon as the tasks of peace are performed in the same spirit of self-sacrifice and devotion, peace societies will not be necessary. The very organization and spirit of society will be a guaranty of peace.

Therefore this peculiar thing comes about, that we can stand here and praise the memory of these soldiers in the interest of peace. They set us the example of self-sacrifice, which if followed in peace will make it unnecessary that men should follow war any more.

We are reputed to be somewhat careless in our discrimination between words in the use of the English language, and yet it is interesting to note that there are some words about which we are very careful. We bestow the adjective "great" somewhat indiscriminately. A man who has made conquest of his fellow men for his own gain may display such genius in war, such uncommon qualities of organization and leadership that we may call him "great," but there is a word which we reserve for men of another kind and about which we are very careful; that is the word "noble." We never call a man "noble" who serves only himself; and if you will look about through all the nations of the world upon the statues that men have erected—upon the inscribed tablets where they have wished to keep alive the memory of the citizens whom they desire most to honor—you will find that almost without exception they have erected the statue to those who had a splendid surplus of energy and devotion to spend upon their fellow men. Nobility exists in America without patent. We have no House of Lords, but we have a house of fame to which we elevate those who are the noble men of our race, who, forgetful of themselves, study and serve the public interest, who have the courage to face any number and any kind of adversary, to speak what in their hearts they believe to be the truth.

We admire physical courage, but we admire above all things else moral courage. I believe that soldiers will bear me out in saying that both come in time of battle. I take it that the moral courage comes in going in the battle, and the physical courage in staying in. There are battles which are just as hard to go into and just as hard to stay in as the battles of arms, and if the man will but stay and think never of himself there will come a time of grateful recollection when men will speak of him not only with admiration but with that which goes deeper, with affection and with reverence.

So that this flag calls upon us for daily service, and the more quiet and self-denying the service the greater the glory of the flag. We are dedicated to freedom, and that freedom means the freedom of the human spirit. All free spirits ought to congregate on an occasion like this to do homage to the greatness of America as illustrated by the greatness of her sons.

It has been a privilege, ladies and gentlemen, to come and say these simple words, which I am sure are merely putting your thought into language. I thank you for the opportunity to lay this little wreath of mine upon these consecrated graves.

ADDRESS.

[Delivered June 4, 1914, at the unveiling of a monument to Confederate soldiers in Arlington (Va.) National Cemetery.]

Mr. Chairman, Mrs. McLaurin Stevens, Ladies and Gentlemen:

I assure you that I am profoundly aware of the solemn significance of the thing that has now taken place. The Daughters of the Confederacy have presented a memorial of their dead to the Government of the United States. I hope that you have noted the history of the conception of this idea. It was proposed by a President of the United States who had himself been a distinguished officer in the Union Army. It was authorized by an act of Congress of the United States. The cornerstone of the monument was laid by a President of the United States,. elevated to his position by the votes of the party which had chiefly prided itself upon sustaining the war for the Union. And now it has fallen to my lot to accept, in the name of the great Government which I am privileged for the time to represent, this emblem of a reunited people.

I am not so much happy as proud to participate in this capacity on such an occasion; proud that I should represent such a people. Am I mistaken, ladies and gentlemen, in supposing that nothing of this sort could have occurred in anything but a democracy? The people of a democracy are not related to their rulers as subjects are related to a Government. They are themselves the sovereign authority, and as they are neighbors of each other, quickened by the same influences and moved by the same motives, they can understand each other. They are shot through with some of the deepest and profoundest instincts of human sympathy. They choose their Governments. They select their rulers. They live their own life and they will not have that life disturbed and discolored by fraternal misunderstandings.

I know that a reuniting of spirits like this can take place more quickly in our time than in any other because men are now united by an easier transmission of those influences which make up the foundations of peace and of mutual understanding, but no process can work these effects unless there is a conducting medium. The conducting medium in this instance is the united heart of a great people. I am not going to detain you by trying to repeat any of the eloquent thoughts which have moved us this afternoon, for I rejoice in the simplicity of the task which is assigned to me. My privilege is this, ladies and gentlemen: To declare this chapter in the history of the United States is now closed and ended, and I bid you turn with me your faces to the future, quickened by the memories of the past, but with nothing to do with the contests of the past, knowing, as we have shed our blood upon opposite sides, we now face and admire one another. I do not know how many years ago it was that the Century Dictionary was published, but I remember one day in the Century Cyclopedia of Names I had occasion to turn to the name of Robert E. Lee, and I found him there in that book published in New York City simply described as a great American general. The generosity of our judgment did not begin to-day. The generosity of our judgment was made up soon after this great struggle was over, when men came and sat together again in the Congress and united in all the efforts of peace and of government, and our solemn duty is to see that each one of us is in his own consciousness and in his own conduct a replica of this great reunited people. It is our duty and our privilege to be like the country we represent, and speaking no word of malice, no word of criticism even, standing shoulder to shoulder to lift the burdens of mankind in the future and show the paths of freedom to all the world.

ADDRESS

[To the Graduating Class of the United States Naval Academy at Annapolis, Maryland, June 5, 1914.]

MR. SUPERINTENDENT, YOUNG GENTLEMEN, LADIES AND GENTLEMEN: During the greater part of my life I have been associated with young men, and on occasions it seems to me without number have faced bodies of youngsters going out to take part in the activities of the world, but I have a consciousness of a different significance on this occasion from that which I have felt on other similar occasions. When I have faced the graduating classes at universities I have felt that I was facing a great conjecture. They were going out into all sorts of pursuits and with every degree of preparation for the particular thing they were expecting to do; some without any preparation at all, for they did not know what they expected to do. But in facing you I am facing men who are trained for a special thing. You know what you are going to do, and you are under the eye of the whole Nation in doing it. For you, gentlemen, are to be part of the power of the Government of the United States. There is a very deep and solemn significance in that fact, and I am sure that every one of you feels it. The moral is perfectly obvious. Be ready and fit for anything that you have to do. And keep ready and fit. Do not grow slack. Do not suppose that your education is over because you have received your diplomas from the academy. Your education has just begun. Moreover, you are to have a very peculiar privilege which not many of your predecessors have had. You are yourselves going to become teachers. You are going to teach those 50,000 fellow countrymen of yours who are the enlisted men of the Navy. You are going to make them fitter to obey your orders and to serve the country. You are going to make them fitter to see what the orders mean in their outlook upon life and upon the service; and that is a great privilege, for out of you is going the energy and intelligence which are going to quicken the whole body of the United States Navy.

I congratulate you upon that prospect, but I want to ask you not to get the professional point of view. I would ask it of you if you were lawyers; I would ask it of you if you were merchants; I would ask it of you whatever you expected to be. Do not get the professional point of view. There is nothing narrower or more unserviceable than the professional point of view, to have the attitude toward life that it centers in your profession. It does not. Your profession is only one of the many activities which are meant to keep the world straight, and to keep the energy in its blood and in its muscle. We are all of us in this world, as I understand it, to set forward the affairs of the whole world, though we play a special part in that great function. The Navy goes all over the world, and I think it is to be congratulated upon having that sort of illustration of what the world is and what it contains; and inasmuch as you are going all over the world you ought to be the better able to see the relation that your country bears to the rest of the world.

It ought to be one of your thoughts all the time that you are sample Americans—not merely sample Navy men, not merely sample soldiers, but sample Americans—and that you have the point of view of America with regard to her Navy and her Army; that she is using them as the instruments of civilization, not as the instruments of aggression. The idea of America is to serve humanity, and every time you let the Stars and Stripes free to the wind you ought to realize that that is in itself a message that you are on an errand which other navies have sometimes forgotten; not an errand of conquest, but an errand of service. I always have the same thought when I look at the flag of the United States, for I know something of the history of the struggle of mankind for liberty. When I look at that flag it seems to me as if the white stripes were strips of parchment upon which are written the rights of man, and the red stripes the streams of blood by which those rights have been made good. Then in the little blue firmament in the corner have swung out the stars of the States of the American Union. So it is, as it were, a sort of floating charter that has come down to us from Runnymede, when men said, "We will not have masters; we will be a people, and we will seek our own liberty."

You are not serving a government, gentlemen; you are serving a people. For we who for the time being constitute the Government are merely instruments for a little while in the hands of a great Nation which chooses whom it will to carry out its decrees and who invariably rejects the man who forgets the ideals which it intended him to serve. So that I hope that wherever you go you will have a generous, comprehending love of the people you come into contact with, and will come back and tell us, if you can, what service the United States can render to the remotest parts of the world; tell us where you see men suffering; tell us where you think advice will lift them up; tell us where you think that the counsel of statesmen may better the fortunes of unfortunate men; always having it in mind that you are champions of what is right and fair all 'round for the public welfare, no matter where you are, and that it is that you are ready to fight for and not merely on the drop of a hat or upon some slight punctillio, but that you are champions of your fellow men, particularly of that great body one hundred million strong whom you represent in the United States.

What do you think is the most lasting impression that those boys down at Vera Cruz are going to leave? They have had to use some force—I pray God it may not be necessary for them to use any more—but do you think that the way they fought is going to be the most lasting impression? Have men not fought ever since the world began? Is there anything new in using force? The new things in the world are the things that are divorced from force. The things that show the moral compulsions of the human conscience, those are the things by which we have been building up civilization, not by force. And the lasting impression that those boys are going to leave is this, that they exercise self-control; that they are ready and diligent to make the place where they went fitter to live in than they found it; that they regarded other people's rights; that they did not strut and bluster, but went quietly, like self-respecting gentlemen, about their legitimate work. And the people of Vera Cruz, who feared the Americans and despised the Americans, are going to get a very different taste in their mouths about the whole thing when the boys of the Navy and the Army come away. Is that not something to be proud of, that you know how to use force like men of conscience and like gentlemen, serving your fellow men and not trying to overcome them? Like that gallant gentleman who has so long borne the heats and perplexities and distresses of the situation in Vera Cruz—Admiral Fletcher. I mention him, because his service there has been longer and so much of the early perplexities fell upon him. I have been in almost daily communication with Admiral Fletcher, and I have tested his temper. I have tested his discretion. I know that he is a man with a touch of statesmanship about him, and he has grown bigger in my eye each day as I have read his dispatches, for he has sought always to serve the thing he was trying to do in the temper that we all recognize and love to believe is typically American.

I challenge you youngsters to go out with these conceptions, knowing that you are part of the Government and force of the United States and that men will judge us by you. I am not afraid of the verdict. I can not look in your faces and doubt what it will be, but I want you to take these great engines of force out onto the seas like adventurers enlisted for the elevation of the spirit of the human race. For that is the only distinction that America has. Other nations have been strong, other nations have piled wealth as high as the sky, but they have come into disgrace because they used their force and their wealth for the oppression of mankind and their own aggrandizement; and America will not bring glory to herself, but disgrace, by following the beaten paths of history. We must strike out upon new paths, and we must count upon you gentlemen to be the explorers who will carry this spirit and spread this message all over the seas and in every port of the civilized world.

You see, therefore, why I said that when I faced you I felt there was a special significance. I am not present on an occasion when you are about to scatter on various errands. You are all going on the same errand, and I like to feel bound with you in one common organization for the glory of America. And her glory goes deeper than all the tinsel, goes deeper than the sound of guns and the clash of sabers; it goes down to the very foundations of those things that have made the spirit of men free and happy and content.

ADDRESS

[At Independence Hall, Philadelphia, Pa., July 4, 1914.]

Mr. Chairman and Fellow Citizens: We are assembled to celebrate the one hundred and thirty-eighth anniversary of the birth of the United States. I suppose that we can more vividly realize the circumstances of that birth standing on this historic spot than it would be possible to realize them anywhere else. The Declaration of Independence was written in Philadelphia; it was adopted in this historic building by which we stand. I have just had the privilege of sitting in the chair of the great man who presided over the deliberations of those who gave the declaration to the world. My hand rests at this moment upon the table upon which the declaration was signed. We can feel that we are almost in the visible and tangible presence of a great historic transaction.

Have you ever read the Declaration of Independence or attended with close comprehension to the real character of it when you have heard it read? If you have, you will know that it is not a Fourth of July oration. The Declaration of Independence was a document preliminary to war. It was a vital piece of practical business, not a piece of rhetoric; and if you will pass beyond those preliminary passages which we are accustomed to quote about the rights of men and read into the heart of the document you will see that it is very express and detailed, that it consists of a series of definite specifications concerning actual public business of the day. Not the business of our day, for the matter with which it deals is past, but the business of that first revolution by which the Nation was set up, the business of 1776. Its general statements, its general declarations can not mean anything to us unless we append to it a similar specific body of particulars as to what we consider the essential business of our own day.

Liberty does not consist, my fellow citizens, in mere general declarations of the rights of man. It consists in the translation of those declarations into definite action. Therefore, standing here where the declaration was adopted, reading its business-like sentences, we ought to ask ourselves what there is in it for us. There is nothing in it for us unless we can translate it into the terms of our own conditions and of our own lives. We must reduce it to what the lawyers call a bill of particulars. It contains a bill of particulars, but the bill of particulars of 1776. If we would keep it alive, we must fill it with a bill of particulars of the year 1914.

The task to which we have constantly to readdress ourselves is the task of proving that we are worthy of the men who drew this great declaration and know what they would have done in our circumstances. Patriotism consists in some very practical things—practical in that they belong to the life of every day, that they wear no extraordinary distinction about them, that they are connected with commonplace duty. The way to be patriotic in America is not only to love America, but to love the duty that lies nearest to our hand and know that in performing it we are serving our country. There are some gentlemen in Washington, for example, at this very moment who are showing themselves very patriotic in a way which does not attract wide attention but seems to belong to mere everyday obligations. The Members of the House and Senate who stay in hot Washington to maintain a quorum of the Houses and transact the all-important business of the Nation are doing an act of patriotism. I honor them for it, and I am glad to stay there and stick by them until the work is done.

It is patriotic, also, to learn what the facts of our national life are and to face them with candor. I have heard a great many facts stated about the present business condition of this country, for example—a great many allegations of fact, at any rate, but the allegations do not tally with one another. And yet I know that truth always matches with truth; and when I find some insisting that everything is going wrong and others insisting that everything is going right, and when I know from a wide observation of the general circumstances of the country taken as a whole that things are going extremely well, I wonder what those who are crying out that things are wrong are trying to do. Are they trying to serve the country, or are they trying to serve something smaller than the country? Are they trying to put hope into the hearts of the men who work and toil every day, or are they trying to plant discouragement and despair in those hearts? And why do they cry that everything is wrong and yet do nothing to set it right? If they love America and anything is wrong amongst us, it is their business to put their hand with ours to the task of setting it right. When the facts are known and acknowledged, the duty of all patriotic men is to accept them in candor and to address themselves hopefully and confidently to the common counsel which is necessary to act upon them wisely and in universal concert.

I have had some experiences in the last 14 months which have not been entirely reassuring. It was universally admitted, for example, my fellow citizens, that the banking system of this country needed reorganization. We set the best minds that we could find to the task of discovering the best method of reorganization. But we met with hardly anything but criticism from the bankers of the country; we met with hardly anything but resistance from the majority of those at least who spoke at all concerning the matter. And yet so soon as that act was passed there was a universal chorus of applause, and the very men who had opposed the measure joined in that applause. If it was wrong the day before it was passed, why was it right the day after it was passed? Where had been the candor of criticism not only, but the concert of counsel which makes legislative action vigorous and safe and successful?

It is not patriotic to concert measures against one another; it is patriotic to concert measures for one another.

In one sense the Declaration of Independence has lost its significance. It has lost its significance as a declaration of national independence. Nobody outside of America believed when it was uttered that we could make good our independence; now nobody anywhere would dare to doubt that we are independent and can maintain our independence. As a declaration of independence, therefore, it is a mere historic document. Our independence is a fact so stupendous that it can be measured only by the size and energy and variety and wealth and power of one of the greatest nations in the world. But it is one thing to be independent and it is another thing to know what to do with your independence. It is one thing to come to your majority and another thing to know what you are going to do with your life and your energies; and one of the most serious questions for sober-minded men to address themselves to in the United States is this: What are we going to do with the influence and power of this great Nation? Are we going to play the old rôle of using that power for our aggrandizement and material benefit only? You know what that may mean. It may upon occasion mean that we shall use it to make the peoples of other nations suffer in the way in which we said it was intolerable to suffer when we uttered our Declaration of Independence.

The Department of State at Washington is constantly called upon to back up the commercial enterprises and the industrial enterprises of the United States in foreign countries, and it at one time went so far in that direction that all its diplomacy came to be designated as "dollar diplomacy." It was called upon to support every man who wanted to earn anything anywhere if he was an American. But there ought to be a limit to that. There is no man who is more interested than I am in carrying the enterprise of American business men to every quarter of the globe. I was interested in it long before I was suspected of being a politician. I have been preaching it year after year as the great thing that lay in the future for the United States, to show her wit and skill and enterprise and influence in every country in the world. But observe the limit to all that which is laid upon us perhaps more than upon any other nation in the world. We set this nation up, at any rate we professed to set it up, to vindicate the rights of men. We did not name any differences between one race and another. We did not set up any barriers against any particular people. We opened our gates to all the world and said, "Let all men who wish to be free come to us and they will be welcome." We said, "This independence of ours is not a selfish thing for our own exclusive private use. It is for everybody to whom we can find the means of extending it." We can not with that oath taken in our youth, we can not with that great ideal set before us when we were a young people and numbered only a scant 3,000,000, take upon ourselves, now that we are 100,000,000 strong, any other conception of duty than we then entertained. If American enterprise in foreign countries, particularly in those foreign countries which are not strong enough to resist us, takes the shape of imposing upon and exploiting the mass of the people of that country it ought to be checked and not encouraged. I am willing to get anything for an American that money and enterprise can obtain except the suppression of the rights of other men. I will not help any man buy a power which he ought not to exercise over his fellow beings.

You know, my fellow countrymen, what a big question there is in Mexico. Eighty-five per cent of the Mexican people have never been allowed to have any genuine participation in their own Government or to exercise any substantial rights with regard to the very land they live upon. All the rights that men most desire have been exercised by the other 15 per cent. Do you suppose that that circumstance is not sometimes in my thought? I know that the American people have a heart that will beat just as strong for those millions in Mexico as it will beat, or has beaten, for any other millions elsewhere in the world, and that when once they conceive what is at stake in Mexico they will know what ought to be done in Mexico. I hear a great deal said about the loss of property in Mexico and the loss of the lives of foreigners, and I deplore these things with all my heart. Undoubtedly, upon the conclusion of the present disturbed conditions in Mexico those who have been unjustly deprived of their property or in any wise unjustly put upon ought to be compensated. Men's individual rights have no doubt been invaded, and the invasion of those rights has been attended by many deplorable circumstances which ought some time, in the proper way, to be accounted for. But back of it all is the struggle of a people to come into its own, and while we look upon the incidents in the foreground let us not forget the great tragic reality in the background which towers above the whole picture.

A patriotic American is a man who is not niggardly and selfish in the things that he enjoys that make for human liberty and the rights of man. He wants to share them with the whole world, and he is never so proud of the great flag under which he lives as when it comes to mean to other people as well as to himself a symbol of hope and liberty. I would be ashamed of this flag if it ever did anything outside America that we would not permit it to do inside of America.

The world is becoming more complicated every day, my fellow citizens. No man ought to be foolish enough to think that he understands it all. And, therefore, I am glad that there are some simple things in the world. One of the simple things is principle. Honesty is a perfectly simple thing. It is hard for me to believe that in most circumstances when a man has a choice of ways he does not know which is the right way and which is the wrong way. No man who has chosen the wrong way ought even to come into Independence Square; it is holy ground which he ought not to tread upon. He ought not to come where immortal voices have uttered the great sentences of such a document as this Declaration of Independence upon which rests the liberty of a whole nation.

And so I say that it is patriotic sometimes to prefer the honor of the country to its material interest. Would you rather be deemed by all the nations of the world incapable of keeping your treaty obligations in order that you might have free tolls for American ships? The treaty under which we gave up that right may have been a mistaken treaty, but there was no mistake about its meaning.

When I have made a promise as a man I try to keep it, and I know of no other rule permissible to a nation. The most distinguished nation in the world is the nation that can and will keep its promises even to its own hurt. And I want to say parenthetically that I do not think anybody was hurt. I can not be enthusiastic for subsidies to a monopoly, but let those who are enthusiastic for subsidies ask themselves whether they prefer subsidies to unsullied honor.

The most patriotic man, ladies and gentlemen, is sometimes the man who goes in the direction that he thinks right even when he sees half the world against him. It is the dictate of patriotism to sacrifice yourself if you think that that is the path of honor and of duty. Do not blame others if they do not agree with you. Do not die with bitterness in your heart because you did not convince the rest of the world, but die happy because you believe that you tried to serve your country by not selling your soul. Those were grim days, the days of 1776. Those gentlemen did not attach their names to the Declaration of Independence on this table expecting a holiday on the next day, and that 4th of July was not itself a holiday. They attached their signatures to that significant document knowing that if they failed it was certain that every one of them would hang for the failure. They were committing treason in the interest of the liberty of 3,000,000 people in America. All the rest of the world was against them and smiled with cynical incredulity at the audacious undertaking. Do you think that if they could see this great Nation now they would regret anything that they then did to draw the gaze of a hostile world upon them? Every idea must be started by somebody, and it is a lonely thing to start anything. Yet if it is in you, you must start it if you have a man's blood in you and if you love the country that you profess to be working for.

I am sometimes very much interested when I see gentlemen supposing that popularity is the way to success in America. The way to success in this great country, with its fair judgments, is to show that you are not afraid of anybody except God and his final verdict. If I did not believe that, I would not believe in democracy. If I did not believe that, I would not believe that people can govern themselves. If I did not believe that the moral judgment would be the last judgment, the final judgment, in the minds of men as well as the tribunal of God, I could not believe in popular government. But I do believe these things, and, therefore, I earnestly believe in the democracy not only of America but of every awakened people that wishes and intends to govern and control its own affairs.

It is very inspiring, my friends, to come to this that may be called the original fountain of independence and liberty in America and here drink draughts of patriotic feeling which seem to renew the very blood in one's veins. Down in Washington sometimes when the days are hot and the business presses intolerably and there are so many things to do that it does not seem possible to do anything in the way it ought to be done, it is always possible to lift one's thought above the task of the moment and, as it were, to realize that great thing of which we are all parts, the great body of American feeling and American principle. No man could do the work that has to be done in Washington if he allowed himself to be separated from that body of principle. He must make himself feel that he is a part of the people of the United States, that he is trying to think not only for them, but with them, and then he can not feel lonely. He not only can not feel lonely but he can not feel afraid of anything.

My dream is that as the years go on and the world knows more and more of America it will also drink at these fountains of youth and renewal; that it also will turn to America for those moral inspirations which lie at the basis of all freedom; that the world will never fear America unless it feels that it is engaged in some enterprise which is inconsistent with the rights of humanity; and that America will come into the full light of the day when all shall know that she puts human rights above all other rights and that her flag is the flag not only of America but of humanity.

What other great people has devoted itself to this exalted ideal? To what other nation in the world can all eyes look for an instant sympathy that thrills the whole body politic when men anywhere are fighting for their rights? I do not know that there will ever be a declaration of independence and of grievances for mankind, but I believe that if any such document is ever drawn it will be drawn in the spirit of the American Declaration of Independence, and that America has lifted high the light which will shine unto all generations and guide the feet of mankind to the goal of justice and liberty and peace.

EXECUTIVE ORDERS

[To require ocean-going vessels to be fitted with wireless apparatus.]

THE WHITE HOUSE, *July 9, 1914.*

By virtue of the authority vested in me, I hereby establish the following order for the Canal Zone:

Section 1. From and after the first day of July, 1915, it shall be unlawful for any ocean-going steamer of the United States, or of any foreign country, carrying fifty or more persons including passengers and crew, to leave or attempt to leave any port of the Canal Zone unless such steamer shall be equipped with an efficient apparatus for radio communication in good working order in charge of a person skilled in the use of such apparatus, which apparatus shall be capable of transmitting and receiving messages for a distance of at least one hundred miles, night or day: provided, that the provisions of this order shall not apply to steamers plying only between the Canal Zone and ports less than two hundred miles therefrom.

Sec. 2. The master or other person being in charge of such vessel which leaves or attempts to leave any port of the Canal Zone in violation of any of the provisions of this order shall, upon conviction, be fined in a sum not to exceed Five Thousand Dollars ($5,000.00), and any such fine shall be a lien upon such vessel, and the vessel may be liable therefor in the District Court of the Canal Zone, and the leaving or attempting to leave by any vessel from each and every port of the Canal Zone shall constitute a separate offense.

Sec. 3. This order shall take effect from and after this date.

WOODROW WILSON.

[Establishing Smith Island Reservation for the protection of native birds.]

THE WHITE HOUSE, *June 6, 1914.*

It is hereby ordered that Smith and Minor Islands, situated approximately in latitude 48° 19′ North, longitude 122° 50′ West from Greenwich, as shown on United States Coast Survey chart No. 6380, in the Strait of Juan de Fuca, about fourteen miles north by west from Port Townsend, Washington, be and the same are hereby reserved and set apart for the use of the Department of Agriculture as a preserve, breeding ground and winter sanctuary for native birds. This order is not intended to abrogate the order of September 11, 1854, reserving these islands for lighthouse purposes, nor shall it in any manner interfere with such use of the islands, but rather, in addition to such use, shall insure the protection of the native birds thereon.

It is unlawful for any person to hunt, trap, capture, wilfully disturb or kill any bird of any kind whatever, or take the eggs of any such bird within the limits of this reserve, except under such rules and regulations as may be prescribed by the Secretary of Agriculture.

Warning is expressly given to all persons not to commit any of the acts herein enumerated, under the penalties of Section 84 of the U. S. Penal Code, approved March 4, 1909, 35 Stat., 1088.

This reserve to be known as Smith Island Reservation.

WOODROW WILSON.

[Amending the Civil Service Rules providing for the appointment of aliens when no citizens are available.]

THE WHITE HOUSE, *July 25, 1914.*

Section 1 of Rule V is hereby amended by adding thereto the following proviso:

Provided, That when an examination has been duly announced to fill a vacancy and there is a lack of eligibles who are citizens, the Commission may, in its discretion, examine persons who are not citizens, but they shall not be certified for appointment so long as citizens are eligible.

As amended this section will read:

1. No person shall be admitted to examination unless he be a citizen of or owe allegiance to the United States: *Provided,* That when an examination has been duly announced to fill a vacancy and there is a lack of eligibles who are citizens, the Commission may, in its discretion, examine persons who are not citizens, but they shall not be certified for appointment so long as citizens are eligible.

This order merely transfers to the civil service rules a provision of an Executive order of June 13, 1906.

WOODROW WILSON.

[Governing the inspection of returns of corporations, joint stock companies, associations, or insurance companies.]

THE WHITE HOUSE, *July 28, 1914.*

Pursuant to the provisions of Section 2 of the Tariff Act of October 3, 1913, said section providing for an income tax, and which contains in paragraph G, sub-paragraph (d) the following provision,

"When the assessment shall be made, as provided in this section, the returns, together with any corrections thereof which may have been made by the Commissioner, shall be filed in the office of the Commissioner of Internal Revenue and shall constitute public records and be open to inspection as such: Provided, That any and all such returns shall be open to inspection only upon the order of the President, under rules and regulations to be prescribed by the Secretary of the Treasury and approved by the President: Provided further, That the proper officers of any State imposing a general income tax may, upon the request of the governor thereof, have access to said returns or to any abstract thereof, showing the name and income of each such corporation, joint stock company, association or insurance company, at such times and in such manner as the Secretary of the Treasury may prescribe,"

it is hereby ordered, that all such returns shall be subject to inspection in accordance and upon compliance with rules and regulations prescribed by the Secretary of the Treasury and approved by the President, bearing even date herewith.

WOODROW WILSON.

[This order was accompanied by a ruling of the Secretary of the Treasury, Wm. G. McAdoo, approved by President Wilson, to the effect that returns of individuals are not open to the inspection of any one except the proper officers and employees of the Treasury Department.]

[Establishing a wireless telegraph station in the Canal Zone for use of the Navy.]

THE WHITE HOUSE, *July 30, 1914.*

The area of land hereinafter described, situated in the Canal Zone, is hereby set apart and assigned to the uses and purposes of a radio station and other naval purposes under the control of the Secretary of the Navy; but said area shall be subject to the civil jurisdiction of the Canal Zone authorities in conformity with the Panama Canal Act.

The said area is described as Darien Naval Radio Station and is shown by the blue print No. 3846, dated March 30, 1914, issued by the Department of Construction and Engineering, Isthmian Canal Commission, office of the Assistant to the Chief Engineer.

WOODROW WILSON.

[For the relief, protection and transportation home of Americans in Europe at the outbreak of the European war of 1914.]

THE WHITE HOUSE, *August 5, 1914.*

To the end that there may be proper co-operation as between the Departments of State, Treasury, War and Navy in the accomplishment of the desired results in connection with the relief, protection and transportation of American citizens abroad made necessary by existing disturbed conditions in Europe, it is directed:

1. The heads of the Departments named will co-operate and co-ordinate their work to the extent possible under the general provisions of this order and in accordance with such further instructions as may be given.

2. The Secretary of the Navy will despatch such ships to such ports as may be determined upon for the purpose of carrying those detailed from the various Departments for relief work, together with supplies and money.

3. The Secretary of War will detail officers for the purpose of organizing and conducting the relief work among, and the transportation of, the refugees. He will attend to the chartering of ships, arranging for transportation, payment therefor by those able to pay, and the proper handling of the destitute, after obtaining all the information possible and availing himself of the services of each of the other Departments who can aid in these respects.

4. The Secretary of the Treasury will make arrangements for handling the funds, determining, after such consultation as may be necessary, how much shall be shipped abroad and how the sums which will be required to be expended by the other Departments shall be drawn against and accounted for. He will make arrangements for fiscal agencies at such points in England and on the Continent as may be practicable, and he will provide means for making available for American citizens in Europe and England moneys furnished by their friends, relatives, and banking and express companies in this country.

5. The Secretary of State will detail such diplomatic agents as may be necessary, including an adviser upon diplomatic procedure and law, to accompany the Assistant Secretary of War on the first shipment to sail for the other side. He will use all avenues of communication available to gather and distribute all obtainable facts.

For the purpose of having a complete and unconfused record, all communications to the Navy ship to carry the Assistant Secretary of War and the Army officers will be sent to the Secretary of War, and by him sent to the Navy Department for transmission. This, of course, refers to the relief work, and not to orders to Naval officers, etc.

6. The heads of the Departments above referred to will keep in constant communication with each other and endeavor to agree upon and arrange every question which arises, advising with the President wherever necessary and securing his directions.

WOODROW WILSON.

[To enforce neutrality of wireless stations.]

THE WHITE HOUSE, *August 5, 1914.*

Whereas Proclamations having been issued by me declaring the neutrality of the United States of America in the wars now existing between various European nations; and

Whereas it is desirable to take precautions to insure the enforcement of said Proclamations in so far as the use of radio communication is concerned;

It is now ordered, by virtue of authority vested in me to establish regulations on the subject, that all radio stations within the jurisdiction of the United States of America are hereby prohibited from transmitting or receiving for delivery messages of an unneutral nature, and from in any way rendering to any one of the belligerents any unneutral service, during the continuance of hostilities.

The enforcement of this order is hereby delegated to the Secretary of the Navy, who is authorized and directed to take such action in the premises as to him may appear necessary.

This order to take effect from and after this date.

WOODROW WILSON.

[Establishing Board of Relief for benefit of Americans stranded abroad during the European war, 1914.]

THE WHITE HOUSE, *August 6, 1914.*

Supplementing the Executive Order signed August 5th, in relation to the Relief, Protection and Transportation of American Citizens abroad, it is further directed:

That the Secretary of State, the Secretary of the Treasury, the Secretary of War and the Secretary of the Navy be, and they are hereby constituted a Board of Relief to have general charge of the work to be done under and by virtue of joint resolution No. 314, passed August 5th, and that the Secretary of the Treasury be, and he hereby is designated Chairman of said Board.

WOODROW WILSON.

[Relating to the Customs Service and providing for fines for dishonest manifests in the Canal Zone.]

The White House, *August 8, 1914.*

By Virtue of the Authority Vested in Me, I Hereby Establish the Following Order for the Canal Zone:

1. If the master of a vessel, arriving at any port in the Canal Zone from a foreign port, shall fail or refuse to produce to the proper officer of the customs, upon demand by him, the ship's manifest and copies thereof, or shall fail or refuse to give a true account of the destination of such vessel, he shall be subject to a fine of not exceeding five hundred dollars.

2. If any merchandise be found on board any vessel arriving in the Canal Zone from a foreign port, which is not included in her manifest, the master of such vessel shall be liable to a penalty equal in amount to the value of the merchandise not manifested, and all such merchandise, belonging to or consigned to the officers or crew of the vessel, shall be forfeited, provided, however, that the penalty authorized by this section shall not be imposed if it should be made to appear to the chief customs officer, at the port of entry, or to the court in which the trial shall be held, that no part of the cargo has been unladened, except as accounted for in the master's report, and that the errors and omissions in the manifest were made without fraud or collusion; in such case the master may be allowed to correct his manifest by means of a post-entry. It shall not be lawful to grant a permit to unload any such merchandise, so omitted from the manifest, before such post-entry or addition to report or manifest has been made.

3. If sea stores are found on board of a vessel arriving at the Canal Zone from a foreign port, which are not specified in the list furnished the boarding officer, or if a greater quantity of such articles is found than that specified in such list, or if any of the articles are landed without a permit being first obtained from the customs officer for that purpose, all of such articles omitted from the list or manifest, or so landed, shall be seized and forfeited, and the master of the vessel shall be liable to a penalty of treble the value of the articles so omitted or landed.

4. The officers of the Bureau of Customs are authorized to administer oaths, and to certify invoices covering shipments of merchandise from the Canal Zone to the United States. In the performance of this duty they shall be governed by the United States Consular regulations, and by the circular instructions concerning the certification of invoices issued to consuls of the United States, insofar as they are applicable, provided, however, that any special instructions heretofore issued, or which may be issued by the Treasury Department, concerning the certification of invoices in the Canal Zone, shall be complied with.

5. Any person violating any of the customs laws, or the customs rules and regulations established, or to be established, by the Governor of The Panama Canal in conformity with existing laws and orders, shall be subject to a fine not exceeding five hundred dollars for each violation of such regulations.

6. This order shall take effect from and after this date.

WOODROW WILSON.

[Giving the Treasury Department full authority over all customs officers in the enforcement of the neutrality laws during emergency.]

THE WHITE HOUSE, *August 8, 1914.*

In order to secure a more prompt and effective enforcement of the neutrality laws to meet the emergent conditions now existing, it is hereby ordered that all instructions to customs officers concerning the enforcement of the neutrality laws of the United States, shall, until otherwise directed, be issued by the Treasury Department.

WOODROW WILSON.

[Relating to Postal Crimes in the Canal Zone.]

THE WHITE HOUSE, *August 14, 1914.*

By virtue of the authority vested in me, I hereby establish the following order for the Canal Zone:

Section 1. The Postal Laws and Regulations of the United States, not locally inapplicable, which define crimes against the Postal Service, and prescribe punishments therefor, are hereby extended to the Canal Zone, and shall be enforceable in the courts of the Canal Zone in the manner and form prescribed for other criminal cases by the Canal Zone laws.

Section 2. This order shall take effect from and after this date.

WOODROW WILSON.

[To require security for costs in civil cases in the Canal Zone.]

THE WHITE HOUSE, *August 14, 1914.*

By virtue of the authority vested in me, I hereby establish the following order for the Canal Zone:

Section 1. The plantiff in any civil suit, or special proceeding, may be ruled to give security for the costs upon motion of the defendant, or of any officer of the court interested in the costs accruing in such suit; and if such rule be entered against the plaintiff, and he fail to comply therewith, within the time prescribed by the court or judge thereof, the suit shall be dismissed.

Municipal Building

A new or additional undertaking may be ordered within such time as the court or judge may prescribe, upon proof that the original undertaking is insufficient security, and failure on the part of the plaintiff to comply with the order of the court, or judge, within the time prescribed, shall cause the dismissal of the suit.

This section shall apply to suits in the magistrates' courts, as well as in the district court.

The security for costs required by this section may consist of a money deposit, bond of a surety company, or cost bond with two or more good and sufficient sureties; the form of such security to be determined by the judge or magistrate of the court before whom the proceedings are pending.

Section 2. All bonds given as security for costs shall authorize judgment against all of the obligors of said bonds for such costs, to be entered in the final judgment of the case or special proceedings.

Section 3. Any party to a suit, who is required to give security for costs, may file with the secretary, or his assistant, or with the magistrate, as the case may be, an affidavit to the effect that he is too poor to pay the costs of the court, and is unable to give security therefor. The secretary of the district court, or his assistant, or the magistrate, as the case may be, may contest the inability of the party to pay the costs, or his inability to give security for the same, the contest to be tried before the judge of the district court in cases pending in that court, and before the magistrate in cases pending in one of the magistrates' courts; and the contest shall be heard at such time as the court or magistrate may determine.

If no contest is made upon the affidavit, or if the same is admitted by the court or magistrate after the contest, it shall be the duty of the officers of the court thereafter to issue and serve all processes and perform all duties on behalf of such party as in other cases.

Section 4. The public administrator, and executors, administrators and guardians appointed by the courts of the Canal Zone shall not be required to give security for costs in any suit brought by them in their fiduciary character.

Section 5. No security for costs shall be required of The United States, The Panama Canal, The Canal Zone Government, or any of its dependencies.

Section 6. The provisions of this order, relating to security for costs, shall apply to an intervenor; and shall also apply to a defendant who seeks a judgment against the plaintiff on a counter-claim, after the defendant shall have discontinued his suit.

Section 7. When the costs are secured by the provisions of an attachment or other bond, filed by the party required to give security for costs, no further security shall be required.

Section 8. All laws, orders and decrees, or parts thereof, in conflict with this order, are hereby repealed, provided, that this order shall not be construed to impair the power conferred upon the courts in respect to costs by Article III of the Executive Order of September 29, 1911, "To Amend Sections 51, 62, and 526, And To Repeal Sections 63 and 529 of The Code of Civil Procedure Of The Canal Zone."

Section 9. This order shall take effect sixty days from this date.

WOODROW WILSON.

[Amending the rules governing the granting of passports.]

THE WHITE HOUSE, *August 14, 1914.*

The Secretary of State is hereby authorized, in his discretion, to issue passports to American citizens abroad, in cases of urgent necessity, upon applications made in their behalf by near relatives or legal representatives in this country. To this extent is amended Section 3 of the Rules Governing the Granting and Issuing of Passports in The United States, dated March 10, 1913.

WOODROW WILSON.

[For a lookout station at Twin Sisters Administrative Site (near Colorado National Forest), Colorado.]

THE WHITE HOUSE, *August 14, 1914.*

Under authority of the Act of Congress approved June 25, 1910 (36 Stat., 847), as amended by the Act of August 24, 1912 (37 Stat., 497), and on the recommendation of the Secretary of Agriculture, it is hereby ordered that the following described tract of land, containing 160 acres, be temporarily withdrawn from settlement, location, sale or entry, except as provided in said Acts, and be reserved for use by the Forest Service as a lookout station in connection with the administration of the Colorado National Forest, said tract being located on the summit of Twin Sisters Mountain, N ½ NW ¼ Section 25, S ½ SW ¼ Section 24, Township 4 North, Range 73 West, 6th P. M., in accordance with the official plat thereof.

WOODROW WILSON.

[To Amend the Executive Order of April 15, 1913, entitled: "Executive Order to Provide Maritime Quarantine Regulations for the Canal Zone and the Harbors of the Cities of Panama and Colon, Republic of Panama."]

THE WHITE HOUSE, *August 14, 1914.*

By virtue of the authority vested in me, I hereby establish the following order for the Canal Zone:

I. The certificate to the form of original bill of health prescribed by section 1 of the Executive Order of April 15, 1913, entitled: "Executive Order to Provide Maritime Quarantine Regulations for the Canal Zone and the Harbors of the Cities of Panama and Colon, Republic of Panama," is hereby amended to read as follows:

> I hereby certify that the vessel has complied with the quarantine rules and regulations of the Panama Canal, and that the vessel leaves this port bound for —— ——, Canal zone, or —— ——, Republic of Panama, via —— ——.
> Given under my hand and seal this —— —— day of —— 191—.
> (SEAL)
> _____
> (Signature of Consular Officer.)

II. The certificate to the form of supplemental bills of health prescribed by section 1 of the above mentioned Executive Order is hereby amended to read as follows:

> I certify also that with reference to the passengers, effects and cargo taken on at this port the vessel has complied with the quarantine rules and regulations of the Panama Canal.
> Given under my hand and seal this —— —— day of ——, 191—.
> (SEAL)
> _____
> (Signature of Consular Officer.)

III. Section 1 of the above mentioned Executive Order is hereby amended by adding the following paragraph to said section:

> Vessels clearing from a foreign port to a port in the United States, or one of their dependencies, and touching at any port of the Canal Zone, or Panama or of Colon, Republic of Panama, shall not be required to obtain an additional bill of health under the quarantine rules and regulations of the Panama Canal, but it shall be sufficient that such vessel obtain extra copies of the bill of health and of the supplemental bill of health, if any, issued in the foreign port by the officer authorized by the quarantine laws of the United States. Such extra copies of the bill of health, or of the supplemental bill of health, as the case may be, shall be delivered by the Captain of the vessel to the quarantine officer of the Panama Canal upon arrival of the vessel in ports of the Canal Zone, or the ports of Panama or Colon, Republic of Panama.

IV. Section 16 of the said Executive Order is hereby amended by adding thereto the following paragraph:

> The baggage of cabin passengers embarking at infected ports shall be treated as provided in this section for baggage of steerage passengers.

V. The second paragraph of section 19 of the above mentioned Executive Order is hereby amended to read as follows:

> (a) Vessels from the United States or their dependencies; (b) Vessels from foreign ports; (c) Vessels with sickness aboard; (d)

Vessels from Panamanian ports where any quarantinable disease prevails; (e) Vessels from Panamanian ports carrying passengers or articles suspected by the quarantine officer as being capable of conveying the infection of a transmissible disease.

VI. Section 26 of the above mentioned Executive Order is hereby amended to read as follows:

Section 26. The quarantine officer, after his inspection of the vessel and its documents, shall decide whether said vessel, or its personnel or passengers, or any article aboard said vessel is liable to convey any of the following diseases: plague, yellow fever, cholera, smallpox, typhus fever or leprosy; and, if so, such vessel shall be placed in quarantine and forbidden entry until free from such liability of conveying any such diseases, and he shall take such measures in respect to the vessel, its passengers or personnel or of cargo as in his judgment may be required to prevent the entry of such diseases into the Canal Zone, or the cities of Panama or Colon, Republic of Panama.

VII. Section 34 of said Executive Order is hereby amended to read as follows:

Any person violating any of the provisions of these regulations shall be punished by a fine not exceeding Five Hundred Dollars ($500.00), or by imprisonment in jail not exceeding ninety (90) days, or both such fine and imprisonment at the discretion of the court. The punishment herein prescribed shall be imposed by the district court of the Canal Zone.

VIII. This order shall take effect from and after the date upon which the Panama Canal is officially and formally opened for use and operation by the proclamation of the President of the United States.

WOODROW WILSON.

[Temporarily abolishing fees for passports and providing for certification of same.]

THE WHITE HOUSE, *August 14, 1914.*

It is hereby ordered that paragraphs 159 and 160 of the regulations and instructions prescribed for the use of the consular service of the United States and the instructions to the diplomatic officers of the United States be amended to read as follows:

"159. *Fees.*—Until further notice, no fee shall be collected for the issuance of an emergency passport, nor for the execution of the application therefor. This has no reference to a regular passport issued by the Department upon an application made before a Diplomatic or Consular Officer."

"160. *Visa.*—A Diplomatic Officer or a Consular Officer, including a Consular Agent, may visa or verify regularly issued passports by endorsing thereon the word "Good" in the language of the country and affixing to the endorsement his official signature and seal. A Diplomatic Officer should visa a passport only when there is no American Consulate established in the city where the mission is situated, or when the Consular Officer is absent, or the Government of the country refuses to acknowledge the validity of the Consular Visa. Whenever a passport without signature is presented to be visaed the holder should be required to sign it before it is visaed by a Diplomatic or Consular Officer. Until further notice, no fee shall be collected for the visaing of a passport. No visa shall be attached to a passport after its validity has expired."

Sections 8, 9 and 32 of the Tariff of United States Consular Fees shall be amended to read as follows:

"8. Issuing a passport—Form No. 9—for extending a passport (Fee waived until further notice by Executive Order of August 14, 1914) ....No fee."

"9. Visaing a passport—Form No. 10 (Fee waived until further notice by Executive Order of August 14, 1914) ....No fee."

"32. Administering oath and preparing passport application (Fee waived as to emergency passport applications by Executive Order of August 14, 1914) ....No fee."

This order shall have no effect as to fees collected by diplomatic or consular officers before they shall have actually received notice of its contents.

The Secretary of State may, when he sees fit, without further authorization, terminate the waiver of fees hereby put into effect, and restore the tariff of fees to the condition existing prior to the amendments made herein.

WOODROW WILSON.

NEUTRALITY PROCLAMATIONS

By the President of the United States of America

A PROCLAMATION

[Neutrality—Austria-Hungary and Servia, Germany and Russia, and Germany and France.]

Whereas a state of war unhappily exists between Austria-Hungary and Servia and between Germany and Russia and between Germany and France; And Whereas the United States is on terms of friendship and amity with the contending powers, and with the persons inhabiting their several dominions;

And Whereas there are citizens of the United States residing within the territories or dominions of each of the said belligerents and carrying on commerce, trade, or other business or pursuits therein;

And Whereas there are subjects of each of the said belligerents residing within the territory or jurisdiction of the United States, and carrying on commerce, trade, or other business or pursuits therein;

And Whereas the laws and treaties of the United States, without interfering with the free expression of opinion and sympathy, or with the commercial manufacture or sale of arms or munitions of war, nevertheless impose upon all persons who may be within their territory and jurisdiction the duty of an impartial neutrality during the existence of the contest;

And Whereas it is the duty of a neutral government not to permit or suffer the making of its waters subservient to the purposes of war;

Now, Therefore, I, WOODROW WILSON, President of the United States of America, in order to preserve the neutrality of the United States and of its citizens and of persons within its territory and jurisdiction, and to enforce its laws and treaties, and in order that all persons, being warned of the general tenor of the laws and treaties of the United States in this behalf, and of the law of nations, may thus be prevented from any violation of the same, do hereby declare and proclaim that by certain provisions of the act approved on the 4th day of March, A. D. 1909, commonly known as the "Penal Code of the United States" the following acts are forbidden to be done, under severe penalties, within the territory and jurisdiction of the United States, to wit:—

1. Accepting and exercising a commission to serve either of the said belligerents by land or by sea against the other belligerent.

2. Enlisting or entering into the service of either of the said belligerents as a soldier, or as a marine, or seaman on board of any vessel of war, letter of marque, or privateer.

3. Hiring or retaining another person to enlist or enter himself in the service of either of the said belligerents as a soldier, or as a marine, or seaman on board of any vessel of war, letter of marque, or privateer.

4. Hiring another person to go beyond the limits or jurisdiction of the United States with intent to be enlisted as aforesaid.

5. Hiring another person to go beyond the limits of the United States with intent to be entered into service as aforesaid.

6. Retaining another person to go beyond the limits of the United States with intent to be enlisted as aforesaid.

7. Retaining another person to go beyond the limits of the United States with intent to be entered into service as aforesaid. (But the said act is not to be construed to extend to a citizen or subject of either belligerent who, being transiently within the United States, shall, on

board of any vessel of war, which, at the time of its arrival within the United States, was fitted and equipped as such vessel of war, enlist or enter himself or hire or retain another subject or citizen of the same belligerent, who is transiently within the United States, to enlist or enter himself to serve such belligerent on board such vessel of war, if the United States shall then be at peace with such belligerent.)

8. Fitting out and arming, or attempting to fit out and arm, or procuring to be fitted out and armed, or knowingly being concerned in the furnishing, fitting out, or arming of any ship or vessel with intent that such ship or vessel shall be employed in the service of either of the said belligerents.

9. Issuing or delivering a commission within the territory or jurisdiction of the United States for any ship or vessel to the intent that she may be employed as aforesaid.

10. Increasing or augmenting, or procuring to be increased or augmented, or knowingly being concerned in increasing or augmenting, the force of any ship of war, cruiser, or other armed vessel, which at the time of her arrival within the United States was a ship of war, cruiser, or armed vessel in the service of either of the said belligerents, or belonging to the subjects of either, by adding to the number of guns of such vessels, or by changing those on board of her for guns of a larger calibre, or by the addition thereto of any equipment solely applicable to war.

11. Beginning or setting on foot or providing or preparing the means for any military expedition or enterprise to be carried on from the territory or jurisdiction of the United States against the territories or dominions of either of the said belligerents.

And I do hereby further declare and proclaim that any frequenting and use of the waters within the territorial jurisdiction of the United States by the armed vessels of a belligerent, whether public ships or privateers, for the purpose of preparing for hostile operations, or as posts of observation upon the ships of war or privateers or merchant vessels of a belligerent lying within or being about to enter the jurisdiction of the United States, must be regarded as unfriendly and offensive, and in violation of that neutrality which it is the determination of this government to observe; and to the end that the hazard and inconvenience of such apprehended practices may be avoided, I further proclaim and declare that from and after the fifth day of August instant, and during the continuance of the present hostilities between Austria-Hungary and Servia, and Germany and Russia and Germany and France, no ship of war or privateer of any belligerent shall be permitted to make use of any port, harbor, roadstead, or waters subject to the jurisdiction of the United States from which a vessel of an opposing belligerent (whether the same shall be a ship of war, a privateer, or a merchant ship) shall have previously departed, until after the expiration of at least twenty-four hours from the departure of such last-mentioned vessel beyond the jurisdiction of the United States. If any ship of war or privateer of a belligerent shall, after the time this notification takes effect, enter any port, harbor, roadstead, or waters of the United States, such vessel shall be required to depart and to put to sea within twenty-four hours after her entrance into such port, harbor, roadstead, or waters, except in case of stress of weather or of her requiring provisions or things necessary for the subsistence of her crew, or for repairs; in any of which cases the authorities of the port or of the nearest port (as the case may be) shall require her to put to sea as soon as possible after the expiration of such period of twenty-four hours, without permitting her to take in supplies beyond what may be necessary for her immediate use; and no such vessel which may have been permitted to remain within the waters of the United States for the purpose of repair shall continue within such port, harbor, roadstead, or waters for a longer period than twenty-four hours after her necessary repairs shall have been completed, unless within such twenty-four hours a vessel, whether ship of war, privateer, or merchant ship of an opposing belligerent, shall have departed therefrom, in which case the time limited for the departure of such ship of war or privateer shall be extended so far as may be necessary to secure an interval of not less than twenty-four hours between such departure and that of any ship of war, privateer, or merchant ship of an opposing belligerent which may have previously quit the same port, harbor, roadstead, or waters. No ship of war or privateer of a belligerent shall be detained in any port, harbor, roadstead, or waters of the United States more than twenty-four hours, by reason of the successive departures from such port, harbor, roadstead, or waters of more than one vessel of an opposing belligerent. But if there be several vessels of opposing belligerents in the same port, harbor, roadstead, or waters, the order of their departure therefrom shall be so arranged as to afford the opportunity of leaving alternately to the vessels of the opposing belligerents, and to cause the least detention consistent with the objects of this proclamation. No ship of war or privateer of a belligerent shall be permitted, while in any port, harbor, roadstead, or waters within the jurisdiction of the United States, to take in any supplies except provisions and such other things as may be requisite for the subsistence of her crew, and except so much coal only as may be sufficient to carry such vessel, if without any sail power, to the nearest port of her own country; or in case the vessel is rigged to go under sail, and may also be propelled by steam power, then with half the quantity of coal which she would be entitled to receive, if dependent upon steam alone, and no coal shall be again supplied to any such ship of war or privateer in the same or any other port, harbor, roadstead, or waters of the United States, without special permission, until after the expiration of three months from the time when such coal may have been last supplied to her within the waters of the United States, unless such ship of war or privateer shall, since last thus supplied, have entered a port of the government to which she belongs.

And I do further declare and proclaim that the statutes and the treaties of the United States and the law of nations alike require that no person, within the territory and jurisdiction of the United States, shall take part, directly or indirectly, in the said wars, but shall remain at peace with all of the said belligerents, and shall maintain a strict and impartial neutrality.

And I do hereby enjoin all citizens of the United States, and all persons residing or being within the territory or jurisdiction of the United States, to observe the laws thereof, and to commit no act contrary to the provisions of the said statutes or treaties or in violation of the law of nations in that behalf.

And I do hereby warn all citizens of the United States, and all persons residing or being within its territory or jurisdiction that, while the free and full expression of sympathies in public and private is not restricted by the laws of the United States, military forces in aid of a belligerent cannot lawfully be originated or organized within its jurisdiction; and that, while all persons may lawfully and without restriction by reason of the aforesaid state of war manufacture and sell within the United States arms and munitions of war, and other articles ordinarily known as "contraband of war," yet they cannot carry such articles upon the high seas for the use or service of a belligerent, nor can they transport soldiers and officers of a belligerent, or attempt to break any blockade which may be lawfully established and maintained during the said wars without incurring the risk of hostile capture and the penalties denounced by the law of nations in that behalf.

And I do hereby give notice that all citizens of the United States and others who may claim the protection of this government, who may misconduct themselves in the premises, will do so at their peril, and that they can in no wise obtain any protection from the government of the United States against the consequences of their misconduct.

In witness whereof I have hereunto set my hand and caused the seal of the United States to be affixed.

Done at the city of Washington this fourth day of August in the year of our Lord one thousand nine hundred and fourteen, and [SEAL.] of the independence of the United States of America the one hundred and thirty-ninth.

By the President: · WOODROW WILSON.

WILLIAM JENNINGS BRYAN, *Secretary of State.*

By the President of the United States of America

A PROCLAMATION

[Neutrality—Germany and Great Britain.]

Whereas a state of war unhappily exists between Germany and Great Britain; And Whereas the United States is on terms of friendship and amity with the contending powers, and with the persons inhabiting their several dominions;

[Here follows the identical preamble and warning against violation of quoted law as in the proclamation of neutrality in the case of hostilities between Austria-Hungary and Servia, Germany and Russia, and Germany and France. See pages 7969, 7970, 7971, 7972 and 7973.— Ed.]

Done at the city of Washington this fifth day of August in the year of our Lord one thousand nine hundred and fourteen, and [SEAL.] of the independence of the United States of America the one hundred and thirty-ninth.

WOODROW WILSON.

By the President:

WILLIAM JENNINGS BRYAN, *Secretary of State.*

By the President of the United States of America

A PROCLAMATION

[Neutrality—Austria-Hungary and Russia.]

Whereas a state of war unhappily exists between Austria-Hungary and Russia; and Whereas the United States is on terms of friendship and amity with the contending powers, and with the persons inhabiting their several dominions;

[Here follows the identical preamble and warning against violation of quoted law as in the proclamation of neutrality in the case of hostilities between Austria-Hungary and Servia, Germany and Russia, and Germany and France. See pages 7969, 7970, 7971, 7972 and 7973.— Ed.]

Done at the city of Washington this seventh day of August in the year of our Lord one thousand nine hundred and fourteen, and [SEAL.] of the independence of the United States of America the one hundred and thirty-ninth.

WOODROW WILSON.

By the President:

WILLIAM JENNINGS BRYAN, *Secretary of State.*

By the President of the United States of America

A PROCLAMATION

[Neutrality—Great Britain and Austria-Hungary.]

Whereas a state of war unhappily exists between Great Britain and Austria-Hungary; and Whereas the United States is on terms of friendship and amity with the contending powers, and with the persons inhabiting their several dominions;

> [Here follows the identical preamble and warning against violation of quoted law as in the proclamation of neutrality in the case of hostilities between Austria-Hungary and Servia, Germany and Russia, and Germany and France. See pages 7969, 7970, 7971, 7972 and 7973.— Ed.]

Done at the city of Washington this thirteenth day of August in the year of our Lord one thousand nine hundred and fourteen, [SEAL.] and of the independence of the United States of America the one hundred and thirty-ninth.

WOODROW WILSON.

By the President:

WILLIAM JENNINGS BRYAN, *Secretary of State.*

By the President of the United States of America

A PROCLAMATION

[Neutrality—France and Austria-Hungary.]

Whereas a state of war unhappily exists between France and Austria-Hungary; And Whereas the United States is on terms of friendship and amity with the contending powers, and with the persons inhabiting their several dominions;

> [Here follows the identical preamble and warning against violation of quoted law as in the proclamation of neutrality in the case of hostilities between Austria-Hungary and Servia, Germany and Russia, and Germany and France. See pages 7969, 7970, 7971, 7972 and 7973.— Ed.]

Done at the city of Washington this fourteenth day of August in the year of our Lord one thousand nine hundred and fourteen and of the independence of the United States of America the one hundred and thirty-ninth.

WOODROW WILSON.

By the President:

WLLIAM JENNINGS BRYAN, *Secretary of State.*

BY THE PRESIDENT OF THE UNITED STATES OF AMERICA

A PROCLAMATION

[Neutrality—Belgium and Germany.]

WHEREAS the United States is in fact aware of the existence of a state of war between Belgium and Germany; And Whereas the United States is on terms of friendship and amity with the contending powers, and with the persons inhabiting their several dominions;

[Here follows the identical preamble and warning against violation of quoted law as in the proclamation of neutrality in the case of hostilities between Austria-Hungary and Servia, Germany and Russia, and Germany and France. See pages 7969, 7970, 7971, 7972 and 7973.— *Ed.*]

DONE at the city of Washington this twenty-fourth day of August in the year of our Lord one thousand nine hundred and [SEAL.] fourteen and of the independence of the United States of America the one hundred and thirty-ninth.

WOODROW WILSON.

By the President:

WLLIAM JENNINGS BRYAN, *Secretary of State.*

BY THE PRESIDENT OF THE UNITED STATES OF AMERICA

A PROCLAMATION

[Neutrality—Japan and Germany.]

WHEREAS a state of war unhappily exists between Japan and Germany; And Whereas the United States is on terms of friendship and amity with the contending powers, and with the persons inhabiting their several dominions;

[Here follows the identical preamble and warning against violation of quoted law as in the proclamation of neutrality in the case of hostilities between Austria-Hungary and Servia, Germany and Russia, and Germany and France. See pages 7969, 7970, 7971, 7972 and 7973.— *Ed.*]

DONE at the city of Washington this twenty-fourth day of August in the year of our Lord one thousand nine hundred and [SEAL.] fourteen and of the independence of the United States of America the one hundred and thirty-ninth.

WOODROW WILSON

By the President:

WILLLIAM JENNINGS BRYAN, *Secretary of State.*

By the President of the United States of America.

A PROCLAMATION.

[Neutrality—Japan and Austria-Hungary.]

Whereas a state of war unhappily exists between Japan and Austria-Hungary; And Whereas the United States is on terms of friendship and amity with the contending powers, and with the persons inhabiting their several dominions;

> [Here follows the identical preamble and warning against violation of quoted law as in the proclamation of neutrality in the case of hostilities between Austria-Hungary and Servia, Germany and Russia, and Germany and France. See pages 7969, 7970, 7971, 7972 and 7973.— *Ed.*]

Done at the city of Washington this twenty-seventh day of August in the year of our Lord one thousand nine hundred and fourteen and of the independence of the United States of America the one hundred and thirty-ninth.

[SEAL.]

WOODROW WILSON.

By the President:
W. J. Bryan, *Secretary of State.*

By the President of the United States of America.

A PROCLAMATION.

[Neutrality—Belgium and Austria-Hungary.]

Whereas a state of war unhappily exists between Belgium and Austria-Hungary; And Whereas the United States is on terms of friendship and amity with the contending powers, and with the persons inhabiting their several dominions;

> [Here follows the identical preamble and warning against violation of quoted law as in the proclamation of neutrality in the case of hostilities between Austria-Hungary and Servia, Germany and Russia, and Germany and France. See pages 7969, 7970, 7971, 7972 and 7973.— *Ed.*]

Done at the city of Washington this first day of September in the year of our Lord one thousand nine hundred and fourteen and of the independence of the United States of America the one hundred and thirty-ninth.

[SEAL.]

WOODROW WILSON.

By the President:
W. J. Bryan, *Secretary of State.*

AMERICAN NEUTRALITY

[An Appeal by the President of the United States to the Citizens of the Republic, Requesting Their Assistance in Maintaining a State of Neutrality During the European War.]

WASHINGTON, D. C., *August 20, 1914.*

MY FELLOW COUNTRYMEN: I suppose that every thoughtful man in America has asked himself, during these last troubled weeks, what influence the European war may exert upon the United States, and I take the liberty of addressing a few words to you in order to point out that it is entirely within our own choice what its effects upon us will be and to urge very earnestly upon you the sort of speech and conduct which will best safeguard the Nation against distress and disaster.

The effect of the war upon the United States will depend upon what American citizens say and do. Every man who really loves America will act and speak in the true spirit of neutrality, which is the spirit of impartiality and fairness and friendliness to all concerned. The spirit of the Nation in this critical matter will be determined largely by what individuals and society and those gathered in public meetings do and say, upon what newspapers and magazines contain, upon what ministers utter in their pulpits, and men proclaim as their opinions on the street.

The people of the United States are drawn from many nations, and chiefly from the nations now at war. It is natural and inevitable that there should be the utmost variety of sympathy and desire among them with regard to the issues and circumstances of the conflict. Some will wish one nation, others another, to succeed in the momentous struggle. It will be easy to excite passion and difficult to allay it. Those responsible for exciting it will assume a heavy responsibility, responsibility for no less a thing than that the people of the United States, whose love of their country and whose loyalty to its Government should unite them as Americans all, bound in honor and affection to think first of her and her interests, may be divided in camps of hostile opinion, hot against each other, involved in the war itself in impulse and opinion if not in action.

Such divisions among us would be fatal to our peace of mind and might seriously stand in the way of the proper performance of our duty as the one great nation at peace, the one people holding itself ready to play a part of impartial mediation and speak the counsels of peace and accommodation, not as a partisan, but as a friend.

I venture, therefore, my fellow countrymen, to speak a solemn word of warning to you against that deepest, most subtle, most essential breach of neutrality which may spring out of partisanship, out of passionately taking sides. The United States must be neutral in fact as well as in name during these days that are to try men's souls. We must be impartial in thought, as well as in action, must put a curb upon our sentiments as well as upon every transaction that might be construed as a preference of one party to the struggle before another.

My thought is of America. I am speaking, I feel sure, the earnest wish and purpose of every thoughtful American that this great country of ours, which is, of course, the first in our thoughts and in our hearts, should show herself in this time of peculiar trial a Nation fit beyond others to exhibit the fine poise of undisturbed judgment, the dignity of self-control, the efficiency of dispassionate action; a Nation that neither sits in judgment upon others nor is disturbed in her own counsels and which keeps herself fit and free to do what is honest and disinterested and truly serviceable for the peace of the world.

Shall we not resolve to put upon ourselves the restraints which will bring to our people the happiness and the great and lasting influence for peace we covet for them?　　　WOODROW WILSON.

EXECUTIVE ORDERS

[Appointing Experts for War Risk Insurance in Treasury Department.]

THE WHITE HOUSE, *September 10, 1914.*

Mr. William C. DeLanoy may be appointed Director, and Mr. J. Brooks B. Parker may be appointed Assistant to the Director in the Bureau of War Risk Insurance in the Treasury Department without compliance with Civil Service rules.

The issuance of this order is recommended by the Secretary of the Treasury for the reason that on account of the technical character of the work required, the services of specially qualified men will be necessary in the higher grades and Mr. DeLanoy and Mr. Parker are regarded as Experts in the particular line of work that will be assigned to the new Bureau.　　　WOODROW WILSON.

[Transferring Deadmans Island to the Health Service.]

THE WHITE HOUSE, *August 26, 1914.*

It is hereby ordered that the following-described portion of the Military Reservation of Deadmans Island, situate at Los Angeles harbor, California, be and the same is hereby transferred to the Treasury Department and set aside for the use of the Public Health Service, viz.:

Beginning at U. S. Engineer Station "R," which is U. S. Coast and Geodetic Survey Station "Deadmans Island," thence N. 72° 25′ E. 413.32 feet to a point; thence S. 17° 35′ E. 500 feet to a point; thence S. 72° 25′ W. 522.72 feet to a point; thence N. 17° 35′ W. 500 feet to a point; thence N. 72° 25′ E. 109.4 feet to point of beginning.

Area: 6 acres.　　　WOODROW WILSON.

ADDRESS

[Delivered by President Wilson at a joint session of the two Houses of Congress, September 4, 1914, urging measures to provide additional revenues.]

GENTLEMEN OF THE CONGRESS: I come to you to-day to discharge a duty which I wish with all my heart I might have been spared; but it is a very clear duty, and therefore I perform it without hesitation or apology. I come to ask very earnestly that additional revenue be provided for the Government.

During the month of August there was, as compared with the corresponding month of last year, a falling off of $10,629,538 in the revenues collected from customs. A continuation of this decrease in the same proportion throughout the current fiscal year would probably mean a loss of customs revenues of from sixty to one hundred millions. I need not tell you to what this falling off is due. It is due, in chief part, not to the reductions recently made in the customs duties, but to the great decrease in importations; and that is due to the extraordinary extent of the industrial area affected by the present war in Europe. Conditions have arisen which no man foresaw; they affect the whole world of commerce and economic production; and they must be faced and dealt with.

It would be very unwise to postpone dealing with them. Delay in such a matter and in the particular circumstances in which we now find ourselves as a nation might involve consequences of the most embarrassing and deplorable sort, for which I, for one, would not care to be responsible. It would be very dangerous in the present circumstances to create a moment's doubt as to the strength and sufficiency of the Treasury of the United States, its ability to assist, to steady, and sustain the financial operations of the country's business. If the Treasury is known, or even thought, to be weak, where will be our peace of mind? The whole industrial activity of the country would be chilled and demoralized. Just now the peculiarly difficult financial problems of the moment are being successfully dealt with, with great self-possession and good sense and very sound judgment; but they are only in process of being worked out. If the process of solution is to be completed, no one must be given reason to doubt the solidity and adequacy of the Treasury of the Government which stands behind the whole method by which our difficulties are being met and handled.

The Treasury itself could get along for a considerable period, no doubt, without immediate resort to new sources of taxation. But at what cost to the business of the community? Approximately $75,-000,000, a large part of the present Treasury balance, is now on deposit with national banks distributed throughout the country. It is deposited, of course, on call. I need not point out to you what the probable consequences of inconvenience and distress and confusion would be if the diminishing income of the Treasury should make it necessary rapidly to withdraw these deposits. And yet without additional revenue that plainly might become necessary, and the time when it became necessary could not be controlled or determined by the convenience of the business of the country. It would have to be determined by the operations and necessities of the Treasury itself. Such risks are not necessary and ought not to be run. We can not too scrupulously or carefully safeguard a financial situation which is at best, while war continues in Europe, difficult and abnormal. Hesitation and delay are the worst forms of bad policy under such conditions.

And we ought not to borrow. We ought to resort to taxation, however we may regret the necessity of putting additional temporary burdens on our people. To sell bonds would be to make a most untimely and unjustifiable demand on the money market; untimely, because this is manifestly not the time to withdraw working capital from other uses to pay the Government's bills; unjustifiable, because unnecessary. The country is able to pay any just and reasonable taxes without distress. And to every other form of borrowing, whether for long periods or for short, there is the same objection. These are not the circumstances, this is at this particular moment and in this particular exigency not the market, to borrow large sums of money. What we are seeking is to ease and assist every financial transaction, not to add a single additional embarrassment to the situation. The people of this country are both intelligent and profoundly patriotic. They are ready to meet the present conditions in the right way and to support the Government with generous self-denial. They know and understand, and will be intolerant only of those who dodge responsibility or are not frank with them.

The occasion is not of our own making. We had no part in making it. But it is here. It affects us as directly and palpably almost as if we were participants in the circumstances which gave rise to it. We must accept the inevitable with calm judgment and unruffled spirits, like men accustomed to deal with the unexpected, habituated to take care of themselves, masters of their own affairs and their own fortunes. We shall pay the bill, though we did not deliberately incur it.

In order to meet every demand upon the Treasury without delay or peradventure and in order to keep the Treasury strong, unquestionably strong, and strong throughout the present anxieties, I respectfully urge that an additional revenue of $100,000,000 be raised through internal taxes devised in your wisdom to meet the emergency. The only suggestion I take the liberty of making is that such sources of revenue be chosen as will begin to yield at once and yield with a certain and constant flow.

I can not close without expressing the confidence with which I approach a Congress, with regard to this or any other matter, which has shown so untiring a devotion to public duty, which has responded to the needs of the Nation throughout a long season despite inevitable fatigue and personal sacrifice, and so large a proportion of whose Members have devoted their whole time and energy to the business of the country.

PROCLAMATIONS

By the President of the United States of America.

A PROCLAMATION.

[Convention with Republics of South and Central America for the Arbitration of Pecuniary Claims.]

Whereas a Convention between the United States of America and the Argentine Republic, Brazil, Chile, Colombia, Costa Rica, Cuba, Dominican Republic, Ecuador, Guatemala, Haiti, Honduras, Mexico, Nicaragua, Panama, Paraguay, Peru, Salvador, Uruguay and Venezuela for the arbitration of pecuniary claims, was concluded and signed by their respective Plenipotentiaries at Buenos Aires on the eleventh day of August, one thousand nine hundred and ten, the original of which Convention, being in the Spanish, English, Portuguese, and French languages, is word for word as follows:

1st. The High Contracting Parties agree to submit to arbitration all claims for pecuniary loss or damage which may be presented by their respective citizens and which can not be amicably adjusted through diplomatic channels, when said claims are of sufficient importance to warrant the expense of arbitration.

The decision shall be rendered in accordance with the principles of International Law.

2d. The High Contracting Parties agree to submit to the decision of the permanent Court of Arbitration of The Hague all controversies which are the subject-matter of the present Treaty, unless both parties agree to constitute a special jurisdiction.

If a case is submitted to the Permanent Court of The Hague, the High Contracting Parties accept the provisions of the treaty relating to the organization of that arbitral Tribunal, to the procedure to be followed and to the obligation to comply with the sentence.

3d. If it shall be agreed to constitute a special jurisdiction, there shall be prescribed in the convention by which this is determined the rules according to which the tribunal shall proceed, which shall have cognizance of the questions involved in the claims referred to in Article 1st of the present treaty.

4th. The present Treaty shall come into force immediately after the thirty-first of December, 1912, when the treaty on pecuniary claims, signed at Mexico, on January 31, 1902, and extended by the treaty signed at Rio de Janeiro, on August 13, 1906, expires.

It shall remain in force indefinitely, as well for the nations which shall then have ratified it as those which shall ratify it subsequently.

The ratifications shall be transmitted to the Government of the Argentine Republic, which shall communicate them to the other contracting parties.

5th. Any of the nations ratifying the present Treaty may denounce it, on its own part, by giving two years' notice in writing, in advance, of its intention so to do.

This notice shall be transmitted to the Government of the Argentine Republic and through its intermediation, to the other contracting parties.

6th. The treaty of Mexico shall continue in force after December 31, 1912, as to any claims which may, prior to that date, have been submitted to arbitration under its provisions.

In witness whereof, the Plenipotentiaries and Delegates sign this Convention and affix to it the seal of the Fourth International American Conference.

Made and signed in the city of Buenos Aires, on the eleventh day of August in the year one thousand nine hundred and ten, in the Spanish, English, Portuguese and French languages, and filed in the Ministry of Foreign Affairs of the Argentine Republic, in order that certified copies may be taken to be forwarded through the appropriate Diplomatic channels to each one of the Signatory Nations.

And whereas, the said Convention has been ratified by the Government of the United States of America, by and with the advice and consent of the Senate thereof, and by the Governments of the Dominican Republic, Guatemala, Honduras, Panama, Nicaragua, and Ecuador and the ratifications of the said Governments have been deposited by their respective Plenipotentiaries with the Government of the Argentine Republic;

Now, therefore, be it known that I, Woodrow Wilson, President of the United States of America, have caused the said Convention to be made public, to the end that the same and every article and clause thereof may be observed and fulfilled with good faith by the United States and the citizens thereof.

In testimony whereof, I have hereunto set my hand and caused the seal of the United States to be affixed.

Done at the City of Washington this twenty-ninth day of July in the year of our Lord one thousand nine hundred and fourteen [SEAL.] and of the Independence of the United States of America the one hundred and thirty-ninth.

WOODROW WILSON.

By the President:

W. J. BRYAN, *Secretary of State.*

BY THE PRESIDENT OF THE UNITED STATES OF AMERICA.

A PROCLAMATION.

[Convention with Republics of South and Central America for the Protection of Patents, Designs, and Industrial Models.]

Whereas a Convention between the United States of America and the Argentine Republic, Brazil, Chile, Colombia, Costa Rica, Cuba, Dominican Republic, Ecuador, Guatemala, Haiti, Honduras, Mexico, Nicaragua, Panama, Paraguay, Peru, Salvador, Uruguay and Venezuela for the protection of inventions, patents, designs, and industrial models, was concluded and signed by their respective Plenipotentiaries at Buenos Aires on the twentieth day of August, one thousand nine hundred and ten, the original of which Convention, being in the Spanish, English, Portuguese, and French languages, is word for word as follows:

The subscribing Nations enter into this convention for the protection of patents of invention, designs and industrial models.

Any persons who shall obtain a patent of invention in any of the signatory States shall enjoy in each of the other States all the advantages which the laws relative to patents of invention, designs and industrial models concede. Consequently, they shall have the right to the same protection and identical legal remedies against any attack upon their rights, provided they comply with the laws of each State.

Any person who shall have regularly deposited an application for a patent of invention or design or industrial model in one of the contracting States shall enjoy, for the purposes of making the deposit in the other States, and under the reserve of the rights of third parties, a right of priority during a period of twelve months for patents of invention, and of four months for designs or industrial models.

In consequence of the deposit subsequently made in any other of the signatory States before the expiration of these periods, can not be invalidated by acts performed in the interval, especially by other deposits, by the publication of the invention or its working, or by the sale of copies of the design or of the model.

When, within the terms fixed, a person shall have filed applications in several States for the patent of the same invention, the rights resulting from patents thus applied for shall be independent of each other.

They shall also be independent of the rights arising under patents obtained for the same invention in countries not parties to this Convention.

Questions which may arise regarding the priority of patents of invention, shall be decided with regard to the date of the application for the respective patents in the countries in which they are granted.

The following shall be considered as inventions: A new manner of manufacturing industrial products; a new machine or mechanical or manual apparatus which serves for the manufacture of said products; the discovery of a new industrial product; the application of known methods for the purpose of securing better results; and every new, original and ornamental design or model for an article of manufacture.

The foregoing shall be understood without prejudice to the laws of each State. Any of the signatory States may refuse to recognize patents for any of the following causes:

(a) Because the inventions or discoveries may have been published in any country prior to the date of the invention by the applicant;

(b) Because the inventions have been registered, published, or described in any country more than one year prior to the date of the application in the country in which the patent is sought;

(c) Because the inventions have been in public use, or have been on sale in the country in which the patent has been applied for, one year prior to the date of said application;

(d) Because the inventions or discoveries are in some manner contrary to morals or laws.

The ownership of a patent of invention comprises the right to enjoy the benefits thereof, and the right to assign or transfer it in accordance with the laws of the country.

Persons who incur civil or criminal liabilities, because of injuries or damage to the rights of inventors, shall be prosecuted and punished, in accordance with the laws of the countries wherein the offence has been committed or the damage occasioned.

Copies of patents certified in the country of origin, according to the national law thereof, shall be given full faith and credit as evidence of the right of priority, except as stated in Article VII.

The treaties relating to patents of invention, designs or industrial models, previously entered into between the countries subscribing to the present Convention, shall be superseded by the same from the time of its ratification in so far as the relations between the signatory States are concerned.

The adhesion of the American Nations to the present Convention shall be communicated to the Government of the Argentine Republic in order that it may communicate them to the other States. These communications shall have the effect of an exchange of ratifications.

A signatory Nation that sees fit to retire from the present convention, shall notify the Government of the Argentine Republic, and one year after the receipt of the communication the force of this Convention shall cease, in so far as the nation which shall have withdrawn its adherence is concerned.

In witness whereof, the Plenipotentiaries have signed the present treaty and affixed thereto the seal of the Fourth International American Conference.

Made and signed in the city of Buenos Aires on the twentieth day of August in the year one thousand nine hundred and ten, in Spanish, English, Portuguese, and French, and deposited in the Ministry of Foreign Affairs of the Argentine Republic, in order that certified copies be made for transmission to each of the Signatory Nations through the appropriate diplomatic channels.

And whereas, the said Convention has been ratified by the Government of the United States of America, by and with the advice and consent of the Senate thereof, and by the Governments of the Dominican Republic, Guatemala, Cuba, Honduras, Panama, Nicaragua and Ecuador and the ratifications of the said Governments have been deposited by their respective Plenipotentiaries with the Government of the Argentine Republic;

Now, therefore, be it known that I, Woodrow Wilson, President of the United States of America, have caused the said Convention to be made public, to the end that the same and every article and clause thereof may be observed and fulfilled with good faith by the United States and the citizens thereof.

In testimony whereof, I have hereunto set my hand and caused the seal of the United States to be affixed.

Done at the City of Washington this twenty-ninth day of July in the year of our Lord one thousand nine hundred and fourteen [SEAL.] and of the Independence of the United States of America the one hundred and thirty-ninth.

WOODROW WILSON.

By the President:

W. J. BRYAN, *Secretary of State.*

BY THE PRESIDENT OF THE UNITED STATES OF AMERICA.

A PROCLAMATION.

[Regulations for the Protection of Migratory Birds.]

Whereas, by virtue of the authority and direction contained in the Act of Congress approved March 4, 1913 (37 Stat. 847), entitled "An Act making appropriations for the Department of Agriculture for the fiscal year ending June thirtieth, nineteen hundred and fourteen," the Department of Agriculture has prepared, has finally adopted, and has caused to be engrossed and submitted to the President of the United States for approval, the following regulation:

Regulation 3 of the Regulations for the Protection of Migratory Birds, approved and proclaimed by the President of the United States on October 1, 1913, is hereby amended so as to read as follows:

Regulation 3.   Closed Season on Insectivorous Birds.

A closed season on migratory insectivorous birds shall continue throughout each year, except that the closed season on reedbirds or ricebirds in New Jersey, Pennsylvania, Delaware, Maryland, the District of Columbia, Virginia, and South Carolina, shall commence November 1 and end August 31, next following, both dates inclusive: Provided, That nothing in this or any other of these regulations shall be construed to prevent the issue of permits for collecting birds for scientific purposes in accordance with the laws and regulations in force in the respective States and Territories and the District of Columbia.

And Whereas, the Department of Agriculture after the preparation of said regulation has caused the same to be made public and has allowed a period of three months in which said regulation might be examined and considered before final adoption and has permitted public hearings thereon;

Now, Therefore, I, WOODROW WILSON, President of the United States of America, by virtue of the authority in me vested by the aforesaid Act of Congress, do hereby approve, proclaim and make known the foregoing regulation.

In witness whereof, I have hereunto set my hand and caused the seal of the United States to be affixed.

Done at the city of Washington this thirty-first day of August in the year of our Lord one thousand nine hundred and four-

[SEAL.] teen and of the independence of the United States the one hundred and thirty-ninth.

WOODROW WILSON.

By the President:

W. J. BRYAN, *Secretary of State.*

EXECUTIVE ORDERS

[Combining Manzano and Zuni National Forests in Arizona and New Mexico.]

THE WHITE HOUSE, *September 10, 1914.*

Under authority of the Act of Congress of June 4, 1897 (30 Stat. 11), and upon recommendation of the Secretary of Agriculture, it is hereby ordered that all the lands included within the boundaries of the Zuni National Forest, Arizona and New Mexico, as fixed and defined by proclamation of July 1, 1910, and modified by Executive Order No. 1367 of May 31, 1911, and Executive Order No. 1482 of February 17, 1912, be, and the same hereby transferred to and made a part of the Manzano National Forest.

It is intended by this Executive Order for economy of administration to merge into one national forest, hereafter to be known as the Manzano National Forest, all the lands at the date hereof in the Zuni and Manzano National Forests, and the boundaries of the Manzano

National Forest as they existed at this date are hereby modified accordingly. This Executive Order is not intended to add to the Manzano National Forest any lands which at the date hereof are not embraced in the Zuni National Forest or to release from reservation for national forest purposes any lands at the date hereof within the Zuni National Forest.   WOODROW WILSON.

[To Amend the Canal Zone Law against Gambling.]

THE WHITE HOUSE, *September 19, 1914.*

By virtue of the authority vested in me I hereby establish the following order for the Canal Zone:

Section 1 of Act No. 4, entitled "An Act to Prohibit Gambling in the Canal Zone, Isthmus of Panama, and to Provide for the Punishment of Violations thereof, and for other purposes" enacted by the Isthmian Canal Commission on August 22, 1904, is hereby amended to read as follows:

Section 1. Every person, within the limits of the Canal Zone, who shall play at any game whatever for any sum of money or other property of value, or shall bet any money or property upon any gambling table, bank, or device, or at or upon any other gambling device, or who shall bet upon any game played at or by means of any such gaming table or gambling device, shall, upon conviction, be fined in any sum not exceeding One Hundred Dollars ($100.00), or by imprisonment in jail not exceeding thirty (30) days, or shall suffer both such fine and imprisonment in the court's discretion.

This order shall take effect thirty days from and after its publication in the Canal Record.   WOODROW WILSON.

[Setting aside Public Land for an Elk Refugee.]

THE WHITE HOUSE, *September 15, 1914.*

Under authority of the Act of Congress approved June 25, 1910 (36 Stat., 847), as amended by the Act of August 24, 1912 (37 Stat., 497), and on the recommendation of the Secretary of Agriculture, it is hereby ordered that the public lands in Sec. 22, T. 41 N., R. 116 W., 6th P. M., Wyoming, be temporarily withdrawn subject to the conditions, provisions and limitations of said acts, in order that the Department of Agriculture may select certain lands therein for use as an elk refuge as provided in the Act of March 4, 1913 (37 Stat., 847).

The Executive Order No. 1814, dated August 25, 1913, withdrawing the therein described lands is hereby revoked in so far as it affects Sec. 1, T. 41 N., R. 116 W., 6th P. M.   WOODROW WILSON.

[To Divide Administrative Site Within Oregon National Forest, Oregon.]

THE WHITE HOUSE, *September 15, 1914.*

On the recommendation of the Secretary of Agriculture it is hereby ordered that the withdrawal of the following described tract of unsurveyed land, containing approximately 40 acres, reserved as a ranger station for the use of the Forest Service in connection with the administration of the Oregon National Forest, Oregon, made by Executive Order (1957) of June 6, 1914, under authority of the Act of Congress approved June 25, 1910 (36 Stat., 847), as amended by the Act of August 24, 1912 (37 Stat., 497), be revoked.

In T. 9 S., R. 8 E., W. M., approximately Sec. 25: Beginning at Corner No. 1, which is the same as the 57 mile post of the west boundary of the Warm Springs Indian Reservation:

Thence South 20 chains to corner No. 2
 " East 20 " " " " 3
 " North 20 " " " " 4
 " West 20 "
to Corner No. 1, the place of beginning. Variation 21° East.

WOODROW WILSON.

[Designating Customs Collection Districts.]

THE WHITE HOUSE, *August 27, 1914.*

Hereafter, under the provisions of the Act of Congress approved August 1, 1914, making appropriations for the Sundry Civil expenses of the Government for the fiscal year ending June thirtieth, nineteen hundred and fifteen, the present Customs Collection Districts are officially designated by numbers and will be known as follows:

District No. 1.—Maine and New Hampshire.
No. 2—Eastern Vermont.
No. 3—Western Vermont.
No. 4—Massachusetts.
No. 5—Rhode Island.
No. 6—Connecticut.
No. 7—St. Lawrence.
No. 8—Rochester.
No. 9—Buffalo.
No. 10—New York.
No. 11—Philadelphia.
No. 12—Pittsburgh.
No. 13—Maryland.
No. 14—Virginia.
No. 15—North Carolina.
No. 16—South Carolina.
No. 17—Georgia.
No. 18—Florida.
No. 19—Mobile.
No. 20—New Orleans.
No. 21—Sabine.
No. 22—Galveston.
No. 23—Laredo.
No. 24—El Paso.
No. 25—Eagle Pass.
No. 26—Arizona.
No. 27—Southern California.
No. 28—San Francisco.
No. 29—Oregon.
No. 30—Washington.
No. 31—Alaska.
No. 32—Hawaii.
No. 33—Montana and Idaho.
No. 34—Dakota.
No. 35—Minnesota.
No. 36—Duluth and Superior.
No. 37—Wisconsin.
No. 38—Michigan.
No. 39—Chicago.
No. 40—Indiana.
No. 41—Ohio.
No. 42—Kentucky.
No. 43—Tennessee.
No. 44—Iowa.
No. 45—St. Louis.
No. 46—Omaha.
No. 47—Colorado.
No. 48—Utah and Nevada.
No. 49—Porto Rico.

WOODROW WILSON.

[Ranger Station for Clear Creek Administrative Site near Coconino National Forest, Arizona.]

THE WHITE HOUSE, *September 15, 1914.*

Under authority of the Act of Congress approved June 25, 1910 (36 Stat., 847), as amended by the Act of August 24, 1912 (37 Stat., 497), and on the recommendation of the Secretary of Agriculture, it is hereby ordered that the E½ NE¼ Section 13, Township 13 North, Range 5 East, G. & S. R. M., containing 80 acres, be temporarily withdrawn from settlement, location, sale or entry, except as provided in said acts, and be reserved for use by the Forest Service as a ranger station in connection with the administration of the Coconino National Forest.

WOODROW WILSON.

[To Amend the Executive Order of March 20, 1914, Relating to Compensation to be Paid to Injured Employees of the Panama Canal and Panama Railroad Company.]

THE WHITE HOUSE, *September 19, 1914.*

By virtue of the authority vested in me, I hereby establish the following order for the Canal Zone:

Section 1. Paragraph E of Section 12, of the Executive Order of March 20, 1914, relating to injury compensation to be paid to employees of The Panama Canal, and the Panama Railroad Company, is hereby amended to read as follows:

(E) If the deceased employee leaves a parent, either partially or wholly dependent on him for support; or a brother, sister, grand-parent or grand-child, wholly dependent on him for support, there may be paid to such relation monthly such portion or portions of the monthly pay of the employee as may be determined by the Governor of The Panama Canal, provided that the total compensation to all beneficiaries under this and paragraphs A, B, C and D of this section shall not exceed fifty per cent of the monthly pay of the deceased employee, and provided, that in order to make payment to the relatives under this paragraph, the Governor of The Panama Canal may, if necessary, reduce the proportion payable to widow or children under paragraphs A, B, C and D of this section, and, provided further, that payment for the benefit of a relative under this paragraph shall cease if he dies, marries, or, in the opinion of the Governor, becomes capable of self-support, but in no case shall payment continue more than eight years.

This amendment shall be effective from the date the order of March 20, 1914, became effective, viz.: April 1, 1914.

WOODROW WILSON.

ADDRESSES.

[Before the American Bar Association at Continental Hall, Washington, Oct. 20, 1914.]

MR. PRESIDENT, GENTLEMEN OF THE AMERICAN BAR ASSOCIATION:

I am very deeply gratified by the greeting that your president has given me and by your response to it. My only strength lies in your confidence.

We stand now in a peculiar case. Our first thought, I suppose, as lawyers, is of international law, of those bonds of right and principle which draw the nations together and hold the community of the world to some standards of action. We know that we see in international law, as it were, the moral processes by which law itself came into existence. I know that as a lawyer I have myself at times felt that there was no real comparison between the law of a nation and the law of nations, because the latter lacked the sanction that gave the former strength and validity. And yet, if you look into the matter more closely, you will find that the two have the same foundations, and that those foundations are more evident and conspicuous in our day than they have ever been before.

The opinion of the world is the mistress of the world; and the processes of international law are the slow processes by which opinion works its will. What impresses me is the constant thought that that is the tribunal at the bar of which we all sit. I would call your attention, incidentally, to the circumstance that it does not observe the ordinary rules of evidence; which has sometimes suggested to me that the ordinary rules of evidence had shown some signs of growing antique. Everything, rumor included, is heard in this court, and the standard of judgment is not so much the character of the testimony as the character of the witness. The motives are disclosed, the purposes are conjectured, and that opinion is finally accepted which seems to be, not the best founded in law, perhaps, but the best founded in integrity of character and of morals. That is the process which is slowly working its will upon the world; and what we should be watchful of is not so much jealous interests as sound principles of action. The disinterested course is always the biggest course to pursue not only, but it is in the long run the most profitable course to pursue. If you can establish your character, you can establish your credit.

What I wanted to suggest to this association, in bidding them very hearty welcome to the city, is whether we sufficiently apply these same ideas to the body of municipal law which we seek to administer. Citations seem to play so much larger a rôle now than principle. There was a time when the thoughtful eye of the judge rested upon the changes of social circumstances and almost palpably saw the law arise out of human life. Have we got to a time when the only way to change law is by statute? The changing of law by statute seems to me like mending a garment with a patch; whereas, law should grow by the life that is in it, not by the life that is outside of it.

I once said to a lawyer with whom I was discussing some question of precedent, and in whose presence I was venturing to doubt the rational validity, at any rate, of the particular precedents he cited, "After all, isn't our object justice?" And he said, "God forbid! We should be very much confused if we made that our standard. Our standard is to find out what the rule has been and how the rule that has been applies to the case that is." I should hate to think that the law was based entirely upon "has beens." I should hate to think that the law did not derive its impulse from looking forward rather than from looking backward, or, rather, that it did not derive its instruction from looking about and seeing what the circumstances of man actually are and what the impulses of justice necessarily are.

Understand me, gentlemen, I am not venturing in this presence to impeach the law. For the present, by the force of circumstances, I am in part the embodiment of the law and it would be very awkward to disavow myself. But I do wish to make this intimation, that in this time of world change, in this time when we are going to find out just how, in what particulars, and to what extent the real facts of human life and the real moral judgments of mankind prevail, it is worth while looking inside our municipal law and seeing whether the judgments of the law are made square with the moral judgments of mankind. For I believe that we are custodians, not of commands, but of a spirit. We are custodians of the spirit of righteousness, of the spirit of equal-handed justice, of the spirit of hope which believes in the perfectibility of the law with the perfectibility of human life itself.

Public life, like private life, would be very dull and dry if it were not for this belief in the essential beauty of the human spirit and the belief that the human spirit could be translated into action and into ordinance. Not entire. You can not go any faster than you can advance the average moral judgments of the mass, but you can go at least as fast as that, and you can see to it that you do not lag behind the average moral judgments of the mass. I have in my life dealt with all sorts and conditions of men, and I have found that the flame of moral judgment burned just as bright in the man of humble life and limited experience as in the scholar and the man of affairs. And I would like his voice always to be heard, not as a witness, not as speaking in his own case, but as if he were the voice of men in general, in our courts of justice, as well as the voice of the lawyers, remembering what the law has been. My hope is that, being stirred to the depths by the extraordinary circumstances of the time in which we live, we may recover from those depths something of a renewal of that vision of the law with which men may be supposed to have started out in the old days of the oracles, who communed with the intimations of divinity.

[At Y. M. C. A. Celebration, Pittsburgh, Pa., Oct. 24, 1914.]

MR. PRESIDENT, MR. PORTER, LADIES, AND GENTLEMEN:

I feel almost as if I were a truant, being away from Washington to-day, but I thought that perhaps if I were absent the Congress would have the more leisure to adjourn. I do not ordinarily open my office at Washington on Saturday. Being a schoolmaster, I am accustomed to a Saturday holiday, and I thought I could not better spend a holiday than by showing at least something of the true direction of my affections; for by long association with the men who have worked for this organization I can say that it has enlisted my deep affection.

I am interested in it for various reasons. First of all, because it is an association of young men. I have had a good deal to do with young men in my time, and I have formed an impression of them which I believe to be contrary to the general impression. They are generally thought to be arch radicals. As a matter of fact, they are the most conservative people I have ever dealt with. Go to a college community and try to change the least custom of that little world and find how the conservatives will rush at you. Moreover, young men are embarrassed by having inherited their fathers' opinions. I have often said that the use of a university is to make young gentlemen as unlike their fathers as possible. I do not say that with the least disrespect for the fathers; but every man who is old enough to have a son in college is old enough to have become very seriously immersed in some particular business and is almost certain to have caught the point of view of that particular business. And it is very useful to his son to be taken out of that narrow circle, conducted to some high place where he may see the general map of the world and of the interests of mankind, and there shown how big the world is and how much of it his father may happen to have forgotten. It would be worth while for men, middle-aged and old, to detach themselves more frequently from the things that command their daily attention and to think of the sweeping tides of humanity.

Therefore I am interested in this association, because it is intended to bring young men together before any crust has formed over them, before they have been hardened to any particular occupation, before they have caught an inveterate point of view; while they still have a searchlight that they can swing and see what it reveals of all the circumstances of the hidden world.

I am the more interested in it because it is an association of young

men who are Christians. I wonder if we attach sufficient importance
to Christianity as a mere instrumentality in the life of mankind.
For one, I am not fond of thinking of Christianity as the means of
saving *individual* souls. I have always been very impatient of processes and institutions which said that their purpose was to put every
man in the way of developing his character. My advice is: Do not
think about your character. If you will think about what you ought
to do for other people, your character will take care of itself. Character is a by-product, and any man who devotes himself to its cultivation in his own case will become a selfish prig. The only way your
powers can become great is by exerting them outside the circle of
your own narrow, special, selfish interests. And that is the reason
of Christianity. Christ came into the world to save others, not to
save himself; and no man is a true Christian who does not think constantly of how he can lift his brother, how he can assist his friend,
how he can enlighten mankind, how he can make virtue the rule of
conduct in the circle in which he lives. An association merely of
young men might be an association that had its energies put forth in
every direction, but an association of Christian young men is an association meant to put its shoulders under the world and lift it, so
that other men may feel that they have companions in bearing the
weight and heat of the day; that other men may know that there are
those who care for them, who would go into places of difficulty and
danger to rescue them, who regard themselves as their brother's
keeper.

And, then, I am glad that it is an association. Every word of its
title means an element of strength. Young men are strong. Christian
young men are the strongest kind of young men, and when they associate themselves together they have the incomparable strength of organization. The Young Men's Christian Association once excited,
perhaps it is not too much to say, the hostility of the organized churches
of the Christian world, because the movement looked as if it were
so nonsectarian, as if it were so outside the ecclesiastical field, that
perhaps it was an effort to draw young men away from the churches
and to substitute this organization for the great bodies of Christian
people who joined themselves in the Christian denominations. But
after a while it appeared that it was a great instrumentality that be-
longed to all the churches; that it was a common instrument for sending the light of Christianity out into the world in its most practical form,
drawing young men who were strangers into places where they could
have companionship that stimulated them and suggestions that kept
them straight and occupations that amused them without vicious practice; and then, by surrounding themselves with an atmosphere of purity
and of simplicity of life, catch something of a glimpse of the great ideal
which Christ lifted when He was elevated upon the cross.

I remember hearing a very wise man say once, a man grown old in the service of a great church, that he had never taught his son religion dogmatically at any time; that he and the boy's mother had agreed that if the atmosphere of that home did not make a Christian of the boy, nothing that they could say would make a Christian of him. They knew that Christianity was catching, and if they did not have it, it would not be communicated. If they did have it, it would penetrate while the boy slept, almost; while he was unconscious of the sweet influences that were about him, while he reckoned nothing of instruction, but merely breathed into his lungs the wholesome air of a Christian home. That is the principle of the Young Men's Christian Association—to make a place where the atmosphere makes great ideals contagious. That is the reason that I said, though I had forgotten that I said it, what is quoted on the outer page of the program—that you can test a modern community by the degree of its interest in its Young Men's Christian Association. You can test whether it knows what road is wants to travel or not. You can test whether it is deeply interested in the spiritual and essential prosperity of its rising generation. I know of no test that can be more conclusively put to a community than that.

I want to suggest to the young men of this association that it is the duty of young men not only to combine for the things that are good, but to combine in a militant spirit. There is a fine passage in one of Milton's prose writings which I am sorry to say I can not quote, but the meaning of which I can give you, and it is worth hearing. He says that he has no patience with a cloistered virtue that does not go out and seek its adversary. Ah, how tired I am of the men who are merely on the defensive, who hedge themselves in, who perhaps enlarge the hedge enough to include their little family circle and ward off all the evil influences of the world from that loved and hallowed group! How tired I am of the men whose virtue is selfish because it is merely self-protective! And how much I wish that men by the hundred thousand might volunteer to go out and seek the adversary and subdue him!

I have had the fortune to take part in affairs of a considerable variety of sorts, and I have tried to hate as few persons as possible, but there is an exquisite combination of contempt and hate that I have for a particular kind of person, and that is the moral coward. I wish we could give all our cowards a perpetual vacation. Let them go off and sit on the side lines and see us play the game; and put them off the field if they interfere with the game. They do nothing but harm, and they do it by that most subtle and fatal thing of all, that of taking the momentum and the spirit and the forward dash out of things. A man who is virtuous and a coward has no marketable virtue about him. The virtue, I repeat, which is merely self-defensive is not serviceable even, I suspect, to himself. For how a man can swallow and not taste bad when he is a coward and thinking only of himself I can not imagine.

Be militant! Be an organization that is going to do things! If you can find older men who will give you countenance and acceptable leadership, follow them; but if you can not, organize separately and dispense with them. There are only two sorts of men worth associating with when something is to be done. Those are young men and men who never grow old. Now, if you find men who have grown old, about whom the crust had hardened, whose hinges are stiff, whose minds always have their eye over the shoulder thinking of things as they *were* done, do not have anything to do with them. It would not be Christian to exclude them from your organization, but merely use them to pad the roll. If you can find older men who will lead you acceptably and keep you in countenance, I am bound as an older man to advise you to follow them. But suit yourselves. Do not follow people that stand still. Just remind them that this is not a statical proposition; it is a movement, and if they can not get a move on them they are not serviceable.

Life, gentlemen—the life of society, the life of the world—has constantly to be fed from the bottom. It has to be fed by those great sources of strength which are constantly rising in new generations. Red blood has to be pumped into it. New fiber has to be supplied. That is the reason I have always said that I believed in popular institutions. If you can guess beforehand who your rulers are going to be, you can guess with a very great certainty that most of them will not be fit to rule. The beauty of popular institutions is that you do not know where the man is going to come from, and you do not care so he is the right man. You do not know whether he will come from the avenue or from the alley. You do not know whether he will come from the city or the farm. You do not know whether you will ever have heard that name before or not. Therefore you do not limit at any point your supply of new strength. You do not say it has got to come through the blood of a particular family or through the processes of a particular training, or by anything except the native impulse and genius of the man himself. The humblest hovel, therefore, may produce you your greatest man. A very humble hovel did produce you one of your greatest men. That is the process of life, this constant surging up of the new strength of unnamed, unrecognized, uncatalogued men who are just getting into the running, who are just coming up from the masses of the unrecognized multitude. You do not know when you will see above the level masses of the crowd some great stature lifted head and shoulders above the rest, shouldering its way, not violently but gently, to the front and saying, 'Here am I; follow me." And his voice will be your voice, his

BY THE PRESIDENT OF THE UNITED STATES OF AMERICA,

A PROCLAMATION.

Whereas a state of war unhappily exists between
Austria-Hungary and Servia and between Germany and
Russia and between Germany and France; And Whereas
the United States is on terms of friendship and amity
with the contending powers, and with the persons inhabiting their several dominions;

And Whereas there are citizens of the United States
residing within the territories or dominions of each of
the said belligerents and carrying on commerce, trade,
or other business or pursuits therein;

And Whereas there are subjects of each of the said
belligerents residing within the territory or jurisdiction of the United States, and carrying on commerce,
trade, or other business or pursuits therein;

And Whereas the laws and treaties of the United
States, without interfering with the free expression of
opinion and sympathy, or with the commercial manufacture
or sale of arms or munitions of war, nevertheless impose
upon all persons who may be within their territory and
jurisdiction the duty of an impartial neutrality during
the existence of the contest;

And Whereas it is the duty of a neutral government
not to permit or suffer the making of its waters subservient to the purposes of war;

Now, Therefore, I, Woodrow Wilson, President of the
United States of America, in order to preserve the

WILSON'S NEUTRALITY PROCLAMATION AT THE OUTBREAK OF
THE EUROPEAN WAR OF 1914.

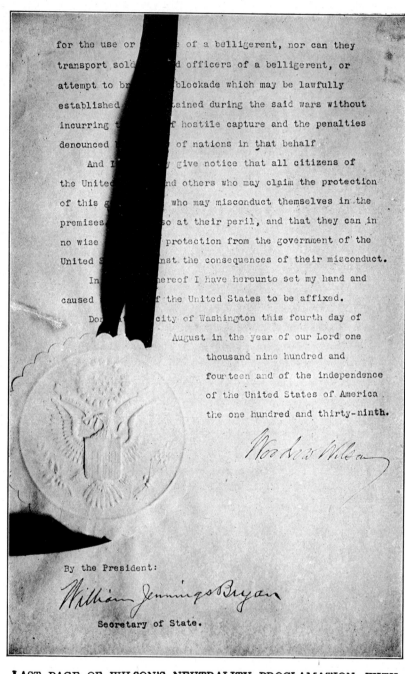

for the use or ___e of a belligerent, nor can they
transport sold___ d officers of a belligerent, or
attempt to br___ blockade which may be lawfully
established___ ained during the said wars without
incurring t___ f hostile capture and the penalties
denounced ___ of nations in that behalf

And I ___ give notice that all citizens of
the United ___ nd others who may claim the protection
of this g___ who may misconduct themselves in the
premises___ o at their peril, and that they can in
no wise ___ protection from the government of the
United S___ nst the consequences of their misconduct.

In ___ ereof I have hereunto set my hand and
caused ___ f the United States to be affixed.

Don___ city of Washington this fourth day of
August in the year of our Lord one
thousand nine hundred and
fourteen and of the independence
of the United States of America
the one hundred and thirty-ninth.

Woodrow Wilson

By the President:

William Jennings Bryan

Secretary of State.

LAST PAGE OF WILSON'S NEUTRALITY PROCLAMATION, WITH
SIGNATURE OF SECRETARY BRYAN.

thought will be your thought, and you will follow him as if you were following the best things in yourselves.

When I think of an association of Christian young men I wonder that it has not already turned the world upside down. I wonder, not that it has done so much, for it has done a great deal, but that it has done so little; and I can only conjecture that it does not realize its own strength. I can only imagine that it has not yet got its pace. I wish I could believe, and I do believe, that at 70 it is just reaching its majority, and that from this time on a dream greater even than George Williams ever dreamed will be realized in the great accumulating momentum of Christian men throughout the world. For, gentlemen, this is an age in which the principles of men who utter public opinion dominate the world. It makes no difference what is done for the time being. After the struggle is over the jury will sit, and nobody can corrupt that jury.

At one time I tried to write history. I did not know enough to write it, but I knew from experience how hard it was to find an historian out, and I trusted I would not be found out. I used to have this comfortable thought as I saw men struggling in the public arena. I used to think to myself, "This is all very well and very interesting. You probably assess yourself in such and such a way. Those who are your partisans assess you thus and so. Those who are your opponents urge a different verdict. But it does not make very much difference, because after you are dead and gone some quiet historian will sit in a secluded room and tell mankind for the rest of time just what to think about you, and his verdict, not the verdict of your partisans and not the verdict of your opponents, will be the verdict of posterity." I say that I used to say that to myself. It very largely was not so. And yet it was true in this sense: If the historian really speaks the judgment of the succeeding generation, then he really speaks the judgment also of the generations that succeed it, and his assessment, made without the passion of the time, made without partisan feeling in the matter—in other circumstances, when the air is cool—is the judgment of mankind upon your actions.

Now, is it not very important that we who shall constitute a portion of the jury should get our best judgments to work and base them upon Christian forbearance and Christian principles, upon the idea that it is impossible by sophistication to establish that a thing that is wrong is right? And yet, while we are going to judge with the absolute standard of righteousness, we are going to judge with Christian feeling, being men of a like sort ourselves, suffering the same temptations, having the same weaknesses, knowing the same passions; and while we do not condemn we are going to seek to say and to live the truth. What I am hoping for is that these 70 years have just been a running start, and that now there will be a great rush of Christian

258

principle upon the strongholds of evil and of wrong in the world. Those strongholds are not as strong as they look. Almost every vicious man is afraid of society, and if you once open the door where he is, he will run. All you have to do is to fight, not with cannon but with light.

May I illustrate it in this way? The Government of the United States has just succeeded in concluding a large number of treaties with the leading nations of the world, the sum and substance of which is this, that whenever any trouble arises the light shall shine on it for a year before anything is done; and my prediction is that after the light has shone on it for a year it will not be necessary to do anything; that after we know what happened, then we will know who was right and who was wrong. I believe that light is the greatest sanitary influence in the world. That, I suppose, is scientific commonplace, because if you want to make a place wholesome the best instrument you can use is the sun; to let his rays in, let him search out all the miasma that may lurk there. So with moral light: It is the most wholesome and rectifying, as well as the most revealing, thing in the world, provided it be genuine moral light; not the light of inquisitiveness, not the light of the man who likes to turn up ugly things, not the light of the man who disturbs what is corrupt for the mere sake of the sensation that he creates by disturbing it, but the moral light, the light of the man who discloses it in order that all the sweet influences of the world may go in and make it better.

That, in my judgment, is what the Young Men's Christian Association can do. It can point out to its members the things that are wrong. It can guide the feet of those who are going astray; and when its members have realized the power of the Christian principle, then they will not be men if they do not unite to see that the rest of the world experiences the same emancipation and reaches the same happiness of release.

I believe in the Young Men's Christian Association because I believe in the progress of moral ideas in the world; and I do not know that I am sure of anything else. When you are after something and have formulated it and have done the very best thing you know how to do, you have got to be sure for the time being that that is the thing to do. But you are a fool if in the back of your head you do not know it is possible that you are mistaken. All that you can claim is that that is the thing as you see it now and that you can not stand still; that you must push forward the things that are right. It may turn out that you made mistakes, but what you do know is your direction, and you are sure you are moving in that way. I was once a college reformer, until discouraged, and I remember a classmate of mine saying, "Why, man, can't you let anything alone?" I said, "I let everything alone that you can show me is not itself moving in the wrong direction, but I am not going to let those things alone that I see are going downhill"; and I borrowed this illustration from an ingenious writer. He says, "If you have a post that is painted white and want to keep it white, you can not let it alone; and if anybody says to you, 'Why don't you let that post alone?' you will say, 'Because I want it to stay white, and therefore I have got to paint it at least every second year.'" There isn't anything in this world that will not change if you absolutely let it alone, and therefore you have constantly to be attending to it to see that it is being taken care of in the right way and that, if it is part of the motive force of the world, it is moving in the right direction.

That means that eternal vigilance is the price, not only of liberty, but of a great many other things. It is the price of everything that is good. It is the price of one's own soul. It is the price of the souls of the people you love; and when it comes down to the final reckoning you have a standard that is immutable. What shall a man give in exchange for his own soul? Will he sell that? Will he consent to see another man sell his soul? Will he consent to see the conditions of his community such that men's souls are debauched and trodden under foot in the mire? What shall he give in exchange for his own soul, or any other man's soul? And since the world, the world of affairs, the world of society, is nothing less and nothing more than all of us put together, it is a great enterprise for the salvation of the soul in this world as well as in the next. There is a text in Scripture that has always interested me profoundly. It says godliness is profitable in this life as well as in the life that is to come; and if you do not start it in this life, it will not reach the life that is to come. Your measurements, your directions, your whole momentum, have to be established before you reach the next world. This world is intended as the place in which we shall show that we know how to grow in the stature of manliness and of righteousness.

I have come here to bid Godspeed to the great work of the Young Men's Christian Association. I love to think of the gathering force of such things as this in the generations to come. If a man had to measure the accomplishments of society, the progress of reform, the speed of the world's betterment, by the few little things that happened in his own life, by the trifling things that he can contribute to accomplish, he would indeed feel that the cost was much greater than the result. But no man can look at the past of the history of this world without seeing a vision of the future of the history of this world; and when you think of the accumulated moral forces that have made one age better than another age in the progress of mankind, then you can open your eyes to the vision. You can see that age by age, though with a blind struggle in the dust of the road, though often mistaking the path and losing its way in the mire, mankind is yet—

sometimes with bloody hands and battered knees—nevertheless struggling step after step up the slow stages to the day when he shall live in the full light which shines upon the uplands, where all the light that illumines mankind shines direct from the face of God.

LETTER.

[To Mr. Underwood, Commending the Work of the Second Session of the Sixty-third Congress.]

THE WHITE HOUSE, *Washington, October 17, 1914.*

MY DEAR MR. UNDERWOOD:

I can not let this session of Congress close without expressing my warm admiration for the fidelity and intelligence with which the program outlined in April and December of last year has been carried out, and my feeling that the people of the country have been served by the members of this Congress as they have seldom, if ever, been served before. The program was a great one, and it is a matter of deep satisfaction to think of the way in which it has been handled.

It had several distinct parts and many items, but, after all, a single purpose, namely, to destroy private control and set business free. That purpose was manifest enough in the case of the tariff and in the legislation affecting trusts; but, though perhaps less evident upon the surface there, it lay at the very heart of the currency bill, too. May I not add, even though it lies outside the field of legislation, that that, and that chiefly, has been the object of the foreign policy of the Government during the last 18 months?

Private control had shown its sinister face on every hand in America, had shown it for a long time, and sometimes very brazenly, in the trusts and in a virtual domination of credit by small groups of men. The safest hiding place and covert of such control was in the tariff. There it for a long time hid very shrewdly. The tariff was a very complicated matter; none but experts thoroughly understood its schedules. Many of the schedules were framed to afford particular advantages to special groups of manufacturers and investors. That was the soil in which trade combinations and combinations of manufacturers most readily grew, and most rankly. High prices did not spring directly out of the tariff. They sprang out of the suppression of domestic, no less than of foreign, competition by means of combinations and trade agreements which could be much more easily contrived and maintained under the protection of a high tariff than without it. The European war came before the withdrawal of this much-coveted opportunity, for monopoly could show its full effects and active competition bring prices to their normal level again; but it is clear enough already that the reduction of the tariff, the simplification of its schedules so as to cut away the jungle in which secret agencies had so long lurked, the correction of its inequalities, and its thorough recasting with the single honest object of revenue, were an indispensable first step to reestablishing competition.

The present Congress has taken that step with courage, sincerity, and effectiveness. The lobby by which some of the worst features of the old tariff had been maintained was driven away by the mere pitiless turning on of the light. The principle was adopted that each duty levied was to be tested by the inquiry whether it was put at such a figure and levied in such a manner as to provoke competition. The soil in which combinations had grown was removed lest some of the seeds of monopoly might be found to remain in it. The thing had needed to be done for a long time, but nobody had ventured before to undertake it in systematic fashion.

The panic that the friends of privilege had predicted did not follow. Business has adready adjusted itself to the new conditions with singular ease and elasticity, because the new conditions are in fact more normal than the old. The revenue lost by the import duties was replaced by an income tax which in part shifted the burden of taxation from the shoulders of every consumer in the country, great or small, to shoulders more certainly able to bear it.

We had time to learn from the actual administration of the law that the revenues resulting from the double change would have been abundant had it not been for the breaking out of the present war in Europe, which affects almost every route of trade and every market in the world outside of the United States. Until the war ends, and until its effects upon manufacture and commerce have been corrected we shall have to impose additional taxes to make up for the loss of such part of our import duties as the war cuts off by cutting off the imports themselves—a veritable war tax, though we are not at war; for war, and only war, is the cause of it.

It is fortunate that the reduction of the duties came first. The import duties collected under the old tariff constituted a much larger proportion of the whole revenue of the Government than to the duties under the new. A still larger proportion of the revenue would have been cut off by the war had the old taxes stood, and a larger war tax would have been necessary as a consequence. No miscalculation, no lack of foresight, has created the necessity for the taxes, but only a great catastrophe world-wide in its operation and effects.

With similar purpose and in a like temper the Congress has sought, in the Trade-Commission bill and in the Clayton bill, to make men in a small way of business as free to succeed as men in a big way, and to kill monopoly in the seed. Before these bills were passed the law was already clear enough that monopolies once formed were illegal and could be dissolved by direct process of law and those who had created them punished as for crime. But there was no law to check the process by which monopoly was built up until the tree was full grown and its fruit developed, or, at any rate, until the full opportunity for monopoly had been created. With this new legislation there is clear and sufficient law to check and destroy the noxious growth in its infancy. Monopolies are built up by unfair methods of competition, and the new Trade Commission has power to forbid and prevent unfair competition, whether upon a big scale or upon a little; whether just begun or grown old and formidable. Monopoly is created also by putting the same men in charge of a variety of business enterprises, whether apparently related or unrelated to one another, by means of interlocking directorates. That the Clayton bill now in large measure prevents. Each enterprise must depend upon its own initiative and effectiveness for success, and upon the intelligence and business energy of the men who officer it. And so all along the line: Monopoly is to be cut off at the roots.

Incidentally, justice has been done the laborer. His labor is no longer to be treated as if it were merely an inanimate object of commerce disconnected from the fortunes and happiness of a living human being, to be dealt with as an object of sale and barter. But that, great as it is, is hardly more than the natural and inevitable corollary of a law whose object is individual freedom and initiative as against any kind of private domination.

The accomplishment of this legislation seems to me a singularly significant thing. If our party were to be called upon to name the particular point of principle in which it differs from its opponents most sharply and in which it feels itself most definitely sustained by experience, we should no doubt say that it was this: That we would have no dealings with monopoly, but reject it altogether; while our opponents were ready to adopt it into the realm of law, and seek merely to regulate it and moderate it in its operation. It is our purpose to destroy monopoly and maintain competition as the only effectual instrument of business liberty.

We have seen the nature of the power of monopoly exhibited. We know that it is more apt to control government than to be controlled by it; for we have seen it control government, dictate legislation, and dominate Executives and courts. We feel that our people are safe only in the fields of free individual endeavor where American genius and initiative are not guided by a few men as in recent years, but made rich by the activities of a multitude, as in days now almost forgotten. We will not consent that an ungovernable giant should be reared to full stature in the very household of the Government itself.

In like manner by the currency bill we have created a democracy of credit such as has never existed in this country before. For a generation or more we have known and admitted that we had the worst banking and currency system in the world, because the volume of our currency was wholly inelastic; that is, because there was more than enough at certain seasons to meet the demands of commerce and credit, and at other times far too little; that we could not lessen the volume when we needed less nor increase it when we needed more. Everybody talked about the absurd system and its quite unnecessary embarrassments, sure to produce periodic panics; and everybody said that it ought to be changed and changed very radically; but nobody took effective steps to change it until the present Congress addressed itself to the task with genuine resolution and an intelligence which expressed itself in definite action. And now the thing is done.

Let bankers explain the technical features of the new system. Suffice it here to say that it provides a currency which expands as it is needed, and contracts when it is not needed; a currency which comes into existence in response to the call of every man who can show a going business and a concrete basis for extending credit to him, however obscure or prominent he may be, however big or little his business transactions.

More than that, the power to direct this system of credits is put into the hands of a public board of disinterested officers of the Government itself who can make no money out of anything they do in connection with it. No group of bankers anywhere can get control; no one part of the country can concentrate the advantages and conveniences of the system upon itself for its own selfish advantage. The board can oblige the banks of one region to go to the assistance of the banks of another. The whole resources of the country are mobilized, to be employed where they are most needed. I think we are justified in speaking of this as a democracy of credit. Credit is at the disposal of every man who can show energy and assets. Each region of the country is set to study its own needs and opportunities and the whole country stands by to assist. It is self-government as well as democracy.

I understand why it was not possible at this session to mature legislation intended specially for the development of a system for handling rural, or rather, agricultural credits; but the Federal Reserve Act itself facilitates and enlarges agricultural credit in an extraordinary degree. The farmer is as much a partner in the new democracy of credit as the merchant or manufacturer. Indeed, special and very liberal provision is made for his need, as will speedily appear when the system has been a little while in operation. His assets are as available as any other man's, and for credits of a longer term.

There have been many other measures passed of extraordinary importance, for the session has been singularly rich in thoughtful and constructive legislation; but I have mentioned the chief acts for which this Congress will be remembered as very notable, indeed. I did not mean when I began to write to make this letter so long, and even to mention the other legislation that is worthy of high praise would extend it to an inordinate length. My purpose in writing was merely to express my own great admiration for the industry and the leadership, as well as the wisdom and constructive skill, which has accomplished all these things.

I wish I could speak by name of the many men who have so honorably shared in these distinguished labors. I doubt if there has ever been a finer exhibition of teamwork or of unhesitating devotion to the fulfillment of party pledges—and yet the best of it is that the great measures passed have shown, I venture to say, no partisan bias, but only a spirit of serious statesmanship. I am proud to have been associated with such men, working in such a spirit through so many months of unremitted labor at trying tasks of counsel. It has been a privilege to have a share in such labors. I wish I could express to every one of the Members who have thus cooperated together my personal appreciation of what he has helped to do. This letter may, I hope, serve in some sort as a substitute for that.

I look forward with confidence to the elections. The voters of the United States have never failed to reward real service. They have never failed to sustain a Congress and administration that were seeking, as this Congress and, I believe, this administration, have sought, to render them a permanent and disinterested benefit in the shape of reformed and rectified laws. They know that, extraordinary as the record is which I have cited, our task is not done; that a great work of constructive development remains to be accomplished, in building up our merchant marine, for instance, and in the completion of a great program for the conservation of our natural resources and the development of the water power of the country—a program which has at this session already been carried several steps toward consummation. They know, too, that without a Congress in close sympathy with the administration a whole scheme of peace and honor and disinterested service to the world, of which they have approved, can not be brought to its full realization. I would like to go into the district of every Member of Congress who has sustained and advanced the plans of the party and speak out my advocacy of his claim for reelection. But, of course, I can not do that; and with so clear a record no Member of Congress needs a spokesman. What he has done speaks for itself. If it be a mere question of political fortunes, I believe the immediate future of the party to be as certain as the past is secure.

The Democratic Party is now in fact the only instrument ready to the country's hand by which anything can be accomplished. It is united, as the Republican Party is not; it is strong and full of the zest of sober achievement, and has been rendered confident by carrying out a great constructive program such as no other party has attempted; it is absolutely free from the entangling alliances which made the Republican Party, even before its rupture, utterly unserviceable as an instrument of reform; its thought, its ambition, its plans are of the vital present and the hopeful future. A practical Nation is not likely to reject such a team, full of the spirit of public service, and substitute, in the midst of great tasks, either a party upon which a deep demoralization has fallen or a party which has not grown to the stature that would warrant its assuming the responsible burdens of state. Every thoughtful man sees that a change of parties made just now would set the clock back, not forward. I have a very complete and very confident belief in the practical sagacity of the American people.

With sincere regard and admiration, faithfully, yours,

WOODROW WILSON.

Hon. OSCAR UNDERWOOD, *House of Representatives, Washington, D. C.*

EXECUTIVE ORDERS.

[Alaskan Townsite Withdrawal No. 4.]

THE WHITE HOUSE, *October 8, 1914.*

Under and pursuant to the provisions of the act of Congress, approved March 12, 1914, entitled "An Act to authorize the President of the United States to locate, construct, and operate railroads in the Territory of Alaska, and for other purposes," it is hereby ordered that the following lands be, and the same are hereby, withdrawn from settlement, location, sale, entry and other disposition, and reserved for townsite purposes, as follows:

All of Sections 22, 23, 26, and 27, in T. 17 N., R. 1 W., Seward Meridian, Territory of Alaska.

WOODROW WILSON.

[Gray's Lake Administrative Site (Near Caribou National Forest) Idaho.]

THE WHITE HOUSE, *October 28, 1914.*

Under authority of the Act of Congress approved June 25, 1910 (36 Stat., 847), as amended by the Act of August 24, 1912 (37 Stat., 497), and on the recommendation of the Secretary of Agriculture, it is hereby ordered that the NE ¼ SE ¼ Sec. 35, T. 4 S., R. 43 E., B. M., containing 40 acres, be temporarily withdrawn from settlement, location, sale or entry, except as provided in said acts, and be reserved for use by the Forest Service as an addition to a ranger station in connection with the administration of the Caribou National Forest, Idaho.

WOODROW WILSON.

[Admitting Foreign-Built Ships to American Registry.]

THE WHITE HOUSE, *September 4, 1914.*

In pursuance of the authority conferred upon the President of the United States by Section 2 of the Act approved August 18, 1914, entitled "An Act to provide for the admission of foreign-built ships to American registry for the foreign trade, and for other purposes," it is hereby ordered:

1. That the provisions of law prescribing that the watch officers of vessels of the United States registered for foreign trade shall be citizens of the United States, are hereby suspended so far and for such length of time as is herein provided, namely,—

All foreign-built ships which shall be admitted to United States registry under said Act may retain the watch officers employed thereon, without regard to citizenship, for seven years from this date, and such watch officers shall be eligible for promotion. Any vacancy occurring among such watch officers within two years from this date may be filled without regard to citizenship; but any vacancy which may occur thereafter shall be filled by a watch officer who is a citizen of the United States.

2. That the provisions of law requiring survey, inspection and measurement, by officers of the United States, of foreign-built ships admitted to United States registry under said Act, are hereby suspended for two years from this date.   WOODROW WILSON.

[Taking Over High-Power Radio Station for Use of the Government.]

THE WHITE HOUSE, *September 5, 1914.*

Whereas an order has been issued by me, dated August 5, 1914, declaring that all radio stations within the jurisdiction of the United States of America were prohibited from transmitting or receiving for delivery messages of an unneutral nature and from in any way rendering to any one of the belligerents any unneutral service; and

Whereas it is desirable to take precautions to insure the enforcement of said order insofar as it relates to the transmission of code and cipher messages by high-powered stations capable of trans-Atlantic communication;

Now, Therefore, it is ordered by virtue of authority vested in me by the radio Act of August 13, 1912, that one or more of the high-powered radio stations within the jurisdiction of the United States and capable of trans-Atlantic communication shall be taken over by the Government of the United States and used or controlled by it to the exclusion of any other control or use for the purpose of carrying on communication with land stations in Europe, including code and cipher messages.

The enforcement of this order and the preparation of regulations therefor is hereby delegated to the Secretary of the Navy, who is authorized and directed to take such action in the premises as to him may appear necessary.

This order shall take effect from and after this date.

WOODROW WILSON.

PROCLAMATIONS

By the President of the United States of America.

A PROCLAMATION

[Setting Apart a Special Day for Prayer and Supplication.]

Whereas great nations of the world have taken up arms against one another and war now draws millions of men into battle whom the counsel of statesmen has not been able to save from the terrible sacrifice;

And Whereas in this as in all things it is our privilege and duty to seek counsel and succor of Almighty God, humbling ourselves before Him, confessing our weakness and our lack of any wisdom equal to these things;

And Whereas is is the especial wish and longing of the people of the United States, in prayer and counsel and all friendliness, to serve the cause of peace;

Therefore, I, Woodrow Wilson, President of the United States of America, do designate Sunday, the fourth day of October next, a day of prayer and supplication and do request all God-fearing persons to repair on that day to their places of worship there to unite their petitions to Almighty God that, overruling the counsel of men, setting straight the things they can not govern or alter, taking pity on the nations now in the throes of conflict, in His mercy and goodness showing a way where men can see none, He vouchsafe His children healing peace again and restore once more that concord among men and nations without which there can be neither happiness nor true friendship nor any wholesome fruit of toil or thought in the world; praying also to this end that He forgive us our sins, our ignorance of His holy will, our wilfulness and many errors, and lead us in the paths of obedience to places of vision and to thoughts and counsels that purge and make wise.

In Witness Whereof I have hereunto set my hand and caused the seal of the United States to be affixed.

Done at the City of Washington this eighth day of September in the year of our Lord one thousand nine hundred and [SEAL] fourteen and of the independence of the United States of America the one hundred and thirty-ninth.

WOODROW WILSON.

By the President:

WILLIAM JENNINGS BRYAN, *Secretary of State.*

BY THE PRESIDENT OF THE UNITED STATES OF AMERICA.

A PROCLAMATION

[Neutrality—Panama Canal Zone.]

Whereas, the United States is neutral in the present war and Whereas the United States exercises sovereignty in the land and waters of the Canal Zone and is authorized by its treaty with Panama of February twenty-sixth, nineteen hundred and four, to maintain neutrality in the cities of Panama and Colon, and the harbors adjacent to the said cities:

Now, Therefore, I, Woodrow Wilson, President of the United States of America, do hereby declare and proclaim the following Rules and Regulations Governing the Use of the Panama Canal by Vessels of Belligerents and the Maintenance of Neutrality by the United States in the Canal Zone, which are in addition to the general "Rules and Regulations for the Operation and Navigation of the Panama Canal and Approaches Thereto, including all Waters under its jurisdiction" put into force by Executive Order of July 9, 1914, and I do bring to the attention of all concerned the Protocol of an Agreement between the United States and the Republic of Panama, signed at Washington, October 10, 1914, which protocol is hereunto annexed.

Rule 1. A vessel of war, for the purposes of these rules, is defined as follows: a public armed vessel, under the command of an officer duly commissioned by the government, whose name appears on the list of officers of the military fleet, and the crew of which are under regular naval discipline, which vessel is qualified by its armament and the character of its personnel to take offensive action against the public or private ships of the enemy.

Rule 2. In order to maintain both the neutrality of the Canal and that of the United States owning and operating it as a government enterprise, the same treatment, except as hereinafter noted, as that given to vessels of war of the belligerents shall be given to every vessel, belligerent or neutral, whether armed or not, that does not fall under the definition of Rule 1, which vessel is employed by a belligerent Power as a transport or fleet auxiliary or in any other way for the direct purpose of prosecuting or aiding hostilities, whether by land or sea; but such treatment shall not be given to a vessel fitted up and used exclusively as a hospital ship.

Rule 3. A vessel of war of a belligerent, or a vessel falling under Rule 2 which is commanded by an officer of the military fleet, shall only be permitted to pass through the Canal after her commanding officer has given written assurance to the Authorities of the Panama Canal that the Rules and Regulations will be faithfully observed.

The authorities of the Panama Canal shall take such steps as may be requisite to insure the observance of the Rules and Regulations by vessels falling under Rule 2 which are not commanded by an officer of the military fleet.

Rule 4. Vessels of war of a belligerent and vessels falling under Rule 2 shall not revictual nor take any stores in the Canal except so far as may be strictly necessary; and the transit of such vessels through the Canal shall be effected with the least possible delay in accordance with the Canal Regulations in force, and with only such intermission as may result from the necessities of the service.

Prizes shall be in all respects subject to the same Rules as vessels of war of the belligerents.

Rule 5. No vessel of war of a belligerent or vessel falling under Rule 2 shall receive fuel or lubricants while within the territorial waters of the Canal Zone, except on the written authorization of the Canal Authorities, specifying the amount of fuel and lubricants which may be received.

Rule 6. Before issuing any authorization for the receipt of fuel and lubricants by any vessel of war of a belligerent or vessel falling under Rule 2, the Canal Authorities shall obtain a written declaration, duly signed by the officer commanding such vessel, stating the amount of fuel and lubricants already on board.

Rule 7. Supplies will not be furnished by the Government of the United States, either directly, or indirectly through the intervention of a corporation, or otherwise, to vessels of war of a belligerent or vessels falling under Rule 2. If furnished by private contractors, or if taken from vessels under the control of a belligerent, fuel and lubricants may be taken on board vessels of war of a belligerent or vessels falling under Rule 2 only upon permission of the Canal Authorities, and then only in such amounts as will enable them, with the fuel and lubricants already on board, to reach the nearest accessible port, not an enemy port, at which they can obtain supplies necessary for the continuation of the voyage. The amounts of fuel and lubricants so received will be deducted from the amounts otherwise allowed in the ports under the jurisdiction of the United States during any time within a period of three months thereafter. Provisions furnished by contractors may be supplied only upon permission of the Canal Authorities, and then only in amount sufficient to bring up their supplies to the peace standard.

Rule 8. No belligerent shall embark or disembark troops, munitions of war, or warlike materials in the Canal, except in case of necessity due to accidental hindrance of the transit. In such cases the Canal Authorities shall be the judge of the necessity, and the transit shall be resumed with all possible dispatch.

Rule 9. Vessels of war of a belligerent and vessels falling under Rule 2 shall not remain in the territorial waters of the Canal Zone under the jurisdiction of the United States longer than twenty-four hours at any one time, except in case of distress; and in such case, shall depart as soon as possible; but a vessel of war of one belligerent shall not depart within twenty-four hours from the departure of a vessel of an opposing belligerent.

The twenty-four hours of this rule shall be construed to be twenty-four hours in addition to the time necessarily occupied in passing through the Canal.

Rule 10. In the exercise of the exclusive right of the United States to provide for the regulation and management of the Canal, and in order to ensure that the Canal shall be kept free and open on terms of entire equality to vessels of commerce and of war, there shall not be, except by special arrangement, at any one time a greater number of vessels of war of any one nation, including those of the allies of a belligerent nation, than three in either terminal port and its adjacent terminal waters, or than three in transit through the Canal; nor shall the total number of such vessels, at any one time, exceed six in all the territorial waters of the Canal Zone under the jurisdiction of the United States.

Rule 11. When vessels of war or vessels falling under Rule 2, belonging to or employed by opposing belligerents, are present simultaneously in the waters of the Canal Zone, a period of not less than twenty-four hours must elapse between the departure of the vessel belonging to or employed by one belligerent and the departure of the vessel belonging to or employed by his adversary.

The order of departure is determined by order of arrival, unless the vessel which arrived first is so circumstanced that an extension of her stay is permissible.

A vessel of war of a belligerent or vessel falling under Rule 2 may not leave the waters of the Canal Zone until twenty-four hours after the departure of a private vessel flying the flag of the adversary.

Rule 12. A vessel of war of a belligerent or vessel falling under Rule 2 which has left the waters of the Canal Zone, whether she has passed through the Canal or not, shall, if she returns within a period of one week after her departure, lose all privileges of precedence in departure from the Canal Zone, or in passage through the Canal, over vessels flying the flag of her adversaries which may enter those waters after her return and before the expiration of one week subsequent to her previous departure. In any such case the time of departure of a vessel which has so returned shall be fixed by the Canal Authorities, who may in so doing consider the wishes of the commander of a public vessel or of the master of a private vessel of the adversary of the returned vessel, which adversary's vessel is then present within the waters of the Canal Zone.

Rule 13. The repair facilities and docks belonging to the United States and administered by the Canal Authorities shall not be used by a vessel of war of a belligerent, or vessels falling under Rule 2, except when necessary in case of actual distress, and then only upon the order of the Canal Authorities, and only to the degree necessary to render the vessel sea-worthy. Any work authorized shall be done with the least possible delay.

Rule 14. The radio installation of any vessel of a belligerent Power, public or private, or of any vessel falling under Rule 2, shall be used only in connection with Canal business to the exclusion of all other business while within the waters of the Canal Zone, including the waters of Colon and Panama Harbors.

Rule 15, Air craft of a belligerent Power, public or private, are forbidden to descend or arise within the jurisdiction of the United States at the Canal Zone, or to pass through the air spaces above the lands and waters within said jurisdiction.

Rule 16. For the purpose of these rules the Canal Zone includes the cities of Panama and Colon and the harbors adjacent to the said cities.

In Witness Whereof, I have hereunto set my hand and caused the seal of the United States to be affixed.

Done at the city of Washington this thirteenth day of November in the year of our Lord one thousand nine hundred and [SEAL] fourteen and of the independence of the United States the one hundred and thirty-ninth.

WOODROW WILSON.

By the President:

W. J. BRYAN, *Secretary of State.*

Protocol of an agreement concluded between Honorable Robert Lansing, Acting Secretary of State of the United States, and Don Eusebio A. Morales, Envoy Extraordinary and Minister Plenipotentiary of the Republic of Panama, signed the tenth day of October, 1914.

The undersigned, the Acting Secretary of State of the United States of America and the Envoy Extraordinary and Minister Plenipotentiary of the Republic of Panama, in view of the close association of the interests of their respective Governments on the Isthmus of Panama, and to the end that these interests may be conserved and that, when a state of war exists, the neutral obligations of both Governments as neutrals may be maintained, after having conferred on the subject and being duly empowered by their respective Governments, have agreed:

That hospitality extended in the waters of the Republic of Panama to a belligerent vessel of war or a vessel belligerent or neutral, whether armed or not, which is employed by a belligerent power as a transport or fleet auxiliary or in any other way for the direct purpose of prosecuting or aiding hostilities, whether by land or sea, shall serve to deprive such vessel of like hospitality in the Panama Canal Zone for a period of three months, and *vice versa.*

In testimony whereof, the undersigned have signed and sealed the present Protocol in the city of Washington, this tenth day of October, 1914.

ROBERT LANSING   [L. S.]
EUSEBIO A. MORALES   [L. S.]

By the President of the United States of America.

A PROCLAMATION.

[Thanksgiving—1914.]

It has long been the honoured custom of our people to turn in the fruitful autumn of the year in praise and thanksgiving to Almighty God for his many blessings and mercies to us as a nation. The year that is now drawing to a close since we last observed our day of national thanksgiving has been, while a year of discipline because of the mighty forces of war and of change which have disturbed the world, also a year of special blessing for us.

It has been vouchsafed to us to remain at peace, with honour, and in some part to succour the suffering and supply the needs of those who are in want. We have been privileged by our own peace and self-control in some degree to steady the counsels and shape the hopes and purposes of a day of fear and distress. Our people have looked upon their own life as a nation with a deeper comprehension, a fuller realization of their responsibilities as well as of their blessings, and a keener sense of the moral and practical significance of what their part among the nations of the world may come to be.

The hurtful effects of foreign war in their own industrial and commercial affairs have made them feel the more fully and see the more clearly their mutual interdependence upon one another and has stirred them to a helpful cooperation such as they have seldom practiced before. They have been quickened by a great moral stimulation. Their unmistakable ardour for peace, their earnest pity and disinterested sympathy for those who are suffering, their readiness to help and to think of the needs of others, has revealed them to themselves as well as to the world.

Our crops will feed all who need food; the self-possession of our people amidst the most serious anxieties and difficulties and the steadiness and resourcefulness of our business men will serve other nations as well as our own.

The business of the country has been supplied with new instrumentalities and the commerce of the world with new channels of trade and intercourse. The Panama Canal has been opened to the commerce of the nations. The two continents of America have been bound in closer ties of friendship. New instrumentalities of international trade have been created which will be also new instrumentalities of acquaintance, intercourse, and mutual service. Never before have the people of the United States been so situated for their own advantage or the advantage of their neighbours or so equipped to serve themselves and mankind.

Now, Therefore, I, Woodrow Wilson, President of the United

States of America, do hereby designate Thursday the twenty-sixth of November next as a day of thanksgiving and prayer, and invite the people throughout the land to cease from their wonted occupations and in their several homes and places of worship render thanks to Almighty God.

In witness whereof, I have hereunto set my hand and caused the seal of the United States to be affixed.

Done at the City of Washington this twenty-eighth day of October in the year of our Lord one thousand nine hundred and [SEAL.] fourteen, and of the Independence of the United States of America the one hundred and thirty-ninth.

WOODROW WILSON.

By the President:

ROBERT LANSING, *Acting Secretary of State.*

BY THE PRESIDENT OF THE UNITED STATES OF AMERICA.

A PROCLAMATION.

[Dispersion of Unlawful Assemblages in Arkansas.]

Whereas by reason of unlawful obstructions, combinations and assemblages of persons, it has become impracticable in the judgment of the President to enforce by the ordinary course of judicial proceedings the laws of the United States within the State of Arkansas and especially within the Western Federal District and in the neighborhood of the towns of Hartford, Midland and Fort Smith in said district;

And whereas for the purpose of enforcing the faithful execution of the laws of the United States and protecting property in the charge of the courts of the United States, the President deems it necessary to employ a part of the military forces of the United States, in pursuance of the statute in that case made and provided;

Now, therefore, I, Woodrow Wilson, President of the United States, do hereby admonish all persons who may be or come within the state, district or towns aforesaid against doing, countenancing, encouraging or taking any part in such unlawful obstructions, combinations and assemblages, and I hereby warn all persons in any manner connected therewith to disperse and retire peaceably to their respective abodes on or before twelve o'clock noon of the sixth day of November instant.

Those who disregard this warning and persist in taking part with a riotous mob in forceably resisting and obstructing the execution of the laws of the United States or interfering with the functions of the Government or destroying or attempting to destroy property in the custody of the courts of the United States or under its directions can not be regarded otherwise than as public enemies.

Troops employed against such combinations and assemblages of persons will act with all the moderation and forbearance consistent with the accomplishment of their duty in the premises; but all citizens must realize that, if they mingle with or become a part of such riotous assemblages, there will be no opportunity for discrimination in the methods employed in dealing with such assemblages. The only safe course, therefore, for those not intentionally participating in such unlawful procedure is to abide at their homes or, at least, not to go or remain in the neighborhood of such riotous assemblages.

In testimony whereof, I have hereunto set my hand and caused the seal of the United States to be affixed.

Done at the City of Washington, this third day of November in the year of our Lord nineteen hundred and fourteen, and of [SEAL.]   the Independence of the United States the one hundred and thirty-ninth.

WOODROW WILSON.

By the President:
ROBERT LANSING, *Acting Secretary of State.*

BY THE PRESIDENT OF THE UNITED STATES OF AMERICA.

A PROCLAMATION.

[Neutrality—Great Britain and Turkey.]

Whereas a state of war unhappily exists between Great Britain and Turkey; And Whereas the United States is on terms of friendship and amity with the contending powers, and with the persons inhabiting their several dominions;

> [Here follows the identical preamble and warning against voilation of quoted law as in the proclamation of neutrality in the case of hostilities between Austria-Hungary and Servia, Germany and Russia, and Germany and France. See pages 7969, 7970, 7971, 7972 and 7973.— *Ed.*]

Done at the City of Washington this sixth day of November in the year of our Lord one thousand nine hundred and fourteen [SEAL.]   and of the independence of the United States of America the one hundred and thirty-ninth.

WOODROW WILSON.

By the President:
ROBERT LANSING, *Acting Secretary of State.*

SECOND ANNUAL ADDRESS

[Delivered at a Joint Session of the two Houses of Congress, December 8, 1914.]

GENTLEMEN OF THE CONGRESS:

The session upon which you are now entering will be the closing session of the Sixty-third Congress, a Congress, I venture to say, which will long be remembered for the great body of thoughtful and constructive work which it has done, in loyal response to the thought and needs of the country. I should like in this address to review the notable record and try to make adequate assessment of it; but no doubt we stand too near the work that has been done and are ourselves too much part of it to play the part of historians toward it.

Our program of legislation with regard to the regulation of business is now virtually complete. It has been put forth, as we intended, as a whole, and leaves no conjecture as to what is to follow. The road at last lies clear and firm before business. It is a road which it can travel without fear or embarrassment. It is the road to ungrudged, unclouded success. In it every honest man, every man who believes that the public interest is part of his own interest, may walk with perfect confidence.

Moreover, our thoughts are now more of the future than of the past. While we have worked at our tasks of peace the circumstances of the whole age have been altered by war. What we have done for our own land and our own people we did with the best that was in us, whether of character or of intelligence, with sober enthusiasm and a confidence in the principles upon which we were acting which sustained us at every step of the difficult undertaking; but it is done. It has passed from our hands. It is now an established part of the legislation of the country. Its usefulness, its effects will disclose themselves in experience. What chiefly strikes us now, as we look about us during these closing days of a year which will be forever memorable in the history of the world, is that we face new tasks, have been facing them these six months, must face them in the months to come,—face them without partisan feeling, like men who have forgotten everything but a common duty and the fact that we are representatives of a great people whose thought is not of us but of what America owes to herself and to all mankind in such circumstances as these upon which we look amazed and anxious.

War has interrupted the means of trade not only but also the processes of production. In Europe it is destroying men and resources wholesale and upon a scale unprecedented and appalling. There is reason to fear that the time is near, if it be not already at hand, when several of the countries of Europe will find it difficult to do for their people what they have hitherto been always easily able to do,—many essential and fundamental things. At any rate, they will need our help and our manifold services as they have never needed them before; and we should be ready, more fit and ready than we have ever been.

It is of equal consequence that the nations whom Europe has usually supplied with innumerable articles of manufacture and commerce of which they are in constant need and without which their economic development halts and stands still can now get only a small part of what they formerly imported and eagerly look to us to supply their all but empty markets. This is particularly true of our own neighbors, the States, great and small, of Central and South America. Their lines of trade have hitherto run chiefly athwart the seas, not to our ports but to the ports of Great Britain and of the older continent of Europe. I do not stop to inquire why, or to make any comment on probable causes. What interests us just now is not the explanation but the fact, and our duty and opportunity in the presence of it. Here are markets which we must supply, and we must find the means of action. The United States, this great people for whom we speak and act, should be ready, as never before, to serve itself and to serve mankind; ready with its resources, its energies, its forces of production, and its means of distribution.

It is a very practical matter, a matter of ways and means. We have the resources, but are we fully ready to use them? And, if we can make ready what we have, have we the means at hand to distribute it? We are not fully ready; neither have we the means of distribution. We are willing, but we are not fully able. We have the wish to serve and to serve greatly, generously; but we are not prepared as we should be. We are not ready to mobilize our resources at once. We are not prepared to use them immediately and at their best, without delay and without waste.

To speak plainly, we have grossly erred in the way in which we have stunted and hindered the development of our merchant marine. And now, when we need ships, we have not got them. We have year after year debated, without end or conclusion, the best policy to pursue with regard to the use of the ores and forests and water powers of our national domain in the rich States of the West, when we should have acted; and they are still locked up. The key is still turned upon them, the door shut fast at which thousands of vigorous men, full of initiative, knock clamorously for admittance. The water power of our navigable streams outside the national domain also, even in the eastern States, where we have worked and planned for generations, is still not used as it might be, because we will and we won't; because the laws we have made do not intelligently balance encouragement against restraint. We withhold by regulation.

I have come to ask you to remedy and correct these mistakes and omissions, even at this short session of a Congress which would certainly seem to have done all the work that could reasonably be expected of it. The time and the circumstances are extraordinary, and so must our efforts be also.

Fortunately, two great measures, finely conceived, the one to unlock, with proper safeguards, the resources of the national domain, the other to encourage the use of the navigable waters outside that domain for the generation of power, have already passed the House of Representatives and are ready for immediate consideration and action by the Senate. With the deepest earnestness I urge their prompt passage. In them both we turn our backs upon hesitation and makeshift and formulate a genuine policy of use and conservation, in the best sense of those words. We owe the one measure not only to the people of that great western country for whose free and systematic development, as it seems to me, our legislation has done so little, but also to the people of the Nation as a whole; and we as clearly owe the other fulfillment of our repeated promises that the water power of the country should in fact as well as in name be put at the disposal of great industries which can make economical and profitable use of it, the rights of the public being adequately guarded the while, and monopoly in the use prevented. To have begun such measures and not completed them would indeed mar the record of this great Congress very seriously. I hope and confidently believe that they will be completed.

And there is another great piece of legislation which awaits and should receive the sanction of the Senate: I mean the bill which gives a larger measure of self-government to the people of the Philippines. How better, in this time of anxious questioning and perplexed policy, could we show our confidence in the principles of liberty, as the source as well as the expression of life, how better could we demonstrate our own self-possession and steadfastness in the courses of justice and disinterestedness than by thus going calmly forward to fulfill our promises to a dependent people, who will now look more anxiously than ever to see whether we have indeed the liberality, the unselfishness, the courage, the faith we have boasted and professed. I can not believe that the Senate will let this great measure of constructive justice await the action of another Congress. Its passage would nobly crown the record of these two years of memorable labor.

But I think that you will agree with me that this does not complete the toll of our duty. How are we to carry our goods to the empty markets of which I have spoken if we have not the ships? How are we to build up a great trade if we have not the certain and constant means of transportation upon which all profitable and useful commerce depends? And how are we to get the ships if we wait for the trade to develop without them? To correct the many mistakes by which we have discouraged and all but destroyed the merchant marine of the country, to retrace the steps by which we have, it seems almost deliberately, withdrawn our flag from the seas, except where, here and there, a ship of war is bidden carry it or some wandering yacht displays it, would take a long time and involve many detailed items of legislation, and the trade which we ought immediately to handle would disappear or find other channels while we debated the items.

The case is not unlike that which confronted us when our own continent was to be opened up to settlement and industry, and we needed long lines of railway, extended means of transportation prepared beforehand, if development was not to lag intolerably and wait interminably. We lavishly subsidized the building of transcontinental railroads. We look back upon that with regret now, because the subsidies led to many scandals of which we are ashamed; but we know that the railroads had to be built, and if we had it to do over again we should of course build them, but in another way. Therefore I propose another way of providing the means of transportation, which must precede, not tardily follow, the development of our trade with our neighbor states of America. It may seem a reversal of the natural order of things, but it is true, that the routes of trade must be actually opened—by many ships and regular sailings and moderate charges—before streams of merchandise will flow freely and profitably through them.

Hence the pending shipping bill, discussed at the last session but as yet passed by neither House. In my judgment such legislation is imperatively needed and can not wisely be postponed. The Government must open these gates of trade, and open them wide; open them before it is altogether profitable to open them, or altogether reasonable to ask private capital to open them at a venture. It is not a question of the Government monopolizing the field. It should take action to make it certain that transportation at reasonable rates will be promptly provided, even where the carriage is not at first profitable; and then, when the carriage has become sufficiently profitable to attract and engage private capital, and engage it in abundance, the Government ought to withdraw. I very earnestly hope that the Congress will be of this opinion, and that both Houses will adopt this exceedingly important bill.

The great subject of rural credits still remains to be dealt with, and it is a matter of deep regret that the difficulties of the subject have seemed to render it impossible to complete a bill for passage at this session. But it can not be perfected yet, and therefore there are no other constructive measures the necessity for which I will at this time call your attention to; but I would be negligent of a very manifest duty were I not to call the attention of the Senate to the fact that the proposed convention for safety at sea awaits its confirmation and that the limit fixed in the convention itself for its acceptance is the last day of the present month. The conference in which this convention originated was called by the United States; the representatives of the United States played a very influential part indeed in framing the provisions of the proposed convention; and those provisions are in themselves for the most part admirable. It would hardly be consistent with the part we have played in the whole matter to let it drop and go by the board as if forgotten and neglected. It was ratified in May by the German Government and in August by the Parliament of Great Britain. It marks a most hopeful and decided advance in international civilization. We should show our earnest good faith in a great matter by adding our own acceptance of it.

There is another matter of which I must make special mention, if I am to discharge my conscience, lest it should escape your attention. It may seem a very small thing. It affects only a single item of appropriation. But many human lives and many great enterprises hang upon it. It is the matter of making adequate provision for the survey and charting of our coasts. It is immediately pressing and exigent in connection with the immense coast line of Alaska, a coast line greater than that of the United States themselves, though it is also very important indeed with regard to the older coasts of the continent. We can not use our great Alaskan domain, ships will not ply thither, if those coasts and their many hidden dangers are not thoroughly surveyed and charted. The work is incomplete at almost every point. Ships and lives have been lost in threading what were supposed to be well-known main channels. We have not provided adequate vessels or adequate machinery for the survey and charting. We have used old vessels that were not big enough or strong enough and which were so nearly unseaworthy that our inspectors would not have allowed private owners to send them to sea. This is a matter which, as I have said, seems small, but is in reality very great. Its importance has only to be looked into to be appreciated.

Before I close may I say a few words upon two topics, much discussed out of doors, upon which it is highly important that our judgments should be clear, definite, and steadfast?

One of these is economy in government expenditures. The duty of economy is not debatable. It is manifest and imperative. In the appropriations we pass we are spending the money of the great people whose servants we are,—not our own. We are trustees and responsible stewards in the spending. The only thing debatable and upon which we should be careful to make our thought and purpose clear is the kind of economy demanded of us. I assert with the greatest confidence that the people of the United States are not jealous of the amount their Government costs if they are sure that they get what they need and desire for the outlay, that the money is being spent for objects of which they approve, and that it is being applied with good business sense and management.

Governments grow, piecemeal, both in their tasks and in the means by which those tasks are to be performed, and very few Governments are organized, I venture to say, as wise and experienced business men would organize them if they had a clean sheet of paper to write upon. Certainly the Government of the United States is not. I think that it is generally agreed that there should be a systematic reorganization and reassembling of its parts so as to secure greater efficiency and effect considerable savings in expense. But the amount of money saved in that way would, I believe, though no doubt considerable in itself, running, it may be, into the millions, be relatively small,—small, I mean, in proportion to the total necessary outlays of the Government. It would be thoroughly worth effecting, as every saving would, great or small. Our duty is not altered by the scale of the saving. But my point is that the people of the United States do not wish to curtail the activities of this Government; they wish, rather, to enlarge them; and with every enlargement, with the mere growth, indeed, of the country itself, there must come, of course, the inevitable increase of expense. The sort of economy we ought to practice may be effected, and ought to be effected, by a careful study and assessment of the tasks to be performed; and the money spent ought to be made to yield the best possible returns in efficiency and achievement. And, like good stewards, we should so account for every dollar of our appropriations as to make it perfectly evident what it was spent for and in what way it was spent.

It is not expenditure but extravagance that we should fear being criticized for; not paying for the legitimate enterprise and undertakings of a great Government whose people command what it should do, but adding what will benefit only a few or pouring money out for what need not have been undertaken at all or might have been postponed or better and more economically conceived and carried out. The Nation is not niggardly; it is very generous. It will chide us only if we forget for whom we pay money out and whose money it is we pay. These are large and general standards, but they are not very difficult of application to particular cases.

The other topic I shall take leave to mention goes deeper into the principles of our national life and policy. It is the subject of national defense.

It can not be discussed without first answering some very searching questions. It is said in some quarters that we are not prepared for war. What is meant by being prepared? Is it meant that we are not ready upon brief notice to put a nation in the field, a nation of men trained to arms? Of course we are not ready to do that; and we shall never be in time of peace so long as we retain our present political principles and institutions. And what is it that it is suggested we should be prepared to do? To defend ourselves against attack? We have always found means to do that, and shall find them whenever it is necessary without calling our people away from their necessary tasks to render compulsory military service in times of peace.

Allow me to speak with great plainness and directness upon this great matter and to avow my convictions with deep earnestness. I have tried to know what America is, what her people think, what they are, what they most cherish and hold dear. I hope that some of their finer passions are in my own heart,—some of the great conceptions and desires which gave birth to this Government and which have made the voice of this people a voice of peace and hope and liberty among the peoples of the world, and that, speaking my own thoughts, I shall, at least in part, speak theirs also, however faintly and inadequately, upon this vital matter.

We are at peace with all the world. No one who speaks counsel based on fact or drawn from a just and candid interpretation of realities can say that there is reason to fear that from any quarter our independence or the integrity of our territory is threatened. Dread of the power of any other nation we are incapable of. We are not jealous of rivalry in the fields of commerce or of any other peaceful achievement. We mean to live our own lives as we will; but we mean also to let live. We are, indeed, a true friend to all the nations of the world, because we threaten none, covet the possessions of none, desire the overthrow of none. Our friendship can be accepted and is accepted without reservation, because it is offered in a spirit and for a purpose which no one need ever question or suspect. Therein lies our greatness. We are the champions of peace and of concord. And we should be very jealous of this distinction which we have sought to earn. Just now we should be particularly jealous of it because it is our dearest present hope that this character and reputation may presently, in God's providence, bring us an opportunity such as has seldom been vouchsafed any nation, the opportunity to counsel and obtain peace in the world and reconciliation and a healing settlement of many a matter that has cooled and interrupted the friendship of nations. This is the time above all others when we should wish and resolve to keep our strength by self-possession, our influence by preserving our ancient principles of action.

From the first we have had a clear and settled policy with regard to military establishments. We never have had, and while we retain our present principles and ideals we never shall have, a large standing army. If asked, Are you ready to defend yourselves? we reply, Most assuredly, to the utmost; and yet we shall not turn

America into a military camp. We will not ask our young men to spend the best years of their lives making soldiers of themselves. There is another sort of energy in us. It will know how to declare itself and make itself effective should occasion arise. And especially when half the world is on fire we shall be careful to make our moral insurance against the spread of the conflagration very definite and certain and adequate indeed.

Let us remind ourselves, therefore, of the only thing we can do or will do. We must depend in every time of national peril, in the future as in the past, not upon a standing army, nor yet upon a reserve army, but upon a citizenry trained and accustomed to arms. It will be right enough, right American policy, based upon our accustomed principles and practices, to provide a system by which every citizen who will volunteer for the training may be made familiar with the use of modern arms, the rudiments of drill and maneuver, and the maintenance and sanitation of camps. We should encourage such training and make it a means of discipline which our young men will learn to value. It is right that we should provide it not only, but that we should make it as attractive as possible, and so induce our young men to undergo it at such times as they can command a little freedom and can seek the physical development they need, for mere health's sake, if for nothing more. Every means by which such things can be stimulated is legitimate, and such a method smacks of true American ideas. It is right, too, that the National Guard of the States should be developed and strengthened by every means which is not inconsistent with our obligations to our own people or with the established policy of our Government. And this, also, not because the time or occasion specially calls for such measures, but because it should be our constant policy to make these provisions for our national peace and safety.

More than this carries with it a reversal of the whole history and character of our polity. More than this, proposed at this time, permit me to say, would mean merely that we had lost our self-possession, that we had been thrown off our balance by a war with which we have nothing to do, whose causes can not touch us, whose very existence affords us opportunities of friendship and disinterested service which should make us ashamed of any thought of hostility or fearful preparation for trouble. This is assuredly the opportunity for which a people and a government like ours were raised up, the opportunity not only to speak but actually to embody and exemplify the counsels of peace and amity and the lasting concord which is based on justice and fair and generous dealing.

A powerful navy we have always regarded as our proper and natural means of defense; and it has always been of defense that we have thought, never of aggression or of conquest. But who shall tell us now what sort of navy to build? We shall take leave to be strong upon the seas, in the future as in the past; and there will be no thought of offense or of provocation in that. Our ships are our natural bulwarks. When will the experts tell us just what kind we should construct—and when will they be right for ten years together, if the relative efficiency of craft of different kinds and uses continues to change as we have seen it change under our very eyes in these last few months?

But I turn away from the subject. It is not new. There is no new need to discuss it. We shall not alter our attitude toward it because some amongst us are nervous and excited. We shall easily and sensibly agree upon a policy of defense. The question has not changed its aspects because the times are not normal. Our policy will not be for an occasion. It will be conceived as a permanent and settled thing, which we will pursue at all seasons, without haste and after a fashion perfectly consistent with the peace of the world, the abiding friendship of states, and the unhampered freedom of all with whom we deal. Let there be no misconception. The country has been mis-informed. We have not been negligent of national defense. We are not unmindful of the great responsibility resting upon us. We shall learn and profit by the lesson of every experience and every new circumstance; and what is needed will be adequately done.

I close, as I began, by reminding you of the great tasks and duties of peace which challenge our best powers and invite us to build what will last, the tasks to which we can address ourselves now and at all times with free-hearted zest and with all the finest gifts of con-structive wisdom we possess. To develop our life and our resources; to supply our own people, and the people of the world as their need arises, from the abundant plenty of our fields and our marts of trade; to enrich the commerce of our own States and of the world with the products of our mines, our farms, and our factories, with the crea-tions of our thought and the fruits of our character,—this is what will hold our attention and our enthusiasm steadily, now and in the years to come, as we strive to show in our life as a nation what liberty and the inspirations of an emancipated spirit may do for men and for societies, for individuals, for states, and for mankind.

Letter to Attorney-General McReynolds

[Directing dissolution proceedings against the New York, New Haven and Hartford Railroad Company and criminal action against directors.]

THE WHITE HOUSE, *July 21, 1914.*

MY DEAR MR. ATTORNEY-GENERAL:

I have your letter of to-day, enclosing a copy of your letter of July 9, to Mr. J. H. Hustis, president of the New York, New Haven and Hartford Railroad Company which, together, disclose the failure of the directors of the New York, New Haven and Hartford Railroad Company to comply with the terms of settlement proposed by them and accepted by us in the matter of their railroad holdings.

Their final decision in this matter causes me the deepest surprise and regret. Their failure upon so slight a pretext to carry out an agreement deliberately and solemnly entered into, and which was manifestly in the common interest, is to me inexplicable and entirely without justification.

You have been kind enough to keep me informed of every step the Department took in this matter and the action of the Department has, throughout, met with my entire approval. It was just, reasonable and efficient. It should have resulted in avoiding what must now be done.

In the circumstances the course you propose is the only one the Government can pursue. I therefore request and direct that a proceeding in equity be filed, seeking the dissolution of unlawful monopolization of transportation in New England territory now sought to be maintained by the New York, New Haven and Hartford Railroad Company, and that the criminal aspects of the case be laid before a Grand Jury. With my regard, sincerely yours,

WOODROW WILSON.

To the Hon. J. C. McReynolds, Attorney-General.

ADDRESSES

[Delivered at Indianapolis, Ind., January 8, 1915.]

GOVERNOR RALSTON, LADIES AND GENTLEMEN:

You have given me a most royal welcome, for which I thank you from the bottom of my heart. It is rather lonely living in Washington. I have been confined for two years at hard labor, and even now I feel that I am simply out on parole. You notice that one of the most distinguished members of the United States Senate is here to see that I go back. And yet, with sincere apologies to the Senate and House of Representatives, I want to say that I draw more inspiration from you than I do from them. They, like myself, are only servants of the people of the United States. Our sinews consist in your sympathy and support, and our renewal comes from contact with you and with the strong movements of public opinion in the country.

That is the reason why I for one would prefer that our thoughts should not too often cross the ocean, but should center themselves upon the policies and duties of the United States. If we think rightly of the United States, when the time comes we shall know how this country can serve the world. I will borrow a very interesting phrase from a distinguished gentleman of my acquaintance and beg that you will "keep your moral powder dry."

But I have come here on Jackson Day. If there are Republicans present, I hope they will feel the compelling influences of such a day. There was nothing mild about Andrew Jackson; that is the reason I spoke of the "compelling influences" of the day. Andrew Jackson was a forthright man who believed everything he did believe in fighting earnest. And really, ladies and gentlemen, in public life that is the only sort of man worth thinking about for a moment. If I was not ready to fight for everything I believe in, I would think it my duty to go back and take a back seat. I like, therefore, to breathe the air of Jackson Day. I like to be reminded of the old militant hosts of Democracy which I believe have come to life again in our time. The United States had almost forgotten that it must keep its fighting ardor in behalf of mankind when Andrew Jackson became President; and you will notice that whenever the United States forgets its ardor for mankind it is necessary that a Democrat should be elected President.

The trouble with the Republican party is that it has not had a new idea for thirty years. I am not speaking as a politician; I am speaking as an historian. I have looked for new ideas in the records and I have not found any proceeding from the Republican ranks. They have had leaders from time to time who suggested new ideas, but they never did anything to carry them out. I suppose there was no harm in their talking, provided they could not do anything. Therefore, when it was necessary to say that we had talked about things long enough which it was necessary to do, and the time had come to do them, it was indispensable that a Democrat should be elected President.

I would not speak with disrespect of the Republican party. I always speak with great respect of the past. The past was necessary to the present, and was a sure prediction of the future. The Republican party is still a covert and refuge for those who are afraid, for those who want to consult their grandfathers about everything. You will notice that most of the advice taken by the Republican party is taken from gentlemen old enough to be grandfathers, and that when they claim that a reaction has taken place, they react to the reelection of the oldest members of their party. They will not trust the youngsters. They are afraid the youngsters may have something up their sleeve.

You will see, therefore, that I have come to you in the spirit of Jackson Day. I got very tired staying in Washington and saying sweet things. I wanted to come out and get in contact with you once more and say what I really thought.

My friends, what I particularly want you to observe is this, that politics in this country does not depend any longer upon the regular members of either party. There are not enough regular Republicans in this country to take and hold national power; and I must immediately add there are not enough regular Democrats in this country to do it, either. This country is guided and its policy is determined by the independent voter; and I have come to ask you how we can best prove to the independent voter that the instrument he needs is the Democratic party, and that it would be hopeless for him to attempt to use the Republican party. I do not have to prove it; I admit it.

What seems to me perfectly evident is this: That if you made a rough reckoning, you would have to admit that only about one-third of the Republican party is progressive; and you would also have to admit that about two-thirds of the Democratic party is progressive. Therefore, the independent progressive voter finds a great deal more company in the Democratic ranks than in the Republican ranks. I say a great deal more, because there are Democrats who are sitting on the breeching strap; there are Democrats who are holding back; there are Democrats who are nervous. I dare say they were born with that temperament. And I respect the conservative temper. I claim to be an animated conservative myself, because being a conservative I understand to mean being a man not only who preserves what is best in the Nation but who sees that in order to preserve it you dare not stand still but must move forward. The virtue of America is not statical; it is dynamic. All the forces of America are forces in action or else they are forces of inertia.

What I want to point out to you—and I believe that this is what the whole country is beginning to perceive—is this, that there is a larger body of men in the regular ranks of the Democratic party who believe in the progressive policies of our day and mean to see them carried forward and perpetuated than there is in the ranks of the Republican party. How can it be otherwise, gentlemen? The Democratic party, and only the Democratic party, has carried out the policies which the progressive people of this country have desired. There is not a single great act of this present great Congress which has not been carried out in obedience to the public opinion of America; and the public opinion of America is not going to permit any body of men to go backward with regard to these great matters.

Let me instance a single thing: I want to ask the business men here present if this is not the first January in their recollection that did not bring a money stringency for the time being, because of the necessity of paying out great sums of money by way of dividends and the other settlements which come at the first of the year? I have asked the bankers if that happened this year, and they say, "No; it did not happen; it could not happen under the Federal Reserve Act." We have emancipated the credits of this country; and is there anybody here who will doubt that the other policies that have given guaranty to this country that there will be free competition are policies which this country will never allow to be reversed? I have taken a long time, ladies and gentlemen, to select the Federal Trade Commission, because I wanted to choose men and be sure that I had chosen men who would be really serviceable to the business men of this country, great as well as small, the rank and the file. These things have been done and will never be undone. They were talked about and talked about with futility until a Democratic Congress attempted and achieved them.

But the Democratic party is not to suppose that it is done with the business. The Democratic party is still on trial. The Democratic party still has to prove to the independent voters of the country not only that it believes in these things, but that it will continue to work along these lines and that it will not allow any enemy of these things to break its ranks. This country is not going to use any party that can not do continuous and consistent teamwork. If any group of men should dare to break the solidarity of the Democratic team for any purpose or from any motive, theirs will be a most unenviable notoriety and a responsibility which will bring deep bitterness to them. The only party that is serviceable to a nation is a party that can hold absolutely together and march with the discipline and with the zest of a conquering host.

I am not saying these things because I doubt that the Democratic party will be able to do this, but because I believe that as leader for the time being of that party I can promise the country that it will do these things. I know my colleagues at Washington; I know their spirit and their purpose; and I know that they have the same emotion, the same high emotion of public service, that I hope I have.

I want at this juncture to pay my tribute of respect and of affectionate admiration for the two great Democratic Senators from the State of Indiana. I have never had to lie awake nights wondering what they were going to do. And the country is not going to trouble itself, ladies and gentlemen, to lie awake nights and wonder what men are going to do. If they have to do that, they will choose other men. Teamwork all the time is what they are going to demand of us, and that is our individual as well as our collective responsibility. That is what Jackson stands for. If a man will not play with the team, then he does not belong to the team. You see, I have spent a large part of my life in college and I know what a team means when I see it; and I know what the captain of a team must have if he is going to win. So it is no idle figure of speech with me.

Now, what is their duty? You say, "Hasn't this Congress carried out a great program?" Yes, it has carried out a great program. It has had the most remarkable record that any Congress since the Civil War has had; and I say since the Civil War because I have not had time to think about those before the Civil War. But we are living at an extraordinary moment. The world has never been in the condition that it is in now, my friends. Half the world is on fire. Only America among the great powers of the world is free to govern her own life; and all the world is looking to America to serve its economic need. And while this is happening what is going on?

Do you know, gentlemen, that the ocean freight rates have gone up in some instances to ten times their ordinary figure? and that the farmers of the United States, those who raise grain and those who raise cotton—these things that are absolutely necessary to the world as well as to ourselves—can not get their due profit out of the great prices that they are willing to pay for these things on the other side of the sea, because practically the whole profit is eaten up by the extortionate charges for ocean carriage? In the midst of this the Democrats propose a temporary measure of relief in a shipping bill. The merchants and the farmers of this country must have ships to carry their goods. Just at the present moment there is no other way of getting them than through the instrumentality that is suggested in the shipping bill. I hear it said in Washington on all hands that the Republicans in the United States Senate mean to talk enough to make the passage of that bill impossible. These self-styled friends of business, these men who say the Democratic party does not know what to do for business, are saying that the Democrats shall do nothing for business. I challenge them to show their right to stand in the way of the release of American products to the rest of the world! Who commissioned them—a minority, a lessening minority? (For they will be in a greater minority in the next Senate than in this.) You know it is the peculiarity of that great body that it has rules of procedure which make it possible for a minority to defy the Nation; and these gentlemen are now seeking to defy the Nation and prevent the release of American products to the suffering world which needs them more than it ever needed them before. Their credentials as friends of business and friends of America will be badly discredited if they succeed. If I were speaking from a selfish, partisan point of view, I could wish nothing better than that they should show their true colors as partisans and succeed. But I am not quite so malevolent as that. Some of them are misguided; some of them are blind; most of them are ignorant. I would rather pray for them than abuse them. The great voice of America ought to make them understand what they are said to be attempting now really means. I have to say "are said to be attempting," because they do not come and tell me that they are attempting them. I do not know why. I would express my opinion of them in parliamentary language, but I would express it, I hope, no less plainly because couched in the terms of courtesy. This country is bursting its jacket, and they are seeing to it that the jacket is not only kept tight but is riveted with steel.

The Democratic party does know how to serve business in this

PRESIDENT WILSON READING PREPAREDNESS MESSAGE

WILSON'S MESSAGE ON PREPAREDNESS

President Wilson's third annual address, which was read to the 64th Congress, December 7, 1915, was devoted largely to questions growing out of the general war in Europe. He counselled strict neutrality toward the belligerent nations, deplored the passionate sympathy of foreign-born citizens for the countries of their nativity, which impelled them to hostile acts against the land of their adoption. He urged Congress to adopt immediate measures for increasing the army and navy and for the enlistment of 400,000 disciplined citizen soldiers.

The Monroe Doctrine was endorsed, and the policy of non-interference in the internal affairs of American republics was reiterated. Abstention from interference in the case of the prolonged revolution in Mexico was cited as an example of the hands-off policy of the United States toward other American republics.

The building of an adequate merchant marine through the purchase and construction of ships with government money was urged upon Congress as the best means to secure immediate success in the extension of our trade with foreign countries, particularly with South and Central America.

Continuance of the existing war tax was suggested, as well as the raising of additional internal revenue by a tax on iron and steel, gasoline, automobiles, and bank checks.

country, and its future program is a program of service. We have cleared the decks. We have laid the lines now upon which business that was to do the country harm shall be stopped and an economic control which was intolerable shall be broken up. We have emancipated America, but America must do something with her freedom. There are great bills pending in the United States Senate just now that have been passed by the House of Representatives, which are intended as constructive measures in behalf of business—one great measure which will make available the enormous water powers of this country for the industry of it; another bill which will unlock the resources of the public domain which the Republicans, desiring to save, locked up so that nobody could use them.

The reason I say the Republicans have not had a new idea in thirty years is that they have not known how to do anything except sit on the lid. If you can release the steam so that it will drive great industries, it is not necessary to sit on the lid. What we are trying to do in the great conservation bill is to carry out for the first time in the history of the United States a system by which the great resources of this country can be used instead of being set aside so that no man can get at them. I shall watch with a great deal of interest what the self-styled friends of business try to do to those bills. Do not misunderstand me. There are some men on that side of the Chamber who understand the value of these things and are standing valiantly by them, but they are a small minority. The majority that is standing by them is on our side of the Chamber, and they are the friends of America.

But there are other things which we have to do. Sometimes when I look abroad, my friends, and see the great mass of struggling humanity on this continent, it goes very much to my heart to see how many men are at a disadvantage and are without guides and helpers. Don't you think it would be a pretty good idea for the Democratic party to undertake a systematic method of helping the workingmen of America? There is one very simple way in which they can help the workingmen. If you were simply to establish a great Federal employment bureau, it would do a vast deal. By the Federal agencies which spread over this country men could be directed to those parts of the country, to those undertakings, to those tasks where they could find profitable employment. The labor of this country needs to be guided from opportunity to opportunity. We proved it the other day. We were told that in two States of the Union 30,000 men were needed to gather the crops. We suggested in a Cabinet meeting that the Department of Labor should have printed information about this in such form that it could be posted up in the post offices all over the United States, and that the Department of Labor should get in touch with the labor departments of the States, so that notice could go out from them, and their co-operation obtained. What was the result? Those 30,000 men were found and were sent to the places where they got profitable employment. I do not know any one thing that has happened in my administration that made me feel happier than that—that the job and the man had been brought together. It will not cost a great deal of money and it will do a great deal of service if the United States were to undertake to do such things systematically and all the year round; and I for my part hope that it will do that. If I were writing an additional plank for a Democratic platform, I would put that in.

There is another thing that needs very much to be done. I am not one of those who doubt either the industry or the learning or the integrity of the courts of the United States, but I do know that they have a very antiquated way of doing business. I do know that the United States in its judicial procedure is many decades behind every other civilized Government in the world, and I say that it is an immediate and an imperative call upon us to rectify that, because the speediness of justice, the inexpensiveness of justice, the ready access to justice, is the greater part of justice itself. If you have to be rich to get justice, because of the cost of the very process itself, then there is no justice at all. So I say this is another direction in which we ought to be very quick to see the signs of the times and to help those who need to be helped.

Then there is something else. The Democrats have heard the Republicans talking about the scientific way in which to handle a tariff, though the Republicans have never given any exhibition of a knowledge of how to handle it scientifically. If it is scientific to put additional profits into the hands of those who are already getting the greater part of the profits, then they have been exceedingly scientific. It has been the science of selfishness; it has been the science of privilege. That kind of science I do not care to know anything about except enough to stop it. But if by scientific treatment of the tariff they mean adjustment to the actual trade conditions of America and the world, then I am with them; and I want to call their attention—for though they voted for it they apparently have not noticed it—to the fact that the bill which creates the new Trade Commission does that very thing. We were at pains to see that it was put in there. That commission is authorized and empowered to inquire into and report to Congress not only upon all the conditions of trade in this country, but upon the conditions of trade, the cost of manufacture, the cost of transportation—all the things that enter into the question of the tariff—in foreign countries and into all those questions of foreign combinations which affect international trade between Europe and the United States. It has the full powers which will guide Congress in the scientific treatment of questions of international trade Being by profession a schoolmaster, I am glad to point that out to the class of uninstructed Republicans, though I have not always taught in the primary grade.

At every turn the things that the progressive Republicans have proposed that were practicable, the Democrats either have done or are immediately proposing to do. If that is not our bill of particulars to satisfy the independent voters of the country, I would like to have one produced. There are things that the Progressive program contained which we, being constitutional lawyers, happened to know can not be done by the Congress of the United States. That is a detail which they seem to have overlooked. But so far as they can be done by State legislatures, I, for one, speaking for one Democrat, am heartily in favor of their being done. Because Democrats do not congregate merely in Washington. They congregate also in the State capitols, and they congregate there in very influential numbers and with very influential organizations.

Just before I came away from Washington I was going over some of the figures of the last elections, the elections of November last. The official returns have not all come in yet. I do not know why they are so slow in getting to us, but so far as they have come in they have given me this useful information, that taking the States where Senators were elected, and where Senators were not elected taking the election of Governors, and where Governors were not elected taking the returns for the State legislatures or for the Congressional delegates, the Democrats, reckoning State by State, would, if it had been a presidential year, have had a majority of about eighty in the Electoral College. Fortunately or unfortunately, this is not a presidential year; but the thing is significant to me for this reason. A great many people have been speaking of the Democratic party as a minority party. Well, if it is, it is not so much of a minority party as the Republican, and as between the minorities I think we can claim to belong to the larger minority. The moral of that is merely what I have already been pointing out to you, that neither party in its regular membership has a majority. I do not want to make the independent voter too proud of himself, but I have got to admit that he is our boss; and I am bound to admit that the things that he wants are, so far as I have seen them mentioned, things that I want.

I am not an independent voter, but I hope I can claim to be an independent person, and I want to say this distinctly: I do not love any party any longer than it continues to serve the immediate and pressing needs of America. I have been bred in the Democratic party; I love the Democratic party; but I love America a great deal more than I love the Democratic party; and when the Democratic party thinks that it is an end in itself, then I rise up and dissent. It is a means to an end, and its power depends, and ought to depend, upon its showing that it knows what America needs and is ready to give it what it needs. That is the reason I say to the independent voter you have got us in the palm of your hand. I do not happen to be one of your number, but I recognize your supremacy, because I read the election returns; and I have this ambition, my Democratic friends—I can avow it on Jackson day—I want to make every independent voter in this country a Democrat. It is a little cold and lonely out where he is, because, though he holds the balance of power, he is not the majority, and I want him to come in where it is warm. I want him to come in where there is a lot of good society, good companionship, where there are great emotions. That is what I miss in the Republican party; they do not seem to have any great emotions. They seem to think a lot of things, old things, but they do not seem to have any enthusiasm about anything.

There is one thing I have got a great enthusiasm about, I might almost say a reckless enthusiasm, and that is human liberty. The Governor has just now spoken about watchful waiting in Mexico. I want to say a word about Mexico, or not so much about Mexico as about our attitude towards Mexico. I hold it as a fundamental principle, and so do you, that every people has the right to determine its own form of government; and until this recent revolution in Mexico, until the end of the Diaz reign, eighty per cent. of the people of Mexico never had a "look in" in determining who should be their governors or what their government should be. Now, I am for the eighty per cent.! It is none of my business, and it is none of your business, how long they take in determining it. It is none of my business, and it is none of yours, how they go about the business. The country is theirs. The Government is theirs. The liberty, if they can get it, and God-speed them in getting it, is theirs. And so far as my influence goes while I am President nobody shall interfere with them.

That is what I mean by a great emotion, the great emotion of sympathy. Do you suppose that the American people are ever going to count a small amount of material benefit and advantage to people doing business in Mexico against the liberties and the permanent happiness of the Mexican people? Have not European nations taken as long as they wanted and spilt as much blood as they pleased in settling their affairs, and shall we deny that to Mexico because she is weak? No, I say! I am proud to belong to a strong nation that says, "This country which we could crush shall have just as much freedom in her own affairs as we have." If I am strong, I am ashamed to bully the weak. In proportion to my strength is my pride in withholding that strength from the oppression of another people. And I know when I speak these things, not merely from the generous response with which they have just met from you, but from my long-time knowledge of the American people, that that is the sentiment of this great people. With all due respect to editors of great newspapers, I have to say to them that I seldom take my opinion of the American people from their editorials. When some great dailies not very far from where I am temporarily residing thundered with rising scorn at watchful waiting, my confidence was not for a moment shaken. I knew what were the temper and prin- ciples of the American people. If I did not at least think I knew, I would emigrate, because I would not be satisfied to stay where I am. There may come a time when the American people will have to judge whether I know what I am talking about or not, but at least for two years more I am free to think that I do, with a great comfort in immunity in the time being.

It is, by the way, a very comforting thought that the next Con- gress of the United States is going to be very safely Democratic and that, therefore, we can all together feel as much confidence as Jack- son did that we know what we are about. You know Jackson used to think that everybody who disagreed with him was an enemy of the country. I have never got quite that far in my thought, but I have ventured to think that they did not know what they were talking about, knowing that my fellow Democrats expected me to live up to the full stature of Jacksonian Democracy.

I feel, my friends, in a very confident mood to-day. I feel con- fident that we do know the spirit of the American people, that we do know the program of betterment which it will be necessary for us to undertake, that we do have a very reasonable confidence in the support of the American people. I have been talking with busi- ness men recently about the present state of mind of American busi- ness. There is nothing the matter with American business except a state of mind. I understand that your chamber of commerce here in Indianapolis is working now upon the motto, "If you are going to buy it, buy it now." That is a perfectly safe maxim to act on. It is just as safe to buy it now as it ever will be, and if you start the buying there will be no end to it, and you will be a seller as well as a buyer. I am just as sure of that as I can be, because I have taken counsel with the men who know. I never was in business and, therefore, I have none of the prejudices of business. I have looked on and tried to see what the interests of the country were in business; I have taken counsel with men who did know, and their counsel is uniform, that all that is needed in America now is to believe in the future; and I can assure you as one of those who speak for the Democratic party that it is perfectly safe to believe in the future. We are so much the friends of business that we were for a little time the enemies of those who were trying to control business. I say "for a little time" because we are now reconciled to them. They have graciously ad- mitted that we had a right to do what we did do, and they have very handsomely said that they were going to play the game.

I believe—I always have believed—that American business men were absolutely sound at heart, but men immersed in business do a lot of things that opportunity offers which in other circumstances they would not do; and I have thought all along that all that was necessary to do was to call their attention sharply to the kind of reforms in business which were needed and that they would acquiesce. Why, I believe they have heartily acquiesced. There is all the more reason, therefore, that, great and small, we should be confident in the future.

And what a future it is, my friends! Look abroad upon the troubled world! Only America at peace! Among all the great powers of the world only America saving her power for her own people! Only America using her great character and her great strength in the interests of peace and of prosperity! Do you not think it likely that the world will some time turn to America and say, "You were right and we were wrong. You kept your head when we lost ours. You tried to keep the scale from tipping, and we threw the whole weight of arms in one side of the scale. Now, in your self-possession, in your coolness, in your strength, may we not turn to you for counsel and for assistance?" Think of the deep-wrought destruction of economic resources, of life, and of hope that is taking place in some parts of the world, and think of the reservoir of hope, the reservoir of energy, the reservoir of sustenance that there is in this great land of plenty! May we not look forward to the time when we shall be called blessed among the nations, because we succored the nations of the world in their time of distress and of dismay? I for one pray God that that solemn hour may come, and I know the solidity of character and I know the exaltation of hope, I know the big principle with which the American people will respond to the call of the world for this service. I thank God that those who believe in America, who try to serve her people, are likely to be also what America herself from the first hoped and meant to be—the servant of mankind.

[Before the United States Chamber of Commerce at the New Willard, Washington, D. C., February 3, 1915.]

MR. PRESIDENT, LADIES AND GENTLEMEN: I feel that it is hardly fair to you for me to come in this casual fashion among a body of men who have been seriously discussing great questions, and it is hardly fair to me, because I come in cold, not having had the advantage of sharing the atmosphere of your deliberations and catching the feeling of your conference. Moreover, I hardly know just how to express my interest in the things you are undertaking. When a man stands outside an organization and speaks to it he is too apt to have the tone of outside commendation, as who should say, "I would desire to pat you on the back and say 'Good boys; you are doing well!'" I would a great deal rather have you receive me as if for the time being I were one of your own number.

The longer I occupy the office that I now occupy the more I regret any lines of separation; the more I deplore any feeling that one set of men has one set of interests and another set of men another set of interests; the more I feel the solidarity of the Nation—the impossibility of separating one interest from another without misconceiving it; the necessity that we should all understand one another, in order that we may understand ourselves.

There is an illustration which I have used a great many times. I will use it again, because it is the most serviceable to my own mind. We often speak of a man who can not find his way in some jungle or some desert as having "lost himself." Did you never reflect that that is the only thing he has not lost? *He* is *there*. He has lost the rest of the world. He has no fixed point by which to steer. He does not know which is north, which is south, which is east, which is west; and if he did know, he is so confused that he would not know in which of those directions his goal lay. Therefore, following his heart, he walks in a great circle from right to left and comes back to where he started—to himself again. To my mind that is a picture of the world. If you have lost sight of other interests and do not know the relation of your own interests to those other interests, then you do not understand your own interests, and have lost yourself. What you want is orientation, relationship to the points of the compass; relationship to the other people in the world; vital connections which you have for the time being severed.

I am particularly glad to express my admiration for the kind of organization which you have drawn together. I have attended banquets of chambers of commerce in various parts of the country and have got the impression at each of those banquets that there was only one city in the country. It has seemed to me that those associations were meant in order to destroy men's perspective, in order to destroy their sense of relative proportions. Worst of all, if I may be permitted to say so, they were intended to boost something in particular. Boosting is a very unhandsome thing. Advancing enterprise is a very handsome thing, but to exaggerate local merits in order to create disproportion in the general development is not a particularly handsome thing or a particularly intelligent thing. A city can not grow on the face of a great state like a mushroom on that one spot. Its roots are throughout the state, and unless the state it is in, or the region it draws from, can itself thrive and pulse with life as a whole, the city can have no healthy growth. You forget the wide rootages of everything when you boost some particular region. There are dangers which probably you all understand in the mere practice of advertisement. When a man begins to advertise himself there are certain points that are somewhat exaggerated, and I have noticed that men who exaggerate most, most quickly lose any proper conception of what their own proportions are. Therefore, these local centers of enthusiasm may be local centers of mistake if they are not very wisely guided and if they do not themselves realize their relations to the other centers of enthusiasm and of advancement.

The advantage about a Chamber of Commerce of the United States is that there is only one way to boost the United States, and that is by seeing to it that the conditions under which business is done throughout the whole country are the best possible conditions. There can not be any disproportion about that. If you draw your sap and your vitality from all quarters, then the more sap and vitality there is in you the more there is in the commonwealth as a whole, and every time you lift at all you lift the whole level of manufacturing and mercantile enterprise. Moreover, the advantage of it is that you can not boost the United States in that way without understanding the United States. You learn a great deal. I agreed with a colleague of mine in the Cabinet the other day that we had never attended in our lives before a school to compare with that we were now attending for the purpose of gaining a liberal education.

Of course, I learn a great many things that are not so, but the interesting thing about that is this: Things that are not so do not match. If you hear enough of them, you see there is no pattern whatever; it is a crazy quilt. Whereas, the truth always matches, piece by piece, with other parts of the truth. No man can lie consistently, and he can not lie about everything if he talks to you long. I would guarantee that if enough liars talked to you, you would get the truth; because the parts that they did not invent would match one another, and the parts that they did invent would *not* match one another. Talk long enough, therefore, and see the connections clearly enough, and you can patch together the case as a whole. I had somewhat that experience about Mexico, and that was about the only way in which I learned anything that was true about it. For there had been vivid imaginations and many special interests which depicted things as they wished me to believe them to be.

Seriously, the task of this body is to match all the facts of business throughout the country and to see the vast and consistent pattern of it. That is the reason I think you are to be congratulated upon the fact that you can not do this thing without common counsel. There isn't any man who knows enough to comprehend the United States. It is a cooperative effort, necessarily. You can not perform the functions of this Chamber of Commerce without drawing in not only a vast number of men, but men, and a number of men, from every region and section of the country. The minute this association falls into the hands, if it ever should, of men from a single section or men with a single set of interests most at heart, it will go to seed and die. Its strength must come from the uttermost parts of the land and must be compounded of brains and comprehensions of every sort. It is a very noble and handsome picture for the imagination, and I have asked myself before I came here to-day, what relation you could bear to the Government of the United States and what relation the Government could bear to you?

There are two aspects and activities of the Government with which you will naturally come into most direct contact. The first is the Government's power of inquiry, systematic and disinterested inquiry, and its power of scientific assistance. You get an illustration of the latter, for example, in the Department of Agriculture. Has it occurred to you, I wonder, that we are just upon the eve of a time when our Department of Agriculture will be of infinite importance to the whole world? There is a shortage of food in the world now. That shortage will be much more serious a few months from now than it is now. It is necessary that we should plant a great deal more; it is necessary that our lands should yield more per acre than they do now; it is necessary that there should not be a plow or a spade idle in this country if the world is to be fed. And the methods of our farmers must feed upon the scientific information to be derived from the State departments of agriculture, and from that taproot of all, the United States Department of Agriculture. The object and use of that department is to inform men of the latest developments and disclosures of science with regard to all the processes by which soils can be put to their proper use and their fertility made the greatest possible. Similarly with the Bureau of Standards. It is ready to supply those things by which you can set norms, you can set bases, for all the scientific processes of business.

I have a great admiration for the scientific parts of the Government of the United States, and it has amazed me that so few men have discovered them. Here in these departments are quiet men, trained to the highest degree of skill, serving for a petty remuneration along lines that are infinitely useful to mankind; and yet in some cases they waited to be discovered until this Chamber of Commerce of the United States was established. Coming to this city, officers of that association found that there were here things that were infinitely useful to them and with which the whole United States ought to be put into communication.

The Government of the United States is very properly a great instrumentality of inquiry and information. One thing we are just beginning to do that we ought to have done long ago: We ought long ago to have had our Bureau of Foreign and Domestic Commerce. We ought long ago to have sent the best eyes of the Government out into the world to see where the opportunities and openings of American commerce and American genius were to be found—men who were not sent out as the commercial agents of any particular set of business men in the United States, but who were eyes for the whole business community. I have been reading consular reports for 20 years. In what I came to regard as an evil day the Congressman from my district began to send me the consular reports, and they ate up more and more of my time. They are very interesting, but they are a good deal like what the old lady said of the dictionary, that it was very interesting but a little disconnected. You get a picture of the world as if a spot light were being dotted about over the surface of it. Here you see a glimpse of this, and here you see a glimpse of that, and through the medium of some consuls you do not see anything at all. Because the consul has to have eyes and the consul has to know what he is looking for. A literary friend of mine said that he used to believe in the maxim that "everything comes to the man who waits," but he discovered after awhile by practical experience that it needed an additional clause, "provided he knows what he is waiting for." Unless you know what you are looking for and have trained eyes to see it when it comes your way, it may pass you unnoticed. We are just beginning to do, systematically and scientifically, what we ought long ago to have done, to employ the Government of the United States to survey the world in order that the American commerce might be guided.

But there are other ways of using the Government of the United States, ways that have long been tried, though not always with conspicuous success or fortunate results. You can use the Government of the United States by influencing its legislation. That has been a very active industry, but it has not always been managed in the interest of the whole people. It is very instructive and useful for the Government of the United States to have such means as you are ready to supply for getting a sort of consensus of opinion which proceeds from no particular quarter and originates with no particular interest. Information is the very foundation of all right action in legislation.

I remember once, a good many years ago, I was attending one of the local chambers of commerce of the United States at a time when everybody was complaining that Congress was interfering with business. If you have heard that complaint recently and supposed that it was original with the man who made it, you have not lived as long as I have. It has been going on ever since I can remember. The complaint came most vigorously from men who were interested in large corporate development. I took the liberty to say to that body of men, whom I did not know, that I took it for granted that there were a great many lawyers among them, and that it was likely that the more prominent of those lawyers were the intimate advisors of the corporations of that region. I said that I had met a great many lawyers from whom the complaint had come most vigorously, not only that there was too much legislation with regard to corporations, but that it was ignorant legislation. I said, "Now, the responsibility is with you. If the legislation is mistaken, you are on the inside and know where the mistakes are being made. You know not only the innocent and right things that your corporations are doing, but you know the other things, too. Knowing how they are done, you can be expert advisors as to how the wrong things can be prevented. If, therefore, this thing is handled ignorantly, there is nobody to blame but yourselves." If we on the outside can not understand the thing and can not get advice from the inside, then we will have to do it with the flat hand and not with the touch of skill and discrimination. Isn't that true? Men on the inside of business know how business is conducted and they can not complain if men on the outside make mistakes about business if they do not come from the inside and give the kind of advice which is necessary.

The trouble has been that when they came in the past—for I think the thing is changing very rapidly—they came with all their bristles out; they came on the defensive; they came to see, not what they could accomplish, but what they could prevent. They did not come to guide; they came to block. That is of no use whatever to the general body politic. What has got to pervade us like a great motive power is that we can not, and must not, separate our interests from one another, but must pool our interests. A man who is trying to fight for his single hand is fighting against the community and not fighting with it. There are a great many dreadful things about war, as nobody needs to be told in this day of distress and of terror, but there is one thing about war which has a very splendid side, and that is the consciousness that a whole nation gets that they must all act as a unit for a common end. And when peace is as handsome as war there will be no war. When men, I mean, engage in the pursuits of peace in the same spirit of self-sacrifice and of conscious service of the community with which, at any rate, the common soldier engages in war, then shall there be wars no more. You have moved the vanguard for the United States in the purposes of this association just a little nearer that ideal. That is the reason I am here, because I believe it.

There is no specific matter about which I, for one, want your advice. Let me say, if I may say it without disrespect, that I do not think you are prepared to give it right away. You will have to make some rather extended inquiries before you are ready to give it. What I am thinking of is competition in foreign markets as between the merchants of different nations.

I speak of the subject with a certain degree of hesitation, because the thing farthest from my thought is taking advantage of nations now disabled from playing their full part in that competition, and seeking a sudden selfish advantage because they are for the time being disabled. Pray believe me that we ought to eliminate all that thought from our minds and consider this matter as if we and the other nations now at war were in the normal circumstances of commerce.

There is a normal circumstance of commerce in which we are apparently at a disadvantage. Our anti-trust laws are thought by some to make it illegal for merchants in the United States to form combinations for the purpose of strengthening themselves in taking advantage of the opportunities of foreign trade. That is a very serious matter for this reason: There are some corporations, and some firms for all I know, whose business is great enough and whose resources are abundant enough to enable them to establish selling agencies in foreign countries; to enable them to extend the long credits which in some cases are necessary in order to keep the trade they desire; to enable them, in other words, to organize their business in foreign territory in a way which the smaller man can not afford to do. His business has not grown big enough to permit him to establish selling agencies. The export commission merchant, perhaps, taxes him a little too highly to make that an available competitive means of conducting and extending his business.

The question arises, therefore, how are the smaller merchants, how are the younger and weaker corporations going to get a foothold as against the combinations which are permitted and even encouraged by foreign governments in this field of competition? There are governments which, as you know, distinctly encourage the formation of great combinations in each particular field of commerce in order to maintain selling agencies and to extend long credits, and to use and maintain the machinery which is necessary for the extension of business; and American merchants feel that they are at a very considerable disadvantage in contending against that. The matter has been many times brought to my attention, and I have each time suspended judgment. I want to be shown this: I want to be shown how such a combination can be made and conducted in a way which will not close it against the use of everybody who wants to use it. A combination has a tendency to exclude new members. When a group of men get control of a good thing, they do not see any particular point in letting other people into the good thing. What I would like very much to be shown, therefore, is a method of cooperation which is not a method of combination. Not that the two words are mutually exclusive, but we have come to have a special meaning attached to the word "combination." Most of our combinations have a safety lock, and you have to know the combination to get in. I want to know how these cooperative methods can be adopted for the benefit of everybody who wants to use them, and I say frankly if I can be shown that, I am for them. If I can not be shown that, I am against them. I hasten to add that I hopefully expect I *can* be shown that.

You, as I have just now intimated, probably can not show it to me off-hand, but by the methods which you have the means of using you certainly ought to be able to throw a vast deal of light on the subject. Because the minute you ask the small merchant, the small banker, the country man, how he looks upon these things and how he thinks they ought to be arranged in order that he can use them, if he is like some of the men in country districts whom I know, he will turn out to have had a good deal of thought upon that subject and to be able to make some very interesting suggestions whose intelligence and comprehensiveness will surprise some city gentlemen who think that only the cities understand the business of the country. As a matter of fact, you do not have time to think in a city. It takes time to think. You can get what you call opinions by contagion in a city and get them very quickly, but you do not always know where the germ came from. And you have no scientific laboratory method by which to determine whether it is a good germ or a bad germ.

There are thinking spaces in this country, and some of the thinking done is very solid thinking indeed, the thinking of the sort of men that we all love best, who think for themselves, who do not see things as they are told to see them, but look at them and see them independently; who, if they are told they are white when they are black, plainly say that they are black—men with eyes and with a courage back of those eyes to tell what they see. The country is full of those men. They have been singularly reticent sometimes, singularly silent, but the country is full of them. And what I rejoice in is that you have called them into the ranks. For your methods are bound to be democratic in spite of you. I do not mean democratic with a big "D," though I have a private conviction that you can not be democratic with a small "d" long without becoming democratic with a big "D." Still that is just between ourselves. The point is that when we have a *consensus* of opinion, when we have this common counsel, then the legislative processes of this Government will be infinitely illuminated.

I used to wonder when I was Governor of one of the States of this great country where all the bills came from. Some of them had a very private complexion. I found upon inquiry—it was easy to find—that practically nine-tenths of the bills that were introduced had been handed to the members who introduced them by some constituent of theirs, had been drawn up by some lawyer whom they might or might not know, and were intended to do something that would be beneficial to a particular set of persons. I do not mean, necessarily, beneficial in a way that would be hurtful to the rest; they may have been perfectly honest, but they came out of cubby-holes all over the State. They did not come out of public places where men had got together and compared views. They were not the products of common counsel, but the products of private counsel, a very necessary process if there is no other, but a process which it would be a very happy thing to dispense with if we could get another. And the only other process is the process of common counsel.

Some of the happiest experiences of my life have been like this. We had once when I was president of a university to revise the whole course of study. Courses of study are chronically in need of revision. A committee of, I believe, 14 men was directed by the faculty of the university to report a revised curriculum. Naturally, the men who had the most ideas on the subject were picked out and, naturally, each man came with a very definite notion of the kind of revision he wanted, and one of the first discoveries we made was that no two of us wanted exactly the same revision. I went in there with all my war paint on to get the revision I wanted, and I dare say, though it was perhaps more skillfully concealed, the other men had their war paint on, too. We discussed the matter for six months. The result was a report which no one of us had conceived or foreseen, but with which we were all absolutely satisfied. There was not a man who had not learned in that committee more than he had ever known before about the subject, and who had not willingly revised his prepossessions; who was not proud to be a participant in a genuine piece of common counsel. I have had several experiences of that sort, and it has led me, whenever I confer, to hold my particular opinion provisionally, as my contribution to go into the final result but not to dominate the final result.

That is the ideal of a government like ours, and an interesting thing is that if you only talk about an idea that will not work long enough, everybody will see perfectly plainly that it will not work; whereas, if you do not talk about it, and do not have a great many people talk about it, you are in danger of having the people who handle it think that it will work. Many minds are necessary to compound a workable method of life in a various and populous country; and as I think about the whole thing and picture the purposes, the infinitely difficult and complex purposes which we must conceive and carry out, not only does it minister to my own modesty, I hope, of opinion, but it also fills me with a very great enthusiasm. It is a splendid thing to be part of a great wide-awake Nation. It is a splendid thing to know that your strength is infinitely multiplied by the strength of other men who love the country as you do. It is a splendid thing to feel that the wholesome blood of a great country can be united in common purposes, and that by frankly looking one another in the face and taking counsel with one another, prejudices will drop away, handsome understandings will arise, a universal spirit of service will be engendered, and that with this increased sense of community of purpose will come a vastly enhanced individual power of achievement; for we will be lifted by the whole mass of which we constitute a part.

Have you never heard a great chorus of trained voices lift the voice of the prima donna as if it soared with easy grace above the whole melodious sound? It does not seem to come from the single throat that produces it. It seems as if it were the perfect accent and crown of the great chorus. So it ought to be with the statesman. So it ought to be with every man who tries to guide the counsels of a great nation. He should feel that his voice is lifted upon the chorus and that it is only the crown of the common theme.

VETO MESSAGE

[Returning to the House of Representatives, without Approval an Act to Regulate the Immigration and Residence of Aliens in the United States.]

THE WHITE HOUSE, *January 28, 1915.*

To THE HOUSE OF REPRESENTATIVES:

It is with unaffected regret that I find myself constrained by clear conviction to return this bill (H. R. 6060, "An act to regulate the immigration of aliens to and the residence of aliens in the United States") without my signature. Not only do I feel it to be a very serious matter to exercise the power of veto in any case, because it involves opposing the single judgment of the President to the judgment of the majority of both the Houses of the Congress, a step which no man who realizes his own liability to error can take without great hesitation, but also because this particular bill is in so many important respects admirable, well conceived, and desirable. Its enactment into law would undoubtedly enhance the efficiency and improve the methods of handling the important branch of the public service to which it relates. But candor and a sense of duty with regard to the responsibility so clearly imposed upon me by the Constitution in matters of legislation leave me no choice but to dissent..

In two particulars of vital consequence this bill embodies a radical departure from the traditional and long-established policy of this country, a policy in which our people have conceived the very character of their Government to be expressed, the very mission and spirit of the Nation in respect of its relations to the peoples of the world outside their borders. It seeks to all but close entirely the gates of asylum which have always been open to those who could find nowhere else the right and opportunity of constitutional agitation for what they conceived to be the natural and inalienable rights of men; and it excludes those to whom the opportunities of elementary education have been denied, without regard to their character, their purposes, or their natural capacity.

Restrictions like these, adopted earlier in our history as a Nation, would very materially have altered the course and cooled the humane ardors of our politics. The right of political asylum has brought to this country many a man of noble character and elevated purpose who was marked as an outlaw in his own less fortunate land, and who has yet become an ornament to our citizenship and to our public councils. The children and the compatriots of these illustrious Americans must stand amazed to see the representatives of their Nation now resolved, in the fullness of our national strength and at the maturity of our great institutions, to risk turning such men back from our shores without test of quality or purpose. It is difficult for me to believe that the full effect of this feature of the bill was realized when it was framed and adopted, and it is impossible for me to assent to it in the form in which it is here cast.

The literacy test and the tests and restrictions which accompany it constitute an even more radical change in the policy of the Nation. Hitherto we have generously kept our doors open to all who were not unfitted by reason of disease or incapacity for self-support or such personal records and antecedents as were likely to make them a menace to our peace and order or to the wholesome and essential relationships of life. In this bill it is proposed to turn away from tests of character and of quality and impose tests which exclude and restrict; for the new tests here embodied are not tests of quality or of character or of personal fitness, but tests of opportunity. Those who come seeking opportunity are not to be admitted unless they have already had one of the chief of the opportunities they seek, the opportunity of education. The object of such provisions is restriction, not selection.

If the people of this country have made up their minds to limit the number of immigrants by arbitrary tests and so reverse the policy of all the generations of Americans that have gone before them, it is their right to do so. I am their servant and have no license to stand in their way. But I do not believe that they have. I respectfully submit that no one can quote their mandate to that effect. Has any political party ever avowed a policy of restriction in this fundamental matter, gone to the country on it, and been commissioned to control its legislation? Does this bill rest upon the conscious and universal assent and desire of the American people? I doubt it. It is because I doubt it that I make bold to dissent from it. I am willing to abide by the verdict, but not until it has been rendered. Let the platforms of parties speak out upon this policy and the people pronounce their wish. The matter is too fundamental to be settled otherwise.

I have no pride of opinion in this question. I am not foolish enough to profess to know the wishes and ideals of America better than the body of her chosen representatives know them. I only want instruction direct from those whose fortunes, with ours and all men's, are involved.   WOODROW WILSON.

PRINCIPAL LEGISLATION

OF THE

SIXTY-THIRD CONGRESS

The House of Representatives of the Sixty-third Congress, chosen coincident with the election of Woodrow Wilson to the Presidency, consisted of 435 members. Of these 291 were Democrats, 124 Republicans, and the remainder were classed as Independents, Progressives and Progressive Republicans. The Senate, of 96 members, 53 of whom were Democrats, was convened in special session at noon March 4, 1913, to confirm the executive appointments of the new President. (For the Cabinet see "Wilson" Encyclopedic Index.) By proclamation of March 17th, President Wilson called upon Congress to assemble April 7th for the purpose of revising the tariff law in accordance with the platform of the Democratic party.

In his opening message Mr. Wilson said (page 7872): "We must abolish everything that bears even the semblance of privilege or of any kind of artificial advantage, and put our business men and producers under the stimulation of a constant necessity to be efficient, economical, and enterprising—masters of competitive supremacy, better workers and merchants than any in the world. Aside from the duties laid upon articles which we do not, and probably can not, produce, therefore, and the duties laid upon luxuries and merely for the sake of the revenues they yield, the object of the tariff duties henceforth laid must be effective competition, the whetting of American wits by contest with the wits of the rest of the world."

The first act of importance was the Underwood Tariff Law, which also included the income and corporation tax provisions. (See Encyclopedic Index, "Tariff of 1913," "Income Tax" and "Corporation Tax.")

Besides enacting the tariff law and getting the currency bill well under way the first session passed the labor arbitration law, increased the number of midshipmen at the Naval Academy, provided for an ambassador to Spain, authorized military intervention in Mexico (page 7934); set apart through presidential proclamation the second Sunday in May as Mothers' Day (page 7941); provided for leasing the coal lands and building a railroad in Alaska and for the relief of the people of the territory, and the Commerce Court was abolished.

The Ministers to Argentina and Chile were promoted to ambassadors. The joint mission to Paraguay and Uruguay was made two separate ministries.

The Federal Reserve Banking and Currency Law was enacted. (See Currency Law.) Two separate laws were passed restricting the sale of opium.

The army enlistment law was improved and an aviation section was added.

American citizens imperilled in Mexico and in the European war zone were provided with means for returning home.

Exemption of American coastwise vessels from payment of tolls was stricken from Panama Canal Law. Foreign built ships were admitted to American registry and insured by the Government against war risks.

Cotton grades were standardized and trading in futures was penalized.

Anti-Trust Legislation.—The President's ideas of anti-monopoly laws were presumed to be legally embodied in the so-called "Seven Sisters" laws of New Jersey (*q.v.*), enacted while he was Governor of that State. Senator Newlands

(Nev.), Feb. 27, 1913, introduced a Democratic measure to create an interstate trade commission with the report of a committee on the amendment of the Sherman act. Two bills to prevent the concentration of corporate capital were introduced with the report of the Pujo committee, which had investigated the so-called Money Trust, and a flood of other bills on the same subject appeared, reflecting for the most part individual opinions.

Mr. Clayton, chairman of the Committee on Judiciary, undertook to compile the suggestions into legal form. For this purpose he prepared four measures which were submitted to the President and agreed to by him as comprehending his ideas of economic reform. These four, with the addition of the Adamson bill, to regulate the issuance of securities by common carriers, became known as the "Five Brothers." His first bill was nearly the same as the Newlands bill of the previous session, and proposed the transfer of the organization, powers and appropriations of the Bureau of Corporations to a Trade Commission of five, to be endowed with inquisitorial powers and to act in an advisory capacity to the Attorney-General in suits under the Sherman act. The second bill prohibited, after two years, interlocking directorates between corporations manufacturing railroad supplies, conducting banks or trust companies or mining or selling coal, and railroad or other corporations engaged in interstate business, and also between banks in the Federal Reserve System. The third Clayton bill specifically defined "contract," "combination in the form of trust or otherwise," "conspiracy in restraint of trade or commerce," and "monopolize," as used in the Sherman act. The fourth proposed new sections to the Sherman act prohibiting unfair competition by means of price discrimination, discounts, rebates, or exclusive agreements, and extended to individuals the right to bring suits in equity against corporations adjudged guilty in suits brought by the government. The fifth brother was the Adamson bill (later the Rayburn bill) to forbid interlocking directorates of common carriers, and extend the powers of the Interstate Commerce Commission to the regulation of the issue of stock and bonds of interstate common carriers.

The four Clayton bills were published immediately after the President's Message of Jan. 20, 1914. (See page 7913) The first introduced in Congress was referred to the Committee on Interstate and Foreign Commerce, and, after extended hearings and discussion, was abandoned in favor of the Covington bill, creating the Federal Trade Commission, which became law Sept. 26, 1914. (See Trade Commission.)

The second, third and fourth "brothers" were finally consolidated into a single measure known as the Clayton anti-trust bill. This was introduced in the House April 14, 1914, as an administration measure and, under insistence by the President, was finally passed Oct. 8th, and signed Oct. 15th.

The fifth "brother," then the Rayburn bill to regulate the issue of securities by interstate corporations was late in August postponed by consent of the President (page 8015, message of Dec. 8th). (See Clayton Anti-Trust Law.)

The Coast Guard was established by consolidating the Revenue Cutter Service and the Life Saving Service. Special war revenue taxes were levied.

Appropriations for the Navy aggregated $150,000,000 and provided for two battleships, six destroyers, two sea-going submarines, sixteen coast defense submarines, one fuel ship, and $1,000,000 for air craft.

The total number of bills introduced in the Senate and House during the three sessions of the Sixty-third Congress was 29,367. In the Senate 7,751 bills were introduced, 573 resolutions and 244 joint resolutions. In the House 21,616 bills were introduced, 751 resolutions, 439 joint resolutions, and 60 concurrent resolutions. About 350 of these various measures became law through the approval of the President.

By the President of the United States

A PROCLAMATION

[Opening of Lands in Standing Rock Indian Reservation.]

I, WOODROW WILSON, President of the United States of America, by virtue of the power and authority vested in me by the Act of Congress approved February 14, 1913 (37 Stat., 675), do hereby prescribe, proclaim and make known that all the non-mineral, unallotted and unreserved lands within the Standing Rock Indian Reservation, in the States of North and South Dakota, shall be disposed of under the general provisions of the homestead laws of the United States and the said Act of Congress, shall be opened to settlement and entry, and shall be settled upon, occupied and entered in the following manner, and not otherwise:

1. *Execution and Presentation of Applications.*—Any person who is qualified to make entry under the general provisions of the homestead laws may swear to and present an application to make homestead entry of these lands on or after May 3, 1915, or any such person who is entitled to the benefits of Sections 2304, 2305 and 2307, of the Revised Statutes of the United States, may file a declaratory statement for these lands on or after said date. Each application to make homestead entry and each declaratory statement filed in person must be sworn to by the applicant before the Register or the Receiver of the United States land office for the district in which the lands are situated, or before a United States Commissioner, or a judge or a clerk of a court of record residing in the county in which the land is situated, or before any such officer who resides outside the county and in the land district and is nearest or most accessible to the land. The agent's affidavit to each declaratory statement filed by agent must be sworn to by the agent before one of such officers on or after May 3, 1915, but the power of attorney appointing the agent may be sworn to by the declarant on or after April 1, 1915, before any officer in the United States having a seal and authority to administer oaths. After applications have been so sworn to, they must be presented to the Register and Receiver of the proper land office. Applicants may present the applications in person, by mail, or otherwise. No person shall be permitted to present more than one application in his own behalf.

2. *Purchase Money, Fees and Commissions.*—One-fifth of the purchase price of the land applied for must be paid at the time of entry and a sum equal thereto must be tendered with all applications to make homestead entry. Such sum will also be required with declaratory statements presented on or before May 17, 1915, and when so tendered will be disposed of as hereinafter provided. In addition, each application to make homestead entry must be accompanied by a fee of $5, if the area is 80 acres or less, or $10, if more than 80 acres, and commissions

at the rate of $.02½ for each acre applied for; and each declaratory statement must be accompanied by a fee of $2.

3. *Disposition of Applications.*—All homestead applications and declaratory statements received by the proper Register and Receiver on or after May 3, 1915, and on or before May 17, 1915, will be treated as filed simultaneously, and where there is no conflict such applications and statements, if in proper form and accompanied by the required payment, will be allowed on May 19, 1915. If such applications or statements conflict in whole or in part, the right of the respective applicants will be determined by public drawings, to be conducted by or under the supervision of the Superintendent of Openings and Sales of Indian Reservations. A drawing will be conducted for lands in North Dakota at the United States land office for the district in which the lands are situated, beginning at 10 o'clock, a. m., on May 19, 1915, and for lands in South Dakota at the United States land office for the district in which the lands are situated, beginning at 10 o'clock, a. m., on May 21, 1915. The names of the persons who presented the conflicting applications and statements will be written on cards and these cards shall be placed in envelopes upon which there are no distinctive or identifying marks. These envelopes shall be thoroughly and impartially mixed, and, after being mixed, shall be drawn one at a time by some disinterested person. As the envelopes are drawn the cards shall be removed, numbered beginning with number one, and fastened to the applications of the proper persons, which shall be the order in which the applications and statements shall be acted upon and disposed of. If homestead application or declaratory statement can not be allowed for any part of the land applied for, it shall be rejected. If it may be allowed for part of, but not for all, the land applied for, the applicant, or the declarant through his agent, shall be allowed thirty days from receipt of notice within which to notify the Register and Receiver what disposition to make thereof. During such time, he may request that the application or statement be allowed for the land not in conflict and rejected as to the land in conflict, or that it be rejected as to all the land applied for; or he may apply to have the application or statement amended to include other land which is subject to entry and to inclusion in his application or statement, provided he is the prior applicant. If it is determined by the drawing that a declaratory statement shall be acted upon and disposed of before a homestead application for the same land, the homestead applicant shall be allowed thirty days from receipt of notice within which to advise the Register and Receiver whether to allow or to reject the application. If an applicant, or a declarant or his agent, fails to notify the Register and Receiver within the time allowed what disposition to make of the application or statement, it will be rejected as to all the land applied for. Homestead applications and declaratory statements which are presented after May 17, 1915, will be received and noted in the order of

their filing, and will be acted upon and disposed of in the usual manner after all such applications and statements presented on or before that date have been acted upon and disposed of.

4. *Disposition of Moneys.*—Moneys tendered with applications and statements presented on or before May 17, 1915, except fees for filing declaratory statements, will be deposited by the Receiver of the proper land office to his official credit and properly accounted for. The fee for filing a declaratory statement must be paid even though the application is rejected, and such fee will be properly applied when the statement is filed. When a homestead application is allowed in whole or in part, the sums required as fees, commissions and purchase money will be properly applied, and any sum in excess of the required amount will be returned to the applicant. When a declaratory statement is allowed in whole or in part, the sum which will be required as purchase money if entry is made under the declaratory statement will be held until entry has been allowed under the statement or the time has expired within which entry may be made and any sum in excess of the required amount will be returned to the declarant. The moneys held will not be returned until the time has expired within which entry may be made under the statement but will be returned as soon as possible thereafter if entry is not made. Moneys tendered with applications and statements which are rejected in whole, except fees for filing declaratory statements, will be returned. If an applicant or declarant fails to secure all the land applied for and amends his application or statement to embrace other lands, the moneys theretofore tendered will be applied on account of the required payment under the amended application. If it is not sufficient, the applicant or declarant will be required to pay the deficiency, and if it is more than sufficient, the excess will be returned. Moneys returned to applicants or declarants will be returned by the official check of the Receiver of the proper United States land office. Moneys tendered with applications or statements presented after May 17, 1915, will be deposited by the Receiver of the proper land office in the usual manner.

5. *Price of Lands.*—Lands entered or filed upon prior to August 19, 1915, must be paid for at the rate of $5 per acre; those entered or filed upon on or after that date and prior to November 19, 1915, at the rate of $3.50 per acre; and those entered or filed upon on or after November 19, 1915, at the rate of $2.50 per acre. Should land be re-entered or re-filed upon, the price will be that fixed by the first entry or filing.

6. *Residence and Cultivation.*—The residence, cultivation and improvements which will be required in connection with entries of these lands will be the same as are required in connection with other lands entered under the general provisions of the homestead laws.

7. *Deferred Payments.*—The portion of the purchase price of the land which is not required when entry is made, may be paid in five

equal installments, the first within two years from the date of entry and the remainder annually in three, four, five and six years, respectively, thereafter, unless commutation proof is submitted. If commutation proof is submitted, final payment must be made at that time. If three-year proof is submitted, final payment may be made then or at any time thereafter before the payments become due in the annual installments. Neither final certificate nor patent will issue under a three-year proof until final payment of purchase money has been made.

8. *Forfeitures.*—If an entryman fails to make any payment when it becomes due, or fails to comply with the requirements as to residence, cultivation or improvement, his entry will be canceled and all payments theretofore made by him under the entry will be forfeited.

9. *Settlement in Advance of Entry.*—Claims may be initiated to these lands by settlement in advance of entry on and after November 19, 1915, and not before then.

10. *Rules and Regulations.*—The Secretary of the Interior is hereby authorized to make and prescribe such forms, rules and regulations as may be necessary to carry the provisions of this Proclamation into full force and effect.

In Witness Whereof I have hereunto set my hand and caused the seal of the United States to be affixed.

Done at the City of Washington this 18th day of March in the
[SEAL.]   year of our Lord nineteen hundred and fifteen and of the
independence of the United States the one hundred and
thirty-ninth.   WOODROW WILSON.
By the President:

W. J. BRYAN, *Secretary of State.*

EXECUTIVE ORDER.

[Changing the name of Culebra Cut to Gaillard Cut.]

THE WHITE HOUSE, *April 27, 1915.*

It is hereby ordered that the portion of the Panama Canal through the continental divide heretofore known as "Culebra Cut" shall hereafter be named "Gaillard Cut" in honor of the late Lieutenant-Colonel D. D. Gaillard, Corps of Engineers, United States Army.

As a member of the Isthmian Canal Commission from March 16, 1907, to December 5, 1913, Lieutenant-Colonel Gaillard was in charge of the work in Culebra Cut until its virtual completion, being compelled to abandon his duties in July, 1913, through an illness which culminated in his death on December 5, 1913. His period of Panama Canal service included the years of most active construction work. He brought to the service trained ability of the highest class, untiring zeal and unswerving devotion to duty.

I deem it a fitting recognition of Lieutenant-Colonel Gaillard's service to the country to re-name in his honor the scene of his life's triumph.   WOODROW WILSON.

ADDRESS

[At the Associated Press Luncheon, New York, N. Y., April 20, 1915.]

MR. PRESIDENT, GENTLEMEN OF THE ASSOCIATED PRESS, LADIES, AND GENTLEMEN: I am deeply gratified by the generous reception you have accorded me. It makes me look back with a touch of regret to former occasions when I have stood in this place and enjoyed a greater liberty than is granted me to-day. There have been times when I stood in this spot and said what I really thought, and I can not help praying that those days of indulgence may be accorded me again. I have come here to-day, of course, somewhat restrained by a sense of responsibility which I can not escape. For I take the Associated Press very seriously. I know the enormous part that you play in the affairs not only of this country but of the world. You deal in the raw material of opinion and, if my convictions have any validity, opinion ultimately governs the world.

It is, therefore, of very serious things that I think as I face this body of men. I do not think of you, however, as members of the Associated Press. I do not think of you as men of different parties or of different racial derivations or of different religious denominations. I want to talk to you as to my fellow citizens of the United States, for there are serious things which as fellow citizens we ought to consider. The times behind us, gentlemen, have been difficult enough; the times before us are likely to be more difficult still, because, whatever may be said about the present condition of the world's affairs, it is clear that they are drawing rapidly to a climax, and at the climax the test will come, not only for the nations engaged in the present colossal struggle—it will come to them, of course—but the test will come for us particularly.

Do you realize that, roughly speaking, we are the only great Nation at present disengaged? I am not speaking, of course, with disparagement of the greatness of those nations in Europe which are not parties to the present war, but I am thinking of their close neighborhood to it. I am thinking how their lives much more than ours touch the very heart and stuff of the business, whereas we have rolling between us and those bitter days across the water 3,000 miles of cool and silent ocean. Our atmosphere is not yet charged with those disturbing elements which must permeate every nation of Europe. Therefore, is it not likely that the nations of the world will some day turn to us for the cooler assessment of the elements engaged? I am not now thinking so preposterous a thought as that we should sit in judgment upon them—no nation is fit to sit in judgment upon any other nation—but that we shall some day have to assist in reconstructing the processes of peace. Our resources are untouched; we are more and more becoming by the force of circumstances the mediating Nation of the world in respect of its finance. We must make up our minds what are the best things to do and what are the best ways to do them. We must put our money, our energy, our enthusiasm, our sympathy into these things, and we must have our judgments prepared and our spirits chastened against the coming of that day.

So that I am not speaking in a selfish spirit when I say that our whole duty, for the present at any rate, is summed up in this motto, "America first." Let us think of America before we think of Europe, in order that America may be fit to be Europe's friend when the day of tested friendship comes. The test of friendship is not now sympathy with the one side or the other, but getting ready to help both sides when the struggle is over. The basis of neutrality, gentlemen, is not indifference; it is not self-interest. The basis of neutrality is sympathy for mankind. It is fairness, it is good will, at bottom. It is impartiality of spirit and of judgment. I wish that all of our fellow citizens could realize that. There is in some quarters a disposition to create distempers in this body politic. Men are even uttering slanders against the United States, as if to excite her. Men are saying that if we should go to war upon either side there would be a divided America—an abominable libel of ignorance! America is not all of it vocal just now. It is vocal in spots, but I, for one, have a complete and abiding faith in that great silent body of Americans who are not standing up and shouting and expressing their opinions just now, but are waiting to find out and support the duty of America. I am just as sure of their solidity and of their loyalty and of their unanimity, if we act justly, as I am that the history of this country has at every crisis and turning point illustrated this great lesson.

We are the mediating Nation of the world. I do not mean that we undertake not to mind our own business and to mediate where other people are quarreling. I mean the word in a broader sense. We are compounded of the nations of the world; we mediate their blood, we mediate their traditions, we mediate their sentiments, their tastes, their passions; we are ourselves compounded of those things. We are, therefore, able to understand all nations; we are able to understand them in the compound, not separately, as partisans, but unitedly as knowing and comprehending and embodying them all. It is in that sense that I mean that America is a mediating Nation. The opinion of America, the action of America, is ready to turn, and free to turn, in any direction. Did you ever reflect upon how almost every other nation has through long centuries been headed in one direction? That is not true of the United States. The United States has no racial momentum. It has no history back of it which makes it run all its energies and all its ambitions in one particular direction. And America is particularly free in this, that she has no hampering ambitions as a world power. We do not want a foot of anybody's territory. If we have been obliged by circumstances, or have considered ourselves to be obliged by circumstances, in the past, to take territory which we otherwise would not have thought of taking, I believe I am right in saying that we have considered it our duty to administer that territory, not for ourselves but for the people living in it, and to put this burden upon our consciences—not to think that this thing is ours for our use, but to regard ourselves as trustees of the great business for those to whom it does really belong, trustees ready to hand it over to the cestui que trust at any time when the business seems to make that possible and feasible. That is what I mean by saying we have no hampering ambitions. We do not want anything that does not belong to us. Is not a nation in that position free to serve other nations, and is not a nation like that ready to form some part of the assessing opinion of the world?

My interest in the neutrality of the United States is not the petty desire to keep out of trouble. To judge by my experience, I have never been able to keep out of trouble. I have never looked for it, but I have always found it. I do not want to walk around trouble. If any man wants a scrap that is an interesting scrap and worth while, I am his man. I warn him that he is not going to draw me into the scrap for his advertisement, but if he is looking for trouble that is the trouble of men in general and I can help a little, why, then, I am in for it. But I am interested in neutrality because there is something so much greater to do than fight; there is a distinction waiting for this Nation that no nation has ever yet got. That is the distinction of absolute self-control and self-mastery. Whom do you admire most among your friends? The irritable man? The man out of whom you can get a "rise" without trying? The man who will fight at the drop of the hat, whether he knows what the hat is dropped for or not? Don't you admire and don't you fear, if you have to contest with him, the self-mastered man who watches you with calm eye and comes in only when you have carried the thing so far that you must be disposed of? That is the man you respect. That is the man who, you know, has at bottom a much more fundamental and terrible courage than the irritable, fighting man. Now, I covet for America this splendid courage of reserve moral force, and I wanted to point out to you gentlemen simply this:

There is news and news. There is what is called news from Turtle Bay that turns out to be falsehood, at any rate in what it is said to signify, but which, if you could get the Nation to believe it true, might disturb our equilibrium and our self-possession. We ought not to deal in stuff of that kind. We ought not to permit that sort of thing to use up the electrical energy of the wires, because its energy is malign, its energy is not of the truth, its energy is of mischief. It is possible to sift truth. I have known some things to go out on the wires as true when there was only one man or one group of men who could have told the originators of that report whether it was true or not, and they were not asked whether it was true or not for fear it might not be true. That sort of report ought not to go out over the wires. There is generally, if not always, somebody who knows whether the thing is so or not, and in these days, above all other days, we ought to take particular pains to resort to the one small group of men, or to the one man if there be but one, who knows whether those things are true or not. The world ought to know the truth; the world ought not at this period of unstable equilibrium to be disturbed by rumor, ought not to be disturbed by imaginative combinations of circumstances, or, rather, by circumstances stated in combination which do not belong in combination. You gentlemen, and gentlemen engaged like you, are holding the balances in your hand. This unstable equilibrium rests upon scales that are in your hands. For the food of opinion, as I began by saying, is the news of the day. I have known many a man to go off at a tangent on information that was not reliable. Indeed, that describes the majority of men. The world is held stable by the man who waits for the next day to find out whether the report was true or not.

We can not afford, therefore, to let the rumors of irresponsible persons and origins get into the atmosphere of the United States. We are trustees for what I venture to say is the greatest heritage that any nation ever had, the love of justice and righteousness and human liberty. For, fundamentally, those are the things to which America is addicted and to which she is devoted. There are groups of selfish men in the United States, there are coteries where sinister things are purposed, but the great heart of the American people is just as sound and true as it ever was. And it is a single heart; it is the heart of America. It is not a heart made up of sections selected out of other countries.

What I try to remind myself of every day when I am almost overcome by perplexities, what I try to remember, is what the people at home are thinking about. I try to put myself in the place of the man who does not know all the things that I know and ask myself what he would like the policy of this country to be. Not the talkative man, not the partisan man, not the man who remembers first that he is a Republican or a Democrat, or that his parents were German or English, but the man who remembers first that the whole destiny of modern affairs centers largely upon his being an American first of all. If I permitted myself to be a partisan in this present struggle, I would be unworthy to represent you. If I permitted myself to forget the people who are not partisans, I would be unworthy to be your spokesman. I am not sure that I am worthy to represent you, but I do claim this degree of worthiness—that before everything else I love America.

CORRESPONDENCE GROWING OUT OF THE EUROPEAN WAR OF 1914-17.

TEXT OF AMERICAN NOTES TO GERMANY AND ENGLAND ON THE SAFETY OF OUR SHIPS AND USE OF OUR FLAG

The full text of the United States Government's notes to Germany and Great Britain in regard to the safety of American ships in the war zone and the use of the American flag, together with the State Department's introductory announcements, are as follows:

To Germany.

February 10, 1915.

The Secretary of State has instructed Ambassador Gerard at Berlin to present to the German Government a note to the following effect:

The Government of the United States, having had its attention directed to the proclamation of the German Admiralty, issued on the 4th of February, that the waters surrounding Great Britain and Ireland, including the whole of the English Channel, are to be considered as comprised within the seat of war; that all enemy merchant vessels found in those waters after the 18th inst. will be destroyed, although it may not always be possible to save crews and passengers; and that neutral vessels expose themselves to danger within this zone of war because, in view of the misuse of neutral flags said to have been ordered by the British Government on the 31st of January and of the contingencies of maritime warfare, it may not be possible always to exempt neutral vessels from attacks intended to strike enemy ships, feels it to be its duty to call the attention of the Imperial German Government, with sincere respect and the most friendly sentiments, but very candidly and earnestly, to the very serious possibilities of the course of action apparently contemplated under that proclamation.

The Government of the United States views those possibilities with such grave concern that it feels it to be its privilege and, indeed, its duty, in the circumstances to request the Imperial German Government to consider before action is taken, the critical situation in respect of the relation between this country and Germany which might arise were the German naval forces, in carrying out the policy foreshadowed in the Admiralty's proclamation, to destroy any merchant vessel of the United States or cause the death of American citizens.

It is, of course, not necessary to remind the German Government that the sole right of a belligerent in dealing with neutral vessels on the high seas is limited to visit and search, unless a blockade is proclaimed and effectively maintained, which this Government does not understand to be proposed in this case. To declare or exercise a right to attack and destroy any vessel entering a prescribed area of the high seas without first certainly determining its belligerent nationality and the contraband character of its cargo would be an act so unprecedented in naval warfare that this Government is reluctant to believe that the Imperial Government of Germany in this case contemplates it as possible.

The suspicion that enemy ships are using neutral flags improperly can create no just presumption that all ships traversing a prescribed area are subject to the same suspicion. It is to determine exactly such questions that this Government understands the right of visit and search to have been recognized.

This Government has carefully noted the explanatory statement issued by the Imperial German Government at the same time with the proclamation of the German Admiralty, and takes this occasion to remind the Imperial German Government very respectfully that the Government of the United States is open to none of the criticisms for unneutral action to which the German Government believes the Governments of certain other neutral nations have laid themselves open; that the Government of the United States has not consented to or acquiesced in any measures which may have been taken by the other belligerent nations in the present war which operate to restrain neutral trade, but has, on the contrary, taken, in all such matters, a position which warrants it in holding those Governments responsible in the proper way for any untoward effects on American shipping which the accepted principles of international law do not justify; and that it, therefore, regards itself as free in the present instance to take with a clear conscience and upon accepted principles the position indicated in this note.

If the commanders of German vessels of war should act upon the presumption that the flag of the United States was not being used in good faith and should destroy on the high seas an American vessel or the lives of American citizens, it would be difficult for the Government of the United States to view the act in any other light than as an indefensible violation of neutral rights,· which it would be very hard, indeed, to reconcile with the friendly relations now happily subsisting between the two Governments.

If such a deplorable situation should arise, the Imperial German Government can readily appreciate that the Government of the United States would be constrained to hold the Imperial Government of Germany to a strict accountability for such acts of their naval authorities, and to take any steps it might be necessary to take to safeguard American lives and property and to secure to American citizens the full enjoyment of their acknowledged rights on the high seas.

The Government of the United States, in view of these considerations, which it urges with the greatest respect and with the sincere purpose of making sure that no misunderstandings may arise, and no circumstances occur, that might even cloud the intercourse of the two Governments, expresses the confident hope and expectation that the Imperial German Government can and will give assurance that American citizens and their vessels will not be molested by the naval forces of Germany otherwise than by visit and search, though their vessels may be traversing the sea area delimited in the proclamation of the German Admiralty.

It is stated for the information of the Imperial Government that representations have been made to his Britannic Majesty's Government in respect to the unwarranted use of the American flag for the protection of British ships.

To England.

February 10, 1915.

The Secretary of State has instructed Ambassador Page at London to present to the British Government a note to the following effect:

The Department has been advised of the declaration of the German Admiralty on February 4, indicating that the British Government had on January 31, explicitly authorized the use of neutral flags on British merchant vessels, presumably for the purpose of avoiding recognition by German naval forces. The Department's attention has also been directed to reports in the press that the Captain of the Lusitania, acting upon orders or information received from the British authorities, raised the American flag as his vessel approached the British coasts, in order to escape anticipated attacks by German submarines. Today's press reports also contain an alleged official statement of the Foreign Office defending the use of the flag of a neutral country by a belligerent vessel in order to escape capture or attack by an enemy.

Assuming that the foregoing reports are true, the Government of the United States, reserving for future consideration the legality and propriety of the deceptive use of the flag of a neutral power in any case for the purpose of avoiding capture, desires very respectfully to point out to his Britannic Majesty's Government the serious consequences which may result to American vessels and American citizens if this practice is continued.

The occasional use of the flag of a neutral or an enemy under the stress of immediate pursuit and to deceive an approaching enemy, which appears by the press reports to be represented as the precedent and justification used to support this action, seems to this Government a very different thing from an explicit sanction by a belligerent Government for its merchant ships generally to fly the flag of a neutral power within certain portions of the high seas, which are presumed to be frequented with hostile warships. The formal declaration of such a policy of general misuse of a neutral's flag jeopardizes the vessels of a neutral visiting those waters in a peculiar degree by raising the presumption that they are of belligerent nationality regardless of the flag which they may carry.

In view of the announced purpose of the German Admiralty to engage in active naval operations in certain delimited sea areas adjacent to the coasts of Great Britain and Ireland, the Government of the United States would view with anxious solicitude any general use of the flag of the United States by British vessels traversing those waters. A policy such as the one which his Majesty's Government is said to intend to adopt, would, if the declaration of the German Admiralty be put in force, it seems clear, afford no protection to British vessels, while it would be a serious and constant menace to the lives and vessels of American citizens.

The Government of the United States, therefore, trusts that his Majesty's Government will do all in their power to restrain vessels of British nationality in the deceptive use of the United States flag in the sea area defined by the German declaration, since such practice would greatly endanger the vessel of a friendly power navigating those waters and would even seem to impose upon the Government of Great Britain a measure of responsibility for the loss of American lives and vessels in case of an attack by a German naval force.

You will impress upon his Majesty's Government the grave concern which this Government feels in the circumstances in regard to the safety of American vessels and lives in the war zone declared by the German Admiralty.

You may add that this Government is making earnest representations to the German Government in regard to the danger to American vessels and citizens if the declaration of the German Admiralty is put into effect.

SUMMARY OF THE AMERICAN NOTE TO GREAT BRITAIN AND GERMANY AND MAIN POINTS OF GERMANY'S REPLY.

An American note to Great Britain and Germany expresses the hope that the belligerents may, by means of reciprocal concessions, discover a basis of understanding, the result of which would tend to free ships engaged in neutral and peaceful commerce from the serious dangers to which they are exposed in passing through the coastal waters of the belligerent countries.

This suggestion, the note proceeds to say, should not be considered as a proposal by the American Government, whom it naturally did not behoove to propose conditions for such an agreement, though the question at issue had a direct and far-reaching interest for the Government and people of the United States.

The note says the United States ventures solely to take a liberty which it is convinced can be conceded to a sincere friend who is actuated by a desire to cause inconvenience to neither of the two nations and possibly serve the common interests of humanity.

The suggestion is made that Germany and Great Britain should agree, first, that isolated drifting mines should be laid by neither party, that anchored mines should be laid exclusively for defensive purposes within gun range of harbors, and that all mines should bear the mark of the Government of origin, and be so constructed as to become harmless after breaking loose from their anchorages.

It is suggested, second, that the submarines of neither of the two Governments should be employed to attack merchant vessels of any nationality except for the purpose of carrying out the right of holding them up and searching them; and, third, that mercantile ships of neither of the parties should employ neutral flags as a war ruse or for the purpose of concealing their identity.

Great Britain, it is suggested, should agree that foodstuffs should not be placed on the list of absolute contraband, and that the British authorities should neither disturb nor hold up cargoes of such goods, when addressed to agencies in Germany, the names of which are communicated by the United States Government, for the purpose of receiving such goods and handing them over to licensed German retailers for further distribution exclusively to the civil population.

Germany, it is contended, should declare her agreement that foodstuffs from the United States, or any other neutral country, should be addressed to such agencies.

Finally, the American Government says it wishes to safeguard itself against the idea that it either acknowledges or repudiates any right on the part of the belligerents or neutrals established on the principles of international law. The American Government would rather regard such an agreement as a *modus vivendi*, which is based more on suitableness than on legal right.

The German Reply.

The German reply to the note of the United States was dispatched shortly after the receipt of the American note. It begins as follows:

The German Government has taken note of the American suggestion with lively interest, and sees therein new proof of friendly feelings, which are fully reciprocated by Germany. The suggestion corresponds also to the German wishes that the naval war should be waged according to rules which, without subjecting one or the other belligerent Power to one-sided restrictions of methods of warfare, would take into consideration the interests of neutrals as well as the laws of humanity.

In this sense, the German note of February 16 already has pointed out that the observance of the London Declaration by Germany's enemies would create a new situation, from which Germany would gladly be prepared to draw conclusions.

Starting from this conception, the German Government has submitted the American suggestion to attentive examination, and believes that it can recognize therein an effectively suitable basis for a practical solution of the questions at issue.

On particular suggestions contained in the American note the following remarks are made:

Germany would be prepared to make the suggested declaration concerning the non-employment of drifting mines and the construction of anchored mines, and further agrees with the suggestion to attach a Government mark to any mines which may be laid. On the other hand, it appears to Germany not to be practicable for the belligerent powers fully to renounce the employment of anchored mines for offensive purpose.

Second—German submarines would employ force against mercantile vessels of whatsoever flag, only in so far as it is required for the purpose of carrying out the right to hold up and search. If the hostile nationality of a ship or the presence of contraband were proved, the submarines would proceed according to the general international rules.

Third—As the American note provides for the above-mentioned restriction in the employment of submarines, it follows that enemy mercantile vessels should abstain from the use of neutral flags and other neutral signs. In this conclusion it is obvious that hostile mercantile vessels should not be armed, and should refrain from offering violent resistance, since such conduct, which is opposed to international law, renders it impossible for submarines to proceed in accordance with international law.

Fourth—The regulation of the legitimate importation of food supplies to Germany, as suggested by the American Government, appears in general to be acceptable. This regulation would, of course, be restricted to importation by sea; but on the other hand, it would also include indirect importation via neutral ports.

Germany would, therefore, be prepared to make declarations such as are provided for in the American note, so that the employment of imported food supplies would be guaranteed to be exclusively for the peaceful civil population.

In this connection Germany must, however, emphasize that the importation also of other raw materials for peaceful economic purposes, and including fodder, should be made possible. For this purpose the hostile Governments would have to allow free passage to Germany of raw materials mentioned in the free list of the London Declaration, and to treat in the same manner as foodstuffs those materials contained in the list of conditional contraband.

The note concludes as follows:

The German Government hopes that the understanding suggested by the American Government will, regard being paid to the foregoing remarks, be realized, and that thereby peaceful neutral shipping and peaceful neutral commerce will not have more to suffer than is absolutely necessary from the effects of the naval warfare.

Such effects, moreover, would be substantially diminished if, as already pointed out in our note of February 16, means and ways could be found to exclude the importation of war material from neutral to belligerent States on ships of whatsoever flag.

The adoption of a definite attitude must, of course, be postponed until the German Government, on the basis of further communication from the American Government, is in a position to see what obligations the British Government, on its side, is prepared to assume.

FULL TEXT OF IDENTIC NOTES SENT BY THE UNITED STATES
TO THE BRITISH AND FRENCH GOVERNMENTS PROTESTING
AGAINST THE INVASION OF NEUTRAL RIGHTS INVOLVED IN
A BRITISH ORDER IN COUNCIL ESTABLISHING A LONG-RANGE
BLOCKADE OF EUROPEAN WATERS.

Washington, March 30, 1915.

The Secretary of State to the American Ambassador at London:

You are instructed to deliver the following to his Majesty's Government in reply to your numbers 1,795 and 1,798 of March 15: The Government of the United States has given careful consideration to the subjects treated in the British notes of March 13 and March 15, and to the British Order in Council of the latter date.

These communications contain matters of grave importance to neutral nations. They appear to menace their rights of trade and intercourse, not only with belligerents but also with one another. They call for frank comment in order that misunderstandings may be avoided. The Government of the United States deems it its duty, therefore, speaking in the sincerest spirit of friendship, to make its own view and position with regard to them unmistakably clear.

The Order in Council of the 15th of March would constitute, were its provisions to be actually carried into effect as they stand, a practical assertion of unlimited belligerent rights over neutral commerce within the whole European area, and an almost unqualified denial of the sovereign rights of the nations now at peace.

The Government takes it for granted that there can be no question what those rights are. A nation's sovereignty over its own ships and citizens under its own flag on the high seas in time of peace is, of course, unlimited, and that sovereignty suffers no diminution in time of war, except in so far as the practice and consent of civilized nations has limited it, by the recognition of certain now clearly determined rights, which it is conceded may be exercised by nations which are at war.

A belligerent nation has been conceded the right of visit and search, and the right of capture and condemnation if upon examination a neutral vessel is found to be engaged in unneutral service or to be carrying contraband of war intended for the enemy's government or armed forces.

It has been conceded the right to establish and maintain a blockade of an enemy's ports and coasts, and to capture and condemn any vessel taken in trying to break the blockade. It is even conceded the right to detain and take to its own ports for judicial examination all vessels which it suspects for substantial reasons to be engaged in unneutral or contraband service and to condemn them if the suspicion is sustained. But such rights, long clearly defined both in doctrine and practice, have hitherto been held to be the only permissible exceptions to the principle of universal quality of sovereignty on the high seas as between belligerents and nations not engaged in war.

It is confidently assumed that his Majesty's Government will not deny that it is a rule sanctioned by general practice that, even though a blockade should exist and the doctrine of contraband as to unblockaded territory be rigidly enforced, innocent shipments may be freely transported to and from the United States through neutral countries to belligerent territory, without being subject to the penalties of contraband traffic or breach of blockade, much less to detention, requisition, or confiscation.

Moreover, the rules of the Declaration of Paris of 1856—among them that free ships make free goods—will hardly at this day be disputed by the signatories of that solemn agreement.

His Majesty's Government, like the Government of the United States, have often and explicitly held that these rights represent the best usage of warfare in the dealings of belligerents with neutrals at sea. In this connection I desire to direct attention to the opinion of the Chief Justice of the United States in the case of the Peterhof, which arose out of the Civil War, and to the fact that that opinion was unanimously sustained in the award of the Arbitration Commission of 1871, to which the case was presented at the request of Great Britain. From that time to the Declaration of London of 1909, adopted with modifications by the Order in Council of the 23d of October last, these rights have not been seriously questioned by the British Government. And no claim on the part of Great Britain of any justification for interfering with the clear rights of the United States and its citizens as neutrals could be admitted. To admit it would be to assume an attitude of unneutrality toward the present enemies of Great Britain, which would be obviously inconsistent with the solemn obligations of this Government in the present circumstances. And for Great Britain to make such a claim would be for her to abandon and set at naught the principles for which she has consistently and earnestly contended in other times and circumstances.

The note of his Majesty's principal Secretary of State for Foreign Affairs, which accompanies the Order in Council, and which bears the same date, notifies the Government of the United States of the establishment of a blockade which is, if defined by the terms of the Order in Council, to include all the coasts and ports of Germany and every port of possible access to enemy territory. But the novel and quite unprecedented feature of that blockade, if we are to assume it to be properly so defined, is that it embraces many neutral ports and coasts, bars access to them, and subjects all neutral ships seeking to approach them to the same suspicion that would attach to them were they bound for the ports of the enemies of Great Britain, and to unusual risks and penalties.

It is manifest that such limitations, risks, and liabilities placed upon the ships of a neutral power on the seas, beyond the right of visit and search and the right to prevent the shipment of contraband already referred to, are a distinct invasion of the sovereign rights of the nation whose ships, trade, or commerce is interfered with.

The Government of the United States is, of course, not oblivious to the great changes which have occurred in the conditions and means of naval warfare since the rules hitherto governing legal blockade were formulated. It might be ready to admit that the old form of "close" blockade, with its cordon of ships in the immediate offing of the blockaded ports is no longer practicable in the face of an enemy possessing the means and opportunity to make an effective defense by the use of submarines, mines and air craft; but it can hardly be maintained that, whatever form of effective blockade may be made use of, it is impossible to conform at least to the spirit and principles of the established rules of war.

If the necessities of the case should seem to render it imperative that the cordon of blockading vessels be extended across the approaches to any neighboring neutral port or country it would seem clear that it would still be easily practicable to comply with the well-recognized and reasonable prohibition of international law against the blockading of neutral ports, by according free admission and exit to all lawful traffic with neutral ports through the blockading cordon.

This traffic would, of course, include all outward-bound traffic from the neutral country and all inward-bound traffic to the neutral country, except contraband in transit to the enemy. Such procedure need not conflict in any respect with the rights of the belligerent maintaining the blockade, since the right would remain with the blockading vessels to visit and search all ships either entering or leaving the neutral territory which they were in fact, but not of right, investing.

The Government of the United States notes that in the Order in Council his Majesty's Government gives as their reason for entering upon a course of action, which they are aware is without precedent in modern warfare, the necessity they conceive themselves to have been placed under to retaliate upon their enemies for measures of a similar nature, which the latter have announced it their intention to adopt and which they have to some extent adopted, but the Government of the United States, recalling the principles upon which his Majesty's Government have hitherto been scrupulous to act, interprets this as merely a reason for certain extraordinary activities on the part of his Majesty's naval forces and not as an excuse for or prelude to any unlawful action.

If the course pursued by the present enemies of Great Britain should prove to be in fact tainted by illegality and disregard of the principles of war sanctioned by enlightened nations, it cannot be supposed, and this Government does not for a moment suppose, that his Majesty's Government would wish the same taint to attach to their own actions or would cite such illegal acts as in any sense or degree a justification for similar practices on their part in so far as they affect neutral rights.

It is thus that the Government of the United States interprets the language of the note of his Majesty's principal Secretary of State for Foreign Affairs,

THE LUSITANIA'S LAST VOYAGE

LAST TRIP OF THE LUSITANIA

The British steamship *Lusitania* of the Cunard Line, one of the largest ocean-going vessels in the world, and valued at $10,000,000, left New York May 1, 1915, for Liverpool, England. May 7th, when off Kinsale, Ireland, she was struck by a torpedo fired by a German undersea boat, which was patroling the war zone declared by Germany to exist around the British Isles.

Besides passengers and crew to the number of 2,159 persons aboard, she carried about 1,500 tons of cargo, valued at $735,579. The principal items of the cargo were for war consumption.

The vessel sank within fifteen minutes after being struck. Of the persons on board only 763 were rescued—462 passengers and 301 of the crew; the number injured was 30 passengers and 17 of crew; of the survivors 45 died from exposure or injuries. The number of Americans lost was 107—23 identified dead and 84 missing and undoubtedly dead.

The upper left panel of the illustration on the reverse page shows the *Lusitania* leaving New York harbor May 1, 1915. The upper right view shows the coffins of American victims of the disaster returning to New York. The lower panel shows the German submarine *U-1*, similar to that which sank the *Lusitania*, replenishing storage batteries by gasoline engine.

which accompanies the copy of the Order in Council, which was handed to the Ambassador of the United States by the Government in London and by him transmitted to Washington.

This Government notes with gratification that "wide discretion is afforded to the prize court in dealing with the trade of neutrals in such manner as may in the circumstances be deemed just, and that full provision is made to facilitate claims by persons interested in any goods placed in the custody of the marshal of the prize court under the order." That "the effect of the Order in Council is to confer certain powers upon executive officers of his Majesty's Government," and that "the extent to which these powers will be actually exercised, and the degree of severity with which the measure of blockade authorized will be put into operation, are matters which will depend on the administrative orders issued by the Government and the decisions of the authorities especially charged with the duty of dealing with individual ships and cargoes, according to the merits of each case."

The Government further notes with equal satisfaction the declaration of the British Government that "the instructions to be issued by his Majesty's Govern· ment to the fleet and to the customs officials and executive committees concerned will impress upon them the duty of acting with the utmost dispatch consistent with the object in view, and of showing in every case such consideration for neutrals as may be compatible with that object, which is succinctly stated, to establish a blockade to prevent vessels from carrying goods for or coming from Germany.

In view of these assurances formally given to this Government it is confidently expected that the extensive powers conferred by the Order in Council on the executive officers of the crown will be restricted by orders issued by the Government, directing the exercise of their discretionary powers in such a manner as to modify in practical application those provisions of the Order in Council which, if strictly enforced, would violate neutral rights and interrupt legitimate trade. Relying on the faithful performance of these voluntary assurances by his Majesty's Government, the United States takes it for granted that the approach of American merchantmen to neutral ports situated upon the long line of coast affected by the Order in Council will not be interfered with when it is known that they do not carry goods which are contraband of war, or goods destined to or proceeding from ports within the belligerent territory affected.

The Government of the United States assumes with the greater confidence that his Majesty's Government will thus adjust their practice to the recognized rules of international law, because it is manifest that the British Government have adopted an extraordinary method of "stopping cargoes destined for or coming from the enemy's territory," which, owing to the existence of unusual conditions in modern warfare at sea, it will be difficult to restrict to the limits which have been heretofore required by the law of nations. Though the area of operations is confined to "European waters including the Mediterranean," so great an area of the high seas is covered, and the cordon of ships is so distant from the territory affected that neutral vessels must necessarily pass through the blockading force in order to reach important neutral ports which Great Britain, as a belligerent, has not the legal right to blockade, and which, therefore, it is presumed she has no intention of claiming to blockade.

The Scandinavian and Danish ports, for example, are open to American trade. They are also free, so far as the actual enforcement of the Order in Council is concerned, to carry on trade with German Baltic ports, although it is an essential element of blockade that it bear with equal severity upon all neutrals.

This Government, therefore, infers that the commanders of his Majesty's ships of war, engaged in maintaining the so-called blockade, will be instructed to avoid an enforcement of the proposed measures of non-intercourse in such a way as to impose restrictions upon neutral trade more burdensome than those which have been regarded as inevitable, when the ports of a belligerent are actually blockaded by the ships of its enemy.

The possibilities of serious interruption of American trade under the Order in Council are so many, and the methods proposed are so unusual, and seem liable to constitute so great an impediment and embarrassment to neutral commerce, that the Government of the United States, if the Order in Council is strictly enforced, apprehends many interferences with its legitimate trade which will impose upon his Majesty's Government heavy responsibilities for acts of the British authorities clearly subversive of the rights of neutral nations on the high seas. It is, therefore, expected that his Majesty's Government, having considered these possibilities, will take the steps necessary to avoid them, and, in the event that they should unhappily occur, will be prepared to make full reparation for every act which under the rules of international law constitutes a violation of neutral rights.

As stated in its communication of Oct. 22, 1914, "this Government will insist that the rights and duties of the United States and its citizens in the present war be defined by the existing rules of international law and the treaties of the United States, irrespective of the provisions of the Declaration of London, and that this Government reserves to itself the right to enter a protest of demand in each case in which those rights and duties so defined are violated or their free exercise interfered with by the authorities of the British Government."

In conclusion, you will reiterate to his Majesty's Government that this statement of the view of the Government of the United States is made in the most friendly spirit, and in accordance with the uniform candor which has characterized the relations of the two Governments in the past, and which has been in large measure the foundation of the peace and amity existing between the two nations without interruption for a century.   BRYAN.

PRESIDENT WILSON'S NOTE TO GERMANY, FOLLOWING THE DESTRUCTION OF THE BRITISH STEAMSHIP LUSITANIA WITH LOSS OF AMERICAN LIVES.

DEPARTMENT OF STATE, Washington, May 13, 1915.

The Secretary of State to the American Ambassador at Berlin:

Please call on the Minister of Foreign Affairs and after reading to him this communication leave with him a copy.

In view of recent acts of the German authorities in violation of American rights on the high seas, which culminated in the torpedoing and sinking of the British steamship Lusitania on May 7, 1915, by which over 100 American citizens lost their lives, it is clearly wise and desirable that the Government of the United States and the Imperial German Government should come to a clear and full understanding as to the grave situation which has resulted.

The sinking of the British passenger steamer Falaba by a German submarine on March 28, through which Leon C. Thrasher, an American citizen, was drowned; the attack on April 28 on the American vessel Cushing by a German aeroplane; the torpedoing on May 1 of the American vessel Gulflight by a German submarine, as a result of which two or more American citizens met their death; and, finally, the torpedoing and sinking of the steamship Lusitania, constitute a series of events which the Government of the United States has observed with growing concern, distress, and amazement.

Recalling the humane and enlightened attitude hitherto assumed by the Imperial German Government in matters of international right, and particularly with regard to the freedom of the seas; having learned to recognize the German views and the German influence in the field of international obligation as always engaged upon the side of justice and humanity; and having understood the instructions of the Imperial German Government to its naval commanders to be upon the same plane of humane action prescribed by the naval codes of other nations, the Government of the United States was loath to believe — it cannot now bring itself to believe — that these acts, so absolutely contrary to the rules, the practices, and the spirit of modern warfare, could have the countenance or sanction of that great Government. It feels it to be its duty, therefore, to address the Imperial German Government concerning them with the utmost frankness and in the earnest hope that it is not mistaken in expecting action on the part of the Imperial German Government, which will correct the unfortunate impressions which have been created, and vindicate once more the position of that Government with regard to the sacred freedom of the seas.

The Government of the United States has been apprised that the Imperial German Government considered themselves to be obliged by the extraordinary circumstances of the present war and the measures adopted by their adversaries

in seeking to cut Germany off from all commerce, to adopt methods of retaliation which go much beyond the ordinary methods of warfare at sea, in the
proclamation of a war zone from which they have warned neutral ships to
keep away. This Government has already taken occasion to inform the Imperial
German Government that it cannot admit the adoption of such measures or
such a warning of danger to operate as in any degree an abbreviation of the
rights of American shipmasters or of American citizens bound on lawful
errands as passengers on merchant ships of belligerent nationality, and that
it must hold the Imperial German Government to a strict accountability for
any infringement of those rights, intentional or incidental. It does not understand the Imperial German Government to question those rights. It assumes,
on the contrary, that the Imperial Government accept, as of course, the
rule that the lives of non-combatants, whether they be of neutral citizenship or
citizens of one of the nations at war, cannot lawfuly or rightfully be put
in jeopardy by the capture or destruction of an unarmed merchantman, and
recognize also, as all other nations do, the obligation to take the usual precaution of visit and search to ascertain whether a suspected merchantman is in
fact of belligerent nationality or is in fact carrying contraband of war under
a neutral flag.

The Government of the United States, therefore, desires to call the attention of the Imperial German Government with the utmost earnestness to the
fact that the objection to their present method of attack against the trade of
their enemies lies in the practical impossibility of employing submarines in
the destruction of commerce without disregarding those rules of fairness,
reason, justice and humanity which all modern opinion regards as imperative.
It is practically impossible for the officers of a submarine to visit a merchantman at sea and examine her papers and cargo. It is practically impossible
for them to make a prize of her; and, if they cannot put a prize crew on board
of her, they cannot sink her without leaving her crew and all on board of
her to the mercy of the sea in her small boats. These facts it is understood
the Imperial German Government frankly admit. We are informed that in the
instances of which we have spoken time enough for even that poor measure of
safety was not given, and in at least two of the cases cited not so much as
a warning was received. Manifestly, submarines cannot be used against merchantmen, as the last few weeks have shown, without an inevitable violation
of many sacred principles of justice and humanity.

American citizens act within their indisputable rights in taking their ships
and in traveling wherever their legitimate business calls them upon the high seas,
and exercise those rights in what should be the well-justified confidence that
their lives will not be endangered by acts done in clear violation of universally
acknowledged international obligations, and certainly in the confidence of their
own Government will sustain them in the exercise of their rights.

There was recently published in the newspapers of the United States,
I regret to inform the Imperial German Government, a formal warning, purporting to come from the Imperial German Embassy at Washington, addressed
to the people of the United States, and stating, in effect, that any citizen of
the United States who exercised his right of free travel upon the seas would
do so at his peril if his journey should take him within the zone of waters
within which the Imperial German Navy was using submarines against the
commerce of Great Britain and France, notwithstanding the respectful but very
earnest protest of this Government, the Government of the United States. I do
not refer to this for the purpose of calling the attention of the Imperial German
Government at this time to the surprising irregularity of a communication
from the Imperial German Embassy at Washington addressed to the people
of the United States through the newspapers, but only for the purpose of
pointing out that no warning that an unlawful and inhumane act will be
committed can possibly be accepted as an excuse or palliation for that act
or as an abatement of the responsibility for its commission.

Long acquainted as this Government has been with the character of the
Imperial Government, and with the high principles of equity by which they
have in the past been actuated and guided, the Government of the United
States cannot believe that the commanders of the vessels which committed
these acts of lawlessness did so except under a misapprehension of the orders
issued by the Imperial German naval authorities. It takes it for granted
that, at least within the practical possibilities of every such case, the commanders even of submarines were expected to do nothing that would involve
the lives of non-combatants or the safety of neutral ships, even at the cost of

failing of their object of capture or destruction. It confidently expects, therefore, that the Imperial German Government will disavow the acts of which the Government of the United States complains; that they will make reparation so far as reparation is possible for injuries which are without measure, and that they will take immediate steps to prevent the recurrence of anything so obviously subversive of the principles of warfare for which the Imperial German Government have in the past so wisely and so firmly contended.

The Government and people of the United States look to the Imperial German Government for just, prompt, and enlightened action in this vital matter with the greater confidence, because the United States and Germany are bound together not only by special ties of friendship, but also by the explicit stipulations of the Treaty of 1828, between the United States and the Kingdom of Prussia.

Expressions of regret and offers of reparation in case of the destruction of neutral ships sunk by mistake, while they may satisfy international obligations, if no loss of life results, cannot justify or excuse a practice the natural and necessary effect of which is to subject neutral nations and neutral persons to new and immeasurable risks.

The Imperial German Government will not expect the Government of the United States to omit any word or any act necessary to the performance of its sacred duty of maintaining the rights of the United States and its citizens and of safeguarding their free exercise and enjoyment.   BRYAN.

PROCLAMATION

BY THE PRESIDENT OF THE UNITED STATES OF AMERICA

A PROCLAMATION

[Exposition to Commemorate the Achievements of the Negro Race During Fifty Years of Freedom.]

A national exposition in commemoration of the achievements of the negro race during the last fifty years will be held in Richmond, Virginia, July fifth to twenty-fifth, 1915. The occasion has been recognized as of national importance by Congress through an appropriation of $55,000 to aid in its promotion and consummation. This sum is being expended by the terms of the appropriation under the direction of the Governor of Virginia. The exposition is under the auspices of the Negro Historical and Industrial Association. The action of Congress in this matter indicates very happily the desire of the nation, as well as of the people of Virginia, to encourage the Negro in his efforts to solve his industrial problem. The National Negro Exposition is designed to demonstrate his progress in the last fifty years and to emphasize his opportunities. As President of the United States, I bespeak the active interest of the nation in the exposition and trust that every facility will be extended to the leaders whose earnest work has made the undertaking possible.

In witness whereof I have hereunto set my hand and caused the seal of the United States to be affixed.

Done at the city of Washington this first day of July in the year
          of our Lord one thousand nine hundred and fifteen and
[SEAL.] of the independence of the United States of America the
          one hundred and thirty-ninth.

By the President: WOODROW WILSON.

ROBERT LANSING, *Secretary of State.*

NEUTRALITY PROCLAMATIONS

By the President of the United States of America

A PROCLAMATION

[Neutrality—Italy and Austria-Hungary.]

Whereas a state of war unhappily exists between Italy and Austria-Hungary; And Whereas the United States is on terms of friendship and amity with the contending powers, and with the persons inhabiting their several dominions;

> [Here follows the identical preamble and warning against violation of quoted law as in the proclamation of neutrality in the case of hostilities between Austria-Hungary and Servia, Germany and Russia, and Germany and France. See pages 7969, 7970, 7971, 7972 and 7973.—*Ed.*]

Done at the city of Washington this twenty-fourth day of May in the year of our Lord one thousand nine hundred and fif-[SEAL.] teen and of the independence of the United States of America the one hundred and thirty-ninth.

WOODROW WILSON.

By the President:

W. J. Bryan, *Secretary of State.*

By the President of the United States of America

A PROCLAMATION

[Neutrality—Italy and Turkey.]

Whereas a state of war unhappily exists between Italy and Turkey; And Whereas the United States is on terms of friendship and amity with the contending powers, and with the persons inhabiting their several dominions;

> [Here follows the identical preamble and warning against violation of quoted law as in the proclamation of neutrality in the case of hostilities between Austria-Hungary and Servia, Germany and Russia, and Germany and France. See pages 7969, 7970, 7971, 7972 and 7973.—*Ed.*]

Done at the city of Washington this twenty-third day of August in the year of our Lord one thousand nine hundred and [SEAL.] fifteen and of the independence of the United States of America the one hundred and fortieth.

WOODROW WILSON.

By the President:

Robert Lansing, *Secretary of State.*

ADDRESSES

[In Convention Hall, Philadelphia, Pa., May 10, 1915, before a Gathering of 4,000 Naturalized American Citizens.]

MR. MAYOR, FELLOW CITIZENS: It warms my heart that you should give me such a reception; but it is not of myself that I wish to think to-night, but of those who have just become citizens of the United States.

This is the only country in the world which experiences this constant and repeated rebirth. Other countries depend upon the multiplication of their own native people. This country is constantly drinking strength out of new sources by the voluntary association with it of great bodies of strong men and forward-looking women out of other lands. And so by the gift of the free will of independent people it is being constantly renewed from generation to generation by the same process by which it was originally created. It is as if humanity had determined to see to it that this great Nation, founded for the benefit of humanity, should not lack for the allegiance of the people of the world.

You have just taken an oath of allegiance to the United States. Of allegiance to whom? Of allegiance to no one, unless it be God— certainly not of allegiance to those who temporarily represent this great Government. You have taken an oath of allegiance to a great ideal, to a great body of principles, to a great hope of the human race. You have said, "We are going to America not only to earn a living, not only to seek the things which it was more difficult to obtain where we were born, but to help forward the great enterprises of the human spirit—to let men know that everywhere in the world there are men who will cross strange oceans and go where a speech is spoken which is alien to them if they can but satisfy their quest for what their spirits crave; knowing that whatever the speech there is but one longing and utterance of the human heart, and that is for liberty and justice." And while you bring all countries with you, you come with a purpose of leaving all other countries behind you—bringing what is best of their spirit, but not looking over your shoulders and seeking to perpetuate what you intended to leave behind in them. I certainly would not be one even to suggest that a man cease to love the home of his birth and the nation of his origin—these things are very sacred and ought not to be put out of our hearts—but it is one thing to love the place where you were born and it is another thing to dedicate yourself to the place to which you go. You cannot dedicate yourself to America unless you become in every respect and with every purpose of your will thorough Americans. You cannot become thorough Americans if you think of yourselves in groups. America does not consist of groups. A man who thinks of himself as belonging to a particular national group in America has not yet become an American, and the man who goes among you to trade upon your nationality is no worthy son to live under the Stars and Stripes.

My urgent advice to you would be, not only always to think first of America, but always, also, to think first of humanity. You do not love humanity if you seek to divide humanity into jealous camps. Humanity can be welded together only by love, by sympathy, by justice, not by jealousy and hatred. I am sorry for the man who seeks to make personal capital out of the passions of his fellow-men. He has lost the touch and ideal of America, for America was created to unite mankind by those passions which lift and not by the passions which separate and debase. We came to America, either ourselves or in the persons of our ancestors, to better the ideals of men, to make them see finer things than they had seen before, to get rid of the things that divide and to make sure of the things that unite. It was but an historical accident no doubt that this great country was called the "United States"; yet I am very thankful that it has that word "United" in its title, and the man who seeks to divide man from man, group from group, interest from interest in this great Union is striking at its very heart.

It is a very interesting circumstance to me, in thinking of those of you who have just sworn allegiance to this great Government, that you were drawn across the ocean by some beckoning finger of hope, by some belief, by some vision of a new kind of justice, by some expectation of a better kind of life. No doubt you have been disappointed in some of us. Some of us are very disappointing. No doubt you have found that justice in the United States goes only with a pure heart and a right purpose as it does everywhere else in the world. No doubt what you found here did not seem touched for you, after all, with the complete beauty of the ideal which you had conceived beforehand. But remember this: If we had grown at all poor in the ideal, you brought some of it with you. A man does not go out to seek the thing that is not in him. A man does not hope for the thing that he does not believe in, and if some of us have forgotten what America believed in, you, at any rate, imported in your own hearts a renewal of the belief. That is the reason that I, for one, make you welcome. If I have in any degree forgotten what America was intended for, I will thank God if you will remind me. I was born in America. You dreamed dreams of what America was to be, and I hope you brought the dreams with you. No man that does not see visions will ever realize any high hope or undertake any high enterprise. Just because you brought dreams with you, America is more likely to realize dreams such as you brought. You are enriching us if you came expecting us to be better than we are.

See, my friends, what that means. It means that Americans must have a consciousness different from the consciousness of every other nation in the world. I am not saying this with even the slightest thought of criticism of other nations. You know how it is with a family. A family gets centered on itself if it is not careful and is less interested in the neighbors than it is in its own members. So a nation that is not constantly renewed out of new sources is apt to have the narrowness and prejudice of a family; whereas, America must have this consciousness, that on all sides it touches elbows and touches hearts with all the nations of mankind. The example of America must be a special example. The example of America must be the example not merely of peace because it will not fight, but of peace because peace is the healing and elevating influence of the world and strife is not. There is such a thing as a man being too proud to fight. There is such a thing as a nation being so right that it does not need to convince others by force that it is right.

You have come into this great Nation voluntarily seeking something that we have to give, and all that we have to give is this: We cannot exempt you from work. No man is exempt from work anywhere in the world. We cannot exempt you from the strife and the heartbreaking burden of the struggle of the day—that is common to mankind everywhere; we cannot exempt you from the loads that you must carry. We can only make them light by the spirit in which they are carried. That is the spirit of hope, it is the spirit of liberty, it is the spirit of justice.

When I was asked, therefore, by the Mayor and the committee that accompanied him to come up from Washington to meet this great company of newly admitted citizens, I could not decline the invitation. I ought not to be away from Washington, and yet I feel that it has renewed my spirit as an American to be here. In Washington men tell you so many things every day that are not so, and I like to come and stand in the presence of a great body of my fellow-citizens, whether they have been my fellow-citizens a long time or a short time, and drink, as it were, out of the common fountains with them and go back feeling what you have so generously given me—the sense of your support and of the living vitality in your hearts of the great ideals which have made America the hope of the world.

[At a Luncheon Tendered to Him by the Mayor's Committee at the Hotel Biltmore, New York, N. Y., May 17, 1915.]

MR. MAYOR, MR. SECRETARY, ADMIRAL FLETCHER, AND GENTLEMEN OF THE FLEET: This is not an occasion upon which, it seems to me, it would be wise for me to make many remarks, but I would deprive myself of a great gratification if I did not express my pleasure in being here, my gratitude for the splendid reception which has been accorded me as the representative of the Nation, and my profound interest in the Navy of the United States. That is an interest with which I was apparently born, for it began when I was a youngster and has ripened with my knowledge of the affairs and policies of the United States.

I think it is a natural, instinctive judgment of the people of the United States that they express their power most appropriately in an efficient navy, and their interest in their ships is partly, I believe, because that Navy is expected to express their character, not within our own borders where that character is understood, but outside our borders where it is hoped we may occasionally touch others with some slight vision of what America stands for.

Before I speak of the Navy of the United States, I want to take advantage of the first public opportunity I have had to speak of the Secretary of the Navy, to express my confidence and my admiration, and to say that he has my unqualified support. For I have counseled with him in intimate fashion; I know how sincerely he has it at heart that everything that the Navy does and handles should be done and handled as the people of the United States wish it handled. Efficiency is something more than organization. Efficiency runs to the extent of lifting the ideals of a service above every personal interest. So when I speak my support of the Secretary of the Navy I am merely speaking my support of what I know every true lover of the Navy to desire and to purpose; for the Navy of the United States is, as I have said, a body specially entrusted with the ideals of America.

I like to imagine in my thought this idea: These quiet ships lying in the river have no suggestion of bluster about them, no intimation of aggression. They are commanded by men thoughtful of the duty of citizens as well as the duty of officers, men acquainted with the traditions of the great service to which they belong, men who know by touch with the people of the United States what sort of purposes they ought to entertain and what sort of discretion they ought to exercise in order to use those engines of force as engines to promote the interests of humanity.

The interesting and inspiring thing about America, gentlemen, is that she asks nothing for herself except what she has a right to ask for humanity itself. We want no nation's property. We mean to question no nation's honor. We do not wish to stand selfishly in the way of the development of any nation. We want nothing that we cannot get by our own legitimate enterprise and by the inspiration of our own example; and, standing for these things, it is not pretension on our part to say that we are privileged to stand for what every nation would wish to stand for, and speak for those things which all humanity must desire.

When I think of the flag which those ships carry, the only touch of color about them, the only thing that moves as if it had a subtle spirit in it in their solid structure, it seems to me that I see alternate strips of parchment upon which are written the rights of liberty and justice, and stripes of blood spilt to vindicate those rights; and, then, in the corner a prediction of the blue serene into which every nation may swim which stands for these things.

The mission of America is the only thing that a sailor or a soldier should think about. He has nothing to do with the formulation of her policy. He is to support her policy whatever it is; but he is to support her policy in the spirit of herself, and the strength of our polity is that we who for the time being administer the affairs of this Nation do not originate her spirit. We attempt to embody it; we attempt to realize it in action; we are dominated by it, we do not dictate it.

So with every man in arms who serves the Nation; he stands and waits to do the thing which the Nation desires. Those who represent America sometimes seem to forget her programmes, but the people never forget them. It is as startling as it is touching to see how whenever you touch a principle you touch the hearts of the people of the United States. They listen to your debates of policy, they determine which party they will prefer to power, they choose and prefer as between men, but their real affection, their real force, their real irresistible momentum is for the ideas which men embody. I never go on the streets of a great city without feeling that somehow I do not confer elsewhere than on the streets with the great spirit of the people themselves, going about their business, attending to the things which immediately concern them, and yet carrying a treasure at their hearts all the while, ready to be stirred not only as individuals but as members of a great union of hearts that constitutes a patriotic people. This sight in the river touches me merely as a symbol of all this; and it quickens the pulse of every man who realizes these things to have anything to do with them. When a crisis occurs in this country, gentlemen, it is as if you put your hand on the pulse of a dynamo, it is as if the things that you were in connection with were spiritually bred, as if you had nothing to do with them except, if you listen truly, to speak the things that you hear.

These things now brood over the river; this spirit now moves with the men who represent the Nation in the Navy; these things will move upon the waters in the maneuvers—no threat lifted against any man, against any nation, against any interest, but just a great solemn evidence that the force of America is the force of moral principle, that there is nothing else that she loves, and that there is nothing else for which she will contend.

[At the Pan-American Financial Conference, Pan-American Building, Washington, D. C., May 24, 1915.]

MR. CHAIRMAN, GENTLEMEN OF THE AMERICAN REPUBLICS, LADIES AND GENTLEMEN: The part that falls to me this morning is a very simple one, but a very delightful one. It is to bid you a very hearty welcome indeed to this conference. The welcome is the more hearty because we are convinced that a conference like this will result in the things that we most desire. I am sure that those who have this conference in charge have already made plain to you its purpose and its spirit. Its purpose is to draw the American Republics together by bonds of common interest and of mutual understanding; and we comprehend, I hope, just what the meaning of that is. There can be no sort of union of interest if there is a purpose of exploitation by any one of the parties to a great conference of this sort. The basis of successful commercial intercourse is common interest, not selfish interest. It is an actual interchange of services and of values: it is based upon reciprocal relations and not selfish relations. It is based upon those things upon which all successful economic intercourse must be based, because selfishness breeds suspicion; suspicion, hostility; and hostility, failure. We are not, therefore, trying to make use of each other, but we are trying to be of use to one another.

It is very surprising to me, it is even a source of mortification, that a conference like this should have been so long delayed, that it should never have occurred before, that it should have required a crisis of the world to show the Americas how truly they were neighbors to one another. If there is any one happy circumstance, gentlemen, arising out of the present distressing condition of the world, it is that it has revealed us to one another: it has shown us what it means to be neighbors. And I cannot help harboring the hope, the very high hope, that by this commerce of minds with one another, as well as commerce in goods, we may show the world in part the path to peace. It would be a very great thing if the Americas could add to the distinction which they already wear this of showing the way to peace, to permanent peace.

The way to peace for us, at any rate, is manifest. It is the kind of rivalry which does not involve aggression. It is the knowledge that men can be of the greatest service to one another, and nations of the greatest service to one another, when the jealousy between them is merely a jealousy of excellence, and when the basis of their intercourse is friendship. There is only one way in which we wish to take advantage of you and that is by making better goods, by doing the things that we seek to do for each other better, if we can, than you do them, and so spurring you on, if we might, by so handsome a jealousy as that to excel us. I am so keenly aware that the basis of personal friendship is this competition in excellence, that I am perfectly certain that this is the only basis for the friendship of nations,—this handsome rivalry, this rivalry in which there is no dislike, this rivalry in which there is nothing but the hope of a common elevation in great enterprises which we can undertake in common.

There is one thing that stands in our way among others—for you are more conversant with the circumstances than I am; the thing I have chiefly in mind is the physical lack of means of communication, the lack of vehicles,—the lack of ships, the lack of established routes of trade,—the lack of those things which are absolutely necessary if we are to have true commercial and intimate commercial relations with one another; and I am perfectly clear in my judgment that if private capital cannot soon enter upon the adventure of establishing these physical means of communication, the government must undertake to do so. We cannot indefinitely stand apart and need each other for the lack of what can easily be supplied, and if one instrumentality cannot supply it, then another must be found which will supply it. We cannot know each other unless we see each other; we cannot deal with each other unless we communicate with each other. So soon as we communicate and are upon a familiar footing of intercourse, we shall understand one another, and the bonds between the Americas will be such bonds that no influence that the world may produce in the future will ever break them.

If I am selfish for America, I at least hope that my selfishness is enlightened. The selfishness that hurts the other party is not enlightened selfishness. If I were acting upon a mere ground of selfishness, I would seek to benefit the other party and so tie him to myself; so that even if you were to suspect me of selfishness, I hope you will also suspect me of intelligence and of knowing the only safe way for the establishment of the things which we covet, as well as the establishment of the things which we desire and which we would feel honored if we could earn and win.

I have said these things because they will perhaps enable you to understand how far from formal my welcome to this body is. It is a welcome from the heart, it is a welcome from the head; it is a welcome inspired by what I hope are the highest ambitions of those who live in these two great continents, who seek to set an example to the world in freedom of institutions, **freedom of trade,** and intelligence of mutual service.

[At G. A. R. Celebration of the Semi-centennial of the Grand Parade of the Union Troops Returning North in 1865, held at Camp Emery, in Washington, D. C., Sept. 27, 1915.]

Mr. Chairman, Gentlemen of the Grand Army of the Republic, Ladies and Gentlemen: I bid you a very cordial welcome to the capital of the Nation, and yet I feel that it is not necessary to bid you welcome here, because you know that the welcome is always warm and always waiting for you.

One could not stand in this presence without many moving thoughts. It is a singular thing that men of a single generation should have witnessed what you have witnessed in the crowded fifty years which you celebrate to-night. You took part when you were young men in a struggle the meaning of which, I dare say, you thought would not be revealed during your lifetime, and yet more has happened in the making of this Nation in your lifetime than has ever happened in the making of any other nation in the lifetime of a dozen generations.

The Nation in which you now live is not the Nation for whose union you fought. You have seen many things come about which have made this Nation one of the representative nations of the world with regard to the modern spirit of that world, and you have the satisfaction, which I dare say few soldiers have ever had, of looking back upon a war absolutely unique in this, that instead of destroying it healed, that instead of making a permanent division it made a permanent union. You have seen something more interesting than that, because there is a sense in which the things of the heart are more interesting than the things of the mind. This Nation was from the beginning a spiritual enterprise, and you have seen the spirits of the two once divided sections of this country absolutely united. A war which seemed as if it had the seed of every kind of bitterness in it has seen a single generation put bitterness absolutely out of its heart, and you feel, as I am sure the men who fought against you feel, that you were comrades even then, though you did not know it, and that now you know that you are comrades in a common love for a country which you are equally eager to serve.

This is a miracle of the spirit, so far as national history is concerned. This is one of the very few wars in which in one sense everybody engaged may take pride. Some wars are to be regretted; some wars mar the annals of history; but some wars, contrasted with those, make those annals distinguished, show that the spirit of man sometimes springs to great enterprises that are even greater than his own mind had conceived.

So it seems to me that, standing in a presence like this, no man, whether he be in the public service or in the ranks of private citizens merely, can fail to feel the challenge to his own heart, can fail to feel the challenge to a new consecration to the things that we all believe in. The thing that sinks deepest in my heart as I try to realize the memories that must be crowding upon you is this: You set the Nation free for that great career of development, of unhampered development, which the world has witnessed since the Civil War; but for my own part I would not be proud of the extraordinary physical development of this country, of its extraordinary development in material wealth and financial power, did I not believe that the people of the United States wished all of this power devoted to ideal ends. There have been other nations as rich as we; there have been other nations as powerful; there have been other nations as spirited; but I hope we shall never forget that we created this Nation, not to serve ourselves, but to serve mankind.

I love this country because it is my home, but every man loves his home. It does not suffice that I should be attached to it because it contains the places and the persons whom I love—because it contains the threads of my own life. That does not suffice for patriotic duty. I should also love it, and I hope I do love it, as a great instrument for the uplift of mankind; and what you, gentlemen, have to remind us of as you look back through a lifetime to the great war in which you took part is that you fought that this instrument meant for the service of mankind should not be impaired either in its material or in its spiritual power.

I hope I may say without even an implication of criticism upon any other great people in the world that it has always seemed to me that the people of the United States wished to be regarded as devoted to the promotion of particular principles of human right. The United States were founded, not to provide free homes, but to assert human rights. This flag meant a great enterprise of the human spirit. Nobody, no large bodies of men, in the time that flag was first set up believed with a very firm belief in the efficacy of democracy. Do you realize that only so long ago as the time of the American Revolution democracy was regarded as an experiment in the world and we were regarded as rash experimenters? But we not only believed in it; we showed that our belief was well founded and that a nation as powerful as any in the world could be erected upon the will of the people; that, indeed, there was a power in such a nation that dwelt in no other nation unless also in that other nation the spirit of the people prevailed.

Democracy is the most difficult form of government, because it is the form under which you have to persuade the largest number of persons to do anything in particular. But I think we were the more pleased to undertake it because it is difficult. Anybody can do what is easy. We have shown that we could do what was hard, and the pride that ought to dwell in your hearts to-night is that you saw to it that that experiment was brought to the day of its triumphant demonstration. We now know, and the world knows, that the thing that we then undertook, rash as it seemed, has been practicable, and that we have set up in the world a government maintained and promoted by the general conscience and the general conviction.

So I stand here not to welcome you to the Nation's capital as if I were your host but merely to welcome you to your own capital, because I am, and am proud to be, your servant. I hope I shall catch, as I hope we shall all catch, from the spirit of this occasion a new consecration to the high duties of American citizenship.

[In Old Census Building, Washington, D. C., Before Veterans of the G. A. R., in Annual Encampment, Sept. 28, 1915.]

It is a singular thing that men of a single generation should have witnessed what you have witnessed in the crowded fifty years which you celebrate to-night. You took part when you were young men in a struggle, the meaning of which, I dare say, you thought would not be revealed during your lifetime, and yet more has happened in the making of this nation in your lifetime than has ever happened in the making of any other nation in the lifetime of a dozen generations.

You have seen many things which have made this nation one of the representative nations of the world, with regard to the modern spirit of that world, and you have the satisfaction, which, I dare say, few soldiers have ever had, of looking back upon a war absolutely unique in this, that, instead of destroying, it has healed; that, instead of making a permanent division, it has made a permanent union.

This nation was from the beginning a spiritual enterprise, and you have seen the spirits of the two once-divided sections of this country absolutely united. A war which seemed as if it had the seed of every kind of bitterness in it has seen a single generation put bitterness absolutely out of its heart, and you feel, as I am sure the men who fought against you feel, that you were comrades even then, though you did not know it, and that now you know that you are comrades in a common love for a country which you are equally eager to serve.

This is a miracle of the spirit, so far as national history is concerned. This is one of the very few wars in which, in one sense, everybody engaged may take pride. Some wars are to be regretted, some wars mar the annals of history, but some wars, contrasted with those, make those annals distinguished and show that the spirit of man sometimes springs to great enterprises that are even greater than his own mind had conceived.

You set the nation free for that great career of development, of unhampered development, which the world has witnessed since the civil war. But, for my part, I would not be proud of the extraordinary physical development of this country, of its extraordinary development in material wealth and financial power, did I not believe that the people of the United States wish all of this power devoted to ideal ends.

There have been other nations as rich as we, there have been other nations as powerful, there have been other nations as spirited; but I hope we shall never forget that we created this nation, not to serve ourselves, but to serve mankind.

I hope I may say without even an implication of criticism upon any other great people in the world that it has always seemed to me that the people of the United States wished to be regarded as devoted to the promotion of particular principles of human rights. The United States were founded, not to provide free homes, but to assert human rights. This flag meant a great enterprise of the human spirit.

Nobody, no large bodies of men, at the time that flag was first set up, believed with a very firm belief in the efficacy of democracy. Do you realize that only so long ago as the time of the American Revolution democracy was regarded as an experiment in the world and we were regarded as rash experimenters? But we not only believed in it, we showed our belief was well founded, and that a nation as powerful as any in the world could be erected upon the will of the people; that, indeed, there was a power in such a nation that dwelt in no other nation, unless also in that other nation the spirit of the people prevailed.

We now know and the world knows that the thing that we then undertook, rash as it seemed, has been practicable, and that we have set up in the world a government maintained and promoted by the general conscience and the general conviction. So I stand here not to welcome you to the nation's capital as if I were your host, but merely to welcome you to your own capital, because I am, and am proud to be, your servant. I hope I shall catch, as I hope we all catch, from the spirit of this occasion a new consecration to the high duties of American citizenship.

[Before the Civilian Advisory Board of the Navy, at the White House. Washington, D. C., Oct. 7, 1915.]

There is very little that I can say to you, except to give you a very cordial welcome and to express my very great pleasure in this association of laymen with the Government. But I do want to say this:

I think the whole nation is convinced that we ought to be prepared, not for war, but for defense, and very adequately prepared, and that the preparation for defense is not merely a technical matter, that it is not a matter that the Army and Navy alone can take care of, but a matter in which we must have the co-operation of the best brains and knowledge of the country, outside the official service of the Government, as well as inside.

For my part, I feel that it is only in the spirit of a true democracy that we get together to lend such voluntary aid, the sort of aid that comes from interest, from a knowledge of the varied circumstances that are involved in handling a nation.

I want you to feel, those of you who are coming to the assistance of the professional officers of the Government, that we have a very serious purpose, that we have not asked you to associate yourself with us except for a very definite and practical purpose—to get you to give us your best independent thoughts as to how we ought to make ready for any duty that may fall upon the nation.

I do not have to expound it to you; you know as well as I do the spirit of America. The spirit of America is one of peace, but one of independence. It is a spirit that is profoundly concerned with peace, because it can express itself best only in peace. It is the spirit of peace and good-will and of human freedom; but it is also the spirit of a nation that is self-conscious, that knows and loves its mission in the world and that knows that it must command the respect of the world.

So it seems to me that we are not working as those who would change anything of America, but only as those who would safeguard everything in America. I know that you will enter into conference with the officers of the Navy in that spirit and with that feeling, and it makes me proud, gentlemen, that the busy men of America—the men who stand at the front of their professions—should be willing in this way to associate themselves voluntarily with the Government in the task in which it needs all sorts of expert and serious advice.

Nothing ought to be done in this by any single group of persons; everything ought to be done by all of us, united together, and I welcome this association in the most serious and grateful spirit.

[Before the Daughters of the American Revolution, in Memorial Continental Hall, Washington, D. C., Oct. 11, 1915.]

There is a very great thrill to be had from the memories of the American Revolution, but the American Revolution was a beginning, not a consummation, and the duty laid upon us by that beginning is the duty of bringing the things then begun to a noble triumph of completion, for it seems to me that the peculiarity of patriotism in America is that it is not a mere sentiment. It is an active principle of conduct. It is something that was born into the world not to leave it, but to regenerate it. It is something that was born into the world to replace systems that had preceded it, to bring them out upon a new plane of privilege.

The American Revolution was the birth of a nation, it was the creation of a great free Republic based upon traditions of personal liberty which heretofore had been confined to a single little island, but which it was purposed should spread to all mankind. And the singular fascination of American history is that it has been a process of constant re-creation, of making over again in each generation the thing which was conceived at first. You know how peculiarly necessary that has been in our case, because America has not grown by the mere multiplication of the original stock. It is easy to preserve tradition with continuity of blood; it is easy in a single family to remember the origins of the race and the purposes of its organization, but it is not so easy when that race is constantly being renewed and augmented from other sources, from stocks that did not carry or originate the same principles.

So from generation to generation strangers have had to be indoctrinated with the principles of the American family, and the wonder and the beauty of it all has been that the infection has been so generously easy, for the principles of liberty are united with the principles of hope. Every individual, as well as every nation, wishes to realize the best thing that is in him, the best thing that can be conceived out of the materials of which his spirit is constructed. It has happened in a way that I think fascinates the imagination that we have not only been augmented by additions from outside, but that we have been greatly stimulated by those additions.

Living in the easy prosperity of a free people, knowing that the sun had always been free to shine upon us and prosper our undertakings, we did not realize how hard the task of liberty is and how rare the privilege of liberty is, and men were drawn out of every climate and out of every race because of an irresistible attraction of their spirits to the American ideal. They thought of America as lifting, like that great statue, in the harbor of New York, a torch to light the pathway of men to the things that they desire, and men of all sorts and conditions struggled toward that light and came to our shores with an eager desire to realize it and a hunger for it such as some of us no longer felt, for we were as if we were satiated and sated and were indulging ourselves after a fashion that did not belong to the ascetic devotion of the early devotees of those great principles. So they came to remind us of what we had promised ourselves and through ourselves had promised mankind. All men came to us and said, "Where is the bread of life with which you promised to feed us, and have you partaken of it yourselves?"

For my part, I believe that the constant renewal of this people out of foreign stocks has been a constant source of reminder to this people of what the inducement was that was offered to men who would come and be of our number. Now we have come to a time of special stress and test. There never was a time when we needed more clearly to conserve the principles of our own patriotism than this present time. The rest of the world from which our politics were drawn seems for the time in the crucible, and no man can predict what will come out of that crucible. We stand apart unembroiled, conscious of our own principles, conscious of what we hope and purpose so far as our powers permit for the world at large, and it is necessary that we should consolidate the American principle. Every political action, every social action, should have for its object in America at this time to challenge the spirit of America; to ask that every man and woman who thinks first of America should rally to the standards of our life. There have been some among us who have not thought first of America, who have thought to use the might of America in some matter not of America's originative, and they have forgotten that the first duty of a nation is to express its principles in the action of the family of nations and not to seek to aid and abet any rival or contrary ideal.

Neutrality is a negative word. It is a word that does not express what America ought to feel. America has a heart, and that heart throbs with all sorts of intense sympathies, but America has schooled its heart to love the things that America believes in, and it ought to devote itself only to the things that America believes in, and, believing that America stands apart in its ideals, it ought not to allow itself to be drawn, so far as its heart is concerned, into anybody's quarrel. Not because it does not understand the quarrel, not because it does not in its head assess the merits of the controversy, but because America has promised the world to stand apart and maintain certain principles of action which are grounded in law and in justice. We are not trying to keep out of trouble, we are trying to preserve the foundations upon which peace can be rebuilt. Peace can be rebuilt only upon the ancient and accepted principles of international law, only upon those things which remind nations of their duties to each other and, deeper than that, of their duties to mankind and to humanity.

America has a great cause which is not confined to the American Continent. It is the cause of humanity itself. I do not mean in anything that I say to imply a judgment upon any nation or upon any policy, for my object here this afternoon is not to sit in judgment upon anybody but ourselves and to challenge you to assist all of us who are trying to make America conscious of nothing so much as her own principles and her own duty. I look forward to the necessity in every political agitation in the years which are immediately at hand of calling upon every man to declare himself, where he stands. Is it America first or is it not? We ought to be very careful about some of the impressions that we are forming just now. There is too general an impression, I fear, that very large numbers of our fellow-citizens born in other lands have not entertained with sufficient intensity and affection the American ideal, but their numbers are not large. Those who would seek to represent them are very vocal, but they are not very influential. Some of the best stuff of America has come out of foreign lands, and some of the best stuff in America is in the men who are naturalized citizens of the United States.

I would not be afraid upon the test of "America first" to take a census of all the foreign-born citizens of the United States, for I know the vast majority of them came here because they believed in America, and their belief in America has made them better citizens than some people who were born in America. They can say that they have bought this privilege with a great price. They have left their homes, they have left their kindred, they have broken all the nearest and dearest ties of human life in order to come to a new land, take a new rootage, begin a new life, and so by self-sacrifice express their confidence in a new principle, whereas, it costs us nothing of these things. We were born into this privilege; we were rocked and cradled in it; we did nothing to create it, and it is, therefore, the greater duty on our part to do a great deal to enhance it and preserve it. I am not deceived as to the balance of opinion among the foreign-born citizens of the United States, but I am in a hurry to have an opportunity to have a line-up and let the men who are thinking first of other countries stand on one side —Biblically, it should be the left—and all those that are for America, first, last and all the time on the other side.

Now, you can do a great deal in this direction. When I was a college officer I used to be very much opposed to hazing, not because hazing is not wholesome, but because sophomores are poor judges. I remember a very dear friend of mine, a professor of ethics on the other side of the water, was asked if he thought it was ever justifiable to tell a lie. He said yes, he thought it was sometimes justifiable to lie, "but," he said, "it is so difficult to judge of the justification that I usually tell the truth." I think that ought to be the motto of the sophomore. There are freshmen who need to be hazed, but the need is to be judged by such nice tests that a sophomore is hardly old enough to determine. But the world can determine them. We are not freshmen at college, but we are con-

stantly hazed. I would a great deal rather be obliged to draw pepper
up my nose than to observe the hostile glances of my neighbors. I
would a great deal rather be beaten than ostracized. I would a
great deal rather endure any sort of physical hardship if I might
have the affection of my fellow-men. We constantly discipline our
fellow-citizens by having an opinion about them. That is the sort
of discipline we ought now to administer to everybody who is not
to the very core of his heart an American. Just have an opinion
about him and let him experience the atmospheric effects of that
opinion. And I know of no body of persons comparable to a body
of ladies for creating an atmosphere of opinion. I have myself in
part yielded to the influence of that atmosphere, for it took me a
long time to observe how I was going to vote in New Jersey.

So it has seemed to me that my privilege this afternoon was not
merely a privilege of courtesy, but the real privilege of reminding
you, for I am sure I am doing nothing more, of the great principles which we stand associated to promote. And I, for my part,
rejoice that we belong to a country in which the whole business of
government is so difficult. We do not take orders from anybody;
it is a universal communication of conviction, the most subtle, delicate and difficult of processes. There is not a single individual's
opinion that is not of some consequence in making up the grand
total. And to be in this great co-operative effort is the most stimulating thing in the world. A man standing alone may well misdoubt
his own judgment. He may mistrust his own intellectual processes;
he may even wonder if his own heart leads him right in matters of
public conduct; but if he finds his heart part of the great throb of
a national life, there can be no doubt about it. If that is his happy
circumstance, then he may know that he is part of one of the great
forces of the world.

I would not feel any exhilaration in belonging to America if I
did not feel that she was something more than a rich and powerful
nation. I should not feel proud to be in some respects and for a little
while her spokesman if I did not believe that there was something
else than physical force behind her. I believe that the glory of
America is that she is a great spiritual conception and that in the
spirit of her institutions dwells not only her distinction but her
power, and that the one thing that the world cannot permanently
resist is the moral force of great and triumphant convictions.

[At Biltmore Hotel (New York) Banquet Celebrating the Fiftieth Anniversary of
the Manhattan Club, Nov. 5, 1915.]

MR. TOASTMASTER AND GENTLEMEN: I warmly felicitate the club
upon the completion of fifty years of successful and interesting life.

Club life may be made to mean a great deal to those who know how to use it. I have no doubt that to a great many of you has come genuine stimulation in the associations of this place and that as the years have multiplied you have seen more and more the useful ends which may be served by organizations of this sort.

But I have not come to speak wholly of that, for there are others of your own members who can speak of the club with a knowledge and an intelligence which no one can have who has not been intimately associated with it. Men band themselves together for the sake of the association, no doubt, but also for something greater and deeper than that—because they are conscious of common interests lying outside their business occupations, because they are members of the same community and in frequent intercourse find mutual stimulation and a real maximum of vitality and power.

I shall assume that here around the dinner table on this memorial occasion our talk should properly turn to the wide and common interests which are most in our thoughts, whether they be the interests of the community or of the nation.

A year and a half ago our thought would have been almost altogether of great domestic questions. They are many and of vital consequence. We must and shall address ourselves to their solution with diligence, firmness and self-possession, notwithstanding we find ourselves in the midst of a world disturbed by great disaster and ablaze with terrible war; but our thought is now inevitably of new things about which formerly we gave ourselves little concern.

We are thinking now chiefly of our relations with the rest of the world—not our commercial relations—about those we have thought and planned always—but about our political relations, our duties as an individual and independent force in the world—to ourselves, our neighbors and the world itself.

Our principles are well known. It is not necessary to avow them again. We believe in political liberty and founded our great Government to obtain it, the liberty of men and of peoples—of men to choose their own lives and of people to choose their own allegiance.

Our ambition, also, all the world has knowledge of. It is not only to be free and prosperous ourselves, but also to be the friend and thoughtful partisan of those who are free or who desire freedom the world over.

If we have had aggressive purposes and covetous ambitions, they were the fruit of our thoughtless youth as a nation and we have put them aside. We shall, I confidently believe, never again take another foot of territory by conquest.

We shall never in any circumstances seek to make an independent people subject to our dominion; because we believe, we passionately believe, in the right of every people to choose their own allegiance and be free of masters altogether. For ourselves we wish nothing but the full liberty of self-development; and with ourselves in this great matter we associate all the peoples of our own hemisphere.

We wish not only for the United States but for them the fullest freedom of independent growth and of action, for we know that throughout this hemisphere the same aspirations are everywhere being worked out, under diverse conditions but with the same impulse and ultimate object.

All this is very clear to us and will, I confidently predict, become more and more clear to the whole world as the great processes of the future unfold themselves. It is with a full consciousness of such principles and such ambitions that we are asking ourselves at the present time what our duty is with regard to the armed force of the nation. Within a year we have witnessed what we did not believe possible— a great European conflict involving many of the greatest nations of the world. The influences of a great war are everywhere in the air. All Europe is embattled.

Force everywhere speaks out with a loud and imperious voice in a titanic struggle of governments, and from one end of our own dear country to the other men are asking one another what our own force is, how far we are prepared to maintain ourselves against any interference with our national action or development.

In no man's mind, I am sure, is there even raised the question of the wilful use of force on our part against any nation or any people. No matter what military or naval force the United States might develop, statesmen throughout the whole world might rest assured that we were gathering that force, not for attack in any quarter, not for aggression of any kind, not for the satisfaction of any political or international ambition, but merely to make sure of our own security.

We have it in mind to be prepared, not for war, but only for defense; and with the thought constantly in our minds that the principles we hold most dear can be achieved by the slow processes of history only in the kindly and wholesome atmosphere of peace, and not by the use of hostile force. The mission of America in the world is essentially a mission of peace and good will among men. She has become the home and asylum of men of all creeds and races. Within her hospitable borders they have found homes and congenial associations and freedom and a wide and cordial welcome, and they have become part of the bone and sinew and spirit of America itself. America has been made up out of the nations of the world and is the friend of the nations of the world.

But we feel justified in preparing ourselves to vindicate our right to independent and unmolested action by making the force that is in us ready for assertion.

And we know that we can do this in a way that will be itself an illustration of the American spirit. In accordance with our American traditions, we want and shall work for only an army adequate to the constant and legitimate uses of times of international peace.

But we do want to feel that there is a great body of citizens who have received at least the most rudimentary and necessary forms of military training; that they will be ready to form themselves into a fighting force at the call of the nation; and that the nation has the munitions and supplies with which to equip them without delay should it be necessary to call them into action. We wish to supply them with the training they need, and we think we can do so without calling them at any time too long away from their civilian pursuits.

It is with this idea, with this conception in mind that the plan had been made which it will be my privilege to lay before the Congress at its next session.

That plan calls for only such an increase in the regular army of the United States as experience has proved to be required for the performance of the necessary duties of the army in the Philippines, in Hawaii, in Porto Rico, upon the borders of the United States, at the coast fortifications and at the military posts of the interior.

For the rest, it calls for the training within the next three years of a force of 400,000 citizen soldiers to be raised in annual contingents of 133,000, who would be asked to enlist for three years with the colors and three years on furlough, but who, during their three years of enlistment with the colors, would not be organized as a standing force, but would be expected merely to undergo intensive training for a very brief period of each year.

Their training would take place in immediate association with the organized units of the regular army. It would have no touch of the amateur about it, neither would it exact of the volunteers more than they could give in any one year from their civilian pursuits.

And none of this would be done in such a way as in the slightest degree to supersede or subordinate our present serviceable and efficient National Guard. On the contrary, the National Guard itself would be used as part of the instrumentality by which training would be given the citizens who enlisted under the new conditions, and I should hope and expect that the legislation by which all this would be accomplished would put the National Guard itself upon a better and more permanent footing than it has ever been before, giving it not only the recognition which it deserves, but a more definite support from the national government and a more definite connection with the military organization of the nation.

What we all wish to accomplish is that the forces of the nation should indeed be part of the nation, and not a separate professional force, and the chief cost of the system would not be in the enlistment or in the training of the men, but in the providing of ample equipment in case it should be necessary to call all forces into the field.

Moreover, it has been American policy time out of mind to look to the Navy as the first and chief line of defense. The Navy of the United States is already a very great and efficient force. Not rapidly, but slowly, with careful attention, our naval force has been developed until the Navy of the United States stands recognized as one of the most efficient and notable of the modern time.

All that is needed in order to bring it to a point of extraordinary force and efficiency as compared with the other navies of the world is that we should hasten our pace in the policy we have long been pursuing, and that chief of all we should have a definite policy of development, not made from year to year, but looking well into the future and planning for a definite consummation.

We can and should profit in all that we do by the experience and example that have been made obvious to us by the military and naval events of the actual present. It is not merely a matter of building battleships and cruisers and submarines, but also a matter of making sure that we shall have the adequate equipment of men and munitions and supplies for the vessels we build and intend to build.

Part of our problem is the problem of what I may call the mobilization of the resources of the nation at the proper time if it should ever be necessary to mobilize them for national defense. We shall study efficiency and adequate equipment as carefully as we shall study the number and size of our ships, and I believe that the plans already in part made public by the Navy Department are plans which the whole nation can approve with rational enthusiasm.

No thoughtful man feels any panic haste in this matter. The country is not threatened from any quarter. She stands in friendly relations with all the world. Her resources are known and her self-respect and her capacity to care for her own citizens and her own rights.

There is no fear amongst us. Under the new-world conditions we have become thoughtful of the things which all reasonable men consider necessary for security and self-defense on the part of every nation confronted with the great enterprise of human liberty and independence. That is all.

Is the plan we propose sane and reasonable and suited to the needs of the hour? Does it not conform to the ancient traditions of America?

Has any better plan been proposed than this programme that we now place before the country? In it there is no pride of opinion. It represents the best professional and expert judgment of the country.

But I am not so much interested in programmes as I am in safeguarding at every cost the good faith and honor of the country. If men differ with me in this vital matter, I shall ask them to make it clear how far and in what way they are interested in making the permanent interests of the country safe against disturbance.

In the fulfillment of the programme I propose I shall ask for the hearty support of the country, of the rank and file of America, of men of all shades of political opinion, for my position in this important matter is different from that of the private individual who is free to speak his own thoughts and to risk his own opinions in this matter.

We are here dealing with things that are vital to the life of America itself. In doing this I have tried to purge my heart of all personal and selfish motives. For the time being I speak as the trustee and guardian of a nation's rights, charged with the duty of speaking for that nation in matters involving her sovereignty—a nation too big and generous to be exacting and yet courageous enough to defend its rights and the liberties of its people wherever assailed or invaded.

I would not feel that I was discharging the solemn obligation I owe the country were I not to speak in terms of the deepest solemnity of the urgency and necessity of preparing ourselves to guard and protect the rights and privileges of our people, our sacred heritage of the fathers who struggled to make us an independent nation.

The only thing within our own borders that has given us grave concern in recent months has been that voices have been raised in America professing to be the voices of Americans which were not indeed and in truth American, but which spoke alien sympathies, which came from men who loved other countries better than they loved America, men who were partisans of other causes than that of America and had forgotten that their chief and only allegiance was to the great government under which they live.

These voices have not been many, but they have been very loud and very clamorous. They have proceeded from a few who were bitter and who were grievously misled. America has not opened its doors in vain to men and women out of other nations. The vast majority of those who have come to take advantage of her hospitality have united their spirits with hers as well as their fortunes.

These men who speak alien sympathies are not their spokesmen, but are the spokesmen of small groups whom it is high time that the nation should call to a reckoning. The chief thing necessary in America in order that she should let all the world know that she is prepared to maintain her own great position is that the real voice of the nation should sound forth unmistakably and in majestic volume in the deep unison of a common, unhesitating national feeling. I do not doubt that upon the first occasion, upon the first opportunity, upon the first definite challenge, that voice will speak forth in tones which no man can doubt and with commands which no man dare gainsay or resist.

May I not say, while I am speaking of this, that there is another danger we should guard against? We should rebuke not only manifestations of racial feeling here in America where there should be none, but also every manifestation of religious and sectarian antagonism. It does not become America that within her borders, where every man is free to follow the dictates of his conscience and worship God as he pleases, men should raise the cry of church against church. To do that is to strike at the very spirit and heart of America.

We are a God-fearing people. We agree to differ about methods of worship, but we are united in believing in Divine Providence and in worshipping the God of Nations. We are the champions of religious right here and everywhere that it may be our privilege to give it our countenance and support. The Government is conscious of the obligation and the nation is conscious of the obligation. Let no man create divisions where there are none.

Here is the nation God has builded by our hands. What shall we do with it? Who is there who does not stand ready at all times to act in her behalf in a spirit of devoted and disinterested patriotism? We are yet only in the youth and first consciousness of our power. The day of our country's life is still but in its fresh morning.

Let us lift our eyes to the great tracts of life yet to be conquered in the interests of righteous peace.

Come, let us renew our allegiance to America, conserve her strength in its purity, make her chief among those who serve mankind, self-reverenced, self-commanded, mistress of all forces of quiet counsel, strong above all others in good will and the might of invincible justice and right.

PROCLAMATIONS

By the President of the United States of America

A PROCLAMATION

[Dinosaur National Monument, Utah.]

Whereas, in section twenty-six, township four south, range twenty-three east of the Salt Lake meridian, Utah, there is located an extraordinary deposit of Dinosaurian and other gigantic reptilian remains of the Juratrias period, which are of great scientific interest and value, and it appears that the public interest would be promoted by reserving these deposits as a National Monument, together with as much land as may be needed for the protection thereof.

Now, therefore, I, Woodrow Wilson, President of the United States of America, by virtue of the power in me vested by Section two of the act of Congress entitled, "An Act for the Preservation of

American Antiquities," approved June 8, 1906, do hereby set aside as the Dinosaur National Monument, the unsurveyed northwest quarter of the southeast quarter and the northeast quarter of the southwest quarter of section twenty-six, township four south, range twenty-three east, Salk Lake meridian, Utah, as shown upon the diagram hereto attached and made a part of this proclamation.

While it appears that the lands embraced within this proposed reserve have heretofore been withdrawn as coal and phosphate lands, the creation of this monument will prevent the use of the lands for the purposes for which said withdrawals were made. Warning is hereby expressly given to all unauthorized persons not to appropriate, excavate, injure or destroy any of the fossil remains contained within the deposits hereby reserved and declared to be a National Monument or to locate or settle upon any of the lands reserved and made a part of this monument by this proclamation.

In witness whereof I have hereunto set my hand and caused the seal of the United States to be affixed.

Done at the city of Washington this fourth day of October in the year of our Lord one thousand nine hundred and [SEAL] fifteen and the Independence of the United States the one hundred and fortieth.

WOODROW WILSON.

By the President:
ROBERT LANSING, *Secretary of State.*

BY THE PRESIDENT OF THE UNITED STATES OF AMERICA

A PROCLAMATION

[Thanksgiving—1915.]

It has long been the honored custom of our people to turn in the fruitful autumn of the year in praise and thanksgiving to Almighty God for his many blessings and mercies to us as a nation. The year that is now drawing to a close since we last observed our day of national thanksgiving has been, while a year of discipline because of the mighty forces of war and of change which have disturbed the world, also a year of special blessing for us.

Another year of peace has been vouchsafed us; another year in which not only to take thought of our duty to ourselves and to mankind but also to adjust ourselves to the many responsibilities thrust upon us by a war which has involved almost the whole of Europe. We have been able to assert our rights and the rights of mankind without breach of friendship with the great nations with whom we have had to deal; and while we have asserted rights we have been able also to perform duties and exercise privileges of succour and helpfulness which should serve to demonstrate our desire to make the offices of friendship the means of truly disinterested and unselfish service. Our ability to serve all who could avail themselves of our services in the midst of crisis has been increased, by a gracious Providence, by more and more abundant crops; our ample financial resources have enabled us to steady the markets of the world and facilitate necessary movements of commerce which the war might otherwise have rendered impossible; and our people have come more and more to a sober realization of the part they have been called upon to play in a time when all the world is shaken by unparalleled distress and disasters. The extraordinary circumstances of such a time have done much to quicken our national consciousness and deepen and confirm our confidence in the principles of peace and freedom by which we have always sought to be guided. Out of darkness and perplexity have come firmer counsels of policy and clearer perceptions of the essential welfare of the nation. We have prospered while other people were at war, but our prosperity has been vouchsafed us, we believe, only that we might the better perform the functions which war rendered it impossible for them to perform.

Now, therefore, I, Woodrow Wilson, President of the United States of America, do hereby designate Thursday the twenty-fifth of November next as a day of thanksgiving and prayer, and invite the people throughout the land to cease from their wonted occupations and in their several homes and places of worship render thanks to Almighty God.

In witness whereof I have hereunto set my hand and caused the seal of the United States to be affixed.

Done at the city of Washington this twentieth day of October in the year of our Lord one thousand nine hundred and fifteen [SEAL] and of the independence of the United States of America the one hundred and fortieth.

By the President: · WOODROW WILSON.

ROBERT LANSING, *Secretary of State.*

BY THE PRESIDENT OF THE UNITED STATES OF AMERICA

A PROCLAMATION

[Forbidding the Export of Arms and Munitions of War to Mexico.]

Whereas, a Joint Resolution of Congress, approved March 14, 1912, reads and provides as follows: "That whenever the President shall find that in any American country conditions of domestic violence exist which are promoted by the use of arms or munitions of war procured from the United States, and shall make proclamation thereof, it shall be unlawful to export except under such limitations and exceptions as the President shall prescribe any arms or munitions of war from any place in the United States to such country until otherwise ordered by the President or by Congress";

And whereas, it is provided by Section II of the said Joint Resolution, "That any shipment of material hereby declared unlawful after such a proclamation shall be punishable by a fine not exceeding ten thousand dollars, or imprisonment not exceeding two years, or both";

Now, therefore, I, Woodrow Wilson, President of the United States of America, acting under and by virtue of the authority conferred on me by the said Joint Resolution of Congress, do hereby declare and proclaim that I have found that there exist in Mexico such conditions of domestic violence promoted by the use of arms or munitions of war procured from the United States as contemplated by the said Joint Resolution; and I do hereby admonish all citizens of the United States and every person to abstain from every violation of the provisions of the Joint Resolution above set forth, hereby made applicable to Mexico, and I do hereby warn them that all violations of such provisions will be rigorously prosecuted. And I do hereby enjoin upon all officers of the United States, charged with the execution of the laws thereof, the utmost diligence in preventing violations of the said Joint Resolution and this my Proclamation issued thereunder, and in bringing to trial and punishment any offenders against the same.

In witness whereof I have hereunto set my hand and caused the seal of the United States to be affixed.

Done at the city of Washington this nineteenth day of October in the year of our Lord one thousand nine hundred and fifteen
[SEAL]   and of the Independence of the United States of America the one hundred and fortieth.

WOODROW WILSON.

By the President:
ROBERT LANSING, *Secretary of State.*

EXECUTIVE ORDERS

[The President's order making an exception in favor of the Carranza de facto government in Mexico took the form of the following letter to Secretary McAdoo:]

THE WHITE HOUSE,
WASHINGTON, D. C., *October 19, 1915.*

MY DEAR MR. SECRETARY: I am informed by the Department of State that the recognized de facto Government of Mexico is now in effective control of all the ports of entry in Mexico, except those along the international boundary in the States of Chihuahua and Sonora, and all the ports in Lower California.

An exception is hereby made to the prohibition against export created by the President's proclamation of October 19, 1915, and you will please instruct the Collectors of Ports and other officers of the Treasury Department to permit to be exported through United States Custom Houses munitions of war for the use of the recognized de facto Government of Mexico, or for industrial or commercial uses within the limits of the territory under its effective control, as above set forth. An embargo, therefore, will be immediately placed against the border ports in the States of Chihuahua and Sonora, as well as all ports in the territory of Lower California, whether or not controlled by the recognized de facto Government of Mexico, and you will so instruct the appropriate Collectors of Customs and other officers of the Treasury Department. Sincerely yours,

WOODROW WILSON.

[Prescribing Consular Regulations for Maintaining the Rights and Enforcing the Duties of American Sailors in Foreign Ports.]

THE WHITE HOUSE, *October 21, 1915.*

The Consular Regulations of 1896 are hereby amended as follows:

192. In case of loss by desertion—In case of desertion or casualty resulting in the loss of one or more of the seamen, the master must ship if obtainable, a number, equal to the number of these, whose services he has been deprived of by desertion or casualty, who must be of the same or of higher grade or rating with those, whose places they fill, and report the same to the United States consul, at the port at which he shall arrive. This section shall not apply to fishing or whaling vessels, or yachts. R. S. sec. 4516. Mar. 4, 1915.

205. Bond for return of seamen—The master of every vessel bound on a foreign voyage or engaged in the whale fishery, is required by law to exhibit a certified copy of the crew list to the first boarding officer at the first port in the United States at which he shall arrive on his return and also to produce the persons named in the crew list. For each failure to produce any person on the certified copy of the crew list, the master and the owner of the vessel are severally liable to a penalty of $400. But the penalty is not incurred for failure to produce any seaman named in the crew list who has been discharged in a foreign country with the consent of a consular officer, certified in writing under his hand and official seal to be produced to the collector with the other persons composing the crew; nor on account of any such persons dying or absconding or being forcibly impressed into other service of which satisfactory proof shall then also be exhibited

to the collector. A master cannot lawfully discharge a seaman in a foreign port without the intervention of the consular officer; and it is not material in such case that the discharge is made with the seaman's consent, or that he has misconducted himself, or is not a citizen of the United States. (R. S. 4576; 7 op. Att. Gen., 349; 1 Low, 107; Tawney's Dec. 24; 29 Stat. L. 688).

207. Cases in which seamen are discharged—Add as section 13. "The seamen shall not be shipped to work alternately on deck and in the fireroom, nor shall those shipped for deck duty be required to work in the fireroom or vice versa, but these provisions shall not limit either the authority of the master, or other officer, or the obedience of the seamen, when in the judgment of the master, or other officer, the whole or any part of the crew are needed for the maneuvering of the vessel or the performance of work necessary for the safety of the vessel or of her cargo, or for the saving of life aboard other vessels in jeopardy, or when in port or at sea, from requiring the whole or any part of the crew to participate in the performance of fire, lifeboat and other drills. While such vessel is in a safe harbor, no seaman shall be required to do any unnecessary work on Sundays, or the following named days: New Year's Day, Fourth of July, Labor Day, Thanksgiving Day and Christmas Day, but this shall not prevent the despatch of a vessel on regular schedule or when ready to proceed on her voyage. And at all times while such vessel is in a safe harbor, nine hours, inclusive of the anchor watch, shall constitute a day's work. Whenever the master of any vessel shall fail to comply with this section, the seaman shall be entitled to discharge from such vessel, and to receive the wages earned. This section shall not apply to fishing vessels, whaling vessels, or to yachts. Sec. 2, Act March 4, 1915.

210. Desertion from cruel treatment—When a consular officer discharges a seaman—in case of desertion caused by unusual or cruel treatment—he must enter upon the crew list, shipping articles and official log, the cause of discharge. In all cases where seamen or. officers are accused, the consular officers shall inquire into the facts, and upon being satisfied of the justice and truth of such complaints, shall require the master to pay such seaman one month's extra wages, over and above the wages due at the time of discharge, and to provide him with adequate employment on board some other vessel, or to provide him with passage on board some other vessel, bound to the port from which he was originally shipped, or to the most convenient port of entry in the United States, or to a port agreed to by the seaman; and the officer discharging such seaman shall enter upon the shipping articles, crew list and official log, the cause of such discharge and the particulars in which the unusual or cruel treatment consisted and subscribe his name thereto, officially. He shall read the entry

THE PRESIDENT'S ENGAGEMENTS

Wednesday, January 12, 1916

10:00 a.m.   John H. Fahey

10:00 a.m.   Committee of the Pittsburgh Chamber of Commerce - to extend invitation. (Joseph F. Guffey)

10:00 a.m.   Senator Hoke Smith

10:00 a.m.   Rep. Tribble, of Georgia

10:00 a.m.   Rep. Heflin, and members Alabama Delegation

10:30 a.m.   Rep. Fitzgerald

10:45 a.m.   Senators Beckham and James

11:00 a.m.   The Speaker

11:30 a.m.   Rep. Eagle, of Texas

11:45 a.m.   Senator Lewis

12:00 noon   Mr. Stevens of Federal Trade Commission

12:15 p.m.   Governor Major, of Missouri

12:30 p.m.   Judge Westcott, New Jersey

5:30 p.m.   THE WHITE HOUSE:
Representative Padgett

Belasco Theatre

FACSIMILE: PAGE OF PRESIDENT WILSON'S ENGAGEMENT BOOK

LIST OF PRESIDENT'S ENGAGEMENTS.

Few persons outside of Washington can conceive of the extent of the various demands upon the time of the President of the United States, especially when Congress is in session. And there can be no doubt that few Presidents have been kept so closely confined to their duties as President Wilson. Even before the outbreak of the European war brought new and perplexing problems before Wilson's administration, the problem of consolidating the Democratic Party for constructive legislative achievements was no easy task. The Party had long been out of power and its majority in Congress was not overwhelming; and many were the interviews and consultations necessary to oil the machinery of government. In this connection, the facsimile of President Wilson's engagements for a typical morning's work must prove most interesting.

made in the official log to the master, and his reply thereto, if any, shall likewise be entered and subscribed in the same manner. R. S. 5483, 1898, and 4600, Mar. 4, 1915.

218. Consular officer to collect wages—If any consular officer when discharging any seaman, shall neglect to require the payment of and collect the arrears of wages and extra wages required to be paid in the case of the discharge of any seaman, he shall be accountable to the United States for the full amount thereof. The master shall provide any seaman so discharged with employment on a vessel agreed to by the seaman, or shall provide him with one month's extra wages, if it shall be shown to the satisfaction of the consul that such seaman was not discharged for neglect of duty, incompetency, or injury incurred on the vessel. If the seaman is discharged by voluntary consent before the consul, he shall be entitled to his wages up to the time of his discharge, but not for any further period. If the seaman is discharged on account of injury or illness, incapacitating him for service, the expenses for his maintenance and return to the United States shall be paid from the fund for the maintenance and transportation of destitute American seamen. Provided, that at the discretion of the Secretary of Commerce, and under such regulations as he may prescribe, if any seaman, incapacitated from service by injury or illness, is on board a vessel so situated that a prompt discharge requiring the personal appearance of the master of the vessel before an American consul, or consular agent is impracticable, such seaman may be sent to a consul or consular agent, who shall care for him and defray the cost of his maintenance and transportation. R. S. 4581—Sec. 19, Act Mar. 4, 1915.

222. Discharge for unusual or cruel treatment—Whenever on the discharge of a seaman in a foreign country by a consular officer, on his complaint against the officers for cruel treatment, it shall be the duty of the consul or consular agent to institute a proper inquiry into the matter, and upon his being satisfied of the truth and justice of such complaint, he shall require the master to pay to such seaman one month's wages over and above the wages due at the time of discharge, *and* to provide him with adequate employment on board some other vessel, *or* to provide him with passage on board some other vessel bound to the port from which he was originally shipped, *or* to the most convenient port of entry in the United States, *or* to a port agreed to by the seaman. R. S. 4583 and 4600.

224. Arrears of wages to be collected and reported—It is the duty of the consular officer to collect all arrears of wages that are due to the seaman at the time of his discharge, and to report the same quarterly together with the extra wages collected, to the Department of State (Form No. 124); and vouchers for wages paid to a seaman,

as prescribed in Form No. 164, must accompany the relief accounts. The arrears of wages and extra wages are not to be applied to the expenses of any discharged seaman after discharge by the consul, but all expenses for his maintenance and return to the United States shall be paid from the fund for the maintenance and transportation of destitute seamen. R. S. 4581 and Cir. Feb. 24, 1910.

228. Loss of vessel—In cases where the services of any seaman terminate before the period contemplated in the agreement, by reason of the loss or wreck of the vessel, such seaman shall be entitled to wages for the time of service prior to such termination, but not for any further period. Such seaman shall be considered as a destitute seaman (R. S. 4526) and it shall be the duty of American consular officers to provide sufficient subsistence and passage to some port in the United States, in the most reasonable manner, at the expense of the United States. The seamen shall, if able, be bound to do duty on board the vessels in which they may be transported, according to their several abilities. (R. S. 4577). This section shall not apply to fishing or whaling vessels, or yachts.

229. Time for payment—The master or owner of any vessel making foreign voyages, or from a port on the Atlantic to a port on the Pacific, or vice versa, shall pay to every seaman his wages within twenty-four hours after the cargo has been discharged, or within four days after the seaman has been discharged, whichever first happens; and in all cases the seaman shall be entitled to be paid at the time of his discharge, on account of wages, a sum equal to one-third part of the balance due him. Every master or owner who refuses or neglects to make payment in the manner hereinbefore mentioned, without sufficient cause, shall pay to the seaman a sum equal to two days' pay for each and every day during which payment is delayed beyond the respective periods, which sum shall be recoverable as wages in any claim made before the court; but this section shall not apply to the masters or owners of any vessel, the seamen of which are entitled to share in the profits of the cruise or voyage. R. S. Sec. 4529.

230. Payment of wages at ports—Every seaman on a vessel of the United States shall be entitled to receive on demand from the master of the vessel to which he belongs, one-half part of the wages, which he shall have then earned, at every port where such vessel, after the voyage has commenced, shall load or deliver cargo before the voyage is ended and all stipulations in the contract shall be void: Provided such demand shall not be made before the expiration of nor oftener than, five days. Any failure of the master to comply with this demand shall release the seaman from his contract, and he shall be entitled to full payment of wages earned. And when the voyage is ended, every such seaman shall be entitled to the remainder of the

wages which shall then be due him, as provided in R. S. 4529. R. S. 4530.

235. Allotment of wages—It shall be lawful for any seaman to stipulate in his shipping agreement for an allotment of any portion of the wages he may earn to his grandparents, parents, wife, sister, or children. No allotment shall be valid unless in writing and signed by and approved by the shipping commissioner. It shall be the duty of the said commissioner to examine such allotments and the parties to them and enforce compliance with the law. All stipulations for the allotment of any part of the wages of a seaman during his absence which are made at the commencement of the voyage shall be inserted in the agreement and shall state the amounts and the times of the payment to be made and the persons to whom the payments are to be made. That no allotment except as provided for in this section shall be lawful. Sec. 10 (b, c, d), Act Mar. 4, 1915.

236. No advance wages—It shall be and is hereby made unlawful in any case to pay any seaman wages in advance of the time when he has actually earned the same, or to pay such advance wages, or to make any order, or note, or other evidence of indebtedness therefor to any other person, or to pay any other person, for the shipment of seamen when payment is deducted from a seaman's wages. Any person violating any of the foregoing provisions of this section shall be deemed guilty of a misdemeanor, and upon conviction, shall be punished by a fine of not less than $25 nor more than $100, and may also be imprisoned for a period of not exceeding six months, at the discretion of the court. The payment of such advance wages or allotment shall in no case except as herein provided, absolve the vessel or the master, or the owner thereof from the full payment of wages, after the same shall have been actually earned, and shall be no defense to a libel suit or action for the recovery of such wages. If any person shall demand or receive, either directly, or indirectly, from any seaman, or other person, seeking employment, as seaman, or from any person in his behalf, any remuneration whatever, for providing him with employment, he shall for every such offense be deemed guilty of a misdemeanor and shall be imprisoned for not more than six months or fined not more than $500. R. S. Sec. 10 (a), Mar. 4, 1915.

238. To be cured at expense of ship—By the general maritime law, a seaman, when he receives any injury when in the service of the ship, or becomes sick during the voyage, and the sickness is not caused by his own fault, is entitled to be cured at the expense of the ship, but if the seaman is discharged on account of illness or injury, incapacitating him for service, the expenses of his maintenance and return to the United States shall be paid from the fund for the maintenance and transportation of destitute American seamen, and pro-

vided, that at the discretion of the Secretary of Commerce, and under such regulations as he may prescribe, if any seaman incapacitated by injury or illness is on board a vessel so situated that a prompt discharge requiring the personal appearance of the master of the vessel before an American consul, or a consular agent is impracticable, such seaman may be sent to a consul or a consular agent, who shall care for him and defray the cost of his maintenance and transportation to the United States. R. S. 4581 and amendments. Sec. 19, Act Mar. 4, 1915. Cir. Feb. 24, 1908.

243. When collected—If any consular officer, when discharging any seaman, shall neglect to require the payment of and collect the arrears of wages and extra wages required to be paid in the case of the discharge of any seaman, he shall be accountable to the United States for the full amount thereof. (R. S. 4581.) Consular officers are required by law to collect one month's extra wages in the following cases, and are prohibited from so doing in any other case.

1. When inspectors appointed by the consul to examine whether the vessel is in a suitable condition to go to sea shall have reported that she was sent to sea unsuitably provided in any important or essential particular by neglect or design, and the consular officer approves of such finding and thereupon the seaman is discharged. But if the master provides the seaman so discharged with passage money to the nearest and most convenient port of the United States or furnishes him with employment on a ship agreed upon, then one month's extra wages should not be collected. R. S. 4561 (paragraphs 207 (6), 208, 315). This section does not apply to fishing or whaling vessels, or yachts. Sec. 11, Dec. 21, 1898.

2. Whenever, on the discharge of a seaman in a foreign country by a consular officer on complaint (his) that the voyage is continued contrary to agreement (paragraph 315) or that the vessel is badly provisioned, or unseaworthy, or against the officers for cruel treatment, it shall be the duty of a consul or a consular agent to institute a proper inquiry into the matter, and, upon his being satisfied of the truth and justice of such complaint, to discharge the seaman. R. S. 4583. The master shall also provide him with adequate employment on board some other vessel, *or* provide him with a passage to the port from which he originally sailed (shipped), *or* to the most convenient port of entry in the United States, *or* to a port agreed to by the seaman.

3. Whenever a seaman is so discharged, if it shall be shown to the satisfaction of the consul that such seaman was not discharged for neglect of duty, incompetency, voluntary consent or injury incurred on the vessel. Sec. 16, R. S. 4581.

247. No waiver of extra wages permitted—A note should be made on the margin of the page opposite the third line from the end, amend-

ing "section 7 of the Act of June 26, 1884," to Section 16 of the Act of December 21, 1898.

252. Vessels sold—Whenever a vessel of the United States is sold in a foreign country and her company discharged, it shall be the duty of the master to produce to the consular officer a certified list of the (the) ship's company, and also the shipping articles, and besides paying to each seaman, or apprentice the wages due him, he shall either provide him with adequate employment on board some other vessel bound for the port at which he was originally shipped, *or* to such other port as may be agreed upon by him, *or* furnish the means of sending him to such port, *or* provide him with a passage home, *or* deposit with the consular officer a sum of money as is by the officer deemed sufficient to defray the expenses of his maintenance and passage home; and the consular officer shall indorse upon the agreement with the crew of the ship which the seaman or apprentice is leaving, the particulars of any payment, provision, or deposit made under this section. A failure to comply with the provisions of this section shall render the owner liable to a fine of not exceeding fifty dollars. Sec. 17, R. S. 4582, Dec. 21, 1898.

254. Discharge for illness or injury—Whenever a seaman is discharged on account of illness or injury incapacitating him for service, the expenses of his maintenance and return to the United States shall be paid from the fund for the maintenance and transportation of destitute seamen. (R. S. 4581; Act of December 21, 1898, Section 17.) At the discretion of the Secretary of Commerce, and under such regulations as he may prescribe, if any seaman incapacitated from service by injury or illness is on board a vessel so situated that a prompt discharge requiring a personal appearance of the master of the vessel before an American consular officer is impracticable, such seaman may be sent to a consular officer who shall care for him and defray the cost of his maintenance and transportation as provided in this paragraph. The personal appearance of the master of the vessel before an American consular officer to consent to the discharge of a seaman who has been incapacitated by injury or illness may be waived by the officer under the following conditions: (a) When the condition of the injured or ill seaman is such that prompt medical attendance is necessary and cannot be furnished on shipboard, and (b) when the master cannot proceed with the seaman to the consul without risk to the crew, the vessel, or the cargo. In such cases the master will address to the consul in writing a full statement of the facts which render necessary the discharge of the seaman, together with a statement of the reasons why he himself is unable to appear before the consul. The statement should cover the usual particulars set forth in a discharge and should be accompanied with an account of the

wages due and with the necessary funds to meet such wages, or (if the cash be not available) with an order on the owner for the amount due. If the consul shall deem the statement satisfactory, he may discharge the seaman as directed in Section 4581, Revised Statutes, as amended by Section 16 of the Act of December 21, 1898, and Section 19 of the Act of March 4, 1915, as if the master were present, attaching to discharge and to his relief account a copy of the statement submitted by the master. If the consul shall deem the statement unsatisfactory, he will decline to grant the discharge and direct that the seaman be returned to the vessel at its expense.

291. Passage money to be paid by the government—In cases where the service of any seaman terminates before the period contemplated in the agreement, by reason of the loss or wreck of the vessel, such seaman shall be entitled to wages for the time of service prior to such termination, but not for any further period. Such seaman shall be considered a destitute seaman and shall be treated and transported to port of shipment as provided in sections 4577 and 4579 of the Revised Statutes. Sec. 3, R. S. 4526. If the seaman is discharged on account of injury or illness, incapacitating him for service, the expenses of his maintenance and return to the United States shall be paid from the fund for the maintenance and transportation of destitute American seamen. Sec. 16, R. S. 4581.

293. Desertion, how punished—It is provided by statute that desertion shall be punished by forfeiture of all or any part of the clothes or effects he leaves on board and of all, or any part of the wages or emoluments he has earned then. For neglecting or refusing without reasonable cause to join his vessel or to proceed to sea in his vessel, or for absence without leave at any time within twenty-four hours of the vessel's sailing from any port, either at the commencement or during the progress of the voyage, or for absence at any time without leave and without sufficient reason from his vessel and from his duty, not amounting to desertion, by forfeiting from his wages not more than two days' pay or sufficient to defray any expenses which shall have been incurred in hiring a substitute. For quitting the vessel without leave, after her arrival at the port of her delivery and before she is placed in security, by forfeiture from his wages of not more than one month's pay. Sec. 7, R. S. 4596, Act March 4, 1915.

299. Arrest of deserters—Cancelled by sections 16 and 17, Act of March 4, 1915.

302. Desertion from cruel treatment—It is by law made the duty of consular officers, in cases where seamen or officers are accused, to inquire into the facts, and, upon his being satisfied of the truth and justice of such complaint, he shall require the master to pay to such

seaman one month's wages over and above the wages due at the time of discharge, and to provide him with adequate employment on board some other vessel, or provide him with a passage on board some other vessel bound for the port from which he was originally shipped, or to the most convenient port of entry in the United States, or to a port agreed to by the seaman; and the officer discharging such seaman shall enter upon the crew list and shipping articles and official log the cause of such discharge and the particulars in which the cruel or unusual treatment consisted, and subscribe his name thereto officially. He shall read the entry made in the official log to the master, and his reply thereto, if any, shall likewise be entered and subscribed in the same manner. Sec. 18, R. S. 4583, Dec. 21, 1898; Sec. 8, R. S. 4600, March 4, 1915.

304. Desertions to be reported within forty-eight hours—Strike out the end of the first sentence beginning at "and consequently no effort is made, or can successfully be made, for the recovery of the deserters, who subsequently come upon the consulate"; and the part of the second sentence reading "In order therefore, to aid in the enforcement of these regulations."

306. Treaty provisions as to desertion—Cancel. Sec. 16 and 17, Act March 4, 1915, forbids the arrest and imprisonment of officers and seamen deserting or charged with desertion from merchant vessels in foreign countries and authorizes the President to give notice of the termination of such treaties to all foreign governments concerned.

315. Complaint of unseaworthiness—Provision has been made by statute for the examination of complaints in respect to the unseaworthy condition of the vessel and insufficient equipment or supplies and for the proceedings of consular officers in such cases. Upon a complaint in writing, signed by the first and second officers, or a majority of the crew of any vessel, while in a foreign port that such vessel is in an unsuitable condition to go to sea, because she is leaky or insufficiently supplied with sails, rigging, anchors, or any other equipment, or that the crew is insufficient to man her, or that her provisions, stores and supplies are not or have not been during the voyage sufficient or wholesome, thereupon in any of these or like cases the consul or consular agent who may discharge any of the duties of a consul shall cause to be appointed three persons of like qualifications with those prescribed in section 4557 of the Revised Statutes, who shall proceed to examine into the cause of complaint and who shall proceed and be governed in all their proceedings as provided by said section (R. S. 4559). The inspectors in their report shall also state whether in their opinion the vessel was sent to sea unsuitably provided in any important or essential particular, by neglect or design, and the consular officer approves of such findings, he shall discharge such of

the crew as request it, and shall require the payment by the master of one month's wages for each seaman over and above the wages then due, or sufficient money for the return of such of the crew as desire to be discharged, or with employment on a ship agreed to by them. But if in the opinion of the inspectors the defects or deficiencies found to exist have been the result of mistake or accident, and could not, in the exercise of ordinary care, have been known and provided against before the sailing of the vessel and the master shall in a reasonable time remove or remedy the cause of complaint, then the crew shall remain and discharge their duty. R. S. 4561, Dec. 21, 1898. (Paragraphs 207 (60, 243). If not so remedied, the consular officer may discharge the crew, on their request, with the arrears of wages, but without any extra wages. The master or commander shall in the first instance pay all the costs of such review, report, or judgment, to be taxed or pay all the costs of such review, report, or judgment, to be taxed or allowed on a fair copy thereof, certified by the judge or justice. But if the complaint of the crew shall appear upon the report and judgment to have been without foundation, the master or commander, or the owner or consignee of such vessel, shall deduct the amount thereof, and of reasonable damages for the detention, to be ascertained by the judge or justice, out of the wages of the complaining seamen. R. S. 4557. In cases of this kind the consular officer will be careful to consult the full text of the statutes. This provision does not apply to fishing or whaling vessels, or yachts.

316. Complaint as to provisions, or water—Amend by changing the last sentence of the paragraph to read: "If the officer to whom any such complaint is made certified in such statement that there was no reasonable ground for such complaint, each of the parties so complaining shall forfeit to the master or owner, his share of the expenses, if any, of the survey." R. S. 4556, Act Dec. 21, 1898. This provision does not apply to fishing or whaling vessels, or yachts (Sec. 26, Act Dec. 21, 1898.)

320. Application to authorities—Strike out form No. 34. ("Requests to Local Authorities for the Arrest of Deserters.") Sec. 16, Act March 4, 1915.

337. Consular Fees—Annote on margin "Section 4559 as amended by section 5 of the Act of March 4, 1915."

352. Insubordination to be discouraged—Amend this paragraph by striking out the first sentence and replacing it with, "It shall be the duty of all consular officers to discountenance by every means in their power and, where the local authorities can be usefully employed for that purpose, to lend their aid and use their exertions to that end in the most effectual manner. In all cases where seamen or officers are accused, the consular officer shall inquire into the facts and proceed

as provided in section 4583 of the Revised Statutes; and the officer discharging such seamen shall enter upon the crew list and shipping articles and official log the cause of such discharge and the particulars in which the cruel or unusual treatment consisted and subscribe his name thereto officially. He shall read the entry made in the official log to the master, and his reply thereto, if any, shall likewise be entered and subscribed in the same manner." The remainder of the paragraph stands as it is.

301. Desertion connived at by master—Strike out the end of the second reading, "and that all proper efforts were made to recover and secure the deserter." Sec. 16, Act Mar. 4, 1915.

Paragraph 89, "The right to reclaim deserters" is cancelled.

WOODROW WILSON.

[Suspending Operation of the Act to Promote the Welfare of American Seamen and to Forbid Their Arrest and Imprisonment for Desertion.]

THE WHITE HOUSE, *November 2, 1915.*

In pursuance of the authority conferred upon the President of the United States by Section 2 of the Act of August 18, 1914, entitled "An Act to provide for the admission of foreign-built ships to American registry for the foreign trade, and for other purposes," it is hereby ordered:

That the provisions of section 4488 of the Revised Statutes, as amended by section 14 of the Act of March 4, 1915, entitled "An Act to promote the welfare of American seamen in the merchant marine of the United States; to abolish arrest and imprisonment as a penalty for desertion and to secure the abrogation of treaty provisions in relation thereto; and to promote safety at sea," are hereby suspended for a period ending September 3d, 1916.

WOODROW WILSON.

[Establishing a United States Sheep Experiment Station.]

THE WHITE HOUSE, *October 30, 1915.*

Pursuant to authority contained in the act of Congress approved June 25, 1910 (36 Stat., 847), as amended by act of August 24, 1912 (37 Stat., 497), and upon the recommendation of the Secretary of Agriculture, it is hereby ordered that the following described areas in the State of Idaho be withdrawn for the use by the Department of Agriculture of the United States as a sheep-breeding and grazing experimental station, excepting from the force and effect of this withdrawal all lands covered by valid adverse claims initiated prior to the date hereof and maintained pursuant to law:

T. 11 N., R. 36 E., all; T. 10 N., R. 36 E., Secs. 1, 2, 11, and 12; and R. 37 E., Secs. 5, 6, 7, and 8, Boise Base and Meridian.

WOODROW WILSON.

THIRD ANNUAL ADDRESS

[Delivered at a Joint Session of the Two Houses of Congress, December 7, 1915.]

GENTLEMEN OF THE CONGRESS: Since I last had the privilege of addressing you on the state of the Union the war of nations on the other side of the sea, which had then only begun to disclose its portentous proportions, has extended its threatening and sinister scope until it has swept within its flame some portion of every quarter of the globe, not excepting our own hemisphere, has altered the whole face of international affairs, and now presents a prospect of reorganization and reconstruction such as statesmen and peoples have never been called upon to attempt before.

We have stood apart, studiously neutral. It was our manifest duty to do so. Not only did we have no part or interest in the policies which seem to have brought the conflict on; it was necessary, if a universal catastrophe was to be avoided, that a limit should be set to the sweep of destructive war and that some part of the great family of nations should keep the processes of peace alive, if only to prevent collective economic ruin and the breakdown throughout the world of the industries by which its populations are fed and sustained. It was manifestly the duty of the self-governed nations of this hemisphere to redress, if possible, the balance of economic loss and confusion in the other, if they could do nothing more. In the day of readjustment and recuperation we earnestly hope and believe that they can be of infinite service.

In this neutrality, to which they were bidden not only by their separate life and their habitual detachment from the politics of Europe but also by a clear perception of international duty, the states of America have become conscious of a new and more vital community of interest and moral partnership in affairs, more clearly conscious of the many common sympathies and interests and duties which bid them stand together.

There was a time in the early days of our own great nation and of the republics fighting their way to independence in Central and South America when the government of the United States looked upon itself as in some sort the guardian of the republics to the south of her as against any encroachments or efforts at political control from the other side of the water; felt it its duty to play the part even without invitation from them; and I think that we can claim that the task was undertaken with a true and disinterested enthusiasm for the freedom of the Americas and the unmolested self-government of her independent peoples. But it was always difficult to maintain such a rôle without offense to the pride of the peoples whose freedom of action we sought to protect, and without provoking serious misconceptions of our motives, and every thoughtful man of affairs must welcome the altered circumstances of the new day in whose light we now stand, when there is no claim of guardianship or thought of wards but, instead, a full and honorable association as of partners between ourselves and our neighbors, in the interest of all America, north and south. Our concern for the independence and prosperity of the states of Central and South America is not altered. We retain unabated the spirit that has inspired us throughout the whole life of our government and which was so frankly put into words by President Monroe. We still mean always to make a common cause of national independence and of political liberty in America. But that purpose is now better understood so far as it concerns ourselves. It is known not to be a selfish purpose. It is known to have in it no thought of taking advantage of any government in this hemisphere or playing its political fortunes for our own benefit. All the governments of America stand, so far as we are concerned, upon a footing of genuine equality and unquestioned independence.

We have been put to the test in the case of Mexico, and we have stood the test. Whether we have benefited Mexico by the course we have pursued remains to be seen. Her fortunes are in her own hands. But we have at least proved that we will not take advantage of her in her distress and undertake to impose upon her an order and government of our own choosing. Liberty is often a fierce and intractable thing, to which no bounds can be set, and to which no bounds of a few men's choosing ought ever to be set. Every American who has drunk at the true fountains of principle and tradition must subscribe without reservation to the high doctrine of the Virginia Bill of Rights, which in the great days in which our government was set up was everywhere amongst us accepted as the creed of free men. That doctrine is, "That government is, or ought to be, instituted for the common benefit, protection, and security of the people, nation, or community"; that "of all the various modes and forms of government, that is the best which is capable of producing the greatest degree of happiness and safety, and is most effectually secured against the danger of maladministration; and that, when any government shall be found inadequate or contrary to these purposes, a majority of the community hath an indubitable, inalienable, and indefeasible right to reform, alter, or abolish it, in such manner as shall be judged most conducive to the public weal." We have unhesitatingly applied that heroic principle to the case of Mexico, and now hopefully await the rebirth of the troubled Republic, which had so much of which to purge itself and so little sympathy from any outside quarter in the radical but necessary process. We will aid and befriend Mexico, but we will not coerce her; and our course with regard to her ought to be sufficient proof to all America that we seek no political suzerainty or selfish control.

The moral is, that the states of America are not hostile rivals but coöperating friends, and that their growing sense of community ot interest, alike in matters political and in matters economic, is likely to give them a new significance as factors in international affairs and in the political history of the world. It presents them as in a very deep and true sense a unit in world affairs, spiritual partners, standing together because thinking together, quick with common sympathies and common ideals. Separated they are subject to all the cross currents of the confused politics of a world of hostile rivalries; united in spirit and purpose they cannot be disappointed of their peaceful destiny.

This is Pan-Americanism. It has none of the spirit of empire in it. It is the embodiment, the effectual embodiment, of the spirit of law and independence and liberty and mutual service.

A very notable body of men recently met in the City of Washington, at the invitation and as the guests of this Government, whose deliberations are likely to be looked back to as marking a memorable turning point in the history of America. They were representative spokesmen of the several independent states of this hemisphere and were assembled to discuss the financial and commercial relations of the republics of the two continents which nature and political fortune have so intimately linked together. I earnestly recommend to your perusal the reports of their proceedings and of the actions of their committees. You will get from them, I think, a fresh conception of the ease and intelligence and advantage with which Americans of both continents may draw together in practical coöperation and of what the material foundations of this hopeful partnership of interest must consist,—of how we should build them and of how necessary it is that we should hasten their building.

There is, I venture to point out, an especial significance just now attaching to this whole matter of drawing the Americans together in bonds of honorable partnership and mutual advantage because of the economic readjustments which the world must inevitably witness within the next generation, when peace shall have at last resumed its healthful tasks. In the performance of these tasks I believe the Americas to be destined to play their parts together. I am interested to fix your attention on this prospect now because unless you take it within your view and permit the full significance of it to command your thought I cannot find the right light in which to set forth the particular matter that lies at the very font of my whole thought as I address you to-day. I mean national defense.

No one who really comprehends the spirit of the great people for whom we are appointed to speak can fail to perceive that their passion is for peace, their genius best displayed in the practice of the arts of peace. Great democracies are not belligerent. They do not seek or desire war. Their thought is of individual liberty and of the free labor that supports life and the uncensored thought that quickens it. Conquest and dominion are not in our reckoning, or agreeable to our principles. But just because we demand unmolested development and the undisturbed government of our own lives upon our own principles of right and liberty, we resent, from whatever quarter it may come, the aggression we ourselves will not practice. We insist upon security in prosecuting our self-chosen lines of national development. We do more than that. We demand it also for others. We do not confine our enthusiasm for individual liberty and free national development to the incidents and movements of affairs which affect only ourselves. We feel it wherever there is a people that tries to walk in these difficult paths of independence and right. From the first we have made common cause with all partisans of liberty on this side the sea, and have deemed it as important that our neighbors should be free from all outside domination as that we ourselves should be; have set America aside as a whole for the uses of independent nations and political freemen.

Out of such thoughts grow all our policies. We regard war merely as a means of asserting the rights of a people against aggression. And we are as fiercely jealous of coercive or dictatorial power within our own nation as of aggression from without. We will not maintain a standing army except for uses which are as necessary in times of peace as in times of war; and we shall always see to it that our military peace establishment is no larger than is actually and continuously needed for the uses of days in which no enemies move against us. But we do believe in a body of free citizens ready and sufficient to take care of themselves and of the governments which they have set up to serve them. In our constitutions themselves we have commanded that "the right of the people to keep and bear arms shall not be infringed," and our confidence has been that our safety in times of danger would lie in the rising of the nation to take care of itself, as the farmers rose at Lexington.

But war has never been a mere matter of men and guns. It is a thing of disciplined might. If our citizens are ever to fight effectively upon a sudden summons, they must know how modern fighting is done, and what to do when the summons comes to render themselves immediately available and immediately effective. And the government must be their servant in this matter, must supply them with the training they need to take care of themselves and of it. The military arm of their government, which they will not allow to direct them, they may properly use to serve them and make their independence secure,—and not their own independence merely but the rights also of those with whom they have made common cause, should they also be put in jeopardy. They must be fitted to play the great rôle in the world, and particularly in this hemisphere, for which they are qualified by principle and by chastened ambition to play.

It is with these ideals in mind that the plans of the Department of War for more adequate national defense were conceived which will be laid before you, and which I urge you to sanction and put into effect as soon as they can be properly scrutinized and discussed. They seem to me the essential first steps, and they seem to me for the present sufficient.

They contemplate an increase of the standing force of the regular army from its present strength of five thousand and twenty-three officers and one hundred and two thousand nine hundred and eighty-five enlisted men of all services to a strength of seven thousand one hundred and thirty-six officers and one hundred and thirty-four thousand seven hundred and seven enlisted men, or 141,843, all told, all services, rank and file, by the addition of fifty-two companies of coast artillery, fifteen companies of engineers, ten regiments of infantry, four regiments of field artillery, and four aero squadrons, besides seven hundred and fifty officers required for a great variety of extra service, especially the all important duty of training the citizen force of which I shall presently speak, seven hundred and ninety-two non-commissioned officers for service in drill, recruiting and the like, and the necessary quota of enlisted men for the Quartermaster Corps, the Hospital Corps, the Ordnance Department, and other similar auxiliary services. These are the additions necessary to render the army adequate for its present duties, duties which it has to perform not only upon our own continental coasts and borders and at our interior army posts, but also in the Philippines, in the Hawaiian Islands, at the Isthmus, and in Porto Rico.

By way of making the country ready to assert some part of its real power promptly and upon a larger scale, should occasion arise, the plan also contemplates supplementing the army by a force of four hundred thousand disciplined citizens, raised in increments of one hundred and thirty-three thousand a year throughout a period of three years. This it is proposed to do by a process of enlistment under which the serviceable men of the country would be asked to bind themselves to serve with the colors for purposes of training for short periods throughout three years, and to come to the colors at call at any time throughout an additional "furlough" period of three years. This force of four hundred thousand men would be provided with personal accoutrements as fast as enlisted and their equipment for the field made ready to be supplied at any time. They would be assembled for training at stated intervals at convenient places in association with suitable units of the regular army. Their period of annual training would not necessarily exceed two months in the year.

It would depend upon the patriotic feeling of the younger men of the country whether they responded to such a call to service or not. It would depend upon the patriotic spirit of the employers of the country whether they made it possible for the younger men in their employ to respond under favorable conditions or not. I, for one, do not doubt the patriotic devotion either of our young men or of those who give them employment,—those for whose benefit and protection they would in fact enlist. I would look forward to the success of such an experiment with entire confidence.

At least so much by way of preparation for defense seems to me to be absolutely imperative now. We cannot do less.

The programme which will be laid before you by the Secretary of the Navy is similarly conceived. It involves only a shortening of the time within which plans long matured shall be carried out; but it does make definite and explicit a programme which has heretofore been only implicit, held in the minds of the Committees on Naval Affairs and disclosed in the debates of the two Houses but nowhere formulated or formally adopted. It seems to me very clear that it will be to the advantage of the country for the Congress to adopt a comprehensive plan for putting the navy upon a final footing of strength and efficiency and to press that plan to completion within the next five years. We have always looked to the navy of the country as our first and chief line of defense; we have always seen it to be our manifest course of prudence to be strong on the seas. Year by year we have been creating a navy which now ranks very high indeed among the navies of the maritime nations. We should now definitely determine how we shall complete what we have begun, and how soon.

The programme to be laid before you contemplates the construction within five years of ten battleships, six battle cruisers, ten scout cruisers, fifty destroyers, fifteen fleet submarines, eighty-five coast submarines, four gunboats, one hospital ship, two ammunition ships, two fuel oil ships, and one repair ship. It is proposed that of this number we shall the first year provide for the construction of two battleships, two battle cruisers, three scout cruisers, fifteen destroyers, five fleet submarines, twenty-five coast submarines, two gunboats, and one hospital ship; the second year, two battleships, one scout cruiser, ten destroyers, four fleet submarines, fifteen coast submarines, one gunboat, and one fuel oil ship; the third year, two battleships, one battle cruiser, two scout cruisers, five destroyers, two fleet sub-

marines, and fifteen coast submarines; the fourth year, two battleships, two battle cruisers, two scout cruisers, ten destroyers, two fleet
submarines, fifteen coast submarines, one ammunition ship, and one
fuel oil ship; and the fifth year, two battleships, one battle cruiser,
two scout cruisers, ten destroyers, two fleet submarines, fifteen coast
submarines, one gunboat, one ammunition ship, and one repair ship.

The Secretary of the Navy is asking also for the immediate addition to the personnel of the navy of seven thousand five hundred
sailors, twenty-five hundred apprentice seamen, and fifteen hundred
marines. This increase would be sufficient to care for the ships which
are to be completed within the fiscal year 1917 and also for the number of men which must be put in training to man the ships which
will be completed early in 1918. It is also necessary that the number of midshipmen at the Naval academy at Annapolis should be
increased by at least three hundred in order that the force of officers
should be more rapidly added to; and authority is asked to appoint,
for engineering duties only, approved graduates of engineering colleges, and for service in the aviation corps a certain number of men
taken from civil life.

If this full programme should be carried out we should have built
or building in 1921, according to the estimates of survival and
standards of classification followed by the General Board of the
Department, an effective navy consisting of twenty-seven battleships
of the first line, six battle cruisers, twenty-five battleships of the
second line, ten armored cruisers, thirteen scout cruisers, five first
class cruisers, three second class cruisers, ten third class cruisers,
one hundred and eight destroyers, eighteen fleet submarines, one hundred and fifty-seven coast submarines, six monitors, twenty gunboats,
four supply ships, fifteen fuel ships, four transports, three tenders to
torpedo vessels, eight vessels of special types, and two ammunition
ships. This would be a navy fitted to our needs and worthy of our
traditions.

But armies and instruments of war are only part of what has to be
considered if we are to provide for the supreme matter of national
self-sufficiency and security in all its aspects. There are other great
matters which will be thrust upon our attention whether we will or
not. There is, for example, a very pressing question of trade and
shipping involved in this great problem of national adequacy. It is
necessary for many weighty reasons of national efficiency and development that we should have a great merchant marine. The great
merchant fleet we once used to make us rich, that great body of sturdy
sailors who used to carry our flag into every sea, and who were the
pride and often the bulwark of the nation, we have almost driven out
of existence by inexcusable neglect and indifference and by a hope-

lessly blind and provincial policy of so-called economic protection.
It is high time we repaired our mistake and resumed our commercial
independence on the seas.

For it is a question of independence. If other nations go to war
or seek to hamper each other's commerce, our merchants, it seems,
are at their mercy, to do with as they please. We must use their
ships, and use them as they determine. We have not ships enough
of our own. We cannot handle our own commerce on the seas. Our
independence is provincial, and is only on land and within our own
borders. We are not likely to be permitted to use even the ships
of other nations in rivalry of their own trade, and are without means
to extend our commerce even where the doors are wide open and
our goods desired. Such a situation is not to be endured. It is
of capital importance not only that the United States should be
its own carrier on the seas and enjoy the economic independence
which only an adequate merchant marine would give it, but also
that the American hemisphere as a whole should enjoy a like independence and self-sufficiency, if it is not to be drawn into the tangle
of European affairs. Without such independence the whole question
of our political unity and self-determination is very seriously clouded
and complicated indeed.

Moreover, we can develop no true or effective American policy
without ships of our own,—not ships of war, but ships of peace,
carrying goods and carrying much more: creating friendships and
rendering indispensable services to all interests on this side the water.
They must move constantly back and forth between the Americas.
They are the only shuttles that can weave the delicate fabric of sympathy, comprehension, confidence, and mutual dependence in which
we wish to clothe our policy of America for Americans.

The task of building up an adequate merchant marine for America private capital must ultimately undertake and achieve, as it has
undertaken and achieved every other like task amongst us in the
past, with admirable enterprise, intelligence, and vigor; and it seems
to me a manifest dictate of wisdom that we should promptly remove
every legal obstacle that may stand in the way of this much to be
desired revival of our old independence and should facilitate in every
possible way the building, purchase, and American registration of
ships. But capital cannot accomplish this great task of a sudden.
It must embark upon it by degrees, as the opportunities of trade
develop. Something must be done at once; done to open routes and
develop opportunities where they are as yet undeveloped; done to
open the arteries of trade where the currents have not yet learned
to run,—especially between the two American continents, where they
are, singularly enough, yet to be created and quickened; and it is

evident that only the government can undertake such beginnings and assume the initial financial risks. When the risk has passed and private capital begins to find its way in sufficient abundance into these new channels, the government may withdraw. But it cannot omit to begin. It should take the first steps, and should take them at once. Our goods must not lie piled up at our ports and stored upon side tracks in freight cars which are daily needed on the roads; must not be left without means of transport to any foreign quarter. We must not await the permission of foreign ship-owners and foreign governments to send them where we will.

With a view to meeting these pressing necessities of our commerce and availing ourselves at the earliest possible moment of the present unparalleled opportunity of linking the two Americas together in bonds of mutual interest and service, an opportunity which may never return again if we miss it now, proposals will be made to the present Congress for the purchase or construction of ships to be owned and directed by the government similar to those made to the last Congress, but modified in some essential particulars. I recommend these proposals to you for your prompt acceptance with the more confidence because every month that has elapsed since the former proposals were made has made the necessity for such action more and more manifestly imperative. That need was then foreseen; it is now acutely felt and everywhere realized by those for whom trade is waiting but who can find no conveyance for their goods. I am not so much interested in the particulars of the programme as I am in taking immediate advantage of the great opportunity which awaits us if we will but act in this emergency. In this matter, as in all others, a spirit of common counsel should prevail, and out of it should come an early solution of this pressing problem.

There is another matter which seems to me to be very intimately associated with the question of national safety and preparation for defense. That is our policy towards the Philippines and the people of Porto Rico. Our treatment of them and their attitude towards us are manifestly of the first consequence in the development of our duties in the world and in getting a free hand to perform those duties. We must be free from every unnecessary burden or embarrassment; and there is no better way to be clear of embarrassment than to fulfil our promises and promote the interests of those dependent on us to the utmost. Bills for the alteration and reform of the government of the Philippines and for rendering fuller political justice to the people of Porto Rico were submitted to the sixty-third Congress. They will be submitted also to you. I need not particularize their details. You are most of you already familiar with them. But I do recommend them to your early adoption with the sincere conviction that there are few measures you could adopt which would more serviceably clear the way for the great policies by which we wish to make good, now and always, our right to lead in enterprises of peace and good will and economic and political freedom.

The plans for the armed forces of the nation which I have outlined, and for the general policy of adequate preparation for mobilization and defense, involve of course very large additional expenditures of money,—expenditures which will considerably exceed the estimated revenues of the government. It is made my duty by law, whenever the estimates of expenditure exceed the estimates of revenue, to call the attention of the Congress to the fact and suggest any means of meeting the deficiency that it may be wise or possible for me to suggest. I am ready to believe that it would be my duty to do so in any case; and I feel particularly bound to speak of the matter when it appears that the deficiency will arise directly out of the adoption by the Congress of measures which I myself urge it to adopt. Allow me, therefore, to speak briefly of the present state of the Treasury and of the fiscal problems which the next year will probably disclose.

On the thirtieth of June last there was an available balance in the general fund of the Treasury of $104,170,105.78. The total estimated receipts for the year 1916, on the assumption that the emergency revenue measure passed by the last Congress will not be extended beyond its present limit, the thirty-first of December, 1915, and that the present duty of one cent per pound on sugar will be discontinued after the first of May, 1916, will be $670,365,500. The balance of June last and these estimated revenues come, therefore, to a grand total of $774,535,605.78. The total estimated disbursements for the present fiscal year, including twenty-five millions for the Panama Canal, twelve millions for probable deficiency appropriations, and fifty thousand dollars for miscellaneous debt redemptions, will be $753,891,000; and the balance in the general fund of the Treasury will be reduced to $20,644,605.78. The emergency revenue act, if continued beyond its present time limitation, would produce, during the half year then remaining, about forty-one millions. The duty of one cent per pound on sugar, if continued, would produce during the two months of the fiscal year remaining after the first of May, about fifteen millions. These two sums, amounting together to fifty-six millions, if added to the revenues of the second half of the fiscal year, would yield the Treasury at the end of the year an available balance of $76,644,605.78.

The additional revenues required to carry out the programme of military and naval preparation of which I have spoken, would, as at present estimated, be for the fiscal year 1917, $93,800,000. Those figures, taken with the figures for the present fiscal year which I have already given, disclose our financial problem for the year 1917. Assuming that the taxes imposed by the emergency revenue act and the present duty on sugar are to be discontinued, and that the balance at the close of the present fiscal year will be only $20,644,605.78, that the disbursements for the Panama Canal will again be about twenty-five millions, and that the additional expenditures for the army and navy are authorized by the Congress, the deficit in the general fund of the Treasury on the thirtieth of June, 1917, will be nearly two hundred and thirty-five millions. To this sum at least fifty millions should be added to represent a safe working balance for the Treasury, and twelve millions to include the usual deficiency estimates in 1917; and these additions would make a total deficit of some two hundred and ninety-seven millions. If the present taxes should be continued throughout this year and the next, however, there would be a balance in the Treasury of some seventy-six and a half millions at the end of the present fiscal year, and a deficit at the end of the next year of only some fifty millions, or, reckoning in sixty-two millions for deficiency appropriations and a safe Treasury balance at the end of the year, a total deficit of some one hundred and twelve millions. The obvious moral of the figures is that it is a plain counsel of prudence to continue all of the present taxes or their equivalents, and confine ourselves to the problem of providing one hundred and twelve millions of new revenue rather than two hundred and ninety-seven millions.

How shall we obtain the new revenue? We are frequently reminded that there are many millions of bonds which the Treasury is authorized under existing law to sell to reimburse the sums paid out of current revenues for the construction of the Panama Canal; and it is true that bonds to the amount of approximately $222,000,000 are now available for that purpose. Prior to 1913, $134,631,980 of these bonds had actually been sold to recoup the expenditures at the Isthmus; and now constitute a considerable item of the public debt. But I, for one, do not believe that the people of this country approve of postponing the payment of their bills. Borrowing money is short-sighted finance. It can be justified only when permanent things are to be accomplished which many generations will certainly benefit by and which it seems hardly fair that a single generation should pay for. The objects we are now proposing to spend money for cannot be so classified, except in the sense that everything wisely done may be said to be done in the interest of posterity as well as in our own. It seems to me a clear dictate of prudent statesmanship and frank finance that in what we are now, I hope, about to undertake we should pay as we go. The people of the country are entitled to know just what burdens of taxation they are to carry, and to know from the outset, now. The new bills should be paid by internal taxation.

To what sources, then, shall we turn? This is so peculiarly a question which the gentlemen of the House of Representatives are expected under the Constitution to propose an answer to that you will hardly expect me to do more than discuss it in very general terms. We should be following an almost universal example of modern governments if we were to draw the greater part or even the whole of the revenues we need from the income taxes. By somewhat lowering the present limits of exemption and the figure at which the surtax shall begin to be imposed, and by increasing, step by step throughout the present graduation, the surtax itself, the income taxes as at present apportioned would yield sums sufficient to balance the books of the Treasury at the end of the fiscal year 1917 without anywhere making the burden unreasonably or oppressively heavy. The precise reckonings are fully and accurately set out in the report of the Secretary of the Treasury which will be immediately laid before you.

And there are many additional sources of revenue which can justly be resorted to without hampering the industries of the country or putting any too great charge upon individual expenditure. A tax of one cent per gallon on gasoline and naphtha would yield, at the present estimated production, $10,000,000; a tax of fifty cents per horse power on automobiles and internal explosion engines, $15,000,000; a stamp tax on bank cheques, probably $18,000,000; a tax of twenty-five cents per ton on pig iron, $10,000,000; a tax of twenty-five cents per ton on fabricated iron and steel, probably $10,000,000. In a country of great industries like this it ought to be easy to distribute the burdens of taxation without making them anywhere bear too heavily or too exclusively upon any one set of persons or undertakings. What is clear is, that the industry of this generation should pay the bills of this generation.

I have spoken to you to-day, Gentlemen, upon a single theme, the thorough preparation of the nation to care for its own security and to make sure of entire freedom to play the impartial rôle in this hemisphere and in the world which we all believe to have been providentially assigned to it. I have had in my mind no thought of any immediate or particular danger arising out of our relations with other nations. We are at peace with all the nations of the world, and there is reason to hope that no question in controversy between this and other Governments will lead to any serious breach of amicable relations, grave as some differences of attitude and policy have been and may yet turn out to be. I am sorry to say that the gravest threats against our national peace and safety have been uttered within our own borders. There are citizens of the United States,

I blush to admit, born under other flags but welcomed under our generous naturalization laws to the full freedom and opportunity of America, who have poured the poison of disloyalty into the very arteries of our national life; who have sought to bring the authority and good name of our Government into contempt, to destroy our industries wherever they thought it effective for their vindictive purposes to strike at them, and to debase our politics to the uses of foreign intrigue. Their number is not great as compared with the whole number of those sturdy hosts by which our nation has been enriched in recent generations out of virile foreign stock; but it is great enough to have brought deep disgrace upon us and to have made it necessary that we should promptly make use of processes of law by which we may be purged of their corrupt distempers. America never witnessed anything like this before. It never dreamed it possible that men sworn into its own citizenship, men drawn out of great free stocks such as supplied some of the best and strongest elements of that little, but how heroic, nation that in a high day of old staked its very life to free itself from every entanglement that had darkened the fortunes of the older nations and set up a new standard here,— that men of such origins and such free choices of allegiance would ever turn in malign reaction against the Government and people who had welcomed and nurtured them and seek to make this proud country once more a hotbed of European passion. A little while ago such a thing would have seemed incredible. Because it was incredible we made no preparation for it. We would have been almost ashamed to prepare for it, as if we were suspicious of ourselves, our own comrades and neighbors! But the ugly and incredible thing has actually come about and we are without adequate federal laws to deal with it. I urge you to enact such laws at the earliest possible moment and feel that in doing so I am urging you to do nothing less than save the honor and self-respect of the nation. Such creatures of passion, disloyalty, and anarchy must be crushed out. They are not many, but they are infinitely malignant, and the hand of our power should close over them at once. They have formed plots to destroy property, they have entered into conspiracies against the neutrality of the Government, they have sought to pry into every confidential transaction of the Government in order to serve interests alien to our own. It is possible to deal with these things very effectually. I need not suggest the terms in which they may be dealt with.

I wish that it could be said that only a few men, misled by mistaken sentiments of allegiance to the governments under which they were born, had been guilty of disturbing the self-possession and misrepresenting the temper and principles of the country during these days of terrible war, when it would seem that every man who was truly an American would instinctively make it his duty and his pride to keep the scales of judgment even and prove himself a partisan of no nation but his own. But it cannot. There are some men among us, and many resident abroad who, though born and bred in the United States and calling themselves Americans, have so forgotten themselves and their honor as citizens as to put their passionate sympathy with one or the other side in the great European conflict above their regard for the peace and dignity of the United States. They also preach and practice disloyalty. No laws, I suppose, can reach corruptions of the mind and heart; but I should not speak of others without also speaking of these and expressing the even deeper humiliation and scorn which every self-possessed and thoughtfully patriotic American must feel when he thinks of them and of the discredit they are daily bringing upon us.

While we speak of the preparation of the nation to make sure of her security and her effective power we must not fall into the patent error of supposing that her real strength comes from armaments and mere safeguards of written law. It comes, of course, from her people, their energy, their success in their undertakings, their free opportunity to use the natural resources of our great home land and of the lands outside our continental borders which look to us for protection, for encouragement, and for assistance in their development; from the organization and freedom and vitality of our economic life. The domestic questions which engaged the attention of the last Congress are more vital to the nation in this its time of test than at any other time. We cannot adequately make ready for any trial of our strength unless we wisely and promptly direct the force of our laws into these all-important fields of domestic action. A matter which it seems to me we should have very much at heart is the creation of the right instrumentalities by which to mobilize our economic resources in any time of national necessity. I take it for granted that I do not need your authority to call into systematic consultation with the directing officers of the army and navy men of recognized leadership and ability from among our citizens who are thoroughly familiar, for example, with the transportation facilities of the country and therefore competent to advise how they may be coördinated when the need arises, those who can suggest the best way in which to bring about prompt coöperation among the manufacturers of the country, should it be necessary, and those who could assist to bring the technical skill of the country to the aid of the Government in the solution of particular problems of defense. I only hope that if I should find it feasible to constitute such an advisory body the Congress would be willing to vote the small sum of money that would be needed to defray the expenses that would probably be necessary to give it the clerical and administrative machinery with which to do serviceable work.

What is more important is, that the industries and resources of the country should be available and ready for mobilization. It is the more imperatively necessary, therefore, that we should promptly devise means for doing what we have not yet done: that we should give intelligent federal aid and stimulation to industrial and vocational education, as we have long done in the large field of our agricultural industry; that, at the same time that we safeguard and conserve the natural resources of the country we should put them at the disposal of those who will use them promptly and intelligently, as was sought to be done in the admirable bills submitted to the last Congress from its committees on the public lands, bills which I earnestly recommend in principle to your consideration; that we should put into early operation some provision for rural credits which will add to the extensive borrowing facilities already afforded the farmer by the Reserve Bank Act, adequate instrumentalities by which long credits may be obtained on land mortgages; and that we should study more carefully than they have hitherto been studied the right adaptation of our economic arrangements to changing conditions.

Many conditions about which we have repeatedly legislated are being altered from decade to decade, it is evident, under our very eyes, and are likely to change even more rapidly and more radically in the days immediately ahead of us, when peace has returned to the world and the nations of Europe once more take up their tasks of commerce and industry with the energy of those who must bestir themselves to build anew. Just what these changes will be no one can certainly foresee or confidently predict. There are no calculable, because no stable, elements in the problem. The most we can do is to make certain that we have the necessary instrumentalities of information constantly at our service so that we may be sure that we know exactly what we are dealing with when we come to act, if it should be necessary to act at all. We must first certainly know what it is that we are seeking to adapt ourselves to. I may ask the privilege of addressing you more at length on this important matter a little later in your session.

In the meantime may I make this suggestion? The transportation problem is an exceedingly serious and pressing one in this country. There has from time to time of late been reason to fear that our railroads would not much longer be able to cope with it successfully, as at present equipped and coördinated. I suggest that it would be wise to provide for a commission of inquiry to ascertain by a thorough canvass of the whole question whether our laws as at present framed and administered are as serviceable as they might be in the solution of the problem. It is obviously a problem that lies at the very foundation of our efficiency as a people. Such an inquiry ought to draw out every circumstance and opinion worth considering and we need to know all sides of the matter if we mean to do anything in the field of federal legislation.

No one, I am sure, would wish to take any backward step. The regulation of the railways of the country by federal commission has had admirable results and has fully justified the hopes and expectations of those by whom the policy of regulation was originally proposed. The question is not what should we undo? It is, whether there is anything else we can do that would supply us with effective means, in the very process of regulation, for bettering the conditions under which the railroads are operated and for making them more useful servants of the country as a whole. It seems to me that it might be the part of wisdom, therefore, before further legislation in this field is attempted, to look at the whole problem of coördination and efficiency in the full light of a fresh assessment of circumstance and opinion, as a guide to dealing with the several parts of it.

For what we are seeking now, what in my mind is the single thought of this message, is national efficiency and security. We serve a great nation. We should serve it in the spirit of its peculiar genius. It is the genius of common men for self-government, industry, justice, liberty and peace. We should see to it that it lacks no instrument, no facility or vigor of law, to make it sufficient to play its part with energy, safety, and assured success. In this we are no partisans but heralds and prophets of a new age.

PRESIDENT WILSON'S NOTE TO AUSTRIA ON THE ANCONA SINKING

DEPARTMENT OF STATE, Washington, Dec. 6, 1915.

The Secretary of State to Ambassador Penfield:

Please deliver a note to the Minister of Foreign Affairs, textually as follows:

Reliable information obtained from American and other survivors who were passengers on the steamship Ancona shows that on Nov. 7 a submarine flying the Austro-Hungarian flag fired a solid shot toward the steamship, that thereupon the Ancona attempted to escape, but, being overhauled by the submarine, she stopped, that after a brief period and before the crew and passengers were all able to take to the boats the submarine fired a number of shells at the vessel and finally torpedoed and sank her while there were yet many persons on board, and that by gunfire and foundering of the vessel a large number of persons lost their lives or were seriously injured, among whom were citizens of the United States.

The public statement of the Austro-Hungarian Admiralty has been brought to the attention of the Government of the United States and received careful consideration. This statement substantially confirms the principal declaration of the survivors, as it admits that the Ancona, after being shelled, was torpedoed and sunk while persons were still on board.

The Austro-Hungarian Government has been advised, through the correspondence which has passed between the United States and Germany, of the attitude of the Government of the United States as to the use of submarines in attacking vessels of commerce, and the acquiescence of Germany in that attitude, yet with full knowledge on the part of the Austro-Hungarian Government of the views of the Government of the United States as expressed in no uncertain terms to the ally of Austria-Hungary, the commander of the submarine which attacked the Ancona failed to put in a place of safety the crew and passengers of the vessel which they purposed to destroy because, it is presumed, of the impossibility of taking it into port as a prize of war.

The Government of the United States considers that the commander violated the principles of international law and of humanity by shelling and torpedoing the Ancona before the persons on board had been put in a place of safety or even given sufficient time to leave the vessel. The conduct of the commander can only be characterized as wanton slaughter of defenseless noncombatants, since at the time when the vessel was shelled and torpedoed she was not, it appears, resisting or attempting to escape, and no other reason is sufficient to excuse such an attack, not even the possibility of rescue.

The Government of the United States is forced, therefore, to conclude either that the commander of the submarine acted in violation of his instructions or that the Imperial and Royal Government failed to issue instructions to the commanders of its submarines in accordance with the law of nations and the principles of humanity. The Government of the United States is unwilling to believe the latter alternative and to credit the Austro-Hungarian Government with an intention to permit its submarines to destroy the lives of helpless men, women and children. It prefers to believe that the commander of the submarine committed this outrage without authority and contrary to the general or special instructions which he had received.

As the good relations of the two countries must rest upon a common regard for law and humanity, the Government of the United States cannot be expected to do otherwise than to demand that the Imperial and Royal Government denounce the sinking of the Ancona as an illegal and indefensible act; that the officer who perpetrated the deed be punished, and that reparation by the payment of an indemnity be made for the citizens of the United States who were killed or injured by the attack on the vessel.

The Government of the United States expects that the Austro-Hungarian Government, appreciating the gravity of the case, will accede to its demand promptly, and it rests this expectation on the belief that the Austro-Hungarian Government will not sanction or defend an act which is condemned by the world as inhumane and barbarous, which is abhorrent to all civilized nations, and which has caused the death of innocent American citizens.

LANSING.

TEXT OF AUSTRIA'S REPLY TO FIRST ANCONA NOTE, ACCEDING TO NO DEMANDS AND INVITING DISCUSSION

American Embassy, Vienna, Dec. 15, 1915.

Secretary of State, Washington:

Following note received from Minister for Foreign Affairs noon today:

In reply to the much esteemed note, No. 4,167, which his Excellency Mr. Frederic Courtland Penfield, Ambassador Extraordinary and Plenipotentiary of the United States of America, directed to him in the name of the American Government under date of the 9th inst., and in the matter of the sinking of the Italian steamer Ancona, the undersigned, preliminary to a thorough, meritorious treatment of the demand, has the honor to observe that the sharpness with which the Government of the United States considers it necessary to blame the commanding officer of the submarine concerned in the affair, and the firmness in which the demands addressed to the Imperial and Royal Government appear to be expressed, might well have warranted the expectation that the Government of the United States should precisely specify the actual circumstances of the affair upon which it bases its case.

As is not difficult to perceive, the presentation of the facts in the case in the aforesaid note leaves room for many doubts, and even if this presentation were correct in all points and the most rigorous legal conception were applied to the judgment of the case, it does not in any way sufficiently warrant attaching blame to the commanding officer of the war vessel or to the Imperial and Royal Government.

The Government of the United States has also failed to designate the persons upon whose testimony it relies and to whom it apparently believes it may attribute a higher degree of credibility than to the commander of the Imperial and Royal Fleet. The note also fails to give any information whatsoever as to the number, names, and more precise fate of the American citizens who were on board of the said steamer at the critical moment.

Moreover, in view of the fact that the Washington Cabinet has now made a positive statement to the effect that citizens of the United States of America came to grief in the incident in question, the Imperial and Royal Government is in principle ready to enter into an exchange of views in the affair with the Government of the United States. It must, however, in the first place, raise the question why that Government failed to give juridical reasons for the demands set forth in its note with reference to the special circumstances of the incriminating events upon which it itself lays stress, and why in lieu thereof it referred to an exchange of correspondence which it has conducted with another Government in other cases.

The Imperial and Royal Government is the less able to follow the Washington Cabinet in this unusual path, since it by no means possesses authentic knowledge of all of the pertinent correspondence of the Government of the United States, nor is it of the opinion that such knowledge might be sufficient for it in the present case, which, in so far as it is informed, is in essential points of another nature than the case or cases to which the Government of the United States seems to allude. The Imperial and Royal Government may, therefore, leave it to the Washington Cabinet to formulate the particular points of law against which the commanding officer of the submarine is alleged to have offended on the occasion of the sinking of the Ancona.

The Government of the United States has also seen fit to refer to the attitude which the Berlin Cabinet assumed in the above mentioned correspondence. The Imperial and Royal Government finds in the much esteemed note no indication whatever of the intent with which this reference was made. Should, however, the Government of the United States thereby have intended to express an opinion to the effect that a prejudice of whatever nature existed for the Imperial and Royal Government with respect to the juridical consideration of the affair in question, this Government must, in order to preclude possible misunderstandings, declare that, as a matter of course, it reserves to itself full freedom of maintaining its own legal views in the discussion of the case of the Ancona.

In having the honor to have recourse to the kindness of his Excellency the Ambassador of the United States of America with the most respectful request to be good enough to communicate the foregoing to the American Government, and on this occasion to state that the Imperial and Royal Government, in no less degree than the American Government, and under all circumstances, most sincerely deplores the fate of the innocent victims of the incident in question, the undersigned at the same time avails himself of this opportunity to renew the expression of his most distinguished consideration to his Excellency the Ambassador. (Signed) BURIAN.

PENFIELD.

TEXT OF THE SECOND ANCONA NOTE TO AUSTRIA, REITERATING OUR DEMANDS AND DECLINING DISCUSSION

DEPARTMENT OF STATE, WASHINGTON, DEC. 19, 1915.

The Secretary of State to Ambassador Penfield:

You are instructed to address a note to the Austro-Hungarian Minister of Foreign Affairs, textually as follows:

The Government of the United States has received the note of Your Excellency relative to the sinking of the Ancona, which was delivered at Vienna on Dec. 15, 1915, and transmitted to Washington, and has given the note immediate and careful consideration.

On Nov. 15, 1915, Baron Zwiedenek, the Chargé d'Affaires of the Imperial and Royal Government at Washington, transmitted to the Department of State a report of the Austro-Hungarian Admiralty with regard to the sinking of the steamship Ancona, in which it was admitted that the vessel was torpedoed after her engines had been stopped and when passengers were still on board.

This admission alone is, in the view of the Government of the United States, sufficient to fix upon the commander of the submarine which fired the torpedo the responsibility for having wilfully violated the recognized law of nations and entirely disregarded those humane principles which every belligerent should observe in the conduct of war at sea.

In view of these admitted circumstances the Government of the United States feels justified in holding that the details of the sinking of the Ancona, the weight and character of the additional testimony corroborating the Admiralty's report, and the number of Americans killed or injured are in no way essential matters of discussion. The culpability of the commander is in any case established, and the undisputed fact is that citizens of the United States were killed, injured, or put in jeopardy by his lawless act.

The rules of international law and the principles of humanity which were thus wilfully violated by the commander of the submarine have been so long and so universally recognized and are so manifest from the standpoint of right and justice that the Government of the United States does not feel called upon to debate them and does not understand that the Imperial and Royal Government questions or disputes them.

The Government of the United States therefore finds no other course open to it but to hold the Imperial and Royal Government responsible for the act of its naval commander and to renew the definite but respectful demands made in its communication of the 6th of December, 1915.

It sincerely hopes that the foregoing statement of its position will enable the Imperial and Royal Government to perceive the justice of those demands and to comply with them in the same spirit of frankness and with the same concern for the good relations now existing between the United States and Austria-Hungary which prompted the Government of the United States to make them.

LANSING.

Reply to Bennet Resolution

After the reading of President Wilson's Third Annual Address, Congressman Bennet of New York introduced and the House passed a resolution asking the President to advise to whom he referred when he said certain citizens born under other flags "had poured the poison of disloyalty into the very arteries of our national life" and had been guilty of attempts to destroy American industry. (Page 8114.)

The President's reply, made public through Chairman Webb of the House Judiciary Committee, was:

I know that you will believe that it goes without saying that I would be delighted to co-operate in any way in attaining the objects which are no doubt sought by the inclosed resolutions which you were kind enough to send me, but I believe it would seriously interfere with the ends of justice if I were at this time to comply with the specific request contained in this suggested action of the House.

I am sure the Department of Justice will be more than willing to put at your disposal any facts whatever that are in its possession which do not block its own processes or embarrass it in its investigation of the intricate and hidden influences.

SPECIAL MESSAGE

[Protesting Against Submarine Warfare Carried On by Germany in War Against the Entente Allies.]

WASHINGTON, D. C., April 19, 1916.

GENTLEMEN OF THE CONGRESS: A situation has arisen in the foreign relations of the country of which it is my duty to inform you frankly.

It will be recalled that in February, 1915, the Imperial German Government announced its intention to treat the waters surrounding Great Britain and Ireland as embraced within the seat of war, and to destroy all merchant ships owned by its enemies that might be found within any part of that portion of the high seas, and that it warned all vessels, of neutral as well as of belligerent ownership, to keep out of the waters it had thus prescribed, or else enter them at their peril.

The Government of the United States earnestly protested. It took the position that such a policy could not be pursued without the practical certainty of gross and palpable violations of the law of nations, particularly if submarine craft were to be employed as its instruments, inasmuch as the rules prescribed by that law, rules founded upon principles of humanity and established for protection of lives of non-combatants at sea, could not in the nature of the case be observed by such vessels.

It based its protest on the ground that persons of neutral nationality and vessels of neutral ownership would be exposed to extreme and intolerable risks, and that no right to close any part of the high seas against their use, or to expose them to such risks, could lawfully be asserted by any belligerent government.

The law of nations in these matters, upon which the Government of the United States based its protest, is not of recent origin or founded upon merely arbitrary principles set up by convention. It is based, on the contrary, upon manifest and imperative principles of humanity and has long been established with the approval and by the express assent of all civilized nations.

Notwithstanding the earnest protest of our Government, the Imperial German Government at once proceeded to carry out the policy it had announced. It expressed the hope that the dangers involved, at any rate the dangers to neutral vessels, would be reduced to a minimum by the instructions which it had issued to its submarine commanders, and assured the Government of the United States that it would take every possible precaution both to respect the rights of neutrals and to safeguard the lives of non-combatants.

What has actually happened in the year which has since elapsed has shown that those hopes were not justified, those assurances insusceptible of being fulfilled. In pursuance of the policy of submarine warfare against the commerce of its adversaries, thus announced and entered upon by the Imperial German Government, in despite of the solemn protest of this Government, the commanders of German under-sea vessels have attacked merchant ships with greater and greater activity, not only upon the high seas surrounding Great Britain and Ireland, but wherever they could encounter them, in a way that has grown more and more ruthless, more and more indiscriminate as the months have gone by, less and less observant of restraints of any kind; and have delivered their attacks without compunction against vessels of every nationality and bound upon every sort of errand.

Vessels of neutral ownership, even vessels of neutral ownership bound from neutral port to neutral port, have been destroyed along with vessels of belligerent ownership in constantly increasing numbers. Sometimes the merchantman attacked has been warned and summoned to surrender before being fired on or torpedoed; sometimes passengers or crews have been vouchsafed the poor security of being allowed to take the ship's boats before she was sent to the bottom. But again and again no warning has been given, no escape even to the ship's boats allowed to those on board. What this Government foresaw must happen has happened.

Tragedy followed tragedy on the seas in such fashion, with such attendant circumstances, as to make it grossly evident that warfare of such a sort, if warfare it be, cannot be carried on without the most palpable violation of the dictates alike of right and of humanity. Whatever the disposition and intention of the Imperial German Government, it has manifestly proved impossible for it to keep such methods of attack upon the commerce of its enemies within the bounds set by either the reason or the heart of mankind.

In February of the present year the Imperial German Government informed this Government and the other neutral governments of the world that it had reason to believe that the Government of Great Britain had armed all merchant vessels of British ownership and had given them secret orders to attack any submarine of the enemy they might encounter upon the seas, and that the Imperial German Government felt justified in the circumstances in treating all armed merchantmen of belligerent ownership as auxiliary vessels of war, which it would have the right to destroy without warning.

The law of nations has long recognized the right of merchantmen to carry arms for protection, to use them to repel attack, though to use them in such circumstances at their own risk, but the Imperial German Government claimed the right to set these understandings aside in circumstances which it deemed extraordinary.

Even the terms in which it announced its purpose thus still further to relax the restraints it had previously expressed its willingness and desire to put upon the operations of its submarines carried the plain implication that at least vessels which were not armed would still be exempt from destruction without warning, and that personal safety would be accorded their passengers and crews; but even that limitation, if it was ever practicable to observe it, has in fact constituted no check at all on the destruction of ships of every sort.

Again and again the Imperial German Government has given this Government its solemn assurances that at least passenger ships would not be thus dealt with, and yet it has again and again permitted its undersea commanders to disregard those assurances with entire impunity.

Great liners like the Lusitania and the Arabic and mere ferryboats like the Sussex have been attacked without a moment's warning, sometimes before they had even become aware that they were in the presence of an armed vessel of the enemy, and the lives of non-combatants, passengers and crew, have been sacrificed wholesale, in a manner which the Government of the United States cannot but regard as wanton and without the slightest color of justification.

No limit of any kind has in fact been set to the indiscriminate pursuit and destruction of merchantmen of all kinds and nationalities within the waters, constantly extending in area, where these operations have been carried on, and the roll of Americans who have lost their lives on ships thus attacked and destroyed has grown month by month until the ominous toll has mounted into the hundreds.

One of the latest and most shocking instances of this method of warfare was the destruction of the French cross-channel steamer Sussex. It must stand forth, as the sinking of the steamer Lusitania did, as so singularly tragical and unjustifiable as to constitute a truly terrible example of the inhumanity of submarine warfare as commanders of German vessels have for the past twelve months been conducting it.

If this instance stood alone some explanation, some disavowal by the German Government, some evidence of criminal mistake or wilful disobedience on the part of the commander of the vessel that fired the torpedo, might be sought or entertained, but unhappily it does not stand alone. Recent events make the conclusion inevitable that it is only one instance, even though it be one of the most extreme and distressing instances, of the spirit and method of warfare which the Imperial German Government has mistakenly adopted, and which from the first exposed that government to the reproach of thrusting all neutral rights aside in pursuit of its immediate objects.

The Government of the United States has been very patient. At every stage of this distressing experience of tragedy after tragedy in which its own citizens were involved it has sought to be restrained from any extreme course of action, or of protest, by a thoughtful consideration of the extraordinary circumstances of this unprecedented war, and actuated in all that it said or did by the sentiments of genuine friendship which the people of the United States have always entertained, and continue to entertain, toward the German nation.

It has, of course, accepted the successive explanations and assurances of the Imperial German Government as given in entire sincerity and good faith, and has hoped, even against hope, that it would prove to be possible for the German Government so to order and control the acts of its naval commanders as to square its policy with the principles of humanity as embodied in the laws of nations.

It has been willing to wait until the significance of the facts became absolutely unmistakable and susceptible of but one interpretation.

That point has now unhappily been reached. The facts are susceptible of but one interpretation: The Imperial German Government has been unable to put any limits or restraints upon its warfare against either freight or passenger ships.

It has therefore become painfully evident that the position which this Government took at the very outset is inevitable, namely, that the use of submarines for the destruction of an enemy's commerce is of a necessity, because of the character of the vessels employed and the methods of attack which their employment of course involves, incompatible with the principles of humanity, the long established and incontrovertible rights of neutrals and the sacred immunities of non-combatants.

I have deemed it my duty to say to the Imperial German Government that if it is still its purpose to prosecute relentless and indiscriminate warfare against vessels of commerce by the use of submarines, notwithstanding the now demonstrated impossibility of conducting that warfare in accordance with what the Government of the United States must consider the sacred and indisputable rules of international law and the universally recognized dictates of humanity, the Government of the United States is at last forced to the conclusion that there is but one course it can pursue; and that unless the Imperial German Government should now immediately declare and effect an abandonment of its present methods of warfare against passenger and freight vessels this Government can have no choice but to sever diplomatic relations with the Government of the German Empire altogether.

This decision I have arrived at with the keenest regret; the possibility of the action contemplated I am sure all thoughtful Americans will look forward to with unaffected reluctance. But we cannot forget that we are in some sort and by the force of circumstances the responsible spokesmen of the rights of humanity, and that we cannot remain silent while those rights seem in process of being swept utterly away in the maelstrom of this terrible war. We owe it to a due regard for our own rights as a nation, to our sense of duty as a representative of the rights of neutrals the world over, and to a just conception of the rights of mankind to take this stand now with the utmost solemnity and firmness.

I have taken it, and taken it in the confidence that it will meet with your approval and support. All sober-minded men must unite in hoping that the Imperial German Government, which has in other circumstances stood as the champion of all that we are now contending for in the interest of humanity, may recognize the justice of our demands and meet them in the spirit in which they are made.

A GERMAN AIRPLANE COMES INTO RANGE

Photo by International Film Service

A GERMAN AIRPLANE COMES INTO RANGE.

The illustration shows the crews of two British anti-aircraft guns rushing to take a shot at a German plane which has ventured within range behind the battlefront.

NOTE TO GERMANY ON THE SINKING OF THE FRENCH STEAMSHIP SUSSEX IN THE ENGLISH CHANNEL.

WASHINGTON, April 19.

The Secretary of State to Ambassador Gerard:

"You are instructed to deliver to the Secretary of Foreign Affairs a communication reading as follows:

"I did not fail to transmit immediately, by telegraph, to my Government Your Excellency's note of the 10th inst. in regard to certain attacks by German submarines, and particularly in regard to the disastrous explosion which on March 24 last wrecked the French steamship Sussex in the English Channel.

"I have now the honor to deliver, under instructions from my Government, the following reply to Your Excellency:"

Information now in the possession of the Government of the United States fully establishes the facts in the case of the Sussex, and the inferences which my Government has drawn from that information it regards as confirmed by the circumstances set forth in Your Excellency's note of the 10th inst.

On the 24th of March, 1916, at about 2:30 o'clock in the afternoon, the unarmed steamer Sussex, with 325 or more passengers on board, among whom were a number of American citizens, was torpedoed while crossing from Folkstone to Dieppe.

The Sussex had never been armed; was a vessel known to be habitually used only for the conveyance of passengers across the English Channel, and was not following the route taken by troop-ships or supply ships. About eighty of her passengers, non-combatants of all ages and sexes, including citizens of the United States, were killed or injured.

A careful, detailed and scrupulously impartial investigation by naval and military officers of the United States has conclusively established the fact that the Sussex was torpedoed without warning or summons to surrender and that the torpedo by which she was struck was of German manufacture.

In the view of the Government of the United States these facts from the first made the conclusion that the torpedo was fired by a German submarine unavoidable. It now considers that conclusion substantiated by the statements of Your Excellency's note. A full statement of the facts upon which the Government of the United States has based its conclusion is enclosed.

The Government of the United States, after having given careful consideration to the note of the Imperial Government of April 10, regrets to state that the impression made upon it by the statements and proposals contained in that note is that the Imperial Government has failed to appreciate the gravity of the situation which has resulted, not alone from the attack on the Sussex, but from the whole method and character of submarine warfare as disclosed by the unrestrained practice of the commanders of German undersea craft during the past twelve-month, and more in the indiscriminate destruction of merchant vessels of all sorts, nationalities and destinations.

If the sinking of the Sussex had been an isolated case the Government of the United States might find it possible to hope that the officer who was responsible for that act had wilfully violated his orders or had been criminally negligent in taking none of the precautions they prescribed, and that the ends of justice might be satisfied by imposing upon him an adequate punishment, coupled with a formal disavowal of the act and payment of a suitable indemnity by the Imperial Government.

But though the attack upon the Sussex was manifestly indefensible and caused a loss of life so tragical as to make it stand forth as one of the most terrible examples of the inhumanity of submarine warfare as the commanders of German vessels are conducting it, it unhappily does not stand alone.

On the contrary, the Government of the United States is forced by recent events to conclude that it is only one instance, even though one of the most extreme and most distressing instances, of the deliberate method and spirit of indiscriminate destruction of merchant vessels of all sorts, nationalities and destination, which have become more and more unmistakable as the activity of German undersea vessels of war has in recent months been quickened and extended.

The Imperial Government will recall that when, in February, 1915, it announced its intention of treating the waters surrounding Great Britain and Ireland as embraced within the seat of war, and of destroying all merchant ships owned by its enemies that might be found within that zone of danger, and warned all vessels, neutral as well as belligerent, to keep out of the waters thus proscribed or to enter them at their peril, the Government of the United States earnestly protested.

It took the position that such a policy could not be pursued without constant gross and palpable violations of the accepted law of nations, particularly if submarine craft were to be employed as its instruments, inasmuch as the rules prescribed by that law, rules founded on the principles of humanity and established for the protection of the lives of non-combatants at sea, could not in the nature of the case be observed by such vessels.

It based its protest on the ground that persons of neutral nationality and vessels of neutral ownership would be exposed to extreme and intolerable risks; and that no right to close any part of the high seas could lawfully be asserted by the Imperial German Government in the circumstances then existing.

The law of nations in these matters, upon which the Government of the United States based that protest, is not of recent origin or founded upon merely arbitrary principles set up by convention.

It is based, on the contrary, upon manifest principles of humanity and has long been established with the approval and by the express assent of all civilized nations.

The Imperial Government, notwithstanding, persisted in carrying out the policy announced, expressing the hope that the dangers involved at any date to neutral vessels would be reduced to a minimum by the instructions which it had issued to the commanders of its submarines, and assuring the Government of the United States that it would take every possible precaution, both to respect the rights of neutrals and to safeguard the lives of non-combatants.

In pursuance of this policy of submarine warfare against the commerce of its adversaries, thus announced and thus entered upon in despite of the solemn protest of the Government of the United States, the commanders of the Imperial Government's undersea vessels have carried on practices of such ruthless destruction which have made it more and more evident as the months have gone by that the Imperial Government has found it impracticable to put any such restraint upon them as it had hoped and promised to put.

Again and again the Imperial Government has given its solemn assurances to the Government of the United States that at least passenger ships would not be thus dealt with, and yet it has repeatedly permitted its undersea commanders to disregard those assurances with entire impunity.

As recently as February last it gave notice that it would regard all armed merchantmen owned by its enemies as part of the armed naval forces of its adversaries and deal with them as with men-of-war, thus, at least by implication, pledging itself to give warning to vessels which were not armed and to accord security of life to their passengers and crews; but even this limitation their submarine commanders have recklessly ignored.

Vessels of neutral ownership, even vessels of neutral ownership bound from neutral port to neutral port, have been destroyed along with vessels of belligerent ownership in constantly increasing numbers.

Sometimes the merchantmen attacked have been warned and summoned to surrender before being fired on or torpedoed; sometimes their passengers and crews have been vouchsafed the poor security of being allowed to take to the ship's boats before the ship was sent to the bottom. But again and again no warning has been given, no escape even to the ship's boats allowed to those on board.

Great liners like the Lusitania and Arabic and mere passenger boats like the Sussex have been attacked without a moment's warning, often before they have even become aware that they were in the presence of an armed ship of the enemy, and the lives of non-combatants, passengers and crew have been destroyed wholesale and in a manner which the Government of the United States can not but regard as wanton and without the slightest color of justification.

No limit of any kind has, in fact, been set to their indiscriminate pursuit and destruction of merchantmen of all kinds and nationalities within the waters which the Imperial Government has chosen to designate as lying within the seat of war. The roll of Americans who have lost their lives upon ships thus attacked and destroyed has grown month by month until the ominous toll has mounted into the hundreds.

The Government of the United States has been very patient. At every stage of this distressing experience of tragedy after tragedy it has sought to be governed by the most thoughtful consideration of the extraordinary circumstances of an unprecedented war and to be guided by sentiments of very genuine friendship for the people and Government of Germany.

It has accepted the successive explanations and assurances of the Imperial Government as, of course, given in entire sincerity and good faith, and has hoped, even against hope, that it would prove to be possible for the Imperial Government so to order and control the acts of its naval commanders as to square its policy with the recognized principles of humanity as embodied in the law of nations.

It has made every allowance for unprecedented conditions, and has been willing to wait until the facts became unmistakable and were susceptible of only one interpretation.

It now owes it to a just regard for its own rights to say to the Imperial Government that that time has come.

It has become painfully evident to it that the position which it took at the very outset is inevitable, namely, the use of submarines for the destruction of an enemy's commerce, is, of necessity, because of the very character of the vessels employed and the very methods of attack which their employment, of course, involves, utterly incompatible with the principles of humanity, the long-established and incontrovertible rights of neutrals and the sacred immunities of non-combatants.

If it is still the purpose of the Imperial Government to prosecute relentless and indiscriminate warfare against vessels of commerce by the use of submarines without regard to what the Government of the United States must consider the sacred and indisputable rules of international law and the universally recognized dictates of humanity, the Government of the United States is at last forced to the conclusion that there is but one course it can pursue.

Unless the Imperial Government should now immediately declare and effect an abandonment of its present methods of submarine warfare against passenger and freight-carrying vessels, the Government of the United States can have no choice but to sever diplomatic relations with the German Empire altogether.

This action the Government of the United States contemplates with the greatest reluctance but feels constrained to take in behalf of humanity and the rights of neutral nations.

GERMANY'S REPLY TO PRESIDENT WILSON'S NOTE ON THE SINKING OF THE SUSSEX

BERLIN, May 5, 1916 (by Wireless to Sayville, L. I.)

Following is the text of the note of the German Government in reply to the American note respecting submarine warfare, delivered yesterday by Gottlieb von Jagow, the Foreign Secretary, to Ambassador Gerard:

The undersigned, on behalf of the Imperial German Government, has the honor to present to his Excellency the Ambassador of the United States, Mr. James W. Gerard, the following reply to the note of April 20 regarding the conduct of German submarine warfare.

The German Government handed over to the proper naval authorities for early investigation the evidence concerning the Sussex, as communicated by the Government of the United States. Judging by the results that the investigation has hitherto yielded, the German Government is alive to the possibility that the ship mentioned in the note of April 10 as having been torpedoed by a German submarine is actually identical with the Sussex.

The German Government begs to reserve further communication on the matter until certain points are ascertained, which are of decisive importance for establishing the facts of the case. Should it turn out that the commander was wrong in assuming the vessel to be a man-of-war, the German Government will not fail to draw the consequence resulting therefrom.

In connection with the case of the Sussex the Government of the United States made a series of statements, the gist of which is the assertion that the incident is to be considered but one instance of a deliberate method of indiscriminate destruction of vessels of all sorts, nationalities, and destinations by German submarine commanders.

The German Government must emphatically repudiate the assertion. The German Government, however, thinks it of little avail to enter into details in the present stage of affairs, more particularly as the Government of the United States omitted to substantiate the assertion by reference to concrete facts.

The German Government will only state that it has imposed far-reaching restraints upon the use of the submarine weapon, solely in consideration of neutrals' interests, in spite of the fact that these restrictions are necessarily of advantage to Germany's enemies. No such consideration has ever been shown neutrals by Great Britain and her allies.

The German submarine forces have had, in fact, orders to conduct the submarine warfare in accordance with the general principles of visit and search and the destruction of merchant vessels recognized by international law, the sole exception being the conduct of warfare against enemy trade carried on enemy freight ships encountered in the war zone surrounding Great Britain. With regard to these, no assurances have ever been given to the Government of the United States. No such assurances are contained in the declaration of Feb. 8, 1916.

The German Government cannot admit any doubt that these orders were given or are executed in good faith. Errors actually occurred. They can in no kind of warfare be avoided altogether. Allowances must be made in the conduct of naval warfare against an enemy resorting to all kinds of ruses, whether permissible or illicit.

But apart from the possibility of errors, naval warfare, just like warfare on land, implies unavoidable dangers for neutral persons and goods entering the fighting zone. Even in cases where the naval action is confined to ordinary forms of cruiser warfare, neutral persons and goods repeatedly come to grief.

The German Government has repeatedly and explicitly pointed out the dangers from mines that have led to the loss of numerous ships.

The German Government has made several proposals to the Government of the United States in order to reduce to a minimum for American travelers and goods the inherent dangers of naval warfare. Unfortunately the Government of the United States decided not to accept the proposals. Had it accepted, the Government of the United States would have been instrumental in preventing the greater part of the accidents that American citizens have met with in the meantime.

The German Government still stands by its offer to come to an agreement along these lines.

As the German Government repeatedly declared, it cannot dispense with the use of the submarine weapon in the conduct of warfare against enemy trade. The German Government, however, has now decided to make a further concession, adapting methods of submarine war to the interests of neutrals. In reaching its decision the German Government is actuated by considerations which are above the level of the disputed question.

The German Government attaches no less importance to the sacred principles of humanity than the Government of the United States. It again fully takes into account that both Governments for many years co-operated in developing international law in conformity with these principles, the ultimate object of which has always been to confine warfare on sea and land to armed forces of belligerents and safeguard as far as possible noncombatants against the horrors of war.

But although these considerations are of great weight, they alone would not under present circumstances have determined the attitude of the German Government. For in answer to the appeal by the Government of the United States on behalf of the sacred principles of humanity and international law, the German Government must repeat once more, with all emphasis, that it was not the German, but the British, Government which ignored all accepted rules of international law and extended this terrible war to the lives and property of noncombatants, having no regard whatever for the interests and rights of neutrals and noncombatants that through this method of warfare have been severely injured.

In self-defense against the illegal conduct of British warfare, while fighting a bitter struggle for national existence, Germany had to resort to the hard but effective weapon of submarine warfare.

As matters stand, the German Government cannot but reiterate regret that the sentiments of humanity, which the Government of the United States extends with such fervor to the unhappy victims of submarine warfare, are not extended with the same warmth of feeling to many millions of women and children who, according to the avowed intention of the British Government, shall be starved.

and who by sufferings shall force the victorious armies of the Central Powers into ignominious capitulation.

The German Government, in agreement with the German people, fails to understand this discrimination, all the more as it has repeatedly and explicitly declared itself ready to use the submarine weapon in strict conformity with the rules of international law as recognized before the outbreak of the war, if Great Britain likewise was ready to adapt the conduct of warfare to these rules.

Several attempts made by the Government of the United States to prevail upon the British Government to act accordingly failed because of flat refusal on the part of the British Government. Moreover, Great Britain again and again has violated international law, surpassing all bounds in outraging neutral rights. The latest measure adopted by Great Britain, declaring German bunker coal contraband and establishing conditions under which English bunker coal alone is supplied to neutrals, is nothing but an unheard-of attempt by way of exaction to force neutral tonnage into the service of British trade war.

The German people knows that the Government of the United States has the power to confine the war to armed forces of the belligerent countries, in the interest of humanity and maintenance of international law. The Government of the United States would have been certain of attaining this end had it been determined to insist, against Great Britain, on the incontrovertible rights to freedom of the seas. But, as matters stand, the German people is under the impression that the Government of the United States, while demanding that Germany, struggling for existence, shall restrain the use of an effective weapon and while making compliance with these demands a condition for maintenance of relations with Germany, confines itself to protests against illegal methods adopted by Germany's enemies. Moreover, the German people knows to what considerable extent its enemies are supplied with all kinds of war material from the United States.

It will, therefore, be understood that the appeal made by the Government of the United States to sentiments of humanity and principles of international law cannot, under the circumstances, meet the same hearty response from the German people which such an appeal otherwise always is certain to find here. If the German Government, nevertheless, is resolved to go to the utmost limit of concessions, it has been guided not alone by the friendship connecting the two great nations for over one hundred years, but also by the thought of the great doom which threatens the entire civilized world should the cruel and sanguinary war be extended and prolonged.

The German Government, conscious of Germany's strength, twice within the last few months announced before the world its readiness to make peace on a basis safeguarding Germany's vital interests, thus indicating that it is not Germany's fault if peace is still withheld from the nations of Europe. The German Government feels all the more justified in declaring that responsibility could not be borne before the forum of mankind and in history if after twenty-one months of the war's duration the submarine question, under discussion between the German Government and the Government of the United States, were to take a turn seriously threatening maintenance of peace between the two nations.

As far as lies with the German Government, it wishes to prevent things from taking such a course. The German Government, moreover, is prepared to do its utmost to confine operations of the war for the rest of its duration to the fighting forces of the belligerents, thereby also insuring the freedom of the seas, a principle upon which the German Government believes, now as before, that it is in agreement with the Government of the United States.

The German Government, guided by this idea, notifies the Government of the United States that German naval forces have received the following order:

"In accordance with the general principles of visit and search and the destruction of merchant vessels, recognized by international law, such vessels, both within and without the area declared a naval war zone, shall not be sunk without warning and without saving human lives unless the ship attempt to escape or offer resistance."

But neutrals cannot expect that Germany, forced to fight for existence, shall, for the sake of neutral interests, restrict the use of an effective weapon, if the enemy is permitted to continue to apply at will methods of warfare violating rules of international law. Such a demand would be incompatible with the character of neutrality, and the German Government is convinced that the Government of the United States does not think of making such a demand, knowing that the Government of the United States repeatedly declares that it is determined to restore the principle of freedom of the seas, from whatever quarter it has been violated.

Accordingly, the German Government is confident that in consequence of the new orders issued to the naval forces the Government of the United States will also now consider all impediments removed which may have been in the way of a mutual co-operation toward restoration of the freedom of the seas during the war, as suggested in the note of July 23, 1915, and it does not doubt that the Government of the United States will now demand and insist that the British Government shall forthwith observe the rules of international law universally recognized before the war, as are laid down in the notes presented by the Government of the United States to the British Government Dec. 28, 1914, and Nov. 5, 1915.

Should steps taken by the Government of the United States not attain the object it desires, to have the laws of humanity followed by all belligerent nations, the German Government would then be facing a new situation in which it must reserve to itself complete liberty of decision.

The undersigned avails himself of this opportunity to renew to the American Ambassador assurances of highest consideration.

VON JAGOW.

NATIONAL GUARD ORDERED TO MEXICAN BORDER

WASHINGTON, June 18, 1916.

Text of the telegram sent by Secretary of War Baker to governors of states calling out the militia:

Having in view the possibility of further aggression upon the territory of the United States from Mexico and the necessity for the proper protection of that frontier, the President has thought proper to exercise the authority vested in him by the Constitution and laws to call out the organized militia and National Guard necessary for that purpose.

I am, in consequence, instructed by the President to call into the service of the United States forthwith through you the following units of the organized militia and the National Guard of the State of ———, which the President directs shall be assembled at the State mobilization point ——— (or at the place to be designated to you by the commanding general, ——— department) for muster into the service of the United States (here is inserted the allotment from each State).

Organizations to be accepted into the Federal service should have the minimum peace strength now prescribed for organized militia. The maximum strength at which organizations will be accepted, and to which they should be raised as soon as possible, is prescribed in Section 2, Tables of Organizations, United States Army.

In case any regular battalion or squadron now recognized as such contains an insufficient number of organizations to enable it to conform at muster to regular army organization tables, the organization necessary to complete such units may be moved to mobilization camp and there inspected under orders of the department commander to determine fitness for recognition as organized militia by the War Department.

Circular 19, Division of Military Affairs, 1914, prescribes the organizations desired from each State as part of the local tactical division, and only these organizations will be accepted into service.

It is requested that all officers of Adjutant General's department, Quartermaster's Corps and Medical Corps, duly recognized as pertaining to State Headquarters, under Table 1, Tables of Organizations, Organized Militia, and not elsewhere required for duty in State administrations, be ordered to camp for duty as camp staff officers.

Such numbers of these staff officers as the department commanders may determine may be mustered into the service of the United States for the purpose of proper camp administration and will be mustered out when their services are no longer required.

Where recognized brigades or divisions are called into service from a State, the staff officers pertaining to these units under Tables of Organizations, United States Army, will be mustered into service and also the authorized inspectors of small arms practise pertaining thereto.

Except for these two purposes of mobilization camp service and of the prescribed staff practice service with tactical units, officers of State Headquarters, under Table 1. above mentioned, will not be mustered into service at this time.

If tactical divisions are later organized, the requisite additional number of staff officers with rank as prescribed for division staff will, as far as practicable, be called into service from those States which have furnished troops to such division. Acknowledge,

NEWTON D. BAKER,
Secretary of War.

NOTE ACCEPTING GENERAL CARRANZA'S PROPOSAL AND STATEMENT DISCLAIMING INTERVENTION

WASHINGTON, March 13, 1916.

Note forwarded to General Carranza by the United States Government accepting his proposal of a reciprocal agreement for the pursuit of bandits across the line dividing the United States and Mexico:

The Government of the United States has received the courteous note of Señor Acuna, [Carranza's Minister of Foreign Affairs,] and has read with satisfaction his suggestion for reciprocal privileges to the American and Mexican authorities in the pursuit and apprehension of outlaws who infest their respective territories lying along the international boundary and who are a constant menace to the lives and property of residents of that region.

The Government of the United States, in view of the unusual state of affairs which has existed for some time along the international boundary, and earnestly desiring to co-operate with the de facto Government of Mexico to suppress this state of lawlessness, of which the recent attack on Columbus, N. M., is a deplorable example, and to insure peace and order in the region contiguous to the boundary between the two republics, readily grants permission for military forces of the de facto Government of Mexico to cross the international boundary in pursuit of lawless bands of armed men who have entered Mexico from the United States, committed outrages on Mexican soil, and fled into the United States, on the understanding that the de facto Government of Mexico grants the reciprocal privilege that the military forces of the United States may pursue across the international boundary into Mexican territory lawless bands of armed men who have entered the United States from Mexico, committed outrages on American soil, and fled into Mexico.

The Government of the United States understands that, in view of its agreement to this reciprocal arrangement proposed by the de facto Government, the arrangement is now complete and in force, and the reciprocal privileges thereunder may accordingly be exercised by either Government without further interchange of views.

It is a matter of sincere gratification to the Government of the United States that the de facto Government of Mexico has evinced so cordial and friendly a spirit of co-operation in the efforts of the authorities of the United States to apprehend and punish the bands of outlaws who seek refuge beyond the international boundary in the erroneous belief that the constituted authorities will resent any pursuit across the boundary by the forces of the Government whose citizens have suffered by the crimes of the fugitives.

With the same spirit of cordial friendship the Government of the United States will exercise the privilege granted by the de facto Government of Mexico, in the hope and confident expectation that by their mutual efforts lawlessness will be eradicated and peace and order maintained in the territories of the United States and Mexico contiguous to the international boundary.

LANSING'S NON-INTERVENTION STATEMENT

Secretary of State Lansing also issued this statement:

In order to remove any misapprehension that may exist either in the United States or in Mexico, the President has authorized me to give in his name the public assurance that the military operations now in contemplation by this Government will be scrupulously confined to the object already announced and that in no circumstances will they be suffered to infringe in any degree upon the sovereignty of Mexico or develop into intervention of any kind in the internal affairs of our sister republic. On the contrary, what is now being done is deliberately intended to preclude the possibility of intervention.

COMPLAINT AGAINST MEXICO

[Delivered by Secretary of State Lansing to Mexican Ambassador Designate Arredondo in reply to General Carranza's message demanding the withdrawal of United States troops from Mexico.]

DEPARTMENT OF STATE,
WASHINGTON, JUNE 20, 1916.

SIR:—I have read your communication, which was delivered to me on May 22, 1916, under instructions of the Chief Executive of the de facto Government of Mexico, on the subject of the presence of American troops in Mexican territory, and I would be wanting in candor if I did not, before making answer to the allegations of fact and the conclusions reached by your Government, express the surprise and regret which have been caused this Government by the discourteous tone and temper of this last communication of the de facto Government of Mexico.

The Government of the United States has viewed with deep concern and increasing disappointment the progress of the revolution in Mexico. Continuous bloodshed and disorders have marked its progress.

For three years the Mexican Republic has been torn with civil strife; the lives of Americans and other aliens have been sacrificed; vast properties developed by American capital and enterprise have been destroyed or rendered non-productive; bandits have been permitted to roam at will through the territory contiguous to the United States and to seize, without punishment or without effective attempt at punishment, the property of Americans, while the lives of citizens of the United States who ventured to remain in Mexican territory or to return there to protect their interests have been taken, and in some cases barbarously taken, and the murderers have neither been apprehended nor brought to justice.

It would be difficult to find in the annals of the history of Mexico conditions more deplorable than those which have existed there during these recent years of civil war.

It would be tedious to recount instance after instance, outrage after outrage, atrocity after atrocity, to illustrate the true nature and extent of the widespread conditions of lawlessness and violence which have prevailed.

During the past nine months in particular, the frontier of the United States along the lower Rio Grande has been thrown into a state of constant apprehension and turmoil because of frequent and sudden incursions into American territory and depredations and murders on American soil by Mexican bandits who have taken the lives and destroyed the property of American citizens, sometimes carrying American citizens across the international boundary with the booty seized.

American garrisons have been attacked at night, American soldiers killed and their equipment and horses stolen; American ranches have been raided, property stolen and destroyed, and American trains wrecked and plundered.

The attacks on Brownsville, Red House Ferry, Progreso Post Office and Las Peledas, all occurring during September last, are typical. In these attacks on American territory Carranzista adherents, and even Carranzista soldiers, took part in the looting, burning and killing. Not only were these murders characterized by ruthless brutality, but uncivilized acts of mutilation were perpetrated.

Representations were made to General Carranza and he was emphatically requested to stop these reprehensible acts in a section which he has long claimed to be under the complete domination of his authority. Notwithstanding these repetitions and the promise of General Nafarrote to prevent attacks along the international boundary, in the following month of October a passenger train was wrecked by bandits and several persons killed seven miles north of Brownsville, and an attack was made upon United States troops at the same place several days later. Since these attacks leaders of the bandits well known to both Mexican civil and military authorities as well as to American officers, have been enjoying with impunity the liberty of towns of Northern Mexico.

So far has the indifference of the de facto Government to these atrocities gone that some of these leaders, as I am advised, have received not only the protection of that Government but encouragement and aid as well.

Depredations upon American persons and property within Mexican jurisdiction have been still more numerous. This Government has repeatedly requested that the de facto Government safeguard the lives and homes of American citizens and furnish the protection which international obligation imposes, to American interests in the Northern States of Tamaulipas, Nuevo Leon, Coahuila, Chihuahua and Sonora, and also in the States to the south. For example, on January 3, troops were requested to punish the bands of outlaws which looted the Cusi Mining property, eighty miles west of Chihuahua, but no effective results came from this request. During the following week the bandit Villa with his bands of about 200 men, was operating without opposition between Rubio and Santa Ysabel, a fact well known to Carranzista authorities.

Meanwhile a party of unfortunate Americans started by train from Chihuahua to visit the Cusi mines, after having received assurances from the Carranzista authorities in the State of Chihuahua that the country was safe and that a guard on the train was not necessary. The Americans held passports or safe conducts issued by authorities of the de facto Government.

On January 10 the train was stopped by Villa bandits and eighteen of the American party were stripped of their clothing and shot in cold blood in what is now known as "the Santa Ysabel massacre."

General Carranza stated to the agent of the Department of State that he had issued orders for the immediate pursuit, capture and punishment of those responsible for this atrocious crime, and appealed to this Government and to the American people to consider the difficulties of according protection along the railroad where the massacre occurred. Assurances were also given by Mr. Arredondo, presumably under instructions from the de facto Government that the murderers would be brought to justice and that steps would also be taken to remedy the lawless conditions existing in the State of Durango.

It is true that Villa, Castro and Lopez were publicly declared to be outlaws and subject to apprehension and execution, but so far as known only a single man personally connected with the massacre has been brought to justice by Mexican authorities.

Within a month after this barbarous slaughter of inoffensive Americans it was notorious that Villa was operating within twenty miles of Cusihuiriachic, and publicly stated that his purpose was to destroy American lives and property. Despite repeated and insistent demands that military protection be furnished Americans, Villa openly carried on his operations, constantly approaching closer and closer to the border.

He was not intercepted, nor were his movements impeded by troops of the de facto Government, and no effectual attempt was made to frustrate his hostile designs against Americans. In fact, as I am informed, while Villa and his band were slowly moving toward the American frontier in the neighborhood of Columbus, New Mexico, not a single Mexican soldier was seen in his vicinity. Yet the Mexican authorities were fully cognizant of his movements, for on March 6, as General Gavira publicly announced, he advised the American military authorities of the outlaw's approach to the border, so that they might be prepared to prevent him from crossing the boundary.

· Villa's unhindered activities culminated in the unprovoked and cold-blooded attack upon American soldiers and citizens in the town of Columbus on the night of March 9, the details of which do not need repetition here in order to refresh your memory with the heinousness of the crime.

After murdering, burning and plundering Villa and his bandits, fleeing south, passed within sight of the Carranzista military post at Casas Grandes, and no effort was made to stop him by the officers and garrison of the de facto Government stationed there.

In the face of these depredations, not only on American lives and property on Mexican soil, but on American soldiers, citizens and homes on American territory, the perpetrators of which General Carranza was unable or, possibly, considered it inadvisable to apprehend and punish, the United States had no recourse other than to employ force to disperse the bands of Mexican outlaws who were with increasing boldness sytematically raiding across the international boundary.

The marauders engaged in the attack on Columbus were driven back across the border by American cavalry, and subsequently, as soon as a sufficient force to cope with the band could be collected were pursued into Mexico in an effort to capture or destroy them.

Without co-operation or assistance in the field on the part of the de facto Government, despite repeated requests by the United States, and without apparent recognition on its part of the desirability of putting an end to these systematic raids, or of punishing the chief perpetrators of the crimes committed, because they menaced the good relations of the two countries, American forces pursued the lawless bands as far as Parral, where the pursuit was halted by the hostility of Mexicans, presumed to be loyal to the de facto Government, who arrayed themselves on the side of outlawry and became in effect the protectors of Villa and his band.

In this manner and for these reasons have the American forces entered Mexican territory. Knowing fully the circumstances set forth the de facto Government cannot be blind to the necessity which compelled this Government to act and yet it has seen fit to recite groundless sentiments of hostility toward the expedition and to impute to this Government ulterior motives for the continued presence of American troops on Mexican soil. It is charged that these troops crossed the frontier without first obtaining the consent or permission of the de facto Government.

Obviously, as immediate action alone could avail, there was no opportunity to reach an agreement (other than that of March 10-13, now repudiated by General Carranza) prior to the entrance of such an expedition into Mexico if the expedition was to be effective. Subsequent events and correspondence have demonstrated to the satisfaction of this Government that General Carranza would not have entered into any agreement providing for an effective plan for the capture and destruction of the Villa bands.

While the American troops were moving rapidly southward in pursuit of the raiders, it was the form and nature of the agreement that occupied the attention of General Carranza rather than the practical object which it was to attain—the number of limitations that could be imposed upon the American forces to impede their progress rather than the obstacles that could be raised to prevent the escape of the outlaws.

It was General Carranza who suspended through your note of April 12 all discussions and negotiations for an agreement along the lines of the protocols between the United States and Mexico concluded during the period 1882-1896, under which the two countries had so successfully restored peaceful conditions on their common boundary.

It may be mentioned here that, notwithstanding the statement in your note that "the American Government gave no answer to the note of the 12th of April," this note was replied to on April 14th, when the Department instructed Mr. Rodgers by telegraph to deliver this Government's answer to General Carranza.

Shortly after this reply the conferences between Generals Scott, Funston and Obregon began at El Paso, during which they signed on May 2 a project of a memorandum ad referendum regarding the withdrawal of American troops.

As an indication of the alleged bad faith of the American Government you state that though General Scott declared in this memorandum that the destruction and dispersion of the Villa band "had been accomplished," yet American forces are not withdrawn from Mexico. It is only necessary to read the memorandum, which is in the English language, to ascertain that this is clearly a misstatement, for the memorandum states that "the American punitive expeditionary forces have destroyed or dispersed many of the lawless elements and bandits, . . . or have driven them far into the interior of the Republic of Mexico," and further, that the United States forces were then "carrying on a vigorous pursuit of such small numbers of bandits or lawless elements as may have escaped."

The context of your note gives the impression that the object of the expedition being admittedly accomplished, the United States had agreed in the memorandum to begin the withdrawal of its troops. The memorandum shows, however, that it was not alone on account of partial dispersion of the bandits that it was decided to begin the withdrawal of American forces, but equally on account of the assurances of the Mexican Government that their forces were "at the present time being augmented and strengthened to such an extent that they will be able to prevent any disorders occurring in Mexico that would in any way endanger American territory," and "that they would continue to diligently pursue, capture or destroy any lawless bands of bandits that may still exist or hereafter exist in the northern part of Mexico," and that it would "make a proper distribution of such of its forces as may be necessary to prevent the possibility of invasion of American territory from Mexico."

It was because of these assurances, and because of General Scott's confidence that they would be carried out, that he stated in the memorandum that the American forces would be "gradually withdrawn." It is to be noted that, while the American Government was willing to ratify this agreement, General Carranza refused to do so, as General Obregon stated, because, among other things, it imposed improper conditions upon the Mexican Government.

Notwithstanding the assurances in the memorandum, it is well known that the forces of the de facto Government have not carried on a vigorous pursuit of the remaining bandits and that no proper distribution of forces to prevent the invasion of American territory has been made, as will be shown by the further facts hereinafter set forth.

I am reluctant to be forced to the conclusion which might be drawn from these circumstances that the de facto Government, in spite of the crimes committed and the sinister designs of Villa and his followers, did not and does not now intend or desire that these outlaws should be captured, destroyed or dispersed by American troops or, at the request of this Government, by Mexican troops.

While the conferences at El Paso were in progress, and after the American conferees had been assured on May 2 that the Mexican forces in the northern part of the republic were then being augmented so as to be able to prevent any disorders that would endanger American territory, a band of Mexicans, on the night of May 5, made an attack at Glenn Springs, Texas, about twenty miles north of the border, killing American soldiers and civilians, burning and sacking property and carrying off two Americans as prisoners.

Subsequent to this event, the Mexican Government, as you state, gave instructions to General Obregon to notify that of the United States that it would not permit the further passage of American troops into Mexico on this account, and that orders had been given to all military commanders along the frontier not to consent to same.

This Government is, of course, not in a position to dispute the statement that these instructions had been given to General Obregon, but it can decisively assert that General Obregon never gave any such information to General Scott or General Funston or, so far as known, to any other American official. General Obregon did, however, inquire as to whether American troops had entered Mexico in pursuit of the Glenn Springs raiders, and General Funston stated that no orders had been issued to American troops to cross the frontier on account of the raid, but this statement was made before any such orders had been issued and not afterward, as the erroneous account of the interview given in your note would appear to indicate.

Moreover, no statement was made by the American generals that "no more American troops would cross into our territory." On the contrary, it was pointed out to General Obregon and to Mr. Juan Amador, who was present at the conference, and pointed out with emphasis, that the bandits De La Rosa and Pedro Vino, who had been instrumental in causing the invasion of Texas above Brownsville, were even reported to be arranging in the neighborhood of Victoria for another raid across the border, and it was made clear to General Obregon that if the Mexican Government did not take immediate steps to prevent another invasion of the United States by these marauders, who were frequently seen in the company of General Nafarroto, the Constitutionalist commander, Mexico would find in Tamaulipas another punitive expedition similar to that then in Chihuahua.

American troops crossed into Mexico on May 10, upon notification to the local military authorities, under the repudiated agreement of March 10-13, or in any event, in accordance with the practice adopted over forty years ago, when there was no agreement regarding pursuit of marauders across the international boundary. These troops penetrated 168 miles into Mexican territory in pursuit of the Glenn Springs marauders without encountering a detachment of Mexican troops or a single Mexican soldier.

Further discussion of this raid, however, is not necessary, because the American forces sent in pursuit of the bandits recrossed into Texas on the morning of May 22, the date of your note under consideration—a further proof of the singleness of purpose of this Government in endeavoring to quell disorder and stamp out lawlessness along the border.

During the continuance of the El Paso conferences General Scott, you assert, did not take into consideration the plan proposed by the Mexican Government for the protection of the frontier by the reciprocal distribution of troops along the boundary.

The proposition was made by General Obregon a number of times, but each time conditioned upon the immediate withdrawal of American troops, and the Mexican conferees were invariably informed that immediate withdrawal could not take place and that, therefore, it was impossible to discuss the project on that basis.

I have noted the fact that your communication is not limited to a discussion of the deplorable conditions existing along the border and their important bearing on the peaceful relations of our governments, but that an effort is made to connect it with other circumstances in order to support, if possible, a mistaken interpretation of the attitude of the Government of the United States toward Mexico.

You state in effect that the American Government has placed every obstacle in the way of attaining the pacification of Mexico, and that this is shown by the volume of diplomatic representations in behalf of American interests which constantly impede efforts to reorganize the political, economical and social conditions of the country; by the decided aid lent at one time to Villa by American officers and by the Department of State; by the aid extended by the American Catholic clergy to that of Mexico; by the constant activity of the American press in favor of intervention and the interests of American business men; by the shelter and supply of rebels and conspirators on American territory; by the detention of shipment of arms and munitions purchased by the Mexican Government, and by the detention of machinery intended for their manufacture.

In reply to this sweeping charge, I can truthfully affirm that the American Government has given every possible encouragement to the de facto Government in the pacification and rehabilitation of Mexico. From the moment of its recognition, it has had the undivided support of this Government.

An embargo was placed upon arms and ammunition going into Chihuahua, Sonora and Lower California, in order to prevent their falling into the hands of the armed opponents of the de facto Government. Permission has been granted from time to time, as requested, for Mexican troops and equipment to traverse American territory from one point to another in Mexico, in order that the operations of Mexican troops against Villa and his forces might be facilitated.

In view of these friendly acts, I am surprised that the de facto Government has construed diplomatic representations in regard to the unjust treatment accorded American interests, private assistance to opponents of the de facto Government by sympathizers in a foreign country, and the activity of a foreign press as interference by the United States Government in the domestic politics of Mexico.

If a denial is needed that this Government has ulterior and improper motives in its diplomatic representations, or has countenanced the activities of American sympathizers and the American press opposed to the de facto Government, I am glad most emphatically to deny it. It is, however, a matter of common knowledge that the Mexican press has been more active than the press in the United States in endeavoring to inflame the two peoples against each other and to force the two countries into hostilities.

With the power of censorship of the Mexican press, so rigorously exercised by the de facto Government, the responsibility for this activity cannot, it would seem, be avoided by that Government and the issue of the appeal of General Carranza himself in the press of March 12, calling upon the Mexican people to be prepared for any emergency which might arise and intimating that war with the United States was imminent, evidences that attitude of the de facto Government toward these publications. It should not be a matter of surprise that, after such manifestations of hostile feeling, the United States was doubtful of the purpose for which the large amount of ammunition was to be used which the de facto Government appeared eager to import from this country.

Moreover, the policy of the de facto Government in refusing to co-operate and in failing to act independently in destroying the Villa bandits, and in otherwise suppressing outlawry in the vicinity of the border so as to remove the danger of war materials, while passing southward through this zone, falling into the hands of the enemies of law and order, is, in the opinion of this Government, a sufficient ground, even if there were no other, for the refusal to allow such materials to cross the boundary into the bandit-infested region. To have permitted these shipments without careful scrutiny would, in the circumstances, have been to manifest a sense of security which would have been unjustified.

Candor compels me to add that the unconcealed hostility of the subordinate military commanders of the de facto Government toward the American troops engaged in pursuing the Villa bands and the efforts of the de facto Government to compel their withdrawal from Mexican territory by threats and show of military force instead of by aiding in the capture of the outlaws constitute a menace to the safety of the American troops and to the peace of the border. As long as this menace continues and there is any evidence of an intention on the part of the de facto Government or its military commanders to use force against the American troops instead of co-operating with them, the Government of the United States will not permit munitions of war or machinery for their manufacture to be exported from this country to Mexico.

As to the shelter and supply of rebels and conspirators on American territory, I can state that vigorous efforts have been and are being made by the agents of the United States to apprehend and bring to justice all persons found to be conspiring to violate the laws of the United States by organizing to oppose with arms the de facto Government of Mexico.

Political refugees have undoubtedly sought asylum in the United States, but this Government has vigilantly kept them under surveillance and has not hesitated to apprehend them upon proof of their criminal intentions, as the arrest of General Huerta and others fully attests.

Having corrected the erroneous statements of fact to which I have adverted, the real situation stands forth in its true light. It is admitted that American troops have crossed the international boundary in hot pursuit of the Columbus raiders and without notice to or the consent of your Government; but, through several protestations on the part of this Government by the President, by this Department and by other American authorities, that the object of the expedition was to capture, destroy or completely disperse the Villa bands of outlaws, or to turn this duty over to the Mexican authorities when assured that it would be effectively fulfilled, have been carried out in perfect good faith by the United States.

Its efforts, however, have been obstructed at every point; first, by insistence on a palpably useless agreement which you admit was either not to apply to the present expedition or was to contain impracticable restrictions on its organization and operation; then, by actual opposition, encouraged and fostered by the de facto Government, to the further advance of the expedition into Villa territory, which was followed by the sudden suspension of all negotiations for an arrangement for the pursuit of Villa and his followers and the protection of the frontier; and finally by a demand for the immediate withdrawal of the American troops. Meantime conditions of anarchy in the border States of Mexico were continually growing worse.

Incursions into American territory were plotted and perpetrated since the Glenn Springs raid was successfully executed, while no effective efforts were being made by General Carranza to improve the conditions and protect American territory from constant threat of invasion.

In view of this increasing menace, of the inactivity of the Carranza forces, of the lack of co-operation in the apprehension of the Villa bandits, and of the known encouragement and aid given to bandit leaders, it is unreasonable to expect the United States to withdraw its forces from Mexican territory or to prevent their entry again when their presence is the only check upon further bandit outrages, and the only efficient means of protecting American lives and homes—safeguards which General Carranza, though internationally obligated to supply, is manifestly unable or unwilling to give.

In view of the actual state of affairs as I have outlined above, I am now in a position to consider the conclusions which you have drawn in your note under acknowledgment from the erroneous statements of the fact which you have set forth.

Your Government intimates, if it does not openly charge, that the attitude of the United States is one of insincerity, distrust and suspicion toward the de facto Government of Mexico, and that the intention of the United States in sending its troops into Mexico is to extend its sovereignty over Mexican territory and not merely for the purpose of pursuing marauders and preventing future raids across the border.

The de facto Government charges by implication, which admits of but one interpretation, that this Government has as its object territorial aggrandizement, even at the expense of a war of aggression against a neighbor weakened by years of civil strife. The Government of the United States, if it had had designs on the territory of Mexico, would have had no difficulty in finding during this period of revolution and disorder many plausible arguments for intervention in Mexican affairs. Hoping, however, that the people of Mexico would, through their own efforts, restore peace and establish an orderly government, the United States has awaited with patience the consummation of the revolution.

When the superiority of the revolutionary faction led by General Carranza became undoubted, the United States, after conferring with six others of the American republics, recognized unconditionally the present de facto Government. It hoped and expected that that Government would speedily restore order and provide the Mexican people and others, who had given their energy and substance to the development of the great resources of the republic, opportunity to rebuild in peace and security their shattered fortunes.

This Government has waited month after month for the consummation of its hope and expectation. In spite of increasing discouragements, in spite of repeated provocations to exercise force in the restoration of order in the northern regions of Mexico, where American interests have suffered most seriously from lawlessness, the Government of the United States has refrained from aggressive action and sought by appeals and moderate though explicit demands to impress upon the de facto Government the seriousness of the situation and to arouse it to its duty to perform its international obligations toward the citizens of the United States who had entered the territory of Mexico, or had vested interests within its boundaries.

In the face of constantly renewed evidences of the patience and restraint of this Government in circumstances which only a government imbued with an unselfish and sincere desire to respect to the full the sovereign rights and national dignity of the Mexican people would have endured, doubts and suspicions as to the motives of the Government of the United States are expressed in your communication of May 22, for which I can imagine no purpose but to impugn the good faith of this Government, for I find it hard to believe that such imputations are not universally known to be without the least shadow of justification.

In fact, can the de facto Government doubt that, if the United States had turned covetous eyes on Mexican territory it could have found many pretexts in the past for the gratification of its desire? Can that Government doubt that months ago, when the war between the revolutionary factions was in progress, a much better opportunity than the present was afforded for American intervention, if such has been the purpose of the United States as the de facto Government now insinuates? What motive could this Government have had in refraining from taking advantage of such opportunities other than unselfish friendship for the Mexican republic.

I have, of course, given consideration to your argument that the responsibility for the present situation rests largely upon this Government. In the first place, you state that even the American forces along the border, whose attention is undivided by other military operations, find themselves physically unable to protect effectively the frontier on the American side.

Obviously, if there is no means of reaching bands roving on Mexican territory and making sudden dashes at night into American territory, it is impossible to prevent such invasions, unless the frontier is protected by a cordon of troops.

No Government could be expected to maintain a force of this strength along the boundary of a nation with which it is at peace for the purpose of resisting the onslaughts of a few bands of lawless men, especially when the neighboring State makes no effort to prevent these attacks. The most effective method of preventing raids of this nature, as past experience has fully demonstrated, is to visit punishment or destruction on the raiders.

It is precisely this plan which the United States desires to follow along the border without any intention of interfering upon the sovereign rights of her neighbor, but which although obviously advantageous to the de facto Government, it refuses to allow or even countenance. It is in fact protection to American lives and property about which the United States is solicitous and not the methods or ways in which that protection shall be accomplished. If the Mexican Government is unwilling or unable to give this protection by preventing its territory from being the rendezvous and refuge of murderers and plunderers, that does not relieve this Government from its duty to take all the steps necessary to safeguard American citizens on American soil.

The United States Government cannot and will not allow bands of lawless men to establish themselves upon its borders with liberty to invade and plunder American territory with impunity, and when pursued to seek safety across the Rio Grande, relying upon the plea of their Government that the integrity of the soil of the Mexican Republic must not be violated.

The Mexican Government further protests that it has "made every effort on its part to protect the frontier" and that it is doing "all possible to avoid a recurrence of such acts." Attention is again invited to the well-known and unrestricted activities of De La Rosa, Ancieto Piscano, Pedro Vinos and others in connection with border raids, and to the fact that, as I am advised, up to June 4, De La Rosa was still collecting troops at Monterey for the openly avowed purpose of making attacks on Texas border towns, and that Pedro Vinos was recruiting at other places for the same avowed purpose.

I have already pointed out the uninterrupted progress of Villa to and from Columbus, and the fact that the American forces in pursuit of the Glenn Springs marauders penetrated 168 miles into Mexican territory without encountering a single Carranzista soldier. This does not indicate that the Mexican Government is "doing all possible" to avoid further raids, and if it is doing "all possible" this is not sufficient to prevent border raids, and there is every reason, therefore, why this Government must take such preventive measures as it deems sufficient.

It is suggested that injuries suffered on account of bandit raids are a matter of "pecuniary reparation" but, never the cause for American forces to invade Mexican soil. The precedents which have been established and maintained by the Government of the Mexican Republic for the last half century do not bear out this statement. It has grown to be almost a custom not to settle depredations of bandits by payments of money alone, but to quell such disorders and prevent such crimes by swift and sure punishment.

The de facto Government finally argues that "if the frontier were duly protected from incursions from Mexico there would be no reason for the existing difficulty"; thus the de facto Government attempts to absolve itself from the first duty of any Government, namely, the protection of life and property. This is the paramount obligation for which governments are instituted, and governments neglecting or failing to perform it are not worthy of the name.

This is the duty for which General Carranza, it must be assumed, initiated his revolution in Mexico and organized the present Government and for which the United States Government recognized his Government as the de facto Government of Mexico. Protection of American lives and property, then, in the United States is first the obligation of this Government and in Mexico is, first, the obligation of Mexico, and second, the obligation of the United States.

In securing this protection along the common boundary, the United States has a right to expect the co-operation of its neighboring republic; and yet, instead of taking steps to check or punish the raiders, the de facto Government demurs and objects to measures taken by the United States.

The United States Government does not wish to believe that the de facto Government approves these marauding attacks, yet as they continue to be made, they show that the Mexican Government is unable to repress them. This inability, as this Government has had occasion in the past to say, may excuse the failure to check the outrages complained of, but it only makes stronger the duty of the United States to prevent them, for if the Government of Mexico cannot protect the lives and property of Americans, exposed to attack from Mexicans, the Government of the United States is in duty bound, so far as it can, to do so.

In conclusion the Mexican Government invites the United States to support "assurances of friendship with real and effective acts," which "can be no other than the immediate withdrawal of the American troops." For the reasons I have herein fully set forth, this request of the de facto Government cannot now be entertained. The United States has not sought the duty which has been forced upon it of pursuing bandits who, under fundamental principles of municipal and international law, ought to be pursued and arrested and punished by Mexican authorities.

Whenever Mexico will assume and effectively exercise that responsibility the United States, as it has many times before publicly declared, will be glad to have this obligation fulfilled by the de facto Government of Mexico. If, on the contrary, the de facto Government is pleased to ignore this obligation and to believe that "in case of a refusal to retire these troops there is no further recourse than to defend its territory by an appeal to arms," the Government of the United States would surely be lacking in sincerity and friendship if it did not frankly impress upon the de facto Government that the execution of this threat will lead to the gravest consequences.

While this Government would deeply regret such a result, it cannot recede from its settled determination to maintain its national rights and to perform its full duty in preventing further invasions of the territory of the United States and in removing the peril which Americans along the international boundary have borne so long with patience and forbearance.

Accept, etc.,

ROBERT LANSING.

ULTIMATUM TO MEXICO

WASHINGTON, June 26, 1916.

The text of the ultimatum to Carranza, given out by the State Department today, follows. This telegram was sent on June 25, 1916, to James Linn Rodgers, Special Representative of the American Government in Mexico City:

Mr. Arredondo yesterday delivered to this Government the following communication:

"I am directed by my Government to inform Your Excellency, with reference to the Carrizal incident, that the chief executive, through the Mexican war department, gave orders to General Jacinto B. Trevino not to permit American forces from General Pershing's column to advance further south, nor to move either east or west from the points where they are located, and to oppose new incursions of American soldiers into Mexican territory.

"These orders were brought by General Trevino to the attention of General Pershing, who acknowledged the receipt of the communication relative thereto.

"On the 22d instant, as Your Excellency knows, an American force moved eastward quite far from its base notwithstanding orders and was engaged by Mexican troops at Carrizal, State of Chihuahua. As a result of the encounter several men on both sides were killed and wounded, and seventeen American soldiers were made prisoners."

You are hereby instructed to hand to the Minister of Foreign Relations of the de facto Government the following:

"The Government of the United States can put no other construction upon the communication handed to the Secretary of State of the United States on the twenty-fourth of June, by Mr. Arredondo, under instruction of your Government, than that it is intended as a formal avowal of deliberate hostile action against the forces of the United States now in Mexico, and of the purpose to attack them without provocation whenever they move from their present position in pursuance of the objects for which they were sent there, notwithstanding the fact that those objects not only involve no unfriendly intention toward the Government and people of Mexico, but are, on the contrary, intended only to assist that Government in protecting itself and the territory and people of the United States against irresponsible and insurgent bands of rebel marauders.

"I am instructed, therefore, by my Government to demand the immediate release of prisoners taken in the encounter at Carrizal, together with any property of the United States taken with them, and to inform you that the Government of the United States expects an early statement from your Government as to the course of action it wishes the Government of the United States to understand it has determined upon; and that it also expects that this statement be made through the usual diplomatic channels, and not through subordinate military commanders."

LANSING.

EXECUTIVE ORDER

[Providing for the Payment of Interest on Deposit Money Orders Issued in the Canal Zone.]

By virtue of the authority vested in me by law, it is hereby ordered:—

1. That deposit money orders issued by the Canal Zone Postal Service shall bear interest at the rate of one-half of one percentum for each period of three full calendar months, from August 21, 1916, or subsequent date of issue. Interest shall be payable when the order is paid but shall not accrue on any order for more than three years.

2. The Governor of The Panama Canal is authorized to prescribe such detailed rules and regulations as may be necessary to carry out this order.

WOODROW WILSON.

THE WHITE HOUSE, *October 22. 1916.*

NEUTRALITY PROCLAMATIONS

By the President of the United States of America

A PROCLAMATION

[Neutrality—France, Great Britain, Italy, Servia, and Bulgaria.]

WHEREAS a state of war unhappily exists between France, Great Britain, Italy and Servia on the one side and Bulgaria on the other; And Whereas the United States is on terms of friendship and amity with the contending powers, and with the persons inhabiting their several dominions;

[Here follows the identical preamble and warning against violation of quoted law as in the proclamation of neutrality in the case of hostilities between Austria-Hungary and Servia, Germany and Russia, and Germany and France. See pages 7969, 7970, 7971, 7972 and 7973.—*Ed.*]

DONE at the City of Washington this eleventh day of November, in the year of our Lord one thousand nine hundred and fifteen [SEAL.] and of the independence of the United States of America the one hundred and fortieth.

WOODROW WILSON.

By the President:
ROBERT LANSING, *Secretary of State.*

By the President of the United States of America

A PROCLAMATION

[Neutrality—Germany and Portugal.]

WHEREAS a state of war unhappily exists between Germany and Portugal; And Whereas the United States is on terms of friendship and amity with the contending powers, and with the persons inhabiting their several dominions;

[Here follows the identical preamble and warning against violation of quoted law as in the proclamation of neutrality in the case of hostilities between Austria-Hungary and Servia, Germany and Russia, and Germany and France. See pages 7969, 7970, 7971, 7972 and 7973.—*Ed.*]

DONE at the City of Washington this thirteenth day of March in the year of our Lord one thousand nine hundred and sixteen [SEAL.] and of the independence of the United States of America the one hundred and fortieth.

WOODROW WILSON.

By the President:
ROBERT LANSING, *Secretary of State.*

By the President of the United States of America

A PROCLAMATION

[Neutrality—Germany and Italy.]

WHEREAS a state of war unhappily exists between Germany and Italy; And Whereas the United States is on terms of friendship and amity with the contending powers, and with the persons inhabiting their several dominions;

[Here follows the identical preamble and warning against violation of quoted law as in the proclamation of neutrality in the case of hostilities between Austria-Hungary and Servia, Germany and Russia, and Germany and France. See pages 7969, 7970, 7971, 7972 and 7973.—*Ed.*]

DONE at the City of Washington this thirtieth day of August in the year of our Lord one thousand nine hundred and sixteen [SEAL.] and of the independence of the United States of America the one hundred and forty-first.

WOODROW WILSON.

By the President:
ROBERT LANSING, *Secretary of State.*

By the President of the United States of America

A PROCLAMATION

[Neutrality—Austria-Hungary, Bulgaria, Germany, Turkey, and Roumania.]

WHEREAS a state of war unhappily exists between Austria-Hungary, Bulgaria, Germany, and Turkey on the one side and Roumania on the other; And Whereas the United States is on terms of friendship and amity with the contending powers, and with the persons inhabiting their several dominions;

[Here follows the identical preamble and warning against violation of quoted law as in the proclamation of neutrality in the case of hostilities between Austria-Hungary and Servia, Germany and Russia, and Germany and France. See pages 7969, 7970, 7971, 7972 and 7973.—*Ed.*]

DONE at the City of Washington this eighteenth day of September in the year of our Lord one thousand nine hundred and [SEAL.] sixteen and of the independence of the United States of America the one hundred and forty-first.

WOODROW WILSON.

By the President:
ROBERT LANSING, *Secretary of State.*

PROTEST AGAINST BRITISH BLACKLISTING OF AMERICAN FIRMS AND INTERFERENCE IN AMERICAN TRADE WITH NEUTRALS.

DEPARTMENT OF STATE, WASHINGTON, July 26, 1916.

The Acting Secretary of State to Ambassador W. H. Page.

You are instructed to deliver to Sir Edward Grey a formal note on the subject of the Enemy Trading Act, textually as follows:

The announcement that his Britannic Majesty's Government has placed the names of certain persons, firms, and corporations in the United States upon a proscriptive "blacklist" and has forbidden all financial or commercial dealings between them and citizens of Great Britain has been received with the most painful surprise by the people and Government of the United States, and seems to the Government of the United States to embody a policy of arbitrary interference with neutral trade against which it is its duty to protest in the most decided terms.

The scope and effect of the policy are extraordinary. British steamship companies will not accept cargoes from the proscribed firms or persons or transport their goods to any port, and steamship lines under neutral ownership understand that if they accept freight from them they are likely to be denied coal at British ports and excluded from other privileges which they have usually enjoyed, and may themselves be put upon the blacklist. Neutral bankers refuse loans to those on the list and neutral merchants decline to contract for their goods, fearing a like proscription. It appears that British officials regard the prohibitions of the blacklist as applicable to domestic commercial transactions in foreign countries as well as in Great Britain and her dependencies, for Americans doing business in foreign countries have been put on notice that their dealings with blacklisted firms are to be regarded as subject to veto by the British Government. By the same principle Americans in the United States might be made subject to similar punitive action if they were found dealing with any of their own countrymen whose names had thus been listed.

The harsh and even disastrous effects of this policy upon the trade of the United States and upon the neutral rights upon which it will not fail to insist are obvious. Upon the list of those proscribed and in effect shut out from the general commerce of the world may be found American concerns which are engaged in large commercial operations as importers of foreign products and materials and as distributors of American products and manufactures to foreign countries and which constitute important channels through which American trade reaches the outside world. Their foreign affiliations may have been fostered for many years, and when once broken cannot easily or promptly be re-established.

Other concerns may be put upon the list at any time and without notice. It is understood that additions to the proscription may be made "whenever on account of enemy nationality or enemy association of such persons or bodies of persons it appears to his Majesty expedient to do so." The possibilities of undeserved injury to American citizens from such measures, arbitrarily taken, and of serious and incalculable interruptions of American trade are without limit.

It has been stated on behalf of his Majesty's Government that these measures were aimed only at the enemies of Great Britain and would be adopted and enforced with strict regard to the rights of neutrals and with the least possible detriment to neutral trade, but it is evident that they are inevitably and essentially inconsistent with the rights of the citizens of all the nations not involved in war. The Government of the United States begs to remind the Government of his Britannic Majesty that citizens of the United States are entirely within their rights in attempting to trade with the people or the Governments of any of the nations now at war, subject only to well-defined international practices and understandings which the Government of the United States deems the Government of Great Britain to have too lightly and too frequently disregarded.

There are well-known remedies and penalties for breaches of blockade, where the blockade is real and in fact effective, for trade in contraband, for every unneutral act by whomsoever attempted. The Government of the United States cannot consent to see those remedies and penalties altered or extended at the will of a single power or group of powers to the injury of its own citizens or in derogation of its own rights. Conspicuous among the principles which the civilized nations of the world have accepted for the safeguarding of the rights of neutrals is the just and honorable principle that neutrals may not be condemned nor their goods confiscated, except upon fair adjudication and after an opportunity to be heard in prize courts or elsewhere. Such safeguards the blacklist brushes aside. It condemns without hearing, without notice, and in advance. It is manifestly out of the question that the Government of the United States should acquiesce in such methods or applications of punishment to its citizens.

What ever may be said with regard to the legality, in the view of international obligation, of the act of Parliament upon which the practice of the blacklist as now employed by his Majesty's Government is understood to be based, the Government of the United States is constrained to regard that practice as inconsistent with that true justice, sincere amity, and impartial fairness which should characterize the dealings of friendly Governments with one another. The spirit of reciprocal trade between the United States and Great Britain, the privilege long accorded to the nationals of each to come and go with their ships and cargoes, to use each the other's shipping, and be served each by the other's merchants is very seriously impaired by arbitrary and sweeping practices such as this.

There is no purpose or inclination on the part of the Government of the United States to shield American citizens or business houses in any way from the legitimate consequences of unneutral acts or practices; it is quite willing that they should suffer the appropriate penalties which international law and the usage of nations have sanctioned; but his Britannic Majesty's Government cannot expect the Government of the United States to consent to see its citizens put upon an ex parte blacklist without calling the attention of his Majesty's Government, in the gravest terms, to the many serious consequences to neutral right and neutral relations which such an act must necessarily involve. It hopes and believes that his Majesty's Government, in its natural absorption in a single pressing object of policy, has acted without a full realization of the many undesired and undesirable results that might ensue.   POLK, Acting.

SPECIAL ADDRESS

[On the Impending Strike of Railroad Employees, Delivered at a Joint Session of the Two Houses of Congress, August 29, 1916.]

GENTLEMEN OF THE CONGRESS:

I have come to you to seek your assistance in dealing with a very grave situation which has arisen out of the demand of the employees of the railroads engaged in freight train service that they be granted an eight-hour working day, safeguarded by payment for an hour and a half of service for every hour of work beyond the eight.

The matter has been agitated for more than a year. The public has been made familiar with the demands of the men and the arguments urged in favor of them, and even more familiar with the objections of the railroads and their counter demand that certain privileges now enjoyed by their men and certain bases of payment worked out through many years of contest be reconsidered, especially in their relation to the adoption of an eight-hour day. The matter came some three weeks ago to a final issue and resulted in a complete deadlock between the parties. The means provided by law for the mediation of the controversy failed and the means of arbitration for which the law provides were rejected. The representatives of the railway executives proposed that the demands of the men be submitted in their entirety to arbitration, along with certain questions of readjustment as to pay and conditions of employment which seemed to them to be either closely associated with the demands or to call for reconsideration on their own merits; the men absolutely declined arbitration, especially if any of their established privileges were by that means to be drawn again in question. The law in the matter put no compulsion upon them. The four hundred thousand men from whom the demands proceeded had voted to strike if their demands were refused; the strike was imminent; it has since been set for the 4th of September next. It affects the men who man the freight trains on practically every railway in the country. The freight service throughout the United States must stand still until their places are filled, if, indeed, it should prove possible to fill them at all. Cities will be cut off from their food supplies, the whole commerce of the nation will be paralyzed, men of every sort and occupation will be thrown out of employment, countless thousands will in all likelihood be brought, it may be, to the very point of starvation, and a tragical national calamity brought on, to be added to the other distresses of the time, because no basis of accommodation or settlement has been found.

Just as soon as it became evident that mediation under the existing law had failed and that arbitration had been rendered impossible by the attitude of the men, I considered it my duty to confer with the representatives of both the railways and the brotherhoods, and myself offer mediation, not as an arbitrator, but merely as spokesman of the nation, in the interest of justice, indeed, and as a friend of both parties, but not as judge, only as the representative of one hundred millions of men, women and children who would pay the price, the incalculable price, of loss and suffering should these few men insist upon approaching and concluding the matters in controversy between them merely as employers and employees, rather than as patriotic citizens of the United States looking before and after and accepting the larger responsibility which the public would put upon them.

It seemed to me, in considering the subject-matter of the controversy, that the whole spirit of the time and the preponderant evidence of recent economic experience spoke for the eight-hour day. It has been adjudged by the thought and experience of recent years a thing upon which society is justified in insisting as in the interest of health, efficiency, contentment, and a general increase of economic vigor. The whole presumption of modern experience would, it seemed to me, be in its favor, whether there was arbitration or not, and the debatable points to settle were those which arose out of the acceptance of the eight-hour day rather than those which affected its establishment. I, therefore, proposed that the eight-hour day be adopted by the railway managements and put into practice for the present as a substitute for the existing ten-hour basis of pay and service; that I should appoint, with the permission of the Congress, a small commission to observe the results of the change, carefully studying the figures of the altered operating costs, not only, but also the conditions of labor under which the men worked and the operation of their existing agreements with the railroads, with instructions to report the facts as they found them to the Congress at the earliest possible day, but without recommendation; and that, after the facts had been thus disclosed, an adjustment should in some orderly manner be sought of all the matters now left unadjusted between the railroad managers and the men.

These proposals were exactly in line, it is interesting to note, with the position taken by the Supreme Court of the United States when appealed to to protect certain litigants from the financial losses which they confidently expected if they should submit to the regulation of their charges and of their methods of service by public legislation. The court has held that it would not undertake to form a judgment upon forecasts, but could base its action only upon actual experience; that it must be supplied with facts, not with calculations and opinions, however scientifically attempted. To undertake to arbitrate the question of the adoption of an eight-hour day in the light of results merely estimated and predicted would be to undertake an enterprise of conjecture. No wise man could undertake it, or, if he did undertake it, could feel assured of his conclusions.

I unhesitatingly offered the friendly services of the administration to the railway managers to see to it that justice was done the railroads in the outcome. I felt warranted in assuring them that no obstacle of law would be suffered to stand in the way of their increasing their revenues to meet the expenses resulting from the change so far as the development of their business and of their administrative efficiency did not prove adequate to meet them. The public and the representatives of the public, I felt justified in assuring them, were disposed to nothing but justice in such cases and were willing to serve those who served them.

The representatives of the brotherhoods accepted the plan; but the representatives of the railroads declined to accept it. In the face of what I cannot but regard as the practical certainty that they will be ultimately obliged to accept the eight-hour day by the concerted action of organized labor, backed by the favorable judgment of society, the representatives of the railway management have felt justified in declining a peaceful settlement which would engage all the forces of justice, public and private, on their side to take care of the event. They fear the hostile influence of shippers, who would be opposed to an increase of freight rates (for which, however, of course, the public itself would pay); they apparently feel no confidence that the Interstate Commerce Commission could withstand the objections that would be made. They do not care to rely upon the friendly assurances of the Congress or the President. They have thought it best that they should be forced to yield, if they must yield, not by counsel, but by the suffering of the country. While my conferences with them were in progress, and when to all outward appearance those conferences had come to a standstill. the representatives of the brotherhoods suddenly acted and set the strike for the 4th of September.

The railway managers based their decision to reject my counsel in this matter upon their conviction that they must at any cost to themselves or to the country stand firm for the principle of arbitration which the men had rejected. I based my counsel upon the indisputable fact that there was no means of obtaining arbitration. The law supplied none; earnest efforts at mediation had failed to influence the men in the least. To stand firm for the principle of arbitration and yet not get arbitration seemed to me futile, and something more than futile, because it involved incalculable distress to the country and consequences in some respects worse than those of war, and that in the midst of peace.

I yield to no man in firm adherence, alike of conviction and of purpose, to the principle of arbitration in industrial disputes; but matters have come to a sudden crisis in this particular dispute and the country had been caught unprovided with any practicable means of enforcing that conviction in practice (by whose fault we will not now stop to inquire). A situation had to be met whose elements and fixed conditions were indisputable. The practical and patriotic course to pursue, as it seemed to me, was to secure immediate peace by conceding the one thing in the demands of the men which society itself and any arbitrators who represented public sentiment were most likely to approve, and immediately lay the foundations for securing arbitration with regard to everything else involved. The event has confirmed that judgment.

I was seeking to compose the present in order to safeguard the future; for I wished an atmosphere of peace and friendly co-operation in which to take counsel with the representatives of the nation with regard to the best means for providing, so far as it might prove possible to provide, against the recurrence of such unhappy situations in the future—the best and most practicable means of securing calm and fair arbitration of all industrial disputes in the days to come. This is assuredly the best way of vindicating a principle, namely, having failed to make certain of its observance in the present, to make certain of its observance in the future.

But I could only propose. I could not govern the will of others who took an entirely different view of the circumstances of the case, who even refused to admit the circumstances to be what they have turned out to be.

Having failed to bring the parties to this critical controversy to an accommodation, therefore, I turn to you, deeming it clearly our duty as public servants to leave nothing undone that we can do to safeguard the life and interests of the nation. In the spirit of such a purpose, I earnestly recommend the following legislation:

First, immediate provision for the enlargement and administrative reorganization of the Interstate Commerce Commission along the lines embodied in the bill recently passed by the House of Representatives and now awaiting action by the Senate; in order that the Commission may be enabled to deal with the many great and various duties now devolving upon it with a promptness and thoroughness which are with its present constitution and means of action practically impossible.

Second, the establishment of an eight-hour day as the legal basis alike of work and of wages in the employment of all railway employees who are actually engaged in the work of operating trains in interstate transportation.

Third, the authorization of the appointment by the President of a small body of men to observe the actual results in experience of the adoption of the eight-hour day in railway transportation alike for the men and for the railroads; its effects in the matter of operating costs, in the application of the existing practices and agreements to the new conditions, and in all other practical aspects, with the provision that the investigators shall report their conclusions to the Congress at the earliest possible date, but without recommendation as to legislative action; in order that the public may learn from an unprejudiced source just what actual developments have ensued.

Fourth, explicit approval by the Congress of the consideration by the Interstate Commerce Commission of an increase of freight rates to meet such additional expenditures by the railroads as may have been rendered necessary by the adoption of the eight-hour day and which have not been offset by administrative readjustments and economies, should the facts disclosed justify the increase.

Fifth, an amendment of the existing federal statute which provides for the mediation, conciliation, and arbitration of such controversies as the present by adding to it a provision that in case the methods of accommodation now provided for should fail, a full public investigation of the merits of every such dispute shall be instituted and completed before a strike or lockout may lawfully be attempted.

And, sixth, the lodgement in the hands of the executive of the power, in case of military necessity, to take control of such portions and such rolling stock of the railways of the country as may be required for military use and to operate them for military purposes, with authority to draft into the military service of the United States such train crews and administrative officials as the circumstances require for their safe and efficient use.

This last suggestion I make because we cannot in any circumstances suffer the nation to be hampered in the essential matter of national defense. At the present moment circumstances render this duty particularly obvious. Almost the entire military force of the nation is stationed upon the Mexican border to guard our territory against hostile raids. It must be supplied, and steadily supplied, with whatever it needs for its maintenance and efficiency. If it should be necessary for purposes of national defense to transfer any portion of it upon short notice to some other part of the country, for reasons now unforeseen, ample means of transportation must be available, and available without delay. The power conferred in this matter should be carefully and explicitly limited to cases of military necessity, but in all such cases it should be clear and ample.

There is one other thing we should do if we are true champions of arbitration. We should make all arbitral awards judgments by record of a court of law in order that their interpretation and enforcement may lie, not with one of the parties to the arbitration, but with an impartial and authoritative tribunal.

These things I urge upon you, not in haste or merely as a means of meeting a present emergency, but as permanent and necessary additions to the law of the land, suggested, indeed, by circumstances we had hoped never to see, but imperative as well as just, if such emergencies are to be prevented in the future. I feel that no extended argument is needed to commend them to your favorable consideration. They demonstrate themselves. The time and the occasion only give emphasis to their importance. We need them now and we shall continue to need them.

SPEECH OF ACCEPTANCE

[Of His Renomination to the Presidency by the Democratic Party. Delivered on the Grounds of Shadow Lawn, at Long Branch, N. J., Sept. 2, 1916.]

SENATOR JAMES, GENTLEMEN OF THE NOTIFICATION COMMITTEE, FELLOW CITIZENS:

I cannot accept the leadership and responsibility which the National Democratic Convention has again, in such generous fashion, asked me to accept without first expressing my profound gratitude to the party for the trust it reposes in me after four years of fiery trial in the midst of affairs of unprecedented difficulty, and the keen sense of added responsibility with which this honor fills (I had almost said burdens) me as I think of the great issues of national life and policy involved in the present and immediate future conduct of our Government. I shall seek, as I have always sought, to justify the extraordinary confidence thus reposed in me by striving to purge my heart and purpose of every personal and of every misleading party motive and devoting every energy I have to the service of the nation as a whole, praying that I may continue to have the counsel and support of all forward looking men at every turn of the difficult business.

For I do not doubt that the people of the United States will wish the Democratic party to continue in control of the Government. They are not in the habit of rejecting those who have actually served them for those who are making doubtful and conjectural promises of service. Least of all are they likely to substitute those who promised to render them particular services and proved false to that promise for those who have actually rendered those very services.

Boasting is always an empty business which pleases nobody but the boaster, and I have no disposition to boast of what the Democratic party has accomplished. It has merely done its duty. It has merely fulfilled its explicit promises. But there can be no violation of good taste in calling attention to the manner in which those promises have been carried out or in adverting to the interesting fact that many of the things accomplished were what the opposition party had again and again promised to do but had left undone. Indeed that is manifestly part of the business of this year of reckoning and assessment. There is no means of judging the future except by assessing the past. Constructive action must be weighed against destructive comment and reaction. The Democrats either have or have not understood the varied interests of the country. The test is contained in the record.

What is that record? What were the Democrats called into power to do? What things had long waited to be done, and how did the Democrats do them? It is a record of extraordinary length and variety, rich in elements of many kinds, but consistent in principle throughout and susceptible of brief recital.

The Republican party was put out of power because of failure, practical failure and moral failure; because it had served special interests and not the country at large; because, under the leadership of its preferred and established guides, of those who still make its choices, it had lost touch with the thoughts and the needs of the nation and was living in a past age and under a fixed illusion, the illusion of greatness. It had framed tariff laws based upon a fear of foreign trade, a fundamental doubt as to American skill, enterprise and capacity, and a very tender regard for the profitable privileges of those who had gained control of domestic markets and domestic credits; and yet had enacted anti-trust laws which hampered the very things they meant to foster, which were stiff and inelastic, and in part unintelligible. It had permitted the country throughout the long period of its control to stagger from one financial crisis to another under the operation of a national banking law of its own framing which made stringency and panic certain and the control of the larger business operations of the country by the bankers of a few reserve centers inevitable; had made as if it meant to reform the law, but had faint heartedly failed in the attempt because it could not bring itself to do the one thing necessary to make the reform genuine and effectual, namely, break up the control of small groups of bankers. It had been oblivious, or indifferent, to the fact that the farmers, upon whom the country depends for its food and in the last analysis for its prosperity, were without standing in the matter of commercial credit, without the protection of standards in their market transactions and without systematic knowledge of the markets themselves; that the laborers of the country, the great army of men who man the industries it was professing to father and promote, carried their labor as a mere commodity to market, were subject to restraint by novel and drastic process in the courts, were without assurance of compensation for industrial accidents, without Federal assistance in accommodating labor disputes and without national aid or advice in finding the places and the industries in which their labor was most needed. The country had no national system of road construction and development. Little intelligent attention was paid to the army, and not enough to the navy. The other republics of America distrusted us because they found that we thought first of the profits of American investors and only as an afterthought of impartial justice and helpful friendship. Its policy was provincial in all things; its purposes were out of harmony with the temper and purpose of the people and the timely development of the nation's interests.

So things stood when the Democratic party came into power. How do they stand now? Alike in the domestic field and in the wide field of the commerce of the world, American business and life and industry have been set free to move as they never moved before.

The tariff has been revised, not on the principle of repelling foreign trade, but upon the principle of encouraging it, upon something like a footing of equality with our own in respect of the terms of competition, and a Tariff Board has been created whose function it will be to keep the relations of American with foreign business and industry under constant observation for the guidance alike of our business men and of our Congress. American energies are now directed toward the markets of the world.

The laws against trusts have been clarified by definition, with a view to making it plain that they were not directed against big business but only against unfair business and the pretense of competition where there was none; and a Trade Commission has been created with powers of guidance and accommodation which have relieved business men of unfounded fears and set them upon the road of hopeful and confident enterprise.

By the Federal reserve act the supply of currency at the disposal of active business has been rendered elastic, taking its volume, not from a fixed body of investment securities, but from the liquid assets of daily trade; and these assets are assessed and accepted, not by distant groups of bankers in control of unavailable reserves, but by bankers at the many centers of local exchange who are in touch with local conditions everywhere.

Effective measures have been taken for the re-creation of an American merchant marine and the revival of the American carrying trade indispensable to our emancipation from the control which foreigners have so long exercised over the opportunities, the routes and the methods of our commerce with other countries.

The Interstate Commerce Commission is about to be reorganized to enable it to perform its great and important functions more promptly and more efficiently. We have created, extended and improved the service of the parcel post.

So much we have done for business. What other party has understood the task so well or executed it so intelligently and energetically? What other party has attempted it at all? The Republican leaders apparently know of no means of assisting business but "protection." How to stimulate it and put it upon a new footing of energy and enterprise they have not suggested.

For the farmers of the country we have virtually created commercial credit by means of the Federal reserve act and the rural credits act. They now have the standing of other business men in the money market. We have successfully regulated speculation in "futures" and established standards in the marketing of grains. By an intelligent warehouse act we have assisted to make the standard crops available as never before both for systematic marketing and as a security for loans from the banks. We have greatly added to the work of neighborhood demonstration on the farm itself of improved methods of cultivation, and, through the intelligent extension of the functions of the Department of Agriculture, have made it possible for the farmer to learn systematically where his best markets are and how to get at them.

The workingmen of America have been given a veritable emancipation by the legal recognition of a man's labor as part of his life, and not a mere marketable commodity; by exempting labor organizations from processes of the courts which treated their members like fractional parts of mobs and not like accessible and responsible individuals; by releasing our seamen from involuntary servitude; by making adequate provision for compensation for industrial accidents; by providing suitable machinery for mediation and conciliation in industrial disputes, and by putting the Federal Department of Labor at the disposal of the workingman when in search of work.

We have effected the emancipation of the children of the country by releasing them from hurtful labor. We have instituted a system of national aid in the building of high roads such as the country has been feeling after for a century. We have sought to equalize taxation by means of an equitable income tax. We have taken the steps that ought to have been taken at the outset to open up the resources of Alaska. We have provided for national defense upon a scale never before seriously proposed upon the responsibility of an entire political party. We have driven the tariff lobby from cover and obliged it to substitute solid argument for private influence.

This extraordinary recital must sound like a platform, a list of sanguine promises, but it is not. It is a record of promises made four years ago and now actually redeemed in constructive legislation.

These things must profoundly disturb the thoughts and confound the plans of those who have made themselves believe that the Democratic party neither understood nor was ready to assist the business of the country in the great enterprise which it is its evident and inevitable destiny to undertake and carry through. The breaking up of the lobby must especially disconcert them, for it was through the lobby that they sought and were sure they had found the heart of things. The game of privilege can be played successfully by no other means.

This record must equally astonish those who feared that the Democratic party had not opened its heart to comprehend the demands of social justice. We have in four years come very near to carrying out the platform of the Progressive party as well as our own; for we also are progressives.

There is one circumstance connected with this program which ought to be very plainly stated. It was resisted at every step by the interests which the Republican party had catered to and fostered at the expense of the country, and these same interests are now earnestly praying for a reaction which will save their privileges—for the restoration of their sworn friends to power before it is too late to recover what they have lost. They fought with particular desperation and infinite resourcefulness the reform of the banking and currency system, knowing that to be the citadel of their control; and most anxiously are they hoping and planning for the amendment of the Federal reserve act by the concentration of control in a single bank which the old familiar group of bankers can keep under their eye and direction. But while the "big men" who used to write the tariffs and command the assistance of the Treasury have been hostile—all but a few with vision—the average business man knows that he has been delivered, and that the fear that was once every day in his heart, that the men who controlled credit and directed enterprise from the committee rooms of Congress would crush him, is there no more, and will not return—unless the party that consulted only the "big men" should return to power—the party of masterly inactivity and cunning resourcefulness in standing pat to resist change.

The Republican party is just the party that cannot meet the new conditions of a new age. It does not know the way and it does not wish new conditions. It tried to break away from the old leaders and could not. They still select its candidates and dictate its policy, still resist change, still hanker after the old conditions, still know no methods of encouraging business but the old methods. When it changes its leaders and its purposes and brings its ideas up to date it will have the right to ask the American people to give it power again; but not until then. A new age, an age of revolutionary change, needs new purposes and new ideas.

In foreign affairs we have been guided by principles clearly conceived and consistently lived up to. Perhaps they have not been fully comprehended because they have hitherto governed international affairs only in theory, not in practice. They are simple, obvious, easily stated, and fundamental to American ideals.

We have been neutral not only because it was the fixed and traditional policy of the United States to stand aloof from the politics of Europe and because we had had no part either of action or of policy in the influences which brought on the present war, but also because it was manifestly our duty to prevent, if it were possible, the indefinite extension of the fires of hate and desolation kindled by that terrible conflict and seek to serve mankind by reserving our strength and our resources for the anxious and difficult days of restoration and healing which must follow, when peace will have to build its house anew.

The rights of our own citizens of course became involved; that was inevitable. Where they did this was our guiding principle; that property rights can be vindicated by claims for damages and no modern nation can decline to arbitrate such claims; but the fundamental rights of humanity cannot be. The loss of life is irreparable. Neither can direct violations of a nation's sovereignty await vindication in suits for damages. The nation that violates these essential rights must expect to be checked and called to account by direct challenge and resistance. It at once makes the quarrel in part our own. These are plain principles and we have never lost sight of them or departed from them, whatever the stress or the perplexity of circumstance or the provocation to hasty resentment. The record is clear and consistent throughout and stands distinct and definite for any one to judge who wishes to know the truth about it.

The seas were not broad enough to keep the infection of the conflict out of our own politics. The passions and intrigues of certain active groups and combinations of men among us who were born under foreign flags injected the poison of disloyalty into our own most critical affairs, laid violent hands upon many of our industries, and subjected us to the shame of divisions of sentiment and purpose in which America was condemned and forgotten. It is part of the business of this year of reckoning and settlement to speak plainly and act with unmistakable purpose in rebuke of these things, in order that they may be forever hereafter impossible. I am the candidate of a party, but I am above all things else an American citizen. I neither seek the favor nor fear the displeasure of that small alien element among us which puts loyalty to any foreign power before loyalty to the United States.

While Europe was at war our own continent, one of our own neighbors, was shaken by revolution. In that matter, too, principle was plain and it was imperative that we should live up to it if we were to deserve the trust of any real partisan of the right as free men see it. We have professed to believe, and we do believe, that the people of small and weak states have the right to expect to be dealt with exactly as the people of big and powerful states would be. We have acted upon that principle in dealing with the people of Mexico.

Our recent pursuit of bandits into Mexican territory was no violation of that principle. We ventured to enter Mexican territory only because there were no military forces in Mexico that could protect our border from hostile attack and our own people from violence, and we have committed there no single act of hostility or interference even with the sovereign authority of the Republic of Mexico herself. It was a plain case of the violation of our own sovereignty which could not wait to be vindicated by damages and for which there was no other remedy. The authorities of Mexico were powerless to prevent it.

Many serious wrongs against the property, many irreparable wrongs against the persons of Americans have been committed within the territory of Mexico herself during this confused revolution, wrongs which could not be effectually checked so long as there was no constituted power in Mexico which was in a position to check them. We could not act directly in that matter ourselves without denying Mexicans the right to any revolution at all which disturbed us and making the emancipation of her own people await our own interest and convenience.

For it is their emancipation that they are seeking—blindly, it may be, and as yet ineffectually, but with profound and passionate purpose and within their unquestionable right, apply what true American principle you will—any principle that an American would publicly avow. The people of Mexico have not been suffered to own their own country or direct their own institutions. Outsiders, men out of other nations and with interests too often alien to their own, have dictated what their privileges and opportunities should be and who should control their land, their lives and their resources—some of them Americans, pressing for things they could never have got in their own country. The Mexican people are entitled to attempt their liberty from such influences, and so long as I have anything to do with the action of our great Government I shall do everything in my power to prevent any one standing in their way. I know that this is hard for some persons to understand, but it is not hard for the plain people of the United States to understand. It is hard doctrine only for those who wish to get something for themselves out of Mexico. There are men and noble women, too, not a few, of our own people, thank God, whose fortunes are invested in great properties in Mexico who yet see the case with true vision and assess its issues with true American feeling. The rest can be left for the present out of the reckoning until this enslaved people has had its day of struggle toward the light. I have heard no one who was free from such influences propose interference by the United States with the internal affairs of Mexico. Certainly no friend of the Mexican people has proposed it.

The people of the United States are capable of great sympathies and a noble pity in dealing with problems of this kind. As their spokesman and representative I have tried to act in the spirit they would wish me show. The people of Mexico are striving for the rights that are fundamental to life and happiness—15,000,000 oppressed men, overburdened women and pitiful children in virtual bondage in their own home of fertile lands and inexhaustible treasure! Some of the leaders of the revolution may often have been mistaken and violent and selfish, but the revolution itself was inevitable and is right. The unspeakable Huerta betrayed the very comrades he served, traitorously overthrew the government of which he was a trusted part, impudently spoke for the very forces that had driven his people to the rebellion with which he had pretended to sympathize. The men who overcame him and drove him out represent at least the fierce passion of reconstruction which lies at the very heart of liberty; and so long as they represent, however imperfectly, such a struggle for deliverance, I am ready to serve their ends when I can. So long as the power of recognition rests with me the Government of the United States will refuse to extend the hand of welcome to any one who obtains power in a sister republic by treachery and violence. No permanency can be given the affairs of any republic by a title passed upon intrigue and assassination. I declared that to be the policy of this Administration within three weeks after I assumed the Presidency. I here again vow it. I am more interested in the fortunes of oppressed men and pitiful women and children than in any property rights whatever. Mistakes I have no doubt made in this perplexing business, but not in purpose or object.

More is involved than the immediate destinies of Mexico and the relations of the United States with a distressed and distracted people. All America looks on. Test is now being made of us whether we be sincere lovers of popular liberty or not and are indeed to be trusted to respect national sovereignty among our weaker neighbors. We have undertaken these many years to play big brother to the republics of this hemisphere. This is the day of our test whether we mean, or have ever meant, to play that part for our own benefit wholly or also for theirs. Upon the outcome of that test (its outcome in their minds, not in ours) depends every relationship of the United States with Latin America, whether in politics or in commerce and enterprise. These are great issues and lie at the heart of the gravest tasks of the future, tasks both economic and political and very intimately inwrought with many of the most vital of the new issues of the politics of the world. The republics of America have in the last three years been drawing together in a new spirit of accommodation, mutual understanding and cordial co-operation.

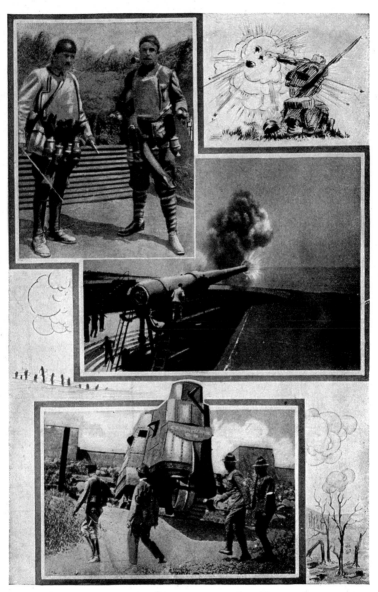

HAND GRENADES, FOURTEEN-INCH GUN AND TANK

AGENTS OF WARFARE.

The preceding picture shows three of the important methods of prosecuting the World War. The tractor, or "tank," is a kind of heavily armored auto-truck, armed with guns and gunners, which made its way through and over all obstacles, into the German trenches. The hand-bombs, shown in the hands of two men especially skilled and trained in their use, caused much destruction of life in the battles in the trenches; but their influence in trench fighting was hardly so great as that of the heavy guns. For hours before a sortie, the heavy guns would pour a veritable rain of steel upon the points to be attacked, often leveling the ground with the trenches, and hence making the latter untenable. When the troops finally advanced to the charge, the big guns would be discharged with unerring aim in advance of them, cloaking them in screens of heavy smoke which made the movements of the troops invisible to the enemy.

Much of the politics of the world in the years to come will depend upon their relationships with one another. It is a barren and provincial statesmanship that loses sight of such things!

The future, the immediate future, will bring us squarely face to face with many great and exacting problems which will search us through and through whether we be able and ready to play the part in the world that we mean to play. It will not bring us into their presence slowly, gently, with ceremonious introduction, but suddenly and at once, the moment the war in Europe is over. They will be new problems, most of them; many will be old problems in a new setting and with new elements which we have never dealt with or reckoned the force and meaning of before. They will require for their solution new thinking, fresh courage and resourcefulness, and in some matters radical reconsiderations of policy. We must be ready to mobilize our resources alike of brains and of materials.

It is not a future to be afraid of. It is, rather, a future to stimulate and excite us to the display of the best powers that are in us. We may enter it with confidence when we are sure that we understand it—and we have provided ourselves already with the means of understanding it.

Look first at what it will be necessary that the nations of the world should do to make the days to come tolerable and fit to live and work in; and then look at our part in what is to follow and our own duty of preparation. For we must be prepared both in resources and in policy.

There must be a just and settled peace, and we here in America must contribute the full force of our enthusiasm and of our authority as a nation to the organization of that peace upon world-wide foundations that cannot easily be shaken. No nation should be forced to take sides in any quarrel in which its own honor and integrity and the fortunes of its own people are not involved; but no nation can any longer remain neutral as against any wilful disturbance of the peace of the world. The effects of war can no longer be confined to the areas of battle. No nation stands wholly apart in interest when the life and interests of all nations are thrown into confusion and peril. If hopeful and generous enterprise is to be renewed, if the healing and helpful arts of life are indeed to be revived when peace comes again, a new atmosphere of justice and friendship must be generated by means the world has never tried before. The nations of the world must unite in joint guarantees that whatever is done to disturb the whole world's life must first be tested in the court of the whole world's opinion before it is attempted.

These are the new foundations the world must build for itself, and we must play our part in the reconstruction, generously and without too much thought of our separate interests. We must make ourselves ready to play it intelligently, vigorously and well.

One of the contributions we must make to the world's peace is this: We must see to it that the people in our insular possessions are treated

263

in their own lands as we would treat them here, and make the rule of the United States mean the same thing everywhere—the same justice, the same consideration for the essential rights of men.

Besides contributing our ungrudging moral and practical support to the establishment of peace throughout the world we must actively and intelligently prepare ourselves to do our full service in the trade and industry which are to sustain and develop the life of the nations in the days to come.

We have already been provident in this great matter and supplied ourselves with the instrumentalities of prompt adjustment. We have created, in the Federal Trade Commission, a means of inquiry and of accommodation in the field of commerce which ought both to co-ordinate the enterprises of our traders and manufacturers and to remove the barriers of misunderstanding and of a too technical interpretation of the law. In the new Tariff Commission we have added another instrumentality of observation and adjustment which promises to be immediately serviceable. The Trade Commission substitutes counsel and accommodation for the harsher processes of legal restraint, and the Tariff Commission ought to substitute facts for prejudices and theories. Our exporters have for some time had the advantage of working in the new light thrown upon foreign markets and opportunities of trade by the intelligent inquiries and activities of the Bureau of Foreign and Domestic Commerce which the Democratic Congress so wisely created in 1912. The Tariff Commission completes the machinery by which we shall be enabled to open up our legislative policy to the facts as they develop.

We can no longer indulge our traditional provincialism. We are to play a leading part in the world drama whether we wish it or not. We shall lend, not borrow; act for ourselves, not imitate or follow; organize and initiate, not peep about merely to see where we may get in.

We have already formulated and agreed upon a policy of law which will explicitly remove the ban now supposed to rest upon co-operation among our exporters in seeking and securing their proper place in the markets of the world. The field will be free, the instrumentalities at hand. It will only remain for the masters of enterprise among us to act in energetic concert, and for the Government of the United States to insist upon the maintenance throughout the world of those conditions of fairness and of evenhanded justice in the commercial dealings of the nations with one another upon which, after all, in the last analysis the peace and ordered life of the world must ultimately depend.

At home also we must see to it that the men who plan and develop and direct our business enterprises shall enjoy definite and settled conditions of law, a policy accommodated to the freest progress. We have set the just and necessary limits. We have put all kinds of unfair competition under the ban and penalty of the law. We have barred monopoly.

These fatal and ugly things being excluded we must now quicken action and facilitate enterprise by every just means within our choice. There will be peace in the business world, and with peace revived confidence and life.

We ought both to husband and to develop our natural resources: our mines, our forests, our water power. I wish we could have made more progress than we have made in this vital matter; and I call once more, with the deepest earnestness and solicitude, upon the advocates of a careful and provident conservation on the one hand and the advocates of a free and inviting field for private capital on the other, to get together in a spirit of genuine accommodation and agreement and set this great policy forward at once.

We must hearten and quicken the spirit and efficiency of labor throughout our whole industrial system by everywhere and in all occupations doing justice to the laborer, not only by paying a living wage, but also by making all the conditions that surround labor what they ought to be. And we must do more than justice. We must safeguard life and promote health and safety in every occupation in which they are threatened or imperiled. That is more than justice and better, because it is humanity and economy.

We must co-ordinate the railway systems of the country for national use, and must facilitate and promote their development with a view to that co-ordination and to their better adaptation as a whole to the life and trade and defense of the nation. The life and industry of the country can be free and unhampered only if these arteries are open, efficient and complete.

Thus shall we stand ready to meet the future as circumstances and international policy affect their unfolding, whether the changes come slowly or come fast and without preface.

I have not spoken explicitly, gentlemen, of the platform adopted at St. Louis; but it has been implicit in all that I have said. I have sought to interpret its spirit and meaning. The people of the United States do not need to be assured now that that platform is a definite pledge, a practical program. We have proved to them that our promises are made to be kept.

We hold very definite ideals. We believe that the energy and initiative of our people have been too narrowly coached and superintended; that they should be set free, as we have set them free, to disperse themselves throughout the nation; that they should not be concentrated in the hands of a few powerful guides and guardians, as our opponents have again and again, in effect if not in purpose, sought to concentrate them. We believe, moreover—who that looks about him now with comprehending eye can fail to believe?—that the day of little Americanism, with its narrow horizons, when methods of "protection" and industrial nursing were the chief study of our provincial statesmen, are past and gone and that a day of enterprise has at last dawned for the United States whose field is the wide world.

We hope to see the stimulus of that new day draw all America, the republics of both continents, on to a new life and energy and initiative in the great affairs of peace. We are Americans for the big America, and rejoice to look forward to the days in which America shall strive to stir the world without irritating it or drawing it on to new antagonisms, when the nations with which we deal shall at last come to see upon what deep foundations of humanity and justice our passion for peace rests, and when all mankind shall look upon our great people with a new sentiment of admiration, friendly rivalry and real affection, as upon a people who, though keen to succeed, seeks always to be at once generous and just and to whom humanity is dearer than profit or selfish power.

Upon this record and in the faith of this purpose we go to the country.

ADDRESSES

[On the occasion of the acceptance by the War Department of a deed of gift to the nation by the Lincoln Farm Association of the Lincoln Birthplace Farm at Hodgenville, Ky., September 4, 1916.]

No more significant memorial could have been presented to the nation than this. It expresses so much of what is singular and noteworthy in the history of the country; it suggests so many of the things that we prize most highly in our life and in our system of government. How eloquent this little house within this shrine is of the vigor of democracy! There is nowhere in the land any home so remote, so humble, that it may not contain the power of mind and heart and conscience to which nations yield and history submits its processes. Nature pays no tribute to aristocracy, subscribes to no creed of caste, renders fealty to no monarch or master of any name or kind. Genius is no snob. It does not run after titles or seek by preference the high circles of society. It affects humble company as well as great. It pays no special tribute to universities or learned societies or conventional standards of greatness, but serenely chooses its own comrades, its own haunts, its own cradle even, and its own life of adventure and of training. Here is proof of it. This little hut was the cradle of one of the great sons of men, a man of singular, delightful, vital genius who presently emerged upon the great stage of the nation's history, gaunt, shy, ungainly, but dominant and majestic, a natural ruler of men, himself inevitably the central figure of the great plot. No man can explain this, but every man can see how it demonstrates the vigor of democracy, where every door is open, in every hamlet and countryside, in city and wilderness alike, for the ruler to emerge when he will and claim his leadership in the free life. Such are the authentic proofs of the validity and vitality of democracy.

Here, no less, hides the mystery of democracy. Who shall guess this secret of nature and providence and a free polity? Whatever the vigor and vitality of the stock from which he sprang, its mere vigor and soundness do not explain where this man got his great heart that seemed to comprehend all mankind in its catholic and benignant sympathy, the mind that sat enthroned behind those brooding, melancholy eyes, whose vision swept many an horizon which those about him dreamed not of,— that mind that comprehended what it had never seen, and understood the language of affairs with the ready ease of one to the manner born,— or that nature which seemed in its varied richness to be the familiar of men of every way of life. This is the sacred mystery of democracy, that its richest fruits spring up out of soils which no man has prepared and in circumstances amidst which they are the least expected. This is a place alike of mystery and of reassurance.

It is likely that in a society ordered otherwise than our own Lincoln could not have found himself or the path of fame and power upon which he walked serenely to his death. In this place it is right that we should remind ourselves of the solid and striking facts upon which our faith in democracy is founded. Many another man besides Lincoln has served the nation in its highest places of counsel and of action whose origins were as humble as his. Though the greatest example of the universal energy, richness, stimulation, and force of democracy, he is only one example among many. The permeating and all-pervasive virtue of the freedom which challenges us in America to make the most of every gift and power we possess every page of our history serves to emphasize and illustrate. Standing here in this place, it seems almost the whole of the stirring story.

Here Lincoln had his beginnings. Here the end and consummation of that great life seem remote and a bit incredible. And yet there was no break anywhere between beginning and end, no lack of natural sequence anywhere. Nothing really incredible happened. Lincoln was unaffectedly as much at home in the White House as he was here. Do you share with me the feeling, I wonder, that he was permanently at home nowhere? It seems to me that in the case of a man,—I would rather say of a spirit,—like Lincoln the question *where* he was is of little significance, that it is always *what* he was that really arrests our thought and takes hold of our imagination. It is the spirit always that is sovereign. Lincoln, like the rest of us, was put through the discipline of the world,—a very rough and exacting discipline for him, and indispensable discipline for every man who would know what he is about in the midst of the world's affairs; but his spirit got only its schooling there. It did not derive its character or its vision from the experiences which brought it to its full revelation. The test of every American must always be, not where he is, but what he is. That, also, is of the essence of democracy, and is the moral of which this place is most gravely expressive.

We would like to think of men like Lincoln and Washington as typical Americans, but no man can be typical who is so unusual as these great men were. It was typical of American life that it should produce such men with supreme indifference as to the manner in which it produced them, and as readily here in this hut as amidst the little circle of cultivated gentlemen to whom Virginia owed so much in leadership and example. And Lincoln and Washington were typical Americans in the use they made of their genius. But there will be few such men at best, and we will not look into the mystery of how and why they come. We will only keep the door open for them always, and a hearty welcome,—after we have recognized them.

I have read many biographies of Lincoln; I have sought out with the greatest interest the many intimate stories that are told of him, the narratives of nearby friends, the sketches at close quarters, in which those who had the privilege of being associated with him have tried to depict for us the very man himself "in his habit as he lived"; but I have nowhere found a real intimate of Lincoln's. I nowhere get the impression in any narrative or reminiscence that the writer had in fact penetrated to the heart of his mystery, or that any man could penetrate to the heart of it. That brooding spirit had no real familiars. I get the impression that it never spoke out in complete self-revelation, and that it could not reveal itself completely to anyone. It was a very lonely spirit that looked out from underneath those shaggy brows and comprehended men without fully communing with them, as if, in spite of all its genial efforts at comradeship, it dwelt apart, saw its visions of duty where no man looked on. There is a very holy and very terrible isolation for the conscience of every man who seeks to read the destiny in affairs for others as well as for himself, for a nation as well as for individuals. That privacy no man can intrude upon. That lonely search of the spirit for the right perhaps no man can assist. This strange child of the cabin kept company with invisible things, was born into no intimacy but that of its own silently assembling and deploying thoughts.

I have come here today, not to utter a eulogy on Lincoln; he stands in need of none, but to endeavor to interpret the meaning of this gift to the nation of the place of his birth and origin. Is not this an altar upon which we may forever keep alive the vestal fire of democracy as upon a shrine at which some of the deepest and most sacred hopes of mankind may from age to age be rekindled? For these hopes must constantly be rekindled, and only those who live can rekindle them. The only stuff that can retain the life-giving heat is the stuff of living hearts. And the hopes of mankind cannot be kept alive by words merely, by constitutions and doctrines of right and codes of liberty.

The object of democracy is to transmute these into the life and action
of society, the self-denial and self-sacrifice of heroic men and women
willing to make their lives an embodiment of right and service and
enlightened purpose. The commands of democracy are as imperative
as its privileges and opportunities are wide and generous. Its compulsion is upon us. It will be great and lift a great light for the guidance
of the nations only if we are great and carry that light high for the
guidance of our own feet. We are not worthy to stand here unless we
ourselves be in deed and in truth real democrats and servants of mankind, ready to give our very lives for the freedom and justice and
spiritual exaltation of the great nation which shelters and nurtures us.

[Before Woman's Suffrage Convention at Atlantic City, N. J., Sept. 8, 1916.]

MADAM PRESIDENT, LADIES OF THE ASSOCIATION:

I have found it a real privilege to be here tonight and to listen to
the addresses which you have delivered. Though you may not all of
you believe it, I would a great deal rather hear somebody else speak
than speak myself; but I should feel that I was omitting a duty if I
did not address you tonight and say some of the things that have been
in my thought as I realized the approach of this evening and the duty
that would fall upon me.

The astonishing thing about the movement which you represent is,
not that it has grown so slowly, but that it has grown so rapidly. No
doubt for those who have been a long time in the struggle, like your
honored president, it seems a long and arduous path that has been
trodden, but when you think of the cumulating force of this movement
in recent decades, you must agree with me that it is one of the most
astonishing tides in modern history. Two generations ago, no doubt
Madam President will agree with me in saying, it was a handful of
women who were fighting this cause. Now it is a great multitude of
women who are fighting it.

And there are some interesting historical connections which I would
like to attempt to point out to you. One of the most striking facts
about the history of the United States is that at the outset it was a
lawyer's history. Almost all of the questions to which America addressed itself, say a hundred years ago, were legal questions, were
questions of method, not questions of what you were going to do with
your Government, but questions of how you were going to constitute
your Government,—how you were going to balance the powers of the
States and the Federal Government, how you were going to balance
the claims of property against the processes of liberty, how you were
going to make your governments up so as to balance the parts against
each other so that the legislature would check the executive, and the
executive the legislature, and the courts both of them put together. The

whole conception of government when the United States became a nation was a mechanical conception of government, and the mechanical conception of government which underlay it was the Newtonian theory of the universe. If you pick up the Federalist, some parts of it read like a treatise on astronomy instead of a treatise on government. They speak of the centrifugal and the centripetal forces, and locate the President somewhere in the rotating system. The whole thing is a calculation of power and an adjustment of parts. There was a time when nobody but a lawyer could know enough to run the Government of the United States, and a distinguished English publicist once remarked, speaking of the complexity of the American Government, that it was no proof of the excellence of the American Constitution that it had been successfully operated, because the Americans could run any constitution. But there have been a great many technical difficulties in running it.

And then something happened. A great question arose in this country which, though complicated with legal elements, was at bottom a human question, and nothing but a question of humanity. That was the slavery question. And is it not significant that it was then, and then for the first time, that women became prominent in politics in America? Not many women; those prominent in that day were so few that you can name them over in a brief catalogue, but, nevertheless, they then began to play a part in writing, not only, but in public speech, which was a very novel part for women to play in America. After the Civil War had settled some of what seemed to be the most difficult legal questions of our system, the life of the nation began not only to unfold but to accumulate. Life in the United States was a comparatively simple matter at the time of the Civil War. There was none of that underground struggle which is now so manifest to those who look only a little way beneath the surface. Stories such as Dr. Davis has told tonight were uncommon in those simpler days. The pressure of low wages, the agony of obscure and unremunerated toil, did not exist in America in anything like the same proportions that they exist now. And as our life has unfolded and accumulated, as the contacts of it have become hot, as the populations have assembled in the cities, and the cool spaces of the country have been supplanted by the feverish urban areas, the whole nature of our political questions has been altered. They have ceased to be legal questions. They have more and more become social questions, questions with regard to the relations of human beings to one another,—not merely their legal relations, but their moral and spiritual relations to one another. This has been most characteristic of American life in the last few decades, and as these questions have assumed greater and greater prominence, the movement which this association represents has gathered cumulative force. So that, if anybody asks himself, "What does this gathering force mean," if he knows anything about the history of the country, he knows that it means something that has not only come to stay, but has come with conquering power.

I get a little impatient sometimes about the discussion of the channels and methods by which it is to prevail. It is going to prevail, and that is a very superficial and ignorant view of it which attributes it to mere social unrest. It is not merely because the women are discontented. It is because the women have seen visions of duty, and that is something which we not only can not resist, but, if we be true Americans, we do not wish to resist. America took its origin in visions of the human spirit, in aspirations for the deepest sort of liberty of the mind and of the heart, and as visions of that sort come up to the sight of those who are spiritually minded in America, America comes more and more into her birthright and into the perfection of her development.

So that what we have to realize in dealing with forces of this sort is that we are dealing with the substance of life itself! I have felt as I sat here tonight the wholesome contagion of the occasion. Almost every other time that I ever visited Atlantic City, I came to fight somebody. I hardly know how to conduct myself when I have not come to fight against anybody, but with somebody. I have come to suggest, among other things, that when the forces of nature are steadily working and the tide is rising to meet the moon, you need not be afraid that it will not come to its flood. We feel the tide; we rejoice in the strength of it; and we shall not quarrel in the long run as to the method of it. Because, when you are working with masses of men and organized bodies of opinion, you have got to carry the organized body along. The whole art and practice of government consists, not in moving individuals, but in moving masses. It is all very well to run ahead and beckon, but, after all, you have got to wait for the body to follow. I have not come to ask you to be patient, because you have been, but I have come to congratulate you that there was a force behind you that will beyond any peradventure be triumphant, and for which you can afford a little while to wait.

REPLY OF THE ENTENTE ALLIES TO AN AMERICAN PROTEST NOT MADE PUBLIC, AGAINST INTERFERENCE WITH AMERICAN MAILS ON THE HIGH SEAS.

OCTOBER 15, 1916.

1—By a letter of May 24 last the Secretary of State of the United States was pleased to give the views of the American Government on the memorandum of the allied Governments concerning mails found on merchant ships on the high seas.

The allied Governments have found that their views agreed with the views of the United States in regard to the Postal Union Convention, which is recognized on both sides to be foreign to the questions now under consideration; post parcels receptively recognized as being under the common rule of merchandise subject to exercise of belligerent right, as provided by international law; the inspection of private mails to the end of ascertaining whether they do not contain contraband goods, and, if carried on an enemy ship, whether they do not contain enemy property. It is clear that that inspection, which necessarily implies the opening of covers so as to verify the contents, could not be carried on on board without being attended with great confusion, causing serious delay to the mails, passengers and cargoes, and without causing for the letters in transit errors, losses, or at least great risk of miscarriage.

That is the reason why the allies had mail bags landed and sent to centers provided with the necessary force and equipment for prompt and regular handling.

2—In all this the allied Governments had no other object in view than to limit, as far as possible, the inconvenience that might result for innocent mails and neutral vessels from the legitimate exercise of their belligerent rights in respect to hostile correspondence.

3—The Government of the United States acknowledges it agrees with the allied Governments as to principle, but expresses certain divergent views and certain criticism as to the methods observed by the allies in applying these principles.

4—These divergencies of views and criticisms are as follows:

5—In the first place, according to the Government of the United States, the practice of the allied Governments is said to be contrary to their own declaration, in that while declaring themselves unwilling to seize and confiscate genuine mail on the high seas, they would obtain the same result by sending, with or without their consent, neutral vessels to allied ports, there to effect the seizures and confiscations above referred to, and thus exercise over those vessels a more extensive belligerent right than that which is theirs on the high seas. According to the Government of the United States there should be, in point of law, no distinction to be made between seizure of mails on the high seas, which the allies have declared they will not apply for the present, and the same seizure practiced on board ships that are, whether willingly or not, in an allied port.

6—On this first point, and as regards vessels summoned on the high seas and compelled to make for an allied port, the allied Governments have the honor to advise the Government of the United States that they have never subjected mails to a different treatment according as they were found on neutral vessels compelled to proceed to an allied port; they have always acknowledged that visits made in port after a forced change of course must in this respect be on the same footing as a visit on the high seas, and the criticism formulated by the Government of the United States does not, therefore, seem warranted.

7—As to ships which of their own accord call at allied ports it is important to point out that in this case they are really "voluntarily" making the call. In calling at an allied port the master acts, not on any order from the allied authorities, but solely carries out the instructions of the owner; neither are those instructions forced upon the said owner.

In consideration of certain advantages derived from the call at an allied port, of which he is at full liberty to enjoy or refuse the benefits, the owner instructs his captain to call at this or that port. He does not in truth undergo any restraint.

As a point of law the allied Governments think it a rule generally accepted, particularly in the United States (United States v. Dickelman, U. S. Supreme Court, 1875; 92 U. S. Rep. 520; Scott's cases, 264), that merchant ships which enter a foreign port thereby place themselves under the laws in force in that port, whether in time of war or of peace, and when martial law is in force in that port.

8—Therefore, legitimate in the case of a neutral merchant ship entering an allied port for the authorities of the allied Government to make sure that the vessel carries nothing inimical to their national defense before granting its clearance.

The note declares the censorship is a necessary precaution against German wiles, and innocent neutrals have nothing to fear. It continues:

In the second place, according to the Government of the United States, the practice now followed by the allied Governments is contrary to the rule of Convention 11 of The Hague, 1907, which they declare their willingness to apply, and would, besides, constitute a violation of the practice heretofore followed by nations.

9—In regard to the value to be attached to the eleventh convention of The Hague, 1907, it may first of all be observed that it refers only to mails found at sea, and that it is entirely foreign to postal correspondence found on board ships in ports.

In the second place, from the standpoint of the peculiar circumstances of the present war, the Government of the United States is aware that that convention, as stated in the memorandum of the allies, has not been signed or ratified by six of the belligerent powers (Bulgaria, Italy, Montenegro, Russia, Serbia and Turkey); that for that very reason Germany availed itself of Article IX. of the convention and denied, so far as it was concerned, the obligatory character in these stipulations, and that for these several reasons the convention possesses in truth but rather doubtful validity in law.

In spite of it all, the allied Governments are guided in the case of mails found on board ships in ports by the intentions expressly manifested in conferences of The Hague sanctioned in the preamble to convention 11, and tending to protect pacific and innocent commerce only. Mails possessing that character are forwarded as quickly as circumstances permit.

In regard to mails found on vessels at sea, the allied Governments have not for the present refused to observe the terms of the convention reasonably interpreted; but they have not admitted and cannot admit that there is therein a final provision legally binding them from which they could not possibly depart. The allied Governments expressly reserve to themselves the right to do so in case enemy abuses and frauds, dissimulations and deceits should make such a measure necessary.

Paragraph 10 points out lack of precedent prohibiting seizure of mails on the high seas. Paragraph 11 details circumstances in which unresisted passage of mails would prove disadvantageous to a belligerent. The note continues:

12—The report adopted by the conference of The Hague in support of convention 11 leaves little doubt as to the former practice in the matter.

"These issues, opening the bags, examination, confiscation, if need be, in all cases delay or even loss, are the fate usually awaiting mail bags carried by sea in time of war. (Second peace conference, acts and documents, Vol. 1, 6, 266.)

13—The American note of May 24, 1916, invokes the practice followed by France in 1870; by the United States in 1898; by Great Britain in the South African war; by Japan and Russia in 1904, and now by Germany.

14—As regards the proceedings of the German Empire toward postal correspondence during the present war, the allied Governments have informed the Government of the United States of the names of some of the mail steamers whose mail bags have been—not examined to be sure—but purely and simply destroyed at sea by the German naval authorities.

Other names could very easily be added—the very recent case of the mail steamer Hudikswell (Swedish) carrying 670 mail bags, may be cited.

15—The allied Governments do not think that the criminal habit of sinking ships, passengers and cargoes, or abandoning on the high seas the survivors of such calamities is, in the eyes of the Government of the United States, any justification for the destruction of the mail bags on board; and they do not deem it to be its purpose to make a comparison between these destructive German proceedings and the acts of the allies in supervising and examining enemy correspondence.

16—As to the practice of Russia and of Japan, it may be permitted to a doubt that it was at variance with the method of the allied Governments in the present war.

Paragraphs 17 and 18 point out procedure adopted by Russia in her war with Turkey in 1877 and the war with Japan in 1904. They cite the seizure of neutral mail by Russian cruisers and its subsequent examination.

19—As regards the practice of Japan, the Japanese rules concerning prizes, dated March 15, 1904, made official enemy correspondence, with certain exceptions, contraband of war. They ordered the examination of mail bags on mail steamers unless there was on board an official of the post office making a declaration in writing and under oath that the bags contained no contraband.

20—The French practice during the war of 1870 is found outlined in the naval instructions of July 26, 1870, under which official dispatches were on principle assimilated to contraband, and official or private letters found on board captured vessels were to be sent immediately to the Minister of Marine.

21—During the South African war the British Government was able to limit its intervention in the forwarding of postal correspondence and mails as far as the circumstances of that war allowed, but it did not cease to exercise its supervision of the mails intended for the enemy.

22—As to the practice followed by the Government of the United States during the American Civil War, particularly in the Peterhoff case, cited in the American memorandum of May 24, 1916, the following instructions issued in that case by the Secretary of State of the United States do not seem to imply anything but the forwarding of correspondence which has been found to be innocent:

"I have, therefore, to recommend that in this case if the District Attorney has any evidence to show the mails are simulated and not genuine it shall be submitted to the court; if there be no reasonable grounds for that belief then that they be put on their way to their original destination."

(Letter of Mr. Seward, Secretary of State, to Mr. Welles, Secretary of the Navy, April 15, 1863; vii. Moore's dig., P. 482.)

Paragraph 23 recounts the American blockade of Tampico during the Mexican War in 1846 and the American naval authorities' permission to neutral mail ships to enter and leave. The note then says no precedent can be based on this, declaring:

24—It seems difficult to compare the blockade of the port of Tampico in 1846 with the measures taken by the allies in the course of this war to reduce the economic resistance of the German Empire, or to find in the method then adopted by the United States a precedent which condemns the practice now put in use by the allied governments.

25—To waive the right to visit mail steamers and mail bags intended for the enemy seemed in the past (Dr. Lushington, "Naval Prize Law," Introd. p. VII.) a sacrifice which could hardly be expected of belligerents.

The allied Governments have again noted in their preceding memorandum how and why, relying on certain declarations of Germany, they had thought in the course of the Second Peace Conference of 1907 they could afford to waive that right. They have also drawn the attention of the Government of the United States to the fraudulent use Germany hastened to make of this waiver of the previous practices above mentioned.

26—After pointing to a certain number of specific cases where American interests happened to be injured from the postal supervision exercised by the British authorities, forming the subject of the special memorandum of the Government of His Majesty, dated July 20, 1916, the Government of the United States was pleased to make known its views as to what is to be and is not to be recognized as not possessing the character of postal correspondence.

27—In this respect the Government of the United States admits that shares, bonds, coupons and other valuable papers, money orders, checks, drafts, bills of exchange and other negotiable papers, being the equivalent of money, may when included in postal shipments be considered as of the same nature as merchandise and other property, and therefore be also subjected to the exercise of belligerent rights.

28—Yet the American memorandum adds that correspondence, including shipping documents, lists of money orders and documents of this nature, even though referring to shipments to or exports by the enemy, must be treated as mail, and pass freely unless they refer to merchandise on the same ship that is liable to capture.

29—As regards shipping documents and commercial correspondence found on neutral vessels, even in an allied port, and offering no interest of consequence as affecting the war, the allied governments have instructed their authorities not to stop them, but to see that they are forwarded with as little delay as possible. Mail matter of that nature must be forwarded to destination as fast as practicable, on the very ship on which it was found, or by a speedier route, as is the case for certain mails inspected in Great Britain.

30—As for the lists of money orders, to which the Government of the United States assigns the character of ordinary mail, the allied governments deem it their duty to draw the attention of the Government of the United States to the following practical consideration:

31—As a matter of fact the list of money orders mailed from the United States to Germany and Austria-Hungary correspond to moneys paid in the United States and payable by the German and Austria-Hungarian post office.

Those lists acquaint those post offices with the sums that have been paid there, which in consequence they have to pay to the addressees. In practice, such payment is at the disposal of such addressees and is effected directly to them as soon as those lists arrive and without the requirement of the individual orders having come into the hands of the addressees. These lists are thus really actually money orders transmitted in lump in favor of several addressees.

Nothing, in the opinion of the allied governments, seems to justify the liberty granted to the enemy country so to receive funds intended to supply by that amount its financial resisting power.

32—The American memorandum sees fit firmly to recall that neutral and belligerent rights are equally sacred, and must be strictly respected. The allied Governments, so far as they are concerned, wholly share that view. They are sincerely striving to avoid an encroachment by the exercise of their belligerent rights on the legitimate exercise of the rights of innocent neutral commerce, but they hold that it is their belligerent right to exercise on the high seas the supervision granted by international law to impede any transportation intended to aid their enemy in the conduct of the war and to uphold his resistance.

The rights of the United States as a neutral power cannot, in our opinion, imply the protection granted by the Federal Government to shipments, invoices, correspondence or communications in any shape whatever having an open or concealed hostile character and with a direct or indirect hostile destination, which American private persons can only effect at their own risk and peril.

That is the very principle which was expressly stated by the President of the United States in his neutrality proclamation.

33—Furthermore, should any abuses, grave errors, or derelictions committed by the allied authorities charged with the duty of inspecting mails be disclosed to the Governments of France and Great Britain, they are now as they ever were ready to settle responsibility therefor in accordance with the principles of law and justice, which it never was and is not now their intention to evade.

MESSAGE TO THE PHILIPPINES

[Congratulating the People of the Islands Upon the Assembling of the First Congress of Natives.]

President Wilson, through Secretary of War Baker, sent to Governor-General Harrison, of the Philippines, a message congratulating him on the convention of the Assembly and Senate of the islands, for the first time composed entirely of natives.

October 16, 1916.

Will you not be kind enough to convey to the members of the Legislature, the first to meet under the new act, my most cordial greetings and best wishes, and will you not express to them the hope that the confidence that has been reposed in them by the people and the Government of the United States will be most abundantly vindicated by their whole course of action and policy? For myself, I look forward with confidence to the growth of self-government in the Philippines under this new and happier order of things and am glad to have had a part in taking the great step in advance which has now been taken.

WOODROW WILSON.

EXECUTIVE ORDERS

[Requiring American Citizens Traveling Abroad to Procure Passports.]

All persons leaving the United States for foreign countries should be provided with passports of the Governments of which they are citizens. These documents are rendered necessary because the regulations of all European countries and of several other foreign countries require passports or other documents of identification of all persons who enter their boundaries. The Secretary of State, in co-operation with the Secretary of the Treasury, will make arrangements for the inspection of passports of all persons, American or foreign, leaving this country, and the fact that these passports have been seen will be stamped thereon.

All applications to the Secretary of State for passports from American citizens must be made in duplicate, and must be accompanied with three copies of the photograph of the applicant. Each applicant for a passport must inform the Department of State at what point he intends to depart, on what date, and by what ship if he sails from an American port.

Applications shall be made in the manner heretofore prescribed by the rules governing the granting and issuing of passports, but the Secretary of State may designate an agent or agents to take applications, and wherever his agent is stationed applications shall be made only before him.

This order will become effective as soon as the Secretary of State and Secretary of the Treasury have made the arrangements necessary for that purpose.

WOODROW WILSON.

THE WHITE HOUSE, December 15, 1915.

[Relating to Cancellation and Reissue of Passports.]

The Secretary of the Treasury is hereby authorized to direct customs officers at ports of entry into the United States to take up passports of American citizens returning to this country. Passports which are not to be used again may be canceled and returned to the owners. Passports which are to be used again should be sent to the Department of State, and the owners informed that they should notify the Department of State, at least five days before they expect to leave this country again, as to the port, name of vessel and date of sailing. If such a person expects to go abroad for an object not mentioned in his passport, or to visit a country not named therein, he should make application in the usual way for a new passport.

WOODROW WILSON.

THE WHITE HOUSE, March 13, 1916.

[Philippines—Requiring Governor General to Report to Secretary of War.]

The following provision is contained in Section 21 of an Act of Congress approved August 29, 1916, entitled:

"An Act to declare the purpose of the people of the United States as to the future political status of the people of the Philippine Islands, and to provide a more autonomous government for those islands."—

. . . "He (the Governor General of the Philippine Islands) shall annually and at such other times as he may be required make such official report of the transactions of the government of the Philippine Islands to an executive department of the United States to be designated by the President, and his said annual report shall be transmitted to the Congress of the United States; And he shall perform such additional duties and functions as may in pursuance of law be delegated or assigned to him by the President."

Under this provision hereafter all official reports which the Governor-General of the Philippine Islands may be required to make of the transactions of the Government of the Philippine Islands will be made to the War Department, and all matters pertaining to the Government of the Philippine Islands, except as otherwise provided by law, are placed in the jurisdiction of that department.

The business of the War Department pertaining to civil government in the Philippine Islands is, pursuant to Section 87 of the Act of Congress approved July 1, 1902, assigned to the Bureau of Insular Affairs. WOODROW WILSON.

THE WHITE HOUSE, September 19, 1916.

[Alaska.—Regulations for sale of the Federal and Cliff Additions to Seward Townsite, Alaska.]

Pursuant to the provisions of the Act of Congress, approved March 12, 1914 (38 Stat., 305), it is hereby ordered that the disposition of the lots in the Federal and Cliff Additions to the townsite of Seward, Alaska, shall be in accordance with the regulations contained in Executive Order No. 2214, issued June 19, 1915, except as to terms of sale, restrictions as to use of lots purchased, forfeiture for failure to comply with restrictions, and time as to issuance of entry and patent, which shall be as follows:

TERMS.—No lot will be sold for less than $25.00, and no bid exceeding that amount will be accepted unless made in multiples of five dollars; the minimum of $25.00 on each lot sold for less than $50.00 must be paid in cash within the time hereinafter specified, and if the price bid is $50.00 or more, one-half of the bid price must be paid in cash within said specified time and the remainder within one year from the date of the register's certificate of sale, or the entire purchase price may be paid at the time of sale. The successful bidder will be given by the Superintendent of Sale a memorandum certificate for identification purposes, showing name and address of bidder, lot, and amount of bid, and the bidder must file it with the Superintendent of Sale before the close of the next succeeding sale day, or the next business day, if bid is accepted on last preceding sale day, together with his application to purchase the lot properly filled and signed and accompanied by the cash payment required by these regulations. The application should be, in substance, as follows:

"I, ..., post office address ...., having been declared the successful bidder for lot No. ...., Block No. ...., in the .... Addition to the townsite of Seward, Alaska, as delineated and designated on the approved plat thereof, containing .... square feet, do hereby apply to purchase said lot, subject to all the regulations governing the sale thereof, and agree to pay therefor the amount bid by me, viz:— .... dollars ($........), on the terms prescribed by said regulations, and upon failure to pay any installment on or before the day the same becomes due, all rights under this application, together with the payments theretofore made, may be forfeited to the United States by the Secretary of the Interior."

WOODROW WILSON.

THE WHITE HOUSE, July 11, 1916.

[Increasing the Strength of the Regular Army.]

Under authority of the Joint Resolution of Congress, approved March 17, 1916, an emergency having arisen making necessary an increase in the enlisted strength of the Regular Army within the continental limits of the United States, the arms of the service are hereby brought up to the statutory maximum enlisted strength as set forth in the following tabulated statement.

Arms of the service.	*Statutory maximum enlisted strength.*
20 regiments of Infantry	36,720
11 regiments, and regimental headquarters and two squadrons of Cavalry	14,469
3 regiments, and regimental headquarters and one battalion of Field Artillery	4,172
Coast Artillery Corps	19,321
Engineers	2,002

WOODROW WILSON.

THE WHITE HOUSE, March 21, 1916.

Establishing Sizes and Proportions of the American Flag and the President's Flag

THE WHITE HOUSE, May 29, 1916.

The Executive Order of October 29, 1912, is hereby revoked, and for it is substituted the following:—

Whereas, "An Act to Establish the Flag of the United States," approved on the 4th of April, 1818, reading as follows:—

"Section 1. Be it enacted, etc., That from and after the fourth day of July next, the flag of the United States be thirteen horizontal stripes, alternate red and white; that the union be twenty stars, white in a blue field.

"Section 2. And be it further enacted, That on the admission of every new State into the Union, one star be added to the union of the flag; and that such addition shall take effect on the fourth of July then next succeeding such admission."

fails to establish proportions;

Whereas, investigation shows some sixty-six different sizes of National flags, and of varying proportions, in use in the Executive Departments;

It is hereby ordered that National Flags and Union Jacks for all Departments of the Government, with the exception noted under (a), shall conform to the following proportions:—

Hoist (width) of Flag.... 1   Fly (length) of Union.... .76
Fly (length) of Flag...... 1.9   Width of each stripe...... 1/13
Hoist (width) of Union... 7/13

(a) Exception: The colors carried by troops, and camp colors, shall be the sizes prescribed for the Military Service (Army and Navy).

Limitation of the number of sizes: With the exception of colors under note (a), the sizes of flags manufactured or purchased for the Government Departments will be limited to those with the following hoists:

(1) .... 20 feet	(7) .... 5.14 feet
(2) ..... (Standard) 19 feet	(8) .... 5 feet
(3) .... 14.35 feet	(9) .... 3.52 feet
(4) .... 12.19 feet	(10) .... 2.90 feet
(5) .... 10 feet	(11) .... 2.37 feet
(6) .... 8.94 feet	(12) .... 1.31 feet

Union Jacks: The size of the Jack shall be the size of the Union of the National Flag with which it is flown.

Position and Size of Stars: The position and size of each star for the Union of the flag shall be as indicated on a plan which will be furnished to the Departments by the Navy Department. From this plan can be determined the location and size of stars for flags of any dimensions. Extra blue-prints of this plan will be furnished upon application to the Navy Department.

Order effective: All National Flags and Union Jacks now on hand or for which contracts have been awarded shall be continued in use until unserviceable, but all those manufactured or purchased for Government use after the date of this order shall conform strictly to the dimensions and proportions herein prescribed.

President's Flag: The President's flag shall be in accordance with the plan accompanying and forming a part of this order. In case sizes are needed other than the two sizes shown on the plan, they shall be manufactured in the same proportions as those shown.

WOODROW WILSON.

[NOTE.—This order was accompanied with illustration (in color) and design of the President's flag, showing solid blue field with eagle in centre bearing shield with red bars; white star at each corner; legend: E Pluribus Unum.]

PROCLAMATIONS

BY THE PRESIDENT OF THE UNITED STATES

A PROCLAMATION

[Flag Day.]

MY FELLOW COUNTRYMEN:

Many circumstances have recently conspired to turn our thoughts to a critical examination of the conditions of our national life, of the influences which have seemed to threaten to divide us in interest and sympathy, of forces within and forces without that seemed likely to draw us away from the happy traditions of united purpose and action of which we have been so proud. It has therefore seemed to me fitting that I should call your attention to the approach of the anniversary of the day upon which the flag of the United States was adopted by the Congress as the emblem of the Union, and to suggest to you that it should this year and in years to come be given special significance as a day of renewal and reminder, a day upon which we should direct our minds with a special desire of renewal to thoughts of the ideals and principles of which we have sought to make our great Government the embodiment.

I therefore suggest and request that throughout the nation and if possible in every community the fourteenth day of June be observed as Flag Day with special patriotic exercises, at which means shall be taken to give significant expression to our thoughtful love of America, our comprehension of the great mission of liberty and justice to which we have devoted ourselves as a people, our pride in the history and our enthusiasm for the political program of the nation, our determination to make it greater and purer with each generation, and our resolution to demonstrate to all the world its vital union in sentiment and purpose, accepting only those as true compatriots who feel as we do the compulsion of this supreme allegiance. Let us on that day rededicate ourselves to the nation, "one and inseparable," from which every thought that is not worthy of our fathers' first vows in independence, liberty, and right shall be excluded and in which we shall stand with united hearts, for an America which no man can corrupt, no influence draw away from its ideals, no force divide against itself,—a nation signally distinguished among all the nations of mankind for its clear, individual conception alike of its duties and its privileges, its obligations and its rights.

In Witness Whereof, I have hereunto set my hand and caused the seal of the United States to be affixed.

Done at the City of Washington this thirtieth day of May, in the year of our Lord one thousand nine hundred and sixteen, [SEAL.] and of the independence of the United States of America the one hundred and fortieth.

By the President: WOODROW WILSON.

Robert Lansing, *Secretary of State.*

By the President of the United States of America

A PROCLAMATION

[Contribution Day for Aid of Stricken Jewish People.]

Whereas, I have received from the Senate of the United States a Resolution, passed January 6, 1916, reading as follows:

"Whereas in the various countries now engaged in war there are nine millions of Jews, the great majority of whom are destitute of food, shelter, and clothing; and

"Whereas millions of them have been driven from their homes without warning, deprived of an opportunity to make provision for their most elementary wants, causing starvation, disease and untold suffering; and

"Whereas the people of the United States of America have learned with sorrow of this terrible plight of millions of human beings and have most generously responded to the cry for help whenever such an appeal has reached them; Therefore be it

"RESOLVED, That, in view of the misery, wretchedness, and hardships which these nine millions of Jews are suffering, the President of the United States be respectfully asked to designate a day on which the citizens of this country may give expression to their sympathy by contributing to the funds now being raised for the relief of the Jews in the war zones."

AND WHEREAS, I feel confident that the people of the United States will be moved to aid the war-stricken people of a race which has given to the United States so many worthy citizens;

Now, therefore, I, Woodrow Wilson, President of the United States, in compliance with the suggestion of the Senate thereof, do appoint and proclaim January 27, 1916, as a day upon which the people of the United States may make such contributions as they feel disposed for the aid of the stricken Jewish people.

Contributions may be addressed to the American Red Cross, Washington, D. C., which will care for their proper distribution.

IN WITNESS WHEREOF, I have hereunto set my hand and caused the seal of the United States to be affixed.

Done at the City of Washington this eleventh day of January, in the year of our Lord one thousand nine hundred and sixteen, [SEAL.] and of the independence of the United States the one hundred and fortieth.

By the President: WOODROW WILSON.

ROBERT LANSING, *Secretary of State.*

[Waiving Citizenship Requirement for Specified Federal Appointment.]

THE WHITE HOUSE, June 30, 1916.

The requirement of the United States citizenship is hereby waived to permit the certification of Mr. Cedric R. Landon for appointment to the position of predatory animal inspector, Bureau of Biological Survey, Department of Agriculture, for service in the State of Texas. Mr. Landon was born in Canada in 1887, was in Texas for a while during his minority, and declared his intention of becoming a citizen of the United States on November 13, 1914. He had been serving temporarily in the position to which appointment is desired, and was admitted to examination conditionally and passed with a rating of 84.75 but can not be certified under existing rules.

The Secretary of Agriculture states that Mr. Landon has had charge of a force of about a dozen hunter-trappers, is a good executive, energetic, resourceful, very tactful in dealing with stockmen with whom he comes in contact, well qualified to handle the accounts and correspondence incident to his position, and very successful in instructing individual hunters. These qualifications together with his intimate knowledge of the country and local conditions (almost indispensable requirements for an inspector) are said to make his services very desirable, particularly in the sparsely settled regions of central and western Texas. He is the only competitor from the section of the country where he is employed.

This order is issued on the recommendation of the Secretary of Agriculture with the concurrence of the Civil Service Commission.

WOODROW WILSON.

[Amending Consular Regulations.]

THE WHITE HOUSE, September 28, 1916.

Paragraph 692 of the Consular Regulations of 1896 is hereby amended to read as follows:

Currency Certificates.—When the price or value of merchandise obtained by purchase, shipped pursuant to an agreement of purchase, or consigned for sale in the United States is expressed in the invoice in depreciated currency, a currency certificate (form 144) must be attached to the invoice showing the percentage of depreciation as compared with the corresponding standard coin currency and the value in such standard coin currency of the total amount of the depreciated currency stated in the invoice. (Rev. Stat., Sec. 2903; T. D. 17252.) This certificate should show, not the value of the depreciated currency in money of account of the United States, but its value in the terms of the standard coin currency in comparison with which the currency stated in the invoice is depreciated. (T. D. 11314, 17170.)

In the assessment of duty the currency of the invoice is reduced to the money of account of the United States upon the basis of the values of foreign coins at the date of shipment, as proclaimed by the Secretary of the Treasury for the first day of January, April, July, and October of each year. (Tariff of 1894, Sec. 25; T. D. 16921.) The date of the consular certification of any invoice shall, for the purposes of this section, be considered the date of exportation. (Tariff of 1894, Sec. 25.) In the absence of a currency certificate no allowance will be made for depreciated currency. (T. D. 15435.)

When an invoice is certified by a consul of a nation at the time in amity with the United States, or by two respectable merchants, as provided by section 2844, Revised Statutes, the currency certificate required by section 2903, Revised Statutes, may be issued by the foreign consul of the two respectable merchants who certify the invoice.

For statistical purposes, currency certificates are required for all invoices of merchandise wherein the price or value is expressed in depreciated currency, without regard to the dutiable or nondutiable character of the merchandise.   WOODROW WILSON.

THE WHITE HOUSE, September 28, 1916.

Paragraph 172 of the Consular Regulations is amended to read as follows:

Registration of American Citizens.—Principal Consular Officers shall keep at their offices a Register of all American citizens residing in their several districts, and will therefore make it known that such a Register is kept and invite all resident Americans to cause their names to be entered therein. Except in cases of emergency no person shall be given a certificate of registration until his application for registration has been approved by the Department. The general principles which govern applications for passports also govern applications for registration. (Paragraph 151.) The forms of application for registration will be prescribed by the Secretary of State.

The Register, which will consist of sworn applications approved by the Department, should show in the case of each person registered the date of registration, the full name of the person registered, the date and place of his birth, the place of his last domicile in the United States, the date of his arrival in the foreign country where he is residing and his place of residence therein, the reasons for his foreign residence, whether or not he is married and if married the name of his wife, her place of birth and residence, if he has children, the name, date and place of birth and residence of each, and any other pertinent information which the Department of State may require. The nature of the proof accepted to establish his citizenship should also appear.

Consuls may issue, upon forms prescribed by the Department, certificates of registration good for one year, for use with the authorities of the place where the persons registered are residing. When a certificate expires a new one may be issued, the old one being surrendered and destroyed, or the original certificate may be renewed for a period of one year if it is clearly shown that the applicant has not expatriated himself. Persons who hold passports which have not expired shall not be furnished with certificates of registration, and it is strictly forbidden to furnish them to be used for traveling in the place of passports, except in cases of extraordinary emergency when the Department of State shall expressly authorize their use for this purpose.

Returns of all registrations and of all certificates of registration issued shall be made at intervals and under regulations to be prescribed by the Secretary of State.

The Secretary of State is authorized to make regulations concerning registration additional to these rules and not inconsistent with them.

No fee shall be required for registration nor for any service connected therewith, except for the issuance of a certificate of registration, for which a fee of one dollar shall be required.

The Tariff of the United States Consular Fees is hereby amended by the addition thereto of the following paragraph:

Certificate of registration of an American citizen. $1.00

This order shall go into effect November 15, 1916.

WOODROW WILSON.

BRITISH REPLY TO THE AMERICAN PROTEST AGAINST THE BLACKLIST.

The British Secretary of State for Foreign Affairs to Ambassador W. H. Page:

FOREIGN OFFICE, *London, Oct. 10, 1916.*

Your Excellency—His Majesty's Government have had under consideration the note which Your Excellency was good enough to communicate to me on the 28th July last, with respect to the addition of certain firms in the United States of America to the statutory list compiled and issued in accordance with "the trading with the Enemy (extension of powers) Act 1915."

You will recall that shortly after this Act became law I had the honor, in my note of the 16th February last, in reply to your note of the 26th January, to explain the object of the Act. It is a piece of purely municipal legislation, and provides that His Majesty may by proclamation prohibit persons in the United Kingdom from trading with any persons in foreign countries who might be specified in such proclamations or in any subsequent orders. It also imposes appropriate penalties upon persons in the United Kingdom who violate the provisions of this statute.

That is all. His Majesty's Government neither purport nor claim to impose any disabilities or penalties upon neutral individuals or upon neutral commerce. The measure is simply one which enjoins those who owe allegiance to Great Britain to cease having trade relations with persons who are found to be assisting or rendering service to the enemy.

I can scarcely believe that the United States Government intend to challenge the right of Great Britain as a sovereign State to pass legislation prohibiting all those who owe her allegiance from trading with any specified persons when such prohibition is found necessary in the public interest. The right to do so is so obvious that I feel sure that the protest which your Excellency handed to me has been founded on a misconception of the scope and intent of the measures which have been taken.

This view is strengthened by some of the remarks which are made in the note. It is, for instance, stated that these measures are "inevitably and essentially inconsistent with the rights of the citizens of all nations not involved in war"

The note then proceeds to point out that citizens of the United States are entirely within their rights in attempting to trade with any of the nations now at war. His Majesty's Government readily admit that the citizens of every neutral nation are free to trade with belligerent countries. The United States Government will, no doubt, equally readily admit that they do so subject to the right of the other belligerent to put an end to that trade by every means within his power which is recognized by international law by such measures, for instance, as the seizure of neutral goods on contraband or for breach of blockade, etc.

The legislation, however, to which exception is taken does not belong to that class of measures. It is purely municipal. It is an exercise of the sovereign right of an independent State over its own citizens, and nothing more.

This fact has not, I feel sure, been fully realized by the Government of the United States of America, for the note maintains that the Government cannot consent to see these remedies and penalties altered and extended at will in derogation of the rights of its citizens, and says that "conspicuous among the principles which the civilized nations of the world have accepted for the safeguarding of the rights of neutrals is the just and honorable principle that neutrals may not be condemned nor their goods confiscated except upon fair adjudication and after an opportunity to be heard in prize courts or elsewhere."

As I have said above, the legislation merely prohibits persons in the United Kingdom from trading with certain specified individuals who, by reason of their nationality or of their association, are found to support the cause of the enemy and trading with whom will therefore strengthen that cause. So far as that legislation is concerned, no rights or property of these specified individuals are interfered with; neither they nor their property are condemned or confiscated; they are as free as they were before to carry on their business. The only disability they suffer is that British subjects are prohibited from giving to them the support and assistance of British credit and British property.

The steps which His Majesty's Government are taking under the above-mentioned act are not confined to the United States of America; the policy is only pursued in all neutral countries. Nay, more, with the full consent of the allied countries, are being placed on the statutory list if they are firms with whom it is necessary to prevent British subjects from trading.

These considerations may, perhaps, serve to convince the Government of the United States that the measures now being taken are not directed against neutral trade in particular; they are part of the general belligerent operations designed to weaken the enemy's resources.

I do not read your note of the 28th July as maintaining that His Majesty's Government are obliged by any rule of international law to give to those who are actively assisting the cause of their enemies, whether they be established in neutral or in enemy territory, the facilities which flow from participation in British commerce. Any such proposition would be so manifestly untenable, that there is no reason to refute it. The feelings which I venture to think have prompted the note under reply must have been that the measures which we have been obliged to take will be expanded to an extent which will result in their interference with genuine neutral commerce; perhaps, also, that they are not exclusively designed for belligerent purposes, but are rather an attempt to forward our own trade interests at the expense of neutral commerce under the cloak of belligerency; and, lastly, that they are, from a military point of view, unnecessary.

Upon these points I am able to give to the Government and people of the United States the fullest assurances. Upon the first point, it is true, as your note says, that the name of a firm may be added to the statutory list of persons with whom British persons may not trade whenever, on account of the enemy association of such firm, it seems expedient to do so. But the Government of the United States can feel confident that this system of prohibition will not be carried further than is absolutely necessary.

It has been forced upon us by the circumstances of the present war. To extend it beyond what is required in order to secure its immediate purpose—the weakening of the resources of our opponents—or to allow it to interfere with what is really the genuine neutral trade of a country with which we desire to have the closest commercial intercourse, would be contrary to British interests.

The advantage derived from a commercial transaction between a British subject and a foreigner is mutual, and for His Majesty's Government to forbid a British subject to trade with the citizen of any foreign country necessarily entails some diminution of commercial opportunity for that British subject, and therefore some loss to both him and his country.

Consequently the United States Government, even if they are willing to ignore the whole tradition and tendency of British policy towards the commerce of other nations, might be confident that self-interest alone would render His Majesty's Government anxious not to place upon the statutory list the name of any firm which carries on a genuine bona fide neutral trade. If they did so, Great Britain herself would be the loser.

As to the second point, there seem to be individuals in the United States and elsewhere whom it is almost impossible to convince that the measures we take are measures against our enemies, and not intended merely to foster our own trade at the expense of that of neutral countries. I can only reiterate, what has been repeatedly explained before, that His Majesty's Government have no such unworthy object in view. We have, in fact, in all the steps we have taken to prevent British subjects from trading with these specified firms, been most careful to cause the least possible dislocation of neutral trade, as much in our interests as in those of the neutral.

I turn now to the question whether the circumstances of the present war are such as to justify resort on the part of His Majesty's Government to novel expedient.

As the United States Government are well aware, the Anglo-American practice has in times past been to treat domicile as the test of enemy character, in contradistinction to the continental practice which has always regarded nationality as the test. The Anglo-American rule, crystallized at the time when means of transport and communication were less developed than now, and when in consequence the actions of a person established in a distant country could have but little influence upon a struggle.

Today the position is very different. The activities of enemy subjects are ubiquitous, and under modern conditions it is easy for them wherever resident to remit money to any place where it may be required for the use of their own government or to act in other ways calculated to assist its purposes and to damage the interests of the powers with whom it is at war. No elaborate exposition of the situation is required to show that full use has been and is being made of these opportunities.

The experience of the war has proved abundantly, as the United States Government will readily admit, that many Germans in neutral countries have done all in their power to help the cause of their own country and to injure that of the allies; in fact, it would be no exaggeration to say that German houses abroad have in a large number of cases, been used as an integral part of an organization deliberately conceived and planned as an engine for the furtherance of German politics and military ambitions.

It is common knowledge that German business establishments in foreign countries have been not merely centers of German trade, but active agents for dissemination of German political and social influence and for the purpose of espionage.

In some cases they have even been used as bases of supply for German cruisers, and in other cases as organizers and paymasters of miscreants employed to destroy by foul means factories engaged in making or ships in carrying supplies required by the allies.

Such operations have been carried out in the territory even of the United States itself, and I am bound to observe what I do not think will be denied, that no adequate action has yet been taken by the Government of the United States to suppress breaches of neutrality of this particularly criminal kind, which I know they are the first to discountenance and deplore.

In the face of enemy activities of this nature it was essential for His Majesty's Government to take steps that should at least deprive interests so strongly hostile to the facilities and advantages of unrestricted trading with British subjects.

The public opinion of this country would not have tolerated the prolonging of the war by the continued liberty of British subjects to trade with and so to enrich the firms in foreign countries whose wealth and influence were alike at the service of the enemy.

Let me repeat that His Majesty's Government make no such claim to dictate to citizens of the United States, nor to those of any other neutral country as to the persons with whom they are or are not to trade. They do, however, maintain the right, which in the present crisis is also their duty toward the people of this country and to their allies, to withhold British facilities from those who conduct their trade for the benefit of our enemies.

If the value to these firms of British facilities is such as to lead them to prefer to give up their trade with our enemies rather than to run the risk of being deprived of such facilities, His Majesty's Government cannot admit that their acceptance of guarantees to that effect is either arbitrary or incompatible with international law or comity.

There is another matter with which I should like to deal.

The idea would seem to be prevalent in some quarters that the military position is now such that it is unnecessary for His Majesty's Government to take any steps which might prejudice, even to a slight extent, the commerce of neutral countries, that the end of the war is in sight, and that nothing which happens in distant neutral countries can effect the ultimate result.

If that were really the position, it is possible that the measures taken by His Majesty's Government might be described as uncalled for, but it is not. We may well wish that it were so. Even though the military situation of the allies has greatly improved, there is still a long and bitter struggle in front of them, and one which in justice to the principles for which they are fighting imposes upon them the duty of employing every opportunity and every measure which they can legitimately use to overcome their opponents.

One observation which is very commonly heard is that certain belligerent acts, even though lawful, are too petty to have any influence upon a struggle of such magnitude. It is, I know, difficult for those who have no immediate contact with war to realize with what painful anxiety men and women in this country must regard even the smallest acts which tend to increase, if only by a hair's breadth, the danger in which their relatives and friends daily stand, or to prolong, if only by a minute, the period during which they are to be exposed to such perils.

Whatever inconvenience may be caused to neutral nations by the exercise of belligerent rights, it is not to be compared for an instant to the suffering and loss occasioned to mankind by the prolongation of the war, even for a week.

One other matter should be mentioned, namely, the exclusion from ships using British coal of goods belonging to firms on the statutory list. This is enforced by rendering it a condition of the supply of bunker coal.

What legal objection can be taken to this course? It is British coal; why should it be used to transport the goods of those who are actively assisting our enemies?

Nor is this the only point. It must be remembered that the German Government by their submarine warfare have sought to diminish the world's tonnage; that they have sunk illegally and without warning hundreds of peaceful merchant ships belonging not only to allied countries, but to neutrals as well. Norwegian, Danish, Swedish, Dutch, Spanish, Greek ships have all been sunk.

Between the first of June and the thirtieth of September, 1916, 262 vessels have been sunk by enemy's submarines; 73 of these were British, 123 allies and 66 neutrals.

These totals include ten British vessels which were sunk without warning and involved the loss of eighty-one lives; two allied, one of which involves the loss of two lives, no information being available as to the other, and three neutral, involving the loss of one life. Even so, the list is incomplete. Probably other vessels were sunk without warning and more lives than those enumerated were lost. It may be added that where those on board did escape it was, as a rule, only by taking to open boats.

One of the first enterprises to feel the loss of tonnage has been the commission for relief in Belgium. Relief ships have themselves been repeatedly sunk, and in spite of all the efforts of His Majesty's Government, in spite of the special facilities given for the supply of coal to ships engaged in the commission's service, that body is constantly unable to import into Belgium the foodstuffs absolutely necessary to preserve the life of the population. Can it, then, be wondered that the British Government are anxious to limit the supply of British coal in such a way as to reserve it as far as possible to ships genuinely employed in allied or neutral trade?

There is, indeed, one preoccupation in regard to this use of coaling advantages by His Majesty's Government which is, no doubt, present in the minds of neutrals, and which I recognize. I refer to the apprehension that the potential control over means of transportation thus possessed by one nation might be used for the disruption of the trade of the world in the selfish interest of that nation.

His Majesty's Government, therefore, take this opportunity to declare that they are not unmindful of the obligations of those who possess sea power, nor of that traditional policy pursued by the British Empire by which such power has been regarded as a trust and has been exercised in the interest of freedom. They require no representations to recall such considerations to mind, but they cannot admit that, in the circumstances of the times, their present use of their coal resources, a use which only differs in extent from that exercised by the United States in the Civil War in the case of vessels proceeding to such ports as Nassau, is obnoxious to their duties or their voluntary professions.

In conclusion, I cannot refrain from calling to mind the instructions issued by Lord Russell on the 5th of July, 1862, to the merchants of Liverpool in regard to trade with the Bahamas. His Lordship there advised British subjects that their "true remedy" would be to "refrain from this species of trade" on the ground that "it exposes innocent commerce to vexatious detention and search by American cruisers."

His Majesty's Government does not ask the Government of the United States to take any such action as this, but they cannot believe that the United States Government will question their right to lay upon British merchants, in the interests of the safety of the British Empire, for which they are responsible, the same prohibition as Lord Russell issued fifty years ago out of consideration for the interests and feelings of a foreign nation.

Suspicions and insinuations which would construe so simple an action as an opening for secret and unavowed design on neutral rights should have no place in the relations between two friendly countries.

I trust that the explanations contained in this note will destroy such suspicions and correct the erroneous views which prevail in the United States on the subject.

I have, etc.,   GREY OF FALLODEN.

BY THE PRESIDENT OF THE UNITED STATES OF AMERICA

A PROCLAMATION

[Thanksgiving—1916.]

It has long been the custom of our people to turn in the fruitful autumn of the year in praise and thanksgiving to Almighty God for His many blessings and mercies to us as a nation. The year that has elapsed since we last observed our day of thanksgiving has been rich in blessings to us as a people, but the whole face of the world has been darkened by war. In the midst of our peace and happiness, our thoughts dwell with painful disquiet upon the struggles and sufferings of the nations at war and of the peoples upon whom war has brought disaster without choice or possibility of escape on their part. We cannot think of our own happiness without thinking also of their pitiful distress.

Now, therefore, I, Woodrow Wilson, President of the United States of America, do appoint Thursday, the thirtieth of November, as a day of National Thanksgiving and Prayer, and urge and advise the people to resort to their several places of worship on that day to render thanks to Almighty God for the blessings of peace and unbroken prosperity which He has bestowed upon our beloved country in such unstinted measure. And I also urge and suggest our duty in this our day of peace and abundance to think in deep sympathy of the stricken peoples of the world upon whom the curse and terror of war has so pitilessly fallen, and to contribute out of our abundant means to the relief of their suffering. Our people could in no better way show their real attitude towards the present struggle of the nations than by contributing out of their abundance to the relief of the suffering which war has brought in its train.

IN WITNESS WHEREOF I have hereunto set my hand and caused the seal of the United States to be affixed.

DONE at the City of Washington this seventeenth day of November, in the year of our Lord one thousand nine hundred and [SEAL.] sixteen and of the independence of the United States the one hundred and forty-first.   WOODROW WILSON.

By the President:

ROBERT LANSING, *Secretary of State.*

FOURTH ANNUAL ADDRESS

[Delivered at a Joint Session of the Two Houses of Congress, December 5, 1916.]

GENTLEMEN OF THE CONGRESS—In fulfilling at this time the duty laid upon me by the Constitution of communicating to you from time to time information of the state of the Union and recommending to your consideration such legislative measures as may be judged necessary and expedient, I shall continue the practice, which I hope has been acceptable to you, of leaving to the reports of the several heads of the executive departments the elaboration of the detailed needs of the public service and confine myself to those matters of more general public policy with which it seems necessary and feasible to deal at the present session of the Congress.

I realize the limitations of time under which you will necessarily act at this session and shall make my suggestions as few as possible; but there were some things left undone at the last session which there will now be time to complete and which it seems necessary in the interest of the public to do at once.

In the first place, it seems to me imperatively necessary that the earliest possible consideration and action should be accorded the remaining measures of the program of settlement and regulation which I had occasion to recommend to you at the close of your last session in view of the public dangers disclosed by the unaccommodated difficulties which then existed, and which still unhappily continue to exist, between the railroads of the country and their locomotive engineers, conductors and trainmen.

I then recommended:

First, immediate provision for the enlargement and administrative reorganization of the Interstate Commerce Commission along the lines embodied in the bill recently passed by the House of Representatives and now awaiting action by the Senate; in order that the Commission may be enabled to deal with the many great and various duties now devolving upon it with a promptness and thoroughness which are, with its present constitution and means of action, practically impossible.

Second, the establishment of an eight-hour day as the legal basis alike of work and wages in the employment of all railway employes who are actually engaged in the work of operating trains in interstate transportation.

Third, the authorization of the appointment by the President of a small body of men to observe actual results in experience of the adoption of the eight-hour day in railway transportation alike for the men and for the railroads.

Fourth, explicit approval by the Congress of the consideration by the Interstate Commerce Commission of an increase of freight rates to meet such additional expenditures by the railroads as may have been rendered necessary by the adoption of the eight-hour day and which have not been offset by administrative readjustments and economies, should the facts disclosed justify the increase.

Fifth, an amendment of the existing Federal statute which provides for the mediation, conciliation and arbitration of such controversies as the present by adding to it a provision that, in case the methods of accommodation now provided for should fail, a full public investigation of the merits of every such dispute shall be instituted and completed before a strike or lockout may lawfully be attempted.

And, sixth, the lodgment in the hands of the Executive of the power, in case of military necessity, to take control of such portions and such rolling stock of the railways of the country as may be required for military use and to operate them for military purposes, with authority to draft into the military service of the United States such train crews and administrative officials as the circumstances require for their safe and efficient use.

The second and third of these recommendations the Congress immediately acted on: it established the eight-hour day as the legal basis of work and wages in train service and it authorized the appointment of a commission to observe and report upon the practical results, deeming these the measures most immediately needed; but it postponed action upon the other suggestions until an opportunity should be offered for a more deliberate consideration of them.

The fourth recommendation I do not deem it necessary to renew. The power of the Interstate Commerce Commission to grant an increase of rates on the ground referred to is indisputably clear and a recommendation by the Congress with regard to such a matter might seem to draw in question the scope of the commission's authority or its inclination to do justice when there is no reason to doubt either.

The other suggestions—the increase in the Interstate Commerce Commission's membership and in its facilities for performing its manifold duties; the provision for full public investigation and assessment of industrial disputes, and the grant to the Executive of the power to control and operate the railways when necessary in time of war or other like public necessity—I now very earnestly renew.

The necessity for such legislation is manifest and pressing. Those who have entrusted us with the responsibility and duty of serving and safeguarding them in such matters would find it hard, I believe, to excuse a failure to act upon these grave matters or any unnecessary postponement of action upon them.

Not only does the Interstate Commerce Commission now find it practically impossible, with its present membership and organization, to perform its great functions promptly and thoroughly, but it is not unlikely that it may presently be found advisable to add to its duties still others equally heavy and exacting. It must first be perfected as an administrative instrument.

The country cannot and should not consent to remain any longer exposed to profound industrial disturbances for lack of additional means of arbitration and conciliation which the Congress can easily and promptly supply.

And all will agree that there must be no doubt as to the power of the Executive to make immediate and uninterrupted use of the railroads for the concentration of the military forces of the nation wherever they are needed and whenever they are needed.

This is a program of regulation, prevention and administrative efficiency which argues its own case in the mere statement of it. With regard to one of its items, the increase in the efficiency of the Interstate Commerce Commission, the House of Representatives has already acted; its action needs only the concurrence of the Senate.

I would hesitate to recommend, and I dare say the Congress would hesitate to act upon the suggestion should I make it, that any man in any occupation should be obliged by law to continue in an employment which he desired to leave.

To pass a law which forbade or prevented the individual workman to leave his work before receiving the approval of society in doing so would be to adopt a new principle into our jurisprudence, which I take it for granted we are not prepared to introduce.

But the proposal that the operation of the railways of the country shall not be stopped or interrupted by the concerted action of organized bodies of men until a public investigation shall have been instituted, which shall make the whole question at issue plain for the judgment of the opinion of the nation, is not to propose any such principle.

It is based upon the very different principle that the concerted action of powerful bodies of men shall not be permitted to stop the industrial processes of the nation, at any rate before the nation shall have had an opportunity to acquaint itself with the merits of the case as between employe and employer, time to form its opinion upon an impartial statement of the merits, and opportunity to consider all practicable means of conciliation or arbitration.

I can see nothing in that proposition but the justifiable safeguarding by society of the necessary processes of its very life. There is nothing arbitrary or unjust in it unless it be arbitrarily and unjustly done. It can and should be done with a full and scrupulous regard for the interests and liberties of all concerned as well as for the permanent interests of society itself.

Three matters of capital importance await the action of the Senate which have already been acted upon by the House of Representatives; the bill which seeks to extend greater freedom of combination to those engaged in promoting the foreign commerce of the country than is now thought by some to be legal under the terms of the laws against monopoly; the bill amending the present organic law of Porto Rico; and the bill proposing a more thorough and systematic regulation of the expenditure of money in elections, commonly called the Corrupt Practices Act.

I need not labor my advice that these measures be enacted into law. Their urgency lies in the manifest circumstances which render their adoption at this time not only opportune but necessary. Even delay would seriously jeopard the interests of the country and of the Government.

Immediate passage of the bill to regulate the expenditure of money in elections may seem to be less necessary than the immediate enactment of the other measures to which I refer, because at least two years will elapse before another election in which Federal offices are to be filled; but it would greatly relieve the public mind if this important matter were dealt with while the circumstances and the dangers to the public morals of the present method of obtaining and spending campaign funds stand clear under recent observation, and the methods of expenditure can be frankly studied in the light of present experience; and a delay would have the further very serious disadvantage of postponing action until another election was at hand and some special object connected with it might be thought to be in the mind of those who urged it. Action can be taken now with facts for guidance and without suspicion of partisan purpose.

I shall not argue at length the desirability of giving a freer hand in the matter of combined and concerted effort to those who shall undertake the essential enterprise of building up our export trade. That enterprise will presently, will immediately assume, has indeed already assumed a magnitude unprecedented in our experience. We have not the necessary instrumentalities for its prosecution; it is deemed to be doubtful whether they could be created upon an adequate scale under our present laws.

We should clear away all legal obstacles and create a basis of undoubted law for it which will give freedom without permitting unregulated license. The thing must be done now, because the opportunity is here and may escape us if we hesitate or delay.

The argument for the proposed amendments of the organic law of Porto Rico is brief and conclusive. The present laws governing the island and regulating the rights and privileges of its people are not just. We have created expectations of extended privilege which we have not satisfied. There is uneasiness among the people of the island and even a suspicious doubt with regard to our intentions concerning them which the adoption of the pending measure would happily remove. We do not doubt what we wish to do in any essential particular. We ought to do it at once.

At the last session of the Congress a bill was passed by the Senate which provides for the promotion of vocational and industrial education, which is of vital importance to the whole country because it concerns a matter, too long neglected, upon which the thorough industrial preparation of the country for the critical years of economic development immediately ahead of us in very large measure depends.

May I not urge its early and favorable consideration by the House of Representatives and its early enactment into law? It contains plans which affect all interests and all parts of the country, and I am sure that there is no legislation now pending before the Congress whose passage the country awaits with more thoughtful approval or greater impatience to see a great and admirable thing set in the way of being done.

There are other matters already advanced to the stage of conference between the two houses of which it is not necessary that I should speak. Some practicable basis of agreement concerning them will no doubt be found and action taken upon them.

Inasmuch as this is, gentlemen, probably the last occasion I shall have to address the Sixty-fourth Congress, I hope that you will permit me to say with what genuine pleasure and satisfaction I have co-operated with you in the many measures of constructive policy with which you have enriched the legislative annals of the country. It has been a privilege to labor in such company. I take the liberty of congratulating you upon the completion of a record of rare serviceableness and distinction.

OFFICIAL NOTES LOOKING TOWARD A TERMINATION OF THE EUROPEAN WAR, FROM THE TEUTONIC ALLIES TO THE NEUTRAL POWERS, THE REPLIES OF THE ENTENTE ALLIES, AND PRESIDENT WILSON'S EFFORTS AT MEDIATION.

Following is the text of the note addressed by Germany and her allies to the neutral powers for transmission to the Entente Allies:

BERLIN, December 12, 1916.

The most terrific war experienced in history has been raging for the last two years and a half over a large part of the world—a catastrophe which thousands of years of common civilization was unable to prevent and which injures the most precious achievements of humanity.

Our aims are not to shatter nor annihilate our adversaries. In spite of our consciousness of our military and economic strength and our readiness to continue the war (which has been forced upon us) to the bitter end, if necessary; at the same time, prompted by the desire to avoid further bloodshed and make an end to the atrocities of war, the four allied powers propose to enter forthwith into peace negotiations.

The propositions which they bring forward for such negotiations, and which have for their object a guarantee of the existence, of the honor and liberty of evolution for their nations, are, according to their firm belief, an appropriate basis for the establishment of a lasting peace.

The four allied powers have been obliged to take up arms to defend justice and the liberty of national evolution. The glorious deeds of our armies have in no way altered their purpose. We always maintained the firm belief that our own rights and justified claims in no way control the rights of these nations.

The spiritual and material progress which were the pride of Europe at the beginning of the twentieth century are threatened with ruin. Germany and her allies, Austria-Hungary, Bulgaria, and Turkey, gave proof of their unconquerable strength in this struggle. They gained gigantic advantages over adversaries superior in number and war material. Our lines stand unshaken against ever-repeated attempts made by armies.

The last attack in the Balkans has been rapidly and victoriously overcome. The most recent events have demonstrated that further continuance of the war will not result in breaking the resistance of our forces, and the whole situation with regard to our troops justifies our expectation of further successes.

If, in spite of this offer of peace and reconciliation, the struggle should go on, the four allied powers are resolved to continue to a victorious end, but they disclaim responsibility for this before humanity and history. The Imperial Government, through the good offices of your Excellency, asks the Government of [here is inserted the name of the neutral power addressed in each instance] to bring this communication to the knowledge of the Government of [here are inserted the names of the belligerents].

TO THE VATICAN.

The note of the German Government, as presented by Dr. von Muhlberg, German Minister to the Vatican, to Cardinal Gasparri, Papal Secretary of State, reads as follows:

BERLIN, December 12, 1916.

According to instructions received, I have the honor to send to your Eminence a copy of the declaration of the Imperial Government today, which by the good offices of the powers intrusted with the protection of German interests in the countries with which the German Empire is in a state of war, transmits to these States, and in which the Imperial Government declares itself ready to enter into peace negotiations. The Austro-Hungarian, Turkish, and Bulgarian Governments also have sent similar notes.

The reasons which prompted Germany and her allies to take this step are manifest. For two years and a half a terrible war has been devastating the European Continent. Unlimited treasures of civilization have been destroyed. Extensive areas have been soaked with blood. Millions of brave soldiers have fallen in battle and millions have returned home as invalids. Grief and sorrow fill almost every house.

Not only upon the belligerent nations, but also upon neutrals, the destructive consequences of the gigantic struggle weigh heavily. Trade and commerce, carefully built up in years of peace, have been depressed. The best forces of the nation have been withdrawn from the production of useful objects. Europe, which formerly was devoted to the propagation of religion and civilization, which was trying to find solutions for social problems, and was the home of science and art and all peaceful labor, now resembles an immense war camp, in which the achievements and works of many decades are doomed to annihilation.

Germany is carrying on a war of defense against her enemies, which aim at her destruction. She fights to assure the integrity of her frontiers and the liberty of the German nation, for the right which she claims to develop freely her intellectual and economic energies in peaceful competition and on an equal footing with other nations. All the efforts of their enemies are unable to shatter the heroic armies of the (Teutonic) allies, which protect the frontiers of their countries, strengthened by the certainty that the enemy shall never pierce the iron wall.

Those fighting on the front know that they are supported by the whole nation, which is inspired by love for its country and is ready for the greatest sacrifices and determined to defend to the last extremity the inherited treasure of intellectual and economic work and the social organization and sacred soil of the country.

Certain of our own strength, but realizing Europe's sad future if the war continues; seized with pity in the face of the unspeakable misery of humanity, the German Empire, in accord with her allies, solemnly repeats what the Chancellor already has declared, a year ago, that Germany is ready to give peace to the world by setting before the whole world the question whether or not it is possible to find a basis for an understanding.

Since the first day of the Pontifical reign his Holiness the Pope has unswervingly demonstrated, in the most generous fashion, his solicitude for the innumer-

THE FIRST DAY AT THE CANTONMENT

THE FIRST DAY AT THE CANTONMENT.

The accompanying illustration, taken at Camp Dix, New Jersey, one of the thirty-two major cantonments utilized during the War to train the American Expeditionary Forces, gives an excellent idea of the civilian appearance of the men drafted into the American army, as they appeared upon arrival at camp.

able victims of this war. He has alleviated the sufferings and ameliorated the fate of thousands of men injured by this catastrophe. Inspired by the exalted ideas of his ministry, his Holiness has seized every opportunity in the interests of humanity to end so sanguinary a war.

The Imperial Government is firmly confident that the initiative of the four powers will find friendly welcome on the part of his Holiness, and that the work of peace can count upon the precious support of the Holy See.

AUSTRIA'S SEPARATE STATEMENT.

An official Austrian statement, referring to the peace offer, says:

When in the summer of 1914 the patience of Austria-Hungary was exhausted by a series of systematically continued and ever increasing provocations and menaces, and the monarchy, after almost fifty years of unbroken peace, found itself compelled to draw the sword, this weighty decision was animated neither by aggressive purposes nor by designs of conquest, but solely by the bitter necessity of self-defense, to defend its existence and safeguard itself for the future against similar treacherous plots of hostile neighbors.

That was the task and aim of the monarchy in the present war. In combination with its allies, well tried in loyal comradeship in arms, the Austro-Hungarian Army and Fleet, fighting, bleeding, but also assailing and conquering, gained such successes that they frustrated the intentions of the enemy. The quadruple alliance not only has won an immense series of victories, but also holds in its power extensive hostile territories. Unbroken is its strength, as our latest treacherous enemy has just experienced.

Can our enemies hope to conquer or shatter this alliance of powers? They will never succeed in breaking it by blockade and starvation measures. Their war aims, to the attainment of which they have come no nearer in the third year of the war, will in the future be proved to have been completely unattainable. Useless and unavailing, therefore, is the prosecution of the fighting on the part of the enemy.

The powers of the Quadruple Alliance, on the other hand, have effectively pursued their aims, namely, defense against attacks on their existence and integrity, which were planned in concert long since, and the achievement of real guarantees, and they will never allow themselves to be deprived of the basis of their existence, which they have secured by advantages won.

The continuation of the murderous war, in which the enemy can destroy much, but cannot—as the Quadruple Alliance is firmly confident—alter fate, is ever more seen to be an aimless destruction of human lives and property, an act of inhumanity justified by no necessity and a crime against civilization.

This conviction, and the hope that similar views may also be begun to be entertained in the enemy camp, has caused the idea to ripen in the Vienna Cabinet—in full agreement with the Governments of the allied [Teutonic] powers—of making a candid and loyal endeavor to come to a discussion with their enemies for the purpose of paving a way for peace.

The Governments of Austria-Hungary, Germany, Turkey, and Bulgaria have addressed today identical notes to the diplomatic representatives in the capitals concerned who are intrusted with the promotion of enemy nationals, expressing an inclination to enter into peace negotiations and requesting them to transmit this overture to enemy States. This step was simultaneously brought to the knowledge of the representatives of the Holy See in a special note, and the active interest of the Pope for this offer of peace was solicited. Likewise the accredited representatives of the remaining neutral States in the four capitals were acquainted with this proceeding for the purpose of informing their Governments.

Austria and her allies by this step have given new and decisive proof of their love of peace. It is now for their enemies to make known their views before the world.

Whatever the result of its proposal may be, no responsibility can fall on the Quadruple Alliance, even before the judgment seat of its own peoples, if it is eventually obliged to continue the war.

264

PEACE NOTE TO THE BELLIGERENT NATIONS

DEPARTMENT OF STATE,
WASHINGTON, D. C., December 18, 1916.

The Secretary of State to the American Ambassadors at the Capitals of the Belligerent Powers:

The President directs me to send you the following communication to be presented immediately to the Minister of Foreign Affairs of the Government to which you are accredited:

The President of the United States has instructed me to suggest to the [here is inserted a designation of the Government addressed] a course of action with regard to the present war, which he hopes that the Government will take under consideration as suggested in the most friendly spirit, and as coming not only from a friend but also as coming from the representative of a neutral nation whose interests have been most seriously affected by the war and whose concern for its early conclusion arises out of a manifest necessity to determine how best to safeguard those interests if the war is to continue.

[*The third paragraph of the note as sent to the four Central Powers— Germany, Austria-Hungary, Turkey, and Bulgaria—is as follows:*]

The suggestion which I am instructed to make the President has long had it in mind to offer. He is somewhat embarrassed to offer it at this particular time, because it may now seem to have been prompted by a desire to play a part in connection with the recent overtures of the Central Powers. It has, in fact, been in no way suggested by them in its origin, and the President would have delayed offering it until those overtures had been independently answered but for the fact that it also concerns the question of peace and may best be considered in connection with other proposals which have the same end in view. The President can only beg that his suggestion be considered entirely on its own merits and as if it had been made in other circumstances.

[*The third paragraph of the note as sent to the ten Entente Allies— Great Britain, France, Italy, Japan, Russia, Belgium, Montenegro, Portugal, Rumania, and Serbia—is as follows:*]

The suggestion which I am instructed to make the President has long had it in mind to offer. He is somewhat embarrassed to offer it at this particular time, because it may now seem to have been prompted by the recent overtures of the Central Powers. It is, in fact, in no way associated with them in its origin, and the President would have delayed offering it until those overtures had been answered but for the fact that it also concerns the question of peace and may best be considered in connection with other proposals which have the same end in view. The President can only beg that his suggestion be considered entirely on its own merits and as if it had been made in other circumstances.

[*Thenceforward the note proceeds identically to all the powers, as follows:*]

The President suggests that an early occasion be sought to call out from all the nations now at war such an avowal of their respective views as to the terms upon which the war might be concluded and the arrangements which would be deemed satisfactory as a guaranty against its renewal or the kindling of any similar conflict in the future as would make it possible frankly to compare them. He is indifferent as to the means taken to accomplish this. He would be happy himself to serve, or even to take the initiative in its accomplishment, in any way that might prove acceptable, but he has no desire to determine the method or the instrumentality. One way will be as acceptable to him as another, if only the great object he has in mind be attained.

He takes the liberty of calling attention to the fact that the objects, which the statesmen of the belligerents on both sides have in mind in this war, are virtually the same, as stated in general terms to their own people and to the world. Each side desires to make the rights and privileges of weak peoples and small States as secure against aggression or denial in the future as the rights and privileges of the great and powerful States now at war. Each wishes itself to be made secure in the future, along with all other nations and peoples, against the recurrence of wars like this and against aggression or selfish interference of any kind. Each would be jealous of the formation of any more rival leagues to preserve an uncertain balance of power amid multiplying suspicions; but each is ready to consider the formation of a league of nations to insure peace and justice throughout the world. Before that final step can be taken, however, each deems it necessary first to settle the issues of the present war upon terms which will certainly safeguard the independence, the territorial integrity, and the political and commercial freedom of the nations involved.

In the measures to be taken to secure the future peace of the world the people and Government of the United States are as vitally and as directly interested as the Governments now at war. Their interest, moreover, in the means to be adopted to relieve the smaller and weaker peoples of the world of the peril of wrong and violence is as quick and ardent as that of any other people or Government. They stand ready, and even eager, to co-operate in the accomplishment of these ends, when the war is over, with every influence and resource at their command. But the war must first be concluded. The terms upon which it is to be concluded they are not at liberty to suggest; but the President does feel that it is his right and his duty to point out their intimate interest in its conclusion, lest it should presently be too late to accomplish the greater things which lie beyond its conclusion, lest the situation of neutral nations, now exceedingly hard to endure, be rendered altogether intolerable, and lest, more than all, an injury be done civilization itself which can never be atoned for or repaired.

The President therefore feels altogether justified in suggesting an immediate opportunity for a comparison of views as to the terms which must precede those ultimate arrangements for the peace of the world, which all desire and in which the neutral nations as well as those at war are ready to play their full responsible part. If the contest must continue to proceed toward undefined ends by slow attrition until the one group of belligerents or the other is exhausted; if million after million of human lives must continue to be offered up until on the one side or the other there are no more to offer; if resentments must be kindled that can never cool and despairs engendered from which there can be no recovery, hopes of peace and of the willing concert of free peoples will be rendered vain and idle.

The life of the entire world has been profoundly affected. Every part of the great family of mankind has felt the burden and terror of this unprecedented contest of arms. No nation in the civilized world can be said in truth to stand outside its influence or to be safe against its disturbing effects. And yet the concrete objects for which it is being waged have never been definitively stated.

The leaders of the several belligerents have, as has been said, stated those objects in general terms. But, stated in general terms, they seem the same on both sides. Never yet have the authoritative spokesmen of either side avowed the precise objects which would, if attained, satisfy them and their people that the war had been fought out. The world has been left to conjecture what definitive results, what actual exchange of guaranties, what political or territorial changes or readjustments, what stage of military success, even, would bring the war to an end.

It may be that peace is nearer than we know; that the terms which the belligerents on the one side and on the other would deem it necessary to insist upon are not so irreconcilable as some have feared; that an interchange of views would clear the way at least for conference and make the permanent concord of the nations a hope of the immediate future, a concert of nations immediately practicable.

The President is not proposing peace; he is not even offering mediation. He is merely proposing that soundings be taken in order that we may learn, the neutral nations with the belligerent, how near the haven of peace may be for which all mankind longs with an intense and increasing longing. He believes that the spirit in which he speaks and the objects which he seeks will be understood by all concerned, and he confidently hopes for a response which will bring a new light into the affairs of the world.   LANSING.

[*Copies of the above will be delivered to all neutral Governments for their information.*]

TEXT OF GERMANY'S NOTE TO PRESIDENT WILSON, PROPOSING PEACE CONFERENCE OF BELLIGERENTS.

BERLIN, December 26, 1916.

Germany and her allies, Austria-Hungary, Bulgaria and Turkey, replied today to the note of President Wilson in which he asked that the belligerent nations state the aims for which they were fighting. The text of the reply, which was handed to James W. Gerard, the American Ambassador, says:

The high-minded suggestion made by the President of the United States of America in order to create a basis for the establishment of a lasting peace has been received and considered by the Imperial Government in the friendly spirit which was expressed in the President's communication.

The President points out that which he has at heart and leaves open the choice of road. To the Imperial Government an immediate exchange of views seems to be the most appropriate road in order to reach the desired result. It begs, therefore, in the sense of the declaration made on Dec. 12, which offered a hand for peace negotiations, to propose an immediate meeting of delegates of the belligerent States at a neutral place.

The Imperial Government is also of the opinion that the great work of preventing future wars can be begun only after the end of the present struggle of the nations. It will, when this moment shall have come, be ready with pleasure to collaborate entirely with the United States in this exalted task.

The answer of the Central Powers concludes with the usual diplomatic terms of politeness.

REPLY OF THE ENTENTE ALLIES TO THE CENTRAL POWERS' OFFER TO OPEN PEACE NEGOTIATIONS.

PARIS, December 30, 1916.

The allied Governments of Belgium, France, Great Britain, Italy, Japan, Montenegro, Portugal, Rumania, Russia, and Serbia, united for the defense of the liberty of their peoples and faithful to engagements taken not to lay down their arms separately, have resolved to reply collectively to the pretended propositions of peace which were addressed to them on behalf of the enemy Governments through the intermediary of the United States, Spain, Switzerland, and Holland.

Before making any reply, the allied powers desire particularly to protest against the two essential assertions of the notes of the enemy powers that pretend to throw upon the Allies responsibility for the war and proclaim the victory of the Central Powers. The allied Governments cannot admit an affirmation doubly inexact and which suffices to render sterile all tentative negotiations. The allied nations have sustained for thirty months a war they did everything to avoid. They have shown by their acts their attachment to peace. That attachment is as strong today as it was in 1914. But it is not upon the word of Germany, after the violation of its engagements, that the peace broken by her may be based.

A mere suggestion without a statement of terms, that negotiations should be opened, is not an offer of peace. The putting forward by the Imperial Government of a sham proposal lacking all substance and precision would appear to be less an offer of peace than a war manoeuvre. It is founded on calculated misinterpretation of the character of the struggle in the past, the present, and the future.

As for the past, the German note takes no account of the facts, dates, and figures, which establish that the war was desired, provoked, and declared by Germany and Austria-Hungary.

At The Hague Conference it was a German delegate who refused all proposals for disarmament. In July, 1914, it was Austria-Hungary, who, after having addressed to Serbia an unprecedented ultimatum, declared war upon her in spite of the satisfaction which had at once been accorded.

The Central Empires then rejected all attempts made by the Entente to bring about a pacific solution of a purely local conflict. Great Britain suggested a conference; France proposed an international commission; the Emperor of Russia asked the German Emperor to go to arbitration, and Russia and Austria-Hungary came to an understanding on the eve of the conflict. But to all these efforts Germany gave neither answer nor effect.

Belgium was invaded by an empire which had guaranteed her neutrality and which had the assurance to proclaim that treaties were "scraps of paper," and that "necessity knows no law."

At the present moment these sham offers on the part of Germany rest on the war map of Europe alone, which represents nothing more than a superficial and passing phase of the situation and not the real strength of the belligerents. A peace concluded upon these terms would be only to the advantage of the aggressors, who, after imagining that they would reach their goal in two months, discovered after two years that they could never attain it.

As for the future, the disasters caused by the German declaration of war and the innumerable outrages committed by Germany and her allies against both belligerents and neutrals demand penalties, reparation and guarantees. Germany avoids mention of any of these.

In reality these overtures made by the Central Powers are nothing more than a calculated attempt to influence the future course of war and to end it by imposing a German peace. The object of these overtures is to create dissension in public opinion in the allied countries. But that public opinion has, in spite of all the sacrifices endured by the Allies, already given its answer with admirable firmness, and has denounced the empty pretense of the declaration of the enemy powers.

They (the peace overtures) have the further object of stiffening public opinion in Germany and in the countries allied to her—one and all severely tried by their losses, worn out by economic pressure and crushed by the supreme effort which has been imposed upon their inhabitants.

They endeavor to deceive and intimidate public opinion in neutral countries, whose inhabitants have long since made up their minds where the initial responsibilities lie and are far too enlightened to favor the designs of Germany by abandoning the defense of human freedom.

Finally, these overtures attempt to justify in advance in the eyes of the world a new series of crimes—submarine warfare, deportations, forced labor and forced enlistment of the inhabitants against their own countries, and violations of neutrality.

Fully conscious of the gravity of this moment, but equally conscious of its requirements, the allied Governments, closely united to one another and in perfect sympathy with their peoples, refuse to consider a proposal which is empty and insincere.

Once again the Allies declare that no peace is possible so long as they have not secured reparation for violated rights and liberties, the recognition of the principle of nationality and of the free existence of small States, so long as they have not brought about a settlement calculated to end once and for all forces which have constituted a perpetual menace to the nations, and to afford the only effective guarantee for the future security of the world.

In conclusion, the Allied Powers think it necessary to put forward the following considerations, which snow tne special situation of Belgium after two and a half years of war. In virtue of the international treaties signed by five great European powers, of which Germany was one, Belgium enjoyed before the war a special status, rendering her territory inviolable and placing her, under the guarantee of the powers, outside all European conflicts. She was, however, in spite of these treaties, the first to suffer the aggression of Germany. For this reason the Belgian Government think it necessary to define the aims which Belgium has never ceased to pursue while fighting side by side with the Entente Powers for right and justice.

Belgium has always scrupulously fulfilled the duties which her neutrality imposed upon her. She has taken up arms to defend her independence and her neutrality violated by Germany and to show that she remains faithful to her international obligations.

On the 4th of August, 1914, in the Reichstag the German Chancellor admitted that this aggression constituted an injustice, contrary to the laws of nations, and pledged himself in the name of Germany to repair it. During two and a half years this injustice has been cruelly aggravated by the proceedings of the occupying forces, which have exhausted the resources of the country, ruined its industries, devastated its towns and villages and have been responsible for innumerable massacres, executions and imprisonments.

At this very moment, while Germany is proclaiming peace and humanity to the world, she is deporting Belgian citizens by thousands and reducing them to slavery.

Belgium before the war asked for nothing but to live in harmony with her neighbors. Her King and her Government have but one aim—the re-establishment of peace and justice. But they only desire peace which would assure to their country legitimate reparation, guarantees and safeguards for the future.

REPLY OF THE ENTENTE ALLIES TO PRESIDENT WILSON'S DIPLOMATIC NOTE PROPOSING A PEACE CONFERENCE OF BELLIGERENTS.

After the reply to the Central Powers printed in the preceding pages, Ambassador Sharp cabled from Paris the following answer of the Entente Allies to the peace proposals of President Wilson:

January 11, 1917.

The allied governments have received the note which was delivered to them in the name of the Government of the United States on the 19th of December, 1916. They have studied it with the care imposed upon them both by the exact realization which they have of the gravity of the hour and by the sincere friendship which attaches them to the American people.

In a general way they wish to declare that they pay tribute to the elevation of the sentiment with which the American note is inspired and that they associate themselves with all their hopes with the project for the creation of a league of nations to insure peace and justice throughout the world. They recognize all the advantages for the cause of humanity and civilization which the institution of international agreements, destined to avoid violent conflicts between nations would prevent; agreements which must imply the sanctions necessary to insure their execution and thus prevent an apparent security from only facilitating new aggressions. But a discussion of future arrangements destined to insure an enduring peace presupposes a satisfactory settlement of the actual conflict. The Allies have as profound a desire as the Government of the United States to terminate as soon as possible a war for which the Central Empires are responsible and which inflicts such cruel sufferings upon humanity.

But they believe that it is impossible at the present moment to attain a peace which will assure them reparation, restitution and such guarantees to which they are entitled by the aggression for which the responsibility rests with the Central Powers and of which the principle itself tended to ruin the security of Europe. A peace which would on the other hand permit the establishment of the future of European nations on a solid basis. The allied nations are conscious that they are not fighting for selfish interests, but above all to safeguard the independence of peoples, of right and of humanity.

The Allies are fully aware of the losses and suffering which the war causes to neutrals, as well as to belligerents, and they deplore them. But they do not hold themselves responsible for them, having in no way either willed or provoked this war, and they strive to reduce these damages in the measure compatible with the inexorable exigencies of their defense against the violence and the wiles of the enemy.

It is with satisfaction, therefore, that they take note of the declaration that the American communication is in nowise associated in its origin with that of the Central Powers, transmitted on the 18th of December by the Government of the United States. They did not doubt, moreover, the resolution of that Government to avoid even the appearance of a support, even moral, of the authors responsible for the war.

The allied governments believe that they must protest in the most friendly but in the most specific manner against the assimilation established in the American note between the two groups of belligerents. This assimilation, based upon public declarations by the Central Powers, is in direct opposition to the evidence, both as regards responsibility for the past and as concerns guarantees for the future. President Wilson in mentioning it certainly had no intention of associating himself with it.

If there is an historical fact established at the present date, it is the willful aggression of Germany and Austria-Hungary to insure their hegemony over Europe and their economic domination over the world. Germany proved by her declaration of war, by the immediate violation of Belgium and Luxemburg and by her manner of conducting the war her simulating contempt for all principles of humanity and all respect for small states; as the conflict developed the attitude of the Central Powers and their allies has been a continual defiance of humanity and civilization.

Is it necessary to recall the horrors which accompanied the invasion of Belgium and of Serbia, the atrocious régime imposed upon the invaded countries, the massacre of hundreds of thousands of inoffensive Armenians, the barbarities perpetrated against the populations of Syria, the raids of Zeppelins on open towns, the destruction by submarines of passenger steamers and of merchantmen even under neutral flags, the cruel treatment inflicted upon prisoners of war, the juridical murder of Miss Cavell and of Captain Fryatt, the deportation and the reduction to slavery of civil populations, etc.? The execution of such a series of crimes perpetrated without any regard for universal reprobation fully explains to President Wilson the protest of the Allies.

They consider that the note which they sent to the United States in reply to the German note, will be a response to the questions put by the American government and, according to the exact words of the latter, constitute "a public declaration as to the conditions upon which the war could be terminated."

President Wilson desires more. He desires that the belligerent Powers openly affirm the objects which they seek by continuing the war. The Allies experience no difficulty in replying to this request. Their objects in the war are well known. They have been formulated on many occasions by the chiefs of their divers governments. Their objects in the war will not be made known in detail with all the equitable compensations and indemnities for damages suffered until the hour of negotiations.

But the civilized world knows that they imply in all necessity and in the first instance the restoration of Belgium, of Serbia and of Montenegro and the indemnities which are due them. The evacuation of the invaded territories of France, of Russia and of Rumania, with just reparation; the reorganization of Europe guaranteed by a stable régime and founded as much upon respect of nationalities and full security and liberty of economic development, which all nations, great or small, possess, as upon territorial conventions and international agreements suitable to guarantee territorial and maritime frontiers against unjustified attacks. The restitution of provinces or territories wrested in the past from the Allies by force or against the will of their populations, the liberation of Italians, of Slavs, of Rumanians and of Tcheco Slovaques from foreign domination. The enfranchisement of populations subject to the bloody tyranny of the Turks; the expulsion from Europe of the Ottoman Empire, which has proved itself so radically alien to western civilization.

The intentions of His Majesty the Emperor of Russia regarding Poland have been clearly indicated in the proclamation which he has just addressed to his armies.

It goes without saying that if the Allies wish to liberate Europe from the brutal covetousness of Prussian militarism, it never has been their design, as has been alleged, to encompass the extermination of the German peoples and their political disappearance. That which they desire above all is to insure a peace upon the principles of liberty and justice, upon the invincible fidelity to international obligation with which the government of the United States has never ceased to be inspired.

United in the pursuits of this supreme object the Allies are determined, individually and collectively, to act with all their power and to consent to all sacrifices to bring to a victorious close the conflict upon which they are convinced not only their own safety and prosperity depend, but also the future of civilization itself.

THE BELGIAN NOTE.

The translation of the Belgian note, which was handed to Mr. Sharp with the Entente reply, follows:

The Government of the King, which has associated itself with the answer handed by the President of the French Council to the American Ambassador on behalf of all, is particularly desirous of paying tribute to the sentiment of humanity which prompted the President of the United States to send his note to the belligerent powers, and it highly esteems the friendship expressed for Belgium through his kindly intermediation. It desires as much as Mr. Woodrow Wilson to see the present war ended as early as possible.

But the President seems to believe that the statesmen of the two opposing camps pursue the same objects of war. The example of Belgium unfortunately demonstrates that this is in no wise the fact. Belgium has never, like the Central Powers, aimed at conquests. The barbarous fashion in which the German government has treated, and is still treating, the Belgian nation, does not permit the supposition that Germany will preoccupy herself with guaranteeing in the future the rights of the weak nations which she has not ceased to trample under foot since the war, let loose by her, began to desolate Europe.

On the other hand, the Government of the King has noted with pleasure and with confidence the assurances that the United States is impatient to co-operate in the measures which will be taken after the conclusion of peace to protect and guarantee the small nations against violence and oppression.

Previous to the German ultimatum Belgian only aspired to live upon good terms with all her neighbors. She practiced with scrupulous loyalty toward each one of them the duties imposed by her neutrality. In the same manner she has been rewarded by Germany for the confidence she placed in her, but from one day to the other, without any plausible reason, her neutrality was violated, and the Chancellor of the Empire when announcing to the Reichstag this violation of right and of treaties was obliged to recognize the iniquity of such an act and predetermine that it would be repaired.

But the Germans, after the occupation of Belgian territory, have displayed no better observance of the rules of international law or the stipulations of The Hague convention. They have, by taxation, as heavy as it is arbitrary, drained the resources of the country. They have intentionally ruined its industries, destroyed whole cities, put to death and imprisoned a considerable number of inhabitants. Even now, while they are loudly proclaiming their desire to put an end to the horrors of war, they increase the rigors of the occupation by deporting into servitude Belgian workers by the thousands.

If there is a country which has the right to say that it has taken up arms to defend its existence it is assuredly Belgium. Compelled to fight or to submit to shame, she passionately desires that an end be brought to the unprecedented sufferings of her population. But she could only accept a peace which would assure her, as well as equitable reparation, security and guarantees for the future.

These facts, entirely to the honor of the American nation, allow the Government of the King to entertain the legitimate hope that at the time of the definite settlement of this long war the voice of the Entente Powers will find in the United States a unanimous echo to claim in favor of the Belgian nation, innocent victim of German ambition and covetousness, the rank and the place which its irreproachable past, the valor of its soldiers, its fidelity to honor and its remarkable faculties for work assign to it among the civilized nations.

GERMANY'S REPLY TO THE CHARGES MADE BY THE ENTENTE ALLIES IN REFUSING TO CONSIDER OVERTURES FOR A CONFERENCE TO END THE WAR.

The same day (January 11, 1917) that the Entente Allies' reply to President Wilson was cabled from Paris Germany handed to neutral governments a note concerning the reply of the Entente to the German peace proposals.

It is first stated, that the German Government has received the reply of the Entente to the note of December 12, containing a proposal to enter at once upon peace negotiations. The note then continues:

Our adversaries declined this proposition, giving as the reason that it is a proposition without sincerity and without importance. The form in which they clothe their communication excludes an answer to them, but the Imperial Government considers it important to indicate to the governments of neutral powers its opinion regarding the situation.

The Central Powers have no reason to enter into any discussion regarding the origin of the world war. History will judge upon whom the immense guilt of the war shall fall. History's verdict will as little pass over the encircling policy of England, the revengeful policy of France and the endeavor of Russia to gain Constantinople as over the instigation of the Serbian assassination in Sarajevo and the complete mobilization of Russia, which meant war against Germany.

Germany and her allies, who had to take up arms for defense of their liberty and their existence, consider this, their aim of war, as obtained.

On the other hand, the hostile Powers always went further away from the realization of their plans, which, according to the declarations of their responsible statesman, were, among others, directed toward the conquest of Alsace-Lorraine and several Prussian provinces, the humiliation and diminution of the Austro-Hungarian monarchy, the partition of Turkey and the mutilation of Bulgaria.

In the face of such war aims, the demand for restitution, reparation and guarantee in the mouth of our adversaries produces a surprising effect.

Our adversaries call the proposal of the four allied (Teutonic) Powers a war manoeuvre. Germany and her allies must protest in the most energetic fashion against such a characterization of their motives, which were frankly explained. They were persuaded that a peace which was just and acceptable to all the belligerents was possible, that it could be brought about by an immediate, spoken exchange of views and that, therefore, the responsibility for further bloodshed could not be taken.

Their readiness was affirmed without reservation to make known their peace conditions when negotiations were entered into, which refutes every doubt as to their sincerity.

Our adversaries, who had it in their hands to examine the proposition as to its contents, neither attempted an examination nor made counter-proposals. Instead, they declared that peace was impossible so long as the re-establishment of violated rights and liberties, the recognition of the principle of nationalities and the free existence of small states were not guaranteed.

The sincerity, which our adversary denies to the proposals of the four allied Powers, will not be conceded by the world to these demands, if the world holds before its eyes the fate of the Irish people, the destruction of the liberty and independence of the Boer Republic, the subjugation of Northern Africa by England, France and Italy, the suppression of Russian alien nations, and also the violation of Greece, which is without precedent in history.

Against the pretended violations of the laws of nations by the four allies (Teutonic), those Powers are not entitled to complain, which from the beginning of the war trampled on justice and tore to pieces the treaties upon which it is built. England already, during the first weeks of the war, repudiated the London Declaration, the contents of which had been recognized by its own delegates as a valid law of nations, and in the further course of the war violated in the most severe fashion, also the Paris Declaration; so that, by her arbitrary measures for warfare, a condition of lawlessness has been created.

The war of starvation against Germany and the pressure exercised in England's interest against neutrals are not less scandalously conflicting with the rules of the laws of nations as with the commands of humanity.

Likewise contrary to the laws of nations and incompatible with the usages of civilization are the use of colored troops in Europe and the extension of the war into Africa, which was done by a breach of existing treaties and which undermines the prestige of the white race on that continent. The barbarous treatment of prisoners, especially in Africa and Russia, and the deportation of the civilian population from Eastern Prussia, Alsace-Lorraine, Galicia and Bukowina are further proof of how our adversaries respect justice and civilization.

At the end of their note of December 30 our adversaries mention the special situation of Belgium. The Imperial Government is unable to acknowledge that the Belgian Government has always observed the duties which were enjoined upon her by her neutrality. Already before the war Belgium, under England's influence, sought support in military fashion from England and France, and thus herself violated the spirit (of the treaty) which she had to guarantee her independence and neutrality.

Twice the Imperial Government declared to the Belgian Government that it did not come as an enemy to Belgium and asked it to spare to the country the terrors of war. Germany offered to guarantee the integrity and independence of the kingdom to the full extent and compensate for all damages which might be caused by the passage of the German troops. It is known that the Royal British Government in 1887 was resolved not to oppose the use of the right of way through Belgium under those conditions.

The Belgian Government declined the repeated offer of the Imperial Government. Upon her and those Powers which instigated her to this attitude falls the responsibility for the fate which befell Belgium.

The accusations about the German warfare in Belgium and the measures taken there in the interest of military safety have been repeatedly refuted by the Imperial Government as untrue. Germany again offers energetic protest against these calumnies.

Germany and her allies have made an honest attempt to terminate the war and open the road for an understanding among the belligerents. The Imperial Government asserts the fact that it merely depended upon the decision of our adversaries whether the road toward peace should be entered upon or not. The hostile governments declined to accept this road. Upon them falls the full responsibility for the continuation of the bloodshed.

Our allied Powers, however, shall continue the struggle in quiet confidence and with firm trust in their right until peace is gained which guarantees to their nations honor, existence and liberty of development, and which to all the nations of the European Continent gives the blessing to co-operate in mutual respect and under equal rights together for the solution of the great problems of civilization.

PEACE WITHOUT VICTORY

[Address Before the Senate Proposing a Policy of International Alliance for the Preservation of Peace and the Racial Autonomy of Nations. Delivered January 22, 1917.]

To the Senate of the United States:

GENTLEMEN OF THE SENATE: On the eighteenth of December last I addressed an identic note to the governments of the nations now at war requesting them to state, more definitely than they had yet been stated by either group of belligerents, the terms upon which they would deem it possible to make peace. I spoke on behalf of humanity and of the rights of all neutral nations like our own, many of whose most vital interests the war puts in constant jeopardy. The Central Powers united in a reply which stated merely that they were ready to meet their antagonists in conference to discuss terms of peace. The Entente Powers have replied much more definitely and have stated, in general terms, indeed, but with sufficient definiteness to imply details, the arrangements, guarantees, and acts of reparation which they deem to be the indispensable conditions of a satisfactory settlement. We are that much nearer a definite discussion of the peace which shall end the present war. We are that much nearer the discussion of the international concert which must thereafter hold the world at peace. In every discussion of the peace that must end this war it is taken for granted that that peace must be followed by some definite concert of power which will make it virtually impossible that any such catastrophe should ever overwhelm us again. Every lover of mankind, every sane and thoughtful man must take that for granted.

I have sought this opportunity to address you because I thought that I owed it to you, as the council associated with me in the final determination of our international obligations, to disclose to you without reserve the thought and purpose that have been taking form in my mind in regard to the duty of our Government in the days to come when it will be necessary to lay afresh and upon a new plan the foundations of peace among the nations.

It is inconceivable that the people of the United States should play no part in that great enterprise. To take part in such a service will be the opportunity for which they have sought to prepare themselves by the very principles and purposes of their polity and the approved practices of their Government ever since the days when they set up a new nation in the high and honourable hope that it might in all that it was and did show mankind the way to liberty. They cannot in honour withhold the service to which they are now about to be challenged. They do not wish to withhold it. But they owe it to themselves and to the other nations of the world to state the conditions under which they will feel free to render it.

That service is nothing less than this, to add their authority and their power to the authority and force of other nations to guarantee peace and justice throughout the world. Such a settlement cannot now be long postponed. It is right that before it comes this Government should frankly formulate the conditions upon which it would feel justified in asking our people to approve its formal and solemn adherence to a League for Peace. I am here to attempt to state those conditions.

The present war must first be ended; but we owe it to candour and to a just regard for the opinion of mankind to say that, so far as our participation in guarantees of future peace is concerned, it makes a great deal of difference in what way and upon what terms it is ended. The treaties and agreements which bring it to an end must embody terms which will create a peace that is worth guaranteeing and preserving, a peace that will win the approval of mankind, not merely a peace that will serve the several interests and immediate aims of the nations engaged. We shall have no voice in determining what those terms shall be, but we shall, I feel sure, have a voice in determining whether they shall be made lasting or not by the guarantees of a universal covenant; and our judgment upon what is fundamental and essential as a condition precedent to permanency should be spoken now, not afterwards when it may be too late.

No covenant of co-operative peace that does not include the peoples of the New World can suffice to keep the future safe against war; and yet there is only one sort of peace that the peoples of America could join in guaranteeing. The elements of that peace must be elements that engage the confidence and satisfy the principles of the American governments, elements consistent with their political faith and with the practical convictions which the peoples of America have once for all embraced and undertaken to defend.

I do not mean to say that any American government would throw any obstacle in the way of any terms of peace the governments now at war might agree upon, or seek to upset them when made, whatever they might be. I only take it for granted that mere terms of peace between the belligerents will not satisfy even the belligerents themselves. Mere agreements may not make peace secure. It will be absolutely necessary that a force be created as a guarantor of the permanency of the settlement so much greater than the force of any nation now engaged or any alliance hitherto formed or projected that no nation, no probable combination of nations could face or withstand it. If the peace presently to be made is to endure, it must be a peace made secure by the organized major force of mankind.

The terms of the immediate peace agreed upon will determine whether it is a peace for which such a guarantee can be secured. The question upon which the whole future peace and policy of the world depends is this: Is the present war a struggle for a just and secure peace, or only for a new balance of power? If it be only a struggle for a new balance of power, who will guarantee, who can guarantee, the stable equilibrium of the new arrangement? Only a tranquil Europe can be a stable Europe. There must be, not a balance of power, but a community of power; not organized rivalries, but an organized common peace.

Fortunately we have received very explicit assurances on this point. The statesmen of both of the groups of nations now arrayed against one another have said, in terms that could not be misinterpreted, that it was no part of the purpose they had in mind to crush their antagonists. But the implications of these assurances may not be equally clear to all,—may not be the same on both sides of the water. I think them to be.

They imply, first of all, that it must be a peace without victory. It is not pleasant to say this. I beg that I may be permitted to put my own interpretation upon it and that it may be understood that no other interpretation was in my thought. I am seeking only to face realities and to face them without soft concealments. Victory would mean peace forced upon the loser, a victor's terms imposed upon the vanquished. It would be accepted in humiliation, under duress, at an intolerable sacrifice, and would leave a sting, a resentment, a bitter memory upon which terms of peace would rest, not permanently, but only as upon quicksand. Only a peace between equals can last. Only a peace the very principle of which is equality and a common participation in a common benefit. The right state of mind, the right feeling between nations, is as necessary for a lasting peace as is the just settlement of vexed questions of territory or of racial and national allegiance.

The equality of nations upon which peace must be founded if it is to last must be an equality of rights; the guarantees exchanged must neither recognize nor imply a difference between big nations and small, between those that are powerful and those that are weak. Right must be based upon the common strength, not upon the individual strength, of the nations upon whose concert peace will depend. Equality of territory or of resources there of course cannot be; nor any other sort of equality not gained in the ordinary peaceful and legitimate development of the peoples themselves. But no one asks or expects anything more than an equality of rights. Mankind is looking now for freedom of life, not for equipoises of power.

And there is a deeper thing involved than even equality of right among organized nations. No peace can last, or ought to last, which does not recognize and accept the principle that governments derive all their just powers from the consent of the governed, and that no right anywhere exists to hand peoples about from sovereignty to sovereignty as if they were property. I take it for granted, for instance, if I may venture upon a single example, that statesmen everywhere are agreed that there should be a united, independent, and autonomous Poland, and that henceforth inviolable security of life, of worship, and of industrial and social development should be guaranteed to all peoples who have lived hitherto under the power of governments devoted to a faith and purpose hostile to their own.

I speak of this, not because of any desire to exalt an abstract political principle which has always been held very dear by those who have sought to build up liberty in America, but for the same reason that I have spoken of the other conditions of peace which seem to me clearly indispensable,—because I wish frankly to uncover realities. Any peace which does not recognize and accept this principle will inevitably be upset. It will not rest upon the affections or the convictions of mankind. The ferment of spirit of whole populations will fight subtly and constantly against it, and all the world will sympathize. The world can be at peace only if its life is stable, and there can be no stability where the will is in rebellion, where there is not tranquility of spirit and a sense of justice, of freedom, and of right.

So far as practicable, moreover, every great people now struggling towards a full development of its resources and of its powers should be assured a direct outlet to the great highways of the sea. Where this cannot be done by the cession of territory, it can no doubt be done by the neutralization of direct rights of way under the general guarantee which will assure the peace itself. With a right comity of arrangement no nation need be shut away from free access to the open paths of the world's commerce.

And the paths of the sea must alike in law and in fact be free. The freedom of the seas is the *sine qua non* of peace, equality, and co-operation. No doubt a somewhat radical reconsideration of many of the rules of international practice hitherto thought to be established may be necessary in order to make the seas indeed free and common in practically all circumstances for the use of mankind, but the motive for such changes is convincing and compelling. There can be no trust or intimacy between the peoples of the world without them. The free, constant unthreatened intercourse of nations is an essential part of the process of peace and of development. It need not be difficult either to define or to secure the freedom of the seas if the governments of the world sincerely desire to come to an agreement concerning it.

It is a problem closely connected with the limitation of naval armaments and the co-operation of the navies of the world in keeping the seas at once free and safe. And the question of limiting naval armaments opens the wider and perhaps more difficult question of the limitation of armies and of all programmes of military preparation. Difficult and delicate as these questions are, they must be faced with the utmost candour and decided in a spirit of real accommodation if peace is to come with healing it its wings, and come to stay. Peace cannot be had without concession and sacrifice. There can be no sense of safety and equality among the nations if great preponderating armaments are henceforth to continue here and there to be built up and maintained. The statesmen of the world must plan for peace and nations must adjust and accommodate their policy to it as they have planned for war and made ready for pitiless contest and rivalry. The question of armaments, whether on land or sea, is the most immediately and intensely practical question connected with the future fortunes of nations and of mankind.

I have spoken upon these great matters without reserve and with the utmost explicitness because it has seemed to me to be necessary if the world's yearning desire for peace was anywhere to find free voice and utterance. Perhaps I am the only person in high authority amongst all the peoples of the world who is at liberty to speak and hold nothing back. I am speaking as an individual, and yet I am speaking also, of course, as the responsible head of a great government, and I feel confident that I have said what the people of the United States would wish me to say. May I not add that I hope and believe that I am in effect speaking for liberals and friends of humanity in every nation and of every programme of liberty? I would fain believe that I am speaking for the silent mass of mankind everywhere who have as yet had no place or opportunity to speak their real hearts out concerning the death and ruin they see to have come already upon the persons and the homes they hold most dear.

And in holding out the expectation that the people and Government of the United States will join the other civilized nations of the world in guaranteeing the permanence of peace upon such terms as I have named I speak with the greater boldness and confidence because it is clear to every man who can think that there is in this promise no breach in either our traditions or our policy as a nation, but a fulfilment, rather, of all that we have professed or striven for.

I am proposing, as it were, that the nations should with one accord adopt the doctrine of President Monroe as the doctrine of the world: that no nation should seek to extend its policy over any other nation or people, but that every people should be left free to determine its own polity, its own way of development, unhindered, unthreatened, unafraid, the little along with the great and powerful.

I am proposing that all nations henceforth avoid entangling alliances which would draw them into competitions of power, catch them in a net of intrigue and selfish rivalry, and disturb their own affairs with influences intruded from without. There is no entangling alliance in a concert of power. When all unite to act in the same sense and with the same purpose all act in the common interest and are free to live their own lives under a common protection.

I am proposing government by the consent of the governed; that freedom of the seas which in international conference after conference representatives of the United States have urged with the eloquence of those who are the convinced disciples of liberty; and that moderation of armaments which makes of armies and navies a power for order merely, not an instrument of aggression or of selfish violence.

These are American principles, American policies. We could stand for no others. And they are also the principles and policies of forward looking men and women everywhere, of every modern nation, of every enlightened community. They are the principles of mankind and must prevail.

NOTE HANDED TO SECRETARY OF STATE LANSING, FEBRUARY 1, 1917, BY THE GERMAN AMBASSADOR, COUNT VON BERNSTORFF, AFTER THE FAILURE OF PEACE PROPOSALS.

Mr. Secretary of State:

Your Excellency was good enough to transmit to the Imperial Government a copy of the message which the President of the United States of America addressed to the Senate on the 22d inst.

The Imperial Government has given it the earnest consideration which the President's statements deserve, inspired, as they are, by a deep sentiment of responsibility.

It is highly gratifying to the Imperial Government to ascertain that the main tendencies of this important statement correspond largely to the desires and principles professed by Germany. These principles especially include self-government and equality of rights for all nations.

Germany would be sincerely glad if in recognition of this principle countries like Ireland and India, which do not enjoy the benefits of political independence, should now obtain their freedom.

The German people also repudiate all alliances which serve to force the countries into a competition for might and to involve them in a net of selfish intrigues. On the other hand, Germany will gladly co-operate in all efforts to prevent future wars.

The freedom of the seas, being a preliminary condition of the free existence of nations and the peaceful intercourse between them, as well as the open door for the commerce of all nations, has always formed part of the leading principles of Germany's political programme.

All the more the Imperial Government regrets that the attitude of her enemies, who are so entirely opposed to peace, makes it impossible for the world at present to bring about the realization of these lofty ideals.

Germany and her allies were ready to enter now into a discussion of peace, and had set down as basis the guaranty of existence, honor and free development of their peoples. Their aims, as has been expressly stated in the note of December 12, 1916, were not directed toward the destruction or annihilation of their enemies, and were, according to their conviction, perfectly compatible with the rights of the other nations.

As to Belgium, for which such warm and cordial sympathy is felt in the United States, the Chancellor had declared only a few weeks previously that its annexation had never formed part of Germany's intentions. The peace to be signed with Belgium was to provide for such conditions in that country, with which Germany desires to maintain friendly neighborly relations, that Belgium should not be used again by Germany's enemies for the purpose of instigating continuous hostile intrigues.

Such precautionary measures are all the more necessary, as Germany's enemies have repeatedly stated not only in speeches delivered by their leading men, but also in the statutes of the economical conference in Paris, that it is their intention not to treat Germany as an equal, even after peace has been restored, but to continue their hostile attitude and especially to wage a systematical economic war against her.

The attempt of the four allied powers to bring about peace has failed owing to the lust of conquest of their enemies, who desired to dictate the conditions of peace. Under the pretense of following the principle of nationality our enemies have disclosed their real aims in this way, viz.: To dismember and dishonor Germany, Austria-Hungary, Turkey and Bulgaria. To the wish of reconciliation they oppose the will of destruction. They desire a fight to the bitter end.

A new situation has thus been created which forces Germany to new decisions. Since two years and a half England is using her naval power for a criminal attempt to force Germany into submission by starvation. In brutal contempt of international law the group of powers led by England does not only curtail the legitimate trade of their opponents, but they also, by ruthless pressure, compel neutral countries either to altogether forego every trade not agreeable to the Entente Powers or to limit it according to their arbitrary decrees. The American Government knows the steps which have been taken to cause England and her allies to return to the rules of international law and to respect the freedom of the seas.

The English Government, however, insists upon continuing its war of starvation, which does not at all affect the military power of its opponents, but compels women and children, the sick and the aged, to suffer for their country pains and privations which endanger the vitality of the nation. Thus British tyranny mercilessly increases the sufferings of the world, indifferent to the laws of humanity, indifferent to the protests of the neutrals whom they severely harm, indifferent even to the silent longing for peace among England's own allies. Each day of the terrible struggle causes new destruction, new sufferings. Each day shortening the war will, on both sides, preserve the life of thousands of brave soldiers and be a benefit to mankind.

The Imperial Government could not justify before its own conscience, before the German people and before history the neglect of any means destined to bring about the end of the war. Like the President of the United States, the Imperial Government had hoped to reach this goal by negotiations. After the attempts to come to an understanding with the Entente Powers have been answered by the latter with the announcement of an intensified continuation of the war, the Imperial Government—in order to serve the welfare of mankind in a higher sense and not to wrong its own people—is now compelled to continue the fight for existence, again forced upon it, with the full employment of all the weapons which are at its disposal.

Sincerely trusting that the people and the Government of the United States will understand the motives for this decision and its necessity, the Imperial Government hopes that the United States may view the new situation from the lofty heights of impartiality and assist, on their part, to prevent further misery and unavoidable sacrifice of human life.

Enclosing two memoranda regarding the details of the contemplated military measures at sea, I remain, etc.,   [Signed]   J. BERNSTORFF.

MEMORANDA ANNEXED.

From February 1, 1917, within barred zones around Great Britain, France, Italy and in the Eastern Mediterranean, as outlined in the following, all sea traffic forthwith will be opposed. Such barred zones are:

In the North Sea, the district around England and France which is limited by a line twenty nautical miles; the district along the Dutch coast as far as the Terschelling lightship, the degree of longitude of the Terschelling lightship to Udir; a line from there across the point 62 degrees north latitude, 5 longitude, westward along 62 degrees to a point three nautical miles south of the south point of Farover (Faroe Islands?), from there across the point 62 degrees north, — degrees west, to 61 degrees north, 15 degrees west; then 57 degrees north, 20 degrees west, to 47 degrees north, 20 degrees west; further, to 43 degrees north, 15 degrees west; then on degree latitude 43 degrees north to the point twenty nautical miles from Cape Finisterre and twenty nautical miles distance along the Spanish north coast as far as the French frontier.

Concerning the south, in the Mediterranean—For neutral shipping there remains open the sea district west of a line from Point de les Paquett to 38 degrees 20 minutes north and 6 degrees east, as well as north and west of a zone sixty sea miles broad along the North African coast, beginning on (?) degrees west longitude.

In order to connect this sea district with Greece, the zone leads twenty sea miles in width north or east, following this line: 38 degrees north and 6 degrees east, 38 degrees north and 11 degrees 30 minutes east to 34 degrees north and 11 degrees 30 minutes east to 34 degrees north and 22 degrees 30 minutes east. From there it leads to a zone twenty sea miles broad west of 22 degrees 30 minutes east longitude into Greek territorial waters.

Neutral ships plying within the barred zones do so at their own risk. Although precautions are being taken to spare neutral ships which on February 1 are on the way to ports in the barred zone, during an appropriate delay, yet it is urgently to be advised that they should be warned and directed to other routes by all means available.

Neutral ships lying in ports of the barred zones can with the same safety abandon the barred zones if they sail before February 5 and take the shortest route into the open district.

Traffic of regular American passenger steamers can go on unmolested if:

A.—Falmouth is taken as the port of destination, and if

B.—On the going and return journey the Scilly Islands, as well as the point 50 degrees north, 20 degrees west, be steered on. Along this route no German mines will be laid.

C.—If steamers on this journey bear the following special signals, which only they will be permitted to display in American ports: A coating of paint on the ship's hull and the superstructure in vertical stripes three metres broad, alternating white and red; on every mast a large flag of checkered white and red, on the stern the American national flag; during darkness the national flag and the coat of paint to be as easily recognizable as possible from a distance, and the ships must be completely and brightly illuminated.

D.—If only one steamer runs each week in each direction, arriving at Falmouth on Sundays, leaving Falmouth on Wednesdays.

E.—If guarantees and assurances are given by the American Government that these steamers carry no contraband (according to the German list of contraband).

Two copies of maps on which the barred zones are outlined are added.

DIPLOMATIC RELATIONS WITH GERMANY SEVERED

[Address Delivered by President Wilson at a Joint Session of the Two Houses of Congress, February 3, 1917.]

GENTLEMEN OF THE CONGRESS:

The Imperial German Government on the thirty-first of January announced to this Government and to the governments of the other neutral nations that on and after the first day of February, the present month, it would adopt a policy with regard to the use of submarines against all shipping seeking to pass through certain designated areas of the high seas, to which it is clearly my duty to call your attention.

Let me remind the Congress that on the eighteenth of April last, in view of the sinking on the twenty-fourth of March the cross-Channel passenger steamer Sussex by a German submarine, without summons or warning, and the consequent loss of the lives of several citizens of the United States who were passengers aboard her, this Government addressed a note to the Imperial German Government in which it made the following declaration:

"If it is still the purpose of the Imperial Government to prosecute relentless and indiscriminate warfare against vessels of commerce by the use of submarines, without regard to what the Government of the United States must consider the sacred and indisputable rules of international law and the universally recognized dictates of humanity, the Government of the United States is at last forced to the conclusion that there is but one course it can pursue.

"Unless the Imperial Government should now immediately declare and effect an abandonment of its present methods of submarine warfare against passenger and freight carrying vessels, the Government of the United States can have no choice but to sever diplomatic relations with the German Empire altogether."

In reply to this declaration the Imperial German Government gave this Government the following assurance:

"The German Government is prepared to do its utmost to confine the operations of war for the rest of its duration to the fighting forces of the belligerents, thereby also insuring the freedom of the seas, a principle upon which the German Government believes, now as before, to be in agreement with the Government of the United States.

"The German Government, guided by this idea, notifies the Government of the United States that the German naval forces have received the following orders: In accordance with the general principles of visit and search and destruction of merchant vessels recognized by international law, such vessels, both within and without the area declared as naval war zone, shall not be sunk without saving human lives, unless these ships attempt to escape or offer resistance.

"But," it added, "neutrals cannot expect that Germany, forced to fight for her existence, shall, for the sake of neutral interest, restrict the use of an effective weapon if her enemy is permitted to continue to apply at will methods of warfare violating the rules of international law. Such a demand would be incompatible with the character of neutrality, and the German Government is convinced that the Government of the United States does not think of making such a demand, knowing that the Government of the United States has repeatedly declared that it is determined to restore the principle of the freedom of the seas from whatever quarter it has been violated."

To this the Government of the United States replied on the 8th of May, accepting, of course, the assurances given, but adding:

"The Government of the United States feels it necessary to state that it takes it for granted that the Imperial German Government does not intend to imply that the maintenance of its newly announced policy is in any way contingent upon the course or result of diplomatic negotiations between the Government of the United States and other belligerent governments, notwithstanding the fact that certain passages in the Imperial Government's note of the fourth instant might appear to be susceptible of that construction.

"In order, however, to avoid any possible misunderstanding, the Government of the United States notifies the Imperial Government that it cannot for a moment entertain, much less discuss, a suggestion that respect by German naval authorities for the rights of citizens of the United States upon the high seas should in any way or in the slightest degree be made contingent upon the conduct of any other Government affecting the rights of neutrals and non-combatants. Responsibility in such matters is single, not joint; absolute, not relative."

To this note of the eighth of May the Imperial German Government made no reply.

On the thirty-first of January, the Wednesday of the present week, the German Ambassador handed to the Secretary of State, along with a formal note, a memorandum which contains the following statement:

"The Imperial Government, therefore, does not doubt that the Government of the United States will understand the situation thus forced upon Germany by the Entente allies' brutal methods of war and by their determination to destroy the Central Powers, and that the Government of the United States will further realize that the now openly disclosed intentions of the Entente allies give back to Germany the freedom of action which she reserved in her note addressed to the Government of the United States on May 4, 1916.

"Under these circumstances Germany will meet the illegal measures of her enemies by forcibly preventing after February 1, 1917, in a zone around Great Britain, France, Italy and in the Eastern Mediterranean, all navigation, that of neutrals included, from and to England and from and to France, etc., etc. All ships met within the zone will be sunk."

I think that you will agree with me that, in view of this declaration, which suddenly and without prior intimation of any kind deliberately withdraws the solemn assurance given in the Imperial Government's note of the fourth of May, 1916, this Government has no alternative consistent with the dignity and honor of the United States but to take the course which, in its note of the eighteenth of April, 1916, it announced that it would take in the event that the German Government did not declare and effect an abandonment of the methods of submarine warfare which it was then employing and to which it now purposes again to resort.

I have, therefore, directed the Secretary of State to announce to His Excellency the German Ambassador that all diplomatic relations between the United States and the German Empire are severed and that the American Ambassador at Berlin will immediately be withdrawn and, in accordance with this decision, to hand to His Excellency his passports.

Notwithstanding this unexpected action of the German Government, this sudden and deeply deplorable renunciation of its assurances, given this Government at one of the most critical moments of tension in the relations of the two Governments, I refuse to believe that it is the intention of the German authorities to do in fact what they have warned us they will feel at liberty to do.

I cannot bring myself to believe that they will indeed pay no regard to the ancient friendship between their people and our own or to the solemn obligations which have been exchanged between them and destroy American ships and take the lives of American citizens in the willful prosecution of the ruthless naval programme they have announced their intention to adopt.

Only actual overt acts on their part can make me believe it even now.

If this inveterate confidence on my part in the sobriety and prudent foresight of their purpose should unhappily prove unfounded; if American ships and American lives should, in fact, be sacrificed by their naval commanders in heedless contravention of the just and reasonable understandings of international law and the obvious dictates of humanity, I shall take the liberty of coming again before the Congress, to ask that authority be given me to use any means that may be necessary for the protection of our seamen and our people in the prosecution of their peaceful and legitimate errands on the high seas. I can do nothing less. I take it for granted that all neutral governments will take the same course.

We do not desire any hostile conflict with the Imperial German Government. We are the sincere friends of the German people and earnestly desire to remain at peace with the Government which speaks for them.

We shall not believe that they are hostile to us unless and until we are obliged to believe it; and we purpose nothing more than the reasonable defense of the undoubted rights of our people. We wish to serve no selfish ends. We seek merely to stand true alike in thought and in action to the immemorial principles of our people, which I sought to express in my address to the Senate only two weeks ago—seek merely to vindicate our rights to liberty and justice and an unmolested life. These are the bases of peace, not war.

God grant we may not be challenged to defend them by acts of willful injustice on the part of the Government of Germany.

[Asking Congress for Authority to Supply Merchant Ships with Defensive Arms, February 26, 1917.]

GENTLEMEN OF THE CONGRESS:

I have again asked the privilege of addressing you because we are moving through critical times during which it seems to me to be my duty to keep in close touch with the Houses of Congress, so that neither counsel nor action shall run at cross purposes between us.

On the third of February I officially informed you of the sudden and unexpected action of the Imperial German Government in declaring its intention to disregard the promises it had made to this Government in April last and undertake immediate submarine operations against all commerce, whether of belligerents or of neutrals, that should seek to approach Great Britain and Ireland, the Atlantic coasts of Europe, or the harbors of the eastern Mediterranean, and to conduct these operations without regard to the established restrictions of international practice, without regard to any considerations of humanity even which might interfere with their object. That policy was forthwith put in practice. It has now been in active execution for nearly four weeks.

Its practical results are not yet fully disclosed. The commerce of other neutral nations is suffering severely, but not, perhaps, very much more severely than it was already suffering before the first of February, when the new policy of the Imperial Government was put into operation. We have asked the cooperation of the other neutral governments to prevent these depredations, but so far none of them has thought it wise to join us in any common course of action. Our own commerce has suffered, is suffering, rather in apprehension than in fact, rather because so many of our ships are timidly keeping to their home ports than because American ships have been sunk.

Two American vessels have been sunk, the Housatonic and the Lyman M. Law. The case of the Housatonic, which was carrying foodstuffs consigned to a London firm, was essentially like the case of the Fry, in which, it will be recalled, the German Government admitted its liability for damages, and the lives of the crew, as in the case of the Fry, were safeguarded with reasonable care. The case of the Law, which was carrying lemon-box staves to Palermo, disclosed a ruthlessness of method which deserves grave condemnation, but was accompanied by no circumstances which might not have been expected at any time in connection with the use of the submarine against merchantmen as the German Government has used it.

In sum, therefore, the situation we find ourselves in with regard to the actual conduct of the German submarine warfare against commerce and its effects upon our own ships and people is substantially the same that it was when I addressed you on the third of February, except for the tying up of our shipping in our own ports because of the unwillingness of our shipowners to risk their vessels at sea without insurance or adequate protection, and the very serious congestion of our commerce which has resulted, a congestion which is growing rapidly more and more serious every day. This in itself might presently accomplish, in effect, what the new German submarine orders were meant to accomplish, so far as we are concerned. We can only say, therefore, that the overt act which I have ventured to hope the German commanders would in fact avoid has not occurred.

But, while this is happily true, it must be admitted that there have been certain additional indications and expressions of purpose on the part of the German press and the German authorities which have increased rather than lessened the impression that, if our ships and our people are spared, it will be because of fortunate circumstances or because the commanders of the German submarines which they may happen to encounter exercise an unexpected discretion and restraint rather than because of the instructions under which those commanders are acting. It would be foolish to deny that the situation is fraught with the gravest possibilities and dangers. No thoughtful man can fail to see that the necessity for definite action may come at any time, if we are in fact, and not in word merely, to defend our elementary rights as a neutral nation. It would be most imprudent to be unprepared.

I cannot in such circumstances be unmindful of the fact that the expiration of the term of the present Congress is immediately at hand, by constitutional limitation; and that it would in all likelihood require an unusual length of time to assemble and organize the Congress which is to succeed it. I feel that I ought, in view of that fact, to obtain from you full and immediate assurance of the authority which I may need at any moment to exercise. No doubt I already possess that authority without special warrant of law, by the plain implication of my constitutional duties and powers; but I prefer, in the present circumstances, not to act upon general implication. I wish to feel that the authority and the power of the Congress are behind me in whatever it may become necessary for me to do. We are jointly the servants of the people and must act together and in their spirit, so far as we can divine and interpret it.

No one doubts what it is our duty to do. We must defend our commerce and the lives of our people in the midst of the present trying circumstances, with discretion but with clear and steadfast purpose. Only the method and the extent remain to be chosen, upon the occasion, if occasion should indeed arise. Since it has unhappily proved impossible to safeguard our neutral rights by diplomatic means against the unwarranted infringements they are suffering at the hands of Germany, there may be no recourse but to *armed* neutrality, which we shall know how to maintain and for which there is abundant American precedent.

It is devoutly to be hoped that it will not be necessary to put armed force anywhere into action. The American people do not desire it, and our desire is not different from theirs. I am sure that they will understand the spirit in which I am now acting, the purpose I hold nearest my heart and would wish to exhibit in everything I do. I am anxious that the people of the nations at war also should understand and not mistrust us. I hope that I need give no further proofs and assurances than I have already given throughout nearly three years of anxious patience that I am the friend of peace and mean to preserve it for America so long as I am able. I am not now proposing or contemplating war or any steps that need lead to it. I merely request that you will accord me by your own vote and definite bestowal the means and the authority to safeguard in practice the right of a great people who are at peace and who are desirous of exercising none but the rights of peace to follow the pursuits of peace in quietness and good will,—rights recognized time out of mind by all the civilized nations of the world. No course of my choosing or of theirs will lead to war. War can come only by the wilful acts and aggressions of others.

You will understand why I make no definite proposals or forecasts of action now and must ask for your supporting authority in the most general terms. The form in which action may become necessary cannot yet be foreseen. I believe that the people will be willing to trust me to act with restraint, with prudence, and in the true spirit of amity and good faith that they have themselves displayed throughout these trying months; and it is in that belief that I request that you will authorize me to supply our merchant ships with defensive arms, should that become necessary, and with the means of using them, and to employ any other instrumentalities or methods that may be necessary and adequate to protect our ships and our people in their legitimate and peaceful pursuits on the seas. I request also that you will grant me at the same time, along with the powers I ask, a sufficient credit to enable me to provide adequate means of protection where they are lacking, including adequate insurance against the present war risks.

I have spoken of our commerce and of the legitimate errands of our people on the seas, but you will not be misled as to my main thought, the thought that lies beneath these phrases and gives them dignity and weight. It is not of material interests merely that we are thinking. It is, rather, of fundamental human rights, chief of all the right of life itself. I am thinking, not only of the rights of Americans to go and come about their proper business by way of the sea, but also of something much deeper, much more fundamental than that. I am thinking of those rights of humanity without which there is no civilization. My theme is of those great principles of compassion and of protection which mankind has sought to throw about human lives, the lives of non-combatants, the lives of men who are peacefully at work keeping the industrial processes of the world quick and vital, the lives of women and children and of those who supply the labor which ministers to their sustenance. We are speaking of no selfish material rights but of rights which our hearts support and whose foundation is that righteous passion for justice upon which all law, all structures alike of family, of state, and of mankind must rest, as upon the ultimate base of our existence and our liberty. I cannot imagine any man with American principles at his heart hesitating to defend these things.

EXECUTIVE ORDERS

[Relating to the Exclusion of Chinese from the Panama Canal Zone.]

The White House, February 6, 1917.

By virtue of the authority vested in me by the provisions of the Act of Congress approved August 21, 1916, entitled "An Act extending certain privileges of Canal employees to other officials on the Canal Zone, and authorizing the President to make rules and regulations affecting the health, sanitation, quarantine, taxation, public roads, self-propelled vehicles and police powers on the Canal Zone, and for other purposes, including provision as to certain fees, money orders and interest deposits", I do hereby establish the following Executive Order for the Canal Zone:

Sec. 1. The Executive Order of January 9, 1908, extending to the Canal Zone Law No. 6 of 1904, of the Republic of Panama, is hereby repealed.

Sec. 2. No Chinese person shall be allowed to enter into or remain in the Canal Zone, except as provided in this order; and any Chinese person found in the Canal Zone in contravention of the provisions of this order, shall be punished as hereinafter prescribed.

Any Chinese person who shall come into the Canal Zone, with the intention of passing into the Republic of Panama, in contravention of the laws of the Republic of Panama, shall be deemed guilty of a violation of this section.

Sec. 3. The master of any vessel, who shall knowingly bring into the Canal Zone on such vessel and land, or attempt to land, or permit to be landed, any Chinese person, except as provided for in this order, shall be punished in the manner hereinafter prescribed, for each Chinese person so brought into and landed in the Canal Zone, or attempted or permitted to be landed therein; provided, however, that when a vessel, having Chinese persons on board, comes within the Canal Zone in distress, or under stress of weather, or when a vessel, having Chinese persons on board, touches at a port of the Canal Zone on its voyage to any foreign port or place, such Chinese persons may be permitted to land when authorized by the Governor of The Panama Canal, but they must depart from the Canal Zone with the vessel on its leaving the port.

Every person who aids or abets in the violation of this order shall be deemed equally guilty with the master of the vessel.

Sec. 4. The master of any vessel from a foreign port, with one or more Chinese persons on board, stopping at a port in the Canal Zone, in addition to the other matters required to be reported by him, shall deliver to the customs official of such Canal port, when he delivers his manifest of cargo, or if there be no cargo when he makes legal entry of his vessel, a descriptive list of all Chinese persons on board of his vessel at the time of its arrival in the Canal Zone. Such list shall contain the names of such Chinese persons, and other particulars regarding them, shown by the ship's papers, and shall be sworn to and subscribed by the master before the customs official to whom the list is delivered; and the customs official is hereby authorized to administer the oath to the master, provided, that when a vessel passes through the Canal, without discharging or taking on cargo or passengers therein, the master of such vessel shall not be required to furnish the list of persons prescribed by this section. If the master of the vessel refuses to deliver the list as required by this section, or fails or refuses to take and subscribe the oath prescribed herein; or if the master of such vessel permits any Chinese person on board the ship to land in the Canal Zone except by authority of the Governor of The Panama Canal, he shall be deemed guilty of a violation of this section.

Sec. 5. Chinese persons, arriving from foreign ports, who desire to enter the Canal Zone in transit to other countries, may be permitted to do so upon such conditions as the Governor of The Panama Canal may prescribe by general or special authorization.

Sec. 6. No Chinese member of the crew of any vessel shall be paid off and discharged within a port of the Canal Zone, without the consent of the Panama Canal authorities, unless it be shown by the ship's articles that said Chinese member of the crew signed said articles at a port in the Canal Zone; and seamen or other members of a ship's crew of the Chinese race, when discharged at any port in the Canal Zone under authority of the Governor, may land and remain temporarily therein until a re-shipment is obtained by them, provided a bond in the sum of $500.00 in each case, is executed by such Chinese person, satisfactory to the shipping commissioner, and payable to the Governor of The Panama Canal, and his successors in office, and conditioned that the principal in the bond, in good faith, will obtain a re-shipment and leave the Canal Zone at the earliest date practicable, to be fixed by the shipping commissioner; and said bond may be forfeited, for the full amount thereof, in favor of The Panama Canal, by judgment in the district court of the Canal Zone, should the principal in said bond fail to comply with any of the conditions thereof.

Sec. 7. This order shall not apply to diplomatic and consular agents of the Chinese government, who shall be entitled to be admitted into the Canal Zone upon proof of their official character; neither shall it apply to Chinese persons lawfully residing in the Canal Zone at the time of the promulgation of this order, but this shall not prevent their removal from the Canal Zone in accordance with the depopulation or deportation laws; neither shall this order apply to a Chinese person who is lawfully residing in the Republic of Panama at the time of the promulgation of this order, and such person shall be authorized to enter into and cross the Canal Zone in a like manner as is permitted to the residents of the Republic of Panama; neither shall this order apply to Chinese persons whose services have been contracted for by the United States, The Panama Canal, or Panama Railroad Company, or any of the auxiliaries of the Canal or the Railroad Company; nor to domestic servants and others employed by persons engaged in the service of the Army or Navy of the United States, stationed in the Canal Zone, when such employment is with the sanction of the respective commanding officers of such forces on the Isthmus; nor shall it apply to any Chinese person coming into the Canal Zone by authority of the Governor of The Panama Canal.

Sec. 8. The Governor of The Panama Canal is hereby authorized to establish rules and regulations to more effectively carry out this order.

Sec. 9. A violation of any of the provisions of this order shall be punished by a fine not to exceed $500.00 or imprisonment not to exceed one year, or both such fine and imprisonment, at the discretion of the court, in conformity with the above mentioned Act of Congress approved August 21, 1916.

Sec. 10. This order shall take effect sixty (60) days from and after its publication in the Panama Canal Record.

WOODROW WILSON.

[Naval Radio Stations for Alaska.]

The White House, February 20, 1917.

By virtue of the power and authority vested in and conferred upon me by the laws of the United States in that behalf made and provided, it is hereby ordered that the tract of land hereinafter described be and the same is hereby withdrawn from settlement, location, sale, entry, or other disposition, and reserved and set aside for the use of the U. S. Navy Department as a Naval Radio Station, namely:

Lots numbered 3 in section numbered 2, in T. 1 S., R. 1 W., containing 38.06 acres in Seward Principal Meridian, Alaska.

WOODROW WILSON.

The White House, February 21, 1917.

It is hereby ordered that all of the lands of the United States hereinafter described be, and the same are hereby, withdrawn from settlement, location, sale, or entry and reserved for the use of the Navy Department of the United States as a distant control receiving station, to be used in conjunction with naval radio station at Mile 31½, near Cordova, Alaska:

All lands of the United States within one-fourth of a mile of that point on the Copper River and Northwestern Railroad, Alaska, designated as Mile 7½, and located on the left side of the tracks of said railroad, traveling from Cordova, Alaska.

WOODROW WILSON.

SPECIAL MESSAGE

To the Senate:

In response to the resolution adopted by the Senate on March 1. 1917, requesting the President to furnish the Senate, if not incompatible with the public interest, whatever information he has concerning the note published in the press of this date purporting to have been sent January 19, 1917, by the German Secretary for Foreign Affairs to the German Minister to Mexico, I transmit herewith a report by the Secretary of State, which has my approval.   WOODROW WILSON.

[Inclosure.]

To the President:

The resolution adopted by the United States Senate on March 1, 1917, requesting that that body be furnished, if not incompatible with the public interest, whatever information you have concerning the note published in the press of this date, purporting to have been sent January 19, 1917, by the German Secretary for Foreign Affairs to the German Minister to Mexico, I have the honor to state that the Government is in possession of evidence which establishes the fact that the note referred to is authentic, and that it is in possession of the Government of the United States, and that the evidence was procured by this Government during the present week, but that it is, in my opinion, incompatible with the public interest to send to the Senate at the present time any further information in possession of the Government of the United States relative to the note mentioned in the resolution of the Senate.

Respectfully submitted.   ROBERT LANSING.

PROCLAMATION

By the President of the United States of America

A PROCLAMATION

[Special Session of the Senate.]

Whereas public interests require that the Senate of the United States be convened at twelve o'clock on the fifth day of March next to receive such communications as may be made by the Executive;

Now, therefore, I, Woodrow Wilson, President of the United States of America, do hereby proclaim and declare that an extraordinary occasion requires the Senate of the United States to convene at the Capitol, in the city of Washington, on the 5th day of March next, at 12 o'clock noon, of which all persons who shall at that time be entitled to act as members of that body are hereby required to take notice.

Given under my hand and the seal of the United States at Washington, the twenty-third of February in the year of our Lord one thousand nine hundred and seventeen, and of the Independence of the United States the one hundred and forty-first.

[SEAL.]

By the President: WOODROW WILSON.

Robert Lansing, Secretary of State.

STATEMENT

[Issued from the White House by the President March 4, 1917, Following the Failure of the Sixty-fourth Congress to Pass the Armed Neutrality Act.]

The termination of the last session of the Sixty-fourth Congress by constitutional limitation discloses a situation unparalleled in the history of the country, perhaps unparalleled in the history of any modern government.

In the immediate presence of a crisis fraught with more subtle and far-reaching possibilities of national danger than any other the Government has known within the whole history of its international relations, the Congress has been unable to act either to safeguard the country or to vindicate the elementary rights of its citizens.

More than five hundred of the five hundred and thirty-one members of the two Houses were ready and anxious to act; the House of Representatives had acted by an overwhelming majority; but the Senate was unable to act because a little group of eleven Senators had determined that it should not.

The Senate has no rules by which debate can be limited or brought to an end, no rules by which dilatory tactics of any kind can be prevented. A single member can stand in the way of action if he have but the physical endurance.

The result in this case is a complete paralysis alike of the legislative and of the executive branches of the Government.

The inability of the Senate to act has rendered some of the most necessary legislation of the session impossible, at a time when the need for it was most pressing and most evident. The bill which would have permitted such combinations of capital and of organization in the export and import trade of the country as the circumstances of international competition have made imperative—a bill which the business judgment of the whole country approved and demanded—has failed.

The opposition of one or two Senators has made it impossible to increase the membership of the Interstate Commerce Commission or to give it the altered organization necessary for its efficiency.

The Conservation bill, which should have released for immediate use the mineral resources which are still locked up in the public lands, now that their release is more imperatively necessary than ever, and the bill which would have made the unused water power of the country immediately available for industry, have both failed, though they have been under consideration throughout the sessions of the two Congresses and have been twice passed by the House of Representatives.

The appropriations for the army have failed, along with the appropriations for the civil establishment of the Government, the appropriations for the Military Academy and the General Deficiency bill.

It has proved impossible to extend the powers of the Shipping Board to meet the special needs of the new situation into which our commerce has been forced, or to increase the gold reserve of our national banking system to meet the circumstances of the existing financial situation.

It would not cure the difficulty to call the Sixty-fifth Congress in extraordinary session. The paralysis of the Senate would remain. The purpose and the spirit of action are not lacking now.

The Congress is more definitely united in thought and purpose at this moment, I venture to say, than it has been within the memory of any man now in its membership. There is not only the most united patriotic purpose, but the objects members have in view are perfectly clear and definite. But the Senate cannot act unless its leaders can obtain unanimous consent. Its majority is powerless, helpless.

In the midst of a crisis of extraordinary peril, when only definite and decided action can make the nation safe or shield it from war itself by the aggression of others, action is impossible.

Although as a matter of fact the nation and the representatives of the nation stand back of the executive with unprecedented unanimity and spirit, the impression made abroad will, of course, be that it is not so and that other governments may act as they please without fear that this Government can do anything at all. We cannot explain.

The explanation is incredible. The Senate of the United States is the only legislative body in the world which cannot act when its majority is ready for action. A little group of wilful men, representing no opinion but their own, have rendered the great Government of the United States helpless and contemptible.

The remedy? There is but one remedy. The only remedy is that the rules of the Senate shall be so altered that it can act. The country can be relied upon to draw the moral. I believe the Senate can be relied on to supply the means of action and save the country from disaster.

EXECUTIVE ORDER

The White House, January 15, 1917.

[Creating an Inter-Departmental Board on Location of Nitrate Plants.]

An Inter-Departmental Board, consisting of the Secretary of War, the Secretary of the Interior, and the Secretary of Agriculture, is hereby organized for the purpose of making the necessary investigations and submitting recommendations relative to the selection of a site or sites suitable for a plant or plants authorized by section one hundred and twenty-four of the act approved June 3, 1916, to be constructed and operated for the production of nitrates and other products needed for munitions of war and useful in the manufacture of fertilizers and other useful products.

This board will consider, through actual examination thereof or otherwise and with such expedition as may be possible, the suitability of water power sites in different parts of the United States for the purposes prescribed by the statute, and will recommend a site or sites for the plant or plants which in its judgment should be established.

This board will have power to direct other representatives of their own or other Departments of the Government to appear before it to give information, aid or advice, and to employ such clerical assistance as may be necessary.

A complete record and minutes of the proceedings of this board will be kept, and a full report of the board, with the record of its proceedings and its recommendations, will be submitted to the President.

WOODROW WILSON.

PROCLAMATIONS

By the President of the United States of America

A PROCLAMATION

[Enlarging Whitman National Forest, Oregon.]

Whereas, it appears that the lands hereinafter described, in the State of Oregon, have been found by the Secretary of Agriculture to be chiefly valuable for the production of timber or for the protection of stream flow; and

Whereas, it appears that such lands should be added to the Whitman National Forest;

Now, therefore, I, WOODROW WILSON, President of the United States of America, by virtue of the power in me vested by section 1 of the Act of Congress approved September 8, 1916 (39 Stat., 852), entitled "An Act Authorizing an adjustment of the boundaries of the Whitman National Forest, in the State of Oregon, and for other purposes," do proclaim that the boundaries of the Whitman National Forest are hereby changed to include the following described lands:

Parts of townships 10, 11 and 12, ranges 34, 35 and 36, east of Willamette meridian, as shown on map submitted.

The withdrawal made by this proclamation shall, as to all lands which are at this date legally appropriated under the public land laws or reserved for any public purpose, be subject to and shall not interfere with or defeat legal rights under such appropriation, nor prevent the use for such public purpose of lands so reserved, so long as such appropriation is legally maintained or such reservation remains in force.

In Witness Whereof, I have hereunto set my hand and caused the seal of the United States to be affixed.

Done at the City of Washington this thirty-first day of January, in the year of our Lord one thousand nine hundred and [SEAL.] seventeen, and of the Independence of the United States the one hundred and forty-first.

By the President: WOODROW WILSON.

ROBERT LANSING, *Secretary of State.*

BY THE PRESIDENT OF THE UNITED STATES OF AMERICA

A PROCLAMATION

[Declaring an Emergency in Water Transportation of the United States.]

Whereas, Congress did by "An Act To establish a United States Shipping Board for the purpose of encouraging, developing and creating a naval auxiliary and naval reserve and a merchant marine to meet the requirements of the commerce of the United States with its Territories and possessions and with foreign countries; to regulate carriers by water engaged in the foreign and interstate commerce of the United States; and for other purposes," approved September 7, 1916, provide that "during any national emergency the existence of which is declared by proclamation of the President, no vessel registered or enrolled and licensed under the laws of the United States shall, without the approval of the board, be sold, leased or chartered to any person not a citizen of the United States, or transferred to a foreign registry or flag";

And whereas, many shipowners of the United States are permitting their ships to pass to alien registers and to foreign trades in which we do not participate, and from which they cannot be bought back to serve the needs of our water-borne commerce without the permission of governments of foreign nations;

Now, therefore, I, WOODROW WILSON, President of the United States of America, acting under and by virtue of the authority conferred in me by said Act of Congress, do hereby declare and proclaim that I have found that there exists a national emergency arising from the insufficiency of maritime tonnage to carry the products of the farms, forests, mines and manufacturing industries of the United States to their consumers abroad and within the United States, and I do hereby admonish all citizens of the United States and every person to abstain from every violation of the provisions of said Act of Congress, and I do hereby warn them that all violations of such provisions will be rigorously prosecuted, and I do hereby enjoin upon all officers of the United States, charged with the execution of the laws thereof, the utmost diligence in preventing violations of said Act, and this my proclamation issued thereunder, and in bringing to trial and punishment any offenders against the same.

In Witness Whereof, I have hereunto set my hand and caused the seal of the United States to be affixed.

Done at the City of Washington this 5th day of February, in the year of our Lord one thousand nine hundred and seventeen, and of the Independence of the United States of America the one hundred and forty-first.

[SEAL.]

By the President: WOODROW WILSON.

ROBERT LANSING, *Secretary of State.*

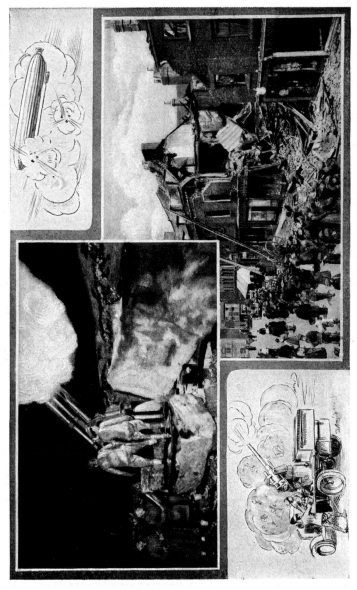

ANTI-AIRCRAFT GUN AND DESTRUCTION BY ZEPPELIN

THE EFFECTS OF A ZEPPELIN RAID ON ENGLAND.

One of the agents of German warfare which was disappointing to those who had expected great achievements from it was the Zeppelin. The Zeppelin, strictly speaking, is not an airplane, but simply a dirigible balloon of great size and complexity. Soon after the outbreak of the World War, Zeppelins bombarded English towns, both defended and undefended, but with seemingly little effect. During the daytime, Zeppelins usually were afraid to approach England's shores because of the fear of counter-attack by English airplanes; and when night fell, England darkened her cities so that the Zeppelins were afforded few marks for bombs. Moreover, powerful searchlights, illuminating the heavens, compelled raiding Zeppelins to climb to great heights to escape observation, and made it practically impossible for the Zeppelin crews to do much more than rain down bombs haphazardly.

SECOND INAUGURAL ADDRESS

[Delivered before the Public on the Front Portico of the Capitol at Washington, D. C., March 5, 1917.]

MY FELLOW CITIZENS:

The four years which have elapsed since last I stood in this place have been crowded with counsel and action of the most vital interest and consequence. Perhaps no equal period in our history has been so fruitful of important reforms in our economic and industrial life or so full of significant changes in the spirit and purpose of our political action. We have sought very thoughtfully to set our house in order, correct the grosser errors and abuses of our industrial life, liberate and quicken the processes of our national genius and energy, and lift our politics to a broader view of the people's essential interests.

It is a record of singular variety and singular distinction. But I shall not attempt to review it. It speaks for itself and will be of increasing influence as the years go by. This is not the time for retrospect. It is time rather to speak our thoughts and purposes concerning the present and the immediate future.

Although we have centered counsel and action with such unusual concentration and success upon the great problems of domestic legislation to which we addressed ourselves four years ago, other matters have more and more forced themselves upon our attention—matters lying outside our own life as a nation and over which we had no control, but which, despite our wish to keep free of them, have drawn us more and more irresistibly into their own current and influence.

It has been impossible to avoid them. They have affected the life of the whole world. They have shaken men everywhere with a passion and an apprehension they never knew before. It has been hard to preserve calm counsel while the thought of our own people swayed this way and that under their influence. We are a composite and cosmopolitan people. We are of the blood of all the nations that are at war. The currents of our thoughts as well as the currents of our trade run quick at all seasons back and forth between us and them. The war inevitably set its mark from the first alike upon our minds, our industries, our commerce, our politics and our social action. To be indifferent to it, or independent of it, was out of the question.

And yet all the while we have been conscious that we were not part of it. In that consciousness, despite many divisions, we have drawn closer together. We have been deeply wronged upon the seas, but we have not wished to wrong or injure in return; have retained throughout the consciousness of standing in some sort apart, intent upon an interest that transcended the immediate issues of the war itself.

As some of the injuries done us have become intolerable we have still been clear that we wished nothing for ourselves that we were not ready to demand for all mankind—fair dealing, justice, the freedom to live and to be at ease against organized wrong.

It is in this spirit and with this thought that we have grown more and more aware, more and more certain that the part we wished to play was the part of those who mean to vindicate and fortify peace. We have been obliged to arm ourselves to make good our claim to a certain minimum of right and of freedom of action. We stand firm in armed neutrality since it seems that in no other way we can demonstrate what it is we insist upon and cannot forget. We may even be drawn on, by circumstances, not by our own purpose or desire, to a more active assertion of our rights as we see them and a more immediate association with the great struggle itself. But nothing will alter our thought or our purpose. They are too clear to be obscured. They are too deeply rooted in the principles of our national life to be altered. We desire neither conquest nor advantage. We wish nothing that can be had only at the cost of another people. We always professed unselfish purpose and we covet the opportunity to prove our professions are sincere.

There are many things still to be done at home, to clarify our own politics and add new vitality to the industrial processes of our own life, and we shall do them as time and opportunity serve, but we realize that the greatest things that remain to be done must be done with the whole world for stage and in co-operation with the wide and universal forces of mankind, and we are making our spirits ready for those things.

We are provincials no longer. The tragic events of the thirty months of vital turmoil through which we have just passed have made us citizens of the world. There can be no turning back. Our own fortunes as a nation are involved whether we would have it so or not.

And yet we are not the less Americans on that account. We shall be the more American if we but remain true to the principles in which we have been bred. They are not the principles of a province or of a single continent. We have known and boasted all along that they were the principles of a liberated mankind. These, therefore, are the things we shall stand for, whether in war or in peace:

That all nations are equally interested in the peace of the world and in the political stability of free peoples, and equally responsible for their maintenance; that the essential principle of peace is the actual equality of nations in all matters of right or privilege; that peace cannot securely or justly rest upon an armed balance of power; that governments derive all their just powers from the consent of the governed and that no other powers should be supported by the common thought, purpose or power of the family of nations; that the seas should be equally free and safe for the use of all peoples, under rules set up by common agreement and consent, and that, so far as practicable, they should be accessible to all upon equal terms; that national armaments shall be limited to the necessities of national order and domestic safety; that the community of interest and of power upon which peace must henceforth depend imposes upon each nation the duty of seeing to it that all influences proceeding from its own citizens meant to encourage or assist revolution in other states should be sternly and effectually suppressed and prevented.

I need not argue these principles to you, my fellow countrymen; they are your own, part and parcel of your own thinking and your own motives in affairs. They spring up native amongst us. Upon this as a platform of purpose and of action we can stand together. And it is imperative that we should stand together. We are being forged into a new unity amidst the fires that now blaze throughout the world. In their ardent heat we shall, in God's Providence, let us hope, be purged of faction and division, purified of the errant humors of party and of private interest, and shall stand forth in the days to come with a new dignity of national pride and spirit. Let each man see to it that the dedication is in his own heart, the high purpose of the nation in his own mind, ruler of his own will and desire.

I stand here and have taken the high and solemn oath to which you have been audience because the people of the United States have chosen me for this august delegation of power and have by their gracious judgment named me their leader in affairs.

I know now what the task means. I realize to the full the responsibility which it involves. I pray God I may be given the wisdom and the prudence to do my duty in the true spirit of this great people. I am their servant and can succeed only as they sustain and guide me by their confidence and their counsel. The thing I shall count upon, the thing without which neither counsel nor action will avail, is the unity of America—an America united in feeling, in purpose and in its vision of duty, of opportunity and of service.

We are to beware of all men who would turn the tasks and the necessities of the nation to their own private profit or use them for the building up of private power.

United alike in the conception of our duty and in the high resolve to perform it in the face of all men, let us dedicate ourselves to the great task to which we must now set our hand. For myself I beg your tolerance, your countenance and your united aid.

The shadows that now lie dark upon our path will soon be dispelled, and we shall walk with the light all about us if we be but true to ourselves—to ourselves as we have wished to be known in the counsels of the world and in the thought of all those who love liberty and justice and the right exalted.

By the President of the United States of America

A PROCLAMATION

[Payment by the United States for the Danish West Indian Islands.]

Whereas, by Article 5 of the Convention between the United States and Denmark for the cession of the Danish West Indian Islands to the United States, the United States agrees to pay, in full consideration of the cession made by the said Convention, within ninety (90) days from the exchange of the ratifications of the said Convention, in the City of Washington, to the diplomatic representative or other agent of His Majesty, the King of Denmark, duly authorized to receive the money, the sum of twenty-five million dollars ($25,000,000) in gold coin of the United States;

And whereas, the ratifications of the said Convention were exchanged at the City of Washington on January 17, 1917;

And whereas, by Section 7 of the Act of Congress, approved March 3, 1917, entitled "An Act to provide a temporary government for the West Indian Islands acquired by the United States from Denmark by the Convention entered into between the said countries on the fourth day of August, nineteen hundred and sixteen, and ratified by the Senate of the United States on the seventh day of September, nineteen hundred and sixteen, and for other purposes" the sum of twenty-five million dollars ($25,000,000) was appropriated to be paid in the City of Washington to the diplomatic representative or other agent of His Majesty the King of Denmark duly authorized to receive said money, in full consideration of the cession of the Danish West Indian Islands to the United States made by the said Convention;

And whereas, in conformity with said Convention and said Act of Congress, the sum of twenty-five million dollars ($25,000,000) was on this day paid to Mr. Constantin Brun, Envoy Extraordinary and Minister Plenipotentiary of Denmark at Washington as the Agent duly authorized by the Government of Denmark to receive the money;

And whereas, by Section 8 of the said Act of Congress approved March 3, 1917, the fact and date of such payment shall be made public by a proclamation issued by the President and published in the said Danish West Indian Islands and in the United States.

Now, therefore, be it known that I, Woodrow Wilson, President of the United States of America, do hereby proclaim and publish that the sum of twenty-five million dollars ($25,000,000) has this day been paid to the authorized Agent of His Majesty the King of Denmark in full consideration of the cession of the Danish West Indian Islands to the United States made by the Convention between the United States of America and His Majesty the King of Denmark, concluded August 4, 1916.

In testimony whereof I have hereunto set my hand and caused the seal of the United States to be affixed.

Done at the City of Washington this 31st day of March in the year of our Lord one thousand nine hundred and seventeen, and [SEAL.] of the Independence of the United States of America, the one hundred and forty-first.

WOODROW WILSON.

By the President:

ROBERT LANSING, *Secretary of State.*

EXECUTIVE ORDERS.

[Establishing civil service in first, second and third classes of postoffices.]

THE WHITE HOUSE, *March 31, 1917.*

Hereafter when a vacancy occurs in the position of postmaster of any office of the first, second, or third class as the result of death, resignation, removal, or, on the recommendation of the First Assistant Postmaster General, approved by the Postmaster General, to the effect that the efficiency or needs of the service requires that a change shall be made, the Postmaster General shall certify the fact to the Civil Service Commission which shall forthwith hold an open competitive examination to test the fitness of applicants to fill such vacancy, and when such examination has been held and the papers in connection therewith have been rated the said Commission shall certify the result thereof to the Postmaster General, who shall submit to the President the name of the highest qualified eligible for appointment to fill such vacancy unless it is established that the character or residence of such applicant disqualifies him for appointment. No person who has passed his sixty-fifth birthday shall be given the examination herein provided for. WOODROW WILSON.

[Amending civil service regulations.]

THE WHITE HOUSE, *April 2, 1917.*

In view of present emergency conditions and until further notice, the Civil Service Commission is directed to refuse examination to any person who is, or who has been within three months of the date of the examination, employed in the Government service, or to certify any such person who is on the eligible register of the Commission, unless such person submits the written assent of the Department or office in which he is or has been employed to his taking such examination or to his being so certified. Such assent shall be based solely upon the finding, after due consideration, by such Department or office that the person can render better service for the Government in the place for which the examination is held.

This order is issued solely because of the present international situation and will be withdrawn when the emergency is past.

WOODROW WILSON.

WAR MESSAGE

[Delivered to Joint Session of Congress, April 2, 1917.]

GENTLEMEN OF THE CONGRESS: I have called the Congress into extraordinary session because there are serious, very serious, choices of policy to be made, and made immediately which it was neither right nor constitutionally permissible that I should assume the responsibility of making.

On the third of February last, I officially laid before you the extraordinary announcement of the Imperial German Government that on and after the first day of February it was its purpose to put aside all restraints of law or of humanity and use its submarines to sink every vessel that sought to approach either the ports of Great Britain and Ireland or the western coast of Europe or any of the ports controlled by the enemies of Germany within the Mediterranean. That had seemed to be the object of the German submarine warfare earlier in the war; but since April of last year the Imperial Government had somewhat restrained the commanders of its undersea craft, in conformity with its promise then given to us that passenger boats should not be sunk, and that due warning would be given to all other vessels which its submarines might seek to destroy, when no resistance was offered or escape attempted, and care taken that their crews were given at least a fair chance to save their lives in their open boats. The precautions taken were meager and haphazard enough, as was proved in distressing instance after instance in the progress of the cruel and unmanly business, but a certain degree of restraint was observed.

The new policy has swept every restriction aside. Vessels of every kind, whatever their flag, their character, their cargo, their destination, their errand, have been ruthlessly sent to the bottom without warning and without thought of help or mercy for those on board—the vessels of friendly neutrals along with those of belligerents. Even hospital ships and ships carrying relief to the sorely bereaved and stricken people of Belgium, though the latter were provided with safe conduct through the proscribed areas by the German Government itself, and were distinguished by unmistakable marks of identity, have been sunk with the same reckless lack of compassion or of principle.

I was for a little while unable to believe that such things would in fact be done by any government that had hitherto subscribed to the humane practices of civilized nations. International law had its origin in the attempt to set up some law which would be respected and observed upon the seas, where no nation had right of dominion and where lay the free highways of the world. By painful stage after stage has that law been built up, with meager enough results, indeed, after all was accomplished that could be accomplished, but always with a clear view, at least, of what the heart and conscience of mankind demanded.

This minimum of right the German Government has swept aside under the plea of retaliation and necessity, and because it had no weapons which it could use at sea except these which it is impossible to employ as it is employing them without throwing to the winds all scruples of humanity or of respect for the understandings that were supposed to underlie the intercourse of the world.

I am not now thinking of the loss of property involved, immense and serious as that is, but only of the wanton and wholesale destruction of the lives of non-combatants, men, women and children, engaged in pursuits which have always, even in the darkest period of modern history, been deemed innocent and legitimate. Property can be paid for; the lives of peaceful and innocent people cannot be.

The present German submarine warfare against commerce is a warfare against mankind. It is a war against all nations. American ships have been sunk, American lives taken in ways which it has stirred us very deeply to learn of, but the ships and people of other neutral and friendly nations have been sunk and overwhelmed in the waters in the same way. There has been no discrimination. The challenge is to all mankind. Each nation must decide for itself how it will meet it. The choice we make for ourselves must be made with a moderation of counsel and a temperateness of judgment befitting our character and our motives as a nation.

We must put excited feeling away. Our motive will not be revenge or the victorious assertion of the physical might of the nation, but only the vindication of right, of human right, of which we are only a single champion.

When I addressed the Congress on the 26th of February last, I thought that it would suffice to assert our neutral right with arms; our right to use the sea against unlawful interference; our right to keep our people safe against unlawful violence. But armed neutrality, it now appears, is impracticable. Because submarines are in effect outlaws when used as the German submarines have been used against merchant shipping, it is impossible to defend ships against their attacks as the law of nations has assumed that merchantmen would defend themselves against privateers or cruisers, visible craft giving chase upon the open sea. It is common prudence in such circumstances, grim necessity indeed, to endeavor to destroy them before they have shown their own intention. They must be dealt with upon sight, if dealt with at all.

The German Government denies the right of neutrals to use arms at all within the areas of the sea which it has prescribed, even in the defense of rights which no modern publicist has ever before questioned their right to defend. The intimation is conveyed that the armed guards which we have placed on our merchant ships will be treated as beyond the pale of law and subject to be dealt with as pirates would be. Armed neutrality is ineffectual enough at best; in such circumstances and in the face of such pretensions, it is worse than ineffectual; it is likely only to produce what it was meant to prevent; it is practically certain to draw us into the war without either the rights or the effectiveness of belligerents.

There is one choice we cannot make, we are incapable of making—we will not choose the path of submission and suffer the most sacred rights of our nation and our people to be ignored or violated. The wrongs against which we now array ourselves are no common wrongs; they cut to the very roots of human life.

With a profound sense of the solemn and even tragical character of the step I am taking and of the grave responsibilities which it involves, but in unhesitating obedience to what I deem my constitutional duty, I advise that the Congress declare the recent course of the Imperial German Government to be, in fact, nothing less than war against the Government and people of the United States; that it formally accept the status of belligerent which has thus been thrust upon it; and that it take immediate steps not only to put the country in a more thorough state of defense, but also to exert all its power and employ all its resources to bring the Government of the German Empire to terms and end the war.

What this will involve is clear. It will involve the utmost practicable co-operation in counsel and action with the governments now at war with Germany; and, as incident to that, the extension to those governments of the most liberal financial credits, in order that our resources may, so far as possible, be added to theirs. It will involve the organization and mobilization of all the material resources of the country to supply the materials of war and serve the incidental needs of the nation in the most abundant and yet the most economical and efficient way possible. It will involve the immediate full equipment of the navy in all respects, but particularly in supplying it with the best means of dealing with the enemy's submarines. It will involve the immediate addition to the armed forces of the United States already provided for by law in case of war at least 500,000 men, who should, in my opinion, be chosen upon the principle of universal liability to service, and also the authorization of subsequent additional increments of equal force so soon as they may be needed and can be handled in training.

It will involve also, of course, the granting of adequate credits to the Government, sustained, I hope, so far as they can equitably be sustained, by the present generation, by well-conceived taxation. I say sustained so far as may be equitable by taxation because it seems to me that it would be most unwise to base the credits which will now be necessary entirely on money borrowed. It is our duty, I most respectfully urge, to protect our people so far as we may against the very serious hardships and evils which would be likely to arise out of the inflation which would be produced by vast loans.

In carrying out the measures by which these things are to be accomplished, we should keep constantly in mind the wisdom of interfering as little as possible in our own preparation and in the equipment of our own military forces with the duty—for it will be a very practical duty—of supplying the nations already at war with Germany with the materials which they can obtain only from us or by our assistance. They are in the field, and we should help them in every way to be effective there.

I shall take the liberty of suggesting, through the several executive departments of the Government, for the consideration of your committees, measures for the accomplishment of the several objects I have mentioned. I hope that it will be your pleasure to-deal with them as having been framed after very careful thought by the branch of the Government upon which the responsibility of conducting the war and safeguarding the nation will most directly fall.

While we do these things, these deeply momentous things, let us be very clear, and make very clear to all the world what our motives and our objects are. My own thought has not been driven from its habitual and normal course by the unhappy events of the last two months, and I do not believe that the thought of the nation has been altered or clouded by them.

I have exactly the same things in mind now that I had in mind when I addressed the Senate on the 22d of January last; the same that I had in mind when I addressed the Congress on the 3d of February and on the 26th of February. Our object now, as then, is to vindicate the principles of peace and justice in the life of the world as against selfish and autocratic power and to set up among the really free and self-governed peoples of the world such a concert of purpose and of action as will henceforth insure the observance of those principles.

Neutrality is no longer feasible or desirable where the peace of the world is involved and the freedom of its peoples, and the menace to that peace and freedom lies in the existence of autocratic governments backed by organized force which is controlled wholly by their will, not by the will of their people. We have seen the last of neutrality in such circumstances.

We are at the beginning of an age where it will be insisted that the same standards of conduct and of responsibility for wrong done shall be observed among nations and their governments that are observed among the individual citizens of civilized states.

We have no quarrel with the German people. We have no feeling toward them but one of sympathy and friendship. It was not upon their impulse that their Government acted in entering this war. It was not with their previous knowledge or approval.

It was a war determined upon as wars used to be determined upon in the old, unhappy days when peoples were nowhere consulted by their rulers and wars were provoked and waged in the interest of dynasties or of little groups of ambitious men who were accustomed to use their fellow-men as pawns and tools.

Self-governed nations do not fill their neighbor states with spies or set the course of intrigue to bring about some critical posture of affairs which will give them an opportunity to strike and make conquest. Such designs can be successfully worked out only under cover and where no one has the right to ask questions.

Cunningly contrived plans of deception or aggression, carried, it may be, from generation to generation, can be worked out and kept from the light only within the privacy of courts or behind the carefully guarded confidences of a narrow and privileged class. They are happily impossible where public opinion commands and insists upon full information concerning all the nation's affairs.

A steadfast concert for peace can never be maintained except by a partnership of democratic nations. No autocratic government could be trusted to keep faith within it or observe its covenants. It must be a league of honor, a partnership of opinion. Intrigue would eat its vitals away; the plottings of inner circles who could plan what they would and render account to no one would be a corruption seated at its very heart. Only free peoples can hold their purpose and their honor steady to a common end and prefer the interests of mankind to any narrow interest of their own.

Does not every American feel that assurance has been added to our hope for the future peace of the world by the wonderful and heartening things that have been happening within the last few weeks in Russia?

Russia was known by those who knew her best to have been always in fact democratic at heart, in all the vital habits of her thought, in all the intimate relationships of her people that spoke their natural instinct, their habitual attitude toward life.

The autocracy that crowned the summit of her political structure, long as it had stood and terrible as was the reality of its power, was not in fact Russian in origin, character or purpose; and now it has been shaken off and the great generous Russian people have been added in all their native majesty and might to the forces that are fighting for a freedom in the world, for justice and for peace. Here is a fit partner for a league of honor.

One of the things that has served to convince us that the Prussian autocracy was not and could never be our friend is that from the very outset of the present war it has filled our unsuspecting communities and even our offices of government with spies and set criminal intrigues everywhere afoot against our national unity of council, our peace within and without, our industries and our commerce.

Indeed, it is now evident that its spies were here even before the war began; and it unhappily is not a matter of conjecture, but a fact proved in our courts of justice, that the intrigues which have more than once come perilously near to disturbing the peace and dislocating the industries of the country have been carried on at the instigation, with the support, and even under the personal direction of official agents of the Imperial Government accredited to the Government of the United States.

Even in checking these things and trying to extirpate them, we have sought to put the most generous interpretation possible upon them because we knew that their source lay, not in any hostile feeling or purpose of the German people toward us (who were, no doubt, as ignorant of them as we ourselves were), but only in the selfish designs of a government that did what it pleased and told its people nothing. But they have played their part in serving to convince us at last that that government entertains no real friendship for us and means to act against our peace and security at its convenience. That it means to stir up enemies against us at our very doors, the intercepted note to the German Minister at Mexico City is eloquent evidence.

We are accepting this challenge of hostile purpose because we know that in such a government, following such methods, we can never have a friend; and that in the presence of its organized power always lying in wait to accomplish we know not what purpose, there can be no assured security for the democratic governments of the world.

We are now about to accept gauge of battle with this natural foe to liberty and shall, if necessary, spend the whole force of the nation to check and nullify its pretensions and end its power. We are glad, now that we see the facts with no veil of false pretense about them, to fight thus for the ultimate peace of the world and for the liberation of its peoples, the German peoples included; for the rights of nations great and small and the privilege of men everywhere to choose their way of life and of obedience. The world must be made safe for democracy. Its peace must be planted upon the tested foundations of political liberty.

We have no selfish ends to serve. We desire no conquest, no dominion. We seek no indemnities for ourselves, no material compensation for the sacrifices we shall freely make. We are but one of the champions of the rights of mankind. We shall be satisfied when those rights have been made as secure as the faith and the freedom of the nations can make them.

Just because we fight without rancor and without selfish object, seeking nothing for ourselves but what we shall wish to share with all free peoples, we shall, I feel confident, conduct our operations as belligerents without passion and ourselves observe with proud punctilio the principles of right and of fair play we profess to be fighting for.

I have said nothing of the Governments allied with the Imperial Government of Germany because they have not made war upon us or challenged us to defend our right and our honor. The Austro-Hungarian Government has, indeed, avowed its unqualified indorsement and acceptance of the reckless and lawless submarine warfare adopted now without disguise by the Imperial German Government, and it has therefore not been possible for this Government to receive Count Tarnowski, the Ambassador recently accredited to this Government by the Imperial and Royal Government of Austria-Hungary; but that Government has not actually engaged in warfare against citizens of the United States on the seas, and I take the liberty, for the present at least, of postponing a discussion of our relations with the authorities at Vienna. We enter this war only where we are clearly forced into it because there are no other means of defending our rights.

It will be all the easier for us to conduct ourselves as belligerents in a high spirit of right and fairness because we act without animus, not in enmity toward a people nor with the desire to bring any injury or disadvantage upon them, but only in armed opposition to an irresponsible Government which has thrown aside all considerations of humanity and of right and is running amuck.

We are, let me say again, the sincere friends of the German people, and shall desire nothing so much as the early re-establishment of intimate relations of mutual advantage between us—however hard it may be for them, for the time being, to believe that this is spoken from our hearts. We have borne with their present Government through all these bitter months because of that friendship—exercising a patience and forbearance which would otherwise have been impossible. We shall, happily, still have an opportunity to prove that friendship in our daily attitude and actions toward the millions of men and women of German birth and native sympathy who live among us and share our life, and we shall be proud to prove it toward all who are in fact loyal to their neighbors and to the Government in the hour of test. They are, most of them, as true and loyal Americans as if they had never known any other fealty or allegiance. They will be prompt to stand with us in rebuking and restraining the few who may be of a different mind and purpose.

If there should be disloyalty, it will be dealt with with a firm hand of stern repression; but if it lifts its head at all, it will lift it only here and there and without countenance, except from a lawless and malignant few.

It is a distressing and oppressive duty, gentlemen of the Congress, which I have performed in thus addressing you. There are, it may be, many months of fiery trial and sacrifice ahead of us. It is a fearful thing to lead this great peaceful people into war, into the most terrible and disastrous of all wars, civilization itself seeming to be in the balance. But the right is more precious than peace, and we shall fight for the things which we have always carried nearest our hearts—for democracy, for the right of those who submit to authority to have a voice in their own governments, for the rights and liberties of small nations, for a universal domination of right by such a concert of free peoples as shall bring peace and safety to all nations and make the world itself at last free. To such a task we can dedicate our lives and our fortunes, everything that we are and everything that we have, with the pride of those who know that the day has come when America is privileged to spend her blood and her might for the principles that gave her birth and happiness and the peace which she has treasured. God helping her, she can do no other.

WOODROW WILSON.

EXECUTIVE ORDERS

[Temporarily suspending eight-hour law provisions in Department of Agriculture.]

THE WHITE HOUSE, *April 3, 1917.*

In order to enable the Department of Agriculture to meet the requirements of law to secure the more expeditious distribution of valuable seeds authorized by law, and by virture of the authority vested in me by the provisions of the Act of Congress approved March 4, 1917, entitled "An Act making appropriations for the naval service for the fiscal year ending June thirtieth, nineteen hundred and eighteen, and for other purposes," whereby it is provided "That in case of national emergency the President is authorized to suspend provisions of law prohibiting more than eight hours labor in any one day of persons engaged upon work covered by contracts with the United States: Provided further, That the wages of persons employed upon such contracts shall be computed on a basic day rate of eight hours' work, with overtime rates to be paid for at not less than time and one-half for all hours work in excess of eight hours," I do hereby authorize the suspension of the provisions of law prohibiting more than eight hours of labor in any one day of persons engaged in such work under contract with the Department of Agriculture for thirty days in order to meet present emergency conditions.

This order shall take effect from and after date.

WOODROW WILSON.

[Establishing defensive sea areas.]

THE WHITE HOUSE, *April 5, 1917.*

In accordance with the authority vested in me by section forty-four of the act entitled "An Act to codify, revise, and amend the penal laws of the United States," approved March fourth, nineteen hundred and nine, as amended by the act "Making appropriations for the naval service for the fiscal year ending June thirtieth, nineteen hundred and eighteen, and for other purposes," approved March fourth, nineteen hundred and seventeen, I, Woodrow Wilson, President of the United States of America, do order that defensive sea areas are hereby established, to be maintained until further notification, at the places and within the limits prescribed as follows, that is to say:—

Mouth of Kennebec River: Outer Limit—Arc of circle with Pond Island Light as center, radius two (2) nautical miles.
Inner Limit—A line East and West (true) through Perkins Island Light.
Portland: Outer Limit—Arc of circle center Portland Head Light, radius two (2) nautical miles.
Inner Limit—Line Portland Breakwater Light to west bastion Fort Gorges.
Portsmouth: Outer Limit—Arc of circle with Whaleback Reef Light as center, radius two and one-half (2½) nautical miles.
Inner Limit—A line South (true) from southwest point of Clarks Island.
Boston: Outer Limit—Line from Strawberry Point to Spouting Horn.
Inner Limit—Line west tangent Sheep Island to wharf on east side of Long Island.
Line from wharf west side Long Island to large wharf west side of Deer Island.
New Bedford: Outer Limit—Arc of circle, center the east point of reef off Clark Point, radius distance to Dumping Rocks Lighthouse.
Inner Limit—Line between Butler Flats Light and Egg Island Beacon.
Newport: Outer Limit—Arc of circle with Beaver Tail Light as center and radius of two (2) nautical miles.
Inner Limit—Fort Adams fog bell to north tangent of North Dumpling.
East and West line through Plum Beach Light.
Long Island East: Outer Limit—Line joining Watch Hill and Montauk Point Lights.
Inner Limit—Line joining Plum Island Light and Mumford Point.
New York East: Outer Limit—Line joining Execution Rocks Light and east tangent of Huckleberry Island.
Inner Limit—A line north (true) through Whitestone Point Light.
New York Main Entrance: Outer Limit—Arc of circle center Romer Shoal Light, radius six (6) nautical miles.
Inner Limit—Line west (true) from flagpole on wharf at Fort Hamilton.
Delaware River: Outer Limit—East and west line through north end of Reedy Island.
Inner Limit—East and west line through Finn's Neck Rear Range Light.
Chesapeake Entrance: Outer Limit—Line parallel to that joining Cape Henry Light and Cape Charles Light and four (4) nautical miles to eastward thereof, and the lines from Cape Charles Light and from Cape Henry Light perpendicular to this line.
Inner Limit—Line parallel to line joining Cape Henry Light and Cape Charles Light and three (3) nautical miles to westward thereof.
Baltimore: Outer Limit—Line from Persimmon Point to Love Point.
Inner Limit—Line joining Leading Point Range Light (Rear) and Sollers Point.
Potomac: Outer Limit—Line from Marshall Hall wharf to south extremity of Ferry Point.
Inner Limit—Line from River View wharf drawn West (true).

Hampton Roads: Outer Limit—Line from Back River Light to point one (1) nautical mile East (true) of Thimble Shoal Light; then South (true) to shore.

Inner Limit—Line tangent to end of wharf on west side of Old Point Comfort and Fort Wool.

Wilmington—Cape Fear: Outer Limit—Oak Island Life Saving Station as center of arc, radius five (5) nautical miles.

Inner Limit—Line joining south end of Fort Caswell and Smith Island Range Beacon (Rear).

Charleston: Outer Limit—Arc of circle with Fort Sumter Light as center, radius six (6) nautical miles.

Inner Limit—Line joining Charleston Light and Fort Sumter Light.

Savannah: Outer Limit—Arc of circle with Tybee Island Light as center, radius ten (10) nautical miles.

Inner Limit—Line across channel through southeast end of Cockspur Island.

Key West: Outer Limit—Arc of circle with Key West Light as center, radius seven (7) nautical miles.

Inner Limit—Line joining south tangent East Crawfish Key, and south tangent of Fort Taylor.

Tampa: Outer Limit—Arc of circle with Egmont Key Light as center, radius six (6) nautical miles.

Inner Limit—Line tangent to southwest point of Mullet Key and east tangent of Passage Key.

Pensacola: Outer Limit—Arc of circle center Cut (Front) Range Light, radius six (6) nautical miles.

Inner Limit—South (true) from east corner of dock at Navy Yard old dry-dock slip.

Mobile: Outer Limit—Arc of circle with Fort Morgan Light as center, radius six (6) nautical miles.

Inner Limit—Fort Gaines to Fort Morgan.

Mississippi: Outer Limit—Lucas Canal.

Inner Limit—Bolivar Point.

Galveston: Outer Limit—Arc of circle with Fort Point Light as center, radius five (5) nautical miles.

Inner Limit—Line joining Boliver Point and Fort Point Lights.

San Diego: Outer Limit—Arc of circle with Point Loma Light as center, radius two (2) nautical miles.

Inner Limit—Line joining Beacons Nos. 3 and 4.

San Francisco: Outer Limit—Arc of circle with center at middle point of line joining Point Bonita Light and Rock at Cliff House, radius four (4) nautical miles.

Inner Limit—Line from Bluff Point to Point Campbell on Angel Island and line from Quarry Point on Angel Island to extreme western point on Goat Island; also line from extreme western point on Goat Island to North Point, San Francisco.

Columbia River: Outer Limit—Arc of circle with center three (3) nautical miles south (true) from North Head Light, radius three (3) nautical miles.

Inner Limit—Line from wharf at Flavel Tansy Point at right angles to axis of channel.

Port Orchard: Outer Limit—Arc of circle, center Orchard Rock Spindle, radius two (2) nautical miles.

Inner Limit—Line from Point White at right angles to axis of channel to opposite bank.

Honolulu: Outer Limit—Arcs of circles centers Diamond Head Light and Honolulu Harbor Light, radii nine (9) nautical miles.

Inner Limit—Line across channel at No. 7 fixed light.

Manila: Outer Limit—Line through Luzon Point and Fuego Point.

Inner Limit—Line through San Nicolas Shoal Light and Mt. Sungay.

The responsibility of the United States of America for any damage inflicted by force of arms with the object of detaining any person or vessel proceeding in contravention to Regulations duly promulgated in accordance with this Executive order shall cease from this date.

WOODROW WILSON.

[Regulations for carrying into effect the executive order of the President establishing defensive sea areas.]

THE WHITE HOUSE, *April 5, 1917.*

Whereas, in accordance with section forty-four of the Act entitled "An Act to codify, revise and amend the penal laws of the United States," approved March fourth, nineteen hundred and nine, as amended by "An Act making appropriations for the Naval Service, for the fiscal year ending June thirtieth, nineteen hundred and eighteen, and for other purposes," approved March fourth, nineteen hundred and seventeen, Defensive Sea Areas have been established by my order of April 5, 1917.

Now, therefore, I, Woodrow Wilson, President of the United States of America, do hereby authorize and promulgate the following orders and regulations for the government of persons and vessels within the limits of Defensive Sea Areas; which orders and regulations are necessary for purposes of national defense.

I. In the neighborhood of each Defensive Sea Area, entrances have been designated for incoming and outgoing vessels, including, in the case of Areas across which more than one channel exists, an entrance for each channel. These entrances are described in Article X of these Regulations in conjunction with the Areas to which they respectively pertain.

II. A vessel desiring to cross a Defensive Sea Area shall proceed to the vicinity of the entrance to the proper channel, flying her national colors, together with International Code number and pilot signal, and there await communication with the Harbor Entrance Patrol. It is expressly prohibited for any vessel to enter the limits of a Defensive Sea Area otherwise than at a designated entrance and after authorization by the Harbor Entrance Patrol.

III. Boats and other craft employed in the Harbor Entrance Patrol will be distinguished by the union jack, which will be shown from a position forward; they will also fly the usual naval pennant. At night, they may show a vertical hoist of three lights—white, red, and white, in the order named.

IV. On receiving permission from the Harbor Entrance Patrol to enter a Defensive Sea Area, a vessel must comply with all instructions as to pilotage and other matters that she may receive from proper authority, either before or during her passage across the Area; it is understood that only upon condition of such compliance is the said permission granted.

V. No permission will be granted to other than a public vessel of the

United States to cross a Defensive Sea Area between sunset and sunrise, nor during the prevalence of weather conditions that render navigation difficult or dangerous. A vessel arriving off a Defensive Sea Area after sunset shall anchor or lie-to at a distance of at least a mile outside its limits until the following sunrise; vessels discovered near the limits of the Areas at night may be fired upon.

VI. No vessel shall be permitted to proceed within the limits of a Defensive Sea Area at a greater speed than five (5) knots per hour.

VII. All matters pertaining to fishery and the passage of small crafts within a Defensive Sea Area shall be regulated by the Senior Officer of the Harbor Entrance Patrol.

VIII. These Regulations are subject to modification by the Senior Officer of the Harbor Entrance Patrol when the public interest may require; and such notification as circumstances may permit will be issued regarding modifications thus made.

IX. Any master of a vessel or other person within the vicinity of a Defensive Sea Area who shall violate these Regulations, or shall fail to obey an order to stop or heave to, or shall perform any act threatening the efficiency of mine or other defenses or the safety of navigation, or shall take any action inimical to the interests of the United States in its prosecution of war, may be detained therein by force of arms and renders himself liable to prosecution as provided for in the Act to codify, revise and amend the penal laws of the United States, approved March 4, 1909, as amended by "the Act making appropriations for the Naval Service for the fiscal year ending June 30, 1918, and for other purposes," approved March 4, 1917.

X. The designated entrances to Defensive Sea Areas referred to in Article 1 of these Regulations shall be as follows:

Defensive Sea Area.	Designated Entrances for Incoming Vessels.	Designated Entrances for Outgoing Vessels.
Kennebec River, Maine.	Seguin Island Light bearing West (true) distant one (1) nautical mile.	In the channel between Perkins Island and Bald Head.
Portland, Maine..	Portland Head Light bearing Northwest (true) distant two and one-half (2½) nautical miles.	In harbor north of Portland Breakwater Light.
Portsmouth, New Hampshire.	At a point one-half (½) nautical mile South (true) of Gunboat Shoal Buoy.	In the channel to the westward of Clark Island.

Defensive Sea Area.	Designated Entrances for In-coming Vessels.	Designated Entrances for Out-going Vessels.
Boston, Massachusetts.	Boston Light Vessel..........	In President Roads west of a line drawn North and South (true), one-half (½) nautical mile west of Deer Island Light.
New Bedford, Massachusetts.	Dumpling Rocks Light bearing Northwest (true) distant one and one-half (1½) nautical miles.	In the channel west of Egg Island Beacon.
Newport, Rhode Island.	Beaver Tail Light bearing North (true) distance two and one-half (2½) nautical miles.	In the channel west of Goat Island. In the channel Northeast (true) of Plum Beach Light.
Long Island Sound, Eastern Entrance.	Watch Hill Light bearing Northwest (true) distant five (5) nautical miles.	Bartlett Reef Light Vessel.
Long Island Sound, West End.	Execution Rocks Light bearing Southwest (true) distant one (1) nautical mile.	In channel west of a line drawn North (true) from Whitestone Light.
New York, Southern Entrance.	Sandy Hook Light bearing West (true) distant ten (10) nautical miles.	In Narrows north of a line drawn West (true) from flagpole on Fort Hamilton wharf.
Delaware River...	In the channel below Reedy Island.	In the channel off Newcastle, Pennsylvania.
Chesapeake Bay Entrance.	Chesapeake Bay Main Ship Channel Entrance Buoy.	In the channel between buoys N2 and No. 3 Gas Buoy.
Baltimore, Md....	At Buoy N2C, entrance to Craighill Channel.	In channel on line between Leading Point and Soller's Point.
Potomac River...	In channel off Dague Creek..	In channel off River View.
Hampton Roads...	In channel two (2) nautical miles to eastward and southward of Thimble Shoal Light.	In channel to Northwestward of entrance buoy of dredged channel, Elizabeth River.

Defensive Sea Area.	Designated Entrances for In-coming Vessels.	Designated Entrances for Out-going Vessels.
Cape Fear, N. C..	At a point four (4) nautical miles Southsouthwest (true) from Bell Buoy at entrance channel.	In channel near Beacon No. 2A, off Battery Island.
Charleston, South Carolina.	Charleston Light Ship.......	Lower anchorage to westward of North and South line (true) through Fort Sumter Light.
Tybee Roads, Savannah, Ga.	Four (4) nautical miles east of Whistling Buoy.	Quarantine anchorage.
Key West, Florida	Sand Key Light bearing West-North-West (true) distant five (5) nautical miles.	In channel off fixed red beacon to North - North - Westward of Fort Taylor.
Tampa, Florida...	Whistling Buoy, at entrance to dredged channel.	Off Quarantine Station.
Pensacola, Florida	Pensacola Light bearing North-North-West (true) distant eight (8) nautical miles.	East corner of dock at Navy Yard bearing Northwest (true), distant one-half (½) nautical mile.
Mobile, Alabama.	Whistling Buoy at entrance bearing North (true) distant two (2) nautical miles.	Near Buoy C5.
Mississippi River.	South Pass Gas and Whistling Buoy.	Buras Church.
Galveston, Texas.	Lighted Buoy No. 1 off South Jetty, bearing West (true) distant two (2) nautical miles.	United States Quarantine Station.
San Diego, California.	Entrance Whistling Buoy.....	Between Beacons 5 and 6.
San Francisco, California.	San Francisco Lightship......	Off Quarry Point, Angel Island; and off Light, Goat Island.

Defensive Sea Area.	Designated Entrances for In-coming Vessels.	Designated Entrances for Outgoing Vessels.
Columbia River...	North Head Light bearing North-East (true) distant six (6) nautical miles.	In channel to eastward of Tansy Point.
Port Orchard, Washington.	In Sound to eastward of line joining Restoration Point and east end of Blake Island and one (1) nautical mile South (true) of Restoration Point.	To westward of Point White.
Honolulu, Hawaii	Honolulu harbor light bearing North-North-East (true) distant ten (10) nautical miles.	In harbor north of Honolulu harbor lighthouse.
Manila, P. I......	Peak of Corregidor Island bearing North North-East (true) distant twelve (12) nautical miles.	San Nicolas Shoal Light bearing South (true) distant one (1) nautical mile.

The Secretary of the Navy will be charged with the publication and enforcement of these Regulations.

WOODROW WILSON.

[Additional defensive sea area.]

THE WHITE HOUSE, *April 14, 1917.*

In accordance with the authority vested in me by section forty-four of the act entitled "An act to codify, revise, and amend the penal laws of the United States," approved March fourth, nineteen hundred and nine, as amended by the act "Making appropriations for the naval service for the fiscal year ending June thirtieth, nineteen hundred and eighteen, and for other purposes," approved March fourth, nineteen hundred and seventeen, I, Woodrow Wilson, President of the United States, do order that in addition to those defensive sea areas established by executive order under date of April fifth, nineteen hundred and seventeen, and subject to the same disclaimer of responsibility for damage inflicted as therein proclaimed, a defensive sea area is hereby established, to be maintained until further notification, at the place and within the limits described as follows; that is to say—

York River:
    Outer Limit—Arc of circle with center at Tue Marshes Light, radius 2¾ nautical miles, to line from North tangent Tue Point to Buoy S "11-H", thence line to Tue Point.
    Inner Limit—A line from Sandy Point to end of wharf on Carmines Island.

And I do further order that the "Regulations for Carrying into Effect the Executive Order of the President Establishing Defensive Sea Areas," approved by me April fifth, nineteen hundred and seventeen, duly promulgated and published, are and shall be considered as of full effect and binding on all persons and vessels within the limits of the defensive sea area hereby established.

The designated entrances to the defensive sea area herein established shall be as follows:

Entrance for incoming vessels, at Buoy N "2A."

Entrance for outgoing vessels, at Buoy N 6.

WOODROW WILSON.

[Taking over necessary and closing unnecessary radio stations.]

THE WHITE HOUSE, *April 6, 1917.*

Whereas, the Senate and House of Representatives of the United States of America, in Congress assembled, have declared that a state of war exists between the United States and the Imperial German Government; and

Whereas it is necessary to operate certain radio stations for radio communication by the Government and to close other radio stations not so operated, to insure the proper conduct of the war against the Imperial German Government and the successful termination thereof

Now, therefore, it is ordered by virtue of authority vested in me by the Act to Regulate Radio Communication, approved August 13, 1912, that such radio stations within the jurisdiction of the United States as are required for naval communications shall be taken over by the Government of the United States and used and controlled by it, to the exclusion of any other control or use; and furthermore that all radio stations not necessary to the Government of the United States for naval communications, may be closed for radio communication.

The enforcement of this order is hereby delegated to the Secretary of the Navy, who is authorized and directed to take such action in the premises as to him may appear necessary.

This order shall take effect from and after this date.

WOODROW WILSON.

THE WHITE HOUSE, *April 30, 1917.*

Whereas the Senate and House of Representatives of the United States of America, in Congress assembled, have declared that a state of war exists between the United States and the Imperial German Government; and

Whereas it is necessary to operate certain radio stations for radio communication by the Government and to close other radio stations not so operated, to insure the proper conduct of the war against the Imperial German Government and the successful termination thereof.

Now, therefore, it is ordered by virtue of authority vested in me under the Constitution under the Joint Resolution of Congress, dated April 6, 1917, and under the Act to Regulate Radio Communication, approved August 13, 1912, that such radio stations within the jurisdiction of the United States as are required for Naval Communications shall be taken over by the Government of the United States and used and controlled by it, to the exclusion of any other control or use; and furthermore, that all radio stations not necessary to the Government of the United States for Naval Communications may be closed for radio communication and all radio apparatus therein may be removed therefrom.

The enforcement of this order is hereby delegated to the Secretary of the Navy, who is authorized and directed to take such action in the premises as to him may appear necessary.

This order shall take effect from and after this date.

WOODROW WILSON.

By the President of the United States of America

A PROCLAMATION

[Existence of war—German Empire.]

Whereas the Congress of the United States in the exercise of the constitutional authority vested in them have resolved, by joint resolution of the Senate and House of Representatives bearing date this day "That the state of war between the United States and the Imperial German Government which has been thrust upon the United States is hereby formally declared;"

Whereas it is provided by Section four thousand and sixty-seven of the Revised Statutes, as follows:

"Whenever there is declared a war between the United States and any foreign nation or government, or any invasion or predatory incursion is perpetrated, attempted, or threatened against the territory of the United States, by any foreign nation or government, and the President makes public proclamation of the event, all natives, citizens, denizens, or subjects of the hostile nation or government, being males of the age of fourteen years and upwards, who shall be within the United States, and not actually naturalized, shall be liable to be apprehended, restrained, secured, and removed, as alien enemies. The President is authorized, in any such event, by his proclamation thereof, or other public act, to direct the conduct to be observed, on the part of the United States, toward the aliens who become so liable; the manner and degree of the restraint to which they shall be subject, and in what cases, and upon what security their residence shall be permitted, and to provide for the removal of those who, not being permitted to reside within the United States, refuse or neglect to depart therefrom; and to establish any other regulations which are found necessary in the premises and for the public safety;"

Whereas, by Sections four thousand and sixty-eight, four thousand and sixty-nine, and four thousand and seventy, of the Revised Statutes, further provision is made relative to alien enemies;

Now, therefore, I, Woodrow Wilson, President of the United States of America, do hereby proclaim to all whom it may concern that a state of war exists between the United States and the Imperial German Government; and I do specially direct all officers, civil or military, of the United States that they exercise vigilance and zeal in the discharge of the duties incident to such a state of war; and I do, moreover, earnestly appeal to all American citizens that they, in loyal devotion to their country, dedicated from its foundation to the principles of liberty and justice, uphold the laws of the land, and give undivided and willing support to those measures which may be adopted by the constitutional authorities in prosecuting the war to a successful issue and in obtaining a secure and just peace;

And, acting under and by virtue of the authority vested in me by the Constitution of the United States and the said sections of the Revised Statutes, I do hereby further proclaim and direct that the conduct to be observed on the part of the United States towards all natives, citizens, denizens, or subjects of Germany, being males of the age of fourteen years and upwards, who shall be within the United States and not actually naturalized, who for the purpose of this proclamation and under such sections of the Revised Statutes are termed alien enemies, shall be as follows:

All alien enemies are enjoined to preserve the peace towards the United States and to refrain from crime against the public safety, and from violating the laws of the United States and of the States and Territories thereof, and to refrain from actual hostility or giving information, aid or comfort to the enemies of the United States, and to comply strictly with the regulations which are hereby or which may be from time to time promulgated by the President; and so long as they shall conduct themselves in accordance with law, they shall be undisturbed in the peaceful pursuit of their lives and occupations and be accorded the consideration due to all peaceful and law-abiding persons, except so far as restrictions may be necessary for their own protection and for the safety of the United States; and towards such alien enemies as conduct themselves in accordance with law, all citizens of the United States are enjoined to preserve the peace and to treat them with all such friendliness as may be compatible with loyalty and allegiance to the United States

And all alien enemies who fail to conduct themselves as so enjoined, in addition to all other penalties prescribed by law, shall be liable to restraint, or to give security, or to remove and depart from the United States in the manner prescribed by Sections four thousand and sixty-nine and four thousand and seventy of the Revised Statutes, and as prescribed in the regulations duly promulgated by the President;

And pursuant to the authority vested in me, I hereby declare and establish the following regulations, which I find necessary in the premises and for the public safety:

(1) An alien enemy shall not have in his possession, at any time or place, any fire-arm, weapon or implement of war, or component part thereof, ammunition, maxim or other silencer, bomb or explosive or material used in the manufacture of explosives;

(2) An alien enemy shall not have in his possession at any time or place, or use or operate any aircraft or wireless apparatus, or any form of signalling device, or any form of cipher code, or any paper, document or book written or printed in cipher or in which there may be invisible writing.

(3) All property found in the possession of an alien enemy in violation of the foregoing regulations shall be subject to seizure by the United States;

(4) An alien enemy shall not approach or be found within one-half of a mile of any Federal or State fort, camp, arsenal, aircraft station, Government or naval vessel, navy yard, factory, or workshop for the manufacture of munitions of war or of any products for the use of the army or navy:

(5) An alien enemy shall not write, print, or publish any attack or threats against the Government or Congress of the United States, or either branch thereof, or against the measures or policy of the United States, or against the person or property of any person in the military, naval, or civil service of the United States, or of the States or Territories, or of the District of Columbia, or of the municipal governments therein;

(6) An alien enemy shall not commit or abet any hostile act against the United States, or give information, aid, or comfort to its enemies;

(7) An alien enemy shall not reside in or continue to reside in, to remain in, or enter any locality which the President may from time to

time designate by Executive Order as a prohibited area in which residence by an alien enemy shall be found by him to constitute a danger to the public peace and safety of the United States, except by permit from the President and except under such limitations or restrictions as the President may prescribe;

(8) An alien enemy whom the President shall have reasonable cause to believe to be aiding or about to aid the enemy, or to be at large to the danger of the public peace or safety of the United States, or to have violated or to be about to violate any of these regulations, shall remove to any location designated by the President by Executive Order, and shall not remove therefrom without a permit, or shall depart from the United States if so required by the President;

(9) No alien enemy shall depart from the United States until he shall have received such permit as the President shall prescribe, or except under order of a court, judge, or justice, under Sections 4069 and 4070 of the Revised Statutes;

(10) No alien enemy shall land in or enter the United States, except under such restrictions and at such places as the President may prescribe;

(11) If necessary to prevent violations of these regulations, all alien enemies will be obliged to register;

(12) An alien enemy whom there may be reasonable cause to believe to be aiding or about to aid the enemy, or who may be at large to the danger of the public peace or safety, or who violates or attempts to violate, or of whom there is reasonable ground to believe that he is about to violate, any regulation duly promulgated by the President, or any criminal law of the United States, or of the States or Territories thereof, will be subject to summary arrest by the United States Marshal, or his deputy, or such other officer as the President shall designate, and to confinement in such penitentiary, prison, jail, military camp, or other place of detention as may be directed by the President.

This proclamation and the regulations herein contained shall extend and apply to all land and water, continental or insular, in any way within the jurisdiction of the United States.

In witness whereof, I have hereunto set my hand and caused the seal of the United States to be affixed.

Done at the City of Washington this sixth day of April, in the year of our Lord one thousand nine hundred and seventeen, and [SEAL.] of the independence of the United States the one hundred and forty-first.

WOODROW WILSON.

By the President:

ROBERT LANSING, *Secretary of State.*

By the President of the United States of America

A PROCLAMATION

[Agencies in the United States of German insurance companies.]

Whereas, certain insurance companies, incorporated under the laws of the German Empire, have been admitted to transact the business of insurance in various States of the United States, by means of separate United States Branches established pursuant to the laws of such States, and are now engaged in business under the supervision of the Insurance Departments thereof, with assets in the United States deposited with Insurance Departments or in the hands of resident trustees, citizens of the United States, for the protection of all policyholders in the United States;

And whereas, the interests of the citizens of the United States in the protection afforded by such insurance are of great magnitude, so that it is deemed to be important that the agencies of such companies in the United States be permitted to continue in business;

Now, therefore, I, Woodrow Wilson, President of the United States of America, by virtue of the powers vested in me as such, hereby declare and proclaim that such branch establishments of German Insurance Companies now engaged in the transaction of business in the United States pursuant to the laws of the several States are hereby authorized and permitted to continue the transaction of their business in accordance with the laws of such States in the same manner and to the same extent as though a state of war did not exist; provided, however, that all funds of such establishments now in the possession of their managers or agents, or which shall hereafter come into their possession, shall be subject to such rules and regulations concerning the payment and disposition thereof as shall be prescribed by the insurance supervising officials of the State in which the principal office of such establishment in the United States is located, but in no event shall any funds belonging to or held for the benefit of such companies be transmitted outside of the United States nor be used as the basis for the establishment directly or indirectly of any credit within or outside of the United States to or for the benefit or use of the enemy or any of his allies without the permission of this Government.

In witness whereof, I have hereunto set my hand and caused the seal of the United States to be affixed.

Done at the City of Washington this sixth day of April in the year of our Lord one thousand nine hundred and seventeen, and

[SEAL.]   of the Independence of the United States the one hundred and forty-first.

WOODROW WILSON.

By the President:

ROBERT LANSING, *Secretary of State.*

EXECUTIVE ORDERS

[Creating Committee on Public Information.]

THE WHITE HOUSE, *April 13, 1917.*

I hereby create a Committee on Public Information, to be composed of the Secretary of State, the Secretary of War, the Secretary of the Navy, and a civilian who shall be charged with the executive direction of the Committee.

As Civilian Chairman of this Committee, I appoint Mr. George Creel.

The Secretary of State, the Secretary of War, and the Secretary of the Navy are authorized each to detail an officer or officers to the work of the Committee. WOODROW WILSON.

[Allowing Treasury Department employees to be appointed on defense organizations.]

THE WHITE HOUSE, *April 14, 1917.*

The provisions of the Executive Order of January 17, 1873, prohibiting Federal employees from holding office under any State, Territorial, or Municipal Government, are hereby waived to permit the appointment of such employees in and under the Treasury Department, with the approval of the Secretary of the Treasury, on any State, county, or municipal council or committee of defense for purposes of mobilizing and conserving the resources of the country.

This order is issued on the recommendation of the Secretary of the Treasury. WOODROW WILSON.

BY THE PRESIDENT OF THE UNITED STATES OF AMERICA

A PROCLAMATION

[Treason and misprision of treason.]

Whereas, all persons in the United States, citizens as well as aliens, should be informed of the penalties which they will incur for any failure to bear true allegiance to the United States;

Now, therefore, I, Woodrow Wilson, President of the United States, hereby issue this proclamation to call especial attention to the following provisions of the Constitution and the laws of the United States:

Section 3 of Article III of the Constitution provides, in part:

Treason against the United States, shall consist only in levying war against them, or in adhering to their Enemies, giving them Aid and Comfort.

The Criminal Code of the United States provides:

Section 1

Whoever, owing allegiance to the United States, levies war against them or adheres to their enemies, giving them aid and comfort within the United States or elsewhere, is guilty of treason.

Section 2

Whoever is convicted of treason shall suffer death; or, at the discretion of the court, shall be imprisoned not less than five years and fined not less than ten thousand dollars, to be levied on and collected out of any or all of his property, real and personal, of which he was the owner at the time of committing such treason, any sale or conveyance to the contrary notwithstanding; and every person so convicted of treason shall, moreover, be incapable of holding any office under the United States.

Section 3

Whoever, owing allegiance to the United States and having knowledge of the commission of any treason against them, conceals and does not, as soon as may be, disclose and make known the same to the President or to some judge of the United States, or to the governor or to some judge or justice of a particular State, is guilty of misprision of treason and shall be imprisoned not more than seven years, and fined not more than one thousand dollars.

Section 6

If two or more persons in any State or Territory, or in any place subject to the jurisdiction of the United States, conspire to overthrow, put down, or to destroy by force the Government of the United States, or to levy war against them, or to oppose by force the authority thereof, or by force to prevent, hinder, or delay the execution of any law of the United States, or by force to seize, take, or possess any property of the United States contrary to the authority thereof, they shall each be fined not more than five thousand dollars, or imprisoned not more than six years, or both.

The courts of the United States have stated the following acts to be treasonable:

The use or attempted use of any force or violence against the Government of the United States, or its military or naval forces;

The acquisition, use, or disposal of any property with knowledge that it is to be, or with intent that it shall be, of assistance to the enemy in their hostilities against the United States;

The performance of any act or the publication of statements or information which will give or supply, in any way, aid and comfort to the enemies of the United States;

The direction, aiding, counseling, or countenancing of any of the foregoing acts.

Such acts are held to be treasonable whether committed within the United States or elsewhere; whether committed by a citizen of the United States or by an alien domiciled, or residing, in the United States, inasmuch as resident aliens, as well as citizens, owe allegiance to the United States and its laws.

Any such citizen or alien who has knowledge of the commission of such acts and conceals and does not make known the facts to the officials named in Section 3 of the Penal Code is guilty of misprision of treason.

And I hereby proclaim and warn all citizens of the United States, and all aliens, owing allegiance to the Government of the United States, to abstain from committing any and all acts which would constitute a violation of any of the laws herein set forth; and I further proclaim and warn all persons who may commit such acts that they will be vigorously prosecuted therefor.

In witness whereof, I have hereunto set my hand and caused the seal of the United States to be affixed.

Done at the City of Washington this sixteenth day of April in the year of our Lord one thousand nine hundred and seventeen,
[SEAL.] and of the Independence of the United States of America the one hundred and forty-first.

WOODROW WILSON.

By the President:
Robert Lansing, *Secretary of State.*

ADDRESS TO HIS FELLOW COUNTRYMEN, APRIL 16, 1917

My Fellow-Countrymen:

The entrance of our own beloved country into the grim and terrible war for democracy and human rights which has shaken the world, creates so many problems of national life and action which call for immediate consideration and settlement that I hope you will permit me to address to you a few words of earnest counsel and appeal with regard to them.

We are rapidly putting our navy upon an effective war footing and are about to create and equip a great army, but these are the simplest parts of the great task to which we have addressed ourselves. There is not a single selfish element, so far as I can see, in the cause we are fighting for. We are fighting for what we believe and wish to be the rights of mankind and for the future peace and security of the world. To do this great thing worthily and successfully we must devote ourselves to the service without regard to profit or material advantage and with an energy and intelligence that will rise to the level of the enterprise itself. We must realize to the full how great the task is and how many things, how many kinds and elements of capacity and service and self-sacrifice, it involves.

These, then, are the things we must do, and do well, besides fighting,—the things without which mere fighting would be fruitless:

We must supply abundant food for ourselves and for our armies and our seamen not only, but also for a large part of the nations with whom we have now made common cause, in whose support and by whose sides we shall be fighting;

We must supply ships by the hundreds out of our shipyards to carry to the other side of the sea, submarines or no submarines, what will every day be needed there, and abundant materials out of our fields and our mines and our factories with which not only to clothe and equip our own forces on land and sea but also to clothe and support our people for whom the gallant fellows under arms can no longer work, to help clothe and equip the armies with which we are cooperating in Europe, and to keep the looms and manufactories there in raw material; coal to keep the fires going in ships at sea and in the furnaces of hundreds of factories across the sea; steel out of which to make arms and ammunition both here and there; rails for worn-out railways back of the fighting fronts; locomotives and rolling stock to take the place of those every day going to pieces; mules, horses, cattle for labor and for military service; everything with which the people of England and France and Italy and Russia have usually supplied themselves but can not now afford the men, the materials, or the machinery to make.

It is evident to every thinking man that our industries, on the farms, in the shipyards, in the mines, in the factories, must be made more prolific and more efficient than ever and that they must be more economically managed and better adapted to the particular requirements of our task than they have been; and what I want to say is that the men and the women who devote their thought and their energy to these things will be serving the country and conducting the fight for peace and freedom just as truly and just as effectively as the men on the battlefield or in the trenches. The industrial forces of the country, men and women alike, will be a great national, a great international, Service Army,—a notable and honored host engaged in the service of the nation and the world, the efficient friends and saviors of free men everywhere. Thousands, nay, hundreds of thousands, of men otherwise liable to military service will of right and of necessity be excused from that service and assigned to the fundamental, sustaining work of the fields and factories and mines, and they will be as much part of the great patriotic forces of the nation as the men under fire.

I take the liberty, therefore, of addressing this word to the farmers of the country and to all who work on the farms: The supreme need of our own nation and of the nations with which we are cooperating is an abundance of supplies, and especially of food stuffs. The importance of an adequate food supply, especially for the present year, is superlative. Without abundant food, alike for the armies and the peoples now at war, the whole great enterprise upon which we have embarked will break down and fail. The world's food reserves are low. Not only during the present emergency but for some time after peace shall have come both our own people and a large proportion of the people of Europe must rely upon the harvests in America. Upon the farmers of this country, therefore, in large measure, rests the fate of the war and the fate of the nations. May the nation not count upon them to omit no step that will increase the production of their land or that will bring about the most effectual cooperation in the sale and distribution of their products? The time is short. It is of the most imperative importance that everything possible be done and done immediately to make sure of large harvests. I call upon young men and old alike and upon the able-bodied boys of the land to accept and act upon this duty—to turn in hosts to the farms and make certain that no pains and no labor is lacking in this great matter.

I particularly appeal to the farmers of the South to plant abundant food stuffs as well as cotton. They can show their patriotism in no better or more convincing way then by resisting the great temptation of the present price of cotton and helping, helping upon a great scale, to feed the nation and the peoples everywhere who are fighting for their liberties and for our own. The variety of their crops will be the visible measure of their comprehension of their national duty.

The Government of the United States and the governments of the several States stand ready to cooperate. They will do everything possible to assist farmers in securing an adequate supply of seed, an adequate force of laborers when they are most needed, at harvest time, and the means of expediting shipments of fertilizers and farm machinery, as well as of the crops themselves when harvested. The course of trade shall be as unhampered as it is possible to make it and there shall be no unwarranted manipulation of the nation's food supply by those who handle it on its way to the consumer. This is our opportunity to demonstrate the efficiency of a great Democracy and we shall not fall short of it!

This let me say to the middlemen of every sort, whether they are handling our food stuffs or our raw materials of manufacture or the products of our mills and factories: The eyes of the country will be especially upon you. This is your opportunity for signal service, efficient and disinterested. The country expects you, as it expects all others, to forego unusual profits, to organize and expedite shipments of supplies of every kind, but especially of food, with an eye to the service you are rendering and in the spirit of those who enlist in the ranks, for their people, not for themselves. I shall confidently expect you to deserve and win the confidence of people of every sort and station.

To the men who run the railways of the country, whether they be managers or operative employees, let me say that the railways are the arteries of the nation's life and that upon them rests the immense responsibility of seeing to it that those arteries suffer no obstruction of any kind, no inefficiency or slackened power. To the merchant let me suggest the motto, "Small profits and quick service;" and to the shipbuilder the thought that the life of the war depends upon him. The food and the war supplies must be carried across the seas no matter how many ships are sent to the bottom. The places of those that go down must be supplied and supplied at once. To the miner let me say that he stands where the farmer does: the work of the world waits on him. If he slackens or fails, armies and statesmen are helpless. He also is enlisted in the great Service Army. The manufacturer does not need to be told, I hope, that the nation looks to him to speed and perfect every process; and I want only to remind his employees that their service is absolutely indispensable and is counted on by every man who loves the country and its liberties.

Let me suggest, also, that everyone who creates or cultivates a garden helps, and helps greatly, to solve the problem of the feeding of the nations; and that every housewife who practices strict economy puts herself in the ranks of those who serve the nation. This is the time for America to correct her unpardonable fault of wastefulness and extravagance. Let every man and every woman assume the duty of careful, provident use and expenditure as a public duty, as a dictate of patriotism which no one can now expect ever to be excused or forgiven for ignoring.

In the hope that this statement of the needs of the nation and of the world in this hour of supreme crisis may stimulate those to whom it comes and remind all who need reminder of the solemn duties of a time such as the world has never seen before, I beg that all editors and publishers everywhere will give as prominent publication and as wide circulation as possible to this appeal. I venture to suggest, also, to all advertising agencies that they would perhaps render a very substantial and timely service to the country if they would give it widespread repetition. And I hope that clergymen will not think the theme of it an unworthy or inappropriate subject of comment and homily from their pulpits.

The supreme test of the nation has come. We must all speak, act, and serve together! WOODROW WILSON.

PHOTO FROM AEROPLANE OF TRENCHES

VIEW OF TRENCHES FROM AEROPLANE.

Volumes have been written in description of the method of fighting in trenches, but no words could reveal the nature of the trenches so vividly as does the preceding illustration. In the view taken from an aeroplane, it is clearly shown how the trenches zig-zag in all directions across the face of a country, not only to take advantage of every favorable contour of the ground, but also to present a jagged line to the guns of the enemy, so that a shot finding the trenches will not mow down a whole column of men. Only the depressions in the preceding picture which are filled with men are trenches; the other holes in the ground show the spots where shells from the large guns have exploded, and give an idea both of the accuracy of the marksmanship and of the ever-constant danger of sudden death at the front.

EXECUTIVE ORDERS

[Employees of Council of National Defense.]

THE WHITE HOUSE, *April 17, 1917.*

In view of the confidential nature of the work of the Council of National Defense and its importance to the Government in the crisis which has arisen, the Council is authorized to employ for the period of the war, without reference to the requirements of the civil service law and rules, such persons as in the judgment of those in responsible charge are best adapted to its work, it being understood that all possible use will be made of the registers of the Civil Service Commission.

The Civil Service Commission recommends the issuance of this order.

WOODROW WILSON.

[Cooperation among civil service commissions.]

THE WHITE HOUSE, *April 18, 1917.*

The cooperation of state, county and municipal civil service commissions with the United States Civil Service Commission is desirable in the existing exigency in meeting the needs of the Federal Government for appointment in the civil service. The United States Civil Service Commission is accordingly authorized in its discretion to adopt as its own any eligible register of any such commission, with the consent of such commission. The United States Civil Service Commission must be satisfied that the examinations by such state, county or municipal commissions conform to the requirements of competition prescribed by the United States Civil Service Act and Rules, and that the examinations are fairly the equivalent of its own. The eligibles thus utilized may be certified and appointed in the order of their grades in the same manner as though they had passed the Federal examination, and shall be entitled to all the rights and privileges pertaining to persons examined under the United States Civil Service Act.   WOODROW WILSON.

[Suspending eight-hour law in contracts under War Department.]

THE WHITE HOUSE, *April 28, 1917.*

Under authority contained in the Naval Appropriation Act approved March 4, 1917 (Public No. 391, 64th Congress) it is hereby ordered that the provisions of the Eight-Hour Act of June 19, 1912, are suspended with respect to persons engaged upon work covered by contracts with the United States, made under the War Department, for the construction of any military building or for any public work which in the judgment of the Secretary of War is important for purposes of national defense in addition to the classes of contracts enumerated in Executive Order of March 24, 1917.

It is further declared that the current status of war constitutes an "extraordinary emergency" within the meaning of that term as used in the Eight-Hour Act of March 3, 1913 (37 Stat., 726), and that laborers and mechanics employed on work of the character set forth above, whether employed by government contractors or by agents of the government, may, when regarded by the Secretary of War as necessary for purposes of national defense, be required to work in excess of eight hours per day, and wages to be computed in accordance with the proviso in the said Act of March 4, 1917.

This order shall take effect from and after this date and shall be operative during the pending emergency or until further orders.

WOODROW WILSON.

[Censorship of submarine cables, telegraph and telephone lines.]

THE WHITE HOUSE, *April 28, 1917.*

Whereas, the existence of a state of war between the United States and the Imperial German Government makes it essential to the public safety that no communication of a character which would aid the enemy or its allies shall be had,

Therefore, by virtue of the power vested in me under the Constitution and by the Joint Resolution passed by Congress on April 6, 1917, declaring the existence of a state of war, it is ordered that all companies or other persons, owning, controlling or operating telegraph and telephone lines or submarine cables, are hereby prohibited from transmitting messages to points without the United States, and from delivering messages received from such points, except those permitted under rules and regulations to be established by the Secretary of War for telegraph and telephone lines, and by the Secretary of the Navy for submarine cables,

To these Departments, respectively, is delegated the duty of preparing and enforcing rules and regulations under this order to accomplish the purpose mentioned.

This order shall take effect from date.

WOODROW WILSON.

ADDRESS

[To States' Defense Council Meeting at White House.]

May 2, 1917.

MR. SECRETARY (SECRETARY OF WAR) AND GENTLEMEN:

It goes without saying that I am very glad to see you and very glad to see you on such an errand. I have no homily to deliver to you, because I know you are as intensely interested as I am in drawing all of our efforts and energies together in a common action. My function has not of recent days been to give advice but to get things coordinated so that there will not be any, or at any rate too much, lost motion, and in order that things should not be done twice by different bodies or done in conflict.

It is for that reason that I particularly welcome a conference such as this you are holding today and tomorrow—the conference which will acquaint you with exactly the task as it is conceived here in Washington and with the ways in which cooperation can be best organized. For, after all, the task is comparatively simple. The means of accomplishing the task are very complicated, because we must draw many pieces of machinery together and we must see that they act not only to a common object but at the same time and in a common spirit. My function, therefore, today is the very pleasant function of saying how much obliged to you I am for having come here and associated yourself with us in the great task of making good what the Nation has promised to do—go to the defense and vindication of the rights of people every-where to live as they have a right to live under the very principles of our Nation.

It is a thing one does not dare to talk about because a certain passion comes into one's thought and one's feeling as one thinks of the nature of the task, the ideal nature of it, of the opportunity that America has now to show to all the world what it means to have been a democracy for 145 years and to mean every bit of the creed which we have so long professed. And in this thing it ought to be easy to act and delightful to cooperate.

I thank you very much indeed for your courtesy in coming here.

ADDRESS

[To general meeting of the Committee on Labor of the Advisory Commission of the Council of National Defense.]

WASHINGTON, *May 15, 1917.*

This is a most welcome visit because it means a most welcome thing— the spontaneous cooperation of men from all walks of life interested to see that we do not forget any of the principles of our lives in meeting the great emergency that has come upon us.

Mr. Gompers has expressed already one of the things that have been very much in my mind of late. I have been very much alarmed at one or two things that have happened—at the apparent inclination of the Legislatures of one or two of our States to set aside even temporarily the laws which have safeguarded standards of labor and of life. I think nothing would be more deplorable than that. We are trying to fight in a cause which means the lifting of the standards of life, and we can fight in that cause best by voluntary cooperation. I do not doubt that any body of men representing labor in this country, speaking for their fellows, will be willing to make any sacrifice that is necessary in order to carry this contest to a successful issue, and in that confidence I feel that it would be inexcusable if we deprived men and women of such a spirit of any of the existing safeguards of law. Therefore I shall exercise my influence so far as it goes to see that that does not happen, and that the sacrifices we make shall be made voluntarily and not under the compulsion which mistakenly is interpreted to mean a lowering of the standards which we have sought through so many generations to bring to their present level.

Mr. Gompers has not overstated the case in saying that we are fighting for democracy in a larger sense than can be expressed in any political terms. There are many forms of democratic government, and we are not fighting for any particular form; but we are fighting for the essential part of it all, namely, that we are all equally interested in our social and political life, and all have a right to a voice in the Government under which we live, and that when men and women are equally admitted to those rights we have the best safeguard of justice and peace that the world affords. There is no other safeguard. Let any group of men, whatever their original intentions, attempt to dictate to their fellow-men what their political fortunes shall be, and the result is injustice and hardship and wrong of the deepest sort. Therefore we are just now feeling as we have never felt before, our sense of comradeship. We shall feel it even more because we have not yet made the sacrifices that we are going to make; we have not yet felt the terrible pressure of suffering and pain of war, and we are going presently to feel it, and I have every confidence that as its pressure comes upon us our spirit will not falter, but rise and be strengthened, and that in the last we shall have a national feeling and a national unity such as never gladdened our hearts before.

I want to thank you for the compliment of this visit and say if there is any way in which I can cooperate with the purposes of this committee or with those with whom you are laboring, it will afford me a sense of privilege and pleasure.

A PROCLAMATION

[Registration for draft.]

EXECUTIVE MANSION, WASHINGTON, D. C., *May 18, 1917.*

Whereas, Congress has enacted and the President has on the 18th day of May, one thousand nine hundred and seventeen, approved a law, which contains the following provisions:

"SECTION 5.—That all male persons between the ages of 21 and

30, both inclusive, shall be subject to registration in accordance with regulations to be prescribed by the President: And upon proclamation by the President or other public notice given by him or by his direction, stating the time and place of such registration, it shall be the duty of all persons of the designated ages, except officers and enlisted men of the regular army, the navy, and the National Guard and Naval Militia while in the service of the United States, to present themselves for and submit to registration under the provisions of this act: And every such person shall be deemed to have notice of the requirements of this act upon the publication of said proclamation or other notice as aforesaid, given by the President or by his direction: And any person who shall willfully fail or refuse to present himself for registration or to submit thereto as herein provided, shall be guilty of a misdemeanor and shall, upon conviction in the District Court of the United States having jurisdiction thereof, be punished by imprisonment for not more than one year, and shall thereupon be duly registered; provided that in the call of the docket precedence shall be given, in courts trying the same, to the trial of criminal proceedings under this act; provided, further, that persons shall be subject to registration as herein provided, who shall have attained their twenty-first birthday and who shall not have attained their thirty-first birthday on or before the day set for the registration; and all persons so registered shall be and remain subject to draft into the forces hereby authorized unless excepted or excused therefrom as in this act provided; provided further, that in the case of temporary absence from actual place of legal residence of any person liable to registration as provided herein, such registration may be made by mail under regulations to be prescribed by the President.

"SECTION 6.—That the President is hereby authorized to utilize the service of any or all departments and any or all officers or agents of the United States and of the several States, territories, and the District of Columbia and subdivisions thereof in the execution of this act, and all officers and agents of the United States and of the several States, territories, and subdivisions thereof, and of the District of Columbia; and all persons designated or appointed under regulations prescribed by the President, whether such appointments are made by the President himself or by the Governor or other officer of any State or territory to perform any duty in the execution of this act, are hereby required to perform such duty as the President shall order or direct, and all such officers and agents and persons so designated or appointed shall hereby have full authority for all acts done by them in the execution of this act by the direction of the President. Correspondence in the execution of this act may be carried in penalty envelopes, bearing the frank of the War Department. Any person charged, as herein provided, with the duty of carrying into effect any of the provisions of this act or the regulations made or directions given thereunder who shall fail or neglect to perform such duty, and any person charged with such duty or having and exercising any authority under said act, regulations, or directions, who shall knowingly make or be a party to the making of any false or incorrect registration, physical examination, exemption, enlistment, enrollment, or muster, and any person who shall make or be a party to the making of any false statement or certificate as to the fitness or liability of himself or any other person for service under the provisions of this act, or regulations made by the President thereunder, or otherwise evades or aids another to evade the requirements of this act or of said regulations, or who, in any manner, shall fail or neglect fully to perform any duty required of him in the execution of this act, shall, if not subject to military law, be guilty of a misdemeanor, and upon conviction in the District Court of the United States, having jurisdiction thereof, be punished by imprisonment for not more than one year, or, if subject to military law, shall be tried by court-martial and suffer such punishment as a court-martial may direct."

Now, therefore, I, Woodrow Wilson, President of the United States, do call upon the Governor of each of the several States and Territories, the Board of Commissioners of the District of Columbia, and all officers and agents of the several States and Territories, of the District of Columbia, and of the counties and municipalities therein, to perform certain duties in the execution of the foregoing law, which duties will be communicated to them directly in regulations of even date herewith.

And I do further proclaim and give notice to all persons subject to registration in the several States and in the District of Columbia in accordance with the above law, that the time and place of such registration shall be between 7 A. M. and 7 P. M. on the fifth day of June, 1917, at the registration place in the precinct wherein they have their permanent homes. Those who shall have attained their twenty-first birthday and who shall not have attained their thirty-first birthday on or before the day here named are required to register, excepting only officers and enlisted men of the regular army, the navy, the Marine Corps, and the National Guard and Naval Militia, while in the service of the United States, and officers in the Officers' Reserve Corps and enlisted men in the Enlisted Reserve Corps while in active service. In the territories of Alaska, Hawaii, and Porto Rico a day for registration will be named in a later proclamation.

And I do charge those who through sickness shall be unable to present themselves for registration that they apply on or before the day of registration to the County Clerk of the County where they may be for instructions as to how they may be registered by agent. Those who expect to be absent on the day named from the counties in which they have their permanent homes may register by mail, but their mailed registration cards must reach the places in which they have their permanent homes by the day named herein. They should apply as soon as practicable to the County Clerk of the county wherein they may be for instructions as to how they may accomplish their registration by mail. In case such persons as, through sickness or absence, may be unable to present themselves personally for registration shall be sojourning in cities of over 30,000 population, they shall apply to the City Clerk of the city wherein they may be sojourning rather than to the Clerk of the County. The Clerks of counties and of cities of over 30,000 population in which numerous applications from the sick and from nonresidents are expected are authorized to establish such agencies and to employ and deputize such clerical force as may be necessary to accommodate these applications.

The Power against which we are arrayed has sought to impose its will upon the world by force. To this end it has increased armament until it has changed the face of war. In the sense in which we have been wont to think of armies, there are no armies in this struggle, there are entire nations armed. Thus, the men who remain to till the soil and man the factories are no less a part of the army that is in France than the men beneath the battle flags. It must be so with us. It is not an army that we must shape and train for war; it is a nation.

To this end our people must draw close in one compact front against a common foe. But this cannot be if each man pursues a private purpose. All must pursue one purpose. The nation needs all men; but it needs each man, not in the field that will most pleasure him, but in the endeavor that will best serve the common good. Thus, though a sharpshooter pleases to operate a trip-hammer for the forging of great guns and an expert machinist desires to march with the flag, the nation is being served only when the sharpshooter marches and the machinist remains at his levers.

The whole nation must be a team, in which each man shall play the part for which he is best fitted. To this end, Congress has provided that the nation shall be organized for war by selection; that each man shall be classified for service in the place to which it shall best serve the general good to call him.

The significance of this cannot be overstated. It is a new thing in our history and a landmark in our progress. It is a new manner of accepting and vitalizing our duty to give ourselves with thoughtful devotion to the common purpose of us all. It is in no sense a conscription of the unwilling; it is, rather, selection from a nation which has volunteered in mass. It is no more a choosing of those who shall march with the colors than it is a selection of those who shall serve an equally necessary and devoted purpose in the industries that lie behind the battle line.

The day here named is the time upon which all shall present themselves for assignment to their tasks. It is for that reason destined to be remembered as one of the most conspicuous moments in our history. It is nothing less than the day upon which the manhood of the country shall step forward in one solid rank in defense of the ideals to which this nation is consecrated. It is important to those ideals no less than to the pride of this generation in manifesting its devotion to them, that there be no gaps in the ranks.

It is essential that the day be approached in thoughtful apprehension of its significance, and that we accord to it the honor and the meaning that it deserves. Our industrial need prescribes that it be not made a technical holiday, but the stern sacrifice that is before us urges that it be carried in all our hearts as a great day of patriotic devotion and obligation, when the duty shall lie upon every man, whether he is himself to be registered or not, to see to it that the name of every male person of the designated ages is written on these lists of honor.

In witness whereof, I have hereunto set my hand and caused the seal of the United States to be affixed.

Done at the City of Washington this 18th day of May in the year of our Lord one thousand nine hundred and seventeen, and [SEAL.] of the independence of the United States of America the one hundred and forty-first.

WOODROW WILSON.

By the President:
ROBERT LANSING, *Secretary of State.*

ANNOUNCEMENT

[Sending U. S. army division abroad.]

WHITE HOUSE, *May 18, 1917.*

The President has directed an expeditionary force of approximately one division of regular troops under command of Major General John J. Pershing to proceed to France at as early a date as practicable. General Pershing and staff will precede the troops abroad. It is requested that no details or speculations with regard to the mobilization of this command, dates of departure, composition, or other items, be carried by the press, other than the official bulletins given out by the War Department relating thereto.

[Statement Regarding Colonel Roosevelt.]

I shall not avail myself, at any rate at the present stage of the war, of the authorization conferred by the act to organize volunteer divisions.

To do so would seriously interfere with the carrying out of the chief and most immediately important purpose contemplated by this legislation, the prompt creation and early use of an effective army, and would contribute practically nothing to the effective strength of the armies now engaged against Germany.

I understand that the section of this act which authorizes the creation of volunteer divisions in addition to the draft was added with a view to providing an independent command for Mr. Roosevelt and giving the military authority an opportunity to use his fine vigor and enthusiasm in recruiting forces now at the Western front.

It would be very agreeable to me to pay Mr. Roosevelt this compliment and the Allies the compliment of sending to their aid one of our most distinguished public men, an ex-President who has rendered many conspicuous public services and proved his gallantry in many striking ways. Politically, too, it would no doubt have a very fine effect and make a profound impression. But this is not the time or the occasion for compliment or for any action not calculated to contribute to the immediate success of the war. The business now in hand is undramatic, practical, and of scientific definiteness and precision. I shall act with regard to it at every step and in every particular under expert and professional advice from both sides of the water.

That advice is that the men most needed are men of the ages contemplated in the draft provision of the present bill, not men of the age and sort contemplated in the section which authorizes the formation of volunteer units, and that for the preliminary training of the men who are to be drafted we shall need all of our experienced officers. Mr. Roosevelt told me, when I had the pleasure of seeing him a few weeks ago, that he would wish to have associated with him some of the most effective officers of the regular army. He named many of those whom he would desire to have designated for the service, and they were men who cannot possibly be spared from the too small force of officers at our command for the much more pressing and necessary duty of training regular troops to be put into the field in France and Belgium as fast as they can be got ready.

The first troops sent to France will be taken from the present forces of the regular army, and will be under the command of trained soldiers only.

The responsibility for the successful conduct of our own part in this great war rests upon me. I could not escape it if I would. I am too much interested in the cause we are fighting for to be interested in anything but success. The issues involved are too immense for me to take into consideration anything whatever except the best, most effective, most immediate means of military action. What these means are I know from the mouths of men who have seen war as it is now conducted, who have no illusions, and to whom grim matter is a matter of business. I shall center my attention upon those means and let everything else wait.

I should be deeply to blame should I do otherwise, whatever the argument of policy for a personal gratification or advantage.

EXECUTIVE ORDER

THE WHITE HOUSE, *May 11, 1917.*

The Civil Service Commission may, in its discretion, authorize the appointment of civilian employees attached to military organizations sent to Europe, without reference to the requirements of the Civil Service Law and Rules.

The Civil Service Commission recommends the issuance of this order.

WOODROW WILSON.

STATEMENT

[Food Control Program.]

THE WHITE HOUSE, *May 19, 1917.*

It is very desirable, in order to prevent misunderstanding or alarms and to assure cooperation in a vital matter, that the country should understand exactly the scope and purpose of the very great powers which I have thought it necessary in the circumstances to ask the Congress to put in my hands with regard to our food supplies. Those powers are very great, indeed, but they are no greater than it has proved necessary to lodge in the other Governments which are conducting this momentous war, and their object is stimulation and conservation, not arbitrary restraint or injurious interference with the normal processes of production. They are intended to benefit and assist the farmer and all those who play a legitimate part in the preparation, distribution, and marketing of foodstuffs.

It is proposed to draw a sharp line of distinction between the normal activities of the Government represented in the Department of Agriculture in reference to food production, conservation, and marketing, on the one hand, and the emergency activities necessitated by the war in reference to the regulation of food distribution and consumption, on the other. All measures intended directly to extend the normal activities of the Department of Agriculture in reference to the production, conservation, and the marketing of farm crops will be administered, as in normal times, through that department, and the powers asked for over distribution and consumption, over exports, imports, prices, purchase, and requisition of commodities, storing, and the like which may require regulation during the war will be placed in the hands of a Commissioner of Food Administration, appointed by the President and directly responsible to him.

The objects sought to be served by the legislation asked for are: Full inquiry into the existing available stocks of foodstuffs and into the costs and practices of the various food producing and distributing trades; the prevention of all unwarranted hoarding of every kind and of the control of foodstuffs by persons who are not in any legitimate sense producers, dealers, or traders; the requisitioning when necessary for the public use of food supplies and of the equipment necessary for handling them properly; the licensing of wholesome and legitimate mixtures and milling percentages, and the prohibition of the unnecessary or wasteful use of foods.

Authority is asked also to establish prices, but not in order to limit the profits of the farmers, but only to guarantee to them when necessary a minimum price which will insure them a profit where they are asked to attempt new crops and to secure the consumer against extortion by breaking up corners and attempts at speculation, when they occur, by fixing temporarily a reasonable price at which middlemen must sell.

I have asked Mr. Herbert Hoover to undertake this all-important task of food administration. He has expressed his willingness to do so on condition that he is to receive no payment for his services and that the whole of the force under him, exclusive of clerical assistance, shall be employed, so far as possible, upon the same volunteer basis. He has expressed his confidence that this difficult matter of food administration can be successfully accomplished through the voluntary cooperation and direction of legitimate distributors of foodstuffs and with the help of the women of the country.

Although it is absolutely necessary that unquestionable powers shall be placed in my hands, in order to insure the success of this administration of the food supplies of the country, I am confident that the exercise of those powers will be necessary only in the few cases where some small and selfish minority proves unwilling to put the nation's interests above personal advantage, and that the whole country will heartily support Mr. Hoover's efforts by supplying the necessary volunteer agencies throughout the country for the intelligent control of food consumption and securing the cooperation of the most capable leaders of the very interests most directly affected, that the exercise of the powers deputed to him will rest very successfully upon the good-will and cooperation of the people themselves, and that the ordinary economic machinery of the country will be left substantially undisturbed.

The proposed food administration is intended, of course, only to meet a manifest emergency and to continue only while the war lasts. Since it will be composed, for the most part, of volunteers, there need be no fear of the possibility of a permanent bureaucracy arising out of it.

All control of consumption will disappear when the emergency has passed. It is with that object in view that the Administration considers it to be of pre-eminent importance that the existing associations of producers and distributers of foodstuffs should be mobilized and made use of on a volunteer basis. The successful conduct of the projected food administration by such means will be the finest possible demonstration of the willingness, the ability, and the efficiency of democracy, and of its justified reliance upon the freedom of individual initiative. The last thing that any American could contemplate with equanimity would be the introduction of anything resembling Prussian autocracy into the food control in this country.

It is of vital interest and importance to every man who produces food and to every man who takes part in its distribution that these policies thus liberally administered should succeed, and succeed altogether. It is only in that way that we can prove it to be absolutely unnecessary to resort to the rigorous and drastic measures which have proved to be necessary in some of the European countries.

A PROCLAMATION

[Red Cross Week.]

THE WHITE HOUSE, *May 26, 1917.*

Inasmuch as our thoughts as a nation are now turned in united purpose toward the performance to the utmost of the services and duties which we have assumed in the cause of justice and liberty;

Inasmuch as but a small proportion of our people can have the opportunity to serve upon the actual field of battle, but all men, women, and children alike may serve and serve effectively by making it possible to care properly for those who do serve under arms at home and abroad.

And inasmuch as the American Red Cross is the official recognized agency for voluntary effort in behalf of the armed forces of the nation and for the administration of relief,

Now, therefore, by virtue of my authority as President of the United States and President of the American Red Cross, I, Woodrow Wilson, do hereby proclaim the week ending June 25, 1917, as Red Cross Week, during which the people of the United States will be called upon to give generously and in a spirit of patriotic sacrifice for the support and maintenance of this work of national need.

WOODROW WILSON.

ADDRESS

[Delivered on Memorial Day before the Grand Army of the Republic at Arlington Cemetery.]

May 30, 1917.

Mr. Commander and Fellow Citizens: The program has conferred an unmerited dignity upon the remarks I am going to make by calling them an address because I am not here to deliver an address. I am here merely to show in my official capacity the sympathy of this great government with the objects of this occasion, and also to state just a word of the sentiment that is in my own heart.

Any Memorial Day of this sort is, of course, a day touched with sorrowful memory, and yet I for one do not see how we can have any thoughts of pity for the men whose memory we honor to-day. I do not pity them. I envy them, rather, because theirs is the great work for liberty accomplished, and we are in the midst of a work unfinished, testing our strength where their strength has already been tested.

There is a touch of sorrow, but there is a touch of reassurance also in a day like this, because we know how the men of America have responded to the call of the cause of liberty, and it fills our minds with a perfect assurance that that response will come again in equal measure, with equal majesty and with a result which will hold the attention of all mankind.

When you reflect upon it, these men who died to preserve the Union died to preserve the instrument which we are now using to serve the world—a free nation espousing the cause of human liberty.

In one sense the great struggle into which we have now entered is an American struggle, because it is in defense of American honor and American rights, but it is something even greater than that— it is a world struggle. It is a struggle of men who love liberty everywhere, and in this cause America will show herself greater than ever because she will rise to a greater thing.

We have said in the beginning that we planted this great government that men who wished freedom might have a place of refuge and a place where their hopes could be realized, and now, having established such a government, having preserved such a government, having vindicated the power of such a government, we are saying to all mankind, "We did not set this government up that we might have a selfish and separate liberty, for we are now ready to come to your assistance and fight out upon the field of the world the cause of human liberty."

In this thing America attains her full dignity and the full fruition of her great purpose.

No man can be glad such things have happened as we have witnessed in these last fateful years, but perhaps it may be permitted to us to be glad that we have an opportunity to show the principles that we profess to be living, principles that live in our hearts, and to have a chance by the pouring out of our blood and treasure to vindicate the thing which we have professed.

For, my friends, the real fruition of life is to do the thing we have said we wished to do. There are times when words seem empty and only action seems great. Such a time has come, and in the providence of God, America will once more have an opportunity to show the world that she was born to serve mankind.

PROCLAMATIONS

By the President of the United States of America

A PROCLAMATION

[Rules and Regulations for the Regulation, Management and Protection of the Panama Canal and the Maintenance of Its Neutrality.]

Whereas the United States exercises sovereignty in the land and waters of the Canal Zone and is responsible for the construction, operation, maintenance, and protection of the Panama Canal:

Now, therefore, I, Woodrow Wilson, President of the United States of America, do hereby declare and proclaim the following Rules and Regulations for the regulation, management and protection of the Panama Canal and the Maintenance of its Neutrality which are in addition to the general "Rules and Regulations for the Operation and Navigation of the Panama Canal and Approaches Thereto, including all Waters under its jurisdiction" put into force by Executive Order of July 9, 1914.

Rule 1. A vessel of war, for the purposes of these rules, is defined as a public armed vessel, under the command of an officer duly commissioned by the government, whose name appears on the list of officers of the military fleet, and the crew of which are under regular naval discipline, which vessel is qualified by its armament and the character of its personnel to take offensive action against the public or private ships of the enemy.

Rule 2. An auxiliary vessel, for the purposes of these rules, is defined as any vessel, belligerent or neutral, armed or unarmed, which does not fall under the definition of Rule 1, which is employed as a transport or fleet auxiliary or in any other way for the direct purpose of prosecuting or aiding hostilities, whether by land or sea; but a vessel fitted up and used exclusively as a hospital ship is excepted.

Rule 3. A vessel of war or an auxiliary vessel of a belligerent, other than the United States, shall only be permitted to pass through the Canal after her commanding officer has given written assurance to the Authorities of the Panama Canal that the Rules and Regulations will be faithfully observed.

The authorities of the Panama Canal shall take such steps as may be requisite to insure the observance of the Rules and Regulations by auxiliary vessels which are not commanded by an officer of the military fleet.

Rule 4. Vessels of war or auxiliary vessels of a belligerent, other than the United States, shall not revictual nor take any stores in the Canal except so far as may be strictly necessary; and the transit of such vessels through the Canal shall be effected with the least possible delay in accordance with the Canal Regulations in force, and with only such intermission as may result from the necessities of the service.

Prizes shall be in all respects subject to the same Rules as vessels of war of a belligerent.

Rule 5. No vessel of war or auxiliary vessel of a belligerent, other than the United States, shall receive fuel or lubricants while within the territorial waters of the Canal Zone, except on the written authorization of the Canal Authorities, specifying the amount of fuel and lubricants which may be received.

Rule 6. Before issuing any authorization for the receipt of fuel and lubricants by any vessel of war or auxiliary vessel of a belligerent, other than the United States, the Canal Authorities shall obtain a written declaration, duly signed by the officer commanding such vessel, stating the amount of fuel and lubricants already on board.

Rule 7. Fuel and lubricants may be taken on board vessels of war or auxiliary vessels of a belligerent, other than the United States, only upon permission of the Canal Authorities, and then only in such amounts as will enable them, with the fuel and lubricants already on board, to reach the nearest accessible port, not an enemy port, at which they can obtain supplies necessary for the continuation of the voyage. Provisions furnished by contractors may be supplied only upon permission of the Canal Authorities, and then only in amount sufficient to bring up their supplies to the peace standard.

Rule 8. No belligerent, other than the United States, shall embark or disembark troops, munitions of war, or warlike materials in the Canal, except in case of necessity due to accidental hindrance of the transit. In such cases the Canal Authorities shall be the judge of the necessity, and the transit shall be resumed with all possible dispatch.

Rule 9. Vessels of war or auxiliary vessels of a belligerent, other than the United States, shall not remain in the territorial waters of the Canal Zone under the jurisdiction of the United States longer than twenty-four hours at any one time, except in case of distress; and in such case, shall depart as soon as possible.

Rule 10. In the exercise of the exclusive right of the United States to provide for the regulation and management of the Canal, and in order to ensure that the Canal shall be kept free and open on terms of entire equality to vessels of commerce and of war, there shall not be, except by special arrangement, at any one time a greater number of vessels of war of any one nation, other than the United States, including those of the allies of such nation, than three in either terminal port and its adjacent terminal waters, or than three in transit through the Canal; nor shall the total number of such vessels, at any one time, exceed six in all the territorial waters of the Canal Zone under the jurisdiction of the United States.

Rule 11. The repair facilities and docks belonging to the United States and administered by the Canal Authorities shall not be used by a vessel of war or an auxiliary vessel of a belligerent, other than the United States, except when necessary in case of actual distress, and then only upon the order of the Canal Authorities, and only to the degree necessary to render the vessel seaworthy. Any work authorized shall be done with the least possible delay.

Rule 12. The radio installation of any public or private vessel or of any auxiliary vessel of a belligerent, other than the United States, shall be used only in connection with Canal business to the exclusion of all other business while within the waters of the Canal Zone, including the waters of Colon and Panama Harbors.

Rule 13. Air craft, public or private, of a belligerent, other than the United States, are forbidden to descend or arise within the jurisdiction of the United States at the Canal Zone, or to pass through the air spaces above the lands and waters within said jurisdiction.

Rule 14. For the purpose of these rules the Canal Zone includes the cities of Panama and Colon and the harbors adjacent to the said cities.

Rule 15. In the interest of the protection of the Canal while the United States is a belligerent no vessel of war, auxiliary vessel, or private vessel of an enemy of the United States or an ally of such enemy shall be allowed to use the Panama Canal nor the territorial waters of the Canal Zone for any purpose, save with the consent of the

Canal authorities and subject to such rules and regulations as they may prescribe.

In witness whereof, I have hereunto set my hand and caused the seal of the United States to be affixed.

Done at the city of Washington this twenty-third day of May in the year of our Lord one thousand nine hundred and seventeen, [SEAL.] and of the Independence of the United States of America the one hundred and forty-first.

By the President: WOODROW WILSON.
ROBERT LANSING, *Secretary of State.*

BY THE PRESIDENT OF THE UNITED STATES OF AMERICA

A PROCLAMATION

[Letters Patent—Germany.]

Whereas, the laws of the German Empire provide that letters patent granted or issued to citizens of other countries shall lapse unless certain taxes, annuities or fees are paid within stated periods;

And whereas, the interests of the citizens of the United States in such letters patent are of great value, so that it is imporant that such payments should be made in order to preserve their rights;

Now, therefore, I, Woodrow Wilson, President of the United States of America, by virtue of the powers vested in me as such, hereby declare and proclaim that citizens of the United States owning letters patent granted or issued by the German Empire are hereby authorized and permitted to make payment of any tax, annuity or fee which may be required by the laws of the German Empire for the preservation of their rights in such letters patent.

In witness whereof, I have hereunto set my hand and caused the seal of the United States to be affixed.

Done at the city of Washington, this 24th day of May, in the year of our Lord Nineteen Hundred and Seventeen and of the [SEAL.] Independence of the United States, the One Hundred and Forty-First.

By the President: WOODROW WILSON.
ROBERT LANSING, *Secretary of State.*

BY THE PRESIDENT OF THE UNITED STATES OF AMERICA

A PROCLAMATION

[Warning Against Evasion of Registration.]

Whereas the President, in a proclamation issued on the 18th day of May, 1917, set apart the 5th day of June, 1917, between the hours of

7 a. m. and 7 p. m. for the registration of all male persons between the ages of twenty-one and thirty, both inclusive, who may be subject to registration in accordance with the Act of Congress approved May 18, 1917, authorizing the President to increase temporarily the military establishment of the United States:

Now therefore I, Woodrow Wilson, President of the United States of America, do hereby give warning that all persons subject to registration under the provisions of the said Act of Congress and the proclamation of the President who withdraw from the jurisdiction of the United States for the purpose of evading said registration, expose themselves upon their return to the jurisdiction of the United States, to prosecution for such evasion of registration pursuant to Section 5 of the Act of Congress approved May 18, 1917, which enacts that "Any person who shall willfully fail or refuse to present himself for registration or to submit thereto as herein provided, shall be guilty of a misdemeanor and shall, upon conviction in a district court of the United States having jurisdiction thereof, be punished by imprisonment for not more than one year, and shall thereupon be duly registered."

In witness whereof, I have hereunto set my hand and caused the seal of the United States to be affixed.

Done at the City of Washington this twenty-sixth day of May in the year of our Lord one thousand nine hundred and seventeen, [SEAL.] and of the Independence of the United States of America the one hundred and forty-first.

WOODROW WILSON.

By the President:
ROBERT LANSING, *Secretary of State.*

MESSAGE

TO THE RUSSIAN GOVERNMENT

[Delivered by Ambassador Francis in Petrograd, June 8, 1917.]

In view of the approaching visit of the American delegation to Russia to express the deep friendship of the American people for the people of Russia and to discuss the best and most practical means of co-operation between the two peoples in carrying the present struggle for the freedom of all peoples to a successful consummation, it seems opportune and appropriate that I should state again in the light of this new partnership the objects the United States has had in mind in entering the war. Those objects have been much beclouded during the past few weeks by mistaken and misleading statements, and the issues at stake are too momentous, too tremendous, too significant for the whole human race to permit any misinterpretations or misunderstandings, however slight, to remain uncorrected for a moment.

The war has begun to go against Germany, and in their desperate desire to escape the inevitable, ultimate defeat those who are in authority in Germany are using every possible instrumentality, are making use even of the influence of groups and parties among their own subjects to whom they have never been just or fair or even tolerant, to promote a propaganda on both sides of the sea which will preserve for them their influence at home and their power abroad, to the undoing of the very men they are using.

The position of America in this war is so clearly avowed that no man can be excused for mistaking it. She seeks no material profit or aggrandizement of any kind. She is fighting for no advantage or selfish object of her own, but for the liberation of peoples everywhere from the aggressions of autocratic force.

The ruling classes in Germany have begun of late to profess a like liberality and justice of purpose, but only to preserve the power they have set up in Germany and the selfish advantages which they have wrongly gained for themselves and their private projects of power all the way from Berlin to Bagdad and beyond. Government after government has by their influence, without open conquest of its territory, been linked together in a net of intrigue directed against nothing less than the peace and liberty of the world. The meshes of that intrigue must be broken, but cannot be broken unless wrongs already done are undone; and adequate measures must be taken to prevent it from ever again being rewoven or repaired.

Of course, the imperial German government and those whom it is using for their own undoing are seeking to obtain pledges that the war will end in the restoration of the status quo ante. It was the status quo ante out of which this iniquitous war issued forth, the power of the imperial German government within the empire and its widespread domination and influence outside of that empire. That status must be altered in such fashion as to prevent any such hideous thing from ever happening again.

We are fighting for the liberty, the self-government and the undictated development of all peoples, and every feature of the settlement that concludes this war must be conceived and executed for that purpose. Wrongs must first be righted and then adequate safeguards must be created to prevent their being committed again. We ought not to consider remedies merely because they have a pleasing and sonorous sound. Practical questions can be settled only by practical means. Phrases will not achieve the result. Effective readjustments will; and whatever readjustments are necessary must be made.

But they must follow a principle, and that principle is plain. No people must be forced under sovereignty under which it does not wish to live. No territory must change hands except for the purpose of securing those who inhabit it a fair chance of life and liberty. No indemnities must be insisted on except those that constitute payment for manifest wrongs done. No readjustments of power must be made except such as will tend to secure the future peace of the world and the future welfare and happiness of its peoples.

And then the free peoples of the world must draw together in some common covenant, some genuine and practical co-operation, that will in effect combine their force to secure peace and justice in the dealings of nations with one another. The brotherhood of mankind must no longer be a fair but empty phrase; it must be given a structure of force and reality. The nations must realize their common life and effect a workable partnership to secure that life against the aggressions of autocratic and self-pleasing power.

For these things we can afford to pour out blood and treasure. For these are the things we have always professed to desire, and unless we pour out blood and treasure now and succeed we may never be able to unite or show conquering force again in the great cause of human liberty. The day has come to conquer or submit. If the forces of autocracy can divide us, they will overcome us; if we stand together, victory is certain and the liberty which victory will secure. We can afford then to be generous, but we cannot afford then or now to be weak or omit any single guarantee of justice and security.

WOODROW WILSON.

EXECUTIVE ORDER

[Authorizing employment of foreign inspectors.]

THE WHITE HOUSE, *June 4, 1917.*

The Civil Service Commission may, in its discretion, when it believes such action to be in the interest of the service, authorize the employment by the War Department, for such time as may be necessary during the period of the present war, of the inspection staffs now or heretofore employed by the British, French, Russian, or Italian Government in munitions factories of this country, including subjects of countries allied with the United States in war. In each case in which the War Department requests authority under this order it shall furnish to the Commission a list giving the name, designation, rate of pay, and nationality of each person proposed for employment.

WOODROW WILSON.

By the President of the United States of America.

A PROCLAMATION

[Contribution Day for Aid of Stricken Ruthenians (Ukrainians).]

Whereas, I approved on March 2, 1917, a Joint Resolution of the Congress of the United States of America, reading as follows:

"Whereas in the countries situated in the eastern part of Europe, the theatre of devastating war, there are at least one million Ruthenians (Ukrainians) in dire need of food, clothing, and shelter; and

"Whereas hundreds of thousands of these people have been forced to abandon their homes and their property, and being deprived of all opportunity to provide even for their most elementary wants have undergone disease, starvation, and indescribable suffering; and

"Whereas the people of the United States of America have learned with sorrow of this terrible plight of great numbers of their fellow beings and have most generously responded to the appeal of humanity for assistance whenever such appeal has reached them: Therefore be it

"Resolved by the Senate and House of Representatives of the United States of America in Congress Assembled, That in view of the wretchedness, misery, and privation which these people are enduring, the President of the United States be respectfully requested to designate and appoint a day on which the citizens of this country may give expression to their sympathy by contributing to the funds now being raised for the relief of the Ruthenians (Ukrainians) in the belligerent countries."

And Whereas, I feel confident that the people of the United States will be moved to aid these people stricken by war, famine and disease;

Now, therefore, I, Woodrow Wilson, President of the United States, in compliance with the request of the Congress of the United States do appoint and proclaim April 21, 1917, as a day upon which the people of the United States may make such contributions as they feel disposed for the aid of the stricken Ruthenians (Ukrainians) in the belligerent countries.

Contributions may be addressed to the American Red Cross, Washington, D. C., which will care for their proper distribution.

In witness whereof, I have hereunto set my hand and caused the seal of the United States to be affixed.

Done at the City of Washington this sixteenth day of March in the year of our Lord one thousand nine hundred and seventeen, and of the Independence of the United States the one hundred and forty-first.

[SEAL.]

WOODROW WILSON.

By the President:

ROBERT LANSING, *Secretary of State.*

EXECUTIVE ORDERS

[Listing alien enemies for International Red Cross.]

THE WHITE HOUSE, *May, 9, 1917*

Whereas Section 4 of the Red Cross Convention signed at Geneva, July 6, 1906, to which the United States is a party, provides:

Belligerents will keep each other mutually advised of internments and transfers, together with admissions to hospitals and deaths which occur among the sick and wounded in their hands. They will collect all objects of personal use, valuables, letters, etc., which are found upon the field of battle, or have been left by the sick or wounded who have died in sanitary formations, or other establishments, for transmission to persons in interest through the authorities of their own country (35 Stat. Pt. 2, 1885, 1891).

And Whereas the Charter of the American Red Cross of January 5, 1905, in Section 3, paragraph 4, provides:

That the purposes of this corporation are and shall be Fourth. To act in matters of voluntary relief and in accord with the military and naval authorities as a medium of communication between the people of the United States of America and their Army and Navy, and to act in such matters between similar national societies of other governments through the "Comité International de Secours" and the Government and the people and the Army and Navy of the United States of America. (33 Stat. 600.)

Now Therefore, in order that the said Conventional provision shall be carried out in good faith by the United States, it is ordered that the Executive Departments of the United States shall furnish to such representative as may be designed by the American Red Cross lists of all alien enemies now interned in the United States, to the end that the said lists may be forwarded to the International Red Cross at Geneva, in pursuance of the said recited provision of the Charter of the American Red Cross.

WOODROW WILSON.

[Amending consular regulations and forms.]

THE WHITE HOUSE, *May, 11, 1917.*

Paragraph 160 of the Consular Regulations is hereby amended to read as follows:

Verifications of American passports and visa of Foreign passports.—A diplomatic officer or a consular officer, including a consular agent, may verify regularly issued American passports by endorsing thereon the word "Good" in the language of the country and affixing to the endorsement his official signature and seal. A diplomatic officer shall verify an American passport only when there is no American consulate established in the city where the mission is situated, or when the consular officer is absent, or the Government of the country refuses to acknowledge the validity of the consular verification. Whenever a passport without signature is presented to be verified the holder should be required to sign it before it is verified by a diplomatic or consular officer. No verification of a passport shall be made after its validity has expired. No fee shall be collected for verifying an American passport or, when instructed to do so by the Department of State, for visaing a foreign passport.

Consular Forms Nos. 10 and 11 are amended to read as follows:

FORM NO. 10.

Form for verification of an American passport.

(Paragraph 160.)

CONSULATE OF THE UNITED STATES OF AMERICA AT . . . .
. . . ., 19. . . . .

Good.

(L. S.)   . . . .,

Consul of the United States of America.

FORM NO. 11.

Form for a visa of a foreign passport.

(Paragraph 160.)

CONSULATE OF THE UNITED STATES OF AMERICA AT . . . .
. . . ., 19. . . . .

Seen.

(L. S.)   . . . .,

Consul of the United States of America.

Sections 8 and 9 of the Tariff of United States Consular Fees are hereby amended to read as follows:

Fee.

8. Issuing a passport—Form No. 9. . . . .$1.00
(No fee shall be collected for extending a passport.)

9. Verifying an American passport (Form No. 10) or visaing a foreign passport (Form No. 11). . . . . .No fee

WOODROW WILSON.

[Reinstating certain persons formerly in the competitive service.]

THE WHITE HOUSE, *May, 22, 1917.*

Civil Service Rule IX is hereby amended by numbering the present rule as a paragraph and adding the following paragraph:

2. A person resigning a scientific, professional, or technical position in the competitive service in which he has acquired training and experience not to be acquired elsewhere, to enter the public service of a State, county, municipality, or foreign government in a similar capacity, may immediately upon the completion of such service be reinstated in the Department in which he formerly served, upon the certificate of the Commission issued upon the requisition of the Department dated within three years from the date of his separation from the competitive service.

As amended the rule will read:

1. A person separated without delinquency or misconduct from a competitive position, or from a position which he entered by transfer or promotion from a competitive position, may be reinstated in the Department or office in which he formerly served, upon certificate of the Commission, subject to the following limitations:

(*a*) The separation must have occurred within one year next preceding the date of the requisition of the nominating or appointing officer for such certificate; but this limitation shall not apply to a person who served in the Civil War or the War with Spain and was honorably discharged, or his widow, or an army nurse of either war.

(*b*) No person may be reinstated to a position requiring an examination different from that required for the position from which he was separated without passing an appropriate examination.

2. A person resigning a scientific, professional, or technical position in the competitive service in which he has acquired training and experience not to be acquired elsewhere, to enter the public service of a State, county, municipality, or foreign government in a similar capacity, may immediately upon the completion of such service be reinstated in the Department in which he formerly served, upon the certificate of the Commission issued upon the requisition of the Department dated within three years from the date of his separation from the competitive service.

WOODROW WILSON.

ADDRESS

[Flag Day Exercises.]

WASHINGTON, D, C., *June 14, 1917.*

MY FELLOW CITIZENS:

We meet to celebrate Flag Day because this flag which we honor and under which we serve is the emblem of our unity, our power, our thought and purpose as a Nation. It has no other character than that which we give it from generation to generation. The choices are ours. It floats in majestic silence above the hosts that execute those choices, whether in peace or in war. And yet, though silent, it speaks to us— speaks to us of the past, of the men and women who went before us and of the records they wrote upon it. We celebrate the day of its birth; and from its birth until now it has witnessed a great history, has floated on high the symbol of great events, of a great plan of life worked out by a great people. We are about to carry it into battle, to lift it where it will draw the fire of our enemies. We are about to bid thousands, hundreds of thousands, it may be millions, of our men, the young, the strong, the capable men of the Nation, to go forth and die beneath it on fields of blood far away—for what? For some unaccustomed thing? For something for which it has never sought the fire before? American armies were never before sent across the seas. Why are they sent now? For some new purpose, for which this great flag has never been carried before, or for some old, familiar, heroic purpose for which it has seen men, its own men, die on every battle field upon which Americans have borne arms since the Revolution?

These are questions which must be answered. We are Americans. We in our turn serve America, and can serve her with no private purpose. We must use her flag as she has always used it. We are accountable at the bar of history and must plead in utter frankness what purpose it is we seek to serve.

It is plain enough how we were forced into the war. The extraordinary insults and aggressions of the Imperial German Government left us no self-respecting choice but to take up arms in defense of our rights as a free people and of our honor as a sovereign government. The military masters of Germany denied us the right to be neutral. They filled our unsuspecting communities with vicious spies and conspirators and sought to corrupt the opinion of our people in their own behalf. When they found that they could not do that their agents diligently spread sedition amongst us and sought to draw our own citizens from their allegiance—and some of those agents were men connected with the official embassy of the German Government itself here in our own Capital. They sought by violence to destroy our industries and arrest our commerce. They tried to incite Mexico to take up arms against us and to draw Japan into a hostile alliance with her— and that, not by indirection, but by direct suggestion from the foreign office in Berlin. They impudently denied us the use of the high seas and repeatedly executed their threat that they would send to their death any of our people who ventured to approach the coasts of Europe. And many of our own people were corrupted. Men began to look upon their own neighbors with suspicion and to wonder in their hot resentment and surprise whether there was any community in which hostile intrigue did not lurk. What great nation in such circumstances would not have taken up arms? Much as we had desired peace, it was denied us, and not of our own choice. This flag under which we serve would have been dishonored had we withheld our hand.

But that is only part of the story. We know now as clearly as we knew before we were ourselves engaged that we are not the enemies of the German people and that they are not our enemies. They did not originate or desire this hideous war or wish that we should be drawn into it; and we are vaguely conscious that we are fighting their cause, as they will some day see it, as well as our own. They are themselves in the grip of the same sinister power that has now at last stretched its ugly talons out and drawn blood from us. The whole world is at war because the whole world is in the grip of that power and is trying out the great battle which shall determine whether it is to be brought under its mastery or fling itself free.

The war was begun by the military masters of Germany, who proved to be also the masters of Austria-Hungary. These men have never regarded nations as peoples, men, women, and children of like blood and frame as themselves, for whom governments existed and in whom governments had their life. They have regarded them merely as serviceable organizations which they could by force or intrigue bend or corrupt to their own purpose. They have regarded the smaller States, in particular, and the peoples who could be overwhelmed by force, as their natural tools and instruments of domination. Their purpose has long been avowed.

The statesmen of other nations, to whom that purpose was incredible, paid little attention; regarded what German professors expounded in their classrooms and German writers set forth to the world as the goal of German policy as rather the dream of minds detached from practical affairs, as preposterous private conceptions of German destiny, than as the actual plans of responsible rulers; but the rulers of Germany themselves knew all the while what concrete plans, what well-advanced intrigues lay back of what the professors and the writers were saying, and were glad to go forward unmolested, filling the thrones of Balkan States with German princes, putting German officers at the service of Turkey to drill her armies and make interest with her government, developing plans of sedition and rebellion in India and Egypt, setting their fires in Persia. The demands made by Austria upon Servia were a mere single step in a plan which compassed Europe and Asia, from Berlin to Bagdad. They hoped those demands might not arouse Europe, but they meant to press them whether they did or not, for they thought themselves ready for the final issue of arms.

Their plan was to throw a broad belt of German military power and political control across the very center of Europe and beyond the Mediterranean into the hearts of Asia; and Austria-Hungary was to be as much their tool and pawn as Servia or Bulgaria or Turkey or the ponderous states of the East. Austria-Hungary, indeed, was to become part of the central German Empire, absorbed and dominated by the same forces and influences that had originally cemented the German states themselves. The dream had its heart at Berlin. It could have had a heart nowhere else! It rejected the idea of solidarity of race entirely. The choice of peoples played no part in it at all. It contemplated binding together racial and political units which could be kept together only by force—Czechs, Magyars, Croats, Serbs, Roumanians, Turks, Armenians—the proud states of Bohemia and Hungary, the stout little commonwealths of the Balkans, the indomitable Turks, the subtile peoples of the East. These peoples did not wish to be united. They ardently desired to direct their own affairs, would be satisfied only by undisputed independence. They could be kept quiet only by the presence or the constant threat of armed men. They would live under a common power only by sheer compulsion and await the day of revolution. But the German military statesmen had reckoned with all that and were ready to deal with it in their own way.

And they have actually carried the greater part of that amazing plan into execution! Look how things stand. Austria is at their mercy. It has acted, not upon its own initiative or upon the choice of its own people, but at Berlin's dictation ever since the war began. Its people now desire peace, but can not have it until leave is granted from Berlin. The so-called Central Powers are in fact but a single power. Servia is at its mercy, should its hands be but for a moment freed. Bulgaria has consented to its will, and Roumania is overrun. The Turkish armies, which Germans trained, are serving Germany, certainly not themselves, and the guns of German warships lying in the harbor at Constantinople remind Turkish statesmen every day that they have no choice but to take their orders from Berlin. From Hamburg to the Persian Gulf the net is spread.

Is it not easy to understand the eagerness for peace that has been manifested from Berlin ever since the snare was set and sprung? Peace, peace, peace has been the talk of her foreign office for now a year and more; not peace upon her own initiative, but upon the initiative of the nations over which she now deems herself to hold the advantage. A little of the talk has been public, but most of it has been private. Through all sorts of channels it has come to me, and in all sorts of guises, but never with the terms disclosed which the German Government would be willing to accept. That government has other valuable pawns in its hands besides those I have mentioned. It still holds a valuable part of France, though with slowly relaxing grasp, and practically the whole of Belgium. Its armies press close upon Russia and overrun Poland at their will. It can not go farther; it dare not go back. It wishes to close its bargain before it is too late and it has little left to offer for the pound of flesh it will demand.

The military masters under whom Germany is bleeding see very clearly to what point fate has brought them. If they fall back or are forced back an inch, their power both abroad and at home will fall to pieces like a house of cards. It is their power at home they are thinking about now more than their power abroad. It is that power which is trembling under their very feet; and deep fear has entered their hearts. They have but one chance to perpetuate their military power or even their controlling political influence. If they can secure peace now, with the immense advantages still in their hands which they have up to this point apparently gained, they will have justified themselves before the German people; they will have gained by force what they promised to gain by it—an immense expansion of German power, an immense enlargement of German industrial and commercial opportunities. Their prestige will be secure, and with their prestige their political power. If they fail, their people will thrust them aside; a government accountable to the people themselves will be set up in Germany as it has been in England, in the United States, in France, and in all the great countries of the modern time except Germany. If they succeed they are safe, and Germany and the world are undone; if they fail, Germany is saved and the world will be at peace. If they succeed, America will fall within the menace. We and all the rest of the world must remain armed, as they will remain, and must make ready for the next step in their aggression; if they fail, the world may unite for peace, and Germany may be of the union.

Do you not now understand the new intrigue, the intrigue for peace, and why the masters of Germany do not hesitate to use any agency that promises to effect their purpose, the deceit of the nations? Their present particular aim is to deceive all those who throughout the world stand for the rights of peoples and the self-government of nations; for they see what immense strength of the forces of justice and of liberalism are gathering out of this war. They are employing liberals in their enterprise. They are using men, in Germany and without, as their spokesmen whom they have hitherto despised and oppressed, using them for their own destruction—socialists, the leaders of labor, the thinkers they have hitherto sought to silence. Let them once succeed and these men, now their tools, will be ground to powder beneath the weight of the great military empire they will have set up; the revolutionists in Russia will be cut off from all succor or cooperation in western Europe and a counter revolution fostered and supported:

Germany herself will lose her chance of freedom; and all Europe will arm for the next, the final struggle.

The sinister intrigue is being no less actively conducted in this country than in Russia and in every country in Europe to which the agents and dupes of the Imperial German Government can get access. That Government has many spokesmen here, in places high and low. They have learned discretion. They keep within the law. It is opinion they utter now, not sedition. They proclaim the liberal purposes of their masters; declare this a foreign war which can touch America with no danger to either her lands or her institutions; set England at the center of the stage and talk of her ambition to assert economic dominion throughout the world; appeal to our ancient tradition of isolation in the politics of the nations; and seek to undermine the Government with false professions of loyalty to its principles.

But they will make no headway. The false betray themselves always in every accent. It is only friends and partisans of the German Government whom we have already identified who utter these thinly disguised disloyalties. The facts are patent to all the world, and nowhere are they more plainly seen than in the United States, where we are accustomed to deal with facts and not with sophistries; and the great fact that stands out above all the rest is that this is a people's war, a war for freedom and justice and self-government amongst all the nations of the world, a war to make the world safe for the peoples who live upon it and have made it their own, the German people themselves included; and that with us rests the choice to break through all these hypocrisies and patent cheats and masks of brute force and help set the world free, or else stand aside and let it be dominated a long age through by sheer weight of arms and the arbitrary choices of self-constituted masters, by the nation which can maintain the biggest armies and the most irresistible armaments—a power to which the world has afforded no parallel and in the face of which political freedom must wither and perish.

For us there is but one choice. We have made it. Woe be to the man or group of men that seeks to stand in our way in this day of high resolution, when every principle we hold dearest is to be vindicated and made secure for the salvation of the nations. We are ready to plead at the bar of history, and our flag shall wear a new luster. Once more we shall make good with our lives and fortunes the great faith to which we were born, and a new glory shall shine in the face of our people.

HOW THE WAR CAME TO AMERICA

[The Red, White and Blue Book.]

PUBLISHED BY THE COMMITTEE ON PUBLIC
INFORMATION, JUNE 25, 1917

In the years when this republic was still struggling for existence, in the face of threatened encroachments by hostile monarchies over the sea, in order to make the New World safe for democracy our forefathers established here the policy that soon came to be known as the Monroe Doctrine. Warning the Old World not to interfere in the political life of the New, our Government pledged itself in return to abstain from interference in the political conflicts of Europe; and history has vindicated the wisdom of this course. We were then too weak to influence the destinies of Europe, and it was vital to mankind that this first great experiment in government of and by the people should not be disturbed by foreign attack.

Reinforced by the experience of our expanding national life, this doctrine has been ever since the dominating element in the growth of our foreign policy. Whether or not we could have maintained it in case of concerted attack from abroad, it has seemed of such importance to us that we were at all times ready to go to war in its defense. And though since it was first enunciated our strength has grown by leaps and bounds, although in that time the vast increase in our foreign trade and of travel abroad, modern transport, modern mails, the cables and the wireless have brought us close to Europe and have made our isolation more and more imaginary, there has been until the outbreak of the present conflict small desire on our part to abrogate or even amend the old familiar tradition which has for so long given us peace.

In both conferences at The Hague, in 1899 and 1907, we reaffirmed this policy. As our delegates signed the first convention in regard to arbitration they read into the minutes this statement:

"Nothing contained in this convention shall be so construed as to require the United States of America to depart from its traditional policy of not intruding upon, interfering with or entangling itself in the political questions or policy or internal administration of any foreign state; nor shall anything contained in the said convention be construed to imply a relinquishment by the United States of America of its traditional attitude toward purely American questions."

At The Hague we pledged ourselves, in case we ever went to war, to observe certain broad general rules of decency and fair fighting. But at the same time we cleared ourselves from any responsibility for forcing other nations to observe similar pledges. And in 1906, when our delegates took part in the Algeciras Conference, which was to regulate the affairs of the distracted Kingdom of Morocco, they followed the same formula there. While acquiescing in the new regime which guaranteed the independence and integrity of Morocco, we explicitly announced that we assumed no police responsibility for the enforcement of the treaty. And if any honest doubt was left as to our attitude in regard to the enforcement of Old World agreements, it was dispelled five years later, when our Government refused to protest against the overthrow of the Acte d'Algeciras.

We declined to be drawn into quarrels abroad which might endanger in any way our traditional policy.

Our second great tradition in international relations has been our persistent effort to secure a stable and equitable agreement of the nations upon such a maritime code as would assure to all the world a just freedom of the seas.

This effort was born of our vital need. For although it was possible for the Republic to keep aloof from the nineteenth century disputes that rent the Continent of Europe, we could not be indifferent to the way in which war was conducted at sea. In those early years of our national life, when we were still but a few communities ranged along the Atlantic coast, we were a sea-faring people. At a time when our frontiersmen had not yet reached the Mississippi, the fame of our daring clipper ships had spread to all the Seven Seas. So while we could watch the triumphant march and the tragic countermarch of Napoleon's grand army with detached indifference, his Continental Blockade and the British Orders in Council at once affected the lives of our citizens intimately and disastrously.

So it was in the case of the Barbary pirates. We had no interest in the land quarrels and civil wars of the Barbary States, but we fought them for obstructing the freedom of the seas.

And in the decades ever since, although the imagination of our people has been engrossed in the immense labor of winning the West, our Department of State has never lost sight of the compelling interest that we have upon the seas, and has constantly striven to gain the assent of all nations to a maritime code which should be framed and enforced by a joint responsibility. Various watchwords have arisen in this long controversy. We have urged the inviolability of private property at sea, we have asked for a liberal free list and a narrow definition of contraband. But our main insistence has not been on any such details. One salient idea has guided our diplomacy. The law of the sea must be founded not on might, but on right and a common accord, upon a code binding all alike, which cannot be changed or set aside by the will of any one nation. Our ideal has been not a weakening but a strengthening of legal restraint by the free will and agreement of all. We have asked nothing for ourselves that we do not ask for the whole world. The seas will never be free, in our American meaning, until all who sail thereon have had a voice in framing sea laws. The just governance of the seas must rest on the consent of the governed.

No other question of international polity has found the great Powers more divided. But in our insistence on this fundamental principle, we have been strengthened by the support of many other countries. At times we have had the support of Great Britain. No one of our Secretaries of State has more clearly defined our ideal than has Viscount Grey, recently British Secretary of State for Foreign Affairs. None of our statesmen has ever gone so far as he in advocating limitation of the rights of belligerents on the sea. It was on his initiative that the international naval conference was summoned to London in 1909, and it was under his guidance that the eminent international lawyers and diplomats and admirals who gathered there drew up the Declaration of London.

While there were in that Declaration sections that did not quite meet our approval and that we should have liked to amend, the document was from our point of view a tremendous step in advance. For although, like any effort to concisely formulate the broad principles of equity, it did not wholly succeed in its purpose, it was at least an honest attempt to arrive at an agreement on a complete international code of sea law, based upon mutual consent and not to be altered by any belligerent in the heat of the conflict.

But the Declaration of London was not ratified by the British Parliament, for the point of view prevailing then in England was that a power dependent almost wholly upon its navy for protection could not safely accept further limitations upon action at sea unless there were compensating limitations on land powers. And this latter concession Germany consistently refused to make. This conference therefore came to naught. And the London Declaration having been rejected by the strongest maritime Power, its indorsement was postponed by all the other countries involved. Our motives, however, remained unchanged; and our Government persisted in its purpose to secure a general ratification either of this declaration or of some similar maritime code.

There has been in our diplomacy one more outstanding aspiration. We have constantly sought to substitute judicial for military settlement of disputes between nations.

The genesis of this idea dates from the discussions over the Federal organizations of our thirteen original States, which were almost as jealous of their sovereignties as are the nations of Europe to-day. The first great step toward the League of Honor, which we hope will at last bring peace to the world, was taken when our thirteen States agreed to disarm and submit all their disputes to the high tribunal of the new federation.

WAR TRAINING AT AN AMERICAN UNIVERSITY

WAR TRAINING AT AN AMERICAN UNIVERSITY.

American colleges and universities were in the forefront of the institutions used to train American youth for the purposes of war. The illustration shows a section of the student body of Harvard University, members of the Reserve Officers' Training Corps, drilling upon the grounds of the University.

And this idea of an interstate court, which except at the time of our Civil War has given this nation internal peace, has profoundly influenced our foreign policy. Of our efforts to bring others to our way of thinking, an historical resume was presented by our delegates at the First Hague Conference. A project was submitted there for the formation of a world court. And a few years later Mr. Root, our Secretary of State, in instructing our delegates to the Second Conference at The Hague, laid especial emphasis on this same international ideal.

We have taken a particular pride in being in the vanguard of the movement for the peaceable settlement by process of law of all disputes between nations. And these efforts have not been without success. For although the last few decades have seen this principle time and again put under a terrific strain, no nation has dared to go to war against the award of a court of arbitration. The stupendous possibilities that lie in arbitration for solving international problems, promoting liberal principles and safeguarding human life had been amply demonstrated before the present war began.

But in the discussions at The Hague, largely through the resistance of the German empire and its satellites, the efforts of our delegates and those of other governments to bring about a general treaty of compulsory arbitration had failed. And therefore this nation, having been thwarted in its attempts to secure a general agreement, began negotiations with all those nations which, like our own, preferred the methods of law and peace, with the purpose of effecting dual arbitration treaties. And before the end of 1914 we had signed far-reaching treaties with thirty nations, twenty of which had been duly ratified and proclaimed. But in this work, too, we were made to feel the same opposition as at The Hague. For, while Great Britain, France, Russia and Italy cordially welcomed our overtures, the German and Austro-Hungarian empires were noticeably absent from the list of those nations who desired, by specific agreements in advance, to minimize the danger of war.

On the eve of the present conflict, our position toward other nations might have been summarized under three heads:

I. The Monroe Doctrine.—We have pledged ourselves to defend the New World from European aggression, and we had by word and deed made it clear that we would not intervene in any European dispute.

II. The Freedom of the Seas.—In every naval conference our influence had been given in support of the principle that sea law to be just and worthy of general respect must be based on the consent of the governed.

III. Arbitration.—As we have secured peace at home by referring interstate disputes to a Federal tribunal, we urged a similar settlement of international controversies. Our ideal was a permanent world court. We had already signed arbitration treaties not only with great powers which might conceivably attack us, but even more freely with weaker neighbors in order to show our good faith in recognizing the equality of all nations both great and small. We had made plain to the nations our purpose to forestall by every means in our power the recurrence of wars in the world.

The outbreak of war in 1914 caught this nation by surprise. The peoples of Europe had had at least some warnings of the coming storm, but to us such a blind, savage onslaught on the ideals of civilization had appeared impossible.

The war was incomprehensible. Either side was championed here by millions living among us who were of European birth. Their contradictory accusations threw our thought into disarray, and in the first chaotic days we could see no clear issue that affected our national policy. There was no direct assault on our rights. It seemed at first to most of us a purely European dispute, and our minds were not prepared to take sides in such a conflict. The President's proclamation of neutrality was received by us as natural and inevitable. It was quickly followed by his appeal to "the citizens of the republic."

"Every man who really loves America will act and speak in the true spirit of neutrality," he said, "which is the spirit of impartiality and fairness and friendliness to all concerned. * * * It will be easy to excite passion and difficult to allay it." He expressed the fear that our nation might become divided in camps of hostile opinion. "Such divisions among us * * * might seriously stand in the way of the proper performance of our duty as the one great nation at peace, the one people holding itself ready to play a part of impartial mediation and speak counsels of peace and accommodation, not as a partisan, but as a friend."

This purpose—the preservation of a strict neutrality in order that later we might be of use in the great task of mediation—dominated all the President's early speeches.

"We are the mediating nation of the world," he declared in an address on April 20, 1915. "We are compounded of the nations of the world; we mediate their blood, we mediate their traditions, we mediate their sentiments, their tastes, their passions; we are ourselves compounded of those things. We are, therefore, able to understand them in the compound, not separately as partisans, but unitedly as knowing and comprehending and embodying them all. It is in that sense that I mean that America is a mediating nation."

American neutrality, in those first months of the great war, was beyond any question real.

But the spirit of neutrality was not easy to maintain. Public opinion was deeply stirred by the German invasion of Belgium and by reports of atrocities there. The Royal Belgian Commission, which came in

September, 1914, to lay their country's cause for complaint before our national Government, was received with sympathy and respect. The President in his reply reserved our decision in the affair. It was the only course he could take without an abrupt departure from our most treasured traditions of non-interference in Old World disputes. But the sympathy of America went out to the Belgians in the heroic tragedy, and from every section of our land money contributions and supplies of food and clothing poured over to the Commission for Relief in Belgium, which was under the able management of our fellow countrymen abroad.

Still, the thought of taking an active part in this European war was very far from most of our minds. The nation shared with the President the belief that by maintaining a strict neutrality we could best serve Europe at the end as impartial mediators.

But in the very first days of the war our Government foresaw that complications on the seas might put us in grave risk of being drawn into the conflict. No neutral nation could foretell what violations of its vital interests at sea might be attempted by the belligerents. And so, on August 6, 1914, our Secretary of State dispatched an identical note to all the powers then at war, calling attention to the risk of serious trouble arising out of this uncertainty of neutrals as to their maritime rights, and proposing that the Declaration of London be accepted by all nations for the duration of the war.

But the British Government's response, while expressing sympathy with the purpose of our suggestion and declaring their "keen desire to consult so far as possible the interests of neutral countries," announced their decision "to adopt generally the rules of the Declaration in question, subject to certain modifications and additions which they judge indispensable to the efficient conduct of their naval operations." The Declaration had not been indorsed by any power in time of peace, and there was no legal obligation on Great Britain to accept it. Her reply, however, was disappointing, for it did nothing to clarify the situation. Great Britain recognized as binding certain long accepted principles of international law and sought now to apply them to the peculiar and unforeseen conditions of this war. But these principles were often vague and therefore full of dangerous possibilities of friction.

Controversies soon arose between Great Britain and this Nation. In practice their ruling sometimes seemed to our Government inconsistent with the spirit of international law, and especially with the established precedents which they invoked. But painful as this divergency of opinion sometimes was, it did not seriously threaten our position of neutrality, for the issues that arose involved only rights of property and were amply covered by the arbitration treaty signed only a short time before by Great Britain and the United States.

And this controversy led to a clearer understanding on our part of the British attitude toward our ideal of the freedom of the seas. They were not willing to accept our classification of the seas as being distinct from the Old World. We had confined our interest to matters affecting rights at sea and had kept carefully aloof from issues affecting the interests of European nations on land. The British were interested in both. They explained that they had participated in the London naval conference in the hope that it would lead to a sound and liberal entente in the interest of the rights of all nations on the sea and on the land as well, and that they had refused to ratify the London Declaration because no compensating accord on the Continent had resulted. They could not afford to decrease the striking power of their navy unless their powerful neighbors on land agreed to decrease their armies.

That this attitude of England deeply impressed our Government is shown by the increasing attention given by the United States to the search for ways and means of insuring at the end of the war a lasting peace for all the world. The address of our President, on May 27, 1916, before the League to Enforce Peace was a milestone in our history.

He outlined the main principles on which a stable peace must rest, principles plainly indicating that this nation would have to give up its position of isolation and assume the responsibilities of a world power. The President said:

"So sincerely do we believe these things that I am sure that I speak the mind and wish of the people of America when I say that the United States is willing to become a partner in any feasible association of nations formed in order to realize these objects and make them secure against violation."

It was a new and significant note in our foreign policy. But the mind of America had learned much in the long bitter months of war. Future historians will make charts of this remarkable evolution in our public opinion: the gradual abandonment of the illusion of isolation; the slow growth of a realization that we could not win freedom on sea—for us a vital interest—unless we consented to do our share in maintaining freedom on land as well, and that we could not have peace in the world— the peace we loved and needed for the perfection of our democracy— unless we were willing and prepared to help to restrain any nation that wilfully endangered the peace of the whole world family.

Had this address of the President come before the war, there would have arisen a storm of protest from all sections of the land. But in May, 1916, the nation's response was emphatic approval.

In the meantime, although our neutral rights were not brought into question by Germany as early as by England, the German controversy was infinitely more serious.

For any dissensions that might arise, no arbitration treaty existed between the United States and the German Government. This was from no fault of ours. We had tried to establish with Germany the same treaty relations we had with Great Britain and nineteen other nations. But these overtures had been rejected. And this action on the part of the Imperial German Government was only one example of its whole system of diplomacy. In both conferences at The Hague, it had been the German delegates who were the most active in blocking all projects for the pacific settlement of disputes between nations.

They had preferred to limit international relations to the old modes of diplomacy and war. It was therefore obvious from the first that any controversy with the German Government would be exceedingly serious; for if it could not be solved by direct diplomatic conversations, there was no recourse except to war.

From such conversations there is small hope of satisfactory results unless the good faith of both sides is profound. If either side lacks good faith, or reveals in all its actions an insidious hostility, diplomacy is of no avail. And so it has proved in the present case.

In the first year of the war the Government of Germany stirred up among its people a feeling of resentment against the United States on account of our insistence upon our right as a neutral nation to trade in munitions with the belligerent powers. Our legal right in the matter was not seriously questioned by Germany. She could not have done so consistently, for as recently as the Balkan wars of 1912 and 1913 both Germany and Austria sold munitions to the belligerents.

Their appeals to us in the present war were not to observe international law, but to revise it in their interest. And these appeals they tried to make on moral and humanitarian grounds. But upon "the moral issue" involved, the stand taken by the United States was consistent with its traditional policy and with obvious common sense.

For, if, with all other neutrals, we refused to sell munitions to belligerents, we could never in time of a war of our own obtain munitions from neutrals, and the nation which had accumulated the largest reserves of war supplies in time of peace would be assured of victory.

The militarist state that invested its money in arsenals would be at a fatal advantage over the free people who invested their wealth in schools. To write into international law that neutrals should not trade in munitions would be to hand over the world to the rule of the nation with the largest armament factories. Such a policy the United States of America could not accept.

But our principal controversy with the German Government, and the one which rendered the situation at once acute, rose out of their announcement of a sea zone where their submarines would operate in violation of all accepted principles of international law. Our indignation at such a threat was soon rendered passionate by the sinking of the Lusitania. This attack upon our rights was not only grossly illegal; it defied the fundamental concepts of humanity.

Aggravating restraints on our trade were grievances which could be settled by litigation after the war, but the wanton murder of peaceable men and of innocent women and children, citizens of a nation with which Germany was at peace, was a crime against the civilized world which could never be settled in any court.

Our Government, however, inspired still by a desire to preserve peace if possible, used every resource of diplomacy to force the German Government to abandon such attacks. This diplomatic correspondence, which has already been published, proves beyond doubt that our Government sought by every honorable means to preserve faith in that mutual sincerity between nations which is the only basis of sound diplomatic interchange.

But evidence of the bad faith of the Imperial German Government soon piled up on every hand. Honest efforts on our part to establish a firm basis of good neighborliness with the German people were met by their Government with quibbles, misrepresentations and counter accusations against their enemies abroad.

And meanwhile in this country official agents of the Central Powers —protected from criminal prosecution by diplomatic immunity—conspired against our internal peace, placed spies and agents provocateurs throughout the length and breadth of our land, and even in high positions of trust in departments of our Government.

While expressing a cordial friendship for the people of the United States, the Government of Germany had its agents at work both in Latin America and Japan. They bought or subsidized papers and supported speakers there to rouse feelings of bitterness and distrust against us in those friendly nations, in order to embroil us in war. They were inciting to insurrection in Cuba, in Haiti, and in Santo Domingo; their hostile hand was stretched out to take the Danish Islands; and everywhere in South America they were abroad sowing the seeds of dissension, trying to stir up one nation against another and all against the United States.

In their sum these various operations amounted to direct assault upon the Monroe doctrine. And even if we had given up our right to travel on the sea, even if we had surrendered to German threats and abandoned our legitimate trade in munitions, the German offensive in the New World, in our own land and among our neighbors, was becoming too serious to be ignored.

So long as it was possible, the Government of the United States tried to believe that such activities, the evidence of which was already in a large measure at hand, were the works of irresponsible and misguided individuals. It was only reluctantly, in the face of overwhelming proof, that the recall of the Austro-Hungarian ambassador and of the German military and naval attaches was demanded.

Proof of their criminal violations of our hospitality was presented to their Governments. But these Governments in reply offered no apologies nor did they issue reprimands. It became clear that such intrigue was their settled policy.

In the meantime the attacks of the German submarines upon the lives and property of American citizens had gone on; the protests of our Government were now sharp and ominous; and this nation was rapidly being drawn into a state of war.

As the President said in Topeka, on February 2, 1916:

"We are not going to invade any nation's right. But suppose, my fellow countrymen, some nation should invade our rights. What then? * * * I have come here to tell you that the difficulties of our foreign policy * * * daily increase in number and intricacy and in danger, and I would be derelict to my duty to you if I did not deal with you in these matters with the utmost candor, and tell you what it may be necessary to use the force of the United States to do."

The next day, at St. Louis, he repeated his warning:

"The danger is not from within, gentlemen, it is from without; and I am bound to tell you that that danger is constant and immediate, not because anything new has happened, not because there has been any change in our international relationships within recent weeks or months, but because the danger comes with every turn of events."

The break would have come sooner if our Government had not been restrained by the hope that saner counsels might still prevail in Germany. For it was well known to us that the German people had to a very large extent been kept in ignorance of many of the secret crimes of their Government against us.

And the pressure of a faction of German public opinion less hostile to this country was shown when their Government acquiesced to some degree in our demands, at the time of the Sussex outrage, and for nearly a year maintained at least a pretense of observing the pledge they had made to us. The tension was abated.

While the war spirit was growing in some sections of our nation, there was still no widespread desire to take part in the conflict abroad; for the tradition of noninterference in Europe's political affairs was too deeply rooted in our national life to be easily overthrown.

Moreover, two other considerations strengthened our Government in its efforts to remain neutral in this war. The first was our traditional sense of responsibility toward all the republics of the New World. Throughout the crisis our Government was in constant communication with the countries of Central and South America.

They, too, preferred the ways of peace. And there was a very obvious obligation upon us to safeguard their interests with our own.

The second consideration, which had been so often developed in the President's speeches, was the hope that by keeping aloof from the bitter passions abroad, by preserving untroubled here the holy ideals of civilized intercourse between nations, we might be free at the end of this war to bind up the wounds of the conflict, to be the restorers and rebuilders of the wrecked structure of the world.

All these motives held us back, but it was not long until we were beset by further complications. We soon had reason to believe that the recent compliance of the German Government had not been made to us in good faith, and was only temporary, and by the end of 1916 it was plain that our neutral status had again been made unsafe through the ever-increasing aggressiveness of the German autocracy. There was a general agreement here with the statement of our President on October 26, 1916, that this conflict was the last great war involving the world in which we would remain neutral.

It was in this frame of mind, fearing we might be drawn into the war if it did not soon come to an end, that the President began the preparation of his note, asking the belligerent Powers to define their war aims. But before he had completed it the world was surprised by the peace move of the German Government—an identical note on behalf of the German Empire, Austria-Hungary, Bulgaria and Turkey, sent through neutral Powers on December 12, 1916, to the Governments of the Allies, proposing negotiations for peace.

While expressing the wish to end this war—"a catastrophe which thousands of years of common civilization was unable to prevent and which injures the most precious achievements of humanity"—the greater portion of the note was couched in terms that gave small hope of a lasting peace.

Boasting of German conquests, "the glorious deeds of our armies," the note implanted in neutral minds the belief that it was the purpose of the Imperial German Government to insist upon such conditions as would leave all Central Europe under German dominance and so build up an empire which would menace the whole liberal world.

Moreover, the German proposal was accompanied by a thinly veiled threat to all neutral nations; and from a thousand sources, official and unofficial, the word came to Washington that unless the neutrals used their influence to bring the war to an end on terms dictated from Berlin, Germany and her allies would consider themselves henceforth free from any obligations to respect the rights of neutrals.

The Kaiser ordered the neutrals to exert pressure on the entente to bring the war to an abrupt end, or to beware of the consequences. Clear warnings were brought to our Government that if the German peace move should not be successful, the submarines would be unleashed for a more intense and ruthless war upon all commerce.

On the 18th of December the President dispatched his note to all the belligerent powers, asking them to define their war aims. There was still hope in our minds that the mutual suspicions between the warring powers might be decreased, and the menace of future German aggression and dominance be removed, by finding a guaranty of good faith in a league of nations.

There was a chance that by the creation of such a league as part of the peace negotiations the war could now be brought to an end before our nation was involved. Two statements issued to the press by our Secretary of State, upon the day the note was dispatched, threw a clear light on the seriousness with which our Government viewed the crisis.

From this point, events moved rapidly. The powers of the Entente replied to the German peace note. Neutral nations took action on the note of the President, and from both belligerents replies to this note were soon in our hands.

The German reply was evasive—in accord with their traditional preference for diplomacy behind closed doors. Refusing to state to the world their terms, Germany and her allies merely proposed a conference. They adjourned all discussion of any plan for a league of peace until after hostilities should end.

The response of the Entente Powers was frank and in harmony with our principal purpose. Many questions raised in the statement of their aims were so purely European in character as to have small interest for us; but our great concern in Europe was the lasting restoration of peace, and it was clear that this was also the chief interest of the Entente nations.

As to the wisdom of some of the measures they proposed toward this end, we might differ in opinion, but the trend of their proposals was the establishment of just frontiers based on the rights of all nations, the small as well as the great, to decide their own destinies.

The aims of the belligerents were now becoming clear. From the outbreak of hostilities the German Government had claimed that it was fighting a war of defense. But the tone of its recent proposals had been that of a conqueror. It sought a peace based on victory.

The Central Empires aspired to extend their domination over other races. They were willing to make liberal terms to any one of their enemies, in a separate peace which would free their hands to crush other opponents. But they were not willing to accept any peace which did not, all fronts considered, leave them victors and the dominating imperial power of Europe.

The war aims of the Entente showed a determination to thwart this ambition of the Imperial German Government. Against the German peace to further German growth and aggression the Entente Powers offered a plan for a European peace that should make the whole Continent secure.

At this juncture the President read his address to the Senate on January 22, 1917, in which he outlined the kind of peace the United States of America could join in guaranteeing. His words were addressed not only to the Senate and this nation, but to people of all countries:

"May I not add that I hope and believe that I am in effect speaking for liberals and friends of humanity in every nation and of every programme of liberty? I would fain believe that I am speaking for the silent mass of mankind everywhere who have as yet had no place or opportunity to speak their real hearts out concerning the death and ruin they see to have come already upon the persons and the homes they hold most dear."

The address was a rebuke to those who still cherished dreams of a world dominated by one nation. For the peace he outlined was not that of a victorious emperor, it was not the peace of Caesar. It was in behalf of all the world, and it was a Peace of the People:

"No peace can last, or ought to last, which does not recognize and accept the principle that governments derive all their just powers from the consent of the governed, and that no right anywhere exists to hand people about from sovereignty to sovereignty as if they were property.

"I am proposing, as it were, that the nations should with one accord adopt the doctrine of President Monroe as the doctrine of the world; that no nation should seek to extend its policy over any other nation or people, but that every people should be left free to determine its own polity, its own way of development, unhindered, unthreatened, unafraid, the little along with the great and powerful.

"I am proposing that all nations henceforth avoid entangling alliances which would draw them into competitions of power, catch them in a net of intrigue and selfish rivalry and disturb their own affairs with influences intruded from without. There is no entangling alliance in a concert of power. When all unite to act in the same sense and with the same purpose, all act in the common interest and are free to live their own lives under a common protection.

"I am proposing government by the consent of the governed; that freedom of the seas which in international conference after conference representatives of the United States have urged with the eloquence of those who are convinced disciples of liberty, and that moderation of armaments which makes of armies and navies a power for order merely, not an instrument of aggression or of selfish violence.

"And the paths of the sea must, alike in law and in fact, be free. The freedom of the seas is the sine qua non of peace, equality and co-operation.

"It is a problem closely connected with the limitation of naval armament and the co-operation of the navies of the world in keeping the seas at once free and safe. And the question of limiting naval armaments opens the wider and perhaps more difficult question of the limitation of armies and of all programmes of military preparation. . . . There can be no sense of safety and equality among the nations if great preponderating armaments are henceforth to continue here and there to be built up and maintained.

"Mere agreements may not make peace secure. It will be absolutely necessary that a force be created as a guarantor of the supremacy of the settlement so much greater than the force of any nation now engaged or any alliance hitherto formed or projected that no nation, no probable combination of nations, could face or withstand it. If the peace presently to be made is to endure, it must be a peace made secure by the organized major force of mankind."

If there were any doubt in our minds as to which of the great alliances was the more in sympathy with these ideals, it was removed by the popular response abroad to this address of the President. For, while exception was taken to some parts of it in Great Britain and France, it was plain that so far as the peoples of the entente were concerned the President had been amply justified in stating that he spoke for all forward-looking, liberal-minded men and women. It was not so in Germany. The people there who could be reached, and whose hearts were stirred by this enunciation of the principles of a people's peace, were too few or too oppressed to make their voices heard in the councils of their nation. Already, on January 16, 1917, unknown to the people of Germany, Herr Zimmermann, their Secretary of Foreign Affairs, had secretly dispatched a note to their Minister in Mexico, informing him of the German intention to repudiate the Sussex pledge and instructing him to offer to the Mexican Government New Mexico and Arizona if Mexico would join with Japan in attacking the United States.

In the new year of 1917, as through our acceptance of world responsibilities so plainly indicated in the President's utterances in regard to a league of nations, we felt ourselves now drawing nearer to a full accord with the Powers of the entente; and as on the other hand we found ourselves more and more outraged at the German Government's methods of conducting warfare and their brutal treatment of people in their conquered lands; as we more and more uncovered their hostile intrigues against the peace of the new world; and, above all, as the sinister and anti-democratic ideals of their ruling class became manifest in their maneuvres for a peace of conquest—the Imperial German Government abruptly threw aside the mask.

On the last day of January, 1917, Count Bernstorff handed to Mr.

Lansing a note in which his Government announced its purpose to intensify and render more ruthless the operations of their submarines at sea, in a manner against which our Government had protested from the beginning. The German Chancellor also stated before the Imperial Diet that the reason this ruthless policy had not been earlier employed was simply because the Imperial Government had not then been ready to act. In brief, under the guise of friendship and the cloak of false promises, it had been preparing this attack.

This was the direct challenge. There was no possible answer except to hand their Ambassador his passports and so have done with a diplomatic correspondence which had been vitiated from the start by the often proved bad faith of the Imperial Government.

On the same day, February 3, 1917, the President addressed both houses of our Congress and announced the complete severance of our relations with Germany. The reluctance with which he took this step was evident in every word. But diplomacy had failed, and it would have been the hollowest pretense to maintain relations. At the same time, however, he made it plain that he did not regard this act as tantamount to a declaration of war. Here for the first time the President made his sharp distinction between government and people in undemocratic lands:

"We are the sincere friends of the German people," he said, "and earnestly desire to remain at peace with the Government which speaks for them. * * * God grant we may not be challenged by acts of wilful injustice on the part of the Government of Germany."

In this address of the President, and in its indorsement by the Senate, there was a solemn warning; for we still had hope that the German Government might hesitate to drive us to war. But it was soon evident that our warning had fallen on deaf ears. The tortuous ways and means of German official diplomacy were clearly shown in the negotiations opened by them through the Swiss Legation on the 10th of February. In no word of their proposals did the German Government meet the real issue between us. And our State Department replied that no minor negotiations could be entertained until the main issue had been met by the withdrawal of the submarine order.

By the 1st of March it had become plain that the Imperial Government, unrestrained by the warning in the President's address to Congress on February 3, was determined to make good its threat. The President then again appeared before Congress to report the development of the crisis and to ask the approval of the representatives of the nation for the course of armed neutrality upon which, under his constitutional authority, he had now determined. More than 500 of the 531 members of the two houses of Congress showed themselves ready and anxious to act; and the Armed Neutrality Declaration would have beeen accepted if it had not been for the legal death of the Sixty-fourth Congress on March 4.

No "overt" act, however, was ordered by our Government until Count Bernstorff had reached Berlin and Mr. Gerard was in Washington. For the German Ambassador on his departure begged that no irrevocable decision should be taken until he had had the chance to make one final plea for peace to his sovereign. We do not know the nature of his report to the Kaiser; we know only that, even if he kept his pledge and urged an eleventh-hour revocation of the submarine order, he was unable to sway the policy of the Imperial Government.

And so, having exhausted every resource of patience, our Government on the 12th of March finally issued orders to place armed guards on our merchant ships.

With the definite break in diplomatic relations there vanished the last vestige of cordiality toward the Government of Germany. Our attitude was now to change. So long as we had maintained a strict neutrality in the war, for the reason that circumstances might arise in which Europe would have need of an impartial mediator, for us to have given official heed to the accusations of either party would have been to prejudge the case before all the evidence was in. But now at last, with the breaking of friendly relations with the German Government, we were relieved of the oppressive duty of endeavoring to maintain a judicial detachment from the rights and wrongs involved in the war. We were no longer the outside observers striving to hold an even balance of judgment between disputants. One party by direct attack upon our rights and liberties was forcing us into the conflict. And, much as we had hoped to keep out of the fray, it was no little relief to be free at last from that reserve which is expected of a judge.

Much evidence had been presented to us of things so abhorrent to our ideas of humanity that they had seemed incredible, things we had been loath to believe, and with heavy hearts we had sought to reserve our judgment. But with the breaking of relations with the Government of Germany that duty at last was ended. The perfidy of that Government in its dealings with this nation relieved us of the necessity of striving to give them the benefit of the doubt in regard to their crimes abroad. The Government which under cover of profuse professions of friendship had tried to embroil us in war with Mexico and Japan could not expect us to believe in its good faith in other matters. The men whose paid agents dynamited our factories here were capable of the infamies reported against them over the sea. Their Government's protestations, that their purpose was self-defense and the freeing of small nations, fell like a house of cards before the revelation of their "peace terms."

And judging the German Government now in the light of our own experience through the long and patient years of our honest attempt to keep the peace, we could see the great autocracy and read her record through the war. And we found that record damnable. Beginning long before the war in Prussian opposition to every effort that was made by other nations and our own to do away with warfare, the story of the autocracy has been one of vast preparations for war, combined with an attitude of arrogant intolerance toward all other points of view, all other systems of government, all other hopes and dreams of men.

With a fanatical faith in the destiny of German kultur as the system that must rule the world, the Imperial Government's actions have through years of boasting, double dealing, and deceit tended toward aggression upon the rights of others. And if there still be any doubt as to which nation began this war, there can be no uncertainty as to which one was most prepared, most exultant at the chance, and ready instantly to march upon other nations—even those who had given no offense.

The wholesale depredations and hideous atrocities in Belgium and in Serbia were doubtless part and parcel with the Imperial Government's purpose to terrorize small nations into abject submission for generations to come. But in this the Autocracy has been blind. For its record in those countries, and in Poland and in northern France, has given not only to the allies but to liberal peoples throughout the world the conviction that this menace to human liberties everywhere must be utterly shorn of its power for harm.

For the evil it has affected has ranged far out of Europe—out upon the open seas, where its submarines in defiance of law and the concepts of humanity have blown up neutral vessels and covered the waves with the dead and the dying, men and women and children alike. Its agents have conspired against the peace of neutral nations everywhere, sowing the seeds of dissension, ceaselessly endeavoring by tortuous methods of deceit, of bribery, false promises, and intimidation, to stir up brother nations one against the other, in order that the liberal world might not be able to unite, in order that the Autocracy might emerge triumphant from the war.

All this we know from our own experience with the Imperial Government. As they have dealt with Europe, so they have dealt with us and with all mankind. And so out of these years the conviction has grown that until the German Nation is divested of such rulers democracy cannot be safe.

There remained but one element to confuse the issue. One other great autocracy, the Government of the Russian Czar, had long been hostile to free institutions; it had been a stronghold of tyrannies reaching far back into the past; and its presence among the allies had seemed to be in disaccord with the great liberal principles they were upholding in this war. Russia had been a source of doubt. Repeatedly during the conflict liberal Europe had been startled by the news of secret accord between the Kaiser and the Czar.

But now at this crucial time for our nation, on the eve of our entrance into the war, the free men of all the world were thrilled and heartened by the news that the people of Russia had risen to throw off their Government and found a new democracy; and the torch of freedom in Russia lit up the last dark phases of the situation abroad. Here, indeed, was a fit partner for the League of Honor. The conviction was finally crystallized in American minds and hearts that this war across the sea was no mere conflict between dynasties, but a stupendous civil war of all the world; a new campaign in the age-old war, the prize of which is liberty. Here, at last, was a struggle in which all who love freedom have a stake. Further neutrality on our part would have been a crime against our ancestors, who had given their lives that we might be free.

"The world must be made safe for democracy."

On the 2d of April, 1917, the President read to the new Congress his message, in which he asked the Representatives of the Nation to declare the existence of a state of war, and in the early hours of the 6th of April the House by an overwhelming vote accepted the joint resolution which had already passed the Senate:

"Whereas the Imperial German Government has committed repeated acts of war against the Government of the people of the United States of America: Therefore be it

"Resolved by the Senate and House of Representatives of the United States of America in Congress assembled, That the state of war between the United States and the Imperial German Government which has thus been thrust upon the United States is hereby formally declared; and that the President be, and he is hereby, authorized and directed to employ the entire naval and military forces of the United States and the resources of the Government to carry on war against the Imperial German Government, and to bring the conflict to a successful termination all the resources of the country are hereby pledged by the Congress of the United States."

Neutrality was a thing of the past. The time had come when the President's proud prophecy was fulfilled:

"There will come a day when the world will say, 'This America that we thought was full of a multitude of contrary counsels now speaks with the great volume of the heart's accord, and that great heart of America has behind it the supreme moral force of righteousness and hope and the liberty of mankind.'"

EXECUTIVE ORDER

[Amending Alaskan Railroad Townsite Regulations.]

THE WHITE HOUSE, *June 18, 1917.*

WHEREAS certain forfeiture provisions of the Alaskan Railroad Townsite Regulations, hereinafter mentioned, have been found to impair the stability of land titles and, in consequence, the legitimate development of the communities affected, and if effectively enforced will impose hardships upon innocent persons, and

WHEREAS, by reason of the proper enforcement of the penal laws applicable to Alaska, such forfeiture provisions are deemed no longer necessary to accomplish their purpose,

THEREFORE, Executive Order number twenty-two hundred and fourteen, dated June nineteen, nineteen hundred and fifteen, as amended, providing for the sale and disposition of Alaskan railroad townsites pursuant to the Act of Congress approved March twelfth, nineteen hundred and fourteen (thirty-eighth Statutes at Large, page three hundred and five), is hereby further amended by eliminating therefrom all provisions for the forfeiture of lots as a penalty for using the same for the purpose of manufacturing, selling, or otherwise disposing of intoxicating liquors as a beverage, or for gambling, prostitution, or other unlawful purpose, and no lot shall hereafter be forfeited for violation of any of said provisions.   WOODROW WILSON.

EXECUTIVE ORDER

[Creating Exports Council.]

THE WHITE HOUSE, *June 22, 1917.*

By virtue of authority vested in me by Title VII of the Act approved June 15, 1917, entitled, "An Act to punish acts of interference with the foreign relations, the neutrality, and the foreign commerce of the United States, to punish espionage and better to enforce the criminal laws of the United States, and for other purposes," I hereby vest in the Secretary of Commerce the executive administration of all instructions issued by the President under said Title VII and of the proclamations thereunder, and the said Secretary is hereby authorized and directed to take such measures as may be necessary to administer and execute the same and to grant or refuse export licenses thereunder, in accordance with those instructions.

I hereby establish an Exports Council, to be composed of the Secretary of State, the Secretary of Agriculture, the Secretary of Commerce, and the Food Administrator, and I hereby authorize and direct the said Exports Council, thus constituted, to formulate, for the consideration and approval of the President, policies and make the recommendations necessary to carry out the purposes of this Act.

WOODROW WILSON.

STATEMENT

[Explaining Control of Exports during War with Germany.]

WASHINGTON, D. C., *June 26, 1917.*

It is important that the country should understand just what is intended in the control of exports which is about to be undertaken, and since the power is vested by the Congress in the President I can speak with authority concerning it. The Exports Council will be merely advisory to the President.

There will, of course, be no prohibition of exports. The normal course of trade will be interfered with as little as possible, and, so far as possible, only its abnormal course directed. The whole object will be to direct exports in such a way that they will go first and by preference where they are most needed and most immediately needed, and temporarily to withhold them, if necessary, where they can best be spared.

Our primary duty in the matter of foodstuffs and like necessaries is to see to it that the peoples associated with us in the war get as generous a proportion as possible of our surplus; but it will also be our wish and purpose to supply the neutral nations whose peoples depend upon us for such supplies as nearly in proportion to their need as the amount to be divided permits.

There will thus be little check put upon the volume of exports, and the prices obtained for them will not be affected by this regulation.

This policy will be carried out, not by prohibitive regulations, therefore, but by a system of licensing exports which will be as simply organized and administered as possible, so as to constitute no impediment to the normal flow of commerce. In brief, the free play of trade will not be arbitrarily interfered with; it will only be intelligently and systematically directed in the light of full information with regard to needs and market conditions throughout the world and the necessities of our people at home and our armies and the armies of our associates abroad.

The Government is taking, or has taken, steps to ascertain, for example, just what the available present supply of wheat and corn is remaining from the crops of last year; to learn from each of the countries exporting these foodstuffs from the United States what their purchases in this country now are, where they are stored, and what their needs are, in order that we may adjust things so far as possible to our own needs and free stocks; and this information is in course of being rapidly supplied.

The case of wheat and corn will serve as an illustration of all the rest of supplies of all kinds. Our trade can be successfully and profitably conducted now, the war pushed to a victorious issue, and the needs of our own people and of the other people with whom we are still free to trade efficiently met only by systematic direction; and that is what will be attempted.   WOODROW WILSON.

PROCLAMATIONS

By the President of the United States of America

A PROCLAMATION
[Registration Day—Porto Rico.]

Whereas, on the 18th day of May, A. D. 1917, the President of the United States did issue a Proclamation calling upon all persons subject to registration for military purposes to register as provided by the Act of Congress of May 18, 1917, entitled "An Act to authorize the President to increase temporarily the Military Establishment of the United States."

And Whereas, in such Proclamation it was provided among other things that

"In the territories of Alaska, Hawaii and Porto Rico a day for registration will be named in a later Proclamation."

Now, Therefore, I, Woodrow Wilson, President of the United States, for the purpose of fixing the date for registration in the territory of Porto Rico, do hereby set, fix and establish the 5th day of July, A. D., one thousand nine hundred and seventeen, as the date of registration, and I do hereby direct that on such day, between the hours of 7 A. M. and 9 P. M., all male persons subject to registration for military purposes, the same being

* * * "Those who shall have attained their twenty-first birthday and who shall not have attained their thirty-first birthday on or before the day here named are required to register, excepting only officers and enlisted men of the Regular Army, the Regular Army Reserve, the Officers' Reserve Corps, the Enlisted Reserve Corps, the National Guard and National Guard Reserve recognized by the Militia Bureau of the War Department, the Navy, the Marine Corps, the Coast Guard, and the Naval Militia, Naval Reserve Force, Marine Corps Reserve, and National Naval Volunteers recognized by the Navy Department."

do present themselves, for the purpose of registration for military purposes, at such places and to be registered by such officials in each municipality as shall be designated and appointed by the Governor of Porto Rico.

In Witness Whereof, I have hereunto set my hand and caused the seal of the United States to be affixed.

Done at the City of Washington this 27th day of June one thousand nine hundred and seventeen, and of the Independence of the [SEAL.] United States the one hundred and forty-first.

WOODROW WILSON.

By the President:

ROBERT LANSING, *Secretary of State.*

BY THE PRESIDENT OF THE UNITED STATES OF AMERICA

A PROCLAMATION

[Registration Days—Alaska.]

Whereas, on the 18th day of May, A. D. 1917, the President of the United States did issue a Proclamation calling upon all persons subject to registration for military purposes to register as provided by the Act of Congress of May 18, 1917, entitled "An Act to authorize the President to increase temporarily the Military Establishment of the United States."

And Whereas, in such Proclamation it was provided among other things that

"In the Territories of Alaska, Hawaii and Porto Rico a day for registration will be named in a later Proclamation."

Now, Therefore, I, Woodrow Wilson, President of the United States, for the purpose of fixing the date for registration in the territory of Alaska, do hereby set, fix and establish the period between 7 A. M. on the second day of July next to 9 P. M. on the second day of September (Sundays and legal holidays excepted), one thousand nine hundred and seventeen, as the period of registration, and I do hereby direct that during such period all male persons subject to registration for military purposes, the same being

* * * "Those who shall have attained their twenty-first birthday and who shall not have attained their thirty-first birthday on or before the day here named are required to register, excepting only officers and enlisted men of the Regular Army, the Regular Army Reserve, the Officers' Reserve Corps, the Enlisted Reserve Corps, the National Guard and National Guard Reserve recognized by the Militia Bureau of the War Department, the Navy, the Marine Corps, the Coast Guard, and the Naval Militia, Naval Reserve Force, Marine Corps Reserve, and National Naval Volunteers recognized by the Navy Department."

do present themselves, for the purpose of registration for military purposes, at such places and to be registered by such officials in each municipality as shall be designated and appointed by the Governor of the Territory of Alaska.

In Witness Whereof, I have hereunto set my hand and caused the seal of the United States to be affixed.

Done at the City of Washington this thirtieth day of June one thousand nine hundred and seventeen, and of the Independence [SEAL.]   of the United States the one hundred and forty-first.

WOODROW WILSON.

By the President:

ROBERT LANSING, *Secretary of State.*

BY THE PRESIDENT OF THE UNITED STATES OF AMERICA

A PROCLAMATION

[Registration Day—Hawaii.]

Whereas, on the 18th day of May, A. D. 1917, the President of the United States did issue a Proclamation calling upon all persons subject to registration for military purposes to register as provided by the Act of Congress of May 18, 1917, entitled "An Act to Authorize the President to increase temporarily the Military Establishment of the United States."

And Whereas, in such Proclamation it was provided among other things that

"In the territories of Alaska, Hawaii and Porto Rico a day for registration will be named in a later Proclamation."

Now, Therefore, I, Woodrow Wilson, President of the United States, for the purpose of fixing the date for registration in the territory of Hawaii, do hereby set, fix and establish Tuesday, the thirty-first day of July, one thousand nine hundred and seventeen, as the day of registration, and I do hereby direct that upon such day between the hours of 7 o'clock A. M. and 9 o'clock P. M. thereof, all male persons subject to registration for military purposes, the same being

* * * "Those who shall have attained their twenty-first birthday and who shall have not attained their thirty-first birthday on or before the day here named are required to register, excepting only officers and enlisted men of the Regular Army, the Regular Army Reserve, the Officers' Reserve Corps, the Enlisted Reserve Corps, the National Guard and National Guard Reserve recognized by the Militia Bureau of the War Department, the Navy, the Marine Corps, the Coast Guard, and the Naval Militia, Naval Reserve

Force, Marine Corps Reserve, and National Naval Volunteers recognized by the Navy Department."
do present themselves, for the purpose of registration for military purposes, at such places and to be registered by such officials as shall be designated and appointed by the Governor of the Territory of Hawaii for that purpose.

In Witness Whereof, I have hereunto set my hand and caused the seal of the United States to be affixed.

Done at the City of Washington this second day of July, one thousand nine hundred and seventeen, and of the Independence of the [SEAL.] United States the one hundred and forty-first.

WOODROW WILSON.

By the President:
ROBERT LANSING, *Secretary of State.*

LETTER

[Advising Omission of Beer and Wine Provisions from the Administration Food Bill.]

THE WHITE HOUSE, *June 29, 1917.*

MY DEAR DR. CANNON:

I am very glad to respond to the request of Senator Martin, the Democratic floor leader in the Senate, that I give to your legislative committee an expression of my opinion with regard to the wisest and most patriotic policy to be pursued toward the food-administration legislation now pending in the Congress. I regard the immediate passage of the bill as of vital consequence to the safety and defense of the Nation. Time is of the essence, and yet it has become evident that heated and protracted debate will delay the passage of the bill indefinitely if the provisions affecting the manufacture of beer and wines are retained and insisted upon. In these circumstances I have not hesitated to say to members of the Senate who have been kind enough to consult me, that it would undoubtedly be in the public interest in this very critical matter if the friends of these provisions should consent to their elimination from the present measure. Feeling that your committee is actuated by the same patriotic motives which inspire me, I am confident that these considerations will seem to you, as they seem to me, to be imperative.

Sincerely yours,

WOODROW WILSON.

REV. JAMES CANNON, JR., D. D.,
Chairman *Legislative Committee, Anti-Saloon League of America.*

STATEMENT

[Accompanying Announcement of Rules and Regulations Governing the Selective Service Law.]

THE WHITE HOUSE, *July 2, 1917.*

The regulations which I am today causing to be promulgated, pursuant to the direction of the selective service law, cover the remaining steps of the plan for calling into the service of the United States qualified men from those who have registered; those selected as the result of this process to constitute, with the Regular Army, the National Guard, and the Navy, the fighting forces of the Nation, all of which forces are under the terms of the law placed in a position of equal right, dignity, and responsibility with the members of all other military forces.

The regulations have been drawn with a view to the needs and circumstances of the whole country and provide a system which it is expected will work with the least inequality and personal hardship. Any system of selecting men for military service, whether voluntary or involuntary in its operation, necessarily selects some men to bear the burden of danger and sacrifice for the whole Nation. The system here provided places all men of military age upon an even plane and then, by a selection which neither favors the one nor penalizes the other, calls out the requisite number for service.

The successful operation of this law and of these regulations depends necessarily upon the loyalty, patriotism, and justice of the members of the board to whom its operation is committed, and I admonish all members of every local board and of every district board of review that their duty to their country requires an impartial and fearless performance of the delicate and difficult duties intrusted to them. They should remember as to each individual case presented to them that they are called upon to adjudicate the most sacred rights of the individual and to preserve untarnished the honor of the Nation.

Our armies at the front will be strengthened and sustained if they be composed of men free from any sense of injustice in their mode of selection, and they will be inspired to loftier efforts in behalf of a country in which the citizens called upon to perform high public functions perform them with justice, fearlessness, and impartiality.

WOODROW WILSON.

PROCLAMATION

BY THE PRESIDENT OF THE UNITED STATES OF AMERICA

A PROCLAMATION

[Calling the Militia into National Service.]

WASHINGTON, D. C., *July 9, 1917.*

Whereas, The United States of America and the Imperial German Government are now at war, and, having in view the consequent danger of aggression by a foreign enemy upon the territory of the United States and the necessity for proper protection against possible interference with the execution of the laws of the Union by agents of the enemy, I, Woodrow Wilson, President of the United States, by virtue of the authority vested in me by the Constitution and the laws of the United States, and through the Governors of the respective States, call into the service of the United States as of and from the dates hereinafter respectively indicated, all members of the National Guard and all enlisted members of the National Guard Reserve of the following States who are not now in the service of the United States, except members of staff corps and departments not included in the personnel of tactical organizations, and except such officers of the National Guard as have been or may be specifically notified by my authority that they will not be affected by this call, to wit:

On July 15, 1917—New York, Pennsylvania, Ohio, West Virginia, Michigan, Wisconsin, Minnesota, Iowa, North Dakota, South Dakota, and Nebraska.

On July 25, 1917—Maine, New Hampshire, Vermont, Massachusetts, Rhode Island, Connecticut, New Jersey, Delaware, Maryland, District of Columbia, Virginia, North Carolina, South Carolina, Tennessee, Illinois, Montana, Wyoming, Idaho, Washington, and Oregon.

The members of the National Guard of the various States affected by this call will be concentrated at such places as may be designated by the War Department.

II. And under the authority conferred upon me by Clause II of Section I of the Act of Congress "to authorize the President to increase temporarily the military establishment of the United States," approved May 18, 1917, I do hereby draft into the military service of the United States, as of and from the fifth day of August, nineteen hundred and seventeen, all members of the National Guard and all enlisted members of the National Guard Reserve of the following States, except members of staff corps and departments not included in the personnel of tactical organizations and except such other officers of the National Guard as have been or may be especially notified by my authority that they will not be drafted, to wit:

New York, Pennsylvania, Ohio, West Virginia, Michigan, Wisconsin, Minnesota, Iowa, North Dakota, South Dakota, Nebraska, Maine, New Hampshire, Vermont, Massachusetts, Rhode Island, Connecticut, New Jersey, Delaware, Maryland, District of Columbia, Virginia, North Carolina, South Carolina, Tennessee, Illinois, Montana, Wyoming, Idaho, Washington, Oregon, Indiana, Kentucky, Georgia, Florida, Alabama, Mississippi, Arkansas, Louisiana, Oklahoma, Texas, Missouri, Kansas, Colorado, New Mexico, Arizona, Utah, and California.

III. All persons hereby drafted shall, on and from the fifth day of August, 1917, stand discharged from the militia and, under the terms of Section II of the Act of May 18, 1917, be subject to the laws and regulations governing the regular army, except as to promotions, so far as such laws and regulations are applicable to persons whose permanent retention in the military service on the active or retired list is not contemplated by law.

IV. The members of each company, battalion, regiment, brigade, division or other organization of the National Guard hereby drafted into the military service of the United States shall be embodied in organizations corresponding to those of the regular army. The officers not above the rank of Colonel of said organizations of the National Guard, who are drafted and whose offices are provided for in like organizations of the regular army, are hereby appointed officers of the army of the United States in the arm, staff corps or department, and in the grades in which they now hold commissions as officers of the National Guard, such appointments to be effective, subject to acceptance, on and from the fifth day of August, 1917, and each of them, subject to such acceptance, is hereby assigned as of said date to the organization in the army of the United States composed of those who were members of the organization of the National Guard in which at the time of draft he held a commission. The non-commissioned officers of the organizations of the National Guard, the members of which are hereby drafted, are hereby appointed non-commissioned officers in their present grade in the organizations of the army composed of said members, and shall in each case have the same relative rank as heretofore, and all other enlisted men are hereby confirmed in the army of the United States in the grades and ratings held by them in the National Guard in all cases where such grades and ratings correspond to grades and ratings provided for in like organizations of the regular army, all such appointments of non-commissioned officers and confirmations of other enlisted men in their grades to be without prejudice to the authority of subordinate commanders in respect of promotions, reductions and changes in enlisted personnel.

V. Each organization of the military force hereby created will, until further orders, bear the same name and designation as the former organization of the National Guard of whose members it is composed.

VI. All necessary orders for combining the organizations created by embodying therein members of the National Guard and National Guard Reserve hereby drafted in the military service of the United States into complete tactical units will be issued by the War Department.

In Witness Whereof, I have hereunto set my hand and caused the seal of the United States to be affixed.

Done at the City of Washington this third day of July in the year
of our Lord one thousand nine hundred and seventeen, and
[SEAL.]   of the Independence of the United States of America the
one hundred and forty-first.

WOODROW WILSON.

By the President:
ROBERT LANSING, *Secretary of State.*

PROCLAMATION

EXECUTIVE MANSION, WASHINGTON, D. C., *July 9, 1917.*

Whereas, Congress has enacted, and the President has on the fifteenth
day of June, 1917, approved, a law which contains the following provisions:

"Whenever during the present war the President shall find that
the public safety shall require, and shall make proclamation thereof,
it shall be unlawful to export from or ship from or take out of the
United States to any country named in such proclamation any article
or articles mentioned in such proclamation, except at such time or
times and under such regulations and orders and subject to such
limitations and exceptions as the President shall prescribe, until
otherwise ordered by the President or by Congress: Provided,
however, that no preference shall be given to the ports of one State
over those of another.

"Any person who shall export, ship, or take out, or deliver or
attempt to deliver for export, shipment, or taking out, any article in
violation of this title, or of any regulation or order made hereunder,
shall be fined not more than $10,000, or, if a natural person, im-
prisoned for not more than two years, or both; and any article so
delivered or exported, shipped, or taken out, or so attempted to be
delivered or exported, shipped, or taken out, shall be seized and
forfeited to the United States; and any officer, director, or agent of
a corporation who participates in any such violation shall be liable
to like fine or imprisonment, or both.

"Whenever there is a reasonable cause to believe that any vessel,
domestic or foreign, is about to carry out of the United States any
article or articles in violation of the provisions of this title, the
Collector of Customs for the district in which such vessel is located
is hereby authorized and empowered, subject to review by the Secretary of Commerce, to refuse clearance to any such vessel, domestic

or foreign, for which clearance is required by law, and by formal notice served upon the owners, master, or person or persons in command or charge of any domestic vessel for which clearance is not required by law, to forbid the departure of such vessel from the port, and it shall thereupon be unlawful for such vessel to depart. Whoever, in violation of any of the provisions of this section, shall take, or attempt to take, or authorize the taking, of any such vessel out of port or from the jurisdiction of the United States shall be fined not more than $10,000 or imprisoned not more than two years, or both; and, in addition, such vessel, her tackle, apparel, furniture, equipment, and her forbidden cargo shall be forfeited to the United States."

And, Whereas, the public safety requires that succor shall be prevented from reaching the enemy;

Now, Therefore, I, Woodrow Wilson, President of the United States of America, do hereby proclaim to all whom it may concern that, except at such time or times under such regulations, and orders and subject to such limitations and exceptions as the President shall prescribe, until otherwise ordered by the President or by Congress, the following articles, namely: Coal, coke, fuel oils, kerosene and gasoline, including bunkers; food grains, flour and meal therefrom, fodder and feeds, meat and fats; pig iron, steel billets, ship plates and structural shapes, scrap iron and scrap steel; ferro-manganese; fertilizers; arms, ammunitions and explosives, shall not, on and after the fifteenth day of July, 1917, be carried out of or exported from the United States or its territorial possessions to Abyssinia, Afghanistan, Albania, Argentina, Austria-Hungary, Belgium, her colonies, possessions or protectorates, Bolivia, Brazil, Bulgaria, China, Chile, Colombia, Costa Rica, Cuba, Denmark, her colonies, possessions or protectorates, Dominican Republic, Ecuador, Egypt, France, her colonies, possessions, or protectorates, Germany, her colonies, possessions or protectorates, Great Britain, her colonies, possessions, or protectorates, Greece, Guatemala, Haiti, Honduras, Italy, her colonies, possessions or protectorates, Japan, Liberia, Leichtenstein, Luxemburg, Mexico, Monaco, Montenegro, Morocco, Nepal, Nicaragua, The Netherlands, her colonies, possessions or protectorates, Norway, Oman, Panama, Paraguay, Persia, Peru, Portugal, her colonies, possessions or protectorates, Rumania, Russia, Salvador, San Marino, Serbia, Siam, Spain, her colonies, possessions or protectorates, Sweden, Switzerland, Uruguay, Venezuela, or Turkey.

The orders and regulations from time to time prescribed will be administered by and under the authority of the Secretary of Commerce, from whom licenses, in conformity with the said orders and regulations, will issue.

In Witness Whereof, I have hereunto set my hand and caused the seal of the United States to be affixed. Done at the City of Washington, this ninth day of July, in the year of our Lord One Thousand Nine Hundred and Seventeen, and of the independence of the United States of America the One Hundred and Forty-second.

WOODROW WILSON.

By the President:

FRANK L. POLK, *Acting Secretary of State.*

A SUPPLEMENTARY STATEMENT

WASHINGTON, D. C., *July 9, 1917.*

In controlling by license the export of certain indispensable commodities from the United States, the Government has first and chiefly in view the amelioration of the food conditions which have arisen or are likely to arise in our own country before new crops are harvested. Not only is the conservation of our prime food and fodder supplies a matter which vitally concerns our own people, but the retention of an adequate supply of raw materials is essential to our program of military and naval construction and the continuance of our necessary domestic activities. We shall therefore similarly safeguard all our fundamental supplies.

It is obviously the duty of the United States, in liberating any surplus products over and above our own domestic needs, to consider first the necessities of all the nations engaged in war against the Central Empires. As to neutral nations, however, we also recognize our duty. The Government does not wish to hamper them. On the contrary, it wishes and intends, by all fair and equitable means, to cooperate with them in their difficult task of adding from our available surpluses to their own domestic supply and of meeting their pressing necessities or deficits. In considering the deficits of food supplies the Government means only to fulfill its obvious obligation to assure itself that neutrals are husbanding their own resources and that our supplies will not become available, either directly or indirectly, to feed the enemy.

WOODROW WILSON.

ADDRESS TO FELLOW-COUNTRYMEN, JULY 11, 1917

MY FELLOW-COUNTRYMEN:

The Government is about to attempt to determine the prices at which it will ask you henceforth to furnish various supplies which are necessary for the prosecution of the war and various materials which will be needed in the industries by which the war must be sustained. We shall, of course, try to determine them justly and to the best advantage of the nation as a whole, but justice is easier to speak of than to arrive at and there are some considerations which I hope we shall keep steadily in mind while this particular problem of justice is being worked out. I, therefore, take the liberty of stating very candidly my own view of the situation and of the principles which should guide both the Government and the mine owners and manufacturers of the country in this difficult matter.

A just price must, of course, be paid for everything the Government buys. By a just price I mean a price which will sustain the industries concerned in a high state of efficiency, provide a living for those who conduct them, enable them to pay good wages, and make possible the expansions of their enterprises which will from time to time become necessary as the stupendous undertakings of this great war develop. We could not wisely or reasonably do less than pay such prices. They are necessary for the maintenance and development of industry, and the maintenance and development of industry are necessary for the great task we have in hand.

But I trust that we shall not surround the matter with a mist of sentiment. Facts are our masters now. We ought not to put the acceptance of such prices on the ground of patriotism. Patriotism has nothing to do with profits in a case like this. Patriotism and profits ought never in the present circumstances be mentioned together. It is perfectly proper to discuss profits as a matter of business, with a view to maintaining the integrity of capital and the efficiency of labor in these tragical months when the liberty of free men everywhere and of industry itself trembles in the balance, but it would be absurd to discuss them as a motive for helping to serve and save our country.

Patriotism leaves profits out of the question. In these days of our supreme trial, when we are sending hundreds of thousands of our young men across the seas to serve a great cause, no true man who stays behind to work for them and sustain them by his labor will ask himself what he is personally going to make out of that labor. No true patriot will permit himself to take toll of their heroism in money or seek to grow rich by the shedding of their blood. He will give as freely and with as unstinted self-sacrifice as they. When they are giving their lives will he not give at least his money?

I hear it insisted that more than a just price, more than a price that will sustain our industries, must be paid; that it is necessary to pay very liberal and unusual profits in order to "stimulate production;" that nothing but pecuniary rewards will do—rewards paid in money, not in the mere liberation of the world.

I take it for granted that those who argue thus do not stop to think what that means. Do they mean that you must be paid, must be bribed, to make your contribution, a contribution that costs you neither a drop of blood nor a tear, when the whole world is in travail and men everywhere depend upon and call to you to bring them out of bondage and make the world a fit place to live in again amidst peace and justice? Do they mean that you will exact a price, drive a bargain with the men who are enduring the agony of this war on the battlefield, in the trenches, amidst the lurking dangers of the sea, or with the bereaved women and pitiful children, before you will come forward to do your duty and give some part of your life, in easy peaceful fashion, for the things we are fighting for, the things we have pledged our fortunes, our lives, our sacred honor, to vindicate and defend—liberty and justice and fair dealing and the peace of nations?

Of course you will not. It is inconceivable. Your patriotism is of the same self-denying stuff as the patriotism of the men dead or maimed on the fields of France, or else it is no patriotism at all. Let us never speak, then, of profits and of patriotism in the same sentence, but face facts and meet them. Let us do sound business, but not in the midst of a mist. Many a grievous burden of taxation will be laid on this nation, in this generation and in the next, to pay for this war. Let us see to it that for every dollar that is taken from the people's pockets it shall be possible to obtain a dollar's worth of the sound stuffs they need.

Let me turn for a moment to the ship owners of the United States and the other ocean carriers whose example they have followed and ask them if they realize what obstacles, what almost insuperable obstacles, they have been putting in the way of the successful prosecution of this war by the ocean freight rates they have been exacting. They are doing everything that high freight charges can do to make the war a failure, to make it impossible. I do not say that they realize this or intend it. The thing has happened naturally enough, because the commercial processes which we are content to see operate in ordinary times have, without sufficient thought, been continued into a period where they have no proper place. I am not questioning motives. I am merely stating a fact, and stating it in order that attention may be fixed upon it.

The fact is that those who have fixed war freight rates have taken the most effective means in their power to defeat the armies engaged against Germany. When they realize this, we may—I take it for granted—count upon them to reconsider the whole matter. It is high time. Their extra hazards are covered by war risk insurance.

I know, and you know, what response to this great challenge of duty and of opportunity the nation will expect of you; and I know what response you will make. Those who do not respond, who do not respond in the spirit of those who have gone to give their lives for us on bloody fields far away, may safely be left to be dealt with by opinion and the law—for the law must, of course, command these things. I am dealing with the matter thus publicly and frankly, not because I have any doubt or fear as to the result, but only in order that in all our thinking and in all our dealings with one another we may move in a perfectly clear air of mutual understanding.

And there is something more that we must add to our thinking. The public is now as much part of the Government as are the army and navy themselves; the whole people in all their activities are now mobilized and in service for the accomplishment of the nation's task in this war; it is in such circumstances impossible justly to distinguish between industrial purchases made by the Government and industrial purchases made by the managers of individual industries; and it is just as much our duty to sustain the industries of the country, all the industries that contribute to its life, as it is to sustain our forces in the field and on the sea. We must make the prices to the public the same as the prices to the Government.

Prices mean the same thing everywhere now. They mean the efficiency or the inefficiency of the nation, whether it is the Government that pays them or not. They mean victory or defeat. They mean that America will win her place once for all among the foremost free nations of the world, or that she will sink to defeat and become a second-rate power alike in thought and in action. This is a day of her reckoning and every man amongst us must personally face that reckoning along with her.

The case needs no arguing. I assume that I am only expressing your own thoughts—what must be in the mind of every true man when he faces the tragedy and the solemn glory of the present war for the emancipation of mankind. I summon you to a great duty, a great privilege, a shining dignity and distinction. I shall expect every man who is not a slacker to be at my side throughout this great enterprise. In it no man can win honor who thinks of himself.

WOODROW WILSON.

A PROCLAMATION

By the President of the United States of America

[German Insurance Companies' Participation in Marine and War Risk Insurance.]

Whereas, Certain insurance companies incorporated under the laws of the German Empire have been admitted to transact the business of marine and war risk insurance in various States of the United States by means of separate State branches established pursuant to the laws of such States, and are now engaged in such business under the supervision of the Insurance Departments thereof, with assets in the United States deposited with Insurance Departments or in the hands of resident trustees citizens of the United States, for the protection of all policy holders in the United States; and

Whereas, The nature of marine and war risk insurance is such that those conducting it must of necessity be in touch with the movements of ships and cargoes, and it has been considered by the Government of great importance that this information should not be obtained by alien enemies;

Now, therefore, I, Woodrow Wilson, President of the United States of America, by virtue of the powers vested in me as such, hereby decree and proclaim that such branch establishments of German insurance companies now engaged in the transaction of business in the United States, pursuant to the laws of the several States, are hereby prohibited from continuing the transaction of the business of marine and war risk insurance either as direct insurers or reinsurers; and all individuals, firms, and insurance companies incorporated under the laws of any of the States or Territories of the United States, or of any foreign country, and established pursuant to the laws of such States and now engaged in the United States in the business of marine and war risk insurance, either as direct insurers or reinsurers, are hereby prohibited from reinsuring with companies incorporated under the laws of the German Empire, no matter where located; and all persons in the United States are prohibited from insuring against marine or war risks with insurance companies incorporated under the laws of the German Empire or with individuals, firms, and insurance companies incorporated under the laws of any of the States or Territories of the United States or of any foreign country and now engaged in the business of marine or war risk insurance in the United States, which reinsure business originating in the United States with companies incorporated under the laws of the German Empire, no matter where located.

The foregoing prohibitions shall extend and operate as to all existing contracts for insurance and reinsurance which are hereby suspended for the period of the war, except that they shall not operate to vitiate or prevent the insurance or reinsurance of and the payment or receipt of premiums on insurance or reinsurance under existing contracts on vessels or interest at risk on the date of this proclamation, and such insurance or reinsurance, if for a voyage, shall continue in force until arrival at destination, and if for time, until thirty days from the date of this proclamation, but if for a voyage at that time, until the arrival at destination.

Nothing herein shall be construed to operate to prevent the payment or receipt of any premium or claim now due or which may become due on or in respect to insurances or reinsurances not prohibited by this proclamation.

That all funds of such German companies now in the possession of their managers or agents, or which shall hereafter come into their possession, shall be subject to such rules and regulations concerning the payment and disposition thereof as shall be prescribed by the insurance supervising officials of the State in which the principal office of such establishment in the United States is located, but in no event shall any funds belonging to or held for the benefit of such companies be transmitted outside of the United States, nor be used as the basis for the establishment, directly or indirectly, of any credit within or outside of the United States to or for the benefit or use of the enemy or any of his allies without the permission of this Government.

In Witness Whereof, I have hereunto set my hand and caused the seal of the United States to be affixed.

Done at the District of Columbia this thirteenth day of July, in the year of our Lord one thousand nine hundred and seventeen [SEAL.] and of the independence of the United States the one hundred and forty-second.

WOODROW WILSON.

EXECUTIVE ORDER

[Powers of Shipping Board and Emergency Fleet Corporation.]

THE WHITE HOUSE, *July 11, 1917.*

By virtue of the authority vested in me in the section entitled "Emergency Shipping Fund" of an act of Congress entitled "An Act Making Appropriations to Supply Urgent Deficiencies in Appropriations for the Military and Naval Establishments on Account of War Expenses for the Fiscal Year Ending June 30, 1917, and for Other Purposes," approved June 15, 1917, I hereby direct that the United States Shipping Board Emergency Fleet Corporation shall have and exercise all power and authority vested in me in said section of said act, in so far as applicable to and in furtherance of the construction of vessels, the purchase or requisitioning of vessels in process of construction, whether on the ways or already launched, or of contracts for the construction of such vessels, and the completion thereof, and all power and authority applicable to and in furtherance of the production, purchase, and requisitioning of materials for ship construction.

And I do further direct that the United States Shipping Board shall have and exercise all power and authority vested in me in said section of said act, in so far as applicable to and in furtherance of the taking over of title or possession, by purchase or requisition, of constructed vessels, or parts thereof, or charters therein; and the operation, management and disposition of such vessels, and of all other vessels heretofore or hereafter acquired by the United States. The power herein delegated to the United States Shipping Board may in the discretion of said board be exercised directly by the said board or by it through the United States Shipping Board Emergency Fleet Corporation, or through any other corporation organized by it for such purpose.

WOODROW WILSON.

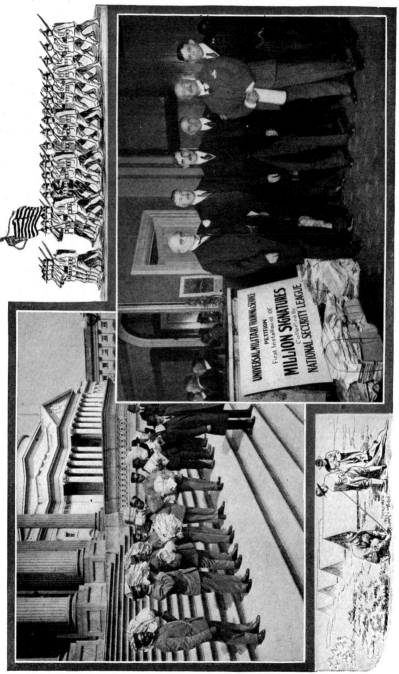

UNIVERSAL TRAINING PETITION

A complete account of the movement for Preparedness and for Compulsory Military Training, together with arguments pro and con, will be found under these heads in the Encyclopedic Index.

By the President of the United States of America

PROCLAMATIONS

[Amnesty and Pardon.]

Whereas, a practice has existed for many years among the judges of certain United States courts of suspending either the imposition or the execution of sentences whenever, in their judgment, the circumstances warranted it, which practice is illegal as has been held by the Supreme Court of the United States in a case entitled "Ex parte United States, petitioner," known as the Killits case, decided December 4, 1916; and

Whereas the practice was widespread, and many thousands of persons are now at liberty under such suspensions, never having served any portion of the sentences duly authorized and required by the statutes; and

Whereas many of these persons are leading blameless lives and have re-established themselves in the confidence of their fellow citizens, and it is believed that the enforcement of the law at this late date would, in most instances, be productive of no good results; and

Whereas the Supreme Court of the United States, in recognition of the necessity for meeting this situation, has stayed the mandate in the Killits case until the end of the present term, to wit, until about June 15, 1917:

Now, therefore, be it known that I, Woodrow Wilson, President of the United States of America, in consideration of the premises, divers, other good and sufficient reasons me thereunto moving, do hereby declare and grant a full amnesty and pardon to all persons under suspended sentences of United States courts liable to penalties as aforesaid, where the sentences imposed were less than the period between the date of imposition and June 15, 1917, and to all persons, defendants in said courts, in cases where pleas of guilty were entered or verdicts of guilty returned prior to June 15, 1916, and in which no sentences have been imposed.

In all other cases of suspension either of the imposition or the execution of sentence by judges of the United States courts occurring prior to December 4, 1916, the date of the decision in the Killits case, a respite of six months is hereby granted from June 15, 1917, in order that the facts and merits of the respective cases may be investigated and considered and appropriate action taken, where warranted, by way of executive clemency.

In testimony whereof, I have hereunto signed my name and caused the seal of the United States to be affixed.

Done in the District of Columbia this fourteenth day of June, in the year of our Lord one thousand nine hundred and seventeen, [SEAL] and of the Independence of the United States the one hundred and forty-first.

WOODROW WILSON.

By the President:

ROBERT LANSING, *Secretary of State.*

[Defining Pardon and Amnesty Proclamation Dated June 14, 1917.]

Whereas, it has become desirable more specifically to define the persons under suspended sentence in United States courts and other persons, defendants in said courts, to whom pardon and amnesty were extended by the Proclamation of the President of the United States which was made and issued on the fourteenth day of June, A. D. 1917; and

Whereas, in a case entitled "Ex parte United States, Petitioner," known as the Killits case, decided December 4, 1916, it was held by the Supreme Court of the United States that United States District judges have no authority to suspend sentence or the imposition thereof; and

Whereas, many judges did not claim such power and others both claimed and exercised it, with the result that there was a lack of uniformity in the administration of the criminal laws, and a large number of persons who had been convicted and were required by acts of Congress to be sentenced and committed had escaped punishment without legal disposition of their cases; and

Whereas, in many instances, defendants in such courts, who had been improperly at large for a number of years, under the circumstances recited, had reestablished themselves in the respective communities wherein they lived; and

Whereas, the object of the aforesaid Proclamation was to meet this situation justly, and the amnesty proposed therein was offered to such defendants and each of them with reference to that object alone;

Now, Therefore, be it known, that I, Woodrow Wilson, President of the United States of America, in order to avoid possible misunderstandings, do hereby proclaim, declare and make known that the aforesaid Proclamation, in purpose and intent, applied and does apply to the following cases, to wit:

(1) Cases of defendants in United States courts, under suspended sentences, wherein the sentences imposed were less than the period between the date of the imposition thereof and June 15, 1917.

(2) Cases of defendants in United States courts, not actually in process of adjudication on June 14, 1917 (the date of the aforesaid Proclamation), wherein pleas of guilty were entered or verdicts of guilty were returned prior to June 15, 1916, and in which the imposition

of sentence had been illegally suspended by the court or in which the court had illegally declined to impose sentence upon proper motion by the prosecuting attorney.

In consideration of the premises, and by virtue of the powers in me vested, I have offered and do now offer amnesty and pardon to all such persons, defendants in said courts, and to no others; on the assumption that the enforcement of sentence would not further the ends of justice in cases where the sentence would have been served when the mandate of the Supreme Court in the aforesaid case entitled "Ex parte United States, Petitioner," should become effective, if such sentence had been properly imposed and its execution begun at the time of its imposition; and, further, on the assumption that, where the imposition of sentence had been designedly suspended, the offense was not a serious one, and that the sentence, if imposed, would not have been for more than a period of one year.

In the remaining cases of illegal suspension, either of the imposition or execution of sentence, by judges of United States courts, occurring prior to December 4, 1916, that being the date of the decision in the so-called Killits case, special application for executive clemency may be made by any person excepted from the benefits of the foregoing provisions, and such application will receive due consideration on the merits, in the course of the general respite of six months granted by the aforesaid Proclamation.

In testimony whereof, I have hereunto signed my name and caused the seal of the United States to be affixed.

Done in the District of Columbia this 21st day of August, in the year of our Lord one thousand nine hundred and seventeen, and [SEAL] of the Independence of the United States the one hundred and forty-second.

WOODROW WILSON.

By the President:

ROBERT LANSING, *Secretary of State.*

EXECUTIVE ORDER

[Lighthouse Service—Virgin Islands.]

THE WHITE HOUSE, *20 July, 1917.*

Whereas, the maintenance of lighthouses and other aids to navigation in the Virgin Islands, West Indies, is necessary for the safe navigation of the waters thereof by the vessels of the Navy and of the merchant marine of the United States, and for the promotion of their commercial interests.

Now, therefore, I, Woodrow Wilson, President of the United States, by virtue of the authority in me vested, and pursuant to Section 1 of the Act approved March 3, 1917, entitled An Act to provide a temporary government for the West Indian Islands acquired by the United States from Denmark, etc., do hereby order that all the public property of the former government of the Virgin Islands ceded heretofore to the United States, consisting of lighthouses and the public lands adjacent thereto and used in connection therewith, to the extent of five acres, or thereabout, adjacent to each lighthouse, when practicable to obtain so much, the exact location of said land and its metes and bounds to be hereafter determined and defined by the Lighthouse Service, light vessels, lighthouse tenders, beacons, buoys, seamarks and their append-ages, and all apparatus, supplies, and materials of all kinds provided therefor, and all the archives, books, documents, drawings, models, returns, and all other things appertaining to any lighthouse establish-ment maintained by the said former government of the Virgin Islands, be and hereby are taken for the uses and purposes of the United States; and the Secretary of Commerce, through the Commissioner of Light-houses, is hereby charged with all administrative duties relating to the said lighthouse service; and said Secretary of Commerce shall have estimates prepared by the Commissioner of Lighthouses and submitted to Congress for an appropriation to defray the expenses of the estab-lishment and maintenance of these aids to navigation.

WOODROW WILSON.

EXECUTIVE ORDER

[Explaining Exemption of Indispensable Government Employees From the Selec-tive Draft.]

THE WHITE HOUSE, *July 28, 1917.*

In view of the high national importance of carrying out the spirit of the Selective Service Act and of securing its fullest effectiveness, by holding to military service all drafted men who are not absolutely in-dispensable to the work of the Civil Executive Departments by reason of their special personal experience and skill, I direct that the greatest care be exercised by Department officials in issuing the affidavits of necessity provided for by the Presidential Regulations Section 20, para-graphs (b), (c), and (d), for the purpose of authorizing the discharge of such persons by local boards.

Those paragraphs provide as follows:

"(c) *Persons employed by the United States in the transmission of the mails.* Any person employed by the United States in the transmis-sion of the mails, upon presentation to such local board, at any time within 10 days after the filing of a claim of discharge by or in respect of such person, of an affidavit signed by the postmaster or some appointee of the President or Postmaster General having direct supervision of such employee, stating that such employee is, in his opinion, necessary to the effective and adequate transmission of the mails and can not be replaced by another person without substantial material loss of efficiency in the effective and adequate transmission of the mails."

"(d) *Artificers and workmen employed in the armories, arsenals, and navy yards of the United States.* Any artificer or workman employed in any armory, arsenal, or navy yard of the United States, upon presentation to such local board, at any time within 10 days after the filing of a claim of discharge by or in respect of such person, of an affidavit signed by the commandant or officer having command of the armory, arsenal, or navy yard of the United States in which such person is employed, stating that such person is, in his opinion, necessary to the efficient and adequate operation of such armory, arsenal, or navy yard of the United States and can not be replaced by another person without substantial material loss of efficiency in the effective and adequate operation of such armory, arsenal, or navy yard of the United States."

"(e) *Persons employed in the service of the United States designated by the President to be exempted.* Any person employed in the service of the United States, upon presentation to such local board at any time within ten days after the filing of a claim of discharge by or in respect of such person, of an affidavit signed by the official of the Government of the United States having direct supervision and control of the department, commission, board, bureau, division, or branch of the Government of the United States in which such person is employed stating that such person is, in his opinion, necessary to the adequate and effective operation of such department, commission, board, bureau, division, or branch in the service of the United States, and can not be replaced by another person without substantial material loss in the adequate and effective operation of said department, commission, board, bureau, division, or branch of the service of the United States."

In the case of a person in the service of a Department within the District of Columbia, who files with the local board a claim of discharge from the selective draft, the affidavit of the Departmental official having direct supervision and control of the branch of the service in which he is employed, as provided for in the above quoted regulations, will be forwarded to the Secretary of that Department accompanied by a memorandum giving sufficient data to enable the Secretary to determine whether or not the case is a proper one for exemption. If on the information furnished he deems the case a proper one for exemption by the board, he will endorse the affidavit "Approved;" if not, "Disapproved." In either case, the affidavit will be returned to the official making it, to be filed with the local board as required by the instructions on the back thereof.

In the case of a person in Departmental service stationed outside of the District of Columbia, the affidavit of the official having direct supervision of the applicant will be forwarded for approval or disapproval to the official, to be designated by the Secretary of the Department, who has jurisdiction or control of the area within which the applicant is stationed at the time, unless the affidavit is originally made by such official.

In the case of a person in the service of the Interstate Commerce Commission, the Smithsonian Institution, or other commission or board or body not organized directly under one of the ten Executive Departments, the same general method will be followed so far as practicable, with a view to reducing the discharges of drafted men to the minimum number consistent with the maintenance of vital national interests during the emergency of war.

It is earnestly hoped, moreover, that, acting in the same spirit as the Federal Departmental officials, all citizens who may be called upon, as employers, under Section 44 of the Regulations, to make affidavits for securing the discharge of persons deemed to be indispensable to national industrial interests during the emergency, will exercise the same conscientious and scrupulous caution to the end that there will appear to be no favored or exempted class among the citizens called by law to the national defense.

WOODROW WILSON.

By the President of the United States of America

A PROCLAMATION

[License of Wheat and Rye Elevators, and Millers.]

Whereas, Under and by virtue of an Act of Congress entitled "An Act to provide further for the national security and defense by encouraging the production, conserving the supply, and controlling the distribution of fuel," approved by the President on the 10th day of August, 1917, it is provided among other things as follows:

"That, by reason of the existence of a state of war, it is essential to the national security and defense, for the successful prosecution of the war, and for the support and maintenance of the Army and Navy, to assure an adequate supply and equitable distribution, and to facilitate the movement, of foods, feeds, fuel, including fuel oil and natural gas, fertilizer and fertilizer ingredients, tools, utensils, implements, machinery, and equipment required for the actual production of foods, feeds, and fuel, hereafter in this Act called necessaries; to prevent, locally or generally, scarcity, monopolization, hoarding, injurious speculation, manipulations, and private controls, affecting such supply, distribution, and movement; and to establish and maintain governmental control of such necessaries during the war. For such purposes the instrumentalities, means, methods, powers, authorities, duties, obligations, and prohibitions hereinafter set forth are created, established, conferred, and prescribed. The President is authorized to make such regulations and to issue such orders as are essential effectively to carry out the provisions of this Act."

And, whereas, it is further provided in said Act as follows:

"That, from time to time, whenever the President shall find it essential to license the importation, manufacture, storage, mining, or distribution of any necessaries, in order to carry into effect any of the purposes of this Act, and shall publicly so announce, no person shall, after a date fixed in the announcement, engage in or carry on any such business specified in the announcement of importation, manufacture, storage, mining, or distribution of any necessaries as set forth in such announcement, unless he shall secure and hold a license issued pursuant to this section. The President is authorized to issue such licenses and to prescribe regulations for systems of accounts and auditing of accounts to be kept by licensees, submission of reports by them, with or without oath or affirmation and the entry and inspection by the President's duly authorized agents of the places of business of licensees."

And, whereas, it is essential in order to carry into effect the provisions of the said Act, and in order to secure an adequate supply and equitable distribution, and to facilitate the movement of certain necessaries hereafter in this proclamation specified that the license powers conferred upon the President by said Act be at this time exercised, to the extent hereinafter set forth.

Now, therefore, I, Woodrow Wilson, President of the United States of America, by virtue of the powers conferred upon me by said Act of Congress, hereby find and determine and by this proclamation do announce that it is essential in order to carry into effect the purposes of said Act, to license the storage and distribution of wheat and rye and the manufacture, storage and distribution of all products derived therefrom to the extent hereinafter specified.

All persons, firms, corporations and associations engaged in the business of either storing or distributing wheat or rye, as owners, lessees or operators of warehouses or elevators, and all persons, firms, corporations and associations engaged in the business of manufacturing any product derived from wheat or rye, (except those operating mills and manufacturing plants of a daily capacity of one hundred barrels or less, and farmers and cooperative association of farmers) are hereby required to secure on or before September 1st, 1917, a license, which license will be issued under such rules and regulations governing the conduct of the business as may be prescribed.

Applications for licenses must be made to the United States Food Administrator, Washington, D. C., upon forms prepared by him for that purpose.

Any person, firm, corporation or association, other than those hereinbefore excepted, who shall engage in, or carry on the business of either storing or distributing wheat or rye as owners, lessees or operators of warehouses or elevators, or manufacturing any products derived from wheat or rye after September 1st, 1917, without first securing such license, will be liable to the penalties prescribed by said Act of Congress.

In witness whereof, I have hereunto set my hand, and caused the seal of the United States to be affixed.

Done in the District of Columbia, this fourteenth day of August in the year of our Lord one thousand nine hundred and seven-

[SEAL] teen, and of the Independence of the United States of America the one hundred and forty-second.

WOODROW WILSON.

By the President:

ROBERT LANSING, *Secretary of State.*

EXECUTIVE ORDERS

[Creating Food Administration Grain Corporation.]

THE WHITE HOUSE, *August 14, 1917.*

Whereas, Under and by virtue of an Act of Congress entitled "An Act to provide for the national security and defense by encouraging the production, conserving the supply and controlling the distribution of food products and fuel," approved August 10th, 1917, it is provided among other things as follows:

"That, by reason of the existence of a state of war, it is essential to the national security and defense, for the successful prosecution of the war, and for the support and maintenance of the Army and Navy, to assure an adequate supply and equitable distribution, and to facilitate the movement, of foods, feeds, fuel, including fuel oil and natural gas, fertilizer and fertilizer ingredients, tools, utensils, implements, machinery and equipment required for the actual production of foods, feeds, and fuel, hereafter in this Act called necessaries; to prevent, locally or generally, scarcity, monopolization, hoarding, injurious speculation, manipulation, and private controls, affecting such supply, distribution, and movement; and to establish and maintain governmental control of such necessaries during the war. For such purposes the instrumentalities, means, methods, powers, authorities, duties, obligations, and prohibitions hereinafter set forth are created, established, conferred, and prescribed. The President is authorized to make such regulations and to issue such orders as are essential effectively to carry out the provisions of this Act."

"That, in carrying out the purposes of this Act the President is authorized * * * to create and use any agency or agencies * * *."

"That, the President is authorized from time to time to purchase, to store, to provide storage facilities for and to sell for cash at reasonable prices, wheat, flour, meal, beans and potatoes."

And, whereas, in order to enable the United States Food Administration acting under the direction of the President to efficiently exercise the authority granted by said Act and to purchase, store, provide storage facilities for and to sell for cash at reasonable prices the commodities above named, and to enable said United States Food Administration to purchase and sell said commodities in the manner and by methods customarily followed in the trade, it is expedient and necessary that a Corporation should be organized, all the stock of which, except the number of shares necessary to qualify directors or incorporators, shall be subscribed for, purchased and owned by the United States.

Now, therefore, under and by virtue of the power conferred upon me by the above entitled Act as hereinbefore set forth, it is hereby ordered that an agency, to-wit, a corporation, under the laws of Delaware be created, said corporation to be named Food Administration Grain Corporation.

That the governing body of said corporation shall consist of a Board of Directors composed of seven members.

That the following persons, having been invited and given their consent to serve, shall be named as four of said directors, to-wit:

Herbert Hoover, of Washington, D. C.

Julius H. Barnes, of Duluth, Minn.

Gates W. McGarrah, of New York, N. Y.

Frank G. Crowell, of Kansas City, Mo.

The remaining three shall be named by the incorporators and be subject to change by and with the approval of the President.

The office and principal place of business of said corporation outside of the State of Delaware shall be at the City of New York, and branch offices shall be established at such places within the United States as may be selected and determined by the United States Food Administrator by and with the consent of the President.

That the capital stock of such corporation shall consist of 500,000 shares of the par value of $100 each.

That the United States shall purchase from time to time at par so much of said capital stock as may be deemed necessary to supply the necessary capital to enable said corporation to carry on its business and none of said capital stock shall be sold to any person other than the United States and to the individual directors or incorporators, for the purpose of qualifying as such directors and incorporators, such qualifying shares to be held by said directors or incorporators in trust for the use and benefit of the United States.

The United States Food Administrator is hereby directed to cause said corporation to be formed, with the powers contained in the articles or certificate of incorporation, and in the by-laws requisite and necessary to define the methods by which said corporation shall conduct its business, which have been approved by the President.

All officers of said corporation shall be selected with the consent and approval of the President.

The United States Food Administrator is hereby authorized and directed to subscribe for and purchase all of said capital stock in the name of and for the use and benefit of the United States and as purchased to pay for the same out of the appropriation of $150,000,000 authorized by Section 19 of the Act of Congress hereinbefore entitled.

Done in the District of Columbia this fourteenth day of August in the year of our Lord one thousand nine hundred and seventeen, and of the Independence of the United States of America the one hundred and forty-second.

WOODROW WILSON.

[Assigning to the Secretary of the Navy Control Over Navy Construction, Supplies and Materials.]

THE WHITE HOUSE, *21 August, 1917.*

By virtue of authority vested in me in the section entitled "Naval Emergency Fund" of an Act of Congress entitled "An Act Making appropriations for the naval service for the fiscal year ending June thirtieth, nineteen hundred and eighteen, and for other purposes," approved March 4, 1917, and in the section entitled "Emergency Shipping Fund" of an Act of Congress entitled "An Act Making appropriations to supply urgent deficiencies in appropriations for the Military and Naval Establishments on account of war expenses for the fiscal year ending June thirtieth, nineteen hundred and seventeen, and for other purposes," approved June 15, 1917, I hereby direct that the Secretary of the Navy shall have and exercise all power and authority vested in me in said sections of said acts, in so far as applicable to and in furtherance of the construction of vessels for the use of the Navy and of contracts for the construction of such vessels and the completion thereof, and all power and authority applicable to and in furtherance of the production, purchase, and requisitioning of materials for construction of vessels for the Navy and of war materials, equipment and munitions required for the use of the Navy, and the more economical and expeditious delivery thereof.

The powers herein delegated to the Secretary of the Navy may, in his discretion, be exercised directly by him, or through any other officer or officers who, acting under his direction, have authority to make contracts on behalf of the Government.

WOODROW WILSON.

STATEMENTS

[Coal Prices.]

WHITE HOUSE, *Aug. 21, 1917.*

The following scale of prices is prescribed for bituminous coal at the mine in the several coal-producing districts. It is provisional only. It is subject to reconsideration when the whole method of administering the fuel supplies of the country shall have been satisfactorily organized and put into operation. Subsequent measures will have as their object a fair and equitable control of the distribution of the supply and of the prices, not only at the mines but also in the hands of the middlemen and the retailers.

The prices provisionally fixed here are fixed by my authority under the provisions of the recent act of Congress regarding administration of the food supply of the country, which also conferred upon the Executive control of the fuel supply. They are based upon the actual cost of production and are deemed to be not only fair and just but liberal as well. Under them the industry should nowhere lack stimulation.

WOODROW WILSON.

Note.—Prices are on f. o. b. mine basis for tons of 2,000 pounds.

	Run of Mine.	Prepared Sizes.	Slack or Screenings.
Pennsylvania	2.00	2.25	1.75
Maryland	2.00	2.25	1.75
West Virigina	2.00	2.25	1.75
West Virginia, (North River)	2.15	2.40	1.90
Virginia	2.00	2.25	1.75
Ohio, (thick vein)	2.00	2.25	1.75
Ohio, (thin vein)	2.35	2.60	2.10
Kentucky	1.95	2.20	1.70
Kentucky, (Jellico)	2.40	2.65	2.15
Alabama, (big seam)	1.90	2.15	1.65
Alabama, (Pratt, Jaeger, and Corona)	2.15	2.40	1.90
Alabama, (Cahaba and Black Creek)	2.40	2.65	2.15
Tennessee, (Eastern)	2.30	2.55	2.05
Tennessee, (Jellico)	2.40	2.65	2.15
Indiana	1.95	2.20	1.70

	Run of Mine.	Prepared Sizes.	Slack or Screenings.
Illinois	1.95	2.20	1.70
Illinois, (third vein)	2.40	2.65	2.15
Arkansas	2.65	2.90	2.40
Iowa	2.70	2.95	2.45
Kansas	2.55	2.80	2.30
Missouri	2.70	2.95	2.45
Oklahoma	3.05	3.30	2.80
Texas	2.65	2.90	2.40
Colorado	2.45	2.70	2.20
Montana	2.70	2.95	2.45
New Mexico	2.40	2.65	2.15
Wyoming	2.50	2.75	2.25
Utah	2.60	2.85	2.35
Washington	3.25	3.50	3.00

[Announcing Coal Regulations and Prices.]

THE WHITE HOUSE, *August 23, 1917.*

The following regulations shall apply to the intrastate, interstate, and foreign commerce of the United States, and the prices and margins referred to herein shall be in force pending further investigation or determination thereof by the President:

1. A coal jobber is defined as a person (or other agency) who purchases and resells coal to coal dealers or to consumers without physically handing it on, over, or through his own vehicle, dock, trestle, or yard.

2. For the buying and selling of bituminous coal a jobber shall not add to his purchase price a gross margin in excess of 15 cents per ton of 2,000 pounds, nor shall the combined gross margins of any number of jobbers who buy and sell a given shipment or shipments of bituminous coal exceed 15 cents per ton of 2,000 pounds.

3. For buying and selling anthracite coal a jobber shall not add to his purchase price a gross margin in excess of 20 cents per ton of 2,240 pounds when delivery of such coal is to be effected at or east of Buffalo. For buying and selling anthracite coal for delivery west of Buffalo a jobber shall not add to his purchase price a gross margin in excess of 30 cents per ton of 2,240 pounds. The combined gross margin of any number of jobbers who buy and sell a given shipment or shipments of anthracite coal for delivery at or east of Buffalo shall not exceed 20 cents per ton of 2,240 pounds, nor shall such combined margins exceed 30 cents per ton of 2,240 pounds for delivery of anthracite coal west of Buffalo. Provided that a jobber's margin realized on a given shipment or shipments of anthracite coal may be increased by not more than 5 cents per ton of 2,240 pounds when the jobber incurs the expense of rescreening it at Atlantic or Lake ports for transshipment by water.

4. Effective September 1, 1917, the maximum prices per ton of 2,240 pounds free on board cars at the mines for the grades and sizes of an-

thracite coal hereinafter specified shall not exceed the prices indicated in paragraph 5 when such coal is produced and sold by the Philadelphia & Reading Coal & Iron Co., Lehigh Coal & Navigation Co., Lehigh & Wilkes-Barre Coal Co., Hudson Coal Co., Delaware & Hudson Co., Scranton Coal Co., Lehigh Valley Coal Co., Coxe Bros. & Co., Pennsylvania Coal Co., Hillside Coal & Iron Co., Delaware, Lackawanna & Western Railroad Co., Delaware, Lackawanna & Western Coal Co., Susquehanna Coal Co., Susquehanna Collieries Co., Lytle Coal Co., or the M. A. Hanna Coal Co.

5. The grades and sizes for which the maximum prices are specified are as follows: White Ash anthracite coal of the grade that between January 1, 1915, and January 1, 1917, was uniformly sold and recognized in the coal trade as coal of White Ash grade; Red Ash anthracite coal of the grade that between January 1, 1915, and January 1, 1917, was uniformly sold and recognized in the trade as coal of Red Ash grade; and Lykens Valley anthracite coal that is mined exclusively from the Lykens Valley seams and of the grade that between January 1, 1915, and January 1, 1917, was uniformly sold and recognized in the coal trade as coal of Lykens Valley grade.

White ash grade:

Broken	$4.55
Egg	4.45
Stove	4.70
Chestnut	4.80
Pea	4.00

Red ash grade:

Broken	$4.75
Egg	4.65
Stove	4.90
Chestnut	4.90
Pea	4.10

Lykens Valley grade:

Broken	$5.00
Egg	4.90
Stove	5.30
Chestnut	5.30
Pea	4.35

6. Producers of anthracite coal who are not specified in paragraph 4 shall not sell the various grades and sizes of anthracite coal at prices that exceed by more than 75 cents per ton of 2,240 pounds free on board cars at the mines the prices enumerated in paragraph 5: Provided, that any producer of anthracite coal who incurs the expense of rescreening it at the Atlantic or lake ports for transshipment by water may increase the price thereof by not more than 5 cents per ton of 2,240 pounds.

7. Producers of anthracite coal specified in paragraph 4 of these regulations shall not sell anthracite coal to producers of anthracite coal not specified in paragraph 4.

8. Dealers and selling agents shall not sell coal produced by the producers included in paragraph 4 on the basis of the prices fixed at the mine for coal produced by producers not specified in said paragraph.

WOODROW WILSON.

EXECUTIVE ORDER

[Appointing Fuel Administrator.]

THE WHITE HOUSE, *23 August, 1917.*

By virtue of the power conferred upon me under the Act of Congress approved August 10, 1917, entitled "An Act to provide further for the national security and defense by encouraging the production, conserving the supply, and controlling the distribution of food products and fuel," and particularly for the purpose of carrying into effect the provisions of said Act relating to fuel, Harry A. Garfield is hereby designated and appointed United States Fuel Administrator, to hold office during the pleasure of the President.

Said fuel administrator shall supervise, direct and carry into effect the provisions of said Act and the powers and authority therein given to the President so far as the same apply to fuel as set forth in said Act, and to any and all practices, procedure and regulations authorized under the provisions of said Act applicable to fuel, including the issuance, regulation and revocation under the name of said United States Fuel Administrator of licenses under said Act. In this behalf he shall do and perform such acts and things as may be authorized and required of him from time to time by direction of the President and under such rules and regulations as may be prescribed.

Said fuel administrator shall also have the authority to employ such assistants and subordinates, including such counsel as may from time to time be deemed by him necessary and to fix the compensation of such assistants, subordinates and counsel.

All departments and established agencies of the Government are hereby directed to cooperate with the United States Fuel Administrator in the performance of his duties as hereinbefore set forth.

WOODROW WILSON.

LETTER

[To School Officials, Requesting Study of New Problems of National Interest.]

THE WHITE HOUSE, *Aug. 23, 1917.*

To SCHOOL OFFICERS:

The war is bringing to the minds of our people a new appreciation of the problems of national life and a deeper understanding of the meaning and aims of democracy. Matters which heretofore have seemed commonplace and trivial are seen in a truer light. The urgent demand for the production and proper distribution of food and other national resources has made us aware of the close dependence of individual on individual and nation on nation. The effort to keep up social and industrial organizations in spite of the withdrawal of men for the army has revealed the extent to which modern life has become complex and specialized.

These and other lessons of the war must be learned quickly if we are intelligently and successfully to defend our institutions. When the war is over we must apply the wisdom which we have acquired in purging and ennobling the life of the world.

In these vital tasks of acquiring a broader view of human possibilities the common school must have a large part. I urge that teachers and other school officers increase materially the time and attention devoted to instruction bearing directly on the problems of community and national life.

Such a plea is in no way foreign to the spirit of American public education or of existing practices. Nor is it a plea for a temporary enlargement of the school program appropriate merely to the period of the war. It is a plea for a realization in public education of the new emphasis which the war has given to the ideals of democracy and to the broader conceptions of national life.

In order that there may be definite material at hand with which the schools may at once expand their teaching, I have asked Mr. Hoover and Commissioner Claxton to organize the proper agencies for the preparation and distribution of suitable lessons for the elementary grades and for the high school classes. Lessons thus suggested will serve the double purpose of illustrating in a concrete way what can be undertaken in the schools and of stimulating teachers in all parts of the country to formulate new and appropriate materials drawn directly from the communities in which they live.

Sincerely yours,

WOODROW WILSON.

EXECUTIVE ORDER

[Rules for Government of Virgin Islands.]

THE WHITE HOUSE, *August 24, 1917.*

Whereas, Section Two of the Act of Congress approved March 3, 1917, entitled "An Act to Provide for a Temporary Government of the Virgin Islands of the United States," provides as follows: "That until Congress shall otherwise provide, in so far as compatible with the changed sovereignty and not in conflict with the provisions of the Act, the laws regulating elections and the electoral franchise as set forth in the code of laws published at Amalienborg the sixth of April, nineteen hundred and six, and the other local laws, in force and effect in said islands on the seventeenth day of January, nineteen hundred and seventeen, shall remain in force and effect in said islands, and the same shall be administered by the civil officials and through the local judicial tribunals established in said islands, respectively; and the orders, judgments, and decrees of said judicial tribunals shall be duly enforced. With the approval of the President, or under such rules and regulations as the President may prescribe, any of said laws may be repealed, altered, or amended by the colonial council having jurisdiction. The jurisdiction of the judicial tribunals of said islands shall extend to all judicial proceedings and controversies in said islands to which the United States or any citizen thereof may be a party. In all cases arising in said West Indian Islands and now reviewable by the courts of Denmark, writs of error and appeals shall be to the Circuit Court of Appeals for the Third Circuit, and, except as provided in sections two hundred and thirty-nine and two hundred and forty of the Judicial Code the judgments, orders, and decrees of such court shall be final in all such cases;"

And whereas, Section Five of the said Act of Congress provides as follows: "That the duties and taxes collected in pursuance of this Act shall not be covered into the general fund of the Treasury of the United States, but shall be used and expended for the government and benefit of said islands under such rules and regulations as the President may prescribe;"

Now, therefore, by virtue of the authority vested in me by the said Sections Two and Five of the said Act of Congress, I do hereby prescribe the following rules: "Repeals, Alterations and Amendments of local laws of Virgin Islands of United States by Colonial Council having jurisdiction, shall be effective and enforced when, and to the extent, said Repeals, Alterations and Amendments are approved by the Governor of said islands, the Governor to state specifically in each case whether his approval is in whole or in part, and if in part only, what part is approved and what part not approved. The President reserves the right to disapprove and set aside any enactments of the Colonial Council;" "The duties and taxes collected in the Virgin Islands of the United States shall be expended for the government and benefit of said islands in accordance with the annual budget prepared and modified as provided by the local laws; provided, that during this current fiscal year of said island, in order to provide for the payments of those expenses of said island formerly paid by Denmark and not provided for in said budgets, and to provide further for other necessary and unforeseen expenses of government, the Governor may authorize such additional expenditures from said funds as, in his discretion, may be necessary for the government and benefit of said islands during this current local fiscal year."

WOODROW WILSON.

By the President of the United States of America

A PROCLAMATION

[Certain Exports In Time of War Unlawful.]

Whereas Congress has enacted, and the President has on the fifteenth day of June, 1917, approved a law which contains the following provisions:

"Whenever during the present war the President shall find that the public safety shall so require, and shall make proclamation thereof, it shall be unlawful to export from or ship from or take out of the United States to any country named in such proclamation any article or articles mentioned in such proclamation, except at such time or times, and under such regulations and orders, and subject to such limitations and exceptions as the President shall prescribe, until otherwise ordered by the President or by Congress: Provided, however, that no preference shall be given to the ports of one State over those of another.

"Any person who shall export, ship, or take out, or deliver or attempt to deliver for export, shipment, or taking out, any article in violation of this title, or of any regulation or order made hereunder, shall be fined not more than $10,000, or, if a natural person, imprisoned for not more than two years, or both; and any article so delivered or exported, shipped or taken out, or so attempted to be delivered or exported, shipped, or taken out, shall be seized and forfeited to the United States; and any officer, director, or agent of a corporation who participates in any such violation shall be liable to like fine or imprisonment, or both.

"Whenever there is reasonable cause to believe that any vessel, domestic or foreign, is about to carry out of the United States any article or articles in violation of the provisions of this title, the collector of customs for the district in which such vessel is located is hereby authorized and empowered, subject to review by the Secretary of Commerce, to refuse clearance to any such vessel, domestic or foreign, for which clearance is required by law, and by formal notice served upon the owners, master, or person or persons in command or charge of any domestic vessel for which clearance is not required by law, to forbid the departure of such vessel from the port, and it shall thereupon be unlawful for such vessel to depart. Whoever, in violation of any of the provisions of this section, shall take, or attempt to take, or authorize the taking of any such vessel out of port or from the jurisdiction of the United States, shall be fined not more than $10,000 or imprisoned for not more than two years, or both; and, in addition, such vessel, her tackle, apparel, furniture, equipment, and her forbidden cargo shall be forfeited to the United States;"

Now, therefore, I, Woodrow Wilson, President of the United States of America, do hereby proclaim to all whom it may concern that the public safety requires that, except at such time or times, and under such regulations and orders, and subject to such limitations and exceptions as the President shall prescribe, until otherwise ordered by the President or by Congress, the following articles, namely: all kinds of arms, guns, ammunition and explosives, machines for their manufacture or repair, component parts thereof, materials or ingredients used in their manufacture, and all articles necessary or convenient for their use; all contrivances for or means of transportation on land or in the water or air, machines used in their manufacture or repair, component parts thereof, materials or ingredients used in their manufacture, and all instruments, articles and animals necessary or convenient for their use; all means of communication, tools, implements, instruments, equipment, maps, pictures, papers and other articles, machines and documents necessary or convenient for carrying on hostile operations; coin, bullion, currency, evidences of debt, and metal, materials, dies, plates, machinery and other articles necessary or convenient for their manufacture; all kinds of fuel, food, food-stuffs, feed, forage and clothing, and all articles and materials used in their manufacture; all chemicals, drugs, dye-stuffs and tanning materials; cotton, wool, silk, flax, hemp, jute, sisal and other fibres and manufactures thereof; all earths, clay, glass, sand and their products; hides, skins and manufactures thereof; non-edible animal and vegetable products; machinery, tools and apparatus; medical, surgical, laboratory and sanitary supplies and equipment; all metals, minerals, mineral oils, ores, and all derivatives and manufactures thereof; paper pulp, books and printed matter; rubber, gums, rosins, tars and waxes, their products, derivatives and substitutes, and all articles containing them; wood and wood manufactures; coffee, cocoa, tea and spices; wines, spirits, mineral waters and beverages: shall not, on and after the 30th day of August, in the year one thousand nine hundred and seventeen, be exported from or shipped from or taken out of the United States or its territorial possessions to Albania, Austria-Hungary, that portion of Belgium occupied by the military forces of Germany, Bulgaria, Denmark, her colonies, possessions or protectorates, Germany, her colonies, possessions or protectorates, Greece, Liechtenstein, Luxembourg, The Kingdom of The Netherlands, Norway, Spain, her colonies, possessions or protectorates, Sweden, Switzerland or Turkey (excluding any portion of the foregoing occupied by the military forces of the United States or the nations associated with the United States in the war), or any territory occupied by the military forces of Germany or her allies; and

I do hereby further proclaim to all whom it may concern that the public safety requires that, except at such time or times, and under such regulations and orders, and subject to such limitations and exceptions as the President shall prescribe, until otherwise ordered by the President or by Congress, the following articles, namely: coal; coke; fuel oils, lubricating oils, hand-lantern oil, naphtha, benzine, red oil, kerosene and gasoline; all bunkers; food grains, flour and meal therefrom, corn flour, barley, rice flour, rice, oat meal and rolled oats; fodder and feeds, oil-cake, oil-meal cake, malt and peanuts; all meats and fats, poultry, cottonseed oil, corn oil, copra, desiccated cocoanuts, butter, fresh, dried and canned fish, edible or inedible grease of animal or vegetable origin, linseed oil, lard, tinned milk, peanut oil and butter, rapeseed oil, tallow, tallow candles and stearic acid; sugar, glucose, syrup and molasses; pig iron, ferro-silicon and spiegeleisen; steel ingots, billets, blooms, slabs and sheet bars; iron and steel plates, including ship, boiler, tank and all other iron and steel plates one-eighth of an inch thick and heavier, and wider than six inches; iron and steel structural shapes, including beams, channels, angles, tees and zees of all sizes; fabricated structural iron and steel, including beams, channels, angles, tees, zees and plates, fabricated and shipped knocked down; scrap iron and scrap steel; ferro-manganese; tool steel, high-speed steel and alloy steels and machine tools; steel-hardening materials; fertilizers, including cattle and sheep manure, nitrate of soda, poudrette, potato manure, potassium salts, land plaster, potash, cyanamide, phosphoric acid, phosphate rock, super-phosphate, chlorate of potash, bone meal, bone flour, ground bone, dried blood, ammonia and ammonia salts, acid phosphates, guano, humus, hardwood ashes, soot, anhydrous ammonia; aeronautical machines and instruments, their parts and accessories thereof; arms and ammunition; all explosives, nitrate of potash, rosin, saltpetre, turpentine, ether, alcohol, sulphur, sulphuric acid and its salts, acetone, nitric acid and its salts, benzol and its derivatives, phenol (carbolic acid) and its derivatives, toluol and its derivatives, mercury and its salts, glycerine, potash and its salts, all cyanides and films; carrier and other pigeons; anti-aircraft instruments, apparatus and accessories; all radio and wireless apparatus and its accessories; optical glass, optical instruments and reflectors; cotton and cotton linters; wool, wool rags, wool and khaki clippings and wool products; flax, sisal, jute, hemp and all manufactures thereof; hides, skins, leather, leather belting, sole and upper leather, leather boots and shoes, harness and saddles and leather clothing; soap and soap powders; all engines and motors operated by steam, gas, electricity or other motive power and their accessories; metal and wood-working machinery; oil well casing, oil well drilling implements and machinery and the accessories thereof; steam boilers, turbines, condensers, pumps and accessories thereof; all electrical equipment; crucibles; emery, emery wheels, carborundum and all artificial abrasives; copper, including copper ingots, bars, rods, plates, sheets, tubes, wire and scrap thereof; lead and white lead; tin, tin plate, tin cans and all articles containing tin; nickel, aluminum, zinc, plumbago and platinum; news-paper, print-paper, wood pulp and cellulose; ash, spruce, walnut, mahogany, oak and birch woods; and industrial diamonds: shall not, on and after the 30th day of August, in the year one thousand nine hundred and seventeen, be exported from, shipped from or taken out of the United States or its territorial possessions to Abyssinia, Afghanistan, Argentina, that portion of Belgium not occupied by the military forces of Germany or the colonies, possessions or protectorates of Belgium, Bolivia, Brazil, China, Chile, Colombia, Costa Rica, Cuba, Dominican Republic, Ecuador, Egypt, France, her colonies, possessions or protectorates, Guatemala, Haiti, Honduras, Italy, her colonies, possessions or protectorates, Great Britain, her colonies, possessions or protectorates, Japan, Liberia, Mexico, Monaco, Montenegro, Morocco, Nepal, Nicaragua, the colonies, possessions or protectorates of The Netherlands, Oman, Panama, Paraguay, Persia, Peru, Portugal, her colonies, possessions or protectorates, Roumania, Russia, Salvador, San Marino, Serbia, Siam, Uruguay, Venezuela (excluding any portion of the foregoing occupied by the military forces of Germany or her allies), or any territory occupied by the military forces of the United States or by the nations associated with the United States in the war.

The regulations, orders, limitations and exceptions prescribed will be administered by and under the authority of the Exports Administrative Board, from whom licenses, in conformity with said regulations, orders, limitations and exceptions, will issue.

In testimony whereof, I have hereunto set my hand and caused the seal of the United States of America to be affixed.

Done in the District of Columbia, this 27th day of August in the
      year of our Lord one thousand nine hundred and seventeen
[SEAL] and of the Independence of the United States of America
      the one hundred and forty-second.

                          WOODROW WILSON.

By the President:
    ROBERT LANSING, *Secretary of State.*

STATEMENT

[Explaining the Above Proclamation.]

The purpose and effect of this proclamation is not export prohibition, but merely export control. It is not the intention to interfere unnecessarily with our foreign trade; but our own domestic needs must be adequately safeguarded and there is the added duty of meeting the necessities of all the nations at war with the Imperial German Government. After these needs are met it is our wish and intention to minister to the needs of the neutral nations as far as our resources permit. This task will be discharged without other than the very proper qualification that the liberation of our surplus products shall not be made the occasion of benefit to the enemy, either directly or indirectly.

The two lists have been prepared in the interests of facility and expediency. The first list, applicable to the enemy and his allies and to the neutral countries of Europe, brings under control practically all articles of commerce, while the second list, applicable to all the other countries of the world, makes only a few additions to the list of commodities controlled by the proclamation of July 9, 1917. It is obvious that a closer supervision and control of exports is necessary with respect to those European neutrals within the sphere of hostilities than is required for those countries farther removed.

The establishment of these distinctions will simplify the administrative processes and enable us to continue our policy of minimizing the interruption of trade.

No licenses will be necessary for the exportation of coin, bullion, currency, and evidences of indebtedness until required by regulations to be promulgated by the Secretary of the Treasury in his discretion.

                          WOODROW WILSON.

EXECUTIVE ORDER

[Establishing Defensive Sea Areas for Terminal Ports of the Panama Canal, and Providing Regulations for the Government of Persons and Vessels Within Said Areas.]

THE WHITE HOUSE, *Aug. 27, 1917.*

By virtue of the authority vested in me by law, the following-described defensive sea areas for the terminal ports of The Panama Canal are hereby established, to be maintained until further notification, at the places and within the limits prescribed as follows, that is to say:

ATLANTIC ENTRANCE:

Outer Limit.—From the northern end of Naranjos Cays to a point two miles due north of the breakwater entrance, thence tangent to the arc of a circle with one-mile radius, having the mouth of the Chagres River as a center, thence along the arc of this circle to the beach.

Inner Limit.—Line joining east end of west breakwater and west end of east breakwater.

PACIFIC ENTRANCE:

Outer Limit.—Line joining Venado Island with north end of Taboguilla Island; thence north 53° east, true for 5 miles; thence north 39° west to a point with San Jose Rock bearing north 53° west, true, distant two nautical miles; thence to Tres Hermanos Beacon; thence to Punta Mala.

Inner Limit.—Line joining Guinea Point with inner end of causeway.

The following orders and regulations for the government of persons and vessels within the limits of said defensive sea areas, which orders and regulations are necessary for the purposes of defense of the Canal Zone, are hereby promulgated:

I. In the neighborhood of each defensive sea area the following entrances are designated for incoming and outgoing vessels:

ATLANTIC:

Designated Entrance for Incoming Vessels:

A patrol boat stationed with end of west breakwater bearing south, true, distant two nautical miles.

Designated Entrance for Outgoing Vessels:

The main entrance to the Panama Canal, between the breakwaters.

PACIFIC:

Designated Entrance for Incoming Vessels:

Patrol boat stationed with north end of Taboguilla Island bearing due west, distant one nautical mile.

Designated Entrance for Outgoing Vessels:

Canal Prism.

II. A vessel desiring to cross a defensive sea area shall proceed to the vicinity of the entrance, flying her national colors, together with International Code number and pilot signal, and there await communication with the Harbor Entrance Patrol. It is expressly prohibited for any vessel to enter the limits of a defensive sea area otherwise than at a designated entrance and after authorization of the Harbor Entrance Patrol.

III. Boats and other craft employed in the Harbor Entrance Patrol will be distinguished by the union jack, which will be shown from a position forward. At night they may show a vertical hoist of three lights—white, red, and white, in the order named.

IV. On receiving permission from the Harbor Entrance Patrol to enter a defensive sea area, a vessel must comply with all instructions as to pilotage and other matters that she may receive from proper authority, either before or during her passage across the area; it is understood that only upon condition of such compliance is the said permission granted.

V. No permission will be granted to other than a public vessel of the United States or a Canal craft to cross a defensive sea area between sunset and sunrise, nor during the prevalence of weather conditions that render navigation difficult or dangerous. A vessel arriving off a defensive sea area after sunset shall anchor or lie-to at a distance of at least a mile outside its limits until the following sunrise; vessels discovered near the limits of the areas at night may be fired upon.

VI. No vessel shall be permitted to proceed within the limits of a defensive sea area at a greater speed than six (6) knots per hour.

VII. All matters pertaining to fishery and the passage of small crafts within a defensive sea area shall be regulated by the senior officer of the Harbor Entrance Patrol.

VIII. These regulations are subject to modification by the senior officer of the Harbor Entrance Patrol when the public interest may require; and such notification as circumstances may permit will be issued regarding modifications thus made.

IX. Any master of a vessel or other person within the vicinity of a defensive sea area who shall violate these regulations, or shall fail to obey an order to stop and heave to, or shall perform any act threatening the efficiency of mine or other defenses or the safety of navigation, or shall take any action inimical to the interests of the United States in its prosecution of war, may be detained therein by force of arms and renders himself liable to prosecution.

X. The responsibility of the United States of America for any damage inflicted by force of arms with the object of detaining any person or vessel proceeding in contravention to regulations duly promulgated in accordance with this executive order shall cease from this date.

XI. This order shall take effect from and after this date.

WOODROW WILSON.

POPE'S OFFER OF MEDIATION.

To the Rulers of the Belligerent Peoples:

From the beginning of our pontificate, in the midst of the horrors of the awful war let loose on Europe, we have had of all things three in mind: To maintain perfect impartiality toward all the belligerents as becomes him who is the common father and loves all his children with equal affection; continually to endeavor to do them all as much good as possible, without exception of person, without distinction of nationality or religion, as is dictated to us by the universal law of charity as well as by the supreme spiritual charge with which we have been intrusted by Christ; finally, as also required by our mission of peace, to omit nothing, as far as it lay in our power, that could contribute to expedite the end of these calamities by endeavoring to bring the people and their rulers to more moderate resolutions, to the serene deliberation of peace, of a "just and lasting" peace.

Whoever has watched our endeavors in these three grievous years that have just elapsed could easily see that while we remained ever true to our resolution of absolute impartiality and beneficent action, we never ceased to urge the belligerent peoples and Governments again to be brothers, although all that we did to reach this very noble goal was not made public.

About the end of the first year of the war we addressed to the contending nations the most earnest exhortations and in addition pointed to the path that would lead to a stable peace honorable to all. Unfortunately our appeal was not heeded and the war was fiercely carried on for two years more with all its horrors. It became even more cruel and spread over land and sea and even to the air, and desolation and death were seen to fall upon defenseless cities, peaceful villages, and their innocent populations. And now no one can imagine how much the general suffering would increase and become worse if other months or, still worse, other years were added to this sanguinary triennium. Is this civilized world to be turned into a field of death and is Europe, so glorious and flourishing, to rush, as carried by a universal folly, to the abyss and take a hand in its own suicide?

In so distressing a situation, in the presence of so grave a menace, we who have no personal political aim, who listen to the suggestions or interests of none of the belligerents, but are solely actuated by the sense of our supreme duty as the common father of the faithful, by the solicitations of our children who implore our intervention and peace-bearing word, uttering the very voice of humanity and reason, we again call for peace and we renew a pressing appeal to those who have in their hands the destinies of the nations. But no longer confining ourselves to general terms, as we were led to do by circumstances in the past, we will now come to more concrete and practical proposals and invite the Governments of the belligerent peoples to arrive at an agreement on the following points, which seem to offer the base of a just and lasting peace, leaving it with them to make them more precise and complete:

First, the fundamental point must be that the material force of arms give way to the moral force of right, whence a just agreement of all upon the simultaneous and reciprocal decease of armaments, according to rules and guarantees to be established, in the necessary and sufficient measure for the maintenance of public order in every State; then, taking the place of arms, the institution of arbitration, with its high pacifying function, according to rules to be drawn in concert and under sanctions to be determined against any State which would decline either to refer international questions to arbitration or to accept its awards.

When supremacy of right is thus established, let every obstacle to ways of communication of the peoples be removed by insuring, through rules to be also determined, the true freedom and community of the seas, which, on the one hand, would eliminate many causes of conflict and, on the other hand, would open to all new sources of prosperity and progress.

As for the damages to be repaid and the cost of the war, we see no other way of solving the question than by setting up the general principle of entire and reciprocal condonation which would be justified by the immense benefit to be derived from disarmament, all the more as one could not understand that such carnage could go on for mere economic reasons. If certain particular reasons stand against this in certain cases, let them be weighed in justice and equity.

But these specific agreements, with the immense advantages that flow from them, are not possible unless territory now occupied is reciprocally restituted. Therefore, on the part of Germany, total evacuation of Belgium, with guarantees of its entire political, military, and economic independence toward any power whatever; evacuation also of the French territory; on the part of the other belligerents a similar restitution of the German colonies.

As regards territorial questions as, for instance, those that are disputed by Italy and Austria, by Germany and France, there is reason to hope that in consideration of the immense advantages of durable peace with disarmaments, the contending parties will examine in a conciliatory spirit, taking into account as far as is just and possible, as we have said formerly, the aspirations of the population, and if occasion arises adjusting private interests to the general good of the great human society.

The same spirit of equity and justice must guide the examination of the other territorial and political questions, notably those relative to Armenia, the Balkan States, and the territories forming part of the old Kingdom of Poland, for which, in particular, its noble historical traditions and the suffering particularly undergone during the present war, must win, with justice, the sympathies of the nations.

These, we believe, are the main bases upon which must rest the future reorganization of the peoples. They are such as to make the recurrence of such conflicts impossible and open the way for the solution of the economic question which is so important for the future and the material welfare of all of the belligerent states. And so, in presenting them to you who, at this tragic hour, guide the destinies of the belligerent nations, we indulge a gratifying hope that they will be accepted and that we shall thus see an early termination of the terrible struggle which has more and more the appearance of a useless massacre. Everybody acknowledges on the other hand that on both sides the honor of arms is safe. Do not, then, turn a deaf ear to our prayer, accept the paternal invitation which we extend to you in the name of the Divine Redeemer, Prince of Peace. Bear in mind your very grave responsibility to God and man; on your decision depend the quiet and joy of numberless families, the lives of thousands of young men, the happiness, in a word, of the peoples to whom it is your imperative duty to secure this boon. May the Lord inspire you with decisions conformable to His very holy will. May Heaven grant that in winning the applause of your contemporaries you will also earn from the future generations the great titles of pacificators.

As for us, closely united in prayer and penitence with all the faithful souls who yearn for peace, we implore for you the divine spirit, enlightenment, and guidance. Given at the Vatican, August 1, 1917.

BENEDICTUS P. M. XV.

REPLY TO THE POPE'S PEACE PROPOSALS

August 27, 1917.

To His Holiness Benedictus XV, Pope.

In acknowledgment of the communication of Your Holiness to the belligerent peoples, dated August 1, 1917, the President of the United States requests me to transmit the following reply:

Every heart that has not been blinded and hardened by this terrible war must be touched by this moving appeal of His Holiness the Pope, must feel the dignity and force of the humane and generous motives which prompted it, and must fervently wish that we might take the path of peace he so persuasively points out. But it would be folly to take it if it does not in fact lead to the goal he proposes. Our response must be based upon the stern facts and upon nothing else. It is not a mere cessation of arms he desires; it is a stable and enduring peace. This agony must not be gone through with again, and it must be a matter of very sober judgment what will insure us against it.

His Holiness in substance proposes that we return to the status quo ante bellum, and that then there be a general condonation, disarmament, and a concert of nations based upon an acceptance of the principle of arbitration; that by a similar concert freedom of the seas be established; and that the territorial claims of France and Italy, the perplexing problems of the Balkan states, and the restitution of Poland be left to such conciliatory adjustments as may be possible in the new temper of such a peace, due regard being paid to the aspirations of the peoples whose political fortunes and affiliations will be involved.

It is manifest that no part of this program can be successfully carried out unless the restitution of the status quo ante furnishes a firm and satisfactory basis for it. The object of this war is to deliver the free peoples of the world from the menace and the actual power of a vast military establishment controlled by an irresponsible government which, having secretly planned to dominate the world, proceeded to carry the plan out without regard either to the sacred obligations of treaty or the long-established practices and long-cherished principles or international action and honor; which chose its own time for the war; delivered its blow fiercely and suddenly; stopped at no barrier either of law or of mercy; swept a whole continent within the tide of blood—not the blood of soldiers only, but the blood of innocent women and children also and of the helpless poor; and now stands balked but not defeated, the enemy of four-fifths of the world. This power is not the German people. It is the ruthless master of the German people. It is no business of ours how that great people came under its control or submitted with temporary zest to the domination of its purpose; but it is our business to see to it that the history of the rest of the world is no longer left to its handling.

To deal with such a power by way of peace upon the plan proposed by His Holiness the Pope would, so far as we can see, involve a recuperation of its strength and a renewal of its policy; would make it necessary to create a permanent hostile combination of nations against the German people, who are its instruments; and would result in abandoning the new-born Russia to the intrigue, the manifold subtle interference, and the certain counter-revolution which would be attempted by all the malign influences to which the German Government has of late accustomed the world. Can peace be based upon a restitution of its power or upon any word of honor it could pledge in a treaty of settlement and accommodation?

Responsible statesmen must now everywhere see, if they never saw before, that no peace can rest securely upon political or economic restrictions meant to benefit some nations and cripple or embarrass others, upon vindictive action of any sort, or any kind of revenge or deliberate injury. The American people have suffered intolerable wrongs at the hands of the Imperial German Government, but they desire no reprisal upon the German people, who have themselves suffered all things in this war, which they did not choose. They believe that peace should rest upon the rights of peoples, not the rights of governments—the rights of peoples great or small, weak or powerful —their equal right to freedom and security and self-government and to a participation upon fair terms in the economic opportunities of the world, the German people of course included if they will accept equality and not seek domination.

The test, therefore, of every plan of peace is this: Is it based upon the faith of all the peoples involved or merely upon the word of an ambitious and intriguing government, on the one hand, and of a group of free peoples, on the other? This is a test which goes to the root of the matter; and it is the test which must be applied.

The purposes of the United States in this war are known to the whole world, to every people to whom the truth has been permitted to come. They do not need to be stated again. We seek no material advantage of any kind. We believe that the intolerable wrongs done in this war by the furious and brutal power of the Imperial German Government ought to be repaired, but not at the expense of the sovereignty of any people—rather a vindication of the sovereignty both of those that are weak and of those that are strong. Punitive damages, the dismemberment of empires, the establishment of selfish and exclusive economic leagues, we deem inexpedient and in the end worse than futile, no proper basis for a peace of any kind, least of all for an enduring peace. That must be based upon justice and fairness and the common rights of mankind.

We can not take the word of the present rulers of Germany as a guarantee of anything that is to endure, unless explicitly supported by such conclusive evidence of the will and purpose of the German people themselves as the other peoples of the world would be justified in accepting. Without such guarantees treaties of settlement, agreements for disarmament, covenants to set up arbitration in the place of force, territorial adjustments, reconstitutions of small nations, if made with the German Government, no man, no nation could now depend on. We must await some new evidence of the purposes of the great peoples of the Central Powers. God grant it may be given soon and in a way to restore the confidence of all peoples everywhere in the faith of nations and the possibility of a covenanted peace.

ROBERT LANSING,
Secretary of State of the United States of America.

TEXT OF GERMAN'S REPLY TO POPE BENEDICT'S PEACE PROPOSAL.

Herr Cardinal: Your Eminence has been good enough, together with your letter of Aug. 2, to transmit to the Kaiser and King, my most gracious master, the note of His Holiness the Pope, in which His Holiness, filled with grief at the devastation of the world war, makes an emphatic peace appeal to the heads of the belligerent peoples. The Kaiser-King has deigned to acquaint me with Your Eminence's letter and intrust the reply to me.

His Majesty has been following for a considerable time, with high respect and sincere gratitude, His Holiness's efforts in a spirit of true impartiality to alleviate as far as possible the sufferings of the war and to hasten the end of hostilities. The Kaiser sees in the latest step of His Holiness fresh proof of his noble and humane feelings, and cherishes a lively desire that for the benefit of the entire world the Papal appeal may meet with success.

The effort of Pope Benedict is to pave the way to an understanding among all peoples, and might surely reckon on a sympathetic reception and the whole-hearted support from His Majesty, seeing that the Kaiser, since taking over the Government, has regarded it as his principal and most sacred task to preserve the blessings of peace for the German people and the world.

In his first speech from the throne at the opening of the German Reichstag on June 25, 1888, the Kaiser promised that his love of the German army and his position toward it should never lead him into temptation to cut short the benefits of peace unless war were a necessity, forced upon us by an attack on the empire or its allies. The German army should safeguard peace for us, and should peace, nevertheless, be broken it would be in a position to win it with honor. The Kaiser has, by his acts, fulfilled the promise he then made in twenty-six years of happy rule, despite provocations and temptations.

In the crisis which led to the present world conflagration His Majesty's efforts were up to the last moment directed toward settling the conflict by peaceful means. After the war had broken out, against his wish and desire, the Kaiser in conjunction with his high Allies was the first solemnly to declare his readiness to enter into peace negotiations. The German people supported His Majesty in his keen desire for peace.

Germany sought within her national frontier the free development of her spiritual and material possessions and outside the imperial territory unhindered competition with nations enjoying equal rights and equal esteem. The free play of forces in the world in peaceable wrestling with one another would lead to the highest perfecting of the noblest human possessions. Disastrous concatenation of events in the year 1914 absolutely broke off all hopeful course of development and transformed Europe into a bloody battle arena.

Appreciating the importance of His Holiness's declaration, the Imperial Government has not failed to submit the suggestion contained therein to earnest and scrupulous examination. Special measures, which the Government has taken in closest contact with representatives of the German people, for discussing and answering the questions raised, prove how earnestly it desires, in accordance with His Holiness's desires, and the peace resolution of the Reichstag on July 19, to find a practical basis for a just and lasting peace.

The Imperial Government greets with special sympathy the leading idea of the peace appeal wherein His Holiness clearly expresses the conviction that in the future the material power of arms must be superseded by the moral power of right. We are also convinced that the sick body of human society can only be healed by fortifying its moral strength of right. From this would follow, according to His Holiness's view, the simultaneous diminution of the armed forces of all states and the institution of obligatory arbitration for international disputes.

We share His Holiness' view that definite rules and a certain safeguard for a simultaneous and reciprocal limitation of armaments on land, on sea, and in the air, as well as for the true freedom of the community and high seas, are the things in treating which the new spirit that in the future should prevail in international relations should find first hopeful expression. The task would then of itself arise to decide international differences of opinion, not by the use of armed forces but by peaceful methods, especially by arbitration, whose high peace-producing effect we together with His Holiness fully recognize.

The Imperial Government will in this respect support every proposal compatible with the vital interest of the German Empire and people.

Germany, owing to her geographical situation and economic requirements, has to rely on peaceful intercourse with her neighbors and with distant countries. No people, therefore, has more reason than the German people to wish that instead of universal hatred and battle a conciliatory fraternal spirit should prevail between nations.

If the nations are guided by this spirit it will be recognized to their advantage that the important thing is to lay more stress upon that which unites them in their relations. They will also succeed in settling individual points of conflict which are still undecided in such a way that conditions of existence will be created which can be satisfactory to every nation, and thereby a repetition of this great world catastrophe would appear impossible.

Only on this condition can a lasting peace be founded which would promote an intellectual rapprochement and a return to the economic prosperity of human society. This serious and sincere conviction encourages our confidence that our enemies also may see a suitable basis in the ideas submitted by His Holiness for approaching nearer to the preparation for future peace under conditions corresponding to a spirit of reasonableness and to the situation in Europe.

The document is signed by the Imperial Chancellor and is addressed to Cardinal Gasparri, Papal Secretary of State.

TEXT OF THE AUSTRIAN EMPEROR'S REPLY TO POPE BENEDICT'S PEACE PROPOSALS.

Holy Father: With due veneration and deep emotion we take cognizance of the new representations which your Holiness, in fulfillment of the holy office intrusted to you by God, makes to us and the heads of the other belligerent States, with the noble intention of leading the heavily tried nations to a unity that will restore peace to them.

With a thankful heart we receive this fresh gift of fatherly care which you, Holy Father, always bestow on all peoples without distinction, and from the depth of our heart we greet the moving exhortation which your Holiness has addressed to the Governments of the belligerent peoples.

During this cruel war we have always looked up to your Holiness as to the highest personage, who, in virtue of his mission, which reaches beyond earthly things, and, thanks to the high conception of his duties laid upon him, stands high above the belligerent peoples, and who, inaccessible to all influence, was able to find a way which may lead to the realization of our own desire for peace, lasting and honorable for all parties.

Since ascending the throne of our ancestors, and fully conscious of the responsibility which we bear before God and men for the fate of the Austro-Hungarian monarchy, we have never lost sight of the high aim of restoring to our peoples, as speedily as possible, the blessings of peace. Soon after our accession to the throne it was vouchsafed to us, in common with our allies, to undertake a step which had been considered and prepared by our exalted predecessor, Francis Joseph, to pave the way for a lasting and honorable peace.

We gave expression to this desire in a speech from the throne delivered at the opening of the Austrian Reichstag, thereby showing that we are striving after a peace that shall free the future life of the nation from rancor and a thirst for revenge, and that shall secure them for generations to come from the employment of armed forces. Our joint Government has in the meantime not failed in repeated and emphatic declarations, which could be heard by all the world, to give expression to our own will and that of the Austro-Hungarian peoples to prepare an end to bloodshed by a peace such as your Holiness has in mind.

Happy in the thought that our desires from the first were directed toward the same object which your Holiness today characterizes as one we should strive for, we have taken into close consideration the concrete and practical suggestions of your Holiness and have come to the following conclusions:

With deep-rooted conviction we agree to the leading idea of your Holiness that the future arrangement of the world must be based on the elimination of armed forces and on the moral force of right and on the rule of international justice and legality.

We, too, are imbued with the hope that a strengthening of the sense of right would morally regenerate humanity. We support, therefore, your Holiness's view that the negotiations between the belligerents should and could lead to an understanding by which, with the creation of appropriate guarantees, armaments on land and sea and in the air might be reduced simultaneously, reciprocally and gradually to a fixed limit, and whereby the high seas, which rightly belong to all the nations of the earth, may be freed from domination or paramountcy, and be opened equally for the use of all.

Fully conscious of the importance of the promotion of peace on the method proposed by your Holiness, namely, to submit international disputes to compulsory arbitration, we are also prepared to enter into negotiations regarding this proposal.

If, as we most heartily desire, agreements should be arrived at between the belligerents which would realize this sublime idea and thereby give security to the Austro-Hungarian monarchy for its unhampered future development, it can then not be difficult to find a satisfactory solution of the other questions which still remain to be settled between the belligerents in a spirit of justice and of a reasonable consideration of the conditions for existence of both parties.

If the nations of the earth were to enter, with a desirable peace, into negotiations with one another in the sense of your Holiness's proposals, then peace could blossom forth from them. The nations could attain complete freedom of movement on the high seas, heavy material burdens could be taken from them, and new sources of prosperity opened to them.

Guided by a spirit of moderation and conciliation, we see in the proposals of your Holiness a suitable basis for initiating negotiations with a view to preparing a peace, just to all and lasting, and we earnestly hope our present enemies may be animated by the same ideas. In this spirit we beg that the Almighty may bless the work of peace begun by your Holiness.

STATEMENT

[Fixing prices of wheat.]

THE WHITE HOUSE, *August 30, 1917.*

Section 11 of the Food Act provides, among other things, for the purchase and sale of wheat and flour by the government, and appropriates money for that purpose. The purchase of wheat and flour for our allies, and to a considerable degree for neutral countries also, has been placed under the control of the Food Administration. I have appointed a committee to determine a fair price to be paid in government purchases. The price now recommended by that committee— $2.20 per bushel at Chicago for the basic grade—will be rigidly adhered to by the Food Administration.

It is the hope and expectation of the Food Administration, and my own also, that this step will at once stabilize and keep within moderate bounds the price of wheat for all transactions throughout the present crop year, and in consequence the prices of flour and bread also. The Food Act has given large powers for the control of storage and exchange operations, and these powers will be fully exercised. An inevitable consequence will be that financial dealings cannot follow their usual course. Whatever the advantages and disadvantages of the ordinary machinery of trade, it cannot function well under such disturbed and abnormal conditions as now exist. In its place, the Food Administration now fixes for its purchases a fair price, as recommended unanimously by a committee representative of all interests and all sections, and believes that thereby it will eliminate speculation, make possible the conduct of every operation in the full light of day, maintain the publicly stated price for all and, through economies made possible by stabilization and control, better the position of consumers also.

Mr. Hoover, at his express wish, has taken no part in the deliberations of the committee on whose recommendation I determine the Government's fair price, nor has he in any way intimated an opinion regarding that price. WOODROW WILSON.

REPORT OF COMMITTEE.

The report of the committee follows:

UNITED STATES FOOD ADMINISTRATION,
Washington, August 30, 1917.

TO THE PRESIDENT OF THE UNITED STATES:

The undersigned committee has been asked by you to recommend the price which the Government should pay for the 1917 crop of wheat.

In its deliberations the committee has kept constantly in mind the three following factors:

First. The fact that the United States is at war.

Second. The need of encouraging the producer.

Third. The necessity of reducing the cost of living to the consumer.

The normal laws of supply and demand have been violently interfered with and Congress has undertaken to offset this disturbance by conferring extraordinary powers upon the President to stabilize prices. Each of the foregoing factors grows out of conditions which have received the careful attention of the committee. Chief among them are: That the wheat yield in a great and important section of the country has this year been below the normal; that over against this situation is the crying need among the whole body of the population, especially the wage earners, that the rising tide of costs shall be stayed and reduced as rapidly as possible consistent with the welfare of the producer; that the Government is at the present time engaged in the great task of reducing and stabilizing costs of other staple commodities; that the wheat of the world is abundant for its needs even disregarding the stores in Russia, but because of lack of shipping and war conditions the burden of supplying wheat to the allies and to neutral nations rests for the time being upon the United States and Canada.

Your committee has also considered the fact that the Government price for the 1917 wheat crop is in effect a continuing guaranty until the minimum price guaranteed by Congress for the crop of 1918 goes into effect (July 1, 1918). It has considered the relation of the 1918 minimum price guaranty to the price here recommended. It has also considered the effect which an early termination of the war would have upon the wheat markets of the world.

In reaching its conclusion the committee has been guided by the principles you have announced, that a fair price should be based upon the cost of production for the entire country, plus a reasonable profit. We have relied upon the cost estimates for the crop of 1917 furnished by the United States Department of Agriculture, checked by the results of our independent investigations and the evidence submitted to the committee by producers and their representatives.

The committee has considered the regulations recently established by the

United States Food Administration Grain Corporation for the different grades of the wheat through which all transactions in wheat are to be standardized and speculation to be entirely eliminated. Also that profits to the grain dealer, miller, and flour dealer have been regulated and reduced by the Grain Corporation, effecting a material reduction in the cost of flour.

In consideration of the foregoing facts and circumstances, this committee respectfully recommends that the price on No. 1 Northern Spring wheat, or its equivalent, at Chicago, be $2.20 per bushel.

Respectfully submitted.

H. A. GARFIELD, *Chairman.*
THEO. N. VAIL.
J. W. SULLIVAN.
E. F. LADD.
F. W. TAUSSIG.
EUGENE E. FUNK.
H. J. WATERS.
C. S. BARRETT.
J. W. SPORTHILL.
L. J. TABER.
W. N. DOAK.

WHEAT DIFFERENTIALS.

The following are differentials between grades and classes of wheat and between the different primary markets of the United States as established by the United States Food Administration upon which the committee on prices based its recommendation of $2.20 for No. 1 Northern Spring wheat at Chicago, or its equivalent:

PRICES AT INTERIOR PRIMARY MARKET.

No. 1 Hard Winter, No. 1 Red Winter, basic grades, equivalent of No. 1 Northern Spring.

	Government price
No. 1, Dark Hard Winter	$2.24
No. 1, Hard Winter, basic	2.20
No. 1, Red Winter, basic	2.20
No. 1, Yellow Hard Winter	2.16
No. 1, Soft Red Winter	2.18
No. 1, Dark Northern Spring	2.24
No. 1, Northern Spring basic	2.20
No. 1, Red Spring	2.18
No. 1, Humpback	2.10
No. 1, Amber Durum	2.24
No. 1, Durum, basic	2.20
No. 1, Red Durum	2.13
No. 1, Red Walla	2.13
No. 1, Hard White, basic	2.20
No. 1, Soft White	2.18
No. 1, White Club	2.16

No. 2 of grade, 3 cents less.
No. 3 of grade, 6 cents less.
No. 4 of grade, 10 cents less.

RELATIVE MARKET BASIS.

Kansas City, 5 cents less.
Omaha, 5 cents less.
Duluth, 3 cents less.
Minneapolis, 3 cents less.
St. Louis, 2 cents less.
Chicago, basis.
New Orleans, basis.
Galveston, basis.
Buffalo, 5 cents more.
Baltimore, 9 cents more.
Philadelphia, 9 cents more.
New York, 10 cents more.

LAUNCHING A WAR TRANSPORT

LAUNCHING A WAR TRANSPORT.

No effort of the United States was of greater value in the final defeat of the Central Powers than shipbuilding. Throughout 1918 and 1919 the German submarine warfare was seriously threatening the ability of the Entente Allies to continue the war; and the presence of American soldiers in large numbers upon the battlefields of Europe was contingent upon the existence of a fleet of transports large enough, not only to carry them across the seas, but also to carry abundant supplies to them despite the activities of the German underseas craft. In the illustration one of the largest transports built for the Army service is seen leaving the ways at Hog Island, the monster shipbuilding plant near Philadelphia erected by the United States during her participation in the War.

LETTERS

[Loyalty of labor and antagonism of certain elements to participation in the
European War.]

August 31, 1917.

MY DEAR MR. GOMPERS:

I am sure that you understand that my inability to accept the invitation to address the Minneapolis conference of the American Alliance for Labor and Democracy is due only to official necessity, and not in any degree to lack of appreciation of the importance of the occasion. The cause you and your fellow patriots uphold is one with the cause we are defending with arms. While our soldiers and sailors are doing their manful work to hold back reaction in its most brutal and aggressive form, we must oppose at home the organized and individual efforts of those dangerous elements who hide disloyalty behind a screen of specious and evasive phrases.

I have read with real pride the names of the men and women who are to take part in the Minneapolis conference. Not one but has a record of devoted service to fundamental democracy; not one but has fought the long, hard fight for equal justice, braving every bitterness that the humblest life might know a larger measure of happiness.

With all my heart I want them to feel that their devotion to country is in no wise a betrayal of principle, and that in serving America today they are serving their cause no less faithfully than in the past. I myself have had sympathy with the fears of the workers of the United States; for the tendency of war is toward reaction, and too often military necessities have been made an excuse for the destruction of laboriously erected industrial and social standards. These fears, happily, have proved to be baseless. With quickened sympathies and appreciation, with a new sense of the invasive and insidious dangers of oppression, our people have not only held every inch of ground that has been won by years of struggle, but have added to the gains of the twentieth century along every line of human betterment. Questions of wages and hours of labor and industrial readjustment have found a solution which gives to the toiler a new dignity and a new sense of social and economic security. I beg you to feel that my support has not been lacking and that the Government has not failed at any point in granting every just request advanced by you and your associates in the name of the American worker.

No one who is not blind can fail to see that the battle line of democracy for America stretches today from the fields of Flanders to every house and workshop where toiling, upward-striving men and women are counting the treasures of right and justice and liberty which are being threatened by our present enemies.

It has not been a matter of surprise to me that the leaders in certain

269

groups have sought to ignore our grievances against the men who have equally misled the German people. Their insistence that a nation whose rights have been grossly violated, whose citizens have been foully murdered under their own flag, whose neighbors have been invited to join in making conquest of its territory, whose patience in pressing the claims of justice and humanity has been met with the most shameful policy of truculence and treachery, their insistence that a nation so outraged does not know its own mind, that it has no comprehensible reason for defending itself, or for joining with all its might in maintaining a free future for itself and its ideals, is of a piece with their deafness to the oft-repeated statement of our national purposes.

Is it, perhaps, that these forces of antagonism have not yet learned to know the voice of that America we love and serve? It may well be that those among us who stand ready to forward the plans of aggression bred in secret do not understand the language of democracy when it proclaims the purposes of war in terms of a peace for the peoples that shall be untroubled by those to whom men are but the pawns in their struggle for power and gain. But true Americans, those who toil here for home and the hope of better things, whose lifted eyes have caught the vision of a liberated world, have said that of the policy of blood and iron there shall be an end and that equal justice, which is the heart of democracy, shall rule in its stead.

May not those who toil and those who have made common cause of the larger hope for the masses of mankind take renewed heart as they think on those days when America has taken its stand for the rights of humanity and the fellowship of social and international justice?

Sincerely yours,

WOODROW WILSON.

Mr. Samuel Gompers, *President American Federation of Labor.*

[Government Insurance for the officers and enlisted men of the Army and Navy.]

U. S. S. Mayflower, *Sept. 1, 1917.*

My Dear Judge:

May I not express to you, and through you to the Committee on Interstate and Foreign Commerce of the House, my sincere gratification at the favorable report the committee has just made on the bill granting family allowances, indemnities, and life insurance for the officers and enlisted men of the Army and Navy; and the hope that the proposed measure may receive the prompt approval of the Congress?

There are so many arguments for the bill that I do not know which to put forward as the most imperative. No doubt you have assembled them in your own mind in their most effective order. But what principally appeals to me about the bill is that it takes into consideration the whole obligation of the soldier not only, but the whole obligation of the Government—the obligations of justice and humanity both to the soldier and to his family. It is one of the most admirable pieces of legislation that has been proposed in connection with the war and I can not too earnestly urge its adoption.

I observe with regret that the limit of life insurance available to the officers and men in the service has been reduced from $10,000 to $5,000. I earnestly hope that the $10,000 limit may be restored.

Cordially and sincerely yours,

WOODROW WILSON.

HON. W. C. ADAMSON, *House of Representatives.*

EXECUTIVE ORDER

[Assigning to the Treasury Department the management of certain portions of the Food Administration Program.]

THE WHITE HOUSE, *2 September, 1917.*

Acting under the authority of Section 2 of the Act of Congress approved August 10, 1917, entitled An Act to provide further for the national security and defense by encouraging the production, conserving the supply and controlling the distribution of food products and fuel, which section reads in part, as follows: "That in carrying out the purposes of this Act the President is authorized * * * to utilize any department or agency of the Government, and to coordinate their activities so as to avoid any preventable loss or duplication of effort or funds;" because the office of the Commissioner of Internal Revenue in the Treasury Department is now regulating the production of distilled spirits throughout the United States and is in control of the machinery necessary to enforce effectively the provisions of Sections 15 and 16 of the aforesaid Act of August 10, 1917, relating to distilled spirits;

Now, in order more effectively to enforce the provisions of said Act, and to avoid preventable duplication of effort and funds, I hereby direct that the Treasury Department shall henceforth supervise, direct and carry into effect the provisions of Sections 15 and 16 of said Act of August 10, 1917, and exercise the powers and authority therein given to the President, subject to such instructions and regulations as may from time to time be issued by the President. For this purpose the Secretary of the Treasury is hereby authorized to assign such duties to the Commissioner of Internal Revenue, the Internal Revenue officers of the United States, and the Division of Customs, and to employ such additional assistants as he may deem necessary therefor.

The Executive Order* dated August 10, 1917, providing for the organization of the United States Food Administration, so far as it is inconsistent herewith, is hereby modified.

WOODROW WILSON.

*Not published.

MESSAGE TO THE NATIONAL ARMY

THE WHITE HOUSE, *Sept. 3, 1917.*

To the Soldiers of the National Army:

You are undertaking a great duty. The heart of the whole country is with you.

Everything that you do will be watched with the deepest interest and with the deepest solicitude, not only by those who are near and dear to you, but by the whole nation besides. For this great war draws us all together, makes us all comrades and brothers, as all true Americans felt themselves to be when we first made good our national independence.

The eyes of all the world will be upon you, because you are in some special sense the soldiers of freedom. Let it be your pride, therefore, to show all men everywhere not only what good soldiers you are, but also what good men you are, keeping yourselves fit and straight in everything and pure and clean through and through.

Let us set for ourselves a standard so high that it will be a glory to live up to it, and then let us live up to it and add a new laurel to the crown of America.

My affectionate confidence goes with you in every battle and every test. God keep and guide you!

WOODROW WILSON.

BY THE PRESIDENT OF THE UNITED STATES OF AMERICA

A PROCLAMATION

[License of Importers, Manufacturers and Refiners of Sugar, Sugar Syrups and Molasses.]

Whereas, Under and by virtue of an Act of Congress entitled "An Act to provide further for the national security and defense by encouraging the production, conserving the supply, and controlling the distribution of food products and fuel," approved by the President on the 10th day of August, 1917, it is provided among other things as follows.

"That by reason of the existence of a state of war, it is essential to the national security and defense, for the successful prosecution of the war, and for the support and maintenance of the Army and Navy, to assure an adequate supply and equitable distribution, and to facilitate the movement, of foods, feeds, fuel, including fuel oil and natural gas, fertilizer and fertilizer ingredients, tools, utensils, implements, machinery, and equipment required for the actual production of foods, feeds, and fuel, hereafter in this Act called necessaries; to prevent, locally or generally, scarcity, monopolization, hoarding, injurious speculation, manipulations, and private controls, affecting such supply, distribution, and movement; and to establish and maintain governmental control of such necessaries during the war. For such purposes the instrumentalities, means, methods, powers, authorities, duties, obligations, and prohibitions hereinafter set forth are created, established, conferred, and prescribed. The President is authorized to make such regulations and to issue such orders as are essential effectively to carry out the provisions of this Act."

And, Whereas, it is further provided in said Act as follows:

"That, from time to time, whenever the President shall find it essential to license the importation, manufacture, storage, mining, or distribution, of any necessaries, in order to carry into effect any of the purposes of this Act, and shall publicly so announce, no person shall, after date fixed in the announcement, engage in or carry on any such business specified in the announcement of importation, manufacture, storage, mining, or distribution of any necessaries as set forth in such announcement, unless he shall secure and hold a license issued pursuant to this section. The President is authorized to issue such licenses and to prescribe regulations for the issuance of licenses and requirements for systems of accounts and auditing of accounts to be kept by licensees, submission of reports by them, with or without oath or affirmation and the entry and inspection by the President's duly authorized agents of the places of business of licensees."

And, Whereas, it is essential in order to carry into effect the provisions of the said Act, and in order to secure an adequate supply and equitable distribution, and to facilitate the movement of certain necessaries hereafter in this proclamation specified that the license powers conferred upon the President by said Act be at this time exercised, to the extent hereinafter set forth.

Now, Therefore, I, Woodrow Wilson, President of the United States of America, by virtue of the powers conferred upon me by said Act of Congress, hereby find and determine and by this proclamation do announce that it is essential in order to carry into effect the purposes of said Act, to license the importation, manufacture and refining of sugar, sugar syrups and molasses, to the extent hereinafter specified.

All persons, firms, corporations and associations engaged in the business either of importing sugar, of manufacturing sugar from sugar cane or beets, or of refining sugar or of manufacturing sugar syrups or molasses, (except those specifically exempted by said Act of Congress), are hereby required to secure on or before October 1, 1917, a license, which license will be issued under such rules and regulations governing the conduct of the business as may be prescribed.

Applications for licenses must be made to the United States Food Administrator, Washington, D. C., upon forms prepared by him for that purpose.

Any person, firm, corporation or association, other than those hereinbefore excepted, who shall engage in or carry on the business either of importing sugar, manufacturing sugar, or refining sugar, or of manufacturing sugar syrups or molasses after October 1, 1917, without first securing such license, will be liable to the penalties prescribed by said Act of Congress.

In Witness Whereof, I have hereunto set my hand and caused the seal of the United States to be affixed.

Done in the District of Columbia, this seventh day of September in the year of our Lord one thousand nine hundred and [SEAL.]   seventeen, and of the Independence of the United States of America, the one hundred and forty-second.

WOODROW WILSON.

By the President:
ROBERT LANSING, *Secretary of State.*

EXECUTIVE ORDER

[Suspending law admitting foreign-built ships to American entry.]

THE WHITE HOUSE, *7 September, 1917.*

In pursuance of the authority conferred upon the President of the United States by Section 2 of the Act approved August 18, 1914, entitled "An Act to provide for the admission of foreign built ships to American registry for the foreign trade, and for other purposes," it is hereby ordered:

That the provisions of law requiring survey, inspection and measurement, by officers of the United States, of foreign built ships admitted to United States registry under said Act are hereby suspended so far and for such length of time as is herein provided, namely: The said provisions shall not apply to any such foreign built ship during the period of two years from September 1, 1917, provided the Secretary of Commerce is satisfied in the case of any such ship that the ship is safe and sea-worthy and that proper effort is being made to comply with the said provision.

WOODROW WILSON,

By the President of the United States of America

A PROCLAMATION

[Exports of Coin, Bullion and Currency Unlawful.]

Whereas Congress has enacted, and the President has on the fifteenth day of June, 1917, approved a law which contains the following provisions:

"Whenever during the present war the President shall find that the public safety shall so require, and shall make proclamation thereof, it shall be unlawful to export from or ship from or take out of the United States to any country named in such proclamation any article or articles mentioned in such proclamation, except at such time or times, and under such regulations and orders, and subject to such limitations and exceptions as the President shall prescribe, until otherwise ordered by the President or by Congress: Provided, however, that no preference shall be given to the ports of one State over those of another.

"Any person who shall export, ship, or take out, or deliver or attempt to deliver for export, shipment, or taking out, any article in violation of this title, or of any regulation or order made hereunder, shall be fined not more than $10,000, or, if a natural person, imprisoned for not more than two years, or both; and any article so delivered or exported, shipped, or taken out, or so attempted to be delivered or exported, shipped, or taken out, shall be seized and forfeited to the United States; and any officer, director, or agent of a corporation who participates in any such violation shall be liable to like fine or imprisonment, or both.

"Whenever there is reasonable cause to believe that any vessel, domestic or foreign, is about to carry out of the United States any article or articles in violation of the provisions of this title, the collector of customs for the district in which such vessel is located is hereby authorized and empowered, subject to review by the Secretary of Commerce, to refuse clearance to any such vessel, domestic or foreign, for which clearance is required by law, and by formal notice served upon the owners, master, or person or persons in command or charge of any domestic vessel for which clearance is not required by law, to forbid the departure of such vessel from the port, and it shall thereupon be unlawful for such vessel to depart. Whoever, in violation of any of the provisions of this section shall take, or attempt to take, or authorize the taking of any such vessel out of port or from the jurisdiction of the United States, shall be fined not more than $10,000 or imprisoned not more than two years, or both; and, in addition, such vessel, her tackle, apparel, furniture, equipment, and her forbidden cargo shall be forfeited to the United States."

And whereas the President has heretofore by proclamation, under date of the twenty-seventh day of August in the year one thousand nine hundred and seventeen, declared certain exports in time of war unlawful, and the President finds that the public safety requires that such proclamation be amended and supplemented in respect to the articles hereinafter mentioned:

Now, Therefore, I, Woodrow Wilson, President of the United States of America, do hereby proclaim to all whom it may concern that the public safety requires that, except at such time or times, and under such regulations and orders, and subject to such limitations and exceptions as the President shall prescribe, until otherwise ordered by the President or by Congress, the following articles, namely: coin, bullion and currency: shall not, on and after the 10th day of September in the year one thousand nine hundred and seventeen, be exported from or shipped from or taken out of the United States or its territorial possessions to Albania, Austria-Hungary, Belgium, Bulgaria, Denmark, her colonies, possessions or protectorates, Germany, her colonies, possessions or protectorates, Greece, Liechtenstein, Luxembourg, The Kingdom of the Netherlands, Norway, Spain, her colonies, possessions or protectorates, Sweden, Switzerland or Turkey, Abyssinia, Afghanistan, Argentina, Bolivia, Brazil, China, Chile, Colombia, Costa Rica, Cuba, Dominican Republic, Ecuador, Egypt, France, her colonies, possessions or protectorates, Guatemala, Haiti, Honduras, Italy, her colonies, possessions or protectorates, Great Britain, her colonies, possessions or protectorates, Japan, Liberia, Mexico, Monaco, Montenegro, Morocco, Nepal, Nicaragua, the colonies, possessions or protectorates of The Netherlands, Oman, Panama, Paraguay, Persia, Peru, Portugal, her colonies, possessions or protectorates, Roumania, Russia, Salvador, San Marino, Serbia, Siam, Uruguay, or Venezuela.

The regulations, orders, limitations and exceptions prescribed will be administered by and under the authority of the Secretary of the Treasury, from whom licenses in conformity with said regulations, orders, limitations and exceptions will issue.

Except as hereby amended and supplemented, the above mentioned proclamation under date of August 27, 1917, shall continue in full force and effect.

In Witness Whereof, I have hereunto set my hand and caused the seal of the United States of America to be affixed.

Done in the District of Columbia, this 7th day of September in the
       year of our Lord one thousand nine hundred and seven-
[SEAL.] teen and of the Independence of the United States of
       America the one hundred and forty-second.

                     WOODROW WILSON.

By the President:
   ROBERT LANSING, *Secretary of State.*

EXECUTIVE ORDER

[Regulations relating to the exportation of coin, bullion and currency.]

              THE WHITE HOUSE, *September 7, 1917.*

By virtue of the authority vested in me, I direct that the regulations, orders, limitations, and exceptions prescribed in relation to the exportation of coin, bullion, and currency shall be administered by and under the authority of the Secretary of the Treasury; and upon the recommendation of the Secretary of the Treasury I hereby prescribe the following regulations in relation thereto:

1. Any individual, firm or corporation desiring to export from the United States or any of its territorial possessions to any foreign country named in the proclamation dated September 7th, 1917, any coin, bullion, or currency, shall first file an application in triplicate with the Federal Reserve Bank of the district in which such individual, firm or corporation is located, such application to state under oath and in detail the nature of the transaction, the amount involved, the parties directly and indirectly interested and such other information as may be of assistance to the proper authorities in determining whether the exportation for which a license is desired will be compatible with the public interest.

2. Each Federal Reserve Bank shall keep a record copy of each application filed with it under the provisions of this regulation and shall forward the original application and a duplicate to the Federal Reserve Board at Washington together with such information or suggestions as it may believe proper in the circumstances and shall in addition make a formal recommendation as to whether or not in its opinion the exportation should be permitted.

3. The Federal Reserve Board, subject to the approval of the Secretary of the Treasury, is hereby authorized and empowered upon receipt of such application and the recommendation of the Federal Reserve Bank to make such ruling as it may deem proper in the circumstances and if in its opinion the exportation in question be compatible with the public interest, to permit said exportation to be made; otherwise to refuse it.   ,WOODROW WILSON.

A PROCLAMATION

[Urging school children to enroll in Red Cross Service.]

September 15, 1917.

To the School Children of the United States:

The President of the United States is also President of the American Red Cross. It is from these offices joined in one that I write you a word of greeting at this time when so many of you are beginning the school year.

The American Red Cross has just prepared a Junior Membership with School Activities in which every pupil in the United States can find a chance to serve our country. The school is the natural center of your life. Through it you can best work in the great cause of freedom to which we have all pledged ourselves.

Our Junior Red Cross will bring to you opportunities of service to your community and to other communities all over the world and guide your service with high and religious ideals. It will teach you how to save in order that suffering children elsewhere may have the chance to live. It will teach you how to prepare some of the supplies which wounded soldiers and homeless families lack. It will send to you through the Red Cross Bulletins the thrilling stories of relief and rescue. And best of all, more perfectly than through any of your other school lessons, you will learn by doing those kind things under your teacher's direction to be the future good citizens of this great country which we all love.

And I commend to all school teachers in the country the simple plan which the American Red Cross has worked out to provide for your cooperation, knowing as I do that school children will give their best service under the direct guidance and instruction of their teachers. Is not this perhaps the chance for which you have been looking to give your time and efforts in some measure to meet our national needs?

(Signed) WOODROW WILSON,
President.

LETTER

[To Mr. Max Eastman, concerning suppression of certain periodicals during the War with Germany.]

THE WHITE HOUSE, *September 18, 1917.*

MY DEAR MR. EASTMAN:

I thank you very warmly for your generous appreciation of my reply to the Pope, and I wish that I could agree with those parts of your letter which concern the other matters we were discussing when you were down here. I think that a time of war must be regarded as wholly exceptional and that it is legitimate to regard things which would in ordinary circumstances be innocent as very dangerous to the public welfare. But the line is manifestly exceedingly hard to draw, and I cannot say that I have any confidence that I know how to draw it. I can only say that a line must be drawn and that we are trying— it may be clumsily, but genuinely—to draw it without favor or prejudice. Cordially and sincerely yours,

WOODROW WILSON.

MEMORANDUM

[To Secretary of Labor, concerning Labor Disputes.]

THE WHITE HOUSE, *September 19, 1917.*

I am very much interested in the labor situation in the mountain region and on the Pacific coast. I have listened with attention and concern to the numerous charges of misconduct and injustice that representatives both of employers and of employees have made against each other. I am not so much concerned, however, with the manner in which they have treated each other in the past as I am desirous of seeing some kind of a working arrangement arrived at for the future, particularly during the period of the war, on a basis that will be fair to all parties concerned. To assist in the accomplishment of that purpose, I have decided to appoint a commission to visit the localities where disagreements have been most frequent as my personal representatives. The commission will consist of William B. Wilson, Secretary of Labor; Col. J. L. Spangler, of Pennsylvania; Verner C. Reed, of Colorado; John H. Walker, of Illinois; and E. P. Marsh, of Washington. Felix Frankfurter, of New York, will act as secretary of the commission.

It will be the duty of the commission to visit, in each instance, the governor of the state, advising him that they are there as the personal representatives of the President with a view to lending sympathetic counsel and aid to the state government in the development of a better understanding between laborers and employers, and also themselves to deal with employers and employees in a conciliatory spirit, seek to compose differences and allay misunderstanding, and in any way that may be open to them to show the active interest of the National Government in furthering arrangements just to both sides. Wherever it is deemed advisable conferences of employers and employees should be called with the purpose of working out a mutual understanding between them which will insure the continued operation of the industry on conditions acceptable to both sides. The commission should also endeavor to learn the real causes for any discontent which may exist on either side, not by the formal process of public hearings but by getting into touch with workmen and employers by the more informal process of personal conversation. I would be pleased to have the commission report to me from time to time such information as may require immediate attention.

WOODROW WILSON.

EXECUTIVE ORDERS

[Suspending eight-hour day in Bureau of Standards.]

THE WHITE HOUSE, *September 20, 1917.*

Under authority contained in the Naval Appropriation Act approved March 4, 1917 (Public No. 391, 64th Congress) whereby it is provided—

"That in case of national emergency the President is authorized to suspend provisions of law prohibiting more than eight hours labor in any one day of persons engaged upon work covered by contracts with the United States: *Provided further,* That the wages of persons employed upon such contracts shall be computed on a basic day rate of eight hours work with overtime rates to be paid for at not less than time and one-half for all hours work in excess of eight hours;"

it is hereby ordered that during the present national emergency the provisions of law limiting the hours of daily service of mechanics and laborers to eight hours in any one day on work under contracts to which the United States is a party are suspended with respect to all contracts of the Bureau of Standards, Department of Commerce, for the construction of an emergency laboratory building to be used for the purpose of standardizing equipment, instruments, and apparatus for the Army and Navy, and other buildings that may be erected and used for research, testing and experimental work in connection with the present national emergency. This order shall take effect from and after this date.

WOODROW WILSON.

[Creating Divisions of Pictures, Films and Publications under Committee on Public Information.]

THE WHITE HOUSE, *25 September, 1917.*

I hereby create, under the jurisdiction of the Committee on Public Information, heretofore established by Executive Order of April 14, 1917, (1) a Division of Pictures; (2) a Division of Films; (3) a Division of Publications; for the purpose of stimulating recruiting and patriotic interest in the war; to the end that the utmost cooperation of all citizens in the successful prosecution of the war be secured.

The Secretary of State, the Secretary of War, and the Secretary of the Navy are authorized each to detail an officer or officers to the work of the committee.

WOODROW WILSON.

[Suspending the eight-hour day in construction of Immigrant Station at Baltimore, Md.]

THE WHITE HOUSE, *September 27, 1917.*

In order to effect the more expeditious construction of the buildings for the new Immigration Station, Baltimore, Maryland, the early completion of the buildings for military purposes creating a national emergency, the same to be turned over to the War Department by the Department of Labor for hospital purposes, etc., and by virtue of the provisions of the Act of Congress approved March 4, 1917, entitled "An Act Making Provisions for the Naval Service for the Fiscal Year Ending June 30, 1918, and for other Purposes," whereby it is provided that in case of national emergency the President is authorized to suspend provisions of law prohibiting more than eight hours labor in any one day by persons engaged upon work covered by contracts with the United States; provided further, that the wages of persons employed upon such contracts shall be computed on a basic day rate of eight hours work with overtime rate to be paid for at not less than time and one-half for all hours work in excess of eight hours, I do hereby suspend the provisions of law prohibiting more than eight hours of labor in any one day by persons engaged in the construction of the new Immigration Station at Baltimore, Maryland. This order shall take effect from and after this date.

WOODROW WILSON.

[Assigning quarantine duties in Virgin Islands to Treasury Department.]

THE WHITE HOUSE, *27 September, 1917.*

Whereas, an Act of Congress approved June 19, 1906, provides "that the Secretary of the Treasury shall have the control, direction, and management of all quarantine stations, grounds, and anchorages, established by authority of the United States * * *."

Now, therefore, I, Woodrow Wilson, President of the United States, by virtue of the authority in me vested, and pursuant to Section 1 of the Act approved March 3, 1917, entitled "An Act to provide a temporary government for the West Indies Islands, acquired by the United States from Denmark, etc.," do hereby order that the provisions of the Act of Congress approved February 15, 1893, entitled "An Act granting additional quarantine powers and imposing additional duties upon the Marine-Hospital Service," and all rules and regulations heretofore prescribed by the Secretary of the Treasury under this Act are to be given full force and effect in the islands of St. Thomas, St. Croix, and St. John, West Indies, and all public property of the former government of the Virgin Islands, ceded heretofore to the United States, consisting of quarantine reservations, buildings, wharves, docks connected therewith, and equipment, be, and hereby are, taken for uses and purposes of the United States, and the Secretary of the Treasury, through the Surgeon General of the Public Health Service, is hereby charged with all administrative duties relating to said quarantine service, and the Secretary of the Treasury shall have estimates prepared by the Surgeon General of the Public Health Service, and submitted to Congress for an appropriation for the maintenance of said quarantine service, and securement of reservations where necessary, and additional facilities for the proper enforcement of quarantine preventive measures.

WOODROW WILSON.

[Giving chief of staff control over War Department in absence of Secretary of War and Assistant Secretary of War.]

THE WHITE HOUSE, *29 September, 1917.*

In accordance with the provisions of Section 179 of the Revised Statutes, as amended by an Act making appropriations for the legislative, executive, and judicial expenses of the Government, approved August 5, 1882 (22 Stats., 238), the Chief of Staff, United States Army, is authorized and directed to perform the duties of Secretary of War during the illness or temporary absence from the seat of Government of the Secretary of War, whenever during such illness or absence the Assistant Secretary of War is also absent.

WOODROW WILSON.

BY THE PRESIDENT OF THE UNITED STATES OF AMERICA

PROCLAMATIONS

[License of Commodities.]

Whereas, under and by virtue of an Act of Congress entitled "An Act to provide further for the national security and defense by encouraging the production, conserving the supply, and controlling the distribution of food products and fuel," approved by the President on the 10th day of August, 1917, it is provided among other things as follows:

"That, by reason of the existence of a state of war, it is essential to the national security and defense, for the successful prosecution of the war, and for the support and maintenance of the

Army and Navy, to assure an adequate supply and equitable distribution, and to facilitate the movement, of foods, feeds, fuel including fuel oil and natural gas, and fertilizer and fertilizer ingredients, tools, utensils, implements, machinery, and equipment required for the actual production of foods, feeds, and fuel, hereafter in this Act called necessaries; to prevent, locally or generally, scarcity, monopolization, hoarding, injurious speculation, manipulations, and private controls, affecting such supply, distribution, and movement; and to establish and maintain governmental control of such necessaries during the war. For such purposes the instrumentalities, means, methods, powers, authorities, duties, obligations, and prohibitions hereinafter set forth are created, established, conferred and prescribed. The President is authorized to make such regulations and to issue such orders as are essential effectively to carry out the provisions of this Act."

And, whereas, it is further provided in said Act as follows:

"That, from time to time, whenever the President shall find it essential to license the importation, manufacture, storage, mining or distribution, of any necessaries, in order to carry into effect any of the purposes of this Act, and shall publicly so announce, no person shall, after a date fixed in the announcement, engage in or carry on any such business specified in the announcement of importation, manufacture, storage, mining, or distribution of any necessaries as set forth in such announcement, unless he shall secure and hold a license issued pursuant to this section. The President is authorized to issue such licenses and to prescribe regulations for the issuance of licenses and requirements for systems of accounts and auditing of accounts to be kept by licensees, submission of reports by them, with or without oath or affirmation, and the entry and inspection by the President's duly authorized agents of the places of business of licensees."

And, Whereas, It is essential, in order to carry into effect the provisions of the said Act, that the powers conferred upon the President by said Act be at this time exercised, to the extent hereinafter set forth,

Now, Therefore, I, Woodrow Wilson, President of the United States of America, by virtue of the powers conferred upon me by said Act of Congress, hereby find and determine and by this proclamation do announce that it is essential, in order to carry into effect the purposes of said Act, to license the importation, manufacture, storage and distribution of necessaries, to the extent hereinafter specified.

All persons, firms, corporations and associations engaged in the business either of (1) operating cold storage warehouses (a cold storage warehouse, for the purposes of this proclamation, being defined as any place artificially or mechanically cooled to or below a temperature of 45 degrees above zero Fahrenheit, in which food products are placed and held for thirty days or more), (2) operating elevators, warehouses or other places for the storage of corn, oats, barley, beans, rice, cotton seed, cottonseed cake, cottonseed meal or peanut meal, or (3) importing, manufacturing (including milling, mixing or packing), or distributing (including buying and selling) any of the following commodities:

Wheat, wheat flour, rye or rye flour; barley or barley flour; oats, oatmeal or rolled oats; corn, corn grits, cornmeal, hominy, corn flour, starch from corn, corn oil, corn syrup or glucose; rice, rice flour; dried beans; pea seed or dried peas; cotton seed, cottonseed oil, cottonseed cake or cottonseed meal; peanut oil or peanut meal; soya bean oil, soya bean meal, palm oil or copra oil; oleomargarine, lard, lard substitutes, oleo oil or cooking fats; milk, butter or cheese; condensed, evaporated or powdered milk; fresh, canned or cured beef, pork or mutton; poultry or eggs; fresh or frozen fish; fresh fruits or vegetables; canned: peas, dried beans, tomatoes, corn, salmon or sardines; dried: prunes, apples, peaches or raisins; sugar, syrups or molasses,—
Excepting, however,

(1) Operators of elevators or warehouses handling wheat or rye, and manufacturers of the derivative products of wheat or rye, who have already been licensed,

(2) Importers, manufacturers and refiners of sugar, and manufacturers of sugar syrups and molasses, who have already been licensed,

(3) Retailers whose gross sales of food commodities do not exceed $100,000.00 per annum,

(4) Common carriers,

(5) Farmers, gardeners, cooperative associations of farmers or gardeners, including live stock farmers, and other persons with respect to the products of any farm, garden or other land owned, leased or cultivated by them,

(6) Fishermen whose business does not extend beyond primary consignment,

(7) Those dealing in any of the above commodities on any exchange, board of trade or similar institution as defined by Section 13 of the Act of August 10th, 1917, to the extent of their dealings on such exchange or board of trade,

(8) Millers of corn, oats, barley, wheat, rye or rice operating only plants of a daily capacity of less than seventy-five barrels,

(9) Canners of peas, dried beans, corn, tomatoes, salmon or sardines whose gross production does not exceed 5,000 cases per annum,

(10) Persons slaughtering, packing and distributing fresh, canned

or cured beef, pork or mutton, whose gross sales of such commodities do not exceed $100,000.00 per annum,

(11) Operators of poultry or egg packing plants, whose gross sales do not exceed $50,000.00 per annum,

(12) Manufacturers of maple syrup, maple sugar and maple compounds,

(13) Ginners, buyers, agents, dealers or other handlers of cotton seed who handle yearly, between September 1st and August 31st, less than one hundred and fifty tons of cotton seed,
are hereby required to secure on or before November 1, 1917, a license, which license will be issued under such rules and regulations governing the conduct of the business as may be prescribed.

Application for license must be made to the United States Food Administration, Washington, D. C., Law Department—License Division, on forms prepared by it for that purpose, which may be secured on request.

Any person, firm, corporation or association other than those hereinbefore excepted, who shall engage in or carry on any business hereinbefore specified after November 1, 1917, without first securing such license will be liable to the penalty prescribed by said Act of Congress.

In Witness Whereof, I have hereunto set my hand and caused the seal of the United States to be affixed.

Done in the District of Columbia, this eighth day of October, in the year of our Lord one thousand nine hundred and [SEAL] seventeen, and of the Independence of the United States of America, the one hundred and forty-second.

WOODROW WILSON.

By the President:

ROBERT LANSING, *Secretary of State.*

[Liberty Day.]

The Second Liberty Loan gives the people of the United States another opportunity to lend their funds to their Government to sustain their country at war. The might of the United States is being mobilized and organized to strike a mortal blow at autocracy in defense of outraged American rights and of the cause of Liberty. Billions of dollars are required to arm, feed and clothe the brave men who are going forth to fight our country's battles and to assist the nations with whom we are making common cause against a common foe. To subscribe to the Liberty Loan is to perform a service of patriotism.

Now, therefore, I, Woodrow Wilson, President of the United States of America, do appoint Wednesday, the twenty-fourth of October, as Liberty Day, and urge and advise the people to assemble in their respective communities and pledge to one another and to the Government that represents them the fullest measure of financial support. On the afternoon of that day I request that patriotic meetings be held in every city, town and hamlet throughout the land, under the general direction of the Secretary of the Treasury and the immediate direction of the Liberty Loan Committees which have been organized by the Federal Reserve Banks. The people responded nobly to the call of the First Liberty Loan with an oversubscription of more than fifty per cent. Let the response to the Second Loan be even greater and let the amount be so large that it will serve as an assurance of unequaled support to hearten the men who are to face the fire of battle for us. Let the result be so impressive and emphatic that it will echo throughout the Empire of our enemy as an index of what America intends to do to bring this war to a victorious conclusion.

For the purpose of participating in Liberty Day celebrations, all employees of the Federal Government throughout the country whose services can be spared, may be excused at twelve o'clock noon, Wednesday, the twenty-fourth of October.

In Witness Whereof, I have hereunto set my hand and caused the seal of the United States to be affixed.

Done in the District of Columbia, this twelfth day of October, in the year of our Lord, one thousand nine hundred and [SEAL] seventeen, and of the Independence of the United States of America the one hundred and forty-second.

WOODROW WILSON.

By the President:
ROBERT LANSING, *Secretary of State.*

EXECUTIVE ORDER

[Vesting power and authority in designated officers and making rules and regulations under Trading with the Enemy Act and Title VII of the act approved June 15, 1917.]

THE WHITE HOUSE, *October 12, 1917.*

By virtue of the authority vested in me by "An Act to Define, Regulate and Punish Trading with the Enemy and for Other Purposes," approved October 6, 1917, and by Title VII of the Act approved June 15, 1917, entitled "An Act to Punish Acts of Interference with the Foreign Relations, the Neutrality and the Foreign Commerce of the United States, to Punish Espionage and Better to Enforce the Criminal Laws of the United States and for Other Purposes," (hereinafter designated as the Espionage Act), I hereby make the following orders and rules and regulations:

WAR TRADE BOARD

I. I hereby establish a War Trade Board to be composed of representatives, respectively, of the Secretary of State, of the Secretary of the Treasury, of the Secretary of Agriculture, of the Secretary of Commerce, of the Food Administrator, and of the United States Shipping Board.

II. I hereby vest in said Board the power and authority to issue licenses under such terms and conditions as are not inconsistent with law, or to withhold or refuse licenses, for the exportation of all articles, except coin, bullion or currency, the exportation or taking of which out of the United States may be restricted by proclamations heretofore or hereafter issued by me under said Title VII of the Espionage Act.

III. I further hereby vest in said War Trade Board the power and authority to issue, upon such terms and conditions as are not inconsistent with law, or to withhold or refuse, licenses for the importation of all articles the importation of which may be restricted by any proclamation hereafter issued by me under Section 11 of the Trading with the Enemy Act.

IV. I further hereby vest in said War Trade Board the power and authority not vested in other officers by subsequent provisions of this order, to issue, under such terms and conditions as are not inconsistent with law, or to withhold or refuse, licenses to trade either directly or indirectly with, to, or from, or for, or on account of, or on behalf of, or for the benefit of, any other person, with knowledge or reasonable cause to believe that such other person is an enemy or ally of enemy, or is conducting or taking part in such trade directly or indirectly for, or on account of, or on behalf of, or for the benefit of, an enemy or ally of enemy.

V. I further hereby vest in said War Trade Board the power and authority, under such terms and conditions as are not inconsistent with law, to issue to every enemy or ally of enemy, other than enemy or ally of enemy insurance or reinsurance companies, doing business within the United States through an agency or branch office, or otherwise, applying therefor within thirty days of October 6, 1917, licenses temporary or otherwise to continue to do business, or said Board may withhold or refuse the same.

VI. And I further hereby vest in said War Trade Board the executive administration of the provisions of Section 4 (b) of the Trading with the Enemy Act relative to granting licenses to enemies and enemy allies to assume or use other names than those by which they were known at the beginning of the war. And I hereby authorize said Board to issue licenses not inconsistent with the provisions of law or to withhold or refuse licenses to any enemy, or ally of enemy, or partnership of which an enemy or ally of enemy is a member or was a member at the beginning of the war, to assume or use any name other than that by which such enemy or ally of enemy or partnership was ordinarily known at the beginning of the war.

VII. I hereby revoke the executive order* of August 21, 1917, creating the Exports Administrative Board. All proclamations, rules, regulations and instructions made or given by me under Title VII of the Espionage Act and now being administered by the Exports Administrative Board are hereby continued, confirmed and made applicable to the War Trade Board, and all employees of the Exports Administrative Board are hereby transferred to and constituted employees of the War Trade Board in the same capacities, and said War Trade Board is hereby authorized to exercise without interruption, the powers heretofore exercised by said Exports Administrative Board.

VIII. The said War Trade Board is hereby authorized and empowered to take all such measures as may be necessary or expedient to administer the powers hereby conferred. And I hereby vest in the War Trade Board the power conferred upon the President by Section 5 (a) to make such rules and regulations, not inconsistent with law, as may be necessary and proper for the exercise of the powers conferred upon said Board.

*Not published.

WAR TRADE COUNCIL

IX. I hereby establish a War Trade Council to be composed of the Secretary of State, Secretary of the Treasury, Secretary of Agriculture, Secretary of Commerce, the Food Administrator and the Chairman of the Shipping Board, and I hereby authorize and direct the said War Trade Council thus constituted to act in an advisory capacity in such matters under said Acts as may be referred to them by the President or the War Trade Board.

SECRETARY OF THE TREASURY

X. I hereby vest in the Secretary of the Treasury the executive administration of any investigation, regulation or prohibition of any transaction in foreign exchange, export or earmarking of gold or silver coin, or bullion or currency, transfers of credit in any form (other than credits relating solely to transactions to be executed wholly within the United States) and transfers of evidence of indebtedness or of the ownership of property between the United States and any foreign country, or between residents of one or more foreign countries, by any person within the United States; and I hereby vest in the Secretary of the Treasury the authority and power to require any person engaged in any such transaction to furnish under oath complete information relative thereto, including the production of any books of account, contracts, letters or other papers in connection therewith in the custody or control of such person, either before or after such transaction is completed.

XI. I further hereby vest in the Secretary of the Treasury the executive administration of the provisions of subsection (c) of Section 3 of the Trading with the Enemy Act relative to sending, or taking out of, or bringing into, or attempting to send, take out of, or bring into, the United States, any letter, writing or tangible form of communication, except in the regular course of the mail; and of the sending, taking, or transmitting, or attempting to send, take, or transmit, out of the United States, any letter, or other writing, book, map, plan or other paper, picture, or any telegram, cablegram, or wireless message, or other form of communication intended for or to be delivered, directly or indirectly, to an enemy or ally of enemy. And said Secretary of the Treasury is hereby authorized and empowered to issue licenses to send, take or transmit out of the United States anything otherwise forbidden by said subsection (c) and give such consent or grant such exemption in respect thereto, as is not inconsistent with law, or to withhold or refuse the same.

XII. I further authorize the Secretary of the Treasury to grant a license under such terms and conditions as are not inconsistent with law or to withhold or refuse the same to any "enemy" or "ally of enemy" insurance or reinsurance company doing business within the United States through an agency or branch office or otherwise, which shall make application within thirty days of October 6, 1917.

XIII. I hereby authorize and direct the Secretary of the Treasury, for the purpose of such executive administration, to take such measures, adopt such administrative procedure, and use such agency or agencies as he may from time to time deem necessary and proper for that purpose. The proclamation of the President, dated September 7, 1917, made under authority vested in him by Title VII of said Act of Congress, approved June 15, 1917, shall remain in full force and effect. The executive order, dated September 7, 1917, made under the authority of said title shall remain in full force and effect until new regulations shall have been established by the President, or by the Secretary of the Treasury, with the approval of the President, and thereupon shall be superseded.

CENSORSHIP BOARD

XIV. I hereby establish a Censorship Board to be composed of representatives, respectively, of the Secretary of War, the Secretary of the Navy, the Postmaster General, the War Trade Board, and the Chairman of the Committee on Public Information.

XV. And I hereby vest in said Censorship Board the executive administration of the rules, regulations and proclamations from time to time established by the President under subsection (d) of section 3, of the Trading with the Enemy Act, for the censorship of communications by mail, cable, radio or other means of transmission passing between the United States and any foreign country from time to time specified by the President, or carried by any vessel, or other means of transportation touching at any port, place or territory of the United States and bound to or from any foreign country.

XVI. The said Censorship Board is hereby authorized to take all such measures as may be necessary or expedient to administer the powers hereby conferred.

FEDERAL TRADE COMMISSION

XVII. I further hereby vest in the Federal Trade Commission the power and authority to issue licenses under such terms and conditions as are not inconsistent with law or to withhold or refuse the same, to any citizen of the United States or any corporation organized within the United States to file and prosecute applications in the country of an enemy or ally of enemy for letters patent or for registration of trademark, print, label, or copyright, and to pay the fees required by law and the customary agents' fees, the maximum amount of which in each case shall be subject to the control of such Commission; or to pay to any enemy or ally of enemy any tax, annuity or fee which may be required by the laws of such enemy or ally of enemy nation in relation to patents, trade-marks, prints, labels and copyrights.

XVIII. I hereby vest in the Federal Trade Commission the power and authority to issue, pursuant to the provisions of Section 10 (c) of the Trading with the Enemy Act, upon such terms and conditions as are not inconsistent with law, or to withhold or refuse, a license to any citizen of the United States, or any corporation organized within the United States, to manufacture or cause to be manufactured a machine, manufacture, composition of matter, or design, or to carry on or cause to be carried on a process under any patent, or to use any trade-mark, print, label, or copyrighted matter owned or controlled by an enemy or ally of enemy, at any time during the present war; and also to fix the prices of articles and products manufactured under such licenses necessary to the health of the military and the naval forces of the United States, or the successful prosecution of the war; and to prescribe the fee which may be charged for such license, not exceeding $100.00 and not exceeding 1 per centum of the fund deposited by the licensee with the Alien Property Custodian as provided by law.

XIX. I hereby further vest in the said Federal Trade Commission the executive administration of the provisions of section 10 (d) of the

Trading with the Enemy Act, the power and authority to prescribe the form of, and time and manner of filing statements of the extent of the use and enjoyment of the license and of the prices received and the times at which the licensee shall make payments to the Alien Property Custodian, and the amounts of said payments, in accordance with the Trading with the Enemy Act.

XX. I further hereby vest in the Federal Trade Commission the power and authority, whenever in its opinion the publication of an invention or the granting of a patent may be detrimental to the public safety or defense, or may assist the enemy, or endanger the successful prosecution of the war, to order that the invention be kept secret and the grant of letters patent withheld until the end of the war.

XXI. The said Federal Trade Commission is hereby authorized to take all such measures as may be necessary or expedient to administer the powers hereby conferred.

THE POSTMASTER GENERAL

XXII. I hereby vest in the Postmaster General the executive administration of all the provisions (except the penal provisions) of Section 19, of the Trading with the Enemy Act, relating to the printing, publishing or circulation in any foreign language of any news item, editorial, or other printed matter respecting the Government of the United States or of any nation engaged in the present war, its policies, international relations, the state or conduct of the war or any matter relating thereto, and the filing with the Postmaster at the place of publication, in the form of an affidavit of a true and complete translation of the entire article containing such matter proposed to be published in such print, newspaper or publication, and the issuance of permits for the printing, publication and distribution thereof free from said restriction. And the Postmaster General is authorized and empowered to issue such permits upon such terms and conditions as are not inconsistent with law and to refuse, withhold or revoke the same.

XXIII. The sum of $35,000.00 or so much thereof as may be necessary is hereby allotted out of the funds appropriated by the Trading with the Enemy Act, to be expended by the Postmaster General in the administration of said section 19 thereof.

XXIV. The Postmaster General is hereby authorized to take all such measures as may be necessary or expedient to administer the powers hereby conferred.

SECRETARY OF STATE

XXV. I hereby vest in the Secretary of State the executive administration of the provisions of subsection (b) of Section 3 of the Trading with the Enemy Act relative to any person transporting or attempting to transport any subject or citizen of an enemy or ally of enemy nation, and relative to transporting or attempting to transport by any owner, master or other person in charge of a vessel of American registry, from any place to any other place, such subject or citizen of an enemy or enemy ally.

XXVI. And I hereby authorize and empower the Secretary of State to issue licenses for such transportation of enemies and enemy allies or to withhold or refuse the same.

XXVII. And said Secretary of State is hereby authorized and empowered to take all such measures as may be necessary or expedient to administer the powers hereby conferred and to grant, refuse, withhold or revoke licenses thereunder.

SECRETARY OF COMMERCE

XXVIII. I hereby vest in the Secretary of Commerce the power to review the refusal of any Collector of Customs under the provisions of Sections 13 and 14 of the Trading with the Enemy Act, to clear any vessel, domestic or foreign, for which clearance is required by law.

ALIEN PROPERTY CUSTODIAN

XXIX. I hereby vest in an Alien Property Custodian, to be hereafter appointed, the executive administration of all the provisions of Section 7 (a), Section 7 (c), and Section 7 (d) of the Trading with the Enemy Act, including all power and authority to require lists and reports, and to extend the time for filing the same, conferred upon the President by the provisions of said Section 7 (a), and including the power and authority conferred upon the President by the provisions of said Section 7 (c), to require the conveyance, transfer, assignment, delivery or payment to himself, at such time and in such manner as he shall prescribe, of any money or other properties owing to or belonging to or held for, by or on account of, or on behalf of, or for the benefit of any enemy or ally of an enemy, not holding a license granted under the provisions of the Trading with the Enemy Act, which, after investigation, said Alien Property Custodian shall determine is so owing, or so belongs, or is so held.

XXX. Any person who desires to make conveyance, transfer, payment, assignment or delivery, under the provisions of Section 7 (d) of the Trading with the Enemy Act, to the Alien Property Custodian of any money or other property owing to or held for, by or an account of, or on behalf of, or for the benefit of an enemy or ally of enemy, not holding a license granted as provided in the Trading with the Enemy Act, or to whom any obligation or form of liability to such enemy or ally of enemy is presented for payment, shall file application with the Alien Property Custodian for consent and permit to so convey, transfer, assign, deliver or pay such money or other property to him and said Alien Property Custodian is hereby authorized to exercise the power and authority conferred upon the President by the provisions of said Section 7 (d) to consent and to issue permit upon such terms and conditions as are not inconsistent with law, or to withhold or refuse *the same.*

XXXI. I further vest in the Alien Property Custodian the executive administration of all the provisions of Section 8 (a), Section 8 (b), and Section 9 of the Trading with the Enemy Act, so far as said Sections relate to the powers and duties of said Alien Property Custodian.

XXXII. I vest in the Attorney General all powers and authority conferred upon the President by the provisions of Section 9 of the Trading with the Enemy Act.

XXXIII. The Alien Property Custodian to be hereafter appointed is hereby authorized to take all such measures as may be necessary or expedient, and not inconsistent with law, to administer the powers hereby conferred; and he shall further have the power and authority to make such rules and regulations not inconsistent with law as may be necessary and proper to carry out the provisions of said Section 7 (a), Section 7 (c), Section 7 (d), Section 8 (a), and Section 8 (b), conferred upon the President by the provisions thereof and by the provisions of Section 5 (a), said rules and regulations to be duly approved by the Attorney General.

XXXIV. The Alien Property Custodian to be hereafter appointed shall, "under the supervision and direction of the President, and under such rules and regulations as the President shall prescribe," have administration of all moneys (including checks and drafts payable on demand) and of all property, other than money which shall come into his possession in pursuance of the provisions of the Trading with the Enemy Act, in accordance with the provisions of Section 6, Section 10, and Section 12 thereof.

WOODROW WILSON.

EXECUTIVE ORDER

[Free consular services.]

THE WHITE HOUSE, *October 13, 1917.*
During the continuance of the war and until further orders, any services which American consular officers shall be called upon to perform under items 8, 12, 31, 32, 33, 38, 39, 40, 41, 42, and 43 of the Tariff of United States Consular Fees for any person in the military or naval service of the United States, shall be rendered free of charge.
WOODROW WILSON.

STATEMENT·

[Urging State Banks to join Federal Reserve System.]

THE WHITE HOUSE, *Oct. 13, 1917.*

It is manifestly imperative that there should be a complete mobilization of the banking resources of the United States. All who are familiar with financial operations must appreciate the importance of developing to the maximum our banking power and of providing financial machinery adequate for meeting the very great financial requirements imposed upon our country by reason of the war.

A vigorous prosecution and satisfactory termination of the war will depend in no small degree upon the ability of the Government not only to finance itself, but also to aid the governments associated with it in the war, which must be kept supplied with munitions, fuel, food, and supplies of all kinds.

The banking problem involved is one which concerns all banks alike. Its solution does not depend upon the national banks alone, nor upon the State banks. The burden and the privilege must be shared by every banking institution in the country. The important functions of the Federal Reserve Banks in the sale of the Government's securities, in receiving and transferring the billions of dollars involved, in supplying credit facilities, and in protecting the reserves of the country have become so familiar to all that I am sure it is unnecessary to dwell upon or expound them.

The extent to which our country can withstand the financial strains for which we must be prepared will depend very largely upon the strength and staying power of the Federal Reserve Banks. The Federal Reserve act is the only constructive financial legislation which we have ever had which was broad enough to accommodate at the same time banks operating under powers granted by the general Government and banks whose charters are granted by the respective States. The unification of our banking system and the complete mobilization of reserves are among the fundamental principles of the act.

The State banking institutions for some reason have until recently seemed inclined to hold aloof. Congress a few months ago prescribed very generous terms for the admission of the State banks into the Federal Reserve system, which have removed the objections heretofore raised by State banks when considering membership. As the law now stands, it leaves member State banks and trust companies practically undisturbed in the exercise of all the banking powers conferred upon them by the States. The law provides also in definite terms the conditions upon which any State bank or trust company may withdraw from the system.

Many of the largest State banks and trust companies are now becoming members, realizing that to win the war we must conserve all of the physical, financial, and moral resources of our country; that our finances must rest on the firmest possible foundation, and that they must be adequately and completely conserved so as to respond instantly to every legitimate demand. How can this necessary condition be brought about and be made permanently effective better than by the concentration of the banking strength of our country in the Federal Reserve system?

May I not, therefore, urge upon the officers and directors of all non-member State banks and trust companies which have the required amount of capital and surplus to make them eligible for membership to unite with the Federal Reserve system now, and thereby contribute their share to the consolidated gold reserves of the country? I feel sure that as member banks they will aid to a greater degree than is possible otherwise in promoting the national welfare, and that at the same time, by securing for themselves the advantages offered by the Federal Reserve system, they will best serve their own interest and the interest of their customers. I believe that co-operation on the part of the banks is a patriotic duty at this time and that membership in the Federal Reserve system is a distinct and significant evidence of patriotism.

There are probably eight or nine thousand State banks and trust companies eligible for membership which have not yet united with the system. These institutions have it in their power to add enormously to the resources of the Federal Reserve Banks, thereby broadening and strengthening the foundation upon which our whole financial structure must rest. Permit me to urge that every bank officer and bank director owes a solemn obligation to the country, which I am sure they wish to discharge. I therefore wish again to impress upon them my solemn conviction that they can best measure up to their duties and responsibilities through membership in the Federal Reserve system.

WOODROW WILSON.

LETTER

[To Mrs. Carrie Chapman Catt, concerning the Woman Suffrage Campaign in New York State.]

THE WHITE HOUSE, *October 13, 1917.*

My Dear Mrs. Catt:

May I not express to you my very deep interest in the campaign in New York for the adoption of Woman Suffrage, and may I not say that I hope that no voter will be influenced in his decision with regard to this matter by anything which the so-called pickets may have done here in Washington? However justly they may have laid themselves open to serious criticism, their action represents, I am sure, so small a fraction of the women of the country who are urging the adoption of Woman Suffrage that it would be most unfair and argue a narrow view to allow their actions to prejudice the cause itself. I am very anxious to see the great State of New York set a great example in this matter.

Cordially and sincerely,

WOODROW WILSON.

EXECUTIVE ORDERS

[Suspending civil service rules in training camp activities.]

THE WHITE HOUSE, *October 15, 1917.*

Civilian employees of the Commissions on Training Camp Activities may be appointed without regard to the requirements of the Civil Service rules.

The staffs of employees of the Commissions on Training Camp Activities, heretofore paid from private funds, are to be taken into the service of the War and Navy Departments and paid from Government appropriations, and it is desired that the established organizations be continued. In the opinion of the Secretary of War and the Secretary of the Navy, it is impracticable to secure qualified employees for this work by competitive examination.

WOODROW WILSON.

[Providing for Requisitioning of Foods and Feeds.]

Under and by virtue of an Act of Congress, entitled "An Act to provide further for the national security and defense by encouraging the production, conserving the supply, and controlling the distribution of food products and fuel," approved August 10, 1917, I, Woodrow Wilson, President of the United States, hereby authorize and direct Herbert Hoover, United States Food Administrator, from time to time, to requisition any and all foods and feeds, and storage facilities for the same, that said Herbert Hoover, United States Food Administrator, may deem are necessary for any public use connected with the common defense, other than the support of the Army or the maintenance of the Navy, and to ascertain and pay a just compensation therefor.

Done in the District of Columbia, this twenty-third day of October, in the year of our Lord one thousand nine hundred and seventeen, and of the Independence of the United States of America, the one hundred and forty-second.

WOODROW WILSON.

[Waiving civil service regulations for confidential positions under Trading with the Enemy Act.]

THE WHITE HOUSE, *October 25, 1917.*

Newspaper readers and translators selected by the Postmaster General for filling certain confidential positions under the Trading with the Enemy Act may be appointed during the period of the war with Germany without examination under the civil service law. The Postmaster General states that there are available to the Post Office Department for appointment in these lines men whose loyalty has been proven and who in some cases will accept employment at a nominal salary through patriotic desire to give service at this time.

The Civil Service Commission concurs in the issuance of this order in view of the highly confidential character of the employments and the particular qualifications required.

WOODROW WILSON.

BY THE PRESIDENT OF THE UNITED STATES OF AMERICA

PROCLAMATIONS

[Supplication and prayer.]

Whereas, the Congress of the United States, by a concurrent resolution adopted on the fourth day of the present month of October, in view of the entrance of our nation into the vast and awful war which now afflicts the greater part of the world, has requested me to set apart by official proclamation a day upon which our people should be called upon to offer concerted prayer to Almighty God for His divine aid in the success of our arms;

And, Whereas, it behooves a great free people, nurtured as we have been in the eternal principles of justice and of right, a nation which has sought from the earliest days of its existence to be obedient to the divine teachings which have inspired it in the exercise of its liberties, to turn always to the supreme Master and cast themselves in faith at His feet, praying for His aid and succor in every hour of trial, to the end that the great aims to which our fathers dedicated our power as a people may not perish among men, but be always asserted and defended with fresh ardor and devotion and, through the Divine blessing, set at last upon enduring foundations for the benefit of all the free peoples of the earth:

Now, therefore, I, Woodrow Wilson, President of the United States, gladly responding to the wish expressed by the Congress, do appoint October twenty-eighth, being the last Sunday of the present month, as a day of supplication and prayer for all the people of the nation, earnestly exhorting all my countrymen to observe the appointed day, according to their several faiths, in solemn prayer that God's blessing may rest upon the high task which is laid upon us, to the end that the cause for which we give our lives and treasure may triumph and our efforts be blessed with high achievement.

In Witness Whereof, I have hereunto set my hand and caused the seal of the United States to be affixed.

Done in the District of Columbia this nineteenth day of October, in the year of our Lord one thousand nine hundred and seven-[SEAL] teen, and of the Independence of the United States of America the one hundred and forty-second.

WOODROW WILSON.

By the President:

ROBERT LANSING, *Secretary of State.*

[Manufacture, etc., of explosives in time of war unlawful.]

Whereas, under and by virtue of an Act of Congress entitled "An Act to prohibit the manufacture, distribution, storage, use and possession in time of war of explosives, providing regulations for the safe manufacture, distribution, storage, use and possession of the same, and for other purposes," approved by the President on the 6th day of October, 1917, it is provided among other things that from and after forty days after the passage and approval of said Act no person shall manufacture, distribute, store, use or possess explosives or ingredients thereof, not including explosives for the military or naval service of the United States of America under the authority of the Government or ingredients in small quantities not used or intended to be used in the manufacture of explosives, and not including small arms or shotgun cartridges, unless such person shall obtain a license issued in the name of the Director of the Bureau of Mines, except that any workman may purchase or accept explosives or ingredients thereof under prescribed conditions from a licensed superintendent or foreman.

And, Whereas, it is further provided in said Act as follows:

"That the Director of the Bureau of Mines, with the approval of the President, is hereby authorized to utilize such agents, agencies, and all officers of the United States and of the several States, Territories, dependencies, and municipalities thereof, and the District of Columbia, in the execution of this Act, and all agents, agencies, and all officers of the United States and of the several States and Territories, dependencies, and municipalities thereof, and the District of Columbia, shall hereby have full authority for all acts done by them in the execution of this Act when acting by the direction of the Bureau of Mines."

Now, therefore, I, Woodrow Wilson, President of the United States of America, by this proclamation do announce the following:

That from and after the 15th day of November, 1917, and during the present war with Germany, it will be unlawful to manufacture, distribute, store, use, or possess explosives or ingredients thereof, except as provided in said Act.

That the Director of the Bureau of Mines is hereby authorized to utilize, where necessary for the proper administration of said Act, the services of all officers of the United States and of the several States, Territories, dependencies, and municipalities thereof, and of the District of Columbia, and such other agents and agencies as he may designate, who shall have full authority for all acts done by them in the execution of the said Act when acting under his direction.

In Witness Whereof, I have hereunto set my hand and caused the seal of the United States to be affixed.

Done in the District of Columbia, this twenty-sixth day of October, in the year of our Lord one thousand nine hundred and [SEAL] seventeen, and of the Independence of the United States of America, the one hundred and forty-second.

WOODROW WILSON.

By the President:
ROBERT LANSING. *Secretary of State.*

APPEAL FOR FOOD CONSERVATION

THE WHITE HOUSE, *October 28, 1917.*

The chief part of the burden of finding food supplies for the peoples associated with us in war falls for the present upon the American people, and the drain upon supplies on such a scale necessarily affects the prices of our necessaries of life. Our country, however, is blessed with an abundance of foodstuffs, and if our people will economize in their use of food, providently confining themselves to the quantities required for the maintenance of health and strength; if they will eliminate waste; and if they will make use of those commodities of which we have a surplus, and thus free for export a large proportion of those required by the world now dependent upon us, we shall not only be able to accomplish our obligations to them, but we shall obtain and establish reasonable prices at home.

To provide an adequate supply of food both for our own soldiers on the other side of the seas and for the civil populations and the armies of the Allies, is one of our first and foremost obligations; for, if we are to maintain their constancy in this struggle for the independence of all nations, we must first maintain their health and strength. The solution of our food problems, therefore, is dependent upon the individual service of every man, woman, and child in the United States.

The great voluntary effort in this direction which has been initiated and organized by the Food Administration under my direction offers an opportunity of service in the war which is open to every individual and by which every individual may serve both his own people and the peoples of the world. We cannot accomplish our objects in this great war without sacrifice and devotion, and in no direction can that sacrifice and devotion be shown more than by each home and public eating place in the country pledging its support to the Food Administration and complying with its requests.

WOODROW WILSON.

EXECUTIVE ORDER

[Fixing salary of and vesting certain power and authority in the alien property custodian appointed under Trading-with-the-Enemy Act.]

THE WHITE HOUSE, *October 29, 1917.*

By virtue of the authority vested in me by "An act to define, regulate, and punish trading with the enemy," approved October 6, 1917, I hereby make and establish the following order:

1. I hereby fix the salary of the Alien Property Custodian heretofore appointed at the sum of $5,000 per annum. I direct that said Alien Property Custodian shall give a bond in the amount of $100,000 with security to be approved by the Attorney General, and which bond shall be conditioned to well and faithfully hold, administer, and account for all money and property in the United States due or belonging to an enemy or ally of enemy or otherwise, which may be paid, conveyed, transferred, assigned, or delivered to said custodian under the provisions of the trading-with-the-enemy act.

2. I hereby authorize and empower the Alien Property Custodian to employ and appoint in the manner provided in the trading-with-the-enemy act in the District of Columbia and elsewhere, and to fix the compensation of, such clerks, attorneys, investigators, accountants, and other employees as he may find necessary for the due administration of the powers conferred on such Alien Property Custodian by law or by any order of the President heretofore or hereafter made.

3. I hereby vest in the Alien Property Custodian the executive administration of the provisions of Section 12 of the trading-with-the-enemy act pertaining to the designation of a depositary, or depositaries, and requiring all such designated depositaries to execute and file bonds and prescribing the form, amount, and security thereof. And I authorize and empower the Alien Property Custodian to designate any bank, or banks, or trust company, or trust companies, or other suitable depositary or depositaries located and doing business in the United